Ruthless Compassion

Wrathful Deities
in Early Indo-Tibetan Esoteric Buddhist Art

Ruthless Compassion

Rob Linrothe

Serindia Publications
London

ISBN 0 906026 51 2

First published in 1999 by
Serindia Publications
10 Parkfields, London SW15 6NH

British library Cataloguing in Publication Data
A catalogue record for this book is available through the British Library.

Frontispiece:
Page ii left: detail of **167**, right: **4**. Page iii detail of **2**.

PRINTED AND BOUND IN HONG KONG THROUGH BOOKBUILDERS LTD

Contents

List of Illustrations

(Unless otherwise indicated, all images are stone, and photographs are by the author.)

Black-and-white Figures

Graphs

Color Plates

List of Abbreviations

AIIS American Institute of Indian Studies
ASI Archaeological Survey of India
JIABS Journal of the International Association of Buddhist Studies
KBC *The Korean Buddhist Canon*, Lewis Lancaster, ed
MVS *Mahāvairocana Sūtra*
MMK *Mañjuśrimūlakalpa*
Njo Nanjio, Bunyo *A Catalogue of the Chinese Translation of the Buddhist Tripitaka*
ns new series
SDPS *Sarva-durgati-pariśodhana*
STTS *Savra-tathāgata-tattva-saṃgraha*
T. *Taishō shinshū Daizōkyō*. The number immediately following T. refers to the volume number, followed by the number of the text as order in the *Taishō* edition, and then the page number. The small case letters a, b or c refer to the three columns of text on each page, beginning at the top.
Yamamoto Chikyo Yamamoto, *Mahāvairocana-Sūtra: translated into English from Ta-p'i-lu-che-na ch'eng-fo shen-pien chia-ch'ih ching, the Chinese version of Śubhākarasimha and I-hsing (AD 725)* (New Delhi, 1990)

Note In quotations appearing in the text, material inside parentheses () appear in the original. Material in square brackets [] is added to clarify or explain quoted material.

Acknowledgements

My indebtedness surpasses my space to acknowledge and my powers to express. So many people have aided me personally and professionally that it is challenging to provide a list which is even remotely comprehensive. At the head of any such list are 4 people: my parents, Robert N. and Vida Jane Linrothe, who helped and encouraged my studies, first under the inspiring Robert Poor of the University of Minnesota and then with the incomparable Harrie Vanderstappen S.V.D. at the University of Chicago. To each of them I owe an unrequitable debt of gratitude, but one which at least they know I recognize.

It is a pleasure to single out a few people who have made my travel and study easier and more productive. The Wahid family, especially Siddiq, Susan and Ghafoor have lived up to their distinguished family's ideals of hospitality. They have repeatedly opened up their lives to me and shared comforts and insights at homes in Kashmir and New Delhi. Dr. Wahid's relative Anwar Ullah in Leh extended great generosity there. Bhikkhu Saddhananda Thero, the noble monk and Bhikkhu-in-Charge of the Orissa center of the Mahabodhi Society in Bhubaneswar in 1990 was unforgettably generous in allowing me to stay with him and share his meals, *puja*s and links to the old Buddhist culture of Orissa. Abigail Smith of Chicago, New York, Paris and London provided a place to stay, good food and good cheer in all of those locales. Anthony Aris has been extraordinarily kind in taking this on as publisher and allowing me to take an active role in the layout. Jane Casey Singer along with her husband Jim were very encouraging when they first read sections of a draft, and I am honored by her Foreword. Amy Heller patiently helped me standardize Tibetan words, and called to my attention her ongoing work on Atisha's special form of Acala, which has frequently been identified as Vighnāntaka. I look forward to seeing that important iconographic study in print. The museums, curators and private collectors who have provided photographs or transparencies with permission to publish have a special place in this list and I am grateful to all of them. Lionel Fournier has been especially generous in this regard, and I thank him sincerely, along with Moke Mokotoff and Donald Rubin, Jaro Poncar, Stephen Markel, Steven Kossak, Valrae Reynolds, the Zimmerman family, Carlton Rochell, Jr. of Sotheby's New York, Eberto Lo Bue and Franco Ricca.

A number of people have contributed to the preparation of the manuscript, layout and design. Anthony Aris once again worked long hours to devise a set of parameters and provide me with information and help at critical junctures. Essential technical and design advice was received from John Danison, Cameron Neilson (who designed the cover) and Audrey Donner, while Ben Rubenstein performed miracles with my black-and-white negatives. Yamini Mehta and Hillary Shugrue offered many useful suggestions. The entire Media Services office at Skidmore College, especially Hunt Conard, Judith Redder and Steve Dinyer, were supportive of my requests and provided access at the unusual hours I needed to keep. Phyllis Roth, the Dean of the Faculty, and Bob DeSieno, Assistant Dean of the Faculty for Faculty Development at Skidmore mobilized financial support for this project at several stages of research, writing and production for which I'm deeply grateful. Marilyn Sheffer and Amy Syrell in the Interlibrary Loan office have heroically located and acquired copies of innumerable books and articles on my behalf.

A signal contributor to this effort is Lauren Emilia Knopf who, in Saratoga Springs and in London, undertook the difficult task of editing this book. Her devotion to clarity, accuracy and consistency was severely tested on this project, but the results exceed the author's expectations or ability to recompense. This is a much better book than it was before Ms. Knopf had her way with it.

In Europe, America and in India, especially, literally dozens of people and institutions kindly made their collections and expertise available to me. I can do no more than to list their names in an order which does not reflect importance: The American Institute of Indian Studies in Delhi and Calcutta as well as its Center for Art and Archaeology at Ramnagar (both research library and photo-archive); The Archaeological Survey of India; K.D. Bajpai; Doboom Tulku; Thomas Donaldson; Roger Goepper; Krishna Deva; Lokesh Chandra; Debala Mitra; Jaro Poncar; B.P. Sinha; Gareth Sparham; Kirti Tsenshap Rimpoche; Tarthang Tulku; P.K. Mitra and Tapash Banerjee at the West Bengal State Archaeological Museum; T. Chanda, Government of West Bengal Information and Cultural Affairs Department; the staff of the Asutosh Museum of Indian Art, University of Calcutta; K.C. Mahakud at the Khiching Museum; Prabhakar Burik of Ayodhya; H.C. Das of Baripada; K.C. Bishwal at the Balasore Museum; Dr. S.D. Trivedi and Shailindra Kumar Rastogi at the Lucknow Museum; D.P. Sinha and Brij Raj Singh at the Sarnath Museum; P.K. Jayashwar, O.P. Pandey and Nutan Sinha of the Patna Museum; Dr. Kumar of the Patna University Museum; S.K. Bhatt of the Bharat Kala Bhavan, Varanasi; Manzar Hasan and the staff of the Gaya Museum; Ajaya Srivasta at the Bodh Gaya and Nalanda Museums; Dwija Mallik of Ratnagiri; Nagabhana Panda at Kuruma; Mr. Chakravarti, Mrs. Mukerji, Mrs. S. Chakravarti, Mrs. A. Sengupta and Mr. D. Das at the Indian Museum, Calcutta; the staff at the Nalanda Museum; Shashi Asthana and Jitendra Nath of the National Museum, New Delhi; The Karsha Lonpo Sonam Angchug; M.C. Joshi of The Archaeological Survey of India; T.B. Dissanayaka of The Mahabodhi Society of India, Calcutta branch; H.C. Das and the staff of the Orissa State Museum; Prakash Charan Prasad, Director of the Bihar State Directorate of Archaeology; John Clarke, Victoria and Albert Museum, London; Ulrich Pagel and Mrs. Ghosh of the Oriental and India Office Collections, British Museum; Vidya Dehejia and David Roy.

Author's note: After the completion of this book, an article by Stephen Hodge was brought to my attention: "Considerations on the Dating and Geographical Origins of the *Mahāvairocanābhisaṃbodhi-sūtra*," pp. 57 - 83 in *The Buddhist Forum Volume III, 1991-1993*, edited by Tadeusz Skorupski and Ulrich Pagel (London: School of Oriental and African Studies, 1994). It is a laudable example of what I hope is a trend in Buddhology to make use of Chinese sources for evidence of the evolutionary sequence of Esoteric Buddhist practice in India and Tibet, to critique the reified Tibetan text classification systems, and to study the early Esoteric Buddhist texts and ideas in the context of Mahāyāna practice more broadly. I hope its author will not mind my stating that it is gratifying to find many of the questions and conclusions I came to independently shared or corroborated by a textual scholar.

This book is gratefully dedicated to all those who allowed me access to the works of art in their care.

Rob Linrothe
Saratoga Springs, New York
December 1998

Foreword

Jane Casey Singer

The iconographic development of *krodha-vighnāntaka* — "wrathful destroyers of obstacles" — is the subject of this excellent study. Images of this class of deity first appeared in eastern India during the late sixth-century and gradually came to characterize Indian Esoteric Buddhism by the late tenth or early eleventh century — Indian Buddhism's final and, arguably, most fascinating phase. Ferocious in appearance and often portrayed in explicitly erotic states, these multi-limbed deities have intrigued and puzzled observers of Esoteric Buddhism for centuries. In 1895 an early Western interpreter of Tibetan Buddhism noted "the wild and terrible ... often monstrous" forms assumed by Indian medieval Buddhist deities, a pantheon that he perceived to be evidence of "the distorted form of Buddhism introduced to Tibet."[1]

While twentieth-century scholarship has considerably revised Waddell's assessment, intriguing questions remain. In this richly argued volume, Rob Linrothe presents a new model for the development of Indian Esoteric Buddhism, one which draws upon both visual and literary evidence. In so doing, he breaks new ground, for previous studies have sought to understand Esoteric Buddhism chiefly by analyzing texts; works of art, if used at all, were primarily valued as illustrations of textual ideas.[2] Linrothe demonstrates that an understanding of the development of Esoteric Buddhist iconography can reveal important paradigmatic shifts within Esoteric Buddhism and, when assessed in the light of textual information, presents a more accurate picture of the development of Esoteric Buddhist ideas and practices. He frequently returns to the relationship between Esoteric Buddhist texts and images, concluding: "It is consistently true that the period when images begin to appear falls after the dates attributed to the earliest layer of relevant texts, though the texts are often accepted as the exclusive markers of the beginning of each movement. Sculpted and painted images are more accurate gauges than texts to identify the period when a substantial community of practitioners engaged in the ritual activity described in a text."[3]

Linrothe's study is founded upon an assessment of hundreds of late sixth- to twelfth-century eastern Indian Buddhist wrathful images, a far larger corpus than was previously known. He arranges these objects chronologically and discerns three main phases in their evolution. Phase One *krodha-vighnāntaka* — seen in works dating from the late sixth to the twelfth centuries — appeared as often undifferentiated subsidiary figures within an essentially Mahāyāna context. Accompanying a bodhisattva whose powers they personified, their purpose was to ensure the attainment of mundane goals. Thus, in the earliest stages of Esoteric Buddhist theory, they are "sent by bodhisattva to gather together and to intimidate the recalcitrant beings of the universe and protect the human aspirants."[4] Phase Two *krodha-vighnāntaka* — seen mainly in mid eighth- to tenth-century images and exemplified in deities such as Yamāntaka and Trailokyavijaya — appeared both as independent deities with clearly differentiated iconography and in larger assemblies, for example as subsidiary deities in mandalas associated with the Five Tathagata. Linrothe suggests that Phase Two images herald the emergence of a new paradigm, one that is only fully realized in Phase Three *krodha-vighnāntaka*. This final phase — seen in late tenth- to twelfth-century images — exhibits breathtakingly imaginative, powerful forms, portrayed both independently and as the central deity in large, highly complex mandalas. They are intimately involved in the primary task of Esoteric Buddhism: "the transformation of the passions and ignorance into compassion and wisdom."[5]

Linrothe's primary concern is to document and explain the remarkable iconographic and iconologic transformation of the *krodha-vighnāntaka* and, crucially, to understand what the evolution of this iconographic type can tell us about the development of Indian Esoteric Buddhism as a whole. Linrothe observes that wrathful deities became more prominent as they were increasingly perceived to represent the power by which an adept is transformed into an enlightened being. "Terrifying deities in sexual embrace expose the enigma at the heart of Phase Three Esoteric Buddhism: poison as its own antidote, harnessed obstacles as the liberating force."[6]

Esoteric Buddhism offered a radical reinterpretation of the path to spiritual enlightenment, postulating that one is *already* enlightened, although the untrained, defiled nature of sensory and psychological functions prevents one from realizing this. The *Hevajra Tantra* states: "All beings are buddhas, but this is obscured by … defilement. When this [defilement] is removed, they are buddhas at once, of this there is no doubt."[7] Esoteric Buddhist practice recommended that these defilements be dispelled not through compassionate deeds exercised over many lifetimes (as advocated in Mahāyāna practice), but in this life, or in a few lifetimes, through rigorous meditative practices (yoga).

Linrothe notes the remarkable parallels between the appearance of the *krodha-vighnāntaka* and that of medieval yogins, who also wore bone ornaments and animal skins, who carried skull cups, and who almost certainly participated in the sexual practices that are sometimes portrayed in *krodha-vighnāntaka* iconography. Citing the Dutch scholar Karel van Kooij, Linrothe states: "Heruka's iconography gives support to the observation … that Heruka is more or less a deified hypostasis of the … yogin himself."[8] It is these medieval yogins who could shed perhaps the most valuable light not only on the significance of the *krodha-vighnāntaka*, but on the entire Esoteric Buddhist movement. But their testimonies are not easily obtained. Texts written by them or by their disciples are often intentionally elliptical and obscure.

Medieval Indian Esoteric Buddhist texts are scathing in their assessment of contemporaneous academics (pandits) who sought to understand their practice by intellectual discourse alone. According to Saraha (active ca. second half eighth to early ninth centuries), a leading yogin and Esoteric Buddhist practitioner: "All these pandits expound the treatises,/ But the Buddha who resides within the body is not known./ … But they shamelessly say, 'we are Pandits.'"[9] The difficulty, even for curious contemporaries, in gaining access to Indian medieval Esoteric knowledge is illustrated in an intriguing if anecdotal passage found in the sixteenth century Tibetan historian Pawo Tsuklak Trenghwa's *Scholar's Feast of Religious History* (*chos 'byung mkhas pa'i dga' ston*). A novice Buddhist heard about Batsiker Island, on which all the inhabitants were said to be yogins and yoginis. Drawn by an intense curiosity, he went to the island, but saw and heard nothing extraordinary. However, while sailing back to the Indian mainland in the company of merchants, he overheard them sharing wonderful tales about the island inhabitants and their magical ways. The novice broke in: "[the claim that] there are only siddhas on Batsiker island … I went to see, but it is not true." A yogin called Kusalipunya was amongst the merchants and he wanted to correct the novice's misconception, so he took him aside. "Among yogins, there is mutual recognition (*phan tshun shes pa yin*).

You don't know. The island inhabitants *are* only yogins." Pawo Tsuklak Trenghwa writes that the two became friends and proceeded to Bodh Gaya to meet the Buddhist teacher, Atīśa.[10]

Linrothe makes an impassioned plea to historians of religion, urging them to make greater use of Esoteric Buddhism's visual legacy. Most art historians recognize the complementary nature of image and text, and the importance of learning to read their respective languages. The link between image and culture is even more important in the study of Esoteric Buddhism, for images — and the practice of visualizing imagery — played a pivotal role within Esoteric Buddhist practices. As Linrothe notes, "The adept is to 'visualize' and to become Trailokyavijaya, Acala, Hayagrīva or Ucchusma, and to participate in the subjugation [of corresponding parts] of the self."[11]

Esoteric Buddhist sources suggest that intimate acquaintance with the wrathful, brutal aspects of life is a prerequisite to wisdom. The *Hevajra Tantra* states: "The six faculties of sense, their six spheres of operation, the five *skandhas* and the five elements are pure in essence, but they are obstructed by ignorance (*avidyā*) and emotional disturbance (*kleśa*). Their purification consists in self-experience, and by no other means of purification may one be released."[12] Such passages seem to suggest that the wrathful iconography of the *krodha-vighnāntaka* is intimately linked with self-experience, that is, with our own inner states. Linrothe summarizes similar textual passages when he writes that *krodha-vighnāntaka* are "metaphors for the internal yogic processes employed to gain enlightenment."[13] The *Sarvatathāgata tattvasaṃgraha*, a ca. mid seventh-century text that Linrothe cites as a prime example of Phase Two Esoteric Buddhism, has Mahāvairocana state that Trailokyavijaya is "specially commissioned and equipped to perform those necessary tasks the Tathāgata cannot perform *with only peaceful means*."[14] If Esoteric Buddhism highlights the wrathful, the sexual, and the malevolent, giving them an exalted place in its worldview and in its arts, it does so heuristically. Esoteric imagery enshrines powerful glimpses of man's malevolence within an aesthetic vision, reflecting the Esoteric Buddhist view that — when informed by Buddhist practice — experience of the wrathful, brutal aspects of one's self can become a transformative, ennobling experience. Professor Linrothe's study will serve as an indispensable guide for all who seek to understand the Indian roots of Esoteric Buddhism and its still potent visual and literary manifestations.

Jane Casey Singer
London, December 1998

Notes to Foreword

1 L.A. Waddell, *The Buddhism of Tibet, or Lamaism* (London, 1895, R New York, 1972), pp. 14-15.
2 See Linrothe's "Afterword," in which he compares his model with those of earlier scholars.
3 Infra, p. 327.
4 Infra, p. 155.
5 Infra, p. 155.
6 Infra, p. 330.
7 David Snellgrove, The Hevajra Tantra 2 vols. (London, 1959), p. 107.
8 Infra, p. 251.
9 Infra, p. 224.
10 Pawo Tsuklak Trenghwa, *Scholar's Feast of Religious History (chos 'byung mkhas pa'i dga' ston) Part 2 (da-pa)*, ed. Lokesh Chandra (New Delhi, 1961), pp. 288-89.
11 Infra, p. 216.
12 Infra, p. 304.
13 Infra, p. 153.
14 Infra, p. 186.

Prologue
and
Introduction

1. Heruka, Ratnagiri (Orissa), ca. 11th century

Prologue

Behold, my land, what blessings
Fury kindly,
Gladly brings to pass. Aeschylus, *The Orestia*

The Wrathful Deity Theme

Among the major venerable religious traditions in the world, Esoteric Buddhism is one of the most liable to misunderstanding. From its emergence as a separate tradition in sixth-century India, Esoteric Buddhism has valued oral interpretations of texts which employ intentionally elliptical language and metaphors. Initiation into enlightenment-directed rituals requires the instruction of a lineage master. The secrecy which surrounds its core teachings, the use of a cryptic language for prayers, the centrality of mystic experience and comprehensive many-layered symbols contribute to a system of belief and praxis which has proved almost impenetrable to discursive scholarship. These difficulties were so discouraging that as late as 1974 the Dutch Buddhologist J.W. de Jong accurately observed, "Tantrism is still the most neglected branch of Buddhist studies."[1]

Despite the accent on secrecy and orality, material expressions of the enlightenment experience were produced wherever Esoteric Buddhism spread in Asia. Visual representations were sculpted and painted, molded and cast, by the hands of initiates or under their supervision. Surviving texts make clear that the production of these objects was important enough to necessitate codified guidelines governing such matters as the motivation of the maker, the types of materials used, the forms, colors, attributes and compositional relations of the deities depicted and their symbolic interpretation.[2] The works of visual art made in accordance with ritual requirements were not "merely" decorative, nor were they the passive focus of acts of ritual piety. Art functioned actively for the practitioners of Esoteric Buddhism both as visual triggers of integrated states of realization and as expressions of those states, which beggared verbal description.

Most of these objects were not available to the non-initiated public at the time they were made and are not analogous to "art" as conceived by twentieth century

Euro-American cultures. As they are now considered works of art, however, many are accessible for study in museums, private collections, caves and excavation sites around the world.[3] They provide invaluable and sometimes unique information about Esoteric Buddhist priorities, social relations, iconographic developments and symbolic systems. If the tools of formal analysis are sharpened, images without inscriptions may be accurately dated, providing in many cases relatively precise information about doctrines and practices. Moreover, by arranging the images chronologically and analyzing the resulting patterns, a schematic model of the entire development of Esoteric Buddhism may be generated. This is the project I undertake here.

Works of art are reliable documents which contribute to an ongoing historical reconstruction. To date most research has been textually oriented, focusing on editing and studying the original Indian scriptures along with their Tibetan and Chinese translations. There have been corollary investigations into the understanding of these texts by later Esoteric Buddhists, through the commentaries of Tibetan and to a lesser extent Japanese Buddhists. In the last few decades field work has expanded to include the observation of contemporary ritual practices.

I believe sculpture and painting have been under-utilized by historians of Esoteric Buddhism, though the discrepancy may also be attributed to the fact that art historians have not sufficiently related their findings to broader movements.[4] Nevertheless, analysis of visual evidence in conjunction with other avenues of study provides valuable insights into the evolution of Esoteric Buddhist doctrines and practices.

The study of artistic remains plays a significant role in the understanding of ideas expressed by the Esoteric Buddhist tradition, as well as the *historical* situation in which they are found. Historical evidence is of particular interest because the living tradition of Esoteric Buddhism as it survives today, in the Himalayan regions and in Japan, generally emphasizes the *revelatory*, a-historical nature of inherited texts and teachings. Learned Tibetan scholastics such as Buton Rinpoche (1290-1364), Tsongkhapa (1357-1419) and his disciple Kaygrubjay (1385-1438) composed elaborate explanations of the conflicting priorities of texts and schools within the broader tradition. These schemes have been knit together so as to elide internal contradictions stemming from the evolutionary development of Buddhism.

Disjunctures between very different types of texts, all under the rubric of Esoteric Buddhism, have also been studied by modern scholars using techniques of comparative philology and textual criticism.[5] Linguistic methods are particularly effective in differentiating layers within a single text which were written at separate times and later joined together. Unfortunately, such studies are often hampered by having to work with redactions of texts which were refashioned centuries after the time they were originally composed, or with translations into Tibetan or Chinese of texts which no longer survive in Middle Indic or Sanskrit languages.[6] David Snellgrove has summed up the difficulties of precisely dating Esoteric Buddhist texts:

> *It is also generally known that to date any sūtra or tantra with certainty is practically impossible, because most of them continued to change and develop over long periods of time, and the most that can be done is to date them at a particular stage of development when they happened to be translated into Chinese, or by such references as may be made to them during clearly recorded periods of Tibetan history.*[7]

Even a group of texts which can be placed in rough chronological order constitute unevenly spaced points along a complex line of development. Greater or lesser gaps remain unmapped. A corpus of texts cannot represent a continuous progression, but only stranded markers of quantum leaps of development. Within the voids, works of art are waiting to be recovered and interrogated.

There are hundreds of sculptures and paintings with Esoteric Buddhist themes preserved from South Asia between the seventh and the twelfth centuries. As long as it is granted that works of art carry intelligible meaning, an art historical analysis of the archaeological record can provide a valuable complement to uneven textual evidence. As Edward Conze, the late doyen of Indian Mahāyāna Buddhist textual studies, comments, "To the historian everything is precious that may help him to trace the often obscure development of Indian religious thought between 600 and 1200 AD."[8]

When ideas — which may or may not be recorded in texts — have become so well-accepted by one or another part of the Esoteric Buddhist tradition that they have been given visual form, we have unimpeachable evidence that those ideas were held at a specific place and time. This can contribute to the corrective project Gregory Schopen has initiated by replacing the ready acceptance of what a few people may have *thought* with what groups actually *did*. The replacement forces us to go beyond the preoccupation of historians of religions "with what small, literate, almost exclusively male and certainly atypical professionalized subgroups wrote."[9] By making use of art in the way Schopen uses donative inscriptions, we can also make note of local variations which did not become visually or textually canonical. Most importantly, we can follow the maturation and dissemination of ideas in ways that textual evidence will not permit us to do.

The evidence of art may be useful, but it is discouraging in its very abundance. Some order must be imposed on its disorienting richness before it can shed light on the development of Esoteric Buddhism. Particular Esoteric Buddhist themes may be grouped systematically to organize the mass of material left by the exigencies of chance survival. The second-level order imposed by thematic grouping, however, should not be merely an artificial system which reveals meaning only in ways which would have been irrelevant or tangential to the aims of the creators. In order to consider the treatment which the theme receives over time, the theme must be continuously present in every period under examination.

Beyond these rather practical constraints, it is essential that the theme selected as a focus be in the nature of an "operative metaphor."[10] While it need not be the single dominant trope, it should be at least what Mircea Eliade points to when he notes the capacity of symbols to express paradoxical situations and structures of ultimate reality;[11] in other words, an integrative symbol as opposed to a subsidiary symbol. A homologous notion is what in art historical studies has been referred to as "symbolic form,"[12] or, necessarily, an *interpretable* paradigm.[13] The vehicle of meaning must reveal certain fundamental attitudes and developmental phenomena or structures ("processes"), while on the local scale it describes the diverse incidences of individual events that embody existential events: the macro-process on a microcosmic scale (i.e., a "pattern").[14]

As embodiments of the "demonic divine," wrathful deities provide just such an appropriate perspective from which to study change in the development of Esoteric Buddhism and to explore its doctrinal commitments. The wrathful deities are present from the sixth to seventh centuries, the very beginning of the period in which Esoteric Buddhist sculptures appear in South Asia. The theme has formal and doctrinal connections with Mahāyāna, early Buddhism and non-Buddhist imagery. It endures without hiatus throughout the period of Esoteric Buddhism in India, at least until the end of the twelfth century. The deities were important enough to occur in all of the cultures outside of India which received Esoteric Buddhist transmission of texts, images, doctrines and rituals; that is, in China and Japan, in Southeast Asia and in Mongolia, Tibet and Nepal.

While the wrathful deity theme can be identified in hundreds of works of art, it is not present in all art which may be considered Esoteric Buddhist in inspiration. This absence works in a positive way, serving to limit the scope of inquiry without narrowing it excessively. The "demonic-divine" theme is compatible with surviving texts which can be used to unpack the wrathful symbolic form. Most importantly, the theme allows us to witness distinct changes over periods in the treatment of the subject matter, in ways which are meaningful and consistent with textual traditions assigned to the same period through other types of evidence. The wrathful deity theme is an extremely sensitive marker of doctrinal change because its significance continues to be reformulated along with Esoteric Buddhism itself. The coherence between the evolution reflected in imagery and in surviving texts seems to belie Bharati's observation that there was "no modification of icons, but constant elaboration of philosophical concepts."[15]

The perception that icons were scarcely modified actually sets into relief the usefulness of the wrathful deity compared to other potential themes. The Buddha image, for instance, has proved to be a suitable topic for general surveying of Buddhism,[16] but is not sufficiently distinctive to Esoteric Buddhism. The special form known as the "adorned Buddha" is a topic which stands in clear need of study with greater reference to extant images. Moreover, the adorned Buddha does seem to be one of the defining characteristics of the Esoteric Buddhist visual program. The central issue in the case of the adorned Buddha, however, is essentially one of dating its origin and cataloguing the settings in which it occurs. The image itself underwent little change once it appeared in the late seventh or eighth century in both India and China. The textual problems and iconographic meanings have been studied in some depth by Paul Mus and others.[17] Scholars generally seem to have agreed that adornment of crown and jewelry "are emblematic of the Buddha's spiritual kingship, reflecting the ritualistic elements of royal consecration ceremonies practiced in Vajrayāna Buddhism."[18]

The bodhisattva image in general, or individual bodhisattva such as Mañjuśrī, Avalokiteśvara, Ākāśagarbha, Maitreya and Vajrapāṇi, would seem to be fruitful topics of study.[19] Once again, however, the bodhisattva are by no means associated with Esoteric Buddhism in any exclusive sense, and a study of any one of them, however valuable, must cover a great deal of ground outside the realm of Esoteric Buddhism. The wrathful deity theme proves to be much more efficient in profiling the distinct character of evolving Esoteric Buddhism.

One of the primary defining characteristics of Esoteric Buddhism, at least in its later South Asian variety, is its "polarity symbolism." The sexual content of this symbolism has generated a great deal of controversy, which is still not resolved. Scholarship has tended to fit into three principal camps with regard to images or textual descriptions of a deity embracing his consort. The first confines itself to expressions of abhorrence and disgust with a tradition which would deem such images religious. The second interprets sexual imagery purely as philosophical metaphors, while the third insists that it reflects actual practices of Esoteric Buddhists.[20] As appropriate as sexual imagery may be as an integrating symbol for Esoteric Buddhism, its appearance in both texts and art is extremely limited in South Asia before the emergence of the third stage of Esoteric Buddhism. In earlier stages of the tradition, notably those which were imported into China and Japan before the mid-ninth century, polarity symbolism is only implicit. Historical data suggest that sexual imagery is a later development and therefore this particular aspect is less fruitful for the study of Esoteric Buddhism's overall development.

It has been persuasively argued that the *maṇḍala* is the ultimate defining and integrating symbol of Esoteric Buddhism.[21] There is considerable valildity in that thesis. It is not a practical theme to take up in an investigation of the visual remains of Esoteric Buddhism, however, because except for a few ninth-century East Asian painted *maṇḍala* and a tiny sample of unusual sculpted ones no *maṇḍala* survive from before the tenth or eleventh century. Therefore a study of *maṇḍala* will either depend on written texts from before the tenth century, or will be confined to the later periods of Esoteric Buddhism.[22]

The wrathful deity theme by contrast has much to recommend it. Its importance will become fully apparent only as the evidence unfolds. It is nonetheless not out of place here to demonstrate the centrality of the wrathful deity to the later forms of Esoteric Buddhism. In his discussion of the texts of the later period, known as *anuttara yoga tantra*, Giuseppe Tucci writes, "Nearly all the Tantras of the Anuttara class centre round the symbol of Akṣobhya or of his hypostases: Heruka, Hevajra, Guhyasamāja."[23] This is significant. Tucci has observed that the important texts and images of the later period put at the very center of their teachings, not the historical Buddha, not cosmic Buddha forms, not the popular bodhisattva, but wrathful deities such as Hevajra and Heruka (also known as Saṃvara). Saṃvara, Hevajra and Caṇḍamahāroṣaṇa along with another wrathful lord, Kālacakra, have elaborate ritual texts named after them which feature them at the center of complex *maṇḍala*.[24]

Others have also noted the position of centrality of wrathful deities in the history of Esoteric Buddhism and its art. R.A. Ray observes that "the integration and hierarchical arrangement of [the *maṇḍala*'s] terrible deities [indicates] not only their fundamental importance to the Tantric process of transformation, but also the different stages of awareness bound up with this process."[25] According to P.H. Pott, one of the two significant and distinctive aspects of Mahāyāna iconography is "the demonizing of its most effective figures."[26] Stephen Beyer has likewise taken note of the paramount position of the later forms of the wrathful deity class:

> *[T]hey belong to the type of Heruka — multitudinous arms bearing attributes of power and ferocity, three-eyed faces distorted in scowls of rage . . . . These Herukas are perhaps the most potent and symbolically evocative of all the Tibetan deities.*[27]

In his treatment of the career of one wrathful deity, Étienne Lamotte states that "Vajrapāṇi in the end rose to the summit of metaphysical reality and acceded to the rank of the supreme being."[28]

It may be argued, then, that the wrathful deity is one of the central paradigms of *late* Esoteric Buddhism. Yet wrathful deities like Vajrapāṇi did not start out competing with the Buddha for the central position. We find in the phase immediately preceding the culminating period that the wrathful deity plays an important but not always central role. During the earliest period his role is definitely subsidiary. Yet even then he is consistently present. Therefore the theme satisfies the requirements of both consistency and volatility and can thus reflect meaningful change over time.

The theme of the wrathful deity in Esoteric Buddhist art has additional advantages in the project of clarifying the history of Esoteric Buddhism. A number of studies over the last seventy years have elucidated the evolution of specific wrathful deities within the Esoteric Buddhist system. For example, Robert Duquenne has illuminated the career of one of this group, known as Yamāntaka.[29] He has made use of Indian Sanskritic as well as Chinese and Japanese sources. Similar analyses of South Asian, Tibetan and East Asian texts have been produced by Robert van Gulik for the horse-necked wrathful deity Hayagrīva, by Lamotte and Lalou for Vajra-pāṇi, by Iyanaga Nobumi for Trailokyavijaya, by Frédéric A. Bischoff for Ucchusma-Mahābala and Roger Goepper for Aizen-Myōō.[30] In addition, there have been recent translations of a number of texts dealing with various wrathful deities.[31] All of these sources, along with the studies of the ritual cycles of Saṃvara, Caṇḍamahāroṣaṇa and Hevajra mentioned above, provide a solid foundation for the study of this class of deities.

Given the recent strides made in this area, it is perhaps now an overstatement to say with Ray that "Unlike the problem of sexual symbolism, Tantric Buddhist horrific symbolism has received, as Pott has noted, hardly any attention at all in Western interpretations of the tradition."[32] Nevertheless, since few of the previous studies have made more than incidental use of actual images, it is still very much a productive area for research.

Finally, the theme of the wrathful deities, apart from its value for the historical study of Esoteric Buddhism, is of interest in other ways for the history of religion, ideas and art. The forms found in Esoteric Buddhist images seem to share a great deal with other traditions of the "grotesque" in that as a "species of confusion" they violate the expectations of reason and natural order.[33] The grotesque is often occupied with the transgression of the boundaries between the sacred and the profane and appears in a number of other religious and secular traditions.[34] What is rather unique to these wrathful deities is that Esoteric Buddhism has infused forms which are expressly violent and threatening (and, at least to the unfamiliar, troubling and offensive[35]) with divine rather than demonic significance. They do not represent merely the darker, destructive side of nature. Instead, by fusing an outer expression of malevolence with an inner valency of compassion, they enfold chaos into the sacred. The are visual expressions of the *coincidentia oppositorum*. For the adept, the fusion paralyzes or transcends dichotomizing cognition, and dualism is subverted. Thus fundamental questions concerning the nature and function of images of the holy are brought into relief by these works.

In this context there is no question of attempting an analysis of the greater "demonic-divine" category as a pattern of human thought and experience. However, it is my hope that by disclosing the main structural outlines of one particular set of expressions — that of eastern Indian Esoteric Buddhism — this work will contribute materials which the historian of religion can at some future time integrate into a broader study.

The present research, then, is a systematic study of the images of wrathful deities in the Esoteric Buddhist art of eastern India. It utilizes prior studies, along with a number of primary sources in the form of texts translated into Chinese in the eighth and ninth centuries.[36] The most important primary sources, however, are a large stock of wrathful deity images compiled on three continents over the past fifteen years. From a narrowly aesthetic point of view, only a few might be considered "masterpieces." Many are fragmentary and of mediocre quality, yet we can still readily recover from them information of considerable historical value.[37] Most are sculptures, which were located, studied and photographed in eastern India. Despite their uneven quality from a technical point of view, the images gathered here represent a nearly continuous record from the seventh through the twelfth centuries. Passages of relevant texts translated into Chinese in the seventh, eighth and ninth centuries bearing on the subject are related to contemporary South Asian images. Early western Tibetan images are also utilized to a lesser extent to solidify the dates of the predominance of one phase over another and to provide a context which rarely survives elsewhere. A total of more than one hundred and fifty images of wrathful deities dating between the sixth and thirteenth centuries creates a collection of visual data of both local and general value.[38]

Together these materials will allow us to survey the development of the class of deities as a whole. We can document their rise in importance from subsidiary deities with roots in non-Buddhist imagery to their height of independence, which rivals the Buddha in terms of immediacy and status within praxis. A continuous narrative emerges from the systematic analysis of extant visual images. These are supplemented by inscriptions and texts which allow for the identification and interpretation of individual images.

With this narrative history of the wrathful deities in place, we can propose a model of the historical development of Esoteric Buddhism itself. This model is then superimposed on the model emerging primarily from textual studies. We will see that the two models coincide in broad outlines. The artistic record fills in gaps in the textual model but fails to reflect certain distinctions made in the scriptural model. There are also a number of interesting temporal disparities between the two models which call attention to the need for a refinement in the periodization of Esoteric Buddhist movements. The disparities recall Oleg Grabar's distinction between absolute and relative time, between the time of events and cultural time.[39] In our case we must distinguish when an idea is formulated and recorded among a localized group of initiates, and when that idea is accepted on a broader scale within the tradition. It is dangerous to give a date to an Esoteric Buddhist movement when that date derives solely from the earliest layer of its most important texts or commentators. Works of art may prove to be better historical markers than texts in such cases.

The primary purpose of this work is to systematically discover patterns within the group of wrathful deity images, identify these patterns along coordinates of time and geography, disclose the relationships between the patterns and reconcile the results with what is already known about the historical and doctrinal development of Esoteric Buddhism. On this basis, a model is generated and analyzed for its potential for integrating new information of different natures.

In sum, to paraphrase R.A. Ray's prediction by substituting the phrase "wrathful deity" for "*maṇḍala*," the "central importance of the [wrathful deity] through the long history of the Vajrayāna is such that, at some future time, it may prove possible to write a detailed history of the Diamond Vehicle through detailing the changes and transformations undergone by the [wrathful deity] image."[40] Notwithstanding an awareness of my own linguistic and conceptual inadequacies, the present work represents an attempt to do just that.

Geographic and Temporal Parameters

At this point it may be appropriate to briefly outline the spread of Esoteric Buddhism, at least for the cultural areas which provide relevant images for this study. To begin with India, it is apparent from texts and from concentrations of archaeological remains that Esoteric Buddhism found a home in the monastic institutions of eastern India during the period of the eighth century through the twelfth or thirteenth century, after which Indian Buddhism declined sharply.[41] These monastic centers sponsored a significant share of the surviving Esoteric Buddhist art, alongside more conventional Mahāyāna art. Bihar and Bengal were the most prominent, and Orissa is increasingly recognized as an important site of Esoteric Buddhist activity.[42]

Most of the South Asian objects presented here come from eastern India (i.e., modern Bihar, Bengal, Orissa). The majority of them are stone stele, "the medium most commonly met with in the art of eastern India."[43] They are currently located either in museums or excavation sites. These include the collections of the major museums in New Delhi, Lucknow, Sarnath, Patna, Calcutta and Bhubaneswar, as well as many large and small sites in Bihar and Orissa, the larger ones including Bodh Gaya, Nalanda, Sarnath, Ratnagiri, Udayagiri and Lalitagiri. The concentration of wrathful deity images available for study there justifies eastern India's importance for this subject.

Field work was concentrated in eastern India and in Indian Tibet (Ladakh, Zanskar, Spiti), though it was also conducted in Nepal and in Maharashtra, at Aurangabad, Ellora and Kanheri, not to mention East and Southeast Asia. However, it is well known that Esoteric Buddhism spread through a wide area of South Asia. This is illustrated in a very concrete way by the fact that *dhāranī* inscriptions have been recovered from different sites in Bengal, Bihar and also northwest India, all deriving from the same or similar texts.[44] Other areas of India, notably Kashmir and southern and western India, also participated to some degree in the development of Esoteric Buddhism.

There are a number of indications in the textual record that major centers were located in the south of India and in Sri Lanka.[45] The Tibetan historian of Esoteric Buddhism, Tāranātha, mentions Dramil (Tamil), while inferences from the Tamil epic *Manimekalai* have suggested to some the influence of Esoteric Buddhism.[46] Līlapa, Nāgārjuna and perhaps others of the eighty-four Mahāsiddhas were originally from southern India.[47] There are also numerous references to South India and Sri Lanka in the biographies of the three major Esoteric Buddhist masters who came to China in the eighth century. Unfortunately, very little in the way of material artifacts remains to support this tradition, although such "late" deities as Heruka, Tārā and Ugra-Tārā were recovered at Amaravati in southeast India.[48] An inscription on an image of Prajñāpāramitā in a style of the ninth or tenth century found at Nalanda which records the gift of a man from Karnataka[49] also underscores the connection between South India and Esoteric Buddhism, albeit indirectly. Von Schroeder has recently gathered together textual and visual data for Mahāyāna and Esoteric Buddhism in Sri Lanka. Despite the textual and inscriptional evidence for a significant if limited presence of Esoteric Buddhism there, the extant images are precious but few.[50] Whatever its role may have been, because of the dearth of visual material, the south can play very little part in this study.

Western Indian cave sites are now being interpreted as early Esoteric Buddhist sites. In particular, Geri H. Malandra has studied the Buddhist caves at Ellora in Maharashtra. The caves date to the seventh and eighth centuries, and she concludes, "Ellora is a remarkably rich resource for the study of early Tantric Buddhist iconography."[51] Caves Six and Seven at Aurangabad, datable to the late sixth or seventh century, have also recently been reinterpreted as early Esoteric Buddhist sites.[52] The western Indian cave sites of Ellora, Aurangabad and Ajanta, however, did not continue to be sites for the production of mature Esoteric Buddhist art. While they are generally fertile fields for the early development of Esoteric Buddhist art, one cannot follow a single theme through a long period of time. Thus their value as comparative material in the development of wrathful deities is restricted to the early period.

The present study also includes images from Kashmir, which was an important center of Buddhism, although "documentation is strangely lacking for study of the strictly historic aspect of this problem."[53] Surviving images, mostly metal sculptures of middle and late period Esoteric Buddhist wrathful deities, are particularly numerous.[54] Kashmir was also important because of the regard in which it was held among Buddhists along the land route to China, at such Central Asian centers as Khotan and Dunhuang. Kashmiri Esoteric Buddhist masters and artists were also critical for the transmission of Esoteric Buddhism to Tibet.[55]

After a severe persecution of Buddhism in Tibet in the mid-ninth century, Yeshe Ö, king of western Tibet, sent a mission to Kashmir in the late tenth century. In good measure due to the efforts of Rinchen Zangpo (958-1055 CE), one of the mission's returning members, Esoteric Buddhism was again ascendant in western Tibet. In Ladakh temple sites like Alchi, Sumda and Mangyu house rare *maṇḍala* paintings featuring wrathful deities which date to the twelfth or early thirteenth century.[56] They can be associated with Rinchen Zangpo's school and bear distinct Kashmiri stylistic and iconographic features.[57] The results obtained through field work will play a role in the present study.

In the middle of the eleventh century, Atiśa (982-1054) came to western Tibet and became Rinchen Zangpo's teacher.[58] He brought with him the doctrinal innovations associated with the legendary Mahāsiddhas of eastern India. He was also a highly respected senior monk who had links with the major monasteries of eastern India, including Nalanda and Vikramaśila. Moreover, he represents the wider, nearly global, perspective of Esoteric Buddhism. Atiśa is recorded as having left India in 1012, returning in 1025. During the intervening years he studied with an Esoteric Buddhist master in Suvarnadvipa. The exact location of Suvarnadvipa is still a matter for debate, but it is most likely in Sumatra and at any rate was within the large Southeast Asian maritime empire known as Srivijaya.[59] Atiśa thus also represents the movement of Esoteric Buddhist practice and imagery into West and central Tibet from eastern India.[60]

Although East Asian Esoteric Buddhist art is not included in the present work, I have made extensive use of the texts transmitted from India and translated and preserved in China and Japan. A sketch of the history of Esoteric Buddhism in East Asia may be helpful here. Interest in South Asian proto-Tantric or *zomitsu* ("diffuse esotericism") texts is attested in China from the fifth century.[61] The introduction of early mature Esoteric Buddhism into China took place in the late seventh and early eighth centuries.[62] Several Chinese pilgrims went to India to study, bringing back Esoteric Buddhist texts and, we must assume, images.[63] Yijing's *Gaoseng zhuan* commemorates fifty-six Chinese and Korean Buddhist monks who left China for India in the seventh century,[64] and there is no reason to believe that the flow of Buddhist travelers slackened in the next century. The systematic beginnings of Esoteric Buddhism in China, however, revolve around the work of several charismatic Esoteric Buddhist masters who came to China from South Asia, where they had studied at such important centers as Nalanda and Vikramaśila.[65] During the eighth and the first half of the ninth centuries, Esoteric Buddhism received the patronage of the Tang Dynasty emperors and high officials at court.[66] The court financed Esoteric Buddhist art of great quality, which prominently features wrathful deities.[67]

Following a severe persecution of Buddhism between 842 and 845 CE, Esoteric Buddhist activities in China were extremely restricted. South Asian texts continued to be translated in the tenth and eleventh centuries, though the texts were not promulgated nor their rituals widely practiced.[68] In a few pockets, mostly on the fringes of China, Esoteric Buddhist ideas continued to have a certain influence and crop up in later Chinese art, as at the Mogao caves at Dunhuang.[69] Such is the case in Yunnan into the twelfth century, and a number of wrathful images in painting and sculpture survive from that milieu.[70] In the territories of western China ruled by the Tangut Xia (1038-1227 CE) and by the Mongols during the Yuan Dynasty (1260-1367 CE), there was a reintroduction of Esoteric Buddhist themes into China under the auspices of the Tibetans. Not only are there Esoteric Buddhist murals painted during that time at Dunhuang, but at other sites in western China as well, in northern China at the Feilai Feng near Hangzhou, and even in central coastal China.[71]

While still riding a tide of imperial patronage in China during the early ninth century, Esoteric Buddhism was brought to Japan. The most important Japanese monk in this process was Kūkai, or Kōbō Daishi, as he was titled after his death in 835 CE.[72] Esoteric Buddhism found a permanent home in Japan under the name of Shingon ("True Word," i.e., *mantra*).[73] Its character was shaped by two factors: first, the stage of Indian Esoteric Buddhism which Japan received through China in the ninth century; and second, reformulations in China and Japan. The Indian basis is recognizable, especially in artistic products of the early centuries (i.e., the ninth to twelfth centuries).

There is therefore justification in using East Asian texts to amplify the South Asian textual record for the purpose of interpreting Esoteric Buddhist developments in South Asia. In turn, clarification of the early history of Esoteric Buddhism in India will shed light on the patterns inherited by East Asian practitioners. Both Robert Buswell and R.A. Stein have pointed out the importance of comprehensive approaches that transcend national traditions.[74] It is hoped that the present work will be of use to those interested in both sides of the transmission.

The Schematic Model

> *[I]n order to draw a general outline of the history of Tantrik ideas in Buddhist literature and life, we must disregard the traditional divisions as embodied in the Tibetan catalogues or the Western theories on the subject and build a classification of our own.*
>
> Louis de La Vallée Poussin, "Tantrism"

I define the Esoteric Buddhist group of deities that I label *krodha-vighnāntaka* on the basis of a fundamental expressive characteristic (*krodha*, wrathfulness) and a primary identifying function (*vighnāntaka*, destroyer of obstacles). The members of this group share the aspect of wrath with other types of deities within the Buddhist pantheon, such as the *dvārapāla* gate guardians, the Lokapāla (guardians of the four directions) and the *dharmapāla* protectors. The *krodha-vighnāntaka* group may also be charged with the same functions as these groups. However, the *krodha-vighnāntaka* group is entrusted with additional functions and attains a higher status. These added functions involve "inner and outer practices," destroying both the inner obstacles to enlightenment (greed, anger, sloth, etc.) and demonic projections which attack the meditator with diseases of mind and body.

The first artists to depict the *krodha-vighnāntaka* in the sixth century in India drew on prior depictions of Yakṣa, *āyudhapuruṣa* (personified attributes, such as Viṣṇu's wheel, Śiva's trident) and Śiva-Gaṇa (Śiva's auspicious dwarf attendants). The Yakṣa image as it appears in early Buddhist art was the ultimate source for the image of the *krodha-vighnāntaka*. Two types of Yakṣa images were created: the dwarfish, big-bellied type (here called *vāmana*-Yakṣa), and the heroic warrior type (here known as *vīra*-Yakṣa). Following this twin tradition, the *krodha-vighnāntaka* are also found in both forms, though the *vāmana*-Yakṣa body-type is more common in the early period of Esoteric Buddhist art in India.

Analysis of the images reveals large-scale patterns in the course of development of the *krodha-vighnāntaka*, suggesting three main phases which I argue correspond closely to the historical stages of Esoteric Buddhism. They will be treated separately in Sections One through Three. The origins of the three stages may be considered diachronically, though after the eighth century Phase One and Two are contemporaneous, and after the tenth century all three are contiguous. Nevertheless, one may say that Phase One dominates the period between the late sixth to the eighth centuries, Phase Two presides from roughly the eighth to the late tenth century and Phase Three from the late tenth century through to the twelfth.

Phase One

The Phase One *krodha-vighnāntaka* is subordinated to a bodhisattva, who is worshipped with offerings and *dhāraṇī*-prayers for specific ends, such as the removal of misfortune. [2] The *krodha-vighnāntaka* performs tasks like gathering together sentient beings to whom the bodhisattva preaches, subduing rowdy elements, or personifying attributes of the bodhisattva, such as his adamantine wisdom or the power of his voice. This phase has links to the traditional Tibetan classification of *kriyā tantra* (action tantras; rites of magic) and *caryā tantra* (performance tantras; rites of religious practice) and can be related to the *trikula* (three family) system. Phase One grows directly out of orthodox Mahāyāna belief and practice, making it difficult to distinguish the two. Important texts for this phase which are discussed in relation to the *krodha-vighnāntaka* are the *Mañjuśrīmūlakalpa* (*MMK*) and the *Mahāvairocana ābhisambodhi sūtra* (*MVS*, transitional between Phases One and Two) as well as a number of minor texts translated into Chinese in the seventh and eighth centuries. The first is the most enduring phase, continuing into the twelfth century in India, by which time it had been transmitted to Nepal, Tibet, Southeast Asia and to a lesser degree East Asia. Because of the length of time over which Phase One images were produced, the *krodha-vighnāntaka* image can be followed through several stages of growth, florescence and finally stylization accompanied by diminished importance. The principal Phase One *krodha-vighnāntaka* deities whose careers are followed here are Hayagrīva, Yamāntaka, Mahābala, and Vajrapuruṣa.

2. *Avalokiteśvara with Hayagrīva, Ratnagiri (Orissa), ca. 9th century*

Phase Two

Particular members of the Phase Two *krodha-vighnāntaka* group become important independent images, often with their own attendants, or are fitted into centrally-ordered schemes of deities (i.e., *maṇḍala*). [3] Throughout this period the *krodha-vighnāntaka* himself performs the tasks of conversion, aversion of misfortune and destruction of obstacles. The wrathful deities are no longer paired off in a subordinate relationship with a bodhisattva; they now correspond to one or another aspect of the Five Directional Buddhas, either one of the five wisdoms or each Buddha's "commanding power." Some Phase Two *krodha-vighnāntaka* appeared earlier in Phase One imagery, but others are new creations. Phase Two may be compared with the traditional Tibetan classification of *yoga tantra* (Yoga tantras; rites of yoga), and can be related to the development of the *pañcakula* (five family) system. Important texts for this phase include the *MVS*, the *Sarvatathāgata Tattvasaṃgrha* (*STTS*), the *Sarvadurgatipariśodhana* (*SDPS*), and sections of the *Guhyasamāja Tantra*, as well as a number of minor texts translated into Chinese in the eighth century. The principal Phase Two *krodha-vighnāntaka* deities whose careers are followed here are Yamāntaka and Vajrapāṇi-Trailokyavijaya.

3. *Trailokyavijaya , Achutrajpur (Orissa), ca. 10th century*

Phase Three

The Phase Three *krodha-vighnāntaka* ranks together with the Buddha among the most important deities in Esoteric Buddhism. He is considered a form of the Buddha who plays a more prominent role in Esoteric Buddhist art than the historical Buddha. The *krodha-vighnāntaka* appears at the center of the dominant *maṇḍala* cycles. As such he supplants both the bodhisattva and the Buddha as the primary *yidam*, or initiatory deity. The *krodha-vighnāntaka* embodies the enlightenment and all the power of the Buddha and, further, the supreme bliss and reality itself. Most of the Phase Three *krodha-vighnāntaka* have new identities which at a deep level are reformulations of Phase Two deities in Phase Three terms. The third phase correlates with the traditional Tibetan classification of *anuttara yoga tantra* (supreme yoga tantras), and its formation had close links with the Hindu tantric *śmaśāna* (cemetery) cult. Important texts for this phase are the *Hevajra Tantra* and the *Saṁvarodaya Tantra*. Outside of Tibetan-inspired instances under the Tanguts, Mongols and Manchus, this phase did not exercise much influence in China or Japan, though some of its texts were translated into Chinese in the late tenth and eleventh centuries. The principal Phase Three *krodha-vighnāntaka* deities whose careers are followed here are Heruka [4], Hevajra, and Saṃvara.

4. *Heruka, Ratnagiri (Orissa), ca. 11th century*

The tripartite outline demonstrates that the *krodha-vighnāntaka* deities have undergone a radical development in tandem with Esoteric Buddhism itself, which gradually began to infuse the *krodha-vighnāntaka* deities with greater meaning. This development is reflected graphically in artistic representations.

The conceptual model is derived from the study of wrathful deity images, which will proceed as follows. The introduction investigates terminology used for this class of deities. It also defines the identity of the group in contradistinction to other groups of deities with partially overlapping functions and formal appearance. The chapters of Section One focus on the evolution of Phase One *krodha-vighnāntaka* imagery, following the careers of four of its members. Two important issues dealt with in the course of this section are a) the origins of the forms used for Phase One wrathful deities in earlier Buddhist, Brahmanical, and cultic art; and b) the religious context of mixed Mahāyāna-Esoteric Buddhism in which Phase One images are found. The chapters of Section Two deal with Phase Two images, and Section Three treats Phase Three wrathful deities. In the Afterword I compare the historical model based on the *krodha-vighnāntaka* material with other models of Esoteric Buddhism and summarize the results of the investigation.

Notes to Prologue

1 J.W. De Jong, "A Brief History of Buddhist Studies in Europe and America," *Eastern Buddhist* 7, no. 2 (1974): 74. (Indian reprint, 2nd revised edition, Delhi, 1987).

2 Marcelle Lalou, *Iconographie des Étoffes Peintes (Pata) dans le Mañjuśrīmūlakalpa* (Paris, 1930).

3 The appropriation of cultural objects in modern educational and art institutions and their transformation into art objects in the modern sense (the "museum effect") is far beyond the scope of this work. Recent thoughtful attempts to grapple with this issue are found in Steven D. Lavine and Ivan Karp, eds., *Exhibiting Cultures: The Poetics and Politics of Museum Display* (Washington, 1991); Philip Fisher, *Making and Effacing Art: Modern American Art in a Culture of Museums* (New York: Oxford University Press, 1991); James Clifford, *The Predicament of Culture* (Cambridge, 1988); Clifford Geertz, "Art as a Cultural System," in *Local Knowledge: Further Essays in Interpretive Anthropology* (New York, 1983), 94-120; Stanley Abe, "Inside the Wonder House: Buddhist Art and the West," in *Curators of the Buddha: The Study of Buddhism under Colonialism*, ed. Donald S. Lopez, Jr. (Chicago: University of Chicago Press, 1995), 63-106; Bernard S. Cohn, "The Transformation of Objects into Artifacts, Antiquities, and Art in Nineteenth-Century India," in *Colonialism and Its Forms of Knowledge: The British in India* (Princeton: Princeton University Press, 1996), 76-105.

4 There is a preoccupation with written records on the part of historians of religion as well. As S.G.F. Brandon observes, "The importance of such literary evidence is not to be minimized; but the almost exclusive attention given to it has resulted in a serious neglect of the witness of art and ritual." *Man and God in Art and Ritual: A Study of Iconography, Architecture and Ritual Action as Primary Evidence of Religious Belief and Practice* (New York, 1975), ix. For the predisposition among scholars to privilege texts over archaeological data, see Gregory Schopen, "Archaeology and Protestant Presuppositions in the Study of Indian Buddhism," *History of Religions* 31, no.1 (1991): 1-23.

5 See E.J. Kenney, "Textual Criticism," *The New Encyclopædia Britannica 15th ed.* (1974) Vol. 18: 189-195; Edward Hobbs, "Prologue: An Introduction to Methods of Textual Criticism," in *The Critical Study of Sacred Texts*, ed. Wendy Doniger O'Flaherty (Berkeley, 1979), 1-27. For an introduction to the special problems of Buddhist texts, see Lewis Lancaster, "Buddhist Literature: Its Canons, Scribes, and Editors," ibid., 215-229.

6 The value of Tibetan translations in reconstructing the wording of a lost Sanskrit original and of Chinese translations for their faithful preservation of content is discussed in Lewis R. Lancaster, "The Editing of Buddhist Texts," in *Buddhist Thought and Asian Civilization: Essays in Honor of Herbert V. Guenther on His Sixtieth Birthday* (Emeryville, 1977), 145-151. For the difficulties in editing Indian Buddhist texts not in "classical" Sanskrit, see John Brough, "The Language of the Buddhist Sanskrit Texts," *Bulletin of the School of Oriental and African Studies* 16 (1954): 351-375.

7 David L. Snellgrove, "Categories of Buddhist Tantras," *Orientalia Iosephi Tucci Memoriae Dicata* (Rome, 1988) 3:1382.

8 Edward Conze, "Tantric Prajñāpāramitā Texts," *Sino-Indian Studies* 5 (1956): 101.

9 Gregory Schopen, *Bones, Stones, and Buddhist Monks: Collected Papers on the Archaeology, Epigraphy, and Texts of Monastic Buddhism in India* (Honolulu: University of Hawaii, 1997), 114; see also 30.

10 Michel Foucault, *Madness and Civilization: A History of Insanity in the Age of Reason*, trans. Richard Howard (New York, 1973), 169.

11 Mircea Eliade, "Methodological Remarks on the Study of Religious Symbolism," in *The History of Religions: Essays in Methodology*, ed. Mircea Eliade and Joseph M. Kitagawa (Chicago, 1959), 101.

12 Erwin Panofsky, "Iconography and Iconology: An Introduction to the Study of Renaissance Art," in *Meaning in the Visual Arts* (Chicago, 1955), 26-54; idem, *Perspective as Symbolic Form* (New York, 1991).

13 Clifford Geertz, "Religion As a Cultural System," Chapter 4 in *The Interpretation of Cultures* (New York, 1973), 100; idem, "Art as a Cultural System," 118. Paradigm used in this sense is analogous to its use in Thomas S. Kuhn, *The Structure of Scientific Revolutions*, 2nd enlarged ed. (Chicago, 1970).

14 Edward Farmer et al, *Comparative History of Civilizations in Asia*, 2 vols. (Menlo Park, 1977), xix-xx.

15 Agehananda Bharati, *The Tantric Tradition* (London, 1965; Indian ed., New Delhi, 1976), 24.

16 See Pratapaditya Pal, ed., *Light of Asia: Buddha Sakyamuni in Asian Art* (Los Angeles, 1984); and, David Snellgrove, ed., *The Image of the Buddha* (Paris, 1978).

17 See Paul Mus, "Le buddha paré, son origine indienne, Cakyamuni dans le Mahayanisme moyen," *Bulletin de l'École Française d'Extrême-Orient* 28 (1928): 1-2, 153-278; Dorothy H. Fickle, "Crowned Buddha Images in Southeast Asia," in *Art and Archaeology in Thailand* (Bangkok, 1974), 85-120; and, Amy Heller, "Early Ninth Century Images of Vairochana from Eastern Tibet," *Orientations* 25, no. 6 (1994): 74-79.

18 Pal, *Light of Asia*, 106. Also see David Snellgrove, "The Notion of Divine Kingship in Tantric Buddhism," in *Studies in the History of Religions, no. 4: Sacral Kingship* (Leiden, 1959), 204-218.

19 See Raoul Birnbaum, *Studies on the Mysteries of Mañjuśrī: A Group of East Asian Maṇḍalas and their Traditional Symbolism*, Society for the Study of Chinese Religions, Monograph no. 2 (Boulder, 1983); R. A. Stein, "Avalokiteśvara/Kouan-Yin: Exemple de Transformation d'un Dieu en Déesse," *Cahiers d'Extrême-Asie* 2 (1986): 17-80; M.W. de Visser, *The Bodhisattva Akaśagarbha (Kokuzo) in China and Japan* (Amsterdam, 1931); Lee Yu-min, "The Maitreya Cult and its Art in Early China," (Ph.D. dissertation, Ohio State University, 1983); and, Étienne Lamotte, "Vajrapāṇi en Inde," *Mélanges de Sinologie offerts à Monsieur Paul Demiéville*, Bibliothèque de l'Institut des Hautes Études Chinoises, no. 20 (Paris, 1966), 113-161.

20 See David Snellgrove, *Indo-Tibetan Buddhism*, 2 vols. (Boston, 1987), 170-176; Reginald Alden Ray, "*Maṇḍala* Symbolism in Tantric Buddhism," (Ph.D. dissertation, University of Chicago, 1973), 185-190; and, Bharati, *Tantric Tradition*, 199-278.

21 Ray, "*Maṇḍala* Symbolism."

22 See Giuseppe Tucci, *The Theory and Practice of the Maṇḍala*, trans. A.H. Broderick (New York, 1969).

23 Giuseppe Tucci, *Tibetan Painted Scrolls* (Rome, 1949), 224.

24 Shinīchi Tsuda, *The Saṁvarodaya-Tantra: Selected Chapters* (Tokyo, 1974); Lama Kazi Dawa-Samdup, *Shrīchakrasaṁbhāra Tantra*, Tantrik Texts, vol. 7, gen. ed. Sir John Woodroffe (London, 1919); David Snellgrove, *The Hevajra Tantra*, 2 vols. (London, 1959); Christopher S. George, *The Caṇḍamahāroṣaṇa Tantra: A Critical Edition and English Translation, Chapters I-VIII*, American Oriental Series, no. 56 (New Haven, 1974); Mario E. Carelli, *Sekoddeśaṭikā of Nādapada (Nāropa)*, Gaekwad's Oriental Series, no. 90 (Baroda, 1941) for a study in English of a commentary on a section of the *Kālacakra Tantra;* H.H. the Dalai Lama, the Fourteenth, and Jeffrey Hopkins, *The Kālachakra Tantra: Rite of Initiation for the Stage of Generation* (London, 1985).

25 Ray, "*Maṇḍala* Symbolism," 194-195.

26 P.H. Pott, "Plural Forms of Buddhist Iconography," *India Antiqua* (Leyden, 1947), 284.

27 Stephen Beyer, *The Cult of Tārā* (Berkeley, 1973), 42.

28 Lamotte, "Vajrapāṇi en Inde," 149 (my translation from the French).

29 Robert Duquenne, "Daiitoku Myōō," in *Hōbōgirin: Dictionnaire Encyclopédique du Bouddhisme D'Après Les Sources Chinoises et Japonaises Fasc. 6: Da-Daijizaiten* (Tokyo/Paris, 1983), 652-670. Despite sophisticated studies like that of Duquenne and others, some contemporary scholars still dismiss the wrathful deities as "weird male and female icons." Debjani Paul, *The Art of Nālndā: Development of Buddhist Sculpture AD 600-1200* (New Delhi, 1995), 103.

30 See Robert van Gulik, *Hayagrīva: The Mantrayanic Aspect of Horse-cult in China and Japan* (Leiden, 1935); Lamotte, "Vajrapāṇi en Inde;" Marcelle Lalou, "Four Notes on Vajrapāṇi," *The Adyar Library Bulletin* 20 (1956):

287-293; idem, "A Fifth Note on Vajrapāṇi," *The Adyar Library Bulletin* 25 (1961): 242-249; Iyanaga Nobumi, "Recits de la soumission de Mahesvara par Trailokyavijaya," in *Tantric and Taoist Studies III*, ed. M. Strickmann (Brussels, 1985), 633-745; Frédéric A. Bischoff, *Ārya Mahābala-Nāma-Mahāyānasūtra, Tibétain (MSS. de Touen-Houang) et Chinois: Contribution à l'étude des divinités mineures du bouddhisme tantrique Buddhica, no.* 10 (Paris, 1956); and, Roger Goepper, *Aizen-Myōō, The Esoteric King of Lust: An Iconographic Study* (Zurich: Artibus Asiae, 1993).

31 Bulcsu Siklós, *The Vajrabhairava Tantras: Tibetan and Mongolian Versions, English Translation and Annotations* (Tring: The Institute of Buddhist Studies, 1996); Martin J. Boord, *The Cult of the Deity Vajrakīla: According to the Texts of the Northern Treasures Tradition of Tibet (Byang-gter phur-ba)* (Tring: The Institute of Buddhist Studies, 1993); and, Robert Mayer, *A Scripture of The Ancient Tantra Collection: The Phur-pa bcu-gnyis* (Oxford: Kiscadale Publications, 1996).

32 Ray, "*Maṇḍala* Symbolism," 191.

33 Geoffrey Harpham, *On the Grotesque: Strategies of Contradiction in Art and Literature* (Princeton, 1982).

34 E.H. Gombrich discusses "The Edge of Chaos" in *The Sense of Order* (Ithaca, 1979), 251-284.

35 This has misled many interpreters of Esoteric Buddhism. L. Austine Waddell, for instance, writes, "Each Lamaist sect has its own special tutelary fiend. . . . Even the purest of all the Lamaist sects . . . are thorough-paced devil-worshippers, and value Buddhism chiefly because it gives them the whip-hand over the devils which everywhere vex humanity with disease and disaster, and whose ferocity weighs heavily upon all." *Tibetan Buddhism, with Its Mystic Cults, Symbolism and Mythology* (reprint, New York: Dover, 1972), 152; first published in 1895 as *The Buddhism of Tibet, or Lamaism.*

36 Most of these have been edited from printed manuscripts and compiled in volumes 18-21 of the standard edition of the Chinese Buddhist canon, *Taishō shinshū daizōkyō*, ed. J. Takakusu and K. Watanabe (Tokyo, 1924-34).

37 For the historical value of images which are aesthetically "worthless," see Giulio Carlo Argan, "Ideology and Iconology," in *The Language of Images*, ed. W.J.T. Mitchell (Chicago: University of Chicago, 1980), 15-23.

38 This is by no means an exhaustive compilation. Many images have been left out of discussion to save space and avoid repetition. Images which are less well-known or accessible have been chosen over prominent examples in major western museum collections.

39 Oleg Grabar, *Formation of Islamic Art* (New Haven, 1973), 6-12.

40 Ray, "*Maṇḍala* Symbolism," 148.

41 Debala Mitra, *Buddhist Monuments* (Calcutta, 1971).

42 For Bihar, see Steven Darian, "Buddhism in Bihar from the Eighth to the Twelfth Century with Special Reference to Nālandā," *Asiatische Studien* 25 (1971): 335-352; Pushpa Niyogi, "Organisation of Buddhist Monasteries in Ancient Bengal and Bihar," *Journal of Indian History* 51 (1973): 531-557; idem, "Some Buddhist Monasteries in Ancient Bengal and Bihar," *Journal of Indian History* 54 (1976): 273-298; K. M. Srivastava, "The Lost University of Vikramaśila," *Arts of Asia* 17, no. 4 (1987): 44-55. For Orissa, see Thomas Donaldson, "Iconography of the Buddhist Sculpture of Orissa" (manuscript, 1990); and, Debala Mitra, *Bronzes from Achutrajpur, Orissa* (Delhi, 1978). The present work maintains, with Jacob N. Kinnard, that Esoteric Buddhist art was only a small part of the monastic art at these sites and that it is found alongside cult Mahāyāna art during its early stages of development. See Kinnard's "Reevaluating the Eight-Ninth Century Pāla Milieu: Icono-Conserva-tism and the Persistence of Śākyamuni," *Journal of the International Association of Buddhist Studies* 19, no. 2 (1996): 281-300.

43 Claudine Bautze-Picron, "Between men and gods: small motifs in the Buddhist art of eastern India, an interpretation," in *Function and Meaning in Buddhist Art*, ed. K.R. van Kooij and H. van der Veere (Groningen: Egbert Forsten, 1995), 59.

44 Gregory Schopen, "The Bodhigarbhālaṅkaralakṣa and Vimaloṣṇīsa Dhāraṇīs in Indian Inscriptions: Two Sources for the Practice of Buddhism in Medieval India," *Journal of the International Association of Buddhist Studies* 3 (1980): 142.

45 See Lokesh Chandra, "Oḍḍiyāna: A New Interpretation," in *Tibetan Studies in Honour of Hugh Richardson*, ed. Michael Aris and Aung San Suu Kyi (Oxford, 1979), 73-78. Lokesh Chandra identifies Oḍḍiyāna, known from texts as a great center of Esoteric Buddhism, with Kanchi, capital of the Pallavas. For implicit evidence of Sri Lanka as an early center of Esoteric Buddhism, see Lin Likouang, "Puṇyodaya (Na-t'i), un propagateur du Tantrisme en Chine et au Cambodge à l'Époque de Hiuan-Tsang," *Journal Asiatique* 227 (1935): 83-100. Amoghavajra found Esoteric Buddhist texts and a master in Sri Lanka. Raffaello Orlando, "A Study of Chinese Documents concerning the Life of the Tantric Buddhist Patriarch Amoghavajra (AD 705-774)," (Ph.D. dissertation, Princeton University, 1981), 140-142, 162-164. Diran Kavork Dohanian suggets the Esoteric Buddhism in Sri Lanka was close to that of South India, particularly at Kanchi, in *The Mahāyāna Buddhist Sculpture of Ceylon* (New York, 1977), 18-19, 26-27.

46 See R. Poongundran, "Tantric Buddhism in Tamil Nadu," *Tamil Civilization* 4.1-2 (1986): 180-185; and, S.N. Kandaswamy, "Tantric Buddhism in Tamil Literature," *Tamil Civilization* 4.1-2 (1986): 86-99.

47 See Abhayadatta's *Caturaśīti-siddha-pravṛtti*, trans. James B. Robinson under the title, *Buddha's Lions: The Lives of the Eighty-Four Siddhas* (Berkeley, 1979).

48 Archaeological Survey of India (hereafter, ASI), *Indian Archaeology 1958-59: Review* (New Delhi, 1959), 5.

49 Acquired by the Indian Museum, Calcutta. ASI, *Annual Report 1930-34* (Delhi, 1936), 238, 257, pl. CXXVII.A.

50 Ulrich von Schroeder, *Buddhist Sculptures of Sri Lanka* (Hong Kong: Visual Dharma, 1990), 209-241. Interestingly, based on what little evidence there is for Esoteric Buddhism in Sri Lanka, von Schroeder concludes, "It is noteworthy that the Sinhalese traditions of Mahāyāna Buddhism did not particularly stress the fierce emanations of the *Vajra* Family." Ibid, 233. Also see idem, *The Golden Age of Sculpture in Sri Lanka* (Hong Kong: Visual Dharma Publications, 1992).

51 Geri H. Malandra, "Buddhist Caves at Ellora," (Ph.D. dissertation, University of Minnesota, 1983), 296. See also idem, "Ellora: the 'Archaeology' of a Maṇḍala," *Ars Orientalis* 15 (1985): 67-94; idem, *Unfolding a Maṇḍala: The Buddhist Cave Temples at Ellora* (Albany: SUNY, 1993); Carmel Berkson, *Ellora: Concept and Style* (New Delhi: Indira Gandhi National Centre for the Arts, 1992); and, Ramesh Shankar Gupte, *The Iconography of the Buddhist Sculptures (Caves) of Ellora* (Aurangabad: Marathwada University, 1964).

52 Carmel Berkson, *The Caves at Aurangabad: Early Buddhist Tantric Art in India* (New York/Ahmedabad, 1986); and, John C. Huntington, "Cave Six at Aurangabad: A Tantrayana Monument?," in *Kaladarsana*, ed. Joanna Williams (New Delhi, 1981), 47-55.

53 Jean Naudou, *Buddhists of Kasmīr*, trans. Brereton and Picron [sic] (Delhi, 1980), 78.

54 Pratapaditya Pal, *Bronzes of Kashmir* (New York, 1975); idem, "Kashmiri-Style Bronzes and Tantric Buddhism," *Annali dell'Istituto Orientale di Napoli* ns 39 (1979): 253-73.

55 David Snellgrove and Tadeusz Skorupski, *The Cultural Heritage of Ladakh*, 2 vols. (Warminster, 1979-1980) 1:15-18ff.; and, Pratapaditya Pal, "Kashmir and the Tibetan Connection," *Marg* 40 no. 2 (nd): 57-75.

56 See Roger Goepper, "Clues for a Dating of the Three-Storeyed Temple (Sumtsek) in Alchi, Ladakh," *Asiatische Studien* 44.2 (1990): 159-169; idem, *Alchi, Ladakh's Hidden Buddhist Sanctuary: The Sumtsek* (London: Serindia, 1996); and, Rob Linrothe, "The Murals of Mangyu: A Distillation of Mature Esoteric Buddhist Iconography," *Orientations* 25, no. 11 (1994): 92-102.

57 See Roger Goepper, with photographs by Jaro Poncar, *Alchi: Buddhas, Goddesses, Maṇḍalas*, English ed. (Köln, 1984); Snellgrove and Skorupski, *Cultural Heritage of Ladakh*; and, Pratapaditya Pal, *A Buddhist Paradise: The Murals of Alchi, Western Himalayas* (Basel/Hong Kong, 1982).

58 For Atiśa's life, see Alaka Chattopadhyaya, *Atiśa and Tibet: Life and Works of Dipaṃkara Śrijñāna* (Calcutta, 1968; reprint ed., Delhi 1981); but also see the cautionary note in Snellgrove, *Indo-Tibetan Buddhism*, 479, note 172. For the most recent and thorough treatment of the early history of Buddhism in western Tibet, see Roberto Vitali, *Gu.ge mkhan.chen Ngag.dbang grags.pa* (Dharamsala, 1996).

59 M.C. Subhadradis Diskul, ed., *The Art of Srivijaya* (Paris, 1980).

60 The importance of eastern Indian monasteries for central Tibetan art in the 11th c. and 12th c. is being increasingly scrutinized. See Claudine Bautze-Picron, "Lakhi Sarai, An Indian Site of Late Buddhist Iconography and Its Position within the Asian Buddhist World," *Silk Road Art and Archaeology* 1 (1990): 123-176; and, idem, "Śākyamuni in Eastern India and Tibet in the 11th to the 13th Centuries," *Silk Road Art and Archaeology* 4 (1995/96): 355-408.

61 Michel Strickmann, "The Consecration Sūtra: A Buddhist Book of Spells," in *Chinese Buddhist Apocrypha*, ed. Robert Buswell, (Honolulu, 1990), 79-81.

62 See Chou I-Liang, "Tantrism in China," *Harvard Journal of Asiatic Studies* 8 (1944-45): 241-331. The classic Japanese work on the subject of Esoteric Buddhism in China is Omura Seigai, *Mikkyō hattatsu-shi* (Tokyo, 1918).

63 See Yijing, *A Record of the Buddhist Religion as Practiced in India and the Malay Archipelago*, trans. J. Takakusu (Oxford, 1896; reprint ed., Taipei, 1970); and, Lo Hsiang-lin, *Tang dai Guangzhou Guangxiao si yu Zhong-Yin jiaotong zhi guanxi* (Guangxiao Monastery of Canton during the Tang with reference to Sino-Indian relations) (Hong Kong, 1960). Two examples intimate pilgrims' interest in images: Wang Xuance reported back to Tang China the precise measurements of the image within the Mahabodhi temple at Bodh Gaya and mentioned repeated attempts to obtain a reproduction; Vajrabodhi is recorded as bringing a Sanskrit edition of the *Mahaprajñāpāramitā sūtra* as well as art objects when he came to China from Sri Lanka. Sylvain Lévi, *The Mission of Wang Hiuen-ts'e in India*, trans. S.P. Chatterjee (Calcutta, 1967), 16-17, 45.

64 Yijing, *Chinese Monks in India: Biography of eminent monks who went to the Western world in search of the Law during the great T'ang Dynasty*, trans. Latika Lahiri (Delhi, 1986).

65 See Raffaello Orlando, "A Study of Chinese Documents Concerning the Life of the Buddhist Patriarch Amoghavajra (AD 705-774)," (Ph.D. dissertation, Princeton, 1981); Antonino Forte, "The Activities in China of the Tantric Master Manicintana (Pao-ssu-wei, ?-721 CE) from Kasmir and of his Northern Indian Collaborators," *East and West* ns 34 (1984): 301-345; and, Lokesh Chandra, "The Tripitaka-Translator Pao-ssu-wei (Cintamani)," in *Śramana Vidyā Studies in Buddhism* (Sarnath, 1987), 283-286.

66 Stanley Weinstein, *Buddhism Under the T'ang* (Princeton, 1987).

67 Cheng Xuehua, "Tang tiejin huacai shike zao xiang" (Tang Dynasty gilt and polychromed statuary), *Wenwu* 7 (1961): 61-63.

68 Jan Yun-hua, "Buddhist Relations Between India and Sung China," *History of Religions* 6 (1966): 24-42, 135-168.

69 See Dunhuang Wenwu Yanjiusuo, ed., *Dunhuang Mogaoku, 5 Vols.*, vols. 4, 5 (Tokyo, 1982); and, Rob Linrothe, "Ushnīshavijayā and the Tangut Cult of the Stūpa at Yü-lin Cave 3," *National Palace Museum Bulletin* 31, nos. 4/5 (1996): 1-24.

70 See Moritaka Matsumoto "Chang Sheng-wen's Long Roll of Buddhist Images: A Reconstruction and Iconology," (Ph.D. Dissertation, Princeton University, 1976); Yunnan sheng wenwu gongzuo dui (Archaeological Team of Yunnan Province), "Dali Congsheng si santa zhuta de shice he qingli" (Survey and Renovation of the Main Pagoda at the Chongsheng Temple in Dali), *Kaogu xuebao* 2 (1981): 245-67; and, Albert Lutz, *Der Tempel der Drei Pagoden* (Zurich: Museum Rietberg, 1991).

71 Dunhuang Yanjiu Yuan (Dunhuang Research Institute) and Sun Xiushen, *Mogao ku bihua yishu: Yuandai* (The Art of Mural Painting in the Mogao Caves: Yuan Dynasty), Dunhuang Art Booklet Series, no. 13 (Lanzhou, 1986). For western China, see Heather Karmay, *Early Sino-Tibetan Art* (Warminster, 1975); for northern China, see the Juyong Guan, datable to 1343-1345, in Akira Fujieda and Jiro Murata, *Chü-yung kuan: The Buddhist Arch of the fourteenth century at the pass of the Great Wall, north-west of Peking 2 vols.* (Kyoto, 1957); for Feilai Feng, see Richard Edwards, "Pu-tai-Maitreya and a Reintroduction to Hangchou's Fei-lai-feng," *Ars Orientalis* 14 (1984): 5-50; and, Hong Huizhen, "Hangzhou Feilai feng 'Fan shi' zaoxiang chutan" (Preliminary Investigation of the "Buddhist style" sculptures of Hangzhou's Feilai feng), *Wenwu* 1 (1986): 50-61.

72 See Yoshito S. Hakeda, *Kūkai: Major Works* (New York, 1972); and, Tokyo National Museum et al, *Kōbō Daishi and The Art of Esoteric Buddhism* (Tokyo: Asahi, 1983).

73 Taikō Yamasaki, *Shingon: Japanese Esoteric Buddhism*, trans. Richard and Cynthia Peterson, ed. Yasuyoshi Morimoto and David Kidd (Boston/London, 1988).

74 See Robert E. Buswell, Jr., "Introduction: Prolegomenon to the Study of Buddhist Apocryphal Scriptures," in *Chinese Buddhist Apocrypha* (Honolulu, 1990), 22; R. A. Stein, "Quelques problèmes du tantrisme chinois," *Annuaire du Collège de France* 74 (1974): 499; and, idem, "Nouveaux problèmes du tantrisme sino-japonais," *Annuaire du Collège de France* 75 (1975): 486-487.

5. Yamāntaka, Kurkihar (Bihar), ca. 10th century, detail of 53

Introduction

Distinctions, Definitions and Terminology

It is obvious, then, that while a definition cannot take the place of inquiry, in the absence of definitions there can be no inquiry — for it is the definition, either ostensive or nominal, which designates the phenomenon to be investigated.

Melford E. Spiro, "Religion: Problems of Definition and Explanation"

Krodha-vighnantaka

The choice of appropriate terminology is determined by two fundamental aspects of the phenomena subject to analysis: form and action, or appearances and functions. They configure both the term used to refer to the group under consideration and the course of the entire investigation. Only seperable in theory, the two aspects are bound up one with the other, just as "Meaning and artistic form are not easily separated in representations."[1] Together they encompass the significance of the wrathful deity of Esoteric Buddhism as the "demonic-divine."

Esoteric Buddhist literature uses a host of terms to refer to the deities I have named *krodha-vighnāntaka*. These include various combinations of *vajra* (adamantine, diamond wisdom), *krodha* (wrath), *vidyā* (wisdom, *dhāraṇī*) *mahā* (great) and *rāja* (king) such as "Vajrakrodha," "Krodharāja," "Vidyārāja," "Krodha Vidyārāja" and "Mahā Vajra Krodha." Any of these is appropriate for Phase One and Two wrathful deities, but not for Phase Three. For example, "Vidyārāja" applies to personifications of *dhāraṇī*, which appropriately describes many of the Phase One and Two wrathful deities. Despite the distinct conceptual and formal relationships between Phase Two and Phase Three *krodha-vighnāntaka*, however, Phase Three deities like Hevajra and Saṃvara are not personifications of particular *dhāraṇī*. Vidyārāja is thus inaccurate in the case of Phase Three. Both *vajra* and *rāja* are laudatories which are neither descriptive of nor specific to the underlying iconography. "*Krodha*" by itself, though used frequently enough in the texts, is also ambiguous because it does not distinguish between wrathful protectors of a lower order of importance and the *krodha-vighnāntaka*. There is then no satisfactory term with a usage sufficiently consistent, descriptive, unambiguous and appropriately comprehensive to be of heuristic value.

I have therefore coined the term "*krodha-vighnāntaka*" to designate the class of deities in Esoteric Buddhism made up of named deities of wrathful appearance who overcome obstacles to enlightenment and may or may not act as apotropaic guardians. The binomial term combines an essential formal attribute (*krodha*) with a primary identifying function (*vighnāntaka*). The Sanskrit term *krodha* means "wrathful"[2] and is one among a number of different terms used inconsistently by the Esoteric Buddhist texts to refer to a shifting group of such deities.[3] The Sanskrit *vighnāntaka* means literally "destroyer of obstacles."[4] In the evolving Esoteric Buddhist system, these obstacles vary from the external threats of demons and disease to the internal resistance to enlightenment caused by sloth, anger or lust.

The destruction of obstacles is the primary Buddhist function the *krodha-vighnāntaka* deities perform. More than one member of the group integrates this into the etymology of their Sanskrit names. For instance, Ucchusma's name means "he who burns up impurities."[5] Another member of the *krodha-vighnāntaka* class is known as Vighnāntaka.[6] He and other members of the group sometimes trample the elephant-headed Vināyaka, the demon who comes to represent obstacles of all kinds. To avoid confusion, *krodha-vighnāntaka* is used to refer to the class of deities and Vighnāntaka to refer to the individual deity of that name.

Krodha as formal attribute

A wrathful appearance is one of the characteristic qualities of the group and its primary formal attribute. As part of the process of defining the *krodha-vighnāntaka*, we must distinguish other types of deities who share this formal trait. Other deities who are characterized by a wrathful demeanor are not included in the class because of the different status and functions which the Esoteric Buddhist system confers on them. Since a wrathful appearance does not belong exclusively to the *krodha-vighnāntaka* group, the term *krodha* is not by itself sufficiently accurate as the name for a rigorously defined class.[7]

Among the most important of the groups who share a wrathful demeanor but have different functions are the Lokapāla and the *dvārapāla*. The Lokapāla (Chinese *tianwang*, "Heavenly Kings") are four in number, and each is associated with one of the four cardinal directions. Dhṛtarāṣṭra, Virūḍhaka, Virūpākṣa and Vaiśravana correspond with east, south, west and north respectively. As for representations of the Lokapāla within a monastic or temple setting, "since each sanctuary represents a 'realm of the Buddha,' they also serve to protect the temple in which they are situated, and especially the central group of Buddhas in the main hall, against inimical forces."[8] They each command armies of demonic beings who are sworn to uphold the Buddha's teaching within their assigned direction. The Lokapāla set is relatively stable and may be traced back to early Mahāyāna in India, though individual members appear in inscriptions at Bharhut of the ca. early first century BCE, and so may be even older.[9] Like the *krodha-vighnāntaka*, they derive from Yakṣa figures, the localized earth deities who were incorporated into Buddhism as protectors at an early period. Vaiśravana in the form of Kubera was the focus of a cult in India, Central Asia, China and Japan. In the latter he was known as Tobatsu Bishamonten.[10]

Reflecting their identity as generals, the Lokapāla invariably wear armor. The Lokapāla's armor visually distinguishes them immediately from *krodha-vighnāntaka* images, whose figures are never similarly clad. Like the *krodha-vighnātaka*, however, the Lokapāla usually hold weapons and sometimes trample on demonic figures. Despite general similarities in their function of protection and wrathful demeanor, the Lokapāla are lower than the *krodha-vighnāntaka* in the hierarchy of Buddhist beings. Lessing comments that the Lokapāla play a menial role, "as the lamas sometimes facetiously put it, 'merely as policemen in the major services.'"[11] The lamas would never admit such a thing in relation to the *krodha-vighnāntaka* deities such as Saṃvara, who stands at the center of an altar the Lokapāla might guard.

Compared to the four Lokapāla, the *dvārapāla* ("Gate Guardians," Chinese: *lishi* or *menshen*) are even lower on the hieratic scale. This is not to imply their role is unimportant. They too ward off enemies. The *dvārapāla* has an aggressive stance, usually with one hand raised, naked to the waist, with bulging eyes, a grotesque facial expression and, at least in East Asia, emphatically developed musculature.[12] *Dvārapāla* are found in pairs, guarding the entryways to temple compounds or to the shrines and temples within the grounds. They are the markers which signify transition between profane and sacred space.[13]

Some *krodha-vighnāntaka* appear like the *dvārapāla*, with only one head and two arms. One major difference distinguishing the appearance of the *krodha-vighnāntaka* from the *dvārapāla* is that the former do not have the hyper-developed muscular physique found in the latter. Otherwise they are often quite similar in appearance. Since the *krodha-vighnāntaka* are higher on hierarchical scale of Esoteric Buddhism, their greater status and doctrinal importance is evident in their larger size in a composition with *dvārapāla*.

The variations in visual characteristics (e.g., armor for the Lokapāla, developed musculature for the *dvārapāla*) reflect differences in function among the various categories of deities with wrathful appearance. The *dvārapāla*, as already indicated, are charged with the protection of the sacred enclosure. They stand in pairs outside the sanctum and ensure that only the deserving are allowed inside. Unlike the *krodha-vighnāntaka*, they are rarely named individually and have only minimal identities apart from being one of a pair of gate guardians. The contexts in which they are found are very limited, which helps to distinguish representations of them from the more adaptable *krodha-vighnāntaka*.

The Lokapāla have a more generalized defensive function of keeping recalcitrant non-human, non-Buddhist beings from devastating an area. They come to the aid of righteousness in general, and in particular to exemplary human kings who support Buddhism. The worship of Vaiśravana in a special cult of Central and East Asia "was focused upon procuring for the devotee purely mundane benefits — chiefly security from enemy attacks and wealth."[15] As we shall shortly see, in addition to the mundane benefits which characterize the Lokapāla, the *krodha-vighnāntaka* possess transcendent effects.

Other groups who are both protective and wrathful are the *kṣetrapāla*, the *dharmapāla* and in part the *dikpāla*. The iconography of the two former groups is relatively unstable. Functionally, however, their tasks are clear. *Kṣetra* means "field" or "territory" and *pāla* means "protector," so these deities are also guardians of locales.[16] The main function of the *kṣetrapāla* appears to be "protection of the field or rather plots of land."[17] *Kṣetrapāla* were also considered to be in the class of *dvārapāla*. Later Tibetan Buddhism enlists a set of eight *kṣetrapāla* to guard the eight cemeteries found along the perimeters of Tibetan paintings,[18] but they do not appear in non-Lamaist East Asian contexts.

The *dikpāla*, like *dvārapāla*, *kṣetrapāla* and the Lokapāla, are also guardians of territory or the directions.[19] *Dikpāla* are the guardians of the eight directions (the four cardinal directions plus the four intermediate directions). They are part of a pan-Indian tradition, but compared to their status in Buddhism they are much more prominent in later Hindu temple architecture.[20] Nevertheless, they are also included in the outer regions of some Esoteric Buddhist *maṇḍala,* including the Garbhadhātu *maṇḍala* as it appears in Japan.[21] Many of them are Vedic gods, like Indra, Agni and Varuṇa, who have fallen from pre-eminence but are not totally forgotten. Yama, the guardian of the south who is associated with death, is often shown in a wrathful form with a huge belly and weapons, standing or sitting on a buffalo.[22] As we will see, these characteristics, as well as his name, relate him directly to the important *krodha-vighnāntaka,* Yamāntaka ("the destroyer of Yama"). Obviously the *krodha-vighnāntaka* group must be distinguished from the *dikpāla,* who are exclusively apotropaic guards of the eight directions. Apart from Yama and Agni's importance in Esoteric Buddhist *homa* rites,[23] the *dikpāla* do not have a great deal of added prominence in the Esoteric Buddhist system.

As for the *dharmapāla,* since *dharma* refers to the Buddha's teachings, and *pāla* to protector, the *dharmapāla* must also be protective deities, not of space or of territory, but of the Buddha's teachings. Outside of the Tibetan context, the term *dharmapāla* (Chinese *hufa dashi*) seems to be used as a generalized title for any of the classes of protective deities already discussed. In Tibetan literature the term takes on more specific associations. In Tibet *dharmapāla* (Tib. Ch'os-skyon) are still considered defenders of the faith but there are ranks within this class. Stephen Beyer describes the main distinction quite clearly:

> *The highest of the protecting deities is called simply the "Lord," or sometimes the "Lord of Knowledge," to indicate his status as a fully enlightened Buddha and to distinguish him from the lesser oath-bound guardians who are occasionally addressed as lords; this generic distinction is sometimes expressed as the difference between mundane and supramundane deities.*[24]

Wrathful deities belonging to the upper supramundane stratum of the *dharmapāla* with status equal to the "fully enlightened Buddha," also belong to the *krodha-vighnāntaka* class. This would include Mahākāla and others like Acala, Yamāntaka and Hayagrīva, who are sometimes classed as *dharmapāla.*[25] Others within the *dharmapāla* category confined to the lower mundane ranks are largely indigenous chthonic Tibetan deities in origin.[26] Owing to their local origin, lower status and limited responsibilities within the Esoteric Buddhism system, they do not belong to the group of *krodha-vighnāntaka,* despite their wrathful appearance.

On the other hand, our category does include certain figures who in the Tibetan pantheon are members of a class known as *yidam.* The *yidam* are the "high patrons of the Tantras, the deities who preside over the great Tantras of the Highest Yoga."[27] Saṃvara, Hevajra and Vajrabhairava are examples. Not all Tibetan *yidam* deities are wrathful and not all belong to the *krodha-vighnāntaka* class, but all wrathful *yidam* deities do belong to the class of *krodha-vighnāntaka.* In other words, the Tibetan classification system divides the class we are calling *krodha-vighnāntaka* into two subgroups of the *yidam* and the *dharmapāla.* Each subgroup in the Tibetan system also includes deities other than *krodha-vighnāntaka.* [Graph 1] Complicated as this may seem at first, I believe there is a simple explanation.

In the Prologue I alluded to the fundamentally a-historical exigetical methods, which are geared toward practice, of the Tibetan tradition. As Bharati notes in his discussion of the evolution of *mantra,* "the believer . . . must deny the very possibility of its having been 'constructed' at any time — for being eternal and only revealed in time, 'construction' is precluded."[28] In the same way, to say that texts of one sort — let us call them Phase One texts — are "earlier" than Phase Three

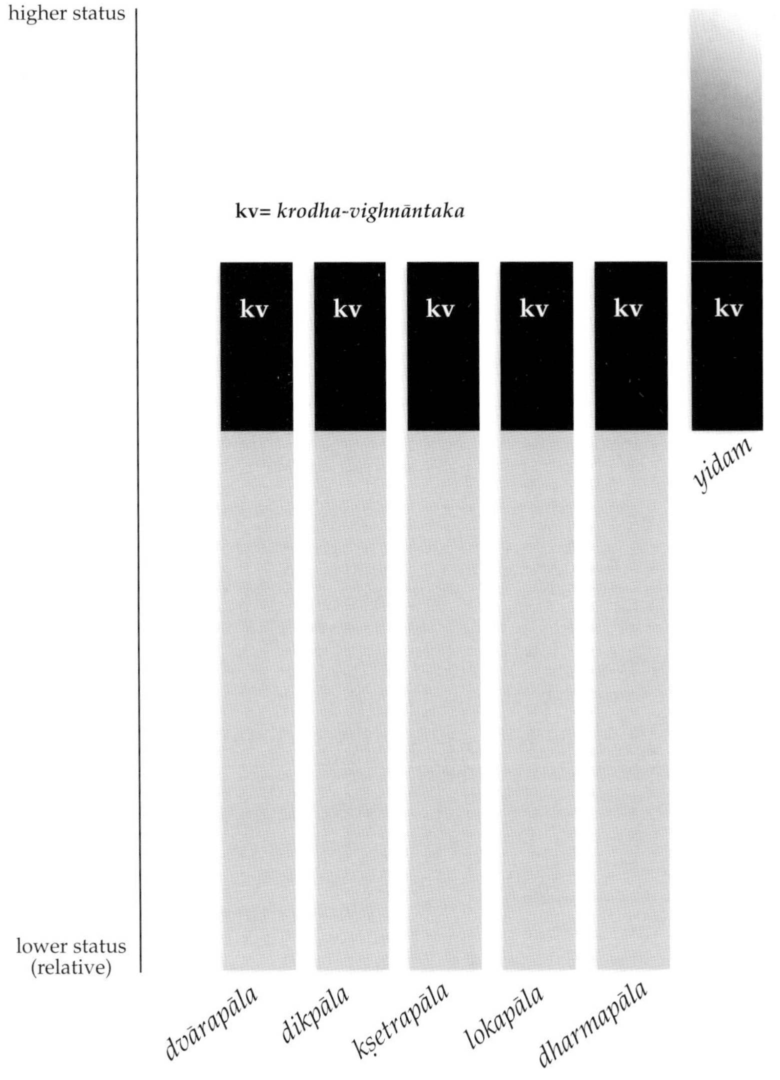

Graph 1: The relationships among the krodha-vighnāntaka and other groups of wrathful deities

texts implies that revelation occurred historically, denying its transcendental origin.[29] In order to account for substantial differences the Tibetans themselves observe among Esoteric Buddhist texts, they ascribe the differences not to historical development but to the attainment each text demands of initiates. Loden Sherap Dagyab, who is part of the contemporary tradition of Tibetan scholarship, has restated the traditional explanation:

> *These tantric teachings [of four classes of texts] were given by the Śākyamuni Buddha to meet the requirement of aspirants of varying degrees of mental and intellectual attainment. Of the four classes of tantra the last is the most profound.*[30]

A tradition which holds the texts to be authentic teachings of Buddha Śākyamuni, Buddha Mahāvairocana, or one of the later (*krodha-vighnāntaka*) interlocutors of Tantras, disregards historical circumstances. [Graph 2, COLOR PLATE 17A] We will later attempt to demonstrate that, contrary to the a-historical Tibetan tradition, the Phase Three *krodha-vighnāntaka* are the historical descendants of Phase Two deities. But when texts of both sorts were translated into Tibetan in the eleventh and twelfth centuries, some attempt to come to terms with the differences within the trans-historical framework was necessary. The *krodha-vighnāntaka* deities found in Phase One and Two texts were often placed in the category of *dharmapāla*, while the *krodha-vighnāntaka* deities of Phase Three texts were classified as *yidam*. By this agency, the wrathful deities of every class share the same "a-historical time" and may be arranged synchronically in a hierarchical grid, the *yidam* (which from a historical perspective derive from a later phase of development) being given precedence over the *dharmapāla* (from an earlier phase of development).

Tibetan systems of classification quite rightly recognize basic differences in status among *krodha-vighnāntaka* deities of Phases One, Two and Three. In most Tibetan classificatory systems, the wrathful *yidam* are grouped with "peaceful patrons" (in other words, the Five Directional Buddhas) and afforded a higher status than other Buddhas and bodhisattva, below only the Guru. The *krodha-vighnāntaka* who are classified as *dharmapāla*, on the other hand, from Phases One and Two, are linked with secondary guardian figures and come near the bottom of the hierarchy.[31] This is an ingenious method of categorization as it preserves historical distinctions, while at the same time casting them in non-historical terms. [Graphs 3 and 4, COLOR PLATES 17B-C] It also encapsulates the two poles of status between which the *krodha-vighnāntaka* begin and end their ascendancy in Esoteric Buddhism: from simple guardian figures to deities which in a certain sense are equal to or above the Buddha.

Dvarapāla, *dikpāla*, the lower category of *dharmapāla*, *kṣetrapāla* and the Lokapāla belong to Mahāyāna Buddhism as a whole. (One might even say they belong to the pan-Indian culture widely conceived, including Brahmanical Hinduism and Jainism.) They cannot be particularly associated with one or another movement within Mahāyāna Buddhism. They do, admittedly, appear in Esoteric Buddhist art, but they do not play a large role. In Esoteric Buddhist contexts their functions are all relatively minor.

The fully developed *krodha-vighnāntaka*, on the other hand, are not commonly found in Mahāyāna art outside of that inspired by Esoteric Buddhism. Phase Two and Three *krodha-vighnāntaka* may be said to be exclusive to Esoteric Buddhism. It is true that they are also charged with the tasks of protection and guarding. In many *maṇḍala* we will find them at the four gateways, as well as in the corners, at the zenith and nadir, forming a group known as the "Ten Wrathful Ones."[32] Likewise the "Eight Vajras" are evoked as protective deities in the introduction to tenth century copies of the *Vajracchedikā Prajñāpāramitā Sūtra* preserved at Dunhuang.[33]

The *krodha-vighnāntaka* perform other functions which also recall the apotropaism of the *dvārapāla*, *kṣetrapāla* and Lokapāla in other contexts. For instance, Esoteric Buddhist texts prescribe rituals devoted to one or another of the *krodha-vighnāntaka*s before starting a ritual cycle. The intent is that of purification of the grounds. In the seventh fascicle of the *Mahāvairocana ābhisambodhi sūtra* (*MVS*), the *mudrā* and *dhāraṇī* ritual of the "*krodha* Acala" is recommended for the *bandhaya-sīman* ceremony to delimit the site of the *maṇḍala*-altar and exclude all evil influences from it, and also for *ātmarakṣa*, a ceremony which does the same for the adept's body.[34] There are many more examples of this in Esoteric Buddhist texts of all periods, as we will explore in greater detail.

Vighnantaka as function

We have now seen that the *krodha-vighnāntaka* deities are wrathful, specific to Esoteric Buddhism and that they perform some of the same tasks of protection executed by other classes of wrathful deities. The *krodha-vighnāntaka* deities, however, have more important duties to discharge. Ferdinand Lessing reports that in Tibetan-style Buddhist rituals, "the invocation of Hayagrīva is essential on account of his power 'to dispel demons,' which is a metaphor for 'removing all obstacles,' particularly all distracting thought preventing the efficacious fulfillment of the rites."[35]

Lessing's observation precipitates two important distinctions. The first is between active/positive and passive/defensive activities. The *krodha-vighnāntaka* perform both, while the other wrathful types (Lokapāla, *kṣetrapāla*, etc.) for the most part perform the latter only. The second distinction is more profound, distinguishing between outer and inner obstacles, just as a text on the *krodha-vighnāntaka* Acala explicitly differentiates inner and outer purification of karmic obstructions.[36] The outer obstacles may be objectified as demonic agents, hostile to well-being. The internal obstacles consist of mental tendencies, the *kleśa*, the "poisons," karmic debt, and so forth, which bar the path leading to enlightenment. Without a doubt, these internal obstacles are often garbed in symbols or metaphors and disguised as enemies of Buddhism. This is certainly the case with the Hindu gods who are trampled under the feet of Phase Two and Three *krodha-vighnāntaka*.[37] Similarly, the *Mahābala Sūtra* describes Vajrapāṇi in the form of Mahābala subjugating Śākyamuni's old adversary Māra, the personification of delusion with his host of demons.[38] But as Esoteric Buddhism evolved, progressing from Phase One to Phase

Three, this metaphorical coating becomes increasingly transparent and the inner significance correspondingly apparent.

The dichotomy between outer obstacles to well-being and inner obstacles to enlightenment is pivotal to understanding the distinction between the *krodha-vighnāntaka* in Esoteric Buddhism and other protective figures in Buddhism at large. Esoteric Buddhism has always emphasized praxis, and it should come as no surprise that the functions of the *krodha-vighnāntaka* are bound more closely to enlightenment-winning practice.

The duties of the lesser protectors common to all types of Buddhism are regularly of the outer sort, though the function of marking the passage to sacred space is somewhat ambiguous. Most frequently they are appealed to for the cure of disease, the increase of wealth, the arousal of affection, or the dissolution of enmity. This was the case of the Lokapāla Tobatsu Bishamonten, whose widespread cult is documented by evidence from Dunhuang.[39]

To be sure, the *krodha-vighnāntaka* is also appealed to for the control of objectified demons and the mental and physical diseases demons are believed to cause. One finds long sections of their texts devoted to rituals to cure illnesses, find hidden treasures and the like. What distinguishes them from other classes of protective deities, however, is that ultimately their functions are homologized with the destruction of barriers which prevent the experience of enlightenment. In the Acala text just mentioned, after describing how to paint an image of Acala and use it in rituals, a long list of mundane benefits is given. These range from subjugating evil men and immoblizing enemy armies to arousing love. Notably, however, the very first boon is that "One will attain all the *samādhi*, and rise to the level of the bodhisattvas."[40] Buddhist goals of this nature always remain at the forefront of the *krodha-vighnāntaka* iconography.

The primary activity of the *krodha-vighnāntaka* deities, then, is not merely to protect sacred territory or the aspirant, but to destroy obstacles, both outer and inner, mundane and transcendental. Exactly how these obstacles are conceived, however, changes over time. The importance of the obstacles and their symbolic linkage with inner conditions gradually escalate along with the status of the *krodha-vighnāntaka*. The more essential are their tasks, the greater status they enjoy. We will follow this correlative growth closely as it appears in both Esoteric Buddhist art and texts. The juxtaposition of a few passages and images from each of the three phases will demonstrate the interdependency of text and images as well as establish the specific tasks of the *krodha-vighnāntaka* within the Esoteric Buddhist system.

A text which reflects the early stage of development is the *Mañjuśrimūlakalpa* (*MMK*). By the late tenth century a version of it was translated into Chinese by Tian Xizai (T.20.1191), but according to Lamotte this translation utilized texts which had already been translated at the beginning of the eighth century.[41] The surviving Sanskrit version of the *MMK* shows evidence that it continued to be expanded in India.[42] The sections of it that are relevant for our purposes are considered to have been written by the eighth century. These actually reflect a considerably earlier and formative phase of Esoteric Buddhism, from the seventh or even sixth century. The text casts Yamāntaka as a wrathful attendant to the Bodhisattva Mañjuśrī. The obstacles which Yamāntaka overcomes in the *MMK* are primarily those of time and space. He manifests his magical power by instantaneously gathering together all the various beings in order to form an assembly to listen to the Buddha preach.

Mañjuśrī assembles his "Vidyāgana" and then addresses Yamāntaka as the "grand slayer of Vighna" and commands him to "perform all my work! Remember your vow! . . . Act on my behalf!"[43] Yamāntaka is commanded specifically "to

6. *Mañjuśrī with Yamāntaka, Guneri (Bihar), ca. 9th-10th century*

assemble all the beings by means of magical powers." Mañjuśrī draws a circle over the "King of Krodhas" (i.e., Krodharāja Yamāntaka) with his hand, and then Yamāntaka is dispatched. "In an instant, the king of the Krodhas had gone to all regions of the world where he succeeded, thanks to his magic power, in mastering hostile beings and compelling them to enter into the circle of the Assembly."[44] Mañjuśrī threatens the unruly portions of the host with reprisals by Yamāntaka, and Yamāntaka is repeatedly referred to as one who destroys demoniacal obstacles. The text spells out that these *vighna*-obstacles are human, natural and supernatural.[45]

A sculpture of Mañjuśrī attended by Yamāntaka from the ninth or tenth century **[6]** reflects the relationship between the two we have just encountered in the *MMK*. Instead of drawing a circle over Yamāntaka's head, Mañjuśrī stretches his hand out toward it, a gesture with a similar connotation of investiture. Yamāntaka's pose is much more active than Mañjuśrī's, denoting his ability to move quickly.

The *Mahāvairocana ābhisambodhi sūtra* (*MVS*) is a text which represents the stage of development of Esoteric Buddhism between the *MMK* and the *Sarvatathāgata tattvasaṃgraha* (*STTS*).[46] The *MVS* makes the connection between obstacles and the *krodha-vighnāntaka* explicit. "Now, as for reciting the great protective *dhāraṇī* to remove obstacles, it causes all demons and evil ghosts to be gone. For this reason, one should think of the Vidyarāja [i.e., *krodha-vighnāntaka*] who are 'hard-to-bear,' because those who create obstacles cannot bear them."[47]

Representing a slightly later phase in the development of Esoteric Buddhism is the *STTS*. Parts of it were translated into Chinese in the mid-eighth century, where it was considered among the most important texts.[48] It was not translated into Chinese in full until the late tenth century, but it must reflect trends current in India in the eighth century. In the ninth *juan* of the Chinese text (T.18.882), the first division of the sixth section, we are treated to an extended discussion of the tasks given to the *krodha-vighnāntaka* Trailokyavijaya (lit. "Conqueror of the Three Worlds"), a wrathful form of Vajrapāṇi.

No longer is it a bodhisattva who commands a *krodha-vighnāntaka*. In the case of the *STTS*, Mahāvairocana presides over and directs Trailokyavijaya. Mahāvairocana is the central Buddha of the five directional Buddhas, or Tathāgatas, and may be described as the highest and most enlightened entity of the *dharmakāya*. Trailokyavijaya is ordered to subjugate the most elevated being, Maheśvara, the Lord of the Gods and Master of the Three Worlds. Maheśvara proves to be a difficult "obstacle" to subdue, but Trailokyavijaya succeeds after Mahāvairocana declines to accept Maheśvara's submission directly. As Trailokyavijaya subdues Maheśvara, the latter appeals to the Buddha, asking how it can be that Vajrapāṇi, whom in anger he has called a mere Yakṣa, can be so strong, stronger even than the Tathāgata as Lord of the Trikaya. Mahāvairocana himself calls Vajrapāṇi-Trailokyavijaya the "Supreme Lord of All the Tathagatas."[49]

This is an amazing promotion, from the quasi-coerced, vow-bound assistant of a bodhisattva (as we saw in the *MMK*) to a being who fuses the wisdom of all five cosmic Buddhas in order to subdue the most powerful god of the universe. The task he performs remains the removal of obstacles, for the presence of Śiva-Maheśvara should not be interpreted here merely as the sectarian humiliation of a Hindu divinity. As I have argued elsewhere, Maheśvara is representative, not of a Hinduism which must be humiliated, but of an egoism which must be vanquished.[50]

A ca. tenth century sculpture of Trailokyavijaya is in all ways parallel to the ideas described in the *STTS*. **[7, 141, 162-164]** Trailokyavijaya is no longer an attendant to a bodhisattva, but a powerful independent deity trampling Maheśvara and his consort.

7. Trailokyavijaya, Mahants compound, Bodh Gaya (Bihar), ca. 10th century

8. Yamāntaka, Nalanda (Bihar), ca. 10th century

The dynamism implicit in his newly defined task has been developed visually to project a powerful understanding of the wrathful deity's up-graded role.

Sometimes the obstacles which the texts specify for destruction by the *krodha-vighnāntaka* are karmic in nature. In the *Amṛita kuṇḍali . . . buddha-uṣṇīṣa sūtra*, for instance, translated by Dharmasena sometime during the Tang period and brought to Japan from Changan by Eun in 847,[51] a set of eight *krodha-vighnāntaka* are described as they stand before the Buddha. He tells them, "If there are men or women of good families who hold to this ten-syllable *dhāraṇī*, you should never, day or night, abandon such a person . . . . Their karmic obstructions of the three worlds should be dissolved by your order. By means of the divine power in your weapons, shatter this karma and command them to attain a state of purity."[52]

Ucchusma is another *krodha-vighnāntaka* deity whose very name speaks of burning up impurities ultimately karmic in nature. Bischoff has noted that "Ucchusma, by his pure compassion, attempts to save all beings, without avoiding contact with filth (stains): by his great radiance, like a scorching fire, he burns up the stains of *kleśa*, of false views, of *vikalpa*, and purifies the spirit."[53]

A ca. tenth-century stone sculpture depicts Yamāntaka, who is specifically mentioned as one of the eight *krodha-vighnāntaka* in the *Amṛita kuṇḍali . . . buddha-uṣṇīṣa sūtra* text mentioned above. **[8, 148]** His six arms bristle with weapons, including a hammer to shatter obstacles, a sword to cut them asunder and a noose to fetter them. He stands solidly on the back of the wild black buffalo and makes a threatening gesture with his primary left hand. Mañjuśrī, who is mentioned in the text manifesting as Yamāntaka, is no longer represented as the object of Yamāntaka's reverence.

The *Hevajra Tantra*, a text from the third phase of Esoteric Buddhism, provides another instance of the variously conceived obstacles which the *krodha-vighnāntaka* is capable of destroying. The text was translated into Chinese in the eleventh century, but it is believed to have been current in India before that time. It certainly represents a later development than either the *MMK* or the *STTS*. Buddha and bodhisattva have minor roles in the *Hevajra Tantra*. The chief interlocutor is Vajrasattva, considered to be a kind of "Ādibuddha" whose "form comprises all the Buddhas" and who is ultimately identical with Hevajra himself. Vajrasattva answers the questions of the Vajra-being or bodhisattva, Vajragarbha, and of *yoginī* (female adepts). The text is solely devoted to the *krodha-vighnāntaka* known as Hevajra, along with his troupe of *yoginī*s. We now find a *krodha-vighnāntaka* at the center of the main *maṇḍala* in a ritual cycle, a much more important position than either the assistant to a bodhisattva, as was Yamāntaka in the *MMK*, or even than Trailokyavijaya, who is at the center of one of a group of *maṇḍala* in the *STTS*,[54] but not the *STTS*'s primary *maṇḍala*.

In the *Hevajra tantra*, Vajrasattva tells the *yoginī*s, who are led by Hevajra's primary consort, Nairātmyā:

> *If he drinks strong poison, the simple man who does not understand it, falls senseless. But he who is free from delusion with his mind intent on the truth destroys it altogether. So those who know the means for release and make effort in Hevajra, are not held by the bonds of delusion and so on, by ignorance and the rest . . . . But when one has found Hevajra, who is the Means, O Vajragarbha of great compassion, one purifies the spheres of sense, and gains the highest state.*[55]

From this passage we realize that Hevajra destroys delusion, that which keeps sentient beings from realizing that "no being is not enlightened." This is one of the "inner" *vighna*-obstacles which *krodha-vighnāntaka* eliminate. Moreover the goal of

9. *Heruka, Nalanda (Bihar), ca. 11th century*

destroying karmic bonds of ignorance and delusion provides significant continuity with earlier texts. The theme is paramount throughout the development of the *krodha-vighnāntaka* in Esoteric Buddhism. It is threaded through the images of Hevajra, Saṃvara and Heruka **[9, 175]**, which appear plentifully at the same sites as the earlier Phase Two wrathful deities.

A commentary by Nāropa (956-1040) on a section of the *Kālacakra Tantra*, a text devoted to the third phase *krodha-vighnāntaka* Kālacakra, gives a mythic slant to their functions. The obstacles destroyed by the *krodha-vighnāntaka* evoked during the *krodhāvesā* ritual are conflated with the futile attacks of Māra's host on Śākyamuni.[56] It is highly significant that the deity mentioned by Nāropa is Vajrapāṇi in wrathful form, because Vajrapāṇi forms a bridge between early Buddhism and Esoteric Buddhism. The attack of Māra is one of the most important events in the legend of the Buddha. Māra created a series of obstacles in the way of the Buddha, but all were destroyed by the Buddha's powers of meditation and wisdom, and by the stockpile of merit which he accumulated through lifetimes of self-sacrifice and compassion.[57] In images and texts from Gandhara during the Kushan period (ca. 1-200 CE), Vajrapāṇi assumes the role of companion-protector of the Buddha. Most importantly for our purposes, in his early form Vajrapāṇi destroys opposition in the guise of Nāga or a recalcitrant Yakṣa.[58] He has become, in effect, the personification of the Buddha's defeat of Māra. The *krodha-vighnāntaka* deity is the reincarnation, if you will, of this personification, which is directly traceable to the historical Buddha's legend. At both ends of the development, self-transformation and realization remains the goal, though the means are clothed in radically different garb.

These examples from Esoteric Buddhist texts have served to demonstrate that the destruction of obstacles is at the heart of the *krodha-vighnāntaka*. It also helps to explain and justify the choice of the term "*vighnāntaka*" (destroyer of obstacles) as part of the binomial designation for this class of deities.

In summary, the binomial neologism "*krodha-vighnāntaka*" is a descriptive term which is: 1) not a generalized laudatory epithet; 2) comprehensive enough to include the entire family of related deities from all phases; and 3) specific enough to exclude deities of a different order, however similar in appearance or partially overlapping in function. The term "*krodha-vighnāntaka*" describes the deities' primary attribute (wrath) and function (the destruction of obstacles). It encapsulates a workable definition of the class, which in Esoteric Buddhism is comprised of named deities of wrathful appearance (a necessary but not sufficient condition), male or female,[59] whose function within Esoteric Buddhism relates to the overcoming of obstacles to enlightenment and may include but is not limited to apotropaic duties.

Notes to Introduction

1 Meyer Schapiro, *Words and Pictures: On the Literal and the Symbolic in the Illustration of a Text* (The Hague/Paris, 1973), 37. The epigraph for this chapter comes from Melford E. Spiro, "Religion: Problems of Definition and Explanation," *Anthropological Approaches to the Study of Religion*, ed. Michael Banton (London, 1966), 90.

2 Sir Monier Monier-Williams, *Sanskrit-English Dictionary* (Oxford, 1899; reprint edition, New Delhi, 1988), 322.

3 For an analysis of alternate terminology used in the texts, see Linrothe, "Compassionate Malevolence," 64-72.

4 *Vighna* is defined as "an obstacle, impediment, hindrance, opposition, prevention, interruption, any difficulty or trouble." Monier-Williams, *Sanskrit-English Dictionary*, 957. *Āntaka* means "making an end, causing death." Ibid., 43.

5 Bischoff, *Mahābala*, 9. Also see Mochizuki Shinkō and Tsukamoto Zenryū, *Bukkyō daijiten*, 3rd ed. (Tokyo, 1958-1963), 212.

6 Benoytosh Bhattacharyya, *The Indian Buddhist Iconography*, 2nd rev. ed. (Calcutta, 1968), p. 180.

7 It is met with, however, in Buddhist texts and in secondary literature, such as Marie-Thérèse de Mallmann, *Introduction a l'iconographie du tantrisme bouddhique* (Paris, 1975), 219-222.

8 Dietrich Seckel, *The Art of Buddhism*, rev. ed. (New York, 1968), 248. For the Lokapāla in the Tibetan tradition, see Loden Sherap Dagyab, *Tibetan Religious Art* (Wiesbaden, 1977), 114-118.

9 For an account of the origins of the Lokapāla in Indian images of Yakṣas, their place in Buddhist texts and careers in China and Central Asia, see Alexander C. Soper, *Literary Evidence for Early Buddhist Art in China* (Ascona, 1959), 231-235; and, Simone Gaulier, Robert Jera-Bezard, and Monique Maillard, *Buddhism in Afghanistan and Central Asia*, 2 vols., Iconography of Religions no. 13 (Leiden, 1976), 31-32.

10 See Phyllis Granoff, "Tobatsu Bishamon: Three Japanese Statues in the United States and an Outline of the Rise of This Cult in East Asia," *East and West* ns 20 (1970): 144-167; and the section devoted to images of Vaiśravana from Khotan in Joanna Williams, "The Iconography of Khotanese Painting," *East and West* ns 23 (1973): 132-138.

11 Ferdinand D. Lessing, *Yung-Ho-Kung: An Iconography of the Lamist Cathedral in Peking, With Notes on Lamaist Mythology and Cult* (Stockholm, 1942), 45.

12 Soper, *Literary Evidence*, 240-241.

13 See Mircea Eliade, *The Sacred and the Profane: The Nature of Religion* (New York, 1959); and, Thomas Donaldson, *Hindu Temple Art Of Orissa*, 3 vols. (Leiden, 1985-86), 855-856.

14 Lokapāla and *dvārapāla* are illustrated in Li Lincan, *Nanzhao Daliguo xin cailiao de zonghe yanjiu* (Taipei, 1982), no. 67; a much larger *krodha-vighnāntaka* within a comparable space is illustrated in ibid., no. 120.

15 Granoff, "Tobatsu Bishamon," 153.

16 de Mallmann, *Introduction a l'iconographie*, 223. Also see Gösta Liebert, *Iconographic Dictionary of the Indian Religions: Hinduism-Buddhism-Jainism*, Studies in South Asian Culture no. 5 (Leiden, 1976), 142.

17 H. Chakravarti, "The Saivite Deity Kṣetrapāla," *Indian Historical Quarterly* 9 (1933): 239.

18 Lessing, *Yung-Ho-Kung*, 93-94, 136.

19 See de Mallmann, *Introduction a l'iconographie*, 157-158; and, R.S. Gupte, *Iconography of the Hindus, Buddhists and Jains* (Bombay, 1972), 49-53, 105.

20 See Donaldson, *Hindu Temple Art of Orissa*, 1141-1148.

21 The *Dikpāla* are discussed individually but assigned to the same directions as in their South Asian grouping in Adrian Snodgrass, *The Matrix and Diamond World Maṇḍalas in Shingon Buddhism*, 2 vols. (New Delhi, 1988).

22 Lourens P. van den Bosch, "Yama: The God on the Black Buffalo," *Visible Religion: Annual for Religious Iconography* 1 (1982): 21-64.

23 For details of the rituals of *homa* dedicated to the ostensibly Hindu god Agni, see the 23rd chapter of the *ST* in Tsuda, *Saṁvarodaya-Tantra*, 306-313.

24 Beyer, *Cult of Tara*, 47. For one Tibetan's understanding of the *dharmapāla*, see Dagyab, *Tibetan Religious Art*, 19.

25 See Ursula Toyka-Fuong, *Ikonographie und Symbolik des Tibetischen Buddhismus: Die Kultplastiken der Sammlung Werner Schulemann im Museum für Asiatische Kunst, Köln*, Asiatische Forschungen no. 78B (Wiesbaden, 1983), nos. 48, 49, 52, 53ff; and, Waddell, *Tibetan Buddhism*, 363-365.

26 A brief discussion of the lower status of protective deities of Tibetan origin placed under the command of Mahākāla, who is in turn inferior to Hevajra in the Sakya system, is found in Ramesh Chandra Tewari, "Pre-Buddhist Elements in Himalayan Buddhism: The Institution of Oracles," *JIABS* 10 (1987): 142-143. Also see Réne de Nebesky-Wojkowitz, *Oracles and Demons of Tibet: The Cult and Iconography of the Tibetan Protective Deities* ('S-Gravenhage: Mouton, 1956); and, Ladrang Kalsang, *The Guardian Deities of Tibet* (Dharmsala: Little Lhasa, 1996).

27 Beyer, *Cult of Tara*, 41.

28 Bharati, *Tantric Tradition*, 115.

29 Generally speaking, the Tibetan tradition comes close to recognizing historical factors by categorizing some texts as *gter-ma* (lit: treasure), or "rediscovered texts." However, the origins of these texts are ascribed to one or another pious founder of religion in Tibet, and ultimately to transcendental agency. See the Fifth Dalai Lama's explanation of the discovery of the *Mani bKa'-'bum* in Matthew Kapstein, "Remarks on the *Mani Bka'-'bum* and the Cult of Avalokitesvara in Tibet" (unpublished paper, typewritten), 4; and, Tulku Thondup Rinpoche, *Hidden Teachings of Tibet* (London, 1986).

30 Dagyab, *Tibetan Religious Art*, 15. The attribution of all the teachings to Śākyamuni, their ranking according to profundity and correlation with the stages of the Buddha's preaching career resembles in principle Zhiyi's earlier (6th c.) *sūtra* and teaching classification. The teachings to which the author himself subscribes are inevitably rated the most profound. See Kenneth Ch'en, *Buddhism in China: A Historical Survey* (Princeton, 1964), 305-311; and, Hakeda, *Kūkai*, 66-76.

31 One can follow this hierarchy for instance in the "Tschangstscha Hutuktu" pantheon. Typically, it begins with the lineage masters, then the Yidam, followed by Buddhas, bodhisattva, *ḍākinī*, *dharmapāla* and two categories of local guardians. See Eugen Pander, *Das Pantheon des Tschangstscha Hutuktu: ein Beitrag zur Iconographie des Lamaismus* (Berlin, 1890), 45-46; and, Sushama Lohia, *Lalitavajra's Manual of Buddhist Iconography* (New Delhi: Aditya Prakashan, 1994); 106ff (*yidam*); 206ff (*dharmapāla*). The rNying-ma-pa have a similar system which does not differ as far as the identity and relative positions of wrathful *yidam* and the *dharmapāla* are concerned. See Khempo Sangay Tenzin and Gomchen Oleshey, *Deities and Divinities of Tibet: The Nyingma Icons*, trans. Keith Dowman (Kathmandu, 1988), 2-4.

32 Marie-Thérèse de Mallmann, *Étude Iconographique sur Mañjuśrī* (Paris, 1964), 111 -134.

33 Michel Soymié, "Notes D'Iconographie Bouddhique: Des Vidyārāja et Vajradhara de Touen-Houang," *Cahiers d'Extrême-Asie* 3 (1987): 17-23.

34 T.18.849.57a. The *MVS* was translated in 725 CE by Śubhakarasiṁha and Yixing (T.18.848) as the last part of the entire *sūtra*, and again by Vajrabodhi (d. 741) on its own (T.18.849).

35 Lessing, *Yung-Ho-Kung*, 95.

36 T.21.1200.7b; "Trisamaya Acalanatha Krodharāja," translated in the 8th c. by Amoghavajra.

37 Rob Linrothe, "Beyond Sectarianism: Towards Reinterpreting the Iconography of Esoteric Buddhist Deities Trampling Hindu Gods," *Indian Journal of Buddhist Studies* 2, no. 2 (1990): 16-25.

38 Bischoff, *Mahābala* 54ff.

39 A woodcut of Vaiśravana dated 947 and recovered from Cave 17 at Dunhuang indicates the mundane benefits for which Vaiśravana typically was addressed. The prayer asks for rewards of happiness and prosperity. Lionel Giles, "Dated Chinese Manuscripts in the Stein Collection, part VI. 10th century (AD 947-995)," *Bulletin of the School of Oriental And African Studies* 11 (1943-46): 148-149. The woodcut is illustrated in Roderick Whitfield and Anne Farrer, *Caves of the Thousand Buddhas: Chinese Art from the Silk Route* (London, 1990), no. 85.

40 T.21.1200.11b-c.

41 Lamotte, "Vajrapāṇi en Inde," 151.

42 Ganapati Sastri, ed., *Āryamañjuśrīmūlakalpa*, 3 vols., Trivandrum Sanskrit Series (Trivandrum, 1920-1925), nos. 70, 76, 84. The difficulties of dating various sections of the *MMK* are discussed in Yukei Matsunaga, "On the Date of the *Mañjuśrīmūlakalpa*," in *Tantric and Taoist Studies in Honor of R.A. Stein, Vol. 3*, ed. Michel Strickmann (Brussels, 1985), 882-893.

43 Ariane Macdonald, *Le Maṇḍala du Mañjuśrīmūlakalpa* (Paris, 1962), 25 (my translation from the French).

44 Macdonald, *Mañjuśrīmūlakalpa*, 77-78 (my translation from the French).

45 Ibid., 106.

46 For a discussion of the origin and transmission to China of the *MVS* and the *STTS*, see Minoru Kiyota, *Shingon Buddhism: Theory and Practice* (Los Angeles/Tokyo, 1978), 19-25.

47 T.18.849.57a.

48 For instance, Amoghavajra begins his "*Chief points of the dhāraṇī of all the families*" (T.18.903): "The fundamental scripture of *Yogā*(*cāra*) in all has ten thousand *gātha* (hymns). There are eighteen assemblies. The premier assembly text is called *Sarvatathāgata tattvasaṃgraha*." T.18.903.898c.

49 T.18.882.372a. In both the Tibetan and Chinese versions of the *Mahābala Sūtra* the defeated Māra asks the Buddha who is this Mahābala *krodha-vighnāntaka* who has subdued him. The Buddha answers he is "the Tathagata." Bischoff, *Mahābala*, 18, 60, 74.

50 Linrothe, "Beyond Sectarianism," 16-25.

51 T.19.965. See "Datsumaseina" in the "Table des Auteurs et Tra-ducteurs," *Répertoire du Canon Bouddhique Sino-Japonais: Fascicule Annexe du Hōbōgirin* (Paris/Tokyo, 1978), 242.

52 T.19.965.341a.

53 Bischoff, *Mahābala*, 9 (my translation from the French).

54 Amoghavajra states, "*Yogācāra maṇḍala* number four. First is the Vajradhātu. Second Trailokyavijaya. Third, that of universal subduing. Fourth, that of the fulfillment of all intentions. These four *maṇḍala* represent the four inner wisdoms of Vairocana Buddha, which are: *vajra*, *abhiṣeka* (initiation), *padma* and *karma*." T.18.903.898c.

55 Snellgrove, *Hevajra Tantra*, 1.107.

56 Carelli, *Sekoddeśaṭīkā*, 29.

57 See Alex Wayman, "Studies in Yama and Māra," *Indo-Iranian Journal* 3 (1959): 44-73, 112-131.

58 Lamotte, "Vajrapāṇi en Inde," 120-138; idem, *History of Indian Buddhism From the Origins to the Saka Era*, trans. Sara Webb-Boin (Louvain, 1988), 687-688; and, Snellgrove, *Indo-Tibetan Buddhism*, 134-141.

59 In order to limit the scope of the inquiry, female wrathful deities have been arbitrarily excluded. They appear in all phases, from Bhṛikuṭī to Aparājitā and Mārīcī to Nairātmyā and Vajravārāhī. They deserve a separate examination and a comparison with male *krodha-vighnāntaka*.

Phase One

10. Vajrapāṇi with attendants, Cave 6 Aurangabad, second half of 6th century

1

The Earliest Krodha-vighnantaka

11. Krodha-vighnāntaka, detail of 10

Hundreds of South Asian *krodha-vighnāntaka* images survive. Those which have been examined can be broken down into a few basic groupings. The most obvious division is between independent images and all those in which the *krodha-vighnāntaka* is a subordinate. As a minor subordinate, the *krodha-vighnāntaka* is invariably represented as a smaller attendant accompanying a larger, more important bodhisattva. This category of *krodha-vighnāntaka* image is probably the largest, evidently the earliest, and seemingly the longest-lived. It will be the first to be examined here.

For the sake of convenience I have termed such images Phase One images. Although this phase begins before Phase Two or Three, Phase One images continue to be made alongside the later forms until Buddhism as a whole was curtailed in India in the thirteenth century. The first *krodha-vighnāntaka* images of the Phase One type may date to the second half of the sixth century. Our initial example, of approximately that date, is found on the north side of the vestibule to Cave 6 in Aurangabad, Maharashtra.[1] [**10-11**] Approximately contemporary is a *krodha-vighnāntaka* attending Avalokiteśvara within the shrine of Aurangabad's Cave 7. [**12, 16**] Slightly later in date, probably very early seventh century, is a quite similar *krodha-vighnāntaka*, again on the doorway to a shrine, in Cave 6 of Ellora, also in Maharashtra.[2] [**13, 20**] These *krodha-vighnāntaka* images are among the very earliest Phase One images to survive in their original contexts.[3] Context is an obvious advantage in establishing their original significance, and an extended discussion will be devoted to characterizing this context.

Before analyzing the broader context of the Cave sculptures, however, it will be helpful to introduce a pair of early *krodha-vighnāntaka*, to enlarge our pool of early examples. As with most of our examples, very little contextual evidence survives for either, giving impetus to derive as much as possible from the Aurangabad and Ellora examples. The first of the two is a ca. sixth or seventh century sculpture of a bodhisattva with a *krodha-vighnāntaka* attendant. [**14, 18**] The two may represent Vajrapāṇi and Vajrapuruṣa, though the identifications are tentative. This sculpture, now in the National Museum of New Delhi, is one of a pair from Sarnath, near Benares, the site of the Buddha's first sermon. The wrathful attendant stands on the

12. *Avalokiteśvara with an attendant krodha-vighnāntaka, Cave 7 Aurangabad, late 6th century*

13. *Vajrapāṇi or Maitreya with an attendant krodha-vighnāntaka, Cave 6 Ellora, early 7th century*

14. Bodhisattva with krodha-vighnāntaka, Sarnath, ca. 6th-7th century

15. Vajrapāṇi with krodha-vighnāntaka, Nalanda, ca. 7th-8th century

proper right side of a two-armed bodhisattva who seems to lean on him. He is dwarfish, with the *vāmana*-Yakṣa body type and a plump face. Though he has "bug-eyes," he has a sweet smile.

Like two of the three *krodha-vighnāntaka* already introduced, the Sarnath wrathful deity [**14, 18**] makes the *vinayahasta mudrā*, crossing his arms in front of his chest. He stands with one leg bent behind the other. There is a diamond-shaped crest at the part of his hair, suggestive of an early type of prong-less *vajra*.[4] It seems possible then that the bodhisattva is meant to be Vajrapāṇi, with the personification of his primary symbol, Vajrapuruṣa. The similarities of pose, body type and iconographic configurations among all the sculptures mentioned so far are quite striking.

The Sarnath bodhisattva [**14**] was originally paired with a standing Avalokiteśvara also in the National Museum in New Delhi. The latter sculpture holds the stem of a lotus in his left hand, and there is an image of Amitabha in his headdress.[5] The right arm is extended down, palm out, towards a kneeling female devotee. The Avalokiteśvara figure looks toward his right, the opposite of the Vajrapāṇi (?) figure. Most likely the two sculptures acted as a framing device on either side of a Buddha, such as that we find at Aurangabad and Ellora.

A Vajrapāṇi with a dwarfish wrathful attendant in the Irving collection on loan to the Metropolitan Museum of Art in New York may also be a member of a pair, though its partner has not been identified.[6] [**15, 19**] It is datable to the seventh or eighth century, and the fearsome qualities of the wrathful attendant have been enhanced by weapons and a snake decoration. He leans his elbow on the upturned handle of an axe and holds a flower in his proper right hand at his shoulder. A snake acts as his *upavīta* (sacred thread). He stands with his right leg bent oddly at the knee and ankle, with the other leg straight. His eyes have outlined lids and slanted eyebrows, and they bulge out beneath a mop of curly hair and above a "parrot-beak" nose. He comes up to the mid-thigh of his sweetly-smiling bodhisattva master, who rests his left hand on the *krodha-vighnāntaka*'s head.

We have now assembled five early *krodha-vighnāntaka* images. Two themes will dominate the discussion of these earliest representative *krodha-vighnāntaka* images. First, as subordinate deities, they appear as the personifications of symbols, abilities, powers or attributes of their masters, the bodhisattva. This relationship is sustained in later Phase One imagery as well and will be explored in the next chapters while discussing Yamāntaka and Hayagrīva. Second, their earliest appearances are conditioned by Mahāyāna Buddhism. The formative stages of Esoteric Buddhism gradually emerge from the broad context of Mahāyāna practice. At this early stage, however, Esoteric Buddhism is difficult to extract from Mahāyāna. Later the *krodha-vighnāntaka* become independent images and help to distinguish Esoteric Buddhist practice from that of mainstream cult Mahāyāna. But the leitmotif of this discussion of the earliest examples will be the interaction between Mahāyāna cult practice and early Esoteric Buddhism.

The Aurangabad Cave 6 example [**10**] stands in the *pratyālīḍha* posture (proper left leg extended, right bent at the knee), while that of the Ellora Cave 6 wrathful deity [**13**] stands in the opposite stance: *ālīḍha*. Each crosses his arms over his chest, in the *vinayahasta* gesture of submission. The face above the *vīra*-Yakṣa body of the Aurangabad *krodha-vighnāntaka* has a grotesque expression, a grimace and bulging eyes. His slightly earlier date is supported by his three-tiered hairdo, which closely recalls the Sondni *vidyādhara* datable to the second quarter of the sixth century.[7] The Ellora *krodha-vighnāntaka* [**13**], while also a *vīra*-Yakṣa in body type, has a slightly less grotesque facial expression.[8]

16. *Two-armed krodha-vighnāntaka, detail of* 12

17. *Two-armed krodha-vighnāntaka, detail of* 13

The *krodha-vighnāntaka* [16] in Aurangabad Cave 7 is in some ways distinct from these two. First of all, it takes the form of the *vāmana*-Yakṣa, a pudgy butterball of an attendant. He has his proper left hand placed rather saucily at his hip, while the other hand holds something against his shoulder. A beaded necklace hangs around his neck. Whatever garment he wears looks as much like a diaper as a waist-wrapping *dhoti*. The dominating bodhisattva leans his torso protectively towards his attendant and places his hand on the round head.

These examples were chosen because they represent early *krodha-vighnāntaka* types frequently met with: the ferocious *vīra*-Yakṣa type [11], the less exaggerated, almost heroic *vīra*-Yakṣa type [17], and the mischievous child-like *vāmana*-Yakṣa type. [16, 18-19] Each form evokes a different reaction in the viewer and provides a seed for later growth. The first type (represented by 10) has an awe-inspiring, slightly fearsome character. These incipient features will be fully developed over time in such deities as Yamāntaka, who among others remains grotesque throughout his many incarnations during Phases One to Three. The subdued but dignified type (seen in 17) combines power with grace. Such handsome *krodha-vighnāntaka* are relatively rare in Phase One images, but they will come to the fore with Phase Two *krodha-vighnāntaka* like Trailokyavijaya. Finally, the *vāmana*-Yakṣa type [14-16] evokes not so much awe as humor, a feeling which is the flipside of sacred horror. These three types contain within themselves shoots which will bloom at the hands of Esoteric Buddhist artists and practitioners in the future. As we will see in the next chapter, they also directly reflect the non-Buddhist conceptual and formal strands which informed the earliest *krodha-vighnāntaka* imagery.

Each of the early *krodha-vighnāntaka* for whom the context is known — that is, the ones from Aurangabad and Ellora — attends a standing bodhisattva. Each of these standing bodhisattva are themselves attending, in one way or another, a shrine containing a Buddha seated with both legs pendent, who makes the *dharmacakra mudrā*.[9] The *vāmana*-Yakṣa *krodha-vighnāntaka* attending Avalokiteśvara [12, 16] is actually inside the inner cella of Cave 7, while the two *vīra*-Yakṣa *krodha-vighnāntaka* [11, 17] belong to compositions arranged around a pair of bodhisattva on either side of the entrance to the inner cella of their respective caves. This arrangement describes Ellora Cave 6. [20]

The pudgy *krodha-vighnāntaka* [16] is found on the north wall of the shrine of Aurangabad Cave 7 next to Avalokiteśvara, who shares the wall with Tārā. Across from them is the celebrated dancing Tārā with musicians. On the west wall is the teaching Buddha seated on a lion-decorated throne in *pralambapada āsana*, surrounded by smaller seated Buddhas. Although the female deities in the cella and in the vestibule are often pointed to as harbingers of mature Esoteric Buddhism, the cave's overall structure relates to mature Mahāyāna with its cults devoted to the male and female bodhisattva, notably Avalokiteśvara and Tārā. Based on its similarity to later images and texts to be discussed in forthcoming chapters, the *krodha-vighnāntaka* present here can be identified as Hayagrīva.

On the outer wall leading to the inner shrine of Ellora Cave 6 stand two gateway bodhisattva. [20] The one on the left (north) side is Avalokiteśvara and the other is either Vajrapāṇi or Maitreya. [13] Assuming the latter is Vajrapāṇi, one would expect the bodhisattva to carry his namesake attribute, but it is instead the *krodha-vighnāntaka* who bears the *vajra* in his headdress. Though transferred to his attendant, the presence of the *vajra* lends some credence to the minority interpretation of the bodhisattva as Vajrapāṇi.[10] The mark that primarily contradicts this argument is the distinct *stūpa* in the bodhisattva's headdress, an iconographic marker usually associated with Maitreya.[11] In other respects, however, both figures

18. Krodha-vighnāntaka, detail of **14**

19. Krodha-vighnāntaka, detail of **15**

closely resemble seventh and eighth century stone and metalwork Nepalese sculptures of Vajrapāṇi.[12] The identities of the bodhisattva and his attendant cannot be determined with certainty. If it is Maitreya, an attendant who embodies the *vajra* is unexpected; if it is Vajrapāṇi, the presence of a *stūpa* in the headdress is unusual. Perhaps the ambiguities reflect the iconographic indistinctiveness of the early stage, particularly in terms of the distribution of *krodha-vighnāntaka* with particular bodhisattva.

Two gateway bodhisattva are also found on the wall leading to the inner shrine at Aurangabad Cave 6. The one on the left (south) side has been identified as Mañjuśrī. If the attribution is accurate, his standing attendant, who holds a bowl with both hands, may be Yamāntaka. The bodhisattva on the right (north) side has been identified as Vajrapāṇi.[13] [**10**] The identification of the northern bodhisattva as Vajrapāṇi is widely accepted, as he holds a *vajra* in the left hand placed at his waist.[14] Vajrapāṇi's attendant, who is the counterpart of the presumed Yamāntaka, therefore may be identified confidently as Vajrapuruṣa, the personification of the *vajra*.

Others, however, have identified him differently. Berkson, for instance, suggests the attendant figure is Māra, "the personified Kāma (desire) or evil, whom Gautama Buddha defeated while achieving the supreme knowledge."[15] No reasons are given for this identification, and though I do not believe it is supportable, it is productively provocative. The submissive gesture and the demonic appearance of the Aurangabad attendant figure may have suggested to Berkson the image of a subdued Māra. Furthermore, in the *Ārya Mahābala-Namā-Mahāyāna sūtra*, a Phase One text, Vajrapāṇi's hypostasis, Mahābala, does subjugate Māra.[16] If that were the case here, however, one would have to accept that the ideas in this Phase One text were current already in the sixth century. Were that granted, then one would expect to see Māra trampled underfoot, because the *Ārya Mahābala-Namā-Mahāyāna sūtra* explicitly states that after Mahābala had spoken his *dhāraṇī*, Māra was "frightened, trembling with fear, heart aflutter, and stupefied; bereft of the use of the four limbs, without the appearance of life."[17] The *krodha-vighnāntaka* is not prostrate and imperiled, however; instead a lotus pad supports the *krodha-vighnāntaka*'s proper left foot, marking him as divinity, not a demon. Rather than Māra, the Aurangabad *krodha-vighnāntaka* is more plausibly identified as a furious form of Vajrapāṇi, either Ucchusma or Mahābala himself, but most likely Vajrapuruṣa, the personification of Vajrapāṇi's attribute.[18]

I am reluctant to invest the *krodha-vighnāntaka* at Ellora and Aurangabad with advanced or well-defined Esoteric Buddhist identities. The context in which they appear does not justify it. Their arrangements are classic Mahāyāna compositions: essentially triadic groupings of a central Buddha and one or more pairs of bodhisattva placed on either side of a doorway leading to the Buddha.[19] [**20**] The shrines in fact fit well with what Sheila Weiner calls "the *Mahāyāna* threshold," attained only in the late fifth and early sixth centuries, with the teaching Buddha in *pralambapada āsana*. As John Newman points out, "the icons at Aurangabad . . . are not *prima facie* 'tantric.'"[20] We can extend this conclusion to related works (e.g., **14**), for which a similar triadic context is confirmed by the existence of a companion piece. Inscriptions on the Nalanda Vajrapāṇi [**15**] reinforce the conservative matrix in which it was made. Above Vajrapāṇi's head and proper left shoulder appears, not an Esoteric Buddhist formulation, but the familiar "Buddhist creed."

There is evidence of nascent Esoteric Buddhist thought and imagery at Aurangabad and Ellora, though it is not as decisive or central as some interpreters would have it. Evidence given for the presence of early Esoteric Buddhism at these

20. *Entrance to Cave 6 Ellora*

21. *Vajrapāṇi with attendants, Cave 6 Aurangabad, second half of 6th century, another view of* **10**

caves has included the prominence of female deities in Aurangabad Cave 7, the presence of the wrathful attendants and the "*maṇḍala*" arrangement of nine Buddha figures seated in three horizontal rows on a side wall of Cave 6 at Ellora.[21]

True *maṇḍala*, wrathful deities and certain female deities (not merely Tārā) are inarguably aspects highlighted by mature Esoteric Buddhism. The basic structure, however, of all three caves under consideration is a nuclear triadic form composed of two bodhisattva flanking the teaching Buddha Śākyamuni. The other elements are fitted into the primary structure in a subsidiary fashion. The putative *maṇḍala* are actually seated Buddha figures arranged in registers. These visual programs are regularized extensions of groupings of five, seven, nine or ten Buddhas, or an abbreviation of the 1000-Buddha theme.[22] The female deities are mainly forms of Tārā and not Mārīcī, or the consorts of Buddhas such as those found in the *Sarvatathāgata tattvasaṃgraha*, the primary Phase Two Esoteric Buddhist text. Nor are they female deities such as Nairātmyā or Vajravārāhī, who are featured in later Esoteric Buddhism. Finally, the wrathful deities are personifications of the powers and abilities of the bodhisattva, who remain much more important than their attendants.

It is more accurate to consider Caves 6 and 7 at Aurangabad and Cave 6 at Ellora, *not* as early Esoteric Buddhist, but as the product of newly mature devotional Mahāyāna Buddhism. As Weiner notes, from the late fifth to early sixth centuries greater stress was given to the Buddha image and to its devotional worship.[23] The iconography of these caves is actually conservative, for as Malandra points out, "there is no difficulty in tracing the source of the Buddha images in [Ellora] caves 2 through 10 to earlier protypes at Ajanta and Aurangabad."[24] Both what is portrayed and what is absent in the caves betray a predominant orientation of sixth-century and early seventh-century cultic Mahāyāna. They typically feature in the Mahāyāna mode iconic images of the Buddhas Śākyamuni, Amitabha and Vairocana, a few narrative episodes from Śākyamuni Buddha's life and the principal bodhisattva with their female counterparts.

What is absent here is a focus on the deities featured in early developed Esoteric Buddhism. Vajrapāṇi, for example, is particularly singled out in Esoteric Buddhist imagery and texts, yet in these caves he is peripheral. Even as early as the *Mañjuśrīmūlakalpa* (*MMK*), Vajrapāṇi has considerable importance as one of the principal interlocutors in a text devoted to Mañjuśrī Bodhisattva. Vajrapāṇi is present at Aurangabad, but only as one of several bodhisattva found in pairs at the gateways leading to a cella enshrining a Buddha. If any bodhisattva is featured at Aurangabad, it is Avalokiteśvara, one of the stars of the *Lotus Sūtra*. In addition, there are no fully independent *krodha-vighnāntaka* images, which is a definitive sign that at these sites Esoteric Buddhism has not yet emerged from Mahāyāna.

Academic representations of Mahāyāna Buddhism tend to emphasize the philosophical strain inscribed in the *Prajñāparamitā* literature. But this literature was hardly "popular," a measure of which must surely be that it would have inspired the many images, planned and intrusive, which fill the cave walls. Much more commonly depicted at the western cave sites was the cult of the Buddha and increasingly the bodhisattva. The goal of cultic Mahāyāna was dual: rebirth in paradise and, more immediately, visions of assemblies of Buddhas and bodhisattva in such a paradise.[25] A passage from a slightly later (ca. seventh century) Mahāyāna liturgical text by Śāntideva gives life to these caves with rich descriptions matching the decorative and figurative carvings and the kinds of rituals which were carried out there:

> *In perfumed bathing halls, beautified by columns that shine with encrusted pearls, with awnings that shine with garlanded pearls, and with floors of shining pure crystal, full of urns inlaid with fine gems, full of delicate flowers and perfumed waters, there shall I prepare a bath for the tathāgatas and their sons, accompanied by music and song. . . . With delicate heavenly clothing, soft to the touch, of many colors, and with fine ornaments, I cover Samantabhadra, Ajita [Maitreya], Mañjughoṣa, Lokeśvara [Avalokiteśvara] and the other bodhisattvas. With the best perfumes that fill a billion worlds with their scent I anoint these [bodhisattvas, who are] monarchs among the sages, whose bodies shine with the brightness of well purified, burnished and polished gold.*[26]

The sculptures of Cave 6 at Aurangabad and Ellora are directly related to the themes of Buddhas teaching in paradise and compassionate savior-bodhisattva. The caves at Aurangabad and Ellora are realizations of the meditative visions involving Buddhas preaching to bodhisattva and other beings in celestial assemblies. These celestial assemblies were described by Mahāyāna texts like the *Buddhabalādhana-prātihāryavikurvāṇanirdeśa Sūtra* and the *Saddharmapuṇḍarīka-sūtra* (the *Lotus Sūtra*). The Tibetan version of the former pairs Vajrapāṇi with Avalokiteśvara as they approach Śākyamuni in a celestial assembly at which Śākyamuni preaches.[27] While not suggesting that Cave 6 at Aurangabad or Ellora necessarily illustrates this text, the site and the text share a resemblance because this triadic formation was fundamental to Mahāyāna imagery, visual *and* literary.

Outside the inner shrine of Cave 7 at Aurangabad, which features the preaching Buddha and Avalokiteśvara with Hayagrīva [**12, 16**], we find the Aṣṭamahābhaya Avalokiteśvara surrounded by the eight perils from which Avalokiteśvara has vowed to save those who call on him.[28] The *locus classicus* for this scene is of course the twenty-fifth chapter of the *Lotus Sūtra*, as translated into Chinese by

Kumarajiva in 405-406 CE.[29] The *Lotus Sūtra* is hardly an Esoteric Buddhist, or even a "proto-Tantric" text, but a popular Mahāyāna scripture. The importance of Avalokiteśvara at both cave sites reinforces the linkage with the Mahāyāna bodhisattva cult. The paradise and bodhisattva cults are much more prominent than the elements of Esoteric Buddhism which have been recognized through ingenious and creative, if slightly over-determined, interpretations.

These earliest surviving *krodha-vighnāntaka* images were incorporated into a context of Mahāyāna cult ritual practices performed by laymen and/or clerics,[30] making it very difficult to extricate proto-Esoteric Buddhism from cultic Mahāyāna. Early Esoteric Buddhist texts like the *MMK* similarly are permeated by Mahāyāna Sūtra features.[31] Texts and images alike share a common format, setting and cast of protagonists. The difference between early Esoteric Buddhist (Phase One) texts and images and those of ritualistic cult Mahāyāna is perhaps only a matter of the degree to which emphasis is laid on *dhāraṇī* and its defense, supra-mundane goals of enlightenment in this life and consecration ceremonies. Even these are not unfailing guides. Iyanaga notes that "The borders between exoteric and esoteric [Buddhism] are extremely fluid,"[32] and S.K. De observes:

> *the line of demarcation between a Mahāyānist and a Vajrayānist work is not fixed; for the former often contains Tantric ideas and practices of Vajrayāna, while the latter includes topics essentially Mahāyānist. Thus, Śantideva's Śikṣa-samuccaya, an undoubtedly Mahāyānist work, contains unreserved praise of the use of the dharānīs and traces of other Tantric ideas.*[33]

Both Mahāyāna and Esoteric Buddhism share an interest in mundane accomplishments. Both perform rituals of veneration and meditations with images. Phase One images of *krodha-vighnāntaka* will continue in this realm of mixed cultic Mahāyāna and early Esoteric Buddhism through the thirteenth century and beyond in India. It was necessary at the outset to point out this feature which marked its birth.

Notes to Chapter One

1 For the date of most of the caves at Aurangabad, including Cave 6, see Susan Huntington, *The Art of Ancient India* (New York/Tokyo, 1985), 265. Malandra dates Aurangabad Cave 6 to the late 6th c. in "Buddhist Caves at Ellora," 300.

2 Malandra dates Cave 6 at Ellora to ca. 600 CE in Geri Hockfield Malandra, "Ellora: The 'Archaeology of a *Maṇḍala*,'" *Ars Orientalis* 15 (1985): 67; idem, *Unfolding a Maṇḍala* (Albany, 1993), 25. For early 7th c. dates, see. S. Huntington, *Art of Ancient India*, 268; Aschwin de Lippe, *Indian Mediaeval Sculpture* (Amsterdam, 1978), 10; and, Malandra, "Buddhist Caves at Ellora," 142.

3 Other early *krodha-vighnāntaka* sculptures outside their original contexts are illustrated and discussed in Linrothe, "Compassionate Malevolence," figs. 3-6.

4 Note the *vajra* depicted on the arms of a cosmic Vairocana from Khotan illustrated in Williams, "Khotanese Painting," 109-154, fig. 1; and, Mario Bussagli, *Central Asian Painting* (New York, 1979), 55. A helpful summary with line-drawings of the forms of pre-8th c. *vajra*s is found in John D. LaPlante, "A Pre-Pāla Sculpture and its Significance for the International Bodhisattva Style in Asia," *Artibus Asiae* 26 (1963): 270-272. He notes that "The open-pronged vajra does not appear to have come into wide usage before the 8th century . . . [before which] Vajrapāṇi's vajra is simple and unpronged." Ibid., 272. Also see E. Dale Saunders, Mudrā: *A Study of Symbolic Gestures in Japanese Buddhist Sculpture* (New York, 1960), 184-191, esp. fig. 101.

5 The National Museum acquisition number is 49.118.

6 Published by Gouriswar Bhattacharya, "The Buddhist Deity Vajrapāṇi," *Silk Road Art and Archaeology* 4 (1995/96): 323-354, fig. 1. The inscription, the standard "*ye dharmā hetu* . . .," is transcribed on ibid., 329-330. We can disregard Bhattacharya's tentative identification of the wrathful attendant as Hayagrīva. The same article also includes a related, if slightly later, example of Vajrapāṇi with wrathful attendant in the David Young collection.

7 See Joanna Williams, "The Sculpture of Mandasor," *Archives of Asian Art* XXVI (1972-73), figs. 15-16.

8 These are among the best preserved and most fully articulated of a few related figures from Aurangabad and Ellora, but they can be only representative. Other examples can be found in Berkson, *Caves at Aurangabad*; idem, *Ellora: Concept and Style*. In at least two of the Hindu caves at Ellora there are attendant figures that have a distinct relationship with the *krodha-vighnāntaka* just mentioned. One is a *vāmana*-Yakṣa or Śiva-Gaṇa attending the Goddess Ganga in Cave 21, also datable to the late 6th c.; the second is a *vīra*-Yakṣa attendant to a *dvarapāla*. Both make the *vinayahasta* gesture. See R.S. Gupte and B.D. Mahajan, *Ajanta, Ellora and Aurangabad Caves* (Bombay, 1962), pl. 125 (right), pl. 126 (left); and, Berkson, *Ellora: Concept and Style*, 160-161.

9 For the plan of the Aurangabad Cave 6, see Berkson, *Caves at Aurangabad*, 181.

10 This is not visible in the drawing or photograph, but is confirmed in the description by Gupte and Mahajan, *Ajanta, Ellora and Aurangabad*, 164; and, de Lippe, *Indian Mediaeval Sculpture*, 10. Malandra discusses other evidence for pairing Avalokiteśvara with Vajrapāṇi but considers Maitreya to be the better identification in *Unfolding a Maṇḍala*, 99-100. Sotaro Sato also identifies the bodhisattva as Maitreya in *Ellora Cave Temples* (Tokyo: Satori, 1977), pl. 19. G. Bhattacharya suggests that it might be Vajrapāṇi, not Maitreya, in "The Buddhist Deity Vajrapāṇi," 332-333.

11 Von Schroeder, however, cautions that the *stūpa* is not an infallible marker, noting that it is not attested in the *Sādhanamālā* or *Niṣpannayogāvalī* as a characteristic of Maitreya. See von Schroeder, *Buddhist Sculptures of Sri Lanka*, 216.

12 Note the ca. 7th c. stone *krodha-vighnāntaka* attending Vajrapāṇi illustrated in Pratapaditya Pal, *Arts of Nepal: Part 1, Sculpture* (Leiden/Köln, 1974), pl. 14; a ca. 8th c. metalwork image, idem, *Sensuous Immortals* (Los Angeles, 1977), no. 93; a ca. 8th c. Nepalese gilt copper Vajrapāṇi with wrathful attendant in the Los Angeles County Museum of Art, Pal, *Arts of Nepal, Part 1*, no. S6; and the Vajrapāṇi with *vāmana*-Yakṣa Vajrapuruṣa in an 8th-9th c. sculpture from Patan, ibid., pl. 182.

13 Berkson, *Caves at Aurangabad*, 178-179.

14 See Gupte and Mahajan, *Ajanta, Ellora and Aurangabad*, 232; Malandra, "Buddhist Caves at Ellora," 300; and, Berkson, *Caves at Aurangabad*, 185 (the *vajra* in the bodhisattva's left hand is clearer in the photograph on 179).

15 Berkson, *Caves at Aurangabad*, 185.

16 See Bischoff, *Mahābala*.

17 T.21.1243.209c. Compare Bischoff, *Mahābala*, 54, 69.

18 These three are included in a list of more than 200 of Vajrapāṇi's "own Vidyārāja" at the beginning of the section of the *Mañjuśrīmūlakalpa* (*MMK*) as translated by Tianxizai (sk. Devaśānti ?) in the late 10th c. T.20.1191.840a-841a. Here I take "Vajrāyudha Vidyārāja" to be Vajrapuruṣa. It does not seem that in the *MMK* a single leader of Vajrapāṇi's Vidyaraja is given prominence. Elsewhere Vajrapāṇi is visualized along with all of his Vidyārāja, "the most important of whom immediately surround him." T.20.1191.890a. Interestingly, the Phase Two text *STTS* gives Vajrāyudha as the consecration name accorded to Indra (who from ancient times was given the *vajra* as emblem) upon his conversion. See T.18.882.373a; and, David Snellgrove, "Introduction," ed. Lokesh Chandra and David L. Snellgrove, *Sarva-tathāgata-tattva-saṅgraha: Facsimile reproduction of a Tenth Century Sanskrit Manuscript from Nepal* (New Delhi, 1981), 49. J. Huntington makes an innovative attempt to identify this figure as Krodhacandratilaka on the basis of the name given for Vajrapāṇi's wrathful attendant in the *MVS* in "Cave Six," 50. In order to accept his identification several discrepancies, temporal and iconographic, must be ignored. See Linrothe, "Compassionate Malevolence," 121-124.

19 Hongnam Kim, "The Divine Triad," in *The Story of a Painting: A Korean Buddhist Treasure from the Mary and Jackson Burke Foundation* (New York, 1991), 2-3.

20 John Newman, "On Recent Studies in Buddhist Architecture of Western India: A Review," *Indian Journal of Buddhist Studies* 1 (1989): 111. Also see Sheila L. Weiner, *Ajanta: Its Place in Buddhist Art* (Los Angeles, 1977), 66.

21 John Huntington suggests that Cave 7 can be related to the *vajradhātu maṇḍala* in which sixteen of the thirty-two deities are female, even though the main shrine has an unadorned Buddha. J. Huntington, "Cave Six," 50. For the putative *maṇḍala*, see Malandra, "Buddhist Caves at Ellora," 68.

22 See Berkson, *Caves at Aurangabad*, 60, 201; Malandra, *Unfolding a Maṇḍala*, figs. 58-61, 135, 242-243.

23 Weiner, *Ajanta*, 68.

24 Malandra, "Buddhist Caves at Ellora," 299.

25 See Gregory Schopen, "Sukhāvatī as a Generalized Religious Goal in Sanskrit Mahāyāna Sutra Literature," *Indo-Iranian Journal* 19 (1977): 177-210. Both goals are stated together in a passage from the *Sarvatathāgatādhiṣṭhāna-sattvāvalokana-buddhakṣetra-sandarśana-vyūha Sūtra*, a Mahāyāna text which Schopen states is significantly earlier than the *MMK* but has "proto-tantric" elements and thus can be dated to ca. 4th-5th c. Ibid., 185 (note 13), 202.

26 Luis O. Gomez, "A Mahāyāna Liturgy," in *Buddhism in Practice*, ed. Donald S. Lopez, Jr. (Princeton, 1995), 186.

27 Gregory Schopen, "The Five Leaves of the *Buddhabalādhanaprātihāryavikurvāṇanirdeśa-sūtra* found at Gilgit," *Journal of Indian Philosophy* 5 (1978): 323.

28 Berkson, *Caves at Aurangabad*, 124. The same theme was popular at Dunhuang. For example, see the late 10th-early 11th c. painting from Dunhuang now in the Musée Guimet illustrated in Jeannine Auboyer et al, *Rarities of the Musée Guimet* (New York, 1975), no. 47.

29 T.9.262 (KBC 116). This chapter is the 24th chapter in other versions. See Hajime Nakamura, *Indian Buddhism: A Survey with Bibliographical Notes* (Indian Edition, Delhi, 1987), 180, 183-191.

30 See Gregory Schopen, "Two Problems in the History of Indian Buddhism: The Layman/Monk Distinction and the Doctrines of the

Transference of Merit," *Studien zur Indologie und Iranistik* 10 (1985): 26; idem, "On Monks, Nuns and 'Vulgar' Practices: The Introduction of the Image Cult into Indian Buddhism," *Artibus Asiae* 49 (1988/89): 153-168.

31 Snellgrove broadly classifies Tantras as those relatable to Mahāyāna Sutras (i.e., *MMK*, *STTS*) and those with non-Buddhist associations (i.e., *Hevajra tantra*, *Saṁvarodaya*) in *Indo-Tibetan Buddhism*, 147-160. To oversimplify slightly, he distinguishes them on the basis of where the text was written or circulated, either the monastery or the yogic retreat. A temporal distinction can also be made, in that those which overlap with Mahāyāna Sūtras derive from the ca. 6th c. through 8th c. and those of with non-Buddhist yogic associations from the ca. 8th c. through the 12th c.

32 Iyanaga, "Récits de la Soumission," 638 (my translation from the French).

33 S.K. De, "Buddhist Tantric Literature of Bengal," *New Indian Antiquary* 1 (1938-39): 3 (note 1). Note that Śāntideva is the author of the Mahāyāna liturgical passage cited earlier in this chapter.

22. *Viṣṇu with āyudhapuruṣa, ca. 5th-6th century, Sarnath Museum*

2

Origins of the Krodha-vighnantaka

23. *Śiva-Gaṇa, Madhya Pradesh, ca. 5th century, Bharat Kala Bhavan*

To understand the visible forms taken by the earliest identifiable *krodha-vighnāntaka* we must step back. Mahāyāna Buddhist sculpture at this period was situated within a wide horizon of religious imagery. Indian religious thought manifested a number of similar tendencies at nearly the same time in Hindu, Jain and Mahāyāna Buddhist art. One tendency is to personify divine attributes as *āyudhapuruṣa*. The forms applied to new iconographic categories were borrowed from the ranks of even older types. Two sources are identifiable: Śiva-Gaṇa and Yakṣa. It is clear that the early *krodha-vighnāntaka* images are closely related to these sources.

Yakṣa developed locally throughout a large portion of India as chthonic nature spirits, "usually beneficent powers of wealth and fertility."[1] They are pre- or non-Aryan folk deities who were integrated grudgingly into Vedic culture. Scholars have associated the etymology of the term Yakṣa with a series of meanings, including "apparition," "opposite," "to honour" or "to worship," "to move quickly towards," and "to glimmer."[2] In Vedic literature Yakṣa are perceived as a kind of "primordial occult power, mysterious, wonderful, apparitional, worshipful and horrid and at the same time god, good or evil."[3] Yakṣa are invisible powers which manifest with sudden luminosity and require appeasement. As Coomaraswamy and others have noted, their character is ambivalent, both deified and demonized.

Gradually Yakṣa were included as demi-gods into both orthodox Brahmanical and, by the time of Bharhut (early 1st century BCE), Buddhist contexts. At Sanchi there was already a bifurcation of Yakṣa body-types: "dwarfed and grotesque" (which I refer to as the *vāmana*-Yakṣa) and "graceful" (*vīra* -Yakṣa).[4] One strain of Yakṣa became less malevolent and more mischievous, or even auspicious, like Kubera.[5] Others became part of the decoration of Buddhist sites like Bharhut as partly decorative, partly auspicious fertility motifs. While the malevolent Yakṣa proved formidable opponents even for the Buddha, protective benevolent Yakṣa began to take on the roles of *dvārapāla* and Lokapāla.[6] For the most part the Yakṣa "had lost their independent status and merged in the personalities of greater cult gods such as Śiva, Ganeśa, the Buddha and Bodhisattvas in the Kushana and Gupta periods."[7]

24. Viṣṇu with āyudhapuruṣa, Gaya, ca. 7th-8th century, Gaya Museum

25. Detail of āyudhapuruṣa below Viṣṇu at Deogarh, Uttar Pradesh, mid-6th century

An offshoot of the benevolent type of Yakṣa evolves into the roly-poly dwarfish Gaṇa. [23] Most often found as lesser companions or attendants of Śiva, they are common to Buddhist and Jain art as well.[8] Pratapaditya Pal defines them succinctly:

> *The word gaṇa literally means "multitude" or "people," but in Indian mythology it denotes a class of semidivine, gnomelike beings who are constant companions of Śiva. They are often described as composite creatures with animal heads, and although grotesque are often delightfully humorous as well. Mythology describes them as playmates of Skanda and Ganeśa, whose name literally means "lord of the gaṇas," but when their master is on the warpath they become relentlessly bellicose.*[9]

This is the branch onto which many of the *krodha-vighnāntaka* (e.g., **12, 14, 18** and **19**) were grafted.

The forms of both the relatively formidable Yakṣa and the less fearsome variety were later adopted to depict personifications of certain symbolic aspects of Brahmanical and Buddhist deities. [**22, 24-28**] The personification of attributes seems to occur somewhat earlier in Brahmanical contexts than in Buddhist. One of the earliest instances in South Asia is the personification of Viṣṇu's wheel (*cakra*), Cakrapuruṣa.[10] Cakrapuruṣa images are found in both the *vīra*-Yakṣa and the *vāmana*-Yakṣa forms,[11] and the *vinayahasta mudrā* is frequent for both [**25, 27**]. The practice of personifying implements is attested over a wide area of India. Cakrapuruṣa appears with various forms of Viṣṇu including Narasiṁha; Triśūlapuruṣa was supplied for Śiva; and both were attached to Hari-Hara. Indra and other Brahmanical deities are accompanied by such figures since at least the early fifth century CE, well before the earliest *krodha-vighnāntaka* images.[12]

The Sarnath, Gaya and Kashmiri Cakrapuruṣa [**26-28**], along with the first male *āyudhapuruṣa* on the lower right of the Deogarh Viṣṇu [**25**], have much in common with the Vajrapuruṣa figures of Aurangabad Cave 6 and the Ellora Cave 7 *krodha-vighnāntaka*. [**10-11, 13, 17**] Although their gestures and positions differ slightly, they are all much smaller than the primary deity each attends. The hair of the Cakrapuruṣas are versions of the "Gupta curls" we will encounter in several early *krodha-vighnāntaka* images. The ca. fifth century Śiva-Gaṇa [**23**] also shares a few features with the *krodha-vighnāntaka* [**16, 18-19**], notably the short but heavy *vāmana*-Yakṣa body type. Other early *krodha-vighnāntaka* images are worth noting for their resemblance to Yakṣa, Gaṇa and *āyudhapuruṣa* images (especially **31, 34-35, 41, 67, 71** and **72**).

Formally the similarities are suggestive and the priority of date unassailable, so that we may take it as established that the creators of the Buddhist images drew on the earlier tradition of Yakṣa, Śiva-Gaṇa and *āyudhapuruṣa* when imaging the earliest *krodha-vighnāntaka*.[13] But it was not just the idea and the form of an *āyudhapuruṣa* which Buddhists employed here. As we expand the inquiry to include Phase One Hayagrīva and Yamāntaka, who are personifications of *dhāraṇī* and not of *āyudha* like Vajrapuruṣa, we will see that all the early *krodha-vighnāntaka* derive from these sources. In fact, Buddhist *āyudhapuruṣa* are generally confined to the early period of Phase One imagery. Their presence at the side of bodhisattva is soon supplemented by increasingly independent wrathful manifestations. It seems to have been a symptom of the early period of borrowing that the idea of a personification was appropriated along with the established form. Borrowed forms were then extended to embody forms other than *āyudhapuruṣa*, as with Yamāntaka and Hayagrīva.

The authors of the *Mañjuśrīmūlakalpa* seem conscious of the sources of the wrathful deities, for one of the terms used to refer to the group of attendant *krodha-*

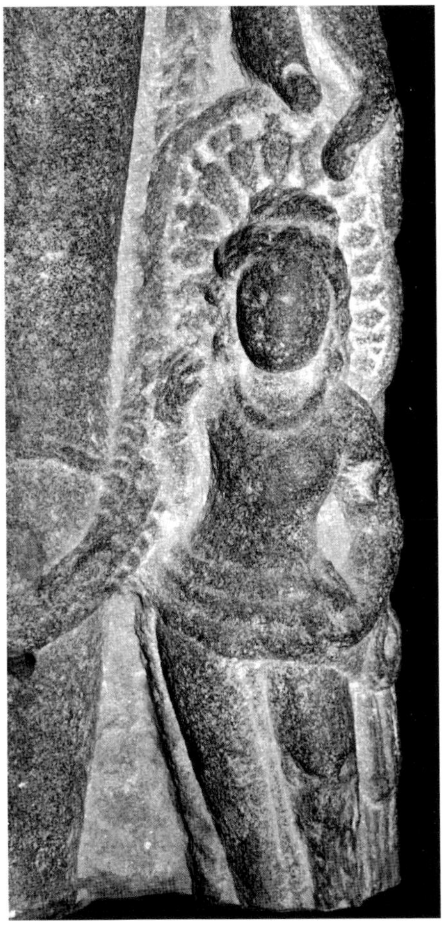

26. *Cakrapuruṣa, detail of* 22

vighnāntaka is "Vidyāgaṇa,"[14] as if to transfer to Buddhism the category of Śiva's auspicious attendants, the Śiva-Gaṇa. It was especially relevant for Vajrapāṇi to have Yakṣa-derived attendants, for his earliest Buddhist incarnation was as a "great yakṣa," then as a "great general of the yakṣas," before becoming a bodhisattva.[15] His origins are not forgotten even in Esoteric Buddhist texts such as the *MMK*, which calls Vajrapāṇi "the master of the Guhyaka, master of the Yakṣa."[16] It is only fitting then that he in particular should have a Yakṣa-like being attending him.

The identification of the *krodha-vighnāntaka*'s visual predecessors also helps to explain a puzzling feature of its history. Rather unexpectedly, the *vīra*-Yakṣa *krodha-vighnāntaka* image appears fully formed from the earliest recognized occurrences. [11, 17] Much larger than any of the other attendant figures, including the female consorts, the posture of the Vajrapuruṣa figures demonstrates more strength and force than any of the other demurely poised figures in their groups. They have several characteristics which we will find repeatedly in Phase One and Phase Two examples of *krodha-vighnāntaka*, including *mudrā, āsana*, body and facial type. Right from the beginning, or as near to a beginning as we are allowed, there was no hesitation on the part of the artist in the manner in which to depict this new Buddhist species. The explanation of course is that the *krodha-vighnāntaka*'s doctrinal *raison d'être* made it appropriate for the artist to fashion a form by drawing on the familiar images of the earlier categories of Yakṣa, Śiva-Gaṇa and *āyudhapuruṣa*.

27. *Cakrapuruṣa, Kashmir, metalwork, 6th century, Los Angeles County Museum of Art*

28. *Āyudhapuruṣa, detail of* 24

29. *Krodha-vighnāntaka, detail of* 13

Notes to Chapter Two

1 Ananda Coomaraswamy, *Yakṣas* (Washington, 1928, 1930; reprint ed., 2 parts in one, New Delhi, 1971), 1:36. Also see Ram Nath Misra, *Yakṣa Cult and Iconography* (New Delhi, 1981); review by Karl Khandalavala, *Lalit Kala* 22 (1985): 39-40.

2 R.N. Misra, "Yakṣa, A Linguistic Complex," *Journal of the U.P. Historical Society* ns 9 (1961): 74-75.

3 Misra, "A Linguistic Complex," 83.

4 For Bharhut and Sanchi examples, see Heinrich Zimmer, *The Art of Indian Asia*, 2 vols. (Princeton, 1955), pls. 34, 19. P.K. Agrawala seems to identify all grotesque Yakṣa as Kumbhanda Gaṇa, though these are a class of Yakṣa. See "The Kumbhanda Figures in Sanchi Sculpture," *East and West* 37 (1987): 179-189; and, Misra, *Yakṣa Cult and Iconography*, 108.

5 Note the ca. 8th-9th c. sculpture of Kubera from Baijnath (Almora), Katyuri, illustrated in de Lippe, *Indian Mediaeval Sculpture*, pl. 47.

6 Misra, *Yakṣa Cult and Iconography*, 37-90; Gail Hinich Sutherland, "The Demon and His Disguises: The Yakṣa in Hindu and Buddhist Art and Literature" (Ph.D. Dissertation, University of Chicago, 1988), 144-147, 157-161; and, idem, *Yakṣa in Hinduism and Buddhism: The Disguises of the Demon* (Albany: SUNY, 1991), 65-68ff.

7 Misra, *Yakṣa Cult and Iconography*, 126.

8 Note the garland bearers attending Avalokiteśvara in Cave 2 of Ellora illustrated in Zimmer, *Art of Indian Asia*, pl. 187.

9 Pratapaditya Pal, *The Ideal Image: The Gupta Sculptural Tradition and Its Influence* (New York 1978), 85.

10 See W.E. Begley, *Visnu's Flaming Wheel: The Iconography of the Sudarśana-Cakra* (New York, 1973); and, V.R. Mani, *The Cult of Weapons: The Iconography of the Āyudhapuruṣas* (Delhi, 1985). Frederick Asher dates the Gaya Viṣṇu (his fig. 12) as late as the late 8th or early 9th c., though he suggests it is based on an earlier type, in *Art of Eastern India* (Minneapolis, 1980), 79-80.

11 See, for instance, the ca. 6th c. metal Viṣṇu Trimurti with a *vāmana* Cakrapuruṣa, from Gandhara or Kashmir, in the Berlin Museum für Indische Kunst illustrated in Pal, *Bronzes of Kashmir*, no. 8.

12 For Triśūlapuruṣa, see N.P. Joshi, "A Note of Triśula-Purusha," *Journal of the U.P. Historical Society* ns 8 (1960): 79-81; and, R.C. Agrawala, "Triśūla Purusa in Indian Sculpture," *Indian Historical Quarterly* 36 (1960): 186-188. The *vāmana*-type Triśūlapuruṣa in the handsome Śivaic guardian figure at Kilchipura (Mandasor) dating to about 525 AD is illustrated in de Lippe, *Indian Mediaeval Sculpture*, pl. 5; and the *vīra*-Yakṣa Lagudapuruṣa and Triśūlapuruṣa attending Śiva at Mandasor, ibid., pl. 6. For the *vāmana*-Yakṣa Lagudapuruṣa of the 6th c. addorsed as Maheśvara Śiva from Fattehgarh, see Pratapaditya Pal, "An Addorsed Śaiva Image from Kashmir and its Cultural Significance," *Art International* 24, nos. 5-6 (1981): fig. 2; Phyllis Granoff, "Maheśvara/Mahākāla: A Unique Buddhist Image from Kasmir," *Artibus Asiae* 41 (1979): fig. 8 (misidentified in the caption as "Small adoring figure"); and, Bansi Lal Malla, *Sculptures of Kashmir (600-1200 A.D.)* (Delhi, 1990), pl. 26. Orissan Triśūlapuruṣa attends the *dvārapāla* Mahākāla on the entrance portal of the Lakśmaneśvara temple (ca. 575 CE). See Donaldson, *Hindu Temple Art of Orissa*, fig. 2674; and, Mani, *Cult of Weapons*, fig. 26 (misidentified as belonging to the Satrughnesvara or Bharateswar temple). For Indra, see the Vajrapuruṣa squatting behind Indra, whose symbol is also the *vajra*, at Buddhist Cave 90 at Kanheri (Maharashtra) illustrated in Pal, *The Arts of Nepal, Part I*, fig. 53; and, S. Huntington, *Art of Ancient India*, 262-264. Also see C. Śivaramamurti, "The Weapons of Viṣṇu," *Artibus Asiae* 18 (1955): 128-136; Bansi Lal Malla, "A Note on Vaishnavite Āyudhapuruṣas in Mediaeval Kashmiri Sculptures," *Indian Museum Bulletin* 20 (1985): 28-31; Gopinatha Rao, *Elements of Hindu Iconography*, (Madras, 1914-16; reprint ed., 2 vols. in 4, New York 1968), 1:1:288-290; 1:2:77-80; and, Begley, *Visnu's Flaming Wheel*, 2. Pal includes a ca. 4th c. Mathuran Viṣṇu with personified attributes in *The Ideal Image*, fig. 3.

13 In working on Mahāyāna and early Esoteric Buddhist imagery, Janice Leoshko has suggested pre-Buddhist imagery was adapted into the language of Buddhism in similar ways, and she claims early Buddhist imagery was transformed into Esoteric Buddhist iconography. See Leoshko, "The Implications of Bodhgaya's Sūrya," in *Aksayanivi: Essays presented to Dr. Debala Mitra* (Delhi: Indian Books, 1991), 231-234; idem, "The Case of the Two Witnesses to the Buddha's Enlightenment," *Marg* 39 (1988): 40-52.

14 Macdonald, *Mañjuśrimūlakalpa*, 110.

15 See Lalou, "Four Notes on Vajrapāṇi," 287-93; idem, "A Fifth Note on Vajrapāṇi," 242-249; Lamotte, "Vajrapāṇi en Inde," 113-159; and, Snellgrove, "Vajrapāṇi (alias Vajradhara) Becomes Preeminent," part of Chapter 3 in *Indo-Tibetan Buddhism*, 134-141.

16 Macdonald, *Mañjuśrimūlakalpa*, 77.

30. *Vajrapāṇi with four-armed krodha-vighnāntaka, Vajragiri (Orissa), ca. 8th century, Orissa State Museum, Bhubaneswar*

3

Mahabala and Mantranaya

The physique of the wrestlers therefore constitutes a basic sign, which like a seed contains the whole fight. But this seed proliferates, for it is at every turn during the fight, in each new situation, that the body of the wrestler casts to the public the magical entertainment of a temperment which finds its natural expression in a gesture.

Roland Barthes, *Mythologies*

1 The Images

31. Four-armed krodha-vighnāntaka, detail of 30

As much as two centuries later than the Aurangabad, Ellora and Sarnath *krodha-vighnāntaka* [**10-14, 16-18**] we find the earliest Esoteric Buddhist wrathful deities so far discovered in Orissan sculpture. Interestingly, two of them are also attendants of Vajrapāṇi. One is now in the Orissa State Museum, Bhubaneswar, but is reported to have come from Vajragiri (or Batragiri), in Cuttack district. [**30-31**] The other, of khondolite,[1] was placed in the east wall of the entrance porch of Ratnagiri's Monastery 1. [**32, 34**]

The two sculptures share the same local Orissan style. The bodies of the bodhisattva are thickset and stocky, with movement that is somewhat tightly controlled and stiff, and facial features are stereotyped, with puffy eyes and small sensual mouths. Though very close in date, the Vajragiri bodhisattva is, if anything, slightly heavier than the Ratnagiri work and might be placed fractionally earlier. The archaeological context of Ratnagiri provides us with a rough date for both of them, as well as for a nearly identical four-armed Avalokiteśvara, who is paired with Vajrapāṇi to the other side of the entrance porch on the west wall of Monastery 1. [**33, 35**]

Debala Mitra, the archaeologist at Ratnagiri, found the Vajrapāṇi [**32**] and Avalokiteśvara sculptures [**33**] *in situ*. She suggests that they belong to the first phase of construction at Monastery 1, which she deems ascribable to the seventh or eighth century.[2] Comparison of the Ratnagiri pair and the Vajragiri Vajrapāṇi [**30-35**] with a number of late eighth or ninth century sculptures of Mañjuśrī at Lalitagiri [**44**] and two four-armed Avalokiteśvara found outside Monastery 1 at Ratnagiri [**2, 70**] reveals that the latter are proportionally much more elongated and

32. *Vajrapāṇi with four-armed krodha-vighnāntaka, Ratnagiri (Orissa), east wall of entrance porch, ca. 7th-8th century*

33. Avalokiteśvara with four-armed krodha-vighnāntaka, Ratnagiri (Orissa), west wall of entrance porch, ca. 7th-8th century

34. Four-armed krodha-vighnāntaka, detail of 32

35. Four-armed Hayagrīva, detail of 33

supple in form and outline. Thus an earlier dating between the seventh and eighth centuries for the two Vajrapāṇi sculptures **[30, 32]** seems acceptable.[3]

The Vajrapāṇi sculptures are both four-armed, though their hand gestures vary. The Vajragiri Vajrapāṇi **[30]** holds a *sūtra* in the upper right hand; the first left arm is broken off below the elbow, but the *chauryī* (flywhisk) it held is still visible against the upper arm and shoulder. The second right hand clutches the stem of a lotus on which rests a horizontally placed *vajra*. This is Vajrapāṇi's primary iconographic mark. His lower left hand is placed on the head of a four-armed *krodha-vighnāntaka* as if in consecration. This last gesture resembles that of older non-Buddhist deities with *āyudhapuruṣa*. **[22, 24]**

Vajrapāṇi's furious attendant **[31]** is stout and close to the *vāmana*-Yakṣa body type. He has a grotesque face with bulging eyes, exaggeratedly curling eyebrows, a leering smile, and a beard and mustache. His hair is piled up into curling tendrils, not unlike the Aurangabad Vajrapuruṣa. **[10]** Adorned with large earrings, he wears a thick necklace and snake bracelets and anklets. The short *dhoti* is scored with a squared pattern, as if to suggest the variegated texture of an animal skin. With his central pair of hands he makes the *añjali mudrā,* a gesture of greeting. His proper upper right hand is turned palm out in the *vandana mudrā* of salutation while his other left hand carries a sword. He stands on a platform, which, unlike that of the attendant figure on the other side of Vajrapāṇi, is not treated with a double row of lotus petals. Craning his head upward to look at the bodhisattva, his legs are placed so as to suggest he is turning toward his superior.

The entire mien of the Phase One *krodha-vighnāntaka* suggests subservience and a willingness to surrender to the will of the bodhisattva. Here we sense an ambiguity which is at the core of the Phase One *krodha-vighnāntaka*. Is he a furious manifestation of the bodhisattva? the personification of Vajrapāṇi's implement? Or is he an unstable oath-bound convert, a powerful outsider Vajrapāṇi has just subjugated and over whom strict control must be maintained?

From one point of view, texts, which are largely unavailable (though more are forthcoming for Hayagrīva and Yamāntaka), are required to answer these questions. From another point of view, the questions themselves reveal much. They require not answers, but only that they be asked, because the artist has created an image which seems to answer "yes" to all these questions. Merely looking up a name in the *Sādhanamālā* or *Niṣpannayogāvalī* does not answer the question of the identity of this *krodha-vighnāntaka*. His essence is not one of neat and easily graspable categories. The unsettling ambiguity suggests the presence of an Esoteric Buddhist element in an otherwise relatively straightforward Mahāyāna context, and it is subtle uncertainty which characterizes the early history of the *krodha-vighnāntaka*. We see here an unstable force which the bodhisattva must restrain, but as time goes on we will watch this force break the bounds of restraint to become larger and more important than the bodhisattva who now employs it.

Turning to the Vajrapāṇi from Ratnagiri [**32**], we find a different set of gestures, which are in fact uncommon for Vajrapāṇi: the upper right hand carries a *mālā* (rosary), the lower right makes *vara mudrā* (the gesture of gift-giving), the lower left holds a long-necked vase and the upper left once again holds the stem of a lotus on which, as in the Vajragiri sculpture, rests a horizontal *vajra*. If we examine the Avalokiteśvara which is placed on the other side of the doorway [**33**], it is clear that the artist has merely duplicated the *mālā, vara mudrā,* and long-necked vase. These implements and gestures are canonical for Avalokiteśvara, not Vajrapāṇi. The same is true for Sūcīmukha, the *preta* or hungry ghost, who kneels on the proper right side of both images in order to assuage his unslakeable thirst with the drops of *amṛit* (nectar) rolling off the bodhisattva's outstretched palm.[4] In converting a four-armed Avalokiteśvara into a matching Vajrapāṇi, the artist has merely changed the fully-blown lotus of Avalokiteśvara into Vajrapāṇi's emblem and substituted gems in Vajrapāṇi's crest for the image of Amitabha nestled in Avalokiteśvara's hair.

The two *krodha-vighnāntaka* images [**34-35**] are even more similar than the Vajrapāṇi and Avalokiteśvara figures. They are iconographically identical, though we know Avalokiteśvara's to be Hayagrīva and Vajrapāṇi's to be a different figure. On the one hand, the likeness must serve to chasten the confidence of our assertions in identifying a Phase One *krodha-vighnāntaka* based on his iconographic characteristics without a verifiable context. On the other hand, it does suggest that at this early period the specific iconographic characteristics of individual *krodha-vighnāntaka* figures were not as strictly determined as were certain shared characteristics of the group as a whole. Within accepted parameters they were formally virtually interchangeable.

Despite similarities, Vajrapāṇi's wrathful attendant [**34**] has a rather more *vāmana*-Yakṣa type body than the Vajragiri figure. [**31**] Their faces, expressions, beard, hair and ornaments are strikingly alike. Instead of making *añjali mudrā,* however, the Ratnagiri *krodha-vighnāntaka* makes the *vinayahasta* gesture with which we are already familiar from the Aurangabad, Nepalese and Sarnath Vajrapuruṣa. His upper right hand also makes the *vandana mudrā,* as if saluting the bodhisattva. In his second left hand he carries a noose. Once again we find a forceful, angular posture, known as *pratyālīḍha,* characteristic of *krodha-vighnāntaka* of all periods: the left leg extended and right leg bent at the knee.

2 Identification

The identities of these two *krodha-vighnāntaka* [**31, 34**] are still in doubt. Possibly they were intended to represent Vajrapuruṣa. It is also possible that at least the Ratnagiri example [**34**] may represent one of Vajrapāṇi's wrathful manifestations, not the personification of his emblem. At this early period (ca. 600-700 CE) a likely candidate is Mahābala, who is in effect identical with Ucchusma.[5]

The *Mahābala Sūtra* was translated into Chinese in 983,[6] but it must have been current in India considerably earlier. The translation into Tibetan is credited to Śilendrabodhi, Jinamitra and the renowned translator Yeshe Day, who worked around the year 800 CE.[7] Mahābala was well represented in fragments of Tibetan texts and *dhāraṇī* prayers at Dunhuang, and he is also mentioned in a Khotanese Buddhist text as the protector of Khotan.[8] Marcelle Lalou points out that the *Mahābala Sūtra* cites *dhāraṇī* from the *Vidyottama-mahātantra*, which is found, along with a Mahābala *dhāraṇī*, in a Tibetan catalogue now accepted as dating to the first quarter of the ninth century.[9] The *Mahābala Sūtra* calls itself a Mahāyāna *sūtra*, and its format, protagonists (Śākyamuni, Vajrapāṇi, Subhūti, etc.) and narrative qualities suggest an origin slightly after the earliest portions of the *MMK* but before the *STTS*, which began to be translated into Chinese in the eighth century.

In his *Sūtra* Mahābala is the primary wrathful manifestation of Vajrapāṇi (along with Trailokyavijaya and Kuṇḍali). He is described as having one head and four arms. The Ratnagiri figure **[34]** conforms to the textual prescriptions by carrying a noose in a left hand, but departs from it by making the *vandana mūdra* with the right rather than the left hand. The club and the *chauryī* mentioned in the text are also absent.[10] Such discrepancies need not deter us from making the identification, however. Even a painted image of Mahābala at the beginning of an early Tibetan translation of the *Mahābala Sūtra* recovered from Dunhuang does not fully follow its own text's prescription.[11]

In the painting of Mahābala from Dunhuang Mahābala stands in *ālīḍha* beside a *vajra* placed on a lotus pedestal. The combination of Mahābala and the *vajra* reinforces the connection with Vajrapāṇi. In accordance with the text and like the Ratnagiri *krodha-vighnāntaka*, Mahābala is one-headed and four-armed. He holds the noose in a lower proper right hand and the club in an upper left, opposite to the text's suggestion. Unfortunately the picture is damaged, so one cannot be sure the *chauryī* was not painted in originally. It appears that he has two fists in front of his chest, not unlike the Ratnagiri and the Vajragiri wrathful figures. **[31, 34]** One hand clearly violates the text's description by neither making the *vandana mudrā* nor holding a *chauryī*. A further similarity with the Orissan versions is the unmistakable *lambodara* belly.

More evidence is found in the *Mahābala Sūtra* to suggest a considerable ideological parallelism with these early sculptures from Ratnagiri. The text describes an assembly around the Buddha. Vajrapāṇi, Mahābala and the other wrathful deities sit on one side of the Buddha while Avalokiteśvara, Hayagrīva and others are placed on the other.[12] The arrangement is very common, reflecting dominant *trikula* thought, which overlaps with earlier Mahāyāna imagery at Ellora and Aurangabad but develops in the direction of Esoteric Buddhism. It also matches rather nicely the arrangement of the entrance porch at Ratnagiri Monastery 1, with Vajrapāṇi and Mahābala (?) on the east wall **[32]** facing Avalokiteśvara and Hayagrīva on the west wall. **[33]**

3 Mantrayana, Mantranaya and Mahayana

Are we justified in suggesting that an early Esoteric Buddhist text is relevant to Orissan art of the seventh and eighth centuries? The evidence of Tibetan translations discussed above places the text at the latest within the eighth century, so temporally we are within reasonable limits. The Tibetans much later classify the *Mahābala Sūtra* as a *kriyā* text. In her highly regarded dissertation, Nancy Hock deduces that *kriyā* texts were utilized at Ratnagiri in relationship to the sculptures. She notes that at Ratnagiri they were "used earlier and more extensively than the *anuttarayoga tantras*."[13] Hock posits that the numerous Amoghapāśa images at Ratnagiri "suggest a cult of this bodhisattva at Ratnagiri and the use of a *kriyā tantra* (probably the *Amoghapāśakalparāja* or its shortened version, the *Amoghapāśahṛdaya-dhāraṇī*) in support of his worship,"[14] and goes on to give reasons why a "*kriyā tantra*" like the *MMK* may have been in circulation there. By her standards the *Mahābala Sūtra* would not be out of place in the context of Ratnagiri.

For the most part I am in agreement with Hock. Specifically I am in accord with her differentiation of early and late Esoteric Buddhism, her suggestion that these distinctions are visible in the art at Ratnagiri, and with her observation that these distinctions have until recently been largely ignored. There are a few differences in our points of view concerning the development of the *krodha-vighnāntaka* and their presence in Phase One imagery at Ratnagiri. My initial reservations may be briefly stated and discussion deferred. First, two distinct strands (here designated Phase Two and Phase Three) can be discerned within what Hock packages singly under the term Vajrayāna; second, each stage in the development of Esoteric Buddhism should not be thought to come to a full stop before the beginning of the next, but to overlap considerably. (Refer to Graph 4, COLOR PLATE 17C.)

The third issue deals with the application of the rubric "Tantric" to sculptures which are thematically of a mixed Mahāyāna and early Esoteric Buddhist strain. This issue has already been broached with our earliest examples of *krodha-vighnāntaka* at Aurangabad and Ellora. Here we must tackle it again for sculpture of between the seventh and eighth centuries at Ratnagiri. Hock insightfully distinguishes later Esoteric Buddhism, classified by the Tibetans as *yoga tantra* and *anuttara yoga tantra* (roughly Phases Two and Three), from an earlier stage, which she deems "transitional" but recognizes as "closer in many respects to Mahāyāna" than to later forms.[15] Despite her acknowledgement of the close relationship with Mahāyāna, Hock isolates the transitional stage as a distinct vehicle called Mantrayāna. While granting an appreciable Esoteric Buddhist influence in Phase One imagery, doctrine and practice, I believe it should be considered no more than a minority movement still within the range of orthodox Mahāyāna ritual.

This less dramatic model is better able to accommodate not only Phase One imagery but also the majority of the imagery at Ratnagiri. Hock states that Ratnagiri is "predominantly a Mantrayāna site," and "The term *tantric* best describes the Buddhism practiced at Ratnagiri."[16] Yet by her count, of sixteen large images of the Buddha, only five are "definitely *tantric*," and even some of these five are "*tantric*" on questionable grounds. For example, the "*tantric*" nature of one is due solely to the presence of elephants on a throne. Others are "*tantric*" because they include or were originally arranged between a pair of bodhisattva, Mañjuśrī and Avalokiteśvara, and Vajrapāṇi and Avalokiteśvara, two-armed in every case.[17] One understands why Hock concludes that the presence of the Buddha with Avalokiteśvara and Vajrapāṇi is "*tantric*" when she reveals, "The only text I know that describes Śākyamuni accompanied by Avalokiteśvara and Vajrapāṇi is the *kriyā tantra*, the *Mañjuśrīmūlakalpa*."[18] As already mentioned above, the Tibetan translation of the Mahāyāna *Buddhabalādhana-prātihārya-vikurvāṇanirdeśa Sūtra* clearly pairs Vajrapāṇi and Avalokiteśvara with the preaching Śākyamuni.[19] Therefore the presence of this pair is not exclusively limited to *kriyā tantra* and is not a definitive signal of Esoteric Buddhism.

Hock similarly infers too much Esoteric Buddhist significance from a two-armed Mañjuśrī in *dharmacakra mudrā*, who sits on a lion and is paired with a two-armed Avalokiteśvara and an unadorned Buddha. The two bodhisattva suggest to Hock "the *tantric* nature of the piece," because this form of Mañjuśrī "explicitly relates to tantric Buddhism. Bu-ston lists the *Mañjuśrītantra* as one of the six *tantras* of the *kriyā* cycle."[20] Neither Mañjuśrī nor Avalokiteśvara are limited to Esoteric Buddhism, and their presence alone need not be a conclusive marker. If only a fraction of the Buddha images (and we could extend it to the bodhisattva images as well) at Ratnagiri display the "*tantric*" mode, how can we accept that Ratnagiri is "predominantly a Mantrayāna site"?

The evidence of visual imagery is corroborated by inscriptional and textual evidence to form a strong argument that the majority practice at Ratnagiri was not separate from the Mahāyāna movement, particularly in the period when the Avalokiteśvara and Vajrapāṇi sculptures **[32-33]** were erected at the outer gate of the largest monastery. Multiple inscriptions of three texts were found at Ratnagiri. All three were enclosed either in large reliquary *stūpa*s or in some of the hundreds of miniature funerary *stūpa*s surrounding the larger ones. The oldest inscriptions, datable to the late fifth or sixth century, appear on several stone slabs and reproduce passages of the *Pratītyasamutpāda Sūtra* in both Sanskrit and Prakrit.[21] This text is a canonical Mahāyāna Mādhyamika text often placed inside *stūpa*s with no particular Esoteric Buddhist association.[22] Hock, however, adduces it to her argument that Ratnagiri is a predominantly "*tantric*" site by affirming that it was "also used by followers of *tantric* Buddhism."[23] Yet there is little evidence for Esoteric Buddhist activity in Orissa in the late fifth or sixth century, and Debala Mitra concludes, "When Monastery 1 was built Ratnagiri was definitely under the grip of Mahāyāna Buddhism."[24]

Extracts from two other texts were discovered at Ratnagiri in the form of *dhāraṇī* inscriptions.[25] The fact that they are *dhāraṇī* inscriptions does not indicate necessarily an Esoteric Buddhist intent, though it is evidence that Esoteric Buddhist ideas were coming to the fore in Mahāyāna ritual practice. Gregory Schopen has identified the texts from which the *dhāraṇī* were extracted to be the *Bodhigarbhālankāralakṣa-dhāraṇī* and either the *Sarvaprajñāntaparāmitāsiddhacaitya-nāma-dhāraṇī* or the *Samantamukhapraveśaraśmivimaloṣṇīsa-prabhāsa-sarvatathāgata-hṛdayasamaya-vilokita-nāma-dhāraṇī*. The *Vimaloṣṇīsa dhāraṇī* as found at Ratnagiri appears in both.[26] The same texts have been found in *stūpa*s at a wide range of sites in India and the northwest. Copies of the *dhāraṇī* found at Ratnagiri date from the ca. ninth century and were also enclosed within *stūpa*s.[27] The *dhāraṇī*s themselves explicitly relate to the practice of making *caitya* and the merit that will be accumulated if the *dhāraṇī* is placed inside.

Schopen is quite clear that if Esoteric Buddhism is characterized by the teachings of a master, by graded initiations, secret doctrines, language and organization, and by highly structured methods involving ritual and meditative techniques, then:

> *there is nothing at all 'Tantric' about these texts. They are texts dealing with ritual forms open to all and religious problems common to all — monks, nuns, lay men and women. Secondly, they show a marked continuity in terms of religious concerns with the literature that preceded them. They are, like much of the canonical Mahāyāna sūtra literature that came before them, preoccupied with death and the problems of rebirth.*[28]

The texts found at Ratnagiri testify to a ritual practice which has very little to do with a separate category of Mantrayāna, despite the use of *dhāraṇī*. The two types of *dhāraṇī* are part of the continuing Buddhist ritual of *caitya* worship, and merely replace the older text of the *Pratītyasamutpāda*, which had been used in both Early Buddhism (Hināyāna) and Mahāyāna. The worship of *caitya* is a venerable

Buddhist practice not particularly associated with Esoteric Buddhism. In fact there is some justification for claiming that *caitya* worship was actually opposed by Esoteric Buddhists.[29]

In another work which identifies a group of *dhāraṇī* inscriptions found associated with a *stūpa* in Sri Lanka, Schopen has called attention to a remark by Arthur Waley,[30] in which the latter presciently notes:

> *European writers have tended to connect . . . the use of dhāraṇī (magic word-formulae) only with the esoteric doctrines of the Vairocana sect . . . In fact, however, scriptures centring round the use of spells figure very largely in the lists of works translated in Chinese even as early as the second century* AD.[31]

As early as 1844 Burnouf discussed *dhāraṇī* in "developed" *sūtras*, including the *Saddharmapuṇḍarīka*, *Gandavyūha* and *Laṇkāvātara*. He argued that the *dhāraṇī* appearing there were not later interpolations but part of the religious milieu at the time of their creation and thus naturally included in the original *sūtra*.[32] Winternitz also stresses the seamlessness of Mahāyāna texts with *dhāraṇī*:

> *A large and essential constituent element of the Mahāyānistical literature is found in the Dhāraṇīs or "Protective Spells."*[33]
>
> *In a similar manner the Dhāraṇīs often appear as constituent elements of the Sūtras, in which the circumstances are stated in which they were proclaimed.*[34]

Schopen groups this type of Mahāyāna text, including the inscriptions found at Ratnagiri, as Mahāyāna "*dhāraṇī sūtras*" and disputes their direct pertinence to "Tantrism" or Vajrayāna.[35] He has also given a lucid survey of a particular theme in *nikāya/āgama* and Mahāyāna literature, which at the same time persuasively demonstrates the harmonization of *dhāraṇī* activity within the realm of Mahāyāna Buddhist goals and practices.[36] There is little in the way of a major conceptual shift from the Mahāyāna rituals of hearing, reciting and copying sacred texts to hearing, reciting, copying and depositing *dhāraṇīs* inside *stūpas*.[37] Schopen suggests that these ideas and the texts which bear them were current "from the 5th/6th century to the 12th century and even later, even though there are indications that some forms of the ideas may have been older."[38]

Admittedly, the origins of early Esoteric Buddhism and its close relationship with Mahāyāna is a difficult problem which has not received a definitive solution.[39] We have reviewed visual, inscriptional and textual evidence. They harmonize in supporting the conclusion that it is appropriate to consider Ratnagiri and by extension other monastic centers like Nalanda as Mahāyāna sites in which cultic Mahāyāna, though inflected by Esoteric Buddhist ideas, continued as the mainstream orthodoxy.[40]

Naturally my position includes reservations about the use of the term Mantrayāna. Hock disagrees with Snellgrove over whether early Esoteric Buddhist texts, including those called *kriyā tantra* by much later Tibetan historians, should be considered Mahāyāna or as belonging to a distinct "vehicle" called Mantrayāna.[41] As already indicated, her inclination is to separate these early texts ideologically from both Mahāyāna and *anuttarayoga tantra*. Thus she creates a three-fold system, which she divides into Mahāyāna, Mantrayāna (*kriyā* and presumably *caryā tantra*) and Vajrayāna (*yoga* and *anuttarayoga tantra*).

There is a great deal of sense in Hock's system, and to a large extent I concur with her distinctions. Still, her clear and ideal boundaries are at the expense of actual overlap between late Mahāyāna and early Esoteric Buddhism. We will have to deal with the daunting question of classification systems at greater length in later chapters, but it is immediately critical to our understanding of the early *krodha-vighnāntaka* images to be as clear as possible about their doctrinal context, even if the effort blurs borders between classifications. Since our interpretation of the visual, inscriptional and textual evidence argues for a predominantly Mahāyāna focus in the seventh and eighth centuries at Ratnagiri, where certain early Esoteric Buddhist practices were accommodated, it is difficult to support the notion that this mixed practice is separable from Mahāyāna as "Mantrayāna."

Rather than assigning early Esoteric Buddhism to a separate vehicle, we may be wiser to follow Jean Naudou, among others, in reviving the term *mantranaya*[42] (practice of *mantra*) rather than Mantrayāna (the vehicle of *mantra*). Unfortunately, Naudou himself does not restrict the term sufficiently. He uses *mantranaya* broadly "to designate *within Mahāyāna*, the progressive method generally called, in modern writing, 'Tantric Buddhism' or 'Vehicle of the Diamond'."[43] As Snellgrove points out, to designate all Esoteric Buddhism with a single term masks the undisputed differences between later Esoteric Buddhism and the early stage presently under discussion.[44] *Mantranaya*, then, may be used to designate *within Mahāyāna* the ritualized use of *dhāraṇī* and certain imagery shared with more developed forms of Esoteric Buddhism (*krodha-vighnātaka* being an example), but used in accord with more traditional Mahāyāna goals.

In treating this issue Snellgrove frames the discourse in terms of textual classification. His system also acknowledges the overlap between Mahāyāna texts and early Esoteric Buddhist texts. He discusses a "progressive tantric development which eventually distinguishes *sūtras* from *tantras*."[45] On a broad scale he divides *tantras* into those relatable to Mahāyāna *sūtras*, (*kriyā*, *caryā* and *yoga tantras*) and those with non-Buddhist associations (basically *anuttarayoga tantras*). He later goes even further to relate the texts, and by implication, also the practices and imagery of early Esoteric Buddhism, with the "normal Mahāyāna world," albeit late Mahāyāna. Snellgrove elsewhere trenchantly observes that the "early tantras (those classed as *kriyā* and *caryā*) . . . were produced in close dependence on Mahāyāna *sūtras* . . . [and] may be regarded as their ritual counterparts."[47] These texts call themselves *sūtras* and describe deities who are familiar from earlier Mahāyāna *sūtras*. For these reasons, both *kriyā* and *caryā tantras* "can best be understood if they are accepted as part of the normal Mahāyāna scene."[48]

36. Four-armed krodha-vighnāntaka, detail of 37

This accords very well with the pair of ca. seventh to eighth-century sculptures of Vajrapāṇi and Avalokiteśvara at the entrance to Monastery 1 at Ratnagiri. [32-33] The fact alone that they were on the outer walls of the entrance passage suggests that the imagery, far from "esoteric," was accessible to all. The cult of the bodhisattva, with which Mahāyāna was by then impregnated, had begun to accommodate the early Esoteric Buddhist ideas, particularly the use of *mantra* and *dhāraṇī*. It expanded the number and elaborated the character of forms of its traditional bodhisattva, like Avalokiteśvara,

Vajrapāṇi, Maitreya and Mañjuśrī. They are given more attributes and hands to hold them, as well as personifications of those attributes.

We feel we are justified then in consulting early Esoteric Buddhist texts to identify the iconography of these early sculptures at Ratnagiri. From them we learn that Mahābala, the four-armed *krodha-vighnāntaka,* is the personification of a *dhāraṇī,* "une formule magique 'furieuse' personnifiée."[49] As in the text, in the Ratnagiri Vajrapāṇi **[36, 37]** Mahābala (?) is still subordinate to Vajrapāṇi bodhisattva in exactly the way that I believe Snellgrove, Naudou and others argue that *mantranaya* was subordinate to Mahāyāna.

37. *Vajrapāṇi with four-armed krodha-vighnāntaka, Ratnagiri (Orissa), entrance porch, ca. 7th-8th century, same as* **32**

Notes to Chapter Three

1 The Ratnagiri sculptures, as well as those at Lalitagiri and Udayagiri, are generally of khondolite, occasionally *muguni* stone. See Padmasri P. Acharya, "Varieties of Stones Used in Building Temples and Making Images in Orissa (Quarries and Method of Transport)," *The Orissa Historical Research Society* 13.2 (1965): 9-20.

2 Debala Mitra, *Ratnagiri (1958-61)*, 2 vols. (New Delhi, 1981-83), 156, 159-160.

3 We can overrule Charles Fabri's opinion that the Vajragiri Vajrapāṇi is a "truly bad example of poor workmanship and lack of aesthetic sense in the squat, top-heavy Bodhisattva Vajrapāṇi. . . . I suggest that it cannot be earlier than the 11th [c.]." Charles Fabri, *History of the Art of Orissa* (New Delhi, 1974), 72.

4 For an image of Sūcīmukha accompanying Avalokiteśvara, see Susan and John Huntington, *Leaves from the* Bodhi *Tree: The Art of Pāla India (8th-12th centuries) and Its International Legacy* (Dayton, 1990), 160.

5 In his introduction to the *Mahābala-sūtra*, Bischoff seems to want to distinguish Mahābala from Ucchusma, but the text itself uses the names interchangeably. For instance, Vajrapāṇi recites a version of Mahābala's *dhāraṇī*, which Bischoff translates as follows: "Om Vajrakrodha Mahābala burn slay ruin, pulverize, O (you of) long hair, O *lambodara*, Ucchusmakrodha *hūṁ*, *phaṭ*, *svāhā*." Bischoff, *Mahābala*, 55 (I have translated it into English from the French, restored the Sanskrit term for "ventre pendant," and added emphasis to indicate the equivalence of Mahābala and Ucchusma). For another *dhāraṇī* which similarly interchanges the two names, see ibid., 56-57.

6 T.21.1243 (Njo 1019, KBC 1097). Lewis Lancaster translates the period of reign as 933, instead of the correct 983. See Lewis R. Lancaster, *The Korean Buddhist Canon: A Descriptive Catalogue* (Berkeley, 1979), 377. In Tibet the *Mahābala sūtra* is classified in the Vajra section of *kriyā-tantra*. See Ferdinand D. Lessing and Alex Wayman, *Introduction to the Buddhist Tantric Systems, translated from Mkhas-grub rje's* Rgyud sde spyihi rnam par gzag pa rgyas par brjod, 2nd ed. (Delhi, 1978), 133, 343.

7 Bischoff, *Mahābala*, 3; Snellgrove, *Indo-Tibetan Buddhism*, 443.

8 See the list given in Bischoff, *Mahābala*, 1-3. Also see Marcelle Lalou, "Documents de Touen-Houang: I. Deux Priāres de Caravaniers Tibétains," *Mélanges chinois et bouddhiques* 8 (1946/47): 217-223; and, H.W. Bailey, "Hvatanica IV," *Bulletin of the School of Oriental and African Studies* 10 (1942): 893.

9 Marcelle Lalou, "Préface," in Bischoff, *Mahābala*, x. On the Tibetan catalogue, see idem, "Les Textes Bouddhiques au temps du roi Khri-Sron-Lde-Bcan: contribution á la Bibiliographie du Kanjur et du Tanjur," *Journal Asiatique* 241 (1953): 313-353. For the accepted date of this catalogue, see Schopen, "Vimaloṣṇīṣa Dhāraṇīs," 125.

10 T.21.1243.207c; Bischoff, *Mahābala*, 50.

11 Bischoff, *Mahābala*, pl. I.

12 T.21.1243.207c.

13 Nancy Hock, "Buddhist ideology and the sculpture of Ratnagiri, seventh through thirteenth centuries" (Ph.D. dissertation, University of California, Berkeley, 1987), 7.

14 Hock, "Buddhist ideology," 37.

15 Ibid., 30.

16 Ibid., 1, 30.

17 Ibid., 49-50, 54.

18 Ibid., 61.

19 Schopen, "Five Leaves," 319-336.

20 Hock, "Buddhist ideology," 55.

21 Mitra, *Ratnagiri*, 25, 29-31, 411-422.

22 Krishna Deva, "Significance of Pratītya-Samutpāda-Sūtra in Buddhist Art and Thought," in *Buddhist Iconography* (New Delhi: Tibet House, 1989), 42-46; and, Jan Fontein, "Relics and reliquaries, texts and artefacts," in *Function and Meaning in Buddhist Art*, ed. K.R. van Kooij and H. van der Veere (Groningen: Egbert Forsten, 1995), 21-31.

23 Hock, "Buddhist ideology," 36.

24 Mitra, *Ratnagiri*, 20.

25 Ibid., 31, 43, 99-100, 104.

26 Schopen, "Vimaloṣṇīṣa Dhāraṇīs," 119-149; and, Hock, "Buddhist ideology," 23-24.

27 Mitra, *Ratnagiri*, 44, 99.

28 Schopen, "Vimaloṣṇīṣa Dhāraṇīs," 147.

29 For example, a verse in the *Guhyasamāja tantra* (an early Phase Three text) states that the yogin "should not engage in the rite of *caitya*." A commentary elaborates: "This refers to the great *yogin* (Mchan: 'belonging to the Stage of Completion'). . . . he should not engage in the rite of *caitya* (e.g., circumambulation), including (preparation of) the site and (removal of) gravel, etc, because it is not right (Mchan: 'for a person on the Stage of Completion who himself is all Tathāgatas') to have craving for *caitya*-worship." Alex Wayman, *Yoga of Guhyasamājatantra: The Arcane Lore of Forty Verses, A Buddhist Tantra Commentary* (Indian ed., Delhi, 1977), 259. It seems this applies to the accomplished one, not the aspirant. Another Phase Three text, the *Advayasiddhi*, repeats the advice against making *stūpas*: "He [the yogin] should not erect *Caityas* of stone or clay . . ." Malati J. Shendge, *Advayasiddhi, Edited with an Introduction* (Baroda, 1964), 29. Gregory Schopen demonstrates that texts like the Vajracchedikā, Aṣṭasāhasrikā Prajñāpāramitā, etc. (texts which were revered as the philosophical underpinning of Esoteric Buddhism) have "an unambiguously negative attitude to the *stūpa* cult." See Schopen, "The Phrase 'sa pṛthivipradeśaś caityabhūto bhavet' in the *Vajracchedikā*: Notes on the Cult of the Book in Mahāyāna," *Indo-Iranian Journal* 17 (1975): 181.

30 Gregory Schopen, "The Text on the 'Dhāraṇī Stones from Abhayagiriya': A Minor Contribution to the Study of Mahāyāna Literature in Ceylon," *JIABS* 5 (1982): 103.

31 Arthur Waley, *A Catalogue of Paintings Recovered from Tun-huang by Sir Aurel Stein, K.C.I.E.* (London, 1931), xiii.

32 Eugène Burnouf, *Introduction a l'histoire du Buddhisme indien* (Paris, 1844), 540-542.

33 Moriz Winternitz, *History of Indian Literature vol. II, Part I: Buddhist Literature*, trans. Bhaskara Jha (Delhi, 1987), 321 (paragraph 393).

34 Winternitz, *History of Indian Literature*, 323 (paragraph 396).

35 Schopen, "'Dhāraṇī Stones from Abhayagiriya'," 105.

36 Gregory Schopen, "The Generalization of an Old Yogic Attainment in Medieval Mahāyāna Sūtra Literature: Some Notes on Jātismara," *JIABS* 6 (1983): 109-47.

37 Schopen, "Old Yogic Attainment," 133.

38 Ibid., 131.

39 "Very little of the genesis of the elements later known as Mantrayāna or Vajrayāna has been adequately explained. Moreover, the extremely close relationship that this tradition in its maturity had with normative Mahāyāna in the monastic setting has been largely ignored." Ronald M. Davidson, "Appendix: An Introduction to the Standards of Scriptural Authenticity in Indian Buddhism," in *Chinese Buddhist Apocrypha*, ed. Robert E. Buswell, Jr. (Honolulu, 1990), 312.

40 Snellgrove suggests that the situation in most Tibetan monasteries may be comparable to that in the monasteries of the late stage of Buddhism in India, in that the majority of the monks "follow the safe but slow way of the sūtras, namely, the practice of conventional morality, the reciting of texts, performing of ceremonies and immersion into bouts of meditation," while only a minority "remain dissatisfied with such methods and aspire to experience here and now the conviction of permanent release [i.e., follow Esoteric Buddhism]." David Snellgrove, *Buddhist Himalaya: Travels and Studies in quest of the origins and nature of Tibetan Religion* (Oxford, 1957), 86.

41 See the discussion in Hock, "Buddhist ideology," 30-43.

42 The *Tattva-ratnavāli* purportedly subdivides Mahāyāna into two schools, *pāramitānaya* (which would include the philosophical texts like the *Prajñāpāramitā* works and meditational practices) and the *mantranaya* (which would include the early ritual texts and practices). See Shashibhusan Dasgupta, *An Introduction to Tantric Buddhism*, 3rd

ed. (Calcutta, 1974), 52-53.

43 Jean Naudou, *Les Bouddhistes Kasmiriens Au Moyen Age* (Paris, 1968), 116 (emphasis added; my translation from the French, with reference to the English translation of Naudou, *Buddhists of Kasmir*, 138).

44 Snellgrove, *Indo-Tibetan Buddhism*, 279.

45 Ibid., 148.

46 Ibid., 147-160.

47 Snellgrove, "Categories of Buddhist Tantras," 1364.

48 Snellgrove, *Indo-Tibetan Buddhism*, 233. Hock quotes this last passage to a fuller degree in "Buddhist ideology," 33. Yet she questions Snellgrove's conclusion. Convinced that Ratnagiri is an exclusively or predominantly Esoteric Buddhist site, she suggests its imagery "is different in character from sculpture at Mahāyāna sites." The example of a Mahāyāna site she gives is Bodh Gaya, which she claims "lacks the iconographically more complex images and program found at Mantrayāna sites." This is difficult to support based on the Yamāntaka and Trailokyavijaya images at the Mahants compound of Bodh Gaya. **[145]**

49 Bischoff, *Mahābala*, 6.

38. Yamāntaka attending Mañjuśrī, Ayodhya (Orissa), ca. late 10th-early 11th century, Ayodhya Mārīcī Mandir, detail of 57

4

Phase One Imagery of Yamantaka

With a nimbus bright as the solar wheel, incinerating (obstacles) like the ultimate fire of destruction, [Yamāntaka] has skin the color of a dark cloud . . . his diamond-sharp fangs protrude, his tongue flashes like lightning.

Māyājāla mahātantra

With Yamāntaka, the wrathful attendant of Mañjuśrī bodhisattva, we are on a firmer path in terms of iconographic identification. We remain in the realm of *mantranaya*, Mahāyāna cult imagery with an admixture of Esoteric Buddhism, but we are on a path which will outlive the lifecycles of Vajrapuruṣa and Mahābala. After the eighth century Vajrapuruṣa, as a personification of an attribute, soon drops from sight outside of Nepal in favor of personifications of *dhāraṇī*. Mahābala too seems to have been replaced in Phase Two imagery by other hypostases of Vajrapāṇi, like Bhūtaḍāmara and Trailokyavijaya. Vajrapāṇi becomes increasingly associated with mature Esoteric Buddhism and seems not to have inspired an enduring cult within Mahāyāna the way that Maitreya, Mañjuśrī and Avalokiteśvara did. As we have already seen, it is the hybrid of Mahāyāna and *mantranaya* which is at the root of Phase One imagery. Phase One style images of Mañjuśrī with Yamāntaka, on the other hand, continue being made into the late eleventh and twelfth centuries.[1] Yamāntaka grows into a mature independent image in Phase Two contexts, to be ultimately transformed during Phase Three into Vajrabhairava and Yamāri.

1 The Iconography of Yamantaka as Attendant to Mañjusri

The identification of Yamāntaka in Phase One imagery is generally dependent on the prior recognition of Mañjuśrī, as only Yamāntaka is consistently paired with Mañjuśrī as his wrathful attendant. De Mallmann notes that Yamāntaka is exclusively the "assistant to bodhisattva Mañjuśrī, of whom he is a wrathful manifestation."[2] The association of the two is well documented in standard iconographic compendia like the *Sādhanamālā* and the *Niṣpannayogāvalī*, and other literature as well. An important early text to make the connection clear is the *Mañjuśrīmūlakalpa*

(*MMK*). This voluminous text has been the subject of a number of studies, including those by Marcelle Lalou and Ariane Macdonald.[3] It was rendered into Chinese by the Kashmiri monk Tianxizai between 980 and 1000, who utilized sections which had already been translated by Amoghavajra in the eighth century.[4] These include chapters thirty through thirty-two of the Chinese version,[5] which deal specifically with the rituals of Yamāntaka. Therefore we may err on the side of caution and say that by the seventh century the portions of the text with which we are concerned had a certain currency in India.

The *MMK* is of direct relevance for Phase One imagery, because it casts the *krodha-vighnāntaka*, and Yamāntaka in particular, as oath-bound power beings who have been converted to Buddhism. Yamāntaka is unequivocally identified as Mañjuśrī's wrathful manifestation.[6] He is portrayed, however, as a being whose power is derived from sources outside of Buddhism (viz., as a Yakṣa, or Yama himself) now harnessed to Buddhist tasks. This is probably nowhere more evident than in the *dhāraṇī* addressed to Yamāntaka. He must be reminded of his oath of allegiance and reprimanded for his procrastination:

> *Om, Khakha khāhikhāhi, Conqueror of evil beings! You with six heads, with four heads [sic], come, come grand slayer of Vighna! Perform, perform all the actions, cut, cut . . . perform all my work! Remember your vow! Hum, Hum! Divide, divide! . . . Why do you delay? Act on my behalf! Svāhā!*[7]

One cannot help recalling here the formal resemblance between the early *krodha-vighnāntaka* images and that of earlier *āyudhapuruṣa*, Śiva-Gaṇa and other Yakṣa figures. This formal "borrowing" by artists is justified by doctrinal connections between the demi-gods outside the Buddhist fold and their new role as "enforcers" who must be reminded of their vows.

The *MMK* goes on to describe in a mythic format the relationship between Mañjuśrī and Yamāntaka in a way that lends itself to pictorialization:

> *Mañjuśrī placed his right hand on the top of the head of the Krodha, and after giving homage to the Buddhas and bodhisattvas, he gave him the order to assemble all the beings by means of magical powers . . . After having drawn a circle over the King of Krodhas with his hand, he [Mañjuśrī] dispatched him [Yamāntaka] to accomplish this mission. In an instant the King of the Krodhas had gone to all regions of the world where he succeeded, thanks to his magical power, in mastering hostile beings and compelling them to enter into the circle of the Assembly.*[8]

Empowered by the gesture of Mañjuśrī's hand over his head, Yamāntaka gathers together all beings to hear the preaching of the Buddha. It would seem Yamāntaka possesses magical powers of rapid flight and swift coercion. These powers are homologized with the powers of *dhāraṇi*, of which Yamāntaka is a personification.[9] It is worth noting that in this instance Yamāntaka is charged with a relatively minor task. Like the other Phase One *krodha-vighnāntaka*, Yamāntaka is more or less a glorified messenger-boy, a servant employed for his speed, cunning and toughness along the byways of the universe.

1.1 Destroyer of obstacles (vighnāntaka)

Besides assembling widespread beings, the *MMK* delineates a few other duties of Yamāntaka. In the fourth chapter of the Sanskrit redaction (seventh *juan* of the Chinese) he is described as "le destructeur de tous les obstacles, sous un aspect extrêmement terrifiant et cruel."[10] The fourth section of the Chinese text later assesses Yamāntaka's powers as follows:

> *He has great abilities, and great power. With great cruelty, he blows up into great wrath. He can destroy all obstacles. If there are those who slander Buddhism and violently compel sentient beings, [Yamāntaka] can effectively convert them and cause them to accept Buddhism. For those who hold and recite his dhāraṇī, performing the rite of protection, even if there are those who slander the dhāraṇī and despise the Three Jewels, who produce all the evil karma, whether in heaven, on earth or below the earth, all these, [Yamāntaka] will subjugate and render them obedient.*[11]

Chapter Two of the *MMK* states explicitly that the *vighna* destroyed by Yamāntaka and his *dhāraṇī* and *homa* rituals are varied enough to include the opposition of evil visions, malicious human acts, demons and the devas. As is typical of Phase One texts, the *MMK* projects them as outward obstacles. Exterior threats of these kinds at least overtly do not share much of the inner significance taken on by obstacles later conceived as anger, egoism and lust.

1.2 Protector

The *MMK* also establishes Yamāntaka's reputation as a protector of the adept. This has both broad and specific applications. His protection applies in a broad sense to all sentient beings who practice Buddhism, particularly those at the Assembly:[12]

> *. . . he protects all sentient beings, along with his countless thousands of krodha minions. Then he sends out in all four directions, up and down, to all places, a great howl. All sentient beings have their hearts pacified in cultivation of the good, by this. They turn to the Three Jewels and don't offend [against Buddhist morality]. If the hearers [of the great howl] want to disobey the commands of the Buddha, their heads split apart into a hundred pieces like a branch of the Arjaka tree.*[13]

Yamāntaka's protective powers are also extended to the protection and purification of the grounds on which the *maṇḍala* is constructed, as well as to the practitioner who performs rituals there. The very first task in purifying the site is to sprinkle it with a mixture which has been sacralized by the recitation of Yamāntaka's *dhāraṇī* 1008 times.[14] This heralds Acalanatha's *bodhi-maṇḍa* purification in the *Mahāvairocana Sūtra*.[15]

1.3 *Abhicāraka*

Mañjuśrī and Vajrapāṇi also threaten recalcitrant beings with reprisals by Yamāntaka. One of the chapters of the *MMK*, translated into Chinese in the eighth century by Amoghavajra, implies that the retaliation of Yamāntaka would be fearsome by giving an account of his effectiveness in magical exorcism, or what may be termed "black magic."[16] The chapter calls itself an "*abhicāraka*" text, which denotes its use in the suppression and exorcism of demons.[17] Generally the *abhicāraka* rites involve painted images of Yamāntaka, but in the *Ārya-yamāntaka-krodharāja . . . mahārddhi . . . adhyāya-dharma*, a "Great Magic" text of which the Chinese translation is also attributed to Amoghavajra, we find mention of metalwork images:

If there is an evil man who harbors resentment against your family, who arouses the evil desire to mortally harm some good man, then one should cast a gilt bronze image of the Krodharāja . . . At some purified spot, make a triangular altar. Place the image in the middle of the altar. . . . The [Yamāntaka] image should face toward the north. Wearing black garb, recite the dhāraṇī. Sit facing toward the south. . . Recite the dhāraṇī three times a day for seventeen days. This evil man will either have a calamitous illness, be plagued with boils, or else his body will succumb.[18]

The *abhicāraka* chapter in the *MMK*, however, focuses on painted images of Yamāntaka. For such images, the painter is to follow the same kinds of rules which Lalou has studied in relation to other chapters of the *MMK*.[19] These include the kind of cloth used, the time of painting, the generosity to the artist and the like.[20] Those images painted personally by the adept are especially potent and their details carefully specified:

Now if the adept . . . should paint/To oppress that which coerces/Then at the beginning of the dark part of the month/The [result will be that the] coercing one will burn himself up./In the second watch, chills and fevers will manifest/His spirit completely stupefied./In the third watch he will forsake his life./After death he will depart this world/ . . . As for painting this image/The likeness of Yamāntaka/Six faces, six arms and feet/Black in color, with a big belly/Bearing a skull, his hair flaring out in anger/A tiger skin wrapped around the hips/Holding all kinds of implements and weapons/Raising his hands in a terrifying manner/Eyes red, with a cruel and evil appearance/Three eyes like pennons/Hair standing up vertically, a mass of flames/Or flying like black smoke/ . . . [Skin] the color of a dark snow or rain cloud/His appearance like that of the cosmic fire of destruction./One should paint him riding a water buffalo./A matter of a wrathful, cruel and dreadful [appearance]/ . . . Anger and cruelty are his eternal calling./Wrathful and fear-inspiring, implacably grasping evil./Amidst cruelty, he is at the extreme of cruelty./He can destroy all sentient beings./Paint him with this anger/Use your own blood for color./Mix it together to make a dull wash of color./With dog's grease mixed with cow butter/Fill up a skull cup./Use a brush-tip made of a dead man's hair./For the handle, use a bone from a dog./Fast, and then one should paint.[21]

Once the painting is finished, one is to submit offerings and recite *dhāraṇī*. Thereby enemies will be shattered, armies dispersed, disasters averted and so on. The *abhicāraka* section is concluded by a remarkable defense of practices certainly foreign to traditional Mahāyāna methods. The defense is framed in a traditional *sūtra* format and testifies to the earliness of such a text, which still felt it must defend itself before a Mahāyāna audience.

Praśamaprajñā (?) Bodhisattva is sitting in the assembly before Śākyamuni where the rites of Yamāntaka and their destructive effects are espoused by Vajrapāṇi. He rises and castigates Vajrapāṇi for promulgating "greed-imbued *dhāraṇī dharma*-teaching." He warns others against following teachings which advocate injury of sentient beings and suggests that the method is no different from what fetters the mind, hardly conducive to freeing it. Vajrapāṇi defends himself in verse:[22]

Reality can't be mentally understood or [fruitfully] discussed (i.e. acintya)/Effect [vs. cause] cannot be mentally understood or discussed/Buddha dharma cannot be mentally understood or discussed/The Bodhisattva cannot be mentally understood or discussed/To discipline the passions is an activity of consciousness/The action of action cannot be mentally understood or discussed/So the bodhisattva's action/Therefore, can be said to be beyond mental understanding or discussion/As for the teaching of all the dhāraṇī/Their meritorious power can't be mentally understood or discussed/The Krodharāja dhāraṇī/

> *Mahātejas Yamāntaka/ The spirit realm, can't be mentally understood or discussed/ Mahātejas, can't be mentally understood or discussed.*[23]

Vajrapāṇi continues in prose:

> *I use skillful means (upāya) in order to perform abhicāraka, in all affairs. One mustn't hold on to the appearances of reality. One mustn't grasp at the imperfect. One ought to study the means (upāya) of subduing the passions in sentient beings. By means of great sin, bind the heart-mind.*[24]

1.4 The hrdaya dhāraṇī

Finally, it is clear that Yamāntaka personifies Mañjuśrī's *dhāraṇī*. His *hrdaya dhāraṇī* (*oṃ āh hūṃ*)[25] has powers identical to those he wields:

> *[The hrdaya dhāraṇī is] all that summons and disperses, puts a stop to disaster, increases prosperity, subjugates all the Māra-demons so that they have a pained, lifeless appearance. . . . [The dhāraṇī] breaks through all the darkness like a huge bright lamp. This great fearless three-character dhāraṇī and the power of its ritual is peerless. For that which is sought, that which is done by all the dhāraṇī, the siddhi accomplishments, just recite the [Yamāntaka] Mahākrodha Vidyārāja hrdaya dhāraṇī.*[26]

Many of the powers and abilities attributed to Yamāntaka and his *dhāraṇī* go much beyond the indications expressed in the earliest sections of the *MMK*. The early sections suggest speed, facility in traveling through all spheres of the universe and the ability to coerce beings to attend the Buddha's assemblies. No doubt later sections of the text elaborate these notions and expand his powers. Phase One images hardly live up to the grandness described by the texts just cited. For images which do express all the puissance with which the texts endow Yamāntaka, we will have to wait for Phase Two imagery. By the time of Phase Two Yamāntaka has accumulated further powers in accordance with changing ideas about the obstacles he eliminates.

Meanwhile, we need to consult the *MMK* once more to discover Yamāntaka's iconographic prescriptions in Phase One visual contexts. We find that he has two arms, one head, black skin, red hair, long nails, knitted brows and a big belly; he wears a tiger-skin apron, long hair and a beard; and he is surrounded by flames that consume obstacles. He looks up at Mañjuśrī in anticipation of commands. "The right hand grasps a *pāśa*-noose, and the left hand holds a *daṇḍa*-club."[27]

2 Yama and Yamantaka

Robert Duquenne has surveyed the etymology of the name Yamāntaka, as well as the evolution of Yamāntaka both in India and in texts translated into Chinese. He notes that Yamāntaka (lit. "the one who puts an end to Yama") assumes many of the characteristics of the god he combats.[28] Yama, the god of death, is converted to the Buddhist pantheon in all his terrifying power and transformed into a new personage of the appelation "He who deals death to the death-dealer." Moreover, as Wayman notes, one of thirteen epithets for Yama current in the first millennium CE is "Antaka" (the End).[29] The compound Yamāntaka is therefore Yama "doubled."

There is significant continuity between the abilities attributed to the Buddhist Yamāntaka and those of the earlier Vedic Yama. One of the characteristics of the

39. Mañjuśrī with Yamāntaka, Nalanda, ca. 8th century, National Museum, New Delhi

40. Śiva-Gaṇa, same as **23**

Vedic Yama that lent itself to recasting as Mañjuśrī's servitor in the *MMK* is Yama's ability to penetrate all corners of the universe. We find for instance in the Rig Veda that Yama "passed beyond along the great, steep straits, spying out the path for many." Animals are likened to Yama because of their speed, or, to emphasize their swiftness, are said to have won a race with Yama. When Agni is lost, it is Yama who discovers him in his watery hiding place.[30] Somewhat like the Western conception of the Grim Reaper, Yama is a "gatherer of the people."[31] As king of the dead, Yama can travel not only underground to the lands of the deceased, with its demons, dark earth-spirits and ghosts, but also to the regions of the gods, which he formerly inhabited.

If we compare these aptitudes with the demands of the tasks assigned to Yamāntaka in the *MMK*, we find a distinct correspondence: the ability to travel rapidly in all directions and to seek out all the inhabited corners of the cosmos, to gather beings together and, it might be added, to terrorize. But it is difficult to extend the comparison to early *images* of Yama and Yamāntaka. Unfortunately, as van den Bosch's study shows, there is very little in the way of a visual description of Yama in the Vedic texts[32] and no surviving images. Epic and Purānic literary descriptions of Yama seem to follow one occuring in two Brahmana texts (*Jaiminīyabrāhmana* and *Śatapathabrāhmana*). The texts speak of a powerful deity of hell named "Wrath" (van den Bosch suspects it was a variant of Yama) who is dark of skin and carries a *daṇḍa*,[33] attributes which correspond with later images of Yama. In the Sanskrit epic period a noose is sometimes added to the *daṇḍa*, and eventually the buffalo mount appears. The buffalo, with which we will find Yamāntaka regularly associated, seems not to appear as Yama's *vāhana* until around the sixth century or perhaps a little earlier.[34] From the earliest times Yama was associated with a sacrificial brown horse.[35]

If the Vedic Yama were depicted, the early association of Yama with virility and vital essence[36] suggests that the powerful *vīra*-Yakṣa image would probably have suited him. The earliest extant images of Yama in Orissa are considerably later. One is part of a set of directional guardians on the Parasuramesvara temple at Bhubaneswar, which Thomas Donaldson dates to the early seventh century. He is seated on his buffalo mount holding a *daṇḍa* and is quite stout.[37] Very quickly Yama attains a standardized form in Orissa, as a *vāmana*-Yakṣa type seated on a buffalo, holding the *daṇḍa* and the *pāśa*-noose. Early images of Yama outside of Orissa are not always *lambodara* but may have *vīra*-Yakṣa type bodies.[38] Since these images are not earlier than the earliest *krodha-vighnāntaka* images, one cannot speak of borrowing, but rather of a common inheritance.

3 Early (8th–9th century) Phase One Images of Yamantaka

One of the earliest recognized images of Yamāntaka depicts him in a manner already familiar to us, as a four-armed attendant of a bodhisattva, who in this case is Mañjuśrī. **[39, 41]** Though found at Nalanda, the sculpture reflects the stylistic influence of the Sarnath school of sculpture, which affected even the choice of materials. The sandstone was imported from the Benares region.[39] Comparison with ca. sixth century bodhisattva from Sarnath[40] shows a figure style much less oriented toward the Gupta compactness, with more attention paid to surface detail. These differences justify a date in the eighth century.

The Mañjuśrī figure is iconographically typical of a number of eighth-century standing Mañjuśrī sculptures.[41] It is the form of Mañjuśrī known as Siddhaikavīra.[42]

41. Four-armed Yamāntaka, detail of 39

42. *(above) Detail of* 43

43. *Mañjuśrī with Yamāntaka, Bihar, ca. 9th century, Los Angeles County Museum of Art*

He holds the stem of an *utpala* (blue lotus) in his raised left hand, while the proper right hand is lowered, palm out, in *vara mudrā*. He wears an elaborate crown and a tiger claw necklace, the latter a distinctive mark of Mañjuśrī images in India.[43]

The *krodha-vighnāntaka* is beardless, of the *vāmana*-Yakṣa body type, and he wears a short *dhoti*. His pose mirrors that of the bodhisattva. He makes no pretence of looking up or gesturing toward Mañjuśrī, but is intently engaged towards the front. A faint smile belies the slight squint and frown that furl his eyebrows. A snake is entwined around his *lambodara*, while other bands of jewelry circle his wrists and neck. His hair is arranged in the same manner as the Ratnagiri *krodha-vighnāntaka* [34-35]: pulled straight back off the forehead in thick striations which release into fat curls on the crown of his head. His upper arms carry a sword and lotus bud in the proper left and right respectively, while the lower left hand grasps a club, and the lower right hand seems to hold something in its palm. Overall he resembles a displeased *vāmana*-Gaṇa. [40] The Mañjuśrī figure lowers his proper right arm, as if to point his hand at Yamāntaka. The gesture recalls the description of the *MMK*.

The gesture is even more precisely depicted in a fine ninth-century stone sculpture in the Los Angeles County Museum of Art. [42-43] Mañjuśrī and Yamāntaka stand within an elaborate architectural niche. Pal observes, "Characteristic of Pāla-period Bihari architecture, the entire segment was probably inserted as a subsidiary shrine in a brick-and-stucco temple, perhaps in Nālanda."[44] Mañjuśrī places his hand on Yamāntaka's head, as the *MMK* describes, though it is the proper left hand instead of the right. Yamāntaka is two-armed, of the *vāmana*-Yakṣa body type. His tightly drawn hair spreads out into a fan around the back of his head. Standing relaxed with one leg bent, he smiles and makes a gesture typical of Phase One *krodha-vighnāntaka*, resting both hands on the upturned handle of the *daṇḍa*.

Among the images of Yamāntaka known to me, the buffalo first makes its appearance in an Orissan sculpture of Mañjuśrī with Yamāntaka. [44-45] This sculpture belongs to a set of eight bodhisattva found in the Lalitagiri area. Thomas Donaldson considers this set, originally placed between Landa and Parabhadi hills, the earliest of four sets of standing bodhisattva found in the Lalitagiri area.[45] Donaldson dates this set (his "C") to the eighth century, but comparison of the bodhisattva from nearby Ratnagiri [32,33] leads us to think the set must have been made quite late in the eighth, if not the early part of the ninth century.

Yamāntaka [45] stands in *ālīḍha* on the back of a rather small buffalo with its face toward Mañjuśrī. Typical of Phase One *krodha-vighnāntaka*, Yamāntaka is two-armed. He is *vāmana*-Yakṣa in body type, with his hair bound into a large flat crown. He carries a skull-tipped *daṇḍa* and a noose — the attributes *par excellence* of his nemesis/ancestor, Yama.

We will find that images subsequent to the Lalitagiri Yamāntaka [44] frequently depict him on the back of the buffalo. These Phase Two representations also tend to multiply the number of arms, heads and legs. The Lalitagiri *krodha-vighnāntaka* images are poised on

44. Mañjuśrī with Yamāntaka, Lalitagiri (Orissa), ca. 8th-9th century, site Museum, Lalitagiri

45. Yamāntaka, detail of **44**

the line of transition; on the one hand they continue to look back to Yakṣa, *āyudha-puruṣa* and Śiva-Gaṇa imagery, and on the other hand they have begun to manifest traits, including Yamāntaka's buffalo, which herald a new individualization and iconographic characterization of members of the group.

4 Middle period (ca. 9th-10th century) Phase One Images of Yamantaka

The *krodha-vighnāntaka* imagery of Orissa seems often to be in advance of other parts of India. For some time after Orissa had adapted the buffalo mount as standard for Yamāntaka, in Bihar his Phase One image was still in flux. He continued to be portrayed there as a generic *krodha-vighnāntaka*, hardly discernible from Hayagrīva or others from the Phase One group.

A ninth or tenth century standing Mañjuśrī sculpture with a two-armed Yamāntaka belongs to the comparatively generalized representation of *krodha-vighnāntaka*. [**46-47**] Found in Guneri, not far from Bodh Gaya in Bihar, it is one of a pair of matching bodhisattva sculptures, the other being Maitreya with his *krodha-vighnāntaka* attendant. [**48**] An old photograph exists of the two set up at Guneri on either side of a seated Buddha in *bhūmisparśa mudrā*.[46] The Buddha remains at Guneri, but both bodhisattva are now in the Archaeological Survey of India's Bodh Gaya Museum. On the sculpture of the Buddha there are small images of Vajrapāṇi and Avalokiteśvara seated on the proper right and left side respectively of the Buddha's head nimbus.[47] The arrangement of the Mañjuśrī and Maitreya sculptures [**46, 48**] originally may have conformed to the symmetrical triadic composition typical of Mahāyāna art, just as the photographer recorded them.

The Guneri Yamāntaka [**47**] is of interest not least because none of the attributes which become his trademarks are included. These attributes seem to be found more consistently in iconographic compilation texts than in actual images. Thus the Guneri Yamāntaka carries neither the club nor the noose, nor does he stand on a buffalo. Instead, with his proper left hand he holds the head of a cobra which acts as his *upavīta*, while the right hand is turned palm out and a lotus bud is grasped by the thumb and middle finger. There is no apparent precedent for the flower, but snakes are often associated with the *krodha-vighnāntaka* group as a whole. In Lalou's translation of the fourth chapter of the *MMK*, we find that, "Une guirlande de serpents se dresse autour de son [i.e., Yamāntaka's] cou."[48]

Another significant aspect of the Guneri image is the hair style, one not yet met with. The hair is drawn back under a low three pointed crown and tied with a snake. The slightly wavy locks spread up and back against the flat nimbus. In fact it recalls the nimbus of flames described in the thirty-first chapter, devoted to *abhicāraka*, of the Chinese translation of the *MMK*: "[Yamāntaka's] hair stands up vertically, [like] a mass of flames/ or flying like black smoke."[49] Later many of the Phase One *krodha-vighnāntaka* deities will have similarly arranged hair, though the tiaras are generally simpler.

Yamāntaka's counterpart at Guneri, who attends Maitreya, has the same three-crested tiara, the same large earrings, nearly the same elaborate folds to the *dhoti* and girdle, but the hair is significantly different. It forms a circle around his head, as if to suggest a full head-aureole, or even a wheel. It is worth comparing the wheel found behind the head of Cakrapuruṣa (see **22, 24, 51**). The identity of Maitreya's wrathful attendant is not yet clear. A late eighth or early ninth-century Maitreya who, like the Guneri bodhisattva, has a *stūpa* in his headdress and carries

46. *Mañjuśrī with Yamāntaka, Guneri (Bihar), ca. 9th-10th century, Bodh Gaya site museum, same as* **6**

47. *(left) Yamāntaka, detail of* **46**

48. *(right) Detail of Cakrapuruṣa (?) attending Maitreya, Guneri (Bihar) ca. 9th-10th century, Bodh Gaya site museum*

49. *(left) Yamāntaka, detail of* **53**

50. *Krodha-vighnāntaka, detail of* **52**

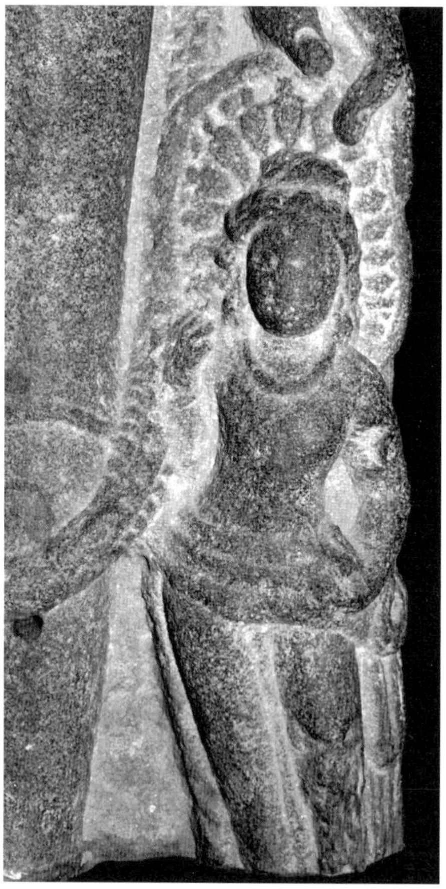

51. *Cakrapuruṣa, detail of 22*

52. *Maitreya with krodha-vighnāntaka, Bodh Gaya (Bihar), ca. 11th century, Mahants compound, Bodh Gaya*

the distinctive *nagapuspa* flower, is also equipped with a *vāmana*-Yakṣa type wrathful attendant. The latter is described merely as "a dwarf" in a recent account.[50] He is quite *retardaire*, with old-style, Gaṇa-like hair. Neither he nor an eleventh- century Maitreya sculpture with a two armed *vāmana*-Yakṣa *krodha-vighnāntaka* **[50, 52]** offer any clue to the identity of Maitreya's *krodha-vighnāntaka.*

The potentially distinctive attribute is once again the peculiar circular arrangement of the Guneri *krodha-vighnāntaka*'s hair. It happens that an Esoteric Buddhist text of the ninth century entitled the *Vajra Mahā-Amrita kundali . . . Buddha-usnisa sūtra* may shed some light on this problem. The text was translated by Dharmasena and brought to Japan in 847.[51] Reference is made to Maitreya's *krodha-vighnāntaka,* "Mahācakra Vajra Vidyārāja," who is described as having an eight-spoked wheel.[52] Perhaps the wheel of hair on the *krodha-vighnāntaka* paired with the Guneri Maitreya **[47]** echoes this specification, and Mahācakra Vidārāja is portrayed here.

His unusual hairstyle aside, the Guneri *krodha-vighnāntaka* is a generalized Phase One type. His posture, leaning with both hands on the up-turned handle of a staff, is frequently met with. But for the wheel of hair, the two Guneri *krodha-vighnāntaka* **[47-48]** would be interchangeable, a telling symptom of Phase One *krodha-vighnāntaka* imagery.

The Guneri Yamāntaka does not correspond to the specific pattern textual descriptions might lead us to expect. Nor is there iconographic consistency among Yamāntaka images of the same region at this period. For instance, one can compare it with another Yamāntaka image from what was probably the same workshop. **[53, 5]** It attends a Mañjuśrī figure who is quite similar to the Guneri Mañjuśrī.[53] **[46]** Now in the storage chambers of the Indian Museum, Calcutta, the museum records indicate that the sculpture came from Kurkihar. The similarity with the Guneri pair in the Bodh Gaya Museum **[46, 48]** may be explained with the help of an observation by Susan Huntington:

> *Since Guneri is so near to Kurkihar, and since Kurkihar was apparently much more of a center of Buddhism than Guneri, it is likely that the craftsmen who executed these works were located at or near Kurkihar and the finished sculptures were then distributed or sold to various other establishments. It is also possible that the craftsmen themselves were itinerant workers and travelled to different sites as building programs required their services at various times.*[54]

The stature of the Kurkihar Yamāntaka **[49]** is more dwarfish and his features more grotesque than the Guneri Yamāntaka. **[47]** Compared to the Guneri wrathful attendants **[47, 48]**, he hearkens even more strongly back to the earliest roots of *krodha-vighnāntaka* imagery. This may reflect a fractionally earlier date than the two of them. All three share a strangely neutral but compelling expression, along with a distinctly pitched angle of the head away from the bodhisattva. The hair of the Kurkihar Yamāntaka is as unusual as that on the Guneri *krodha-vighnāntaka*, though it differs from both. He wears no crown, but a snake has bound the hair away from the forehead, and its hood emerges where the hair begins to fan out asymmetrically against the backdrop. One might expect this Yamāntaka to have the same attributes as the Guneri Yamāntaka, but instead of the snake or the canonical *daṇḍa* and noose, this Yamāntaka holds an axe with its head down, its handle balanced by his right palm. Still in the tenth century a consistent iconography of Yamāntaka had yet to emerge even locally, much less regionally, or over a larger area of India.

By the early to mid-tenth century, the hair style we noticed for the first time on the Guneri wrathful attendants is slightly modified into a form that becomes the standard for the next two centuries of Phase One *krodha-vighnāntaka*. It appears on a sculpture from Bihar Shariff, formerly in the Broadley Collection[55] and now in a storage area beneath the Indian Museum in Calcutta. **[54-55]** Stylistic comparison with datable sculptures of the same area of Bihar allow us to place this Mañjuśrī making the *dharmacakra mudrā* to the first half of the tenth century.[56] The *vāmana*-Yakṣa Yamāntaka is seated in a more casual way than his bodhisattva master, with one leg folded. He drapes his right hand onto the handle of his up-turned club and makes the *tarjanī mudrā* with the left. His face and hair seem particularly stereotyped, with curling mustachios, indications of a beard and a slight point to the "flaming" crest of hair.

Yamāntaka is also given a new partner: instead of the female attendant who often appears on the other side of Mañjuśrī, we have here Sudhanakumāra. Normally Sudhanakumāra is paired with Hayagrīva on either side of Avalokiteśvara, several examples of which we will examine further on. In a *sādhana* for Khasarpaṇa Avalokiteśvara, the *Sādhanamālā* describes Sudhanakumāra exactly as we find him:

> *[H]is two hands joined (añjali), [he] is resplendent like gold, and has the appearance of a prince. He carries the book under his left arm-pit and is decked in all ornaments.*[57]

There are at least two Mañjuśrī *sādhana* in the *Sādhanamālā* which specify Sudhanakumāra with Yamāntaka,[58] but it seems only in the later period, under the influence of the more numerous Avalokiteśvara sculptures, that Sudhanakumāra was regularly added to Mañjuśrī's entourage. The fact that many Phase One images of Yamāntaka and Hayagrīva are virtually indistinguishable would have eased the process of transference.

53. *Mañjuśrī with Yamāntaka, Kurkihar (Bihar), ca. 10th century, Indian Museum, Calcutta*

54. *Mañjuśrī with Yamāntaka, Bihar Shariff, ca. 10th century, Indian Museum, Calcutta*

55. *(above right) Yamāntaka, detail of 54*

5 Late (ca. 10th-11th century) Phase One Images of Yamantaka

Two of the last four Yamāntaka images to be brought into the discussion are somewhat anomalous for the late period in that both still command considerable visual interest. The record of the group as a whole indicates that beginning in the eleventh century the *krodha-vighnāntaka* in sculpture of Orissa, Bihar and Bengal had become something of a tired cliché. The more frequent presence of Hayagrīva, who constitutes our next topic, establishes unambiguously that late Phase One images of Mañjuśrī and Avalokiteśvara routinely include a wrathful deity, albeit a standardized type which the artist (and can we not assume, his co-religionists?) takes for granted. Two eleventh-century examples of Yamāntaka attending Mañjuśrī from Orissa and Bengal prove exceptional in this regard. An extraordinary illuminated manuscript dated by inscription to the late eleventh century and associated with Nalanda indicates that, as one would expect, the same general iconographic trends are shared by painting and sculpture. Our final example, a twelfth-century sculpture, confirms the impression of decline made by late Phase One Yamāntaka and other *krodha-vighnāntaka*.

56. *Yamāntaka, detail of 57, same as 38*

A late tenth or early eleventh-century image of a Phase One Yamāntaka attending Mañjuśrī Bodhisattva [56-57] is located in the Balasore district of northern Orissa. The sculpture belongs to a shrine dedicated to Mārīcī in the village of Ayodhya. At one time this was a Buddhist center of considerable importance which supported more than a hundred shrines. The Mārīcī Mandir, or Khutia temple, as it is also known, houses at the center of the altar a large image of Mārīcī, the Buddhist goddess of the dawn.[59] To one side of the Mārīcī sculpture is Mañjuśrī with Yamāntaka [57], and on the other side is Avalokiteśvara with Hayagrīva. [123] The inhabitants of Ayodhya report there are no longer Buddhists in the village, but the cloth draperies, pigments, ghee and clay horses placed on and around the images reveal they are nevertheless still in worship.

The hardness of the carving, the wide necklaces on Mañjuśrī, the high crowns and the elephant/leogryph throne all speak of a late date. N. Vasu mentions an inscription of around the tenth or eleventh century on the figure of Mārīcī, which Donaldson places at the end of the tenth century.[60] The two bodhisattva do not appear to be earlier, and an early eleventh century date seems justified.

The Yamāntaka image [56] on the bodhisattva's proper right stands sway-hipped, leaning on the up-turned handle of his elaborate *daṇḍa*. The club, the conventional *āyudha* of Yamāntaka, has a *viśva vajra* finial, and an elaborate fitting on the handle as well. His right hand echoes the gesture of Mañjuśrī in a variant of the *vyakhyana mudrā*. Snakes are quite prominent, serving as armlets, crown embellishments and as a *naga*-hood nimbus. His hair is brought up into a high swelling bun, and his face has the curling mustachios and framing beard which we first saw on the Yamāntaka from Bihar Shariff [55], *de rigueur* by the late eleventh century for Phase One *krodha-vighnāntaka*. The most specific identifying attribute, however, is the crouching buffalo on which he stands.

The appearance of the buffalo in turn helps to identify the bodhisattva as Mañjuśrī, whose unusual form might otherwise mislead us. Atop the lotus blossom held by the stem in his left hand, where we would expect the bibliophile Mañjuśrī to carry his copy of the *Prajñāpāramitā* (as in 44, 46 and 54), we find instead a bell. In his right hand he holds at his chest a *vajra*, now somewhat damaged. Whatever he might bear in his crown is obscured by the silver filigree decoration added by modern worshipers. The presence of Yamāntaka, who is exclusively Mañjuśrī's attendant, makes it possible to agree with N.K. Sahu that the central figure is indeed Mañjuśrī.[61] The assumption is confirmed by the stack of books above Yamāntaka's head and by the presence of Sudhanakumāra on Mañjuśrī's right, holding a book under his proper left arm. The Mañjuśrī sculpture from Bihar Shariff [54] pairs Sudhanakumāra with Yamāntaka, and in the *Sādhanamālā* Sudhanakumāra is most commonly present attending either Avalokiteśvara, or else he joins Yamāntaka in attending Mañjuśrī.[62]

The Ayodhya sculpture is only the second Phase One image of Yamāntaka to include his buffalo mount. Significantly, both are from Orissa, where there seems to have been a special interest in Yamāntaka. It may be that Yama's well-developed presence as a *dikpāla* in Orissan Hindu architecture and sculpture[63] eased the enforcement of the Buddhist message. We will also discover that Phase Two imagery of Yamāntaka, in which he is invariably standing on his buffalo *vāhana*, was also prominent in Orissa. The presence of contemporary Phase Two Yamāntaka imagery may have influenced the artist of the Ayodhya sculpture (although it cannot explain the somewhat precocious appearance of Yamāntaka's buffalo on the late eighth-century Yamāntaka of Lalitagiri [44-45]). Orissa will continue to be at the forefront of the development of the *krodha-vighnāntaka*, and we will return there

57. *Mañjuśrī with Yamāntaka, Ayodhya (Orissa), ca. late 10th-early 11th century, Ayodhya Mārīcī Mandir*

time and again, not only for the Phase One Hayagrīva images, but also for Phase Two and Phase Three deities.

A second late Phase One Yamāntaka image is part of a sculpture of Mañjuśrī now in the Asutosh Museum in Calcutta. [58-59] According to the museum records it was found in what is now the 24 Parganas district of West Bengal. Comparison with other sculptures from Bengal and Bihar justifies a date of the mid- to late eleventh century.[64] Once again Sudhanakumāra joins the larger Yamāntaka on the opposite side of Mañjuśrī.[65] Yamāntaka leans his proper left hand on the handle of his *daṇḍa*, which like the Ayodhya sculpture **[56]** has a *viśva vajra* finial and a fitting on the handle-end. With his right hand Yamāntaka makes the *vandana* gesture of salutation. His disproportionately large head crowns a short, swollen body, epitomized by his *lambodara*-belly sagging over the belted animal skin. A cobra wraps itself around his neck and shoulder in imitation of the *upavīta*. His hair is collected in a high-bun, backed by a pointed nimbus of flames. His mouth is open to reveal his fangs, and he also has the mustaches and beard we expect in late figures. All in all, it is a rather hearty representation of Mañjuśrī's attendant, perhaps not as imposing or powerful as the texts describe his potential, but not sapped of all visual interest.

58. *Mañjuśrī with Yamāntaka, 24 Parganas (Bengal), ca. late 11th century, Asutosh Museum, Calcutta*

59. *Yamāntaka, detail of 58*

The Asia Society of New York acquired in 1987 an extraordinary religious document with remarkable eleventh and twelfth-century Sanskrit inscriptions, as well as Tibetan inscriptions mentioning some of the most important Indian and Tibetan scholars of the thirteenth and fourteenth centuries. The *Aṣṭasāhasrikā Prajñāpāramitā* features four illustrated leaves, each with three illuminations.[66] John and Susan Huntington have insightfully discussed the work and identified two phases in the illustrations.[67] To the earlier of the two phases, datable to the late eleventh century, belongs a Mañjuśrī seated on a lion, making the *dharmacakra mudrā,* accompanied by Yamāntaka and Sudhanakumāra. **[60]**

The coyly swaying bodhisattva is attended by a bearded blue Yamāntaka with orange hair and a fiery nimbus. His leopard skin *dhoti* is slung around his hips under his *lambodara*-belly. His gestures are standard for the Phase One class: he leans on an elaborately handled wand or *daṇḍa*, making the *vandana mudrā* with his raised right hand.

What is most significant about this image for our purposes is its demonstration that the *krodha-vighnāntaka* image type was familiar to both painters and sculptors.[68] Such features as the narrow beard lining the jaw, the gestures, the attributes held and body-type of the painted image **[60]** are shared by contemporary sculpted images of Yamāntanka. **[59]** As is characteristic of Phase One imagery, Yamāntaka's gestures and gaze call attention to the larger bodhisattva, and his subsidiary status is further emphasized by his companion attendant, Sudhanakumāra, who is symmetrically paired with him to form a triad.

A ca. twelfth-century sculpture of a seated Mañjuśrī **[61]** illustrates well the marginalisation of the *krodha-vighnāntaka* that occurs in the late period.[69] Mañjuśrī sits with one leg pendent on a lion and makes the *dharmacakra mudrā.* The sculpture was discovered in the Birbhum district of Bengal and later found its way to the Friedrich Hewicker collection, Hamburg. To the proper right of Mañjuśrī sits Sudhanakumāra, who holds the text in his left hand, and at the bodhisattva's proper left

60. *Mañjuśrī with Yamāntaka, Bihar, manuscript illumination, second half of 11th century, Asia Society, New York*

61. *Mañjuśrī with Yamāntaka, Birbhum (Bengal), ca. 12th century, Friedrich Hewicker collection, Hamburg (?)*

knee sits Yamāntaka with his own knee up. Tiny though he is, one can make out his hair spread in a mantle behind him. He has shrunk to almost minuscule proportions and is nearly lost in the other details.

This image is representative of several late eleventh- and twelfth-century examples of Mañjuśrī and Yamāntaka.[70] A certain malaise seems to have set in with regard to the Phase One *krodha-vighnāntaka*. If we compare our very first example of a Phase One *krodha-vighnāntaka* [**10**] with the Birbhum Yamāntaka [**61**], we suspect that the wrathful deities have suffered a steep decline in importance. Where Vajrapuruṣa is nearly half the size of Vajrapāṇi [**10**], this last Yamāntaka is half the size of Mañjuśrī's calf.

Yet we must not be misled to think there was a correlative loss of religious significance. The *krodha-vighnāntaka* grows to such importance by the twelfth century that he is represented both independently and at the center of his own *maṇḍala* (Phases Two and Three). The religious impulse toward the terrifying aspects of life and Buddhist practice, already embodied by early imagery, is now channeled into more distinctly Esoteric Buddhist themes. The bodhisattva, who remains the focus of Mahāyāna cult activity despite the partial influence of Esoteric Buddhist ideas and images, gradually overwhelms his attendant, reducing him to a minor accoutrement. The vitality of the *krodha-vighnāntaka* has been taken up by Phases Two and Three. The Birbhum image of Yamāntaka is merely the dried husk of the *krodha-vighnāntaka* image that has remained, nearly discarded, around the plant that first nurtured it: the bodhisattva cult image.

62. *Vajrapāṇi with krodha-vighnāntaka, Cave 6 Aurangabad, second half of 6th century, detail of* **10**

Notes to Chapter Four

1 Vajrapāṇi does persist, however, in 11th c. and 12th c. manuscript illuminations, such as the early 12th c. "Vredenburg" Perfection of Wisdom manuscript in the Victoria and Albert Museum (IS6-1958, left). Here Vajrapāṇi is one of a set of bodhisattva, each accompanied by virtually identical two-armed *lambodara krodha-vighnāntaka*. The epigraph for this chapter is from T.18.890.566a.

2 De Mallmann, *Introduction a l'iconographie*, 465. Also see idem, *Iconographique sur Mañjuśrī*, 34.

3 Marcelle Lalou, *Iconographie des étoffes Peintes*; idem, "*Mañjuśrīmūlakalpa* and *Tārāmūlakalpa*," *Harvard Journal of Asiatic Studies* 1 (1936): 327-349; idem, "Un Traité de Magie Bouddhique," in *Études d'orientalisme publiées par le Musée Guimet á la memoire de Ray-mond Linossier*, 2 vols. (Paris, 1932) 2:303-322; Macdonald, *Mañjuśrīmūlakalpa*; and, Matsunaga, "Date of the *Mañjuśrīmūlakalpa*," 882-894.

4 See the fascinating account of Tianxizai's collaboration with other Indian and Chinese monks in making translations at the official Song Dynasty "College for Translating the Sūtras," in Robert Hans van Gulik, *Siddham: An Essay on the History of Sanskrit Studies in China and Japan* (New Delhi, 1980), 27-30; and, Lamotte, "Vajrapāṇi en Inde," 151. The sections translated earlier include the *Garudapatalaparivarta* (T.21.1276) and two texts comprising three chapters of the Sanskrit text, dealing with Yamāntaka (T.21.1215 and T.21.1216). The translation of all three texts is attributed to Amoghavajra (d. 774).

5 T.21.1215, 1216. According to Robert Duquenne, these are equivalent to chapters 48 and 49 of the Sanskrit redaction, and chapters 33-35 of the Tibetan translation. See Duquenne, "Daiitoku Myōō," 659.

6 "*Esa bhagavato Mañjuśrīyasya mahākrodharāja yamāntako nāma*," in Chapter 1 of the *MMK*, cited in Macdonald, *Mañjuśrīmūlakalpa*, 100.

7 Macdonald, *Mañjuśrīmūlakalpa*, 25 (my translation from the French).

8 Ibid., 77-78 (my translation from the French).

9 See Jean Przyluski, "Les Vidyārāja: Contribution a l'Histoire de la Magie dans les Sectes Mahāyānistes," *Bulletin de l'Ecole Francaise de Extrême-Orient* 23 (1923): 301-318.

10 Lalou, *Iconographie des étoffes Peintes*, 37.

11 T.20.1191.862a. Compare Lalou, *Iconographie des étoffes Peintes*, 39.

12 Macdonald, *Mañjuśrīmūlakalpa*, 26.

13 T.20.1191.847c-848a. The Arjaka tree is "a tree with white scented flowers, said to fall in seven parts, like an epidendrum." W.E. Soothill and Lewis Hodous, *A Dictionary of Chinese Buddhist Terms* (London, 1937), 288.

14 Macdonald, *Mañjuśrīmūlakalpa*, 81, 99.

15 Ryujun Tajima, "Les Deux Grand Maṇḍalas et la Doctrine de l'Ésotérisme Shingon," *Bulletin de la Maison Franco-Japonaise* ns 6 (1959), 45; and, Chikyō Yamamoto, trans., *Mahāvairocana-Sūtra* (New Delhi, 1990), 16, 41-42.

16 Duquenne provides a concordance between chapter 49 of the Sanskrit *MMK*, chapters 31 and 32 of the Chinese version found in T.21.1216, and chapters 34 and 35 of the Tibetan *MMK* in "Daiitoku Myōō," 659.

17 Soothill and Hodous, *Dictionary of Chinese Buddhist Terms*, 123b.

18 T.21.1214.73b (Njo 1422; KBC 1351).

19 Lalou, *Iconographie des étoffes Peintes*.

20 "Generously reward the painter for his work/Much more than the asking price/Make his heart happy/Nor should one find fault/In this matter of great fierceness/As a valiant man, don't haggle over the price./ . . . Reward the painter of images/Cause his happiness by fulfilling his hopes/One should shelter his body/Don't do injury to yourself through [slighting] him." T.21.1216.78a.

21 T.21.1216.77c.

22 A similar scenario, in which Vajrapāṇi's endorsement of Esoteric Buddhist practices necessitates a protracted defense of those practices, is found in the transitional Phase Two/Phase Three text, the *Guhyasamāja Tantra*. The teachings advocated there are considerably different, however, including the apparent indulgence of sexual pleasure. See Snellgrove, *Indo-Tibetan Buddhism*, 170-173.

23 T.21.1216.79c.

24 Ibid.

25 Macdonald, *Mañjuśrīmūlakalpa*, 77.

26 T.20.1191.848c-849a.

27 T.20.1191.861c. Compare Lalou, *Iconographie des étoffes Peintes*, 37.

28 Duquenne, "Daiitoku Myōō," 654. For the etymology, see ibid., 610-640. This territory is also covered by Yūshō Miyasaka, "Yamāntaka," *Indogaku Bukkyōgaku Kenkyū* 19 no. 2 (1971): 504-512; and, Bulcsu Siklós, "The Evolution of the Buddhist Yama," *The Buddhist Forum* 4 (1996): 165-189.

29 Wayman, "Studies in Yama and Māra," 45, 48.

30 Wendy Doniger O'Flaherty, trans., *The Rig Veda, An Anthology* (New York, 1981), 43, 87, 108, 182.

31 Van den Bosch, "Yama," 24.

32 Ibid., 29.

33 Ibid., 29-30.

34 Ibid., 40-41.

35 Wayman, "Studies in Yama and Māra," 49.

36 Ibid.

37 Donaldson, *Hindu Temple Art of Orissa*, 51, 1145. See also the the numerous images of Yama listed in the photo index under "Dikpālas, Yama," ibid., 1209.

38 See van den Bosch, "Yama," pl. 7, 9, 10.

39 Asher, *Art of Eastern India*, 82.

40 For instance, the ca. 6th c. Avalokiteśvara in the National Museum, New Delhi illustrated in Linrothe, "Compassionate Malevolence," fig. 6.

41 Asher, *Art of Eastern India*, pls. 145, 164-166.

42 De Mallmann, *Étude Iconographique sur Mañjuśrī*, 31-35.

43 In discussing a Mañjuśrī image Pal writes, "Characteristic of a young boy, he wears a necklace of tiger claws, which are regarded as protective charms for children." Pratapaditya Pal, *Indian Sculpture: A Catalogue of the Los Angeles County Museum of Art Collection; Vol. II, 700-1800* (Los Angeles, 1988), 162. The necklace is termed *vyāghranakha*. Also see Adalbert Gail, "Mañjuśrī and his sword," in *Function and Meaning in Buddhist Art*, ed. K.R. van Kooij and H. van der Veere (Groningen: Egbert Forsten, 1995), 135-138.

44 Pal, *Indian Sculpture*, 162. This image is also published in Wayne E. Begley, *Pāla Art: Buddhist and Hindu Sculpture from Eastern India, ca. 800-1200 AD* (Iowa City, 1969), no. 9.

45 Donaldson, "Buddhist Sculptures of Orissa," 224.

46 Muhammad Hamid Kuraishi, *List of Ancient Monuments Protected Under Act VII of 1904 in the Province of Bihar and Orissa, ASI New Imperial Series* no. 51 (Calcutta, 1931), 45.

47 Susan Huntington, *The "Pāla-Sena" Schools of Sculpture* (Leiden, 1984), fig. 118. She also discusses the Guneri Mañjuśrī sculpture **[46]**, noting its similarity with the sculpture of Kurkhihar. Ibid., 104.

48 Lalou, *Iconographie des étoffes Peintes*, 37. I don't find it in the Chinese text.

49 T. 21.1216.77c.

50 S. and J. Huntington, *Leaves*, 128.

51 T. 19.965. See "Datsumaseina" in Paul Demiéville, Hubert Durt, and Anna Seidel, *Repertoire du Canon Bouddhique Sino-Japonais, Édition de Taishō (Taishō Shinshū Daizōkyō), Fascicule Annexe du Hōbōgirin, Édition Révisée et Augmentée* (Paris/Tokyo, 1978), 242

52 T.19.965.340c. The text names the *krodha-vighnāntaka* of the eight great bodhisattva, ibid., 340c-341c: Vajrapāṇi's is Trailokyavijaya, Mañjuśrī's is Yamāntaka, Ākaśagarbha's is Mahāhasa (?), Maitreya's is Mahācakra, Avalokiteśvara's is Hayagrīva, Ksitigarbha's is Aparājita, Sarvanivaranaviskambhin's is Acalanatha, and Samantabhadra's is Padanakśipa. (Ibid., pp. 340c-341c.) However, the "Maitreya Bodhisattva abridged instructions on cultivation of yoga and recitation" invokes Trailokyavijaya in the Maitreya rituals to eliminate all obstructions (T.20.1141.591.b). This text, in two rolls, claims to have been translated by Śubhakarasiṁha at imperial command. It does not appear in the Korean canon, but allegedly was copied by Enchin in Changan, 855 CE.

The Taishō edition is based on several manuscripts including ones dated 1716, 1092, and 1222. Ibid., 590, no. 1; 595a.

53 The entire sculpture is illustrated in S.K. Saraswati, *Tantrayana Art: An Album* (Calcutta, 1977), pl. 14.

54 S. Huntington, *"Pāla-Sena,"* 106.

55 See Frederick Asher, "The Former Broadley Collection, Bihar Sharif," *Artibus Asiae* 32 (1970): 105-24.

56 For a slightly earlier example, see the ca. mid-9th c. Prajñāpāramitā sculpture from the Asian Art Museum of San Francisco, Avery Brundage Collection (B62 S32+) illustrated in S. and J. Huntington, *Leaves*, no. 8. For a slightly later sculpture, see the standing Buddha in the Nalanda site Museum, no. 10515, dated to the mid- to late 10th c., ibid., no. 133

57 Bhattacharyya, *Indian Buddhist Iconography*, 129.

58 See *sādhana* nos. 46, 52 in B. Bhattacharyya, *Indian Buddhist Iconography*, 102, 118; and, de Mallmann, *Introduction a l'iconographie*, 356.

59 See N.K. Sahu, *Buddhism in Orissa* (Cuttack, 1958), 209-212; and, Thomas Donaldson, "Orissan Images of Aṣṭabhujāpīta Mārīcī," *Journal of the Orissa Research Society* 3 (1985): 35-44.

60 N.N. Vasu, *The Archaeological Survey of Mayurbhanja*, 2 vols. (Calcutta, 1912), 90; Donaldson, "Aṣṭabhujāpīta Mārīcī," 39-40.

61 Sahu, *Buddhism in Orissa*, 210. Sahu mistakenly identifies Yamāntaka as a female Yamārī.

62 De Mallmann, *Introduction a l'iconographie*, 356.

63 Donaldson, *Hindu Temple Art of Orissa*, 1145, 1209 (photo index).

64 See S. Huntington, *"Pāla-Sena,"* figs. 74, 80, 137, 225.

65 A similar though slightly smaller Yamāntaka is paired with Sudhanakumāra in attending a 2-armed standing Mañjuśrī. Part of the Nalin collection, the work is also from Bengal and datable to the ca. 11th c., illustrated in S. and J. Huntington, *Leaves*, no. 25.

66 It should be observed that these "illustrations" depict deities in no way connected to the text itself, "whose subject is the purest metaphysics and whose composition is far earlier than the florescence of Tantric Buddhism at the time of the late Pālas." J.P. Losty, "Bengal, Bihar, Nepal? Problems of Provenance in 12th-Century Illuminated Buddhist Manuscripts, Part One," *Oriental Art* ns 35.2 (1989): 90. This "disassociation between text and miniatures" is also commented on by, among others, S. and J. Huntington, *Leaves*, 188-189.

67 S. and J. Huntington, *Leaves*, 185-189, no. 58; color illustrations, 27-29.

68 A Nepalese manuscript of the *Aṣṭasāhasrikā Prajñāpāramitā* dated 1071 CE in the Calcutta Asiatic Society depicts a similar, though not so fine, Mañjuśrī accompanied by a blue Yamāntaka. See Saraswati, *Tantrayana Art*, pl. 217, discussed lxxix-lxxx; a manuscript in the British Library, Or 6902, folio 163; and the related red Phase One Yamāntaka in the "Vredenburg" manuscript in the Victoria and Albert Museum (IS-4-1958, right).

69 B. Bhattacharyya, *Indian Buddhist Iconography*, fig. 83, 169, discussed 117-118. Also see the misidentified "Simhanāda Lokeśvara" in ASI, *Eastern Circle: Annual Report 1920-21* (Patna, 1921), pl. 1 (left), discussed 26-27. For the iconography, see de Mallmann, *Étude Iconographique sur Mañjuśrī*, 23-26, pl. 1.

70 See Saraswati, *Tantrayana Art*, pls. 34, 32. Two other versions of Mañjuśrī on the lion include Sudhanakumāra but go so far as to eliminate Yamāntaka altogether. Ibid., pls. 33, 35.

63. *Hayagrīva attending Tārā, Bihar, ca. early 11th century*

5

Hayagriva: Texts

Hail to Hayagrīva!
Able to destroy all the obstacles of Māra!
It is through the upāya of compassion
That he yet manifests a wrathful appearance.

"Methods and Rules for Incantations and Offerings to Effect a Manifestation of the Great Fierce King, the Holy Hayagrīva"

Hayagrīva is without doubt the most frequently depicted Phase One *krodha-vighnāntaka*. Without attempting an exhaustive survey, we will be acquainted with well over fifty examples of eighth- to twelfth-century images of Hayagrīva from Bihar, Orissa and Bengal. In addition we will expand the scope to take into account a few Southeast Asian, Tibetan and Tibeto-Chinese examples. Hayagrīva's wide currency is unquestionably due in considerable measure to the importance of the cult of his bodhisattva masters. Hayagrīva is linked primarily to several of the various forms of Avalokiteśvara bodhisattva, notably Khasarpaṇa, Padmapāṇi, Lokeśvara and Amoghapāśa. Less well known is Hayagrīva's role as Tārā's wrathful companion. Tārā and Avalokiteśvara may be the most commonly represented of all Buddhist deities after the Buddha himself. The ascendancy of Hayagrīva was assured by their prominence.

Despite its eventual ubiquity, the image of Hayagrīva, like that of any Phase One *krodha-vighnāntaka*, develops only over the course of three stages. The first stage is marked by significant formal dependence on the ancient images of Yakṣa, Gaṇa and *āyudhapuruṣa;* indeed, at this stage Hayagrīva is hardly discernible from these non-Buddhist demigods. The second stage, which spans the ninth and tenth centuries, is one of quite literal growth for Phase One *krodha-vighnāntaka.* Their new size reflects a heightened status, though they never rival their master bodhisattva. A concomitant development of the second stage is greater iconographic differentiation. Both advances are compromised already by the eleventh century, however, when the prominence of the *krodha-vighnāntaka* within Phase One images declines severely. As we saw with Yamāntaka, during the third and final stage Hayagrīva shrinks drastically in relation to Avalokiteśvara or Tārā.

These stages have been illustrated by some of the Phase One *krodha-vighnāntaka* images already discussed. We can recall how some early Yamāntaka [41, 50] resemble Gaṇa. [23] The second stage is exemplified by the stature and developed individuality of Yamāntaka, distinguished by the buffalo. [45] The stage of decline is best illustrated by the diminutive Yamāntaka perched by Mañjuśrī's knee. [61]

Hayagrīva's path of development can be charted much more accurately and in greater depth than any one of the other *krodha-vighnāntaka* discussed so far. It was convenient to begin with others in order to introduce the topic and deal with a number of special problems, notably the roots of the *krodha-vighnāntaka* image in the Yakṣa and the mixed nature of cult Mahāyāna characterized by *mantranaya* practice. Now it will be possible to concentrate on an abundance of Hayagrīva images to isolate more richly the course of development of the *krodha-vighnāntaka.* Equally detailed studies of other Phase One *krodha-vighnāntaka* might confirm or negate the findings we derive from Hayagrīva, but by focusing on Hayagrīva as he appears in Phase One, we avoid distracting iconographic changes. Geographic and temporal differences will still have to be taken into account, but the focus on a single *krodha-vighnāntaka* acts as a control. Before beginning to examine the images, however, we must learn what we can about Hayagrīva from written evidence.

1 The Iconography of Phase One Hayagrīva

Fortunately, understanding Hayagrīva's transformation from a Vedic or Brahmanical deity to a Buddhist one and identifying the kinds of tasks he performs is made much easier by the previous work of several scholars. The seminal work on Hayagrīva is Robert H. van Gulik's *Hayagrīva: The Mantrayanic Aspect of Horse-Cult in China and Japan.* Though the title suggests a singularly East Asian focus, van Gulik also surveys Hayagrīva's pre-Buddhist roots, a theme undertaken by others as well.[1]

1.1 Brahmanical and Buddhist Hayagrīva

Although horses and a horse deity play a significant role in the Vedas, the term Hayagrīva ("the horse-necked one") first appears in the epic period.[2] It is one of several names (Ascacirṣa, Hayacirṣa, Ascamukha, Vaḍavamukha) meaning effectively "horse-headed" or "horse-faced." The most important reference is as an epithet of Viṣṇu, the "loudly-roaring one," a horse-headed incarnation who is "the reader and promulgator of the sacred Vedas."[3] In the *Mahābhārata* Viṣṇu assumes this form in order to recover the four Vedas, which have been stolen by demons. He enters the underworld and begins to recite the *Sama Veda.* The demons are attracted to the sound, and Viṣṇu-Hayagrīva is then able to capture them.

One can see immediately that the qualities of the Brahmanical Hayagrīva lend themselves to the tasks of the Buddhist *krodha-vighnāntaka,* since it will be recalled that at an early stage they were considered personifications of spoken *dhāraṇi.* The vocal character of Hayagrīva, associated perhaps with the sound of a horse's neighing, is stringently preserved in the Esoteric Buddhist tradition. For instance, in a Hayagrīva ritual preserved in Tibet Hayagrīva "yells with dreadful voice, as the horse roaring. This terrible voice subdues all demons and all evils."[4]

For van Gulik, the vocality of the Brahmanical and Buddhist Hayagrīva "can be deduced from the conspicuous physical characteristics of the horse," along with the horse's celerity and phallic potency.[5] While virility may be evident at some deep structural level, the speed of the horse becomes an explicit metaphor for Hayagrīva's ubiquity and his ability to sojourn, like Yamāntaka, in areas otherwise impenetrable. His swiftness was understood this way by the earliest Chinese commentator on the *Mahāvairocana Sūtra*, Yixing, who wrote of Hayagrīva:

> *He is just like the Horse-jewel of a Cakravartin, that wanders about the four continents, nowhere and never giving itself one moment rest, having the great force of all the B[odhisattva]s.*[6]

In the epic and Brahmanical periods Hayagrīva had a second identity apart from that of an incarnation of Viṣṇu. Hayagrīva was also independently the name of an *asura*-demon enemy of Viṣṇu. In the *Harivaṁsa*, for instance, "the terrible, the strong Hayagrīva who, single-handed had fought all the gods during a thousand years," attacks Viṣṇu, "his eyes red with anger," and is only subdued when Viṣṇu responds with a barrage of a thousand arrows. Van Gulik suggests that a gradual amalgamation of the two Hayagrīvas took place, in which the *asura*-demon Hayagrīva is charged with the theft of the Vedas and the Viṣṇu Hayagrīva with vengeance.[7]

One of the earliest Esoteric Buddhist incarnations of the *krodha-vighnāntaka* was as *vidyārāja*, the personifications of a superior class of *dhāraṇī*.[8] *Dhāraṇī* are formulas which derive power not only from the meaning of the words but also their sound. It is for this reason that the Chinese attempted to transliterate, rather than translate, the Sanskrit *dhāraṇī*.[9] Van Gulik quite perceptively argues that because:

> *Viṣṇu-Hayagrīva was celebrated as the Reciter of the Veda's, the Promulgator of the Sacred Word . . . he was exceedingly suitable for a transformation to Vidyārāja. . . . Further all the Vidyārāja's bear a fierce character. Also in this respect the figure of Viṣṇu-Hayagrīva lent itself excellently for the part of a Vidyārāja; for we saw how extensively in Hindu-literature the awe-inspiring shape of Viṣṇu with the horse's head was described, and how closely this figure was connected with the demon Hayagrīva, the strong. This figure fitted in so well in the Mahāyāna, that soon Hayagrīva was wholly dissociated from Viṣṇu.*[10]

As the conceptual link between Brahmanical and early Esoteric Buddhist Hayagrīva is so consistent, it is imperative to note briefly that the appropriation did not extend to the visual form of Hayagrīva. It is not clear whether or how the Brahmanical *asura* Hayagrīva was depicted, but it is known that Hayagrīva as Viṣṇu *avatāra* is portrayed with a horse's head.[11] The Buddhist Hayagrīva, on the other hand, is never portrayed with a horse's head in South Asia.[12] When a horse's head is present in a Hayagrīva image, it appears to emerge from the hair. Even this is rare in South Asia, though common in Tibet and East Asia. We will see that the earliest images of Hayagrīva refer back to the categories of Yakṣa, Gaṇa and *āyudha-puruṣa*, not to the horse-headed incarnation of Viṣṇu.

1.2 Dating the emergence of the Buddhist Hayagrīva

When did this process of appropriation and transformation occur? Van Gulik believes that it took place around the beginning of the sixth century. Like so much of the work of this progressive and versatile scholar, his dating is thoughtfully deduced and may err only slightly on the optimistically early side. In terms of sculptural remains, we have seen that Aurangabad's Cave 7 presents a likely candidate to be identified as Hayagrīva [**12, 16**], datable to the late sixth or early seventh century.[13] The more secure evidence of Vajrapuruṣa images from Aurangabad

64. *Hayagrīva in Cave 7 Aurangabad, ca. late 6th century, detail of* **12**, *same as* **16**

and Ellora [**11, 17**] demonstrate that the *krodha-vighnāntaka* were included in the bodhisattva cult already by the late sixth century.

Textual evidence is also not definitive, offering only a rough *terminus ad quem*. Van Gulik cites three texts which mention Hayagrīva to bolster his claim that "the Horse-headed One was at a rather early date [i.e., early sixth century] incorporated in the Mahāyāna Pantheon."[14] Here we must tread carefully and not allow van Gulik to mislead us, nor abandon him because of uncharacteristic errors of fact. The first text he appeals to is the *MVS*, which he claims was translated into Chinese in the seventh century. In fact it was not translated until the early eighth, in 725 CE.[15] The second text is the voluminous *Dhāraṇī Saṁgraha* (T.18.901), to which reference has already been made. It was translated by Atikuta/Atigupta in 653, and we will return to it and to the *MMK*, as both contain important early dated information on Hayagrīva. First we must correct van Gulik in the dating of the third text which he cites as evidence of Hayagrīva's early absorption into Buddhism. He states that a text on Amoghapāśa which includes a reference to Hayagrīva was translated by Bodhiruci ca. 650 CE.[16] This text (T.20.1092) was actually translated in the early eighth century, in 707 CE, though Bodhiruci did translate the first chapter of it (T.20.1095) in 693 CE .[17]

To these adjustments we can add a little more evidence, some of it negative. The earliest of six Chinese translations of the *Amoghapāśahṛdaya sūtra* (i.e., the first chapter of the *Amoghapāśakalparāja*) was made by Jñānagupta in 587.[18] It is a conventional *dhāraṇī* text, advocating typical Mahāyāna cult goals, such as rebirth in the Pure Land and visions of Avalokiteśvara.[19] The *dhāraṇī* methods are effective in curing illness caused by demons and ensuring births of male children.[20] The *dhāraṇī* text represents an extremely conservative Mahāyāna orientation. It offers reverence to the Śrāvakas, to the Three Jewels, to him who saves from every fear, from flogging, from disasters, to him who expounds moral faculties, the constituents of the path, the four noble truths, to him who dwells in the pure region, who protects, who comforts, and so forth.[21] There is, however, no mention of either Hayagrīva or any other wrathful attendant, not even when the text elaborates on the method of painting Buddha, prescribing Amoghapāśa be seated to his right, wearing a black antelope skin across his shoulder.[22] Nor does Hayagrīva appear seventy-two years later in Xuanzang's translation of the same text.[23]

By the end of the seventh century, two versions of the related *kalpa* text on the ritual used in worshipping Amoghapāśa had been translated in China. Both versions outfit Amoghapāśa with a wrathful attendant, Amoghapāśa Dhāraṇīrāja. He appears in the text translated by the newly arrived Kashmiri, Manicintana, in 693 CE, as well as in the version translated in 700 CE by Li Wuchang, from Lampaka, northwest India.[24] Though Hayagrīva is not named, Amoghapāśa Dhāraṇīrāja's functions and certain details of his appearance are suggestive of Hayagrīva. Amoghapāśa Dhāraṇīrāja is *lambodara*, four-armed and four-tusked, and he gazes up at Avalokiteśvara.[25] He may be interpreted as a harbinger of Hayagrīva's standard association with Amoghapāśa, since, among other consistencies, the Tibetan tradition also maintains the four tusks as canonical.[26] The connection is reinforced by the fact that the text of 700 CE mentions, rather quizzically, that when performing the eighteenth of twenty-two numbered liturgical *mudrā*s, one is to incline the head to the left, "like a horse's head."[27] The Chinese characters are the same as those used for the name Hayagrīva, used appropriately here in connection with a *mudrā* associated with the recitation of *dhāraṇī*.

In 707 CE Bodhiruci completed his translation of the full text in thirty sections (T.20.1092). It includes his second translation of the first chapter, for as mentioned already, in 693 CE he had translated a version (T.20.1095) which, in terms of our interests, is no different from Jñānagupta's of 587 CE. In Bodhiruci's version of 707, Hayagrīva is not yet a part of Amoghapāśa's immediate entourage, but one of the listed forms of Avalokiteśvara. He appears as the "Horse-headed/Hayagrīva Avalokiteśvara Mahā Vidyārāja" in a litany of names of Avalokiteśvara, and simply as "Hayagrīva Avalokiteśvara Bodhisattva," described as holding a hatchet and a flower.[28] As in the slightly earlier version of 700 CE by Li Wuchang, in Bodhiruci's translation, Amoghapāśa is equipped with a wrathful attendant, named Amogha[pāśa's] Aggressive Krodharāja. He is four-armed and holds a noose, a sword, a *tridaṇḍi*, or *triśūla*, and a flower. He sits with Tārā, Bhṛikutī or Vimalajñāna (?) and others beneath a four-armed Amoghapāśa.[29]

These six Chinese translations of Amoghapāśa texts made within 120 years of each other provide more evidence for the dating of the rise of the *krodha-vighnāntaka* in general and Hayagrīva in particular. In the earliest of the six, a text which must have had currency in India by the sixth century (T.20.1093), *krodha-vighnāntaka* are absent in any form. Some advance is shown in the translations of 693 (T.20.1097) and 700 CE (T.20.1096), when not Hayagrīva but a generic *krodha-vighnāntaka* enters the picture. Already by the 707 CE translation (T.20.1092), however, Hayagrīva has a role to play. We can only speculate about the significant promotion of Hayagrīva in the space of just seven years. One explanation might be to assume that both Manicintana (a Kashmiri) and Li Wuchang (from northwest India) had access to the redactions of the *kalpa* texts current in northwest India, while the manuscript which the mysterious Bodhiruci worked on in 707 CE came from central or eastern India. Another reasonable explanation would be that the Sanskrit text of T.20.1096 was current in India around the middle of the seventh century and that of T.20.1092 later on in the century. Perhaps as the "latest" version, newly acquired from India, it induced Bodhiruci to retranslate a text he had already worked on fourteen years earlier. At any rate, between 587 and 707 CE, we see a definite progression toward the inclusion of *krodha-vighnāntaka* into the texts and rituals concerned with Amoghapāśa and incremental advances in the status of wrathful deities.

A similar trail can be followed for the various works concerning Sahasrabhuja-sahasranetra (Thousand-armed thousand-eyed) Avalokiteśvara. In the translation by Zhitong (T.20.1057) in the first half of the seventh century, I find no mention of Hayagrīva. But by the end of the eighth century, between 746 and 774 CE, Amoghavajra included the "Hayagrīva Vidyārāja hook-*mudrā*" and the "Hayagrīva Vidyārāja *dhāraṇī*" in a *kalpa* text on Sahasrabhuja-sahasranetra Avalokiteśvara.[30]

1.3 Hayagrīva with Avalokiteśvara in early Phase One texts

It should not be forgotten that Hayagrīva's gradual inclusion in the entourage and rituals of Amoghapāśa and Sahasrabhuja Avalokiteśvara is merely an expansion of his role as Avalokiteśvara's *krodha-vighnāntaka* and not the basis of it. The *MMK* recognizes Avalokiteśvara as the nominal head of the *padmakula* (lotus family). An assembly of all the *kula* in the first chapter of the *MMK* precipitates a list of all the Mahā-Vidyārāja belonging to the *padmakula*, as named in the late tenth century Chinese translation. The fifth in the list is Amoghapāśa Vidyārāja, who is followed immediately by Hayagrīva Vidyārāja.[31] As discussed above, parts of the *MMK* had already been translated into Chinese in the eighth century, although certain sections seem to be no earlier than the late eighth, and others the tenth.[32] The sections that pertain here, however, are believed to be considerably earlier, and a date of the late sixth or early seventh century is conservatively acceptable.[33]

By the middle of the seventh century, Atigupta had already devoted the sixth of twelve sections of the *Dhāraṇī Saṁgraha* of 653 CE to Hayagrīva. Hayagrīva also appears at least once in the first section and several times in the fourth and twelfth sections as well. He never appears as a "Vidyārāja," because this term did not come into use until the late seventh or early eighth century. He is called instead "Hayagrīva Avalokiteśvara Bodhisattva." Van Gulik has treated this section at length and made a detailed summary.[34] He notes that the previous section deals with various forms of Avalokiteśvara, then Bhṛikutī, and then, section six, "in keeping with the regular order deals with Hayagrīva, as an aspect of Avalokiteśvara."[35] Van Gulik concludes the sixth section forms a self-contained entity, but one well integrated into the *Dhāraṇī Saṁgraha*.

Section six prescribes that Hayagrīva be painted as a four-headed, two-armed deity holding a flower. The text further specifies that the middle head should be crowned with a green-blue horse's head.[36] Some phrases in Hayagrīva's multiple *dhāraṇī* echo Yamāntaka's found in the *MMK*. We find the following phrases: "Devourer of wrong knowledge," "Devour! Devour!," "To the Horse-faced One!," "Scatter! scatter! Disperse, disperse! Devour, svaha! Great Strong One! Guide to all knowledge!"[37] Hayagrīva's *dhāraṇī*s are used for "tying up the Vināyaka's," that is, destroying obstacles. Typical of Phase One texts, these obstacles are interpreted as belonging to the mundane realm. Among the functions listed are the curing of snake bites and headaches, injuries and diseases, caused by devils; rain making; the arousal of love; assistance in winning disputes and in making others powerless, warding off a sword and vanquishing armies; and the prevention of *pollutiones nocturnae*.

The texts are dominated, as Phase One images are, by the mixed Mahāyāna-Esoteric Buddhist cult of the bodhisattva. Although this section of the text is devoted to Hayagrīva, we are never allowed to forget the primacy of Avalokiteśvara. One of the last portions of the Hayagrīva section discusses the creation of a *bodhi-maṇḍa* (altar) "for the initiation to the cult of the Bodhisattva Hayagrīva Avalokiteśvara."[38] In the middle of the altar should be an image of Hayagrīva, on the eastern side should be Ekādaśamukha (eleven-headed) Avalokiteśvara, at the northern side the eight-armed (Amoghapāśa?) Avalokiteśvara, in the south the eight Nāga-rāja. "Then [the aspirant] should enter the *bodhi-maṇḍa* and do *pūjā*-worship. One should concentrate on Avalokiteśvara Bodhisattva. Then in the midst of worship of all the bodhisattva, *siddhis* (powers) will be manifest."[39]

What is significant is that in this, the culminating ritual of the section, the emphasis is on Avalokiteśvara in all his forms, not on Hayagrīva. It is Avalokiteśvara who is of central importance, even though Hayagrīva is at the center of the altar. In Phase One texts and images of Hayagrīva, he is merely an adjunct to the great bodhisattva, Avalokiteśvara, of whom he is, at best, a manifestation, or a *dhāraṇī* personification. Powers to cure, to be victorious and so on ultimately flow from Avalokiteśvara, who "functioned primarily as the center of his own specific and independent cult."[40]

We are left, then, with 653 CE as the earliest date van Gulik discovered for a Sanskrit text mentioning Hayagrīva translated into Chinese. The *Dhāraṇī Saṁgraha* has such a well-developed notion of Hayagrīva and his role that it is unlikely it represents the earliest instance of Hayagrīva's adoption into the cult of Avalokiteśvara. Rather it provides a textual benchmark for the time when Hayagrīva's star had commenced rising. By the eighth century, Hayagrīva is found in both Phase One and Phase Two texts and imagery, and he will continue to be portrayed in India until the late twelfth century and still later outside of India. The Nepalese and Tibetans in particular have preserved Hayagrīva's role as attendant to Avalokiteśvara well into the twentieth century. There does not seem to be a fundamental shift in the iconographic structure of the Phase One Hayagrīva after the twelfth century.[41]

Confirmation of the early sixth century as a *terminus a quo* for the Buddhicization of Hayagrīva can be found in Gilgit manuscripts. These Buddhist Sanskrit manuscripts were discovered in 1931 inside the vault of a *stūpa* near Gilgit, seat of the Shahi rulers. Orthographically they belong to the sixth or seventh century.[42] Much the way it does in the *Dhāraṇī Saṁgraha*, the section on Hayagrīva immediately follows the section devoted to Avalokiteśvara. A short *dhāraṇī* text on Hayagrīva "is written (without any gap) along with the concluding line of the previous ms," which is a text devoted to the Ekādaśamukha form of Avalokiteśvara.[43] The Hayagrīva text begins with a salutation to Avalokiteśvara, and invokes the image of a horse-faced deity (Hayagrīva) above the images of Lokeśvara Avalokiteśvara, who is flanked by Vajradhara (i.e., Vajrapāṇi) and Avalokiteśvara. The fact that the manuscript requires that Hayagrīva be visualized as *vaḍavamukha* (horse-headed) testifies to his relation to the pre-Buddhist Hayagrīva, who is visualized in such a way. As already discussed, no known South Asian images of the Buddhist Hayagrīva provide him with a horse's head for the main head, and images in India which actually depict him with a small horse head in his hair are, as we will discover, quite rare. Once again, it is Avalokiteśvara who dominates the atmosphere, Hayagrīva's section being only an appendix.

1.4 Hayagrīva with Tārā in Phase One texts

Avalokiteśvara in his various forms is not the only bodhisattva of higher status to whom Hayagrīva is subordinated. Tārā, who is both counterpart and emanation of Avalokiteśvara, is also given Hayagrīva as her wrathful subordinate in a number of texts and images.[44] For example, the thirteenth chapter of the *Tārāmūlakalpa* ends with a Hayagrīva ritual.[45] The *Tārā bodhisattva kalpa sūtra*, translated by Amoghavajra in the second half of the eighth century, also provides descriptions of Hayagrīva attending Avalokiteśvara, accompanied by Tārā and Bhṛikuṭi.[46] The Hayagrīva described is four-armed, holding an axe and lotus flower, and he makes his "fundamental *mudrā*."[47]

The later *Ārya Tārābhaṭṭārikāyā-nāmāṣṭottaraśataka* (Sūtra on praising a hundred and eight names of the holy bodhisattva Tārābhadra), translated between 982 and 1000 CE by the same Kashmiri monk who translated the large *MMK* (Tianxizai/Devaśānti), also associates Hayagrīva with Tārā. The text starts off with a hymn of praise, setting the scene around Tārā of a typical Mahāyāna cult vision of a Pure Land, with *cintāmani* trees, heavenly music, colors and scents. Then we read:

> *Ārya Tārā Bodhisattva along with a thousand Vidyarajñi (i.e. female Vidyārāja), Krodha Mahāvidyārājas, Hayagrīva and the others, surrounding her . . .* [48]

It is not by accident that of all the *krodha-vighnāntaka* to be singled out here, it is Hayagrīva who has become associated with Tārā, for he attains prominence as the primary wrathful representative in the *padmakula* through his regular association with the many forms of Avalokiteśvara.

It is by no means my intention to suggest that the textual passages I have selected describing Hayagrīva as a Phase One attendant of Avalokiteśvara and Tārā are complete or comprehensive. They were selected merely to give some idea of Hayagrīva's appearance, function and position in Phase One texts. With the background thus provided, we can begin the examination of images of Hayagrīva in Phase One compositions.

Notes to Chapter Five

1 See N.P. Joshi, "Hayagrīva in Brahmanical Iconography," *Journal of the Indian Society of Oriental Art* ns 5 (1972-73): 36-42. The epigraph for this chapter comes from T.20.1072A.155a.

2 Van Gulik, *Hayagrīva*, 9-10.

3 Ibid., 10. Also see Joshi, "Hayagrīva," 39.

4 From the "Treasury of Percipience" (Dgons-Gter), in *Esoteric Teachings of the Tibetan Tantra: Including Seven Initiation Rituals and the Six Yogas of Nāropa*, trans. Chang Chen Chi and ed. C.A. Muses (York Beach, 1982), 61. The comments by and the attitude of the editor of this volume, C.A. Muses, are unfortunate and offensive, but the translations are useful.

5 Van Gulik, *Hayagrīva*, 95-96.

6 Quoted in van Gulik, *Hayagrīva*, 54. For an earlier translation into French, see "Batōkannon," *Hōbōgirin: Dictionnaire Encyclopédique du Bouddhisme D'Après les Sources Chinoises et Japonaises; Premier Fascicule: A-Bombai*, ed. Paul Demiéville (Tokyo, 1929), 58-59.

7 Van Gulik, *Hayagrīva*, 15, 19.

8 See Przyluski, "Les Vidyārāja."

9 Van Gulik, *Siddham*, 22-24; and, idem, *Hayagrīva*, 48-51.

10 Van Gulik, *Hayagrīva*, 28.

11 Joshi, "Hayagriva," figs. 1, 2; van Gulik, *Hayagrīva*, figs. 1-3.

12 I know of only a few such images from Japan which trace back to the *Taizō Zuzō*, a scroll brought to Japan in the mid-9th c. by Enchin. One appears in the *Kakuzenshō* by Kakuzen (1143-ca. 1218 CE) and is illustrated in T.89.3022.832; in van Gulik, *Hayagrīva* (frontispiece), discussed 47-48; and, in *Hōbōgirin*, 1.58, fig. 27, discussed 60. The relevant section of the *Taizō Zuzō* scroll of images from the *garbhadhātu maṇḍala* now in the Nara National Museum is illustrated in *Nihon Bijutsu Zenshū*, vol. 6: *Mikkyō no Bijutsu: Tōji/Jingōji/Murōji*, ed. Uehara Shoichi (Tokyo, 1980), 169, fig. 59; and, in Hisatoyo Ishida, *Mandara no kenkyū*, 2 vols. (Tokyo, 1975), 2:11, fig. 94.

13 Another candidate is the Gaṇa-like attendant to Tārā in the same cave. See Berkson, *Caves at Aurangabad*, 149, 137. J. Huntington identifies the the attendant figure and the bodhisattva on the other side of the vestibule in Cave 6, opposite Vajrapāṇi **[10]**, as Hayagrīva and Avalokiteśvara respectively in "Cave Six," 50. Berkson, however, identifies the bodhisattva as Mañjuśrī. *Caves at Aurangabad*, 178. The attendant figure stands in a relaxed pose, holding a bowl, perhaps an offering. Unlike Vajrapuruṣa **[10]** he is not aggressive in posture or gesture, making it difficult to identify him with certainty as a *krodha-vighnāntaka*.

14 Van Gulik, *Hayagrīva*, 24.

15 See Lancaster, *Korean Buddhist Canon*, 147, no. 427.

16 Van Gulik, *Hayagrīva*, 24, repeated on 56.

17 For T.20.1092, see Lancaster, *Korean Buddhist Canon*, 106, no. 287 (*Njo*, 317). The earlier version (T.20.1095, *Njo* 315) does not appear in the Korean Buddhist canon.

18 T.20.1093.399a-402b (*KBC* 288, *Njo* 312). Meisezahl, who has studied extensively the Chinese, Tibetan and Sanskrit versions of the Amoghapāśa texts, lists the five Chinese translations. See R.O. Meisezahl, "The Amoghapāśahṛdaya-dhāraṇī: The Early Sanskrit Manuscript of the Reiunji Critically Edited and Translated," *Monumenta Nipponica* 17 (1962): 272. Two errata in Meisezahl should be noted: the text number is misprinted as 1903 instead of 1093; and Meisezahl's no. 4 is dated 602, or 600-664 for Amoghavajra, who worked in the 8th c., not the 7th c. The sixth translation is Bodhiruci's re-translation of 707 CE, as part of the larger *Amoghapāśakalparāja*.

19 T.20.1093.400a, 402a.

20 T.20.1093.401c.

21 See Meisezahl, "Amoghapāśahṛdaya-dhāraṇī," 295-298. Meisezahl retranslates the *dhāraṇī* based on a Tibetan version found at Dunhuang, which was translated into Middle High Tibetan, not from the Sanskrit, but from the Chinese. Also see R.O. Meisezahl, "Amoghapāśa: Some Nepalese Representations and Their Vajrayanic Aspects," *Monumenta Serica* 26 (1967): 494-496.

22 T.20.1093.401c-402a.

23 T.20.1094 (*Njo* 316, *KBC* 289). In an interesting afterword, the text is said to have been translated in 659 CE.

24 T.20.1097.4288a (Manicintana's version; *Njo* 313, *KBC* 290); T.20.1096.415c (Li Wuchang's version; *Njo* 314, *KBC* 291). Manicintana was a Kashmiri monk who arrived in Loyang the year of this translation. The Chinese characters for his name are variously construed into one of the following Sanskrit equivalents: Ratnacinta, Adisena, Manicinta and Cintāmani. For his life and work on translation teams in Loyang and Changan, see Forte, "Tantric Master Manicintana," 301-345; and, Lokesh Chandra, "The Tripitaka-Translator Pao-ssu-Wei (Cintāmani)," 283-286.

25 T.20.1096.415c; T.20.1097.428a.

26 See Pratapaditya Pal, "The Iconography of Amoghapāśa Lokeśvara," Part One: *Oriental Art* 12 (1966): 234-239; Part Two: *Oriental Art* 13 (1967): 20-28; P.H. Pott, "The Amoghapāśa from Bhatgaon and its Parivāra," *Journal of the Indian Society of Oriental Art* ns: 4 (1971-72): 63-65; and, Janice Leoshko, "The Appearance of Amoghapāśa in Pāla Period Art," *Studies in Buddhist Art of South Asia*, ed. A.K. Narain (New Delhi, 1985), 127-135. A *sādhana* preserved in Tibet mentions that Hayagrīva's four canine tusks symbolize the subjugation of the four demons: illness, obstacles to Dharma, Death and *kleśa*. Chang, *Esoteric Teachings*, 64. Stephen Beyer has also studied a ritual visualization, attributed to Atīśa and practiced today, which visualizes Hayagrīva with four fangs. Beyer, *Cult of Tārā*, 351.

27 T.20.1096.420b. See the helpful distinction between liturgical *mudrā* ("indicators of the single phases of the meditation") used in rituals, and iconographic *mudrā* (which indicate "a particular essence or quality of the god or deity to whom it is attributed . . . the idea of *mudrā* thus being inseparable from that of Tantric deity") by which a deity is identified, in Erik Haarh, "Contributions to the Study of Maṇḍala and Mudrā: Analysis of Two Tibetan Manuscripts in the Royal Library in Copenhagen," *Acta Orientalia* 23 (1959): 64.

28 T.20.1092.243a (*mudrā* described 326b); ibid., 271a, 302a, 390c (*mudrā* described 246b and 368c).

29 T.20.1092.266c, 269a.

30 T.20.1056.75c, 81b. On the Phase Two cult of the Thousand-armed Avalokiteśvara in China, see Maria Dorothea Reis, "*The Great Compassion Dhāraṇī* of the Thousand-armed Avalokiteśvara: its Scriptural Source and Cult in China" (typewritten; Kyoto, 1989).

31 T.20.1191.839a.

32 See Przyluski, "Les Vidyārāja," 305-306. K.P. Jayaswal has shown that the historical sections of the text cannot have been written before the end of the 8th c. K.P. Jayaswal, *An Imperial History of India in a Sanskrit Text [c. 700 BC-c. 770 AD]* (Lahore, 1934; reprinted, Patna 1988), 3.

33 See the discussion in Macdonald, *Mañjuśrīmūlakalpa*, 1-20. Benoytosh Bhattacharyya takes the most extreme (and untenable) position of dating the early stratum of the *MMK* to the 2nd c. CE in his introduction to *Guhyasamāja Tantra or Tathāgataguhyaka* (Baroda, 1931), xxxvii; Giuseppe Tucci also pushes for an earlier dating of early Esoteric Buddhist texts in "Animadversiones Indicae," *Journal of the Asiatic Society of Bengal* ns 26 (1930): 128-132. Snellgrove suggests Tucci's placement of the *MMK* in the 5th c. or earlier is plausible with the caveat that "only when all the more important tantras are better known, can we begin to date them with any certainty." Snellgrove, "The Notion of Divine Kingship in Tantric Buddhism,"218. Also see Matsunaga, "On the Date of the *Mañjuśrīmūlakalpa*."

34 Van Gulik, *Hayagrīva*, 62-75.

35 Ibid., 62.

36 T.19.901.837c-838a. Compare van Gulik, *Hayagrīva*, 73.

37 Van Gulik, *Hayagrīva*, 67, 68.

38 Ibid., 74.

39 T.19.901.838b. Compare van Gulik, *Hayagrīva*, 75.

40 Schopen, "Sukhāvatī," 200.

41 Meisezahl has produced a model iconographic study of Amoghapāśa

as he appears in late Sanskrit texts or their Chinese and Tibetan translation and commentaries. The one striking anomaly of several of these later treatments is that Hayagrīva appears as an *āyudhapuruṣa*: he is made to be the personification of the mace. However, this only occurs in the special context where all the deities of a mini-*maṇḍala*, including Amoghapāśa himself, are designated as *āyudhapuruṣa* (Amoghapāśa of the noose, Ekajaṭā of the sword, etc.). See Meisezahl, "Amoghapāśa: Some Nepalese Representations," 475-477; 482 -486.

42 Nalinaksha Dutt, ed., *Gilgit Manuscripts Vol. 1* (Srinagar, 1939), 42. Schopen states that "the manuscripts themselves can be more or less accurately dated on paleographic grounds to the 6th century AD." Schopen, "Sukhāvatī," 202.

43 Dutt, *Gilgit Manuscripts*, 61.

44 K.K. Dasgupta, "Iconography of Tārā," in *The Sakti Cult and Tārā*, ed. D.C. Sircar (Calcutta, 1967), 115; and, Beyer, *Cult of Tārā*, 65.

45 Lalou, "*Mañjuśrīmūlakalpa* et *Tārāmūlakalpa*," 328.

46 T.20.1101.452a, 453b.

47 T.20.1101.453b.

48 T.20.1106.474c.

6

Hayagriva: Images

The study of the few and contradictory texts is insufficient for supplying an answer to these questions and for placing the problems that arise in their right perspective. One must . . . seek out the works of art that bear witness to the passage from one form of Buddhism to another. Giuseppe Tucci

1 Early Phase One (ca. 8th-9th century) South Asian Images of Hayagrıva

The fundamental assumption of this work is that visible remains have as much informative potential as texts have. The textual occurrences of Hayagriva now having been sketched out, it is not my intention to try to find (or to force) iconographic matches between texts and images. More important is to derive from the images a body of evidence which, *independent* of but in tandem with the texts, has something of its own to say about the significance of the *krodha-vighnāntaka* and its modification over time. It is necessary to glean as much as possible from relevant surviving texts, but texts are not the only preserve of religious meaning. We must be willing to jettison the burden of meaning which texts impose when they interfere with the recognition of a different set of values encased in art. Visual depictions arguably have not only a greater impact on the emotional conception of a deity than written material has; visual depictions can shape the written texts as well.[1] Thus images have an unqualified primacy in their demand for our attention, as well as an immediacy and reliability which are at times much less subject to later revision and reformulation than written evidence.

65. *Twelve-armed Avalokiteśvara with Hayagrīva, Nalanda (Bihar), ca. 8th century, Nalanda Museum*

66. *Āyudhapuruṣa, below Viṣṇu at Deogarh (Uttar Pradesh), mid 6th century, same as* 25

67. *Hayagrīva, detail of* 65

1.1 An early Hayagrīva from Nalanda

After the Aurangabad Hayagriva [**12, 64**], one of the earliest recognized images of a Phase One Hayagrīva is included in "one of the great masterworks of Nalanda stone sculpture, recently discovered at Site No. 3, just north of the Great Stupa."[2] [**65, 67**] A standing twelve-armed Avalokiteśvara is accompanied by a substantial entourage. The largest of his companions are Tārā, seated on the proper right holding a lotus and a fruit, and a four-armed Bhṛikuṭī kneeling on the left, making the *vandana mudrā* with the upper right hand and holding a *kalaśa*-bottle against her left thigh. These two are part of a standard set of four or more who often accompany Khasarpaṇa and other forms of Avalokiteśvara.[3] Usually the third is Sudhanakumāra with the book, but he seems to have been rendered redundant by the presence of the small female Prajñāpāramitā seated on a lotus at Avalokiteśvara's waist level on the proper right. Next to Tārā, where Sudhanakumāra usually would be found, we find Sūcīmukha. The *Sādhanamālā* describes him as follows: "[Avalokiteśvara] is an expert in distributing the stream of nectar that flows from his hand, and Sūcīmukha who stands below with an uplifted face, a protruding belly and very pale appearance receives the same."[4]

On the other side, behind and beside Bhṛikuṭī, we find Hayagrīva, the fourth member of Khasarpaṇa Avalokiteśvara's standard accompanying quartet. He stands with one leg bent behind the other, leaning to the side and looking slightly upwards. He appears to be of the *vāmana*-Yakṣa body type. Though he barely emerges from the shadowy background, the features of his distinctly grotesque face are visible: furrowed eyebrows and forehead, a hooked nose and a grin that exposes fangs. He makes the *vinayahasta* gesture, crossing his wrists in front of his chest. The Nalanda Hayagrīva's hair is relatively short, separated into fat "Guptesque" curls that divide in the center and frame his face. The style recalls those of earlier Gaṇa or *āyudhapuruṣa*. [**22-25**] His lower torso is damaged, but he seems to wear a *dhoti,* leaving his upper torso bare. Large earrings hang at his ears, and a bulky necklace circles his neck.

The noteworthy aspects of this early image of Hayagrīva are his relative size and placement, and his Gaṇa-like quality. One notes that of the four attendants on the lower platform, Hayagrīva is not only smaller than Bhṛikuṭī and Tārā, but he is even smaller in scale than his partner, Sūcīmukha. Moreover, he is forced to peek between Avalokiteśvara's *dhoti* and Bhṛikuṭī's elbows, one of which, on the second right arm, originally obscured his figure more but is now broken off. In the future the relative scale and positioning of Hayagrīva and Bhṛikuṭī will be reversed, but in the early period Hayagrīva plays not just a secondary role but one which hardly bears mention. He appears in an exhaustively inclusive depiction of Avalokiteśvara and entourage, an image which masterfully balances intricacy and clarity. The iconographic compexity is impressive in that it has yet to fall into stiff standardization. The shadowy Hayagrīva probably was meant to portray the personification of Avalokiteśvara's *dhāraṇī*, but the composition declares that Hayagrīva represents only one of many means to save those who call on Avalokiteśvara.

While the overall iconography of this powerful sculpture seems quite progressive, the image of Hayagrīva recalls the roots of the *krodha-vighnāntaka* imagery in the Gaṇas and *āyudhapuruṣa* of late Gupta art. The Nalanda Hayagrīva seems to be a mixture of the fifth-century depictions of Śiva-Gaṇa with Viṣṇu's *āyudha-puruṣa.* [**22-25**] Nor is there a great deal of difference from the earliest *krodha-vighnāntaka* treated in Chapter 1. [**10-19**]

68. *Four-armed Hayagrīva, Ratnagiri (Orissa) ca. 7th-8th century, same as 35*

69. *Fragment of Avalokiteśvara with Hayagrīva; Ratnagiri (Orissa), ca. 9th century*

1.2 Hayagrīva images from Ratnagiri

We have previously had occasion to discuss the Avalokiteśvara [33] who is paired with Vajrapāṇi [32] on the entrance porch of Monastery 1 at Ratnagiri. This four-armed form of Avalokiteśvara resembles most closely, perhaps, Jaṭāmukuṭa Lokeśvara, who like him carries the rosary and makes the *vara mudrā* with right hands, holding the lotus and vase in the left.[5] Nearly identical to the *krodha-vighnāntaka* attending Vajrapāṇi, identified provisionally as Mahābala [34, 37], Avalokiteśvara's attendant Hayagrīva [68] is four-armed, he makes the *vandana mudrā* with the upper right hand, holds a noose in the upper left, and makes the *vinayahasta* gesture with the central pair of arms. He stands in an exaggerated *pratyālīḍha*, with a dwarfish *lambodara* figure and bulging eyes. Already he is bearded, with mustaches, and his hair is pulled up into a bun. He stands directly in front of the stalk of a lotus as it emerges from the lotus base on which Avalokiteśvara stands. What is most significant about this Hayagrīva is that in consonance with the early period of *krodha-vighnāntaka* imagery he is relatively small in comparison to Avalokiteśvara. He is, moreover, smaller even than Sūcīmukha on the other side of Avalokiteśvara with whom Hayagrīva is paired. Avalokiteśvara's abilities as a compassionate savior seem to be stressed here, at the expense of his powers to subdue recalcitrant beings or to overcome obstacles with his *dhāraṇī*.

There are a number of Phase One Hayagrīva images dating to the late eighth or late ninth century at Ratnagiri. One of them survives in the lower half of what was most likely a four-armed Avalokiteśvara. [69] It is dated by Debala Mitra as "not later than the ninth century AD."[6] The bodhisattva's hand rests on Hayagrīva's head, and in order for Hayagrīva to be within reach, the artist has propped him up on a special pedestal. Hayagrīva himself is four-armed and of the *vāmana*-Yakṣa type, making the familiar *vinayahasta mudrā* with the central pair of hands, and the *vandana* gesture of salutation with the other right hand.

On several counts the Hayagrīva figure does not seem much of an advance on the earlier one accompanying Jaṭāmukuta Lokeśvara. [68] Their gestures are similar, though the later Hayagrīva has a larger body and a less active pose. There has been a subtle adjustment, however, in the relative size of the two attendants. Not only is the ninth-century Hayagrīva [69] slightly larger in relation to Avalokiteśvara's leg than he was in the earlier composition [68], he is also larger than Tārā, at least in terms of the amount of space devoted to him in the composition. This is the reverse of the relative size of Hayagrīva to Sūcīmukha. [33]

This incremental increase in size of the Phase One *krodha-vighnāntaka* is magnified suddenly when we look at a slightly later, but still ninth-century Avalokiteśvara with "an enormous Hayagrīva." [2, 70, COLOR PLATE 4] If previously Hayagrīva was barely the height of Avalokiteśvara's knee, this Hayagrīva "rises almost to the bodhisattva's waist."[7] In addition, Tārā and Bhṛikutī are reduced to two plaques at the bottom of the lotus pedestal, matching in a way the two Tathāgatas (Amitābha and Akṣobhya) at the upper corners. The four-armed Hayagrīva, with his wicked expression, *lambodara* physique, active posture and expressive gestures, has captured the interest of the artist (and, once again, one can assume, his co-religionists) at the expense of the other members of Avalokiteśvara's entourage.

The elongated proportions, looseness of posture, supple carving and finish suggest that of the two Ratnagiri bodhisattva the complete scuplture [70] was made somewhat later in the ninth century than the relatively stiffer, straighter and less svelte fragmented bodhisattva. [69] His "thrice-broken" *tribhaṇga* posture is more sharply pitched. When the two are viewed together with a third Ratnagiri Avalokiteśvara [33], a coherent developmental sequence emerges, documenting both stylistic factors (most evident in the bodhisattva figures) and the iconographic maturation of the Phase One *krodha-vighnāntaka*. Between the seventh or eighth century [33, 68] and the mid- or late ninth century [70], the growth in stature of the *krodha-vighnāntaka* is visibly measurable.[8]

70. *Avalokiteśvara with Hayagrīva, Ratnagiri (Orissa), ca. 9th century, same as* 2

The Phase One trend toward larger attendants seems to have peaked, at least in Orissa, in the late ninth century. The "enormous Hayagrīva" [COLOR PLATE 4] should be placed at that time. We will appreciate their prominent scale when we return to Orissan images and discover that by the tenth century Phase One *krodha-vighnāntaka* regress to a scale more in keeping with their role as attendants. By the late period they decrease almost to insignificance. The simultaneous growth of Phase One *krodha-vighnāntaka* and the earliest appearance of Phase Two images that took place between the late ninth and early tenth centuries is not merely coincidental. In other words, alongside the more common Mahāyāna bodhisattva cult (Phase One) imagery, we begin to find independent *krodha-vighnāntaka* images, conclusive evidence that mature Esoteric Buddhism was also practiced in Orissa. From that moment on, the Phase One *krodha-vighnāntaka* decline in size and quality, for the later images of Hayagrīva betray a relatively lifeless typing. In the eighth and ninth centuries, on the other hand, artists seem to have lavished a considerable amount of creative energy on highlighting the essence of the Phase One *krodha-vighnāntaka*.

71. *Hayagrīva, detail of 73*

72. *Hayagrīva, detail of 74*

1.3 Early Hayagrīva from Bihar

Returning now to Bihar, it is clear that the early Phase One images of Hayagrīva are also relatively small and insignificant and/or markedly Yakṣa-like. A ca. eighth or ninth-century six-armed Avalokiteśvara from Nalanda [71, 73] includes a minuscule Hayagrīva, resting his hands on the handle of a *daṇḍa* next to Bhṛikuṭī. Neither Sūcīmukha or Sudhanakumāra are present. Hayagrīva is quite chubby and relatively innocuous, his hair in an older style one associates with the Gupta period. He is much smaller than Tārā and Bhṛikuṭī and hardly the size of Avalokiteśvara's foot. Thoroughly subordinated to Amoghapaśa, he looks up with awe and reverence at his spiritual master instead of out at us. His gaze identifies him with the worshiper, since Hayagrīva directs his eyes with us at the main deity, instead of demanding his own reverence.

A slightly later image of a two-armed Lokeśvara Avalokiteśvara, also from Nalanda, affords Hayagrīva greater scope. [72, 74] As the *Sādhanamālā*'s description of Lokeśvara maintains, only Tārā and Hayagrīva accompany the bodhisattva, and Hayagrīva holds the *daṇḍa*.[9] Tārā is larger and placed higher at Lokeśvara's side. Hayagrīva remains below, leaning against a fascinating lion-throne. Its brick-like pattern is a convention for cliffs or boulders. Hayagrīva is quite dwarfish, with a snake *upavita*, heavy earrings, a necklace, and he stands awkwardly. He makes the *vandana* gesture of salutation with his right hand and leans on the upturned handle of a *daṇḍa*, the finial of which is bottommost.

Hayagrīva's dwarfishness and his archaic hairdo are particularly notable aspects of his image type associating him with earlier Yakṣa and their hypostases, the *āyudhapuruṣa* [22, 24] and the more lighthearted, mischievous Gaṇa. [23] Also suggestive is his placement on the throne. There is a long-standing convention, in both Kashmir and eastern India, of placing a Yakṣa-atlantid between two lions to support the throne.[10] Here it seems the Yakṣa has stepped out of the throne, picked up a club and saluted the bodhisattva as Hayagrīva. Once again the Yakṣa origins of the *krodha-vighnāntaka* are reinforced.[11]

An important dated image of Tārā from Hilsa includes a small Hayagrīva. [75, 77] The inscription gives either the twenty-fifth or thirty-fifth year of Devapāla's reign, which lasted from ca. 812 to 850 CE.[12] The twenty-fifth year seems to be the generally accepted reading now,[13] which corresponds to a date of ca. 836 CE. The sculpture was the "religious gift" of a layman, and it mentions "the illustrious great Vihara of Nalanda," which is not far from Hilsa, so it is not unlikely that the piece was commissioned at Nalanda.

There is much concern among iconographers about what to call the Tārā figure. The main figure corresponds with the *Sādhanamālā* description of Khadirāvaṇi Tārā, though in the text she is outfitted with Ekajaṭā and Mārīcī, both female attendants. Here instead we have Ekajaṭā and Hayagrīva.[14] Happily we can leave this question aside, content with the general agreement that it is some form of Tārā. Since we have already shown that Tārā is associated with Hayagrīva in a number of ritual texts, we can accept that the small figure on Tārā's proper left is Hayagrīva.

As is appropriate for an early image of a Phase One *krodha-vighnāntaka*, Hayagrīva is quite diminutive. His standing form leaning against Tārā's thigh is hardly larger than the big-bellied Ekajaṭā who sits on the other side. His long boyish hair pulled back from his forehead cascades onto his shoulders in curly ringlets in a manner which recalls Gupta fashions. His right hand is in front of his chest, making what seems to be the *abhaya mudrā*, the gesture of reassurance. Despite the bulging eyes and swollen cheeks, his countenance is rather benign, an effect reinforced by his

73. *Avalokiteśvara with Hayagrīva, Nalanda (Bihar), ca. 8th-9th century, Indian Museum, Calcutta*

74. *Avalokiteśvara with Hayagrīva, Nalanda (Bihar), ca. 9th century, Indian Museum, Calcutta*

75. *Tārā with Hayagrīva, Hilsa (Bihar), 25th year of Devapāla (ca. 812-850), Patna Museum*

76. *Avalokiteśvara with Hayagrīva, Nalanda (Bihar), ca. 9th century, Indian Museum, Calcutta*

77. *Hayagrīva, detail of 75*

78. *Hayagrīva, detail of 76*

unusual stance, as if he were himself seeking comfort or reassurance. Casually resting his left foot on the blade of the axe, his left hand is placed on the upturned handle. Hardly the ferocious destroyer of obstacles, this early Hayagrīva seems more endearing than threatening.

A stylistically related two-armed Avalokiteśvara, this one actually found at Nalanda, is also seated and features a small Hayagrīva. [76, 78] It belongs to the mid- or late ninth century, certainly somewhat later than the dated example just discussed.[15] Like the Hilsa Tārā's wrathful attendant [77], this *vāmana*-Yakṣa Hayagrīva, perched on the edge of Avalokiteśvara's lotus platform, also nestles against the larger bodhisattva. He is not paired with either Sudhanakumāra or Sūcīmukha, and he is separated from the larger Tārā and Bhṛikuṭī, who sit below the lotus pedestal. Hayagrīva holds a sword upright in his right hand and makes the *tarjanī mudrā* (gesture of admonition) while holding the *pāśa*-noose in his left. His hair is once again pulled back into a series of loose curls. As with the Hilsa-Tārā Hayagrīva [77], the overall effect is neither threatening nor comical but good-natured and, due to his asymmetrical position, visually inviting.

A number of other Phase One Hayagrīva images belong to this stage of development, are datable to about the ninth century and will be referred to only briefly. The figures are all relatively small and somewhat innocuous.[16] They are invariably of the large *vāmana*-Yakṣa body type, and their gestures are limited in variety. Most make the *vandana mudrā* and lean on the handle of a small club or wand. A handsome four-armed Avalokiteśvara from Ghosrawan, Patna District, now in the Indian Museum, Calcutta, portrays a Hayagrīva who is not nearly as large as his counterpart Sūcīmukha, pleading for relief.[17] [79-80]

79. *Avalokiteśvara with Hayagrīva, Ghosrawan (Bihar), ca. 9th century, Indian Museum, Calcutta*

80. *Hayagrīva, detail of* 79

81. Tārā with Ekajaṭā and Hayagrīva, Nalanda (Bihar), ca. 9th century, Indian Museum, Calcutta

82. Hayagrīva, detail of 81

1.4 Images of Hayagrīva with Tārā

Identifying Tārā's attendants in several images has proved problematic in the past. Only by assembling a sufficiently large pool of images and not privileging the *Sādhanamālā* as the primary iconographic authority can the problem be put into perspective. For instance, a Tārā sculpture in the Indian Museum, Calcutta [81] is accompanied by two attendants.[18] The four-armed female holding the elephant skin above her head is, no doubt, Ekajaṭā. She appears in a number of Tārā images, including the Hilsa Tārā [75] and one in the Los Angeles County Museum, about which Pratapaditya Pal rightly comments that the "elephant hide is often given to Ekajaṭā in early images but rarely in texts."[19] In fact a *sādhana* in the Tibetan version of the *Sādhanasamuccaya* mentions a four-armed Ekajaṭā as having an elephant-hide for her upper garment, presumably, as here, a kind of flying cape.[20]

83. *Tārā with Hayagrīva, Baragoan (Bihar), ca. 9th century, Indian Museum, Calcutta*

84. *Hayagrīva, detail of 83*

Who, though, is the male figure on the other side? [82] He seems to be *vīra*-Yakṣa in body type, while all of our Hayagrīva's have been *vāmana*-Yakṣa. On the other hand, he carries an upright sword in the proper right hand, and the left hand placed on the hip grasps a rope, the noose of which is at his left shoulder. Now we have already seen that a wrathful attendant of Avalokiteśvara [76, 78] has the identical attributes. The latter *krodha-vighnāntaka* is *vāmana*-Yakṣa and can only be Hayagrīva. Thus we know that Hayagrīva occasionally appears with sword and noose. Moreover, at least in the Tibetan pantheon, there exists a two-armed Hayagrīva, who holds the sword in the right hand and the noose in the left.[21] This suggests the possibility that it is also Hayagrīva in the Calcutta sculpture. [82] When we further note the fact that Hayagrīva is paired with Ekajaṭā in the Hilsa Tārā [75], the possibility becomes a probability, since the identification of the Hilsa Tārā Hayagrīva is secure.

One of the inconsistencies that delays the identification of Hayagrīva is that he is a *vīra*-Yakṣa type. Another ninth-century Tārā figure in the storage chambers of the Indian Museum in Calcutta may help resolve this problem, since the male attendant paired with the Ekajaṭā also carries the sword and the noose, but has a *lambodara*-belly and a plump face. [83-84] Except for the pose, he seems quite similar iconographically to the *krodha-vighnāntaka* tucked beside Avalokiteśvara [78], who is definitely Hayagrīva. Therefore, we should be able to tentatively identify the wrathful attendants of Tārā [82 and 84] as Hayagrīva.[22] Like Vajrapuruṣa then, Hayagrīva sometimes appears as *vīra*-Yakṣa and sometimes as *vāmana*-Yakṣa.

85. Avalokiteśvara with Hayagrīva, Bihar, ca. 9th century, Rietberg Museum, Zürich

1.5 The Rietberg Hayagrīva

The final South Asian ninth-century Hayagrīva sculpture to be discussed provides no difficulties in identification and is exceptional in depicting the horse's head in Hayagrīva's crown. It is also an extraordinarily handsome sculpture from Telhara, near Nalanda.[23] **[85-86]** A two-armed Avalokiteśvara stands beside a seated Buddha figure situated to the proper right of Avalokiteśvara's nimbus, and at his foot on the same side is a monk who is probably the donor Prajñāsena mentioned in the inscription. On Avalokiteśvara's left, in front of the elaborate stem of the lotus he holds, is a *vāmana*-Yakṣa Hayagrīva making the *vandana mudrā* with his proper right hand. His proper left hand rests on the upturned handle of a hatchet at the same time that it holds the end of a *pāśa*, the loop of which is at his elbow. Hayagrīva's left foot is placed casually on the blade of the hatchet. His right hip is thrust out in an exaggerated stance that is the mirror opposite of the bodhisattva's. Bearded and mustachioed, his long hair falls asymmetrically to his left side. In terms of his relative size, he is larger than both the Buddha figure and the monk-donor, though he is still a minor figure in the composition.

Most significant about this Hayagrīva is the small horse's head emerging out of the center of his loose bun. Although almost all the texts which describe Hayagrīva mention the horse's head, very few images from India proper depict it. According to both van Gulik and B. Bhattacharyya, the horse's head is especially rare when Hayagrīva appears as a "secondary god" or "minor god."[24] That it does occasionally occur in Indian art is demonstrated by this sculpture. With the exception of this sculpture, the horse's head is to the best of my knowledge confined to images outside of India. Within India perhaps the longstanding association of Hayagrīva with Avalokiteśvara or with Tārā made the horse's head superfluous as an iconographic marker. Outside of India, knowledge of Hayagrīva was imported and the textual references were interpreted literally.

The Rietberg sculpture is a valuable anomaly, providing decisive evidence that Avalokiteśvara's attendant *krodha-vighnāntaka*

86. Hayagrīva, detail of 85

deity is in fact Hayagrīva. When we compare this Hayagrīva with others, such as the Hilsa Tārā Hayagrīva, who stands on the hatchet in just the same way, the resemblance is close enough that we may be sure that, with or without the horse's head, the *krodha-vighnāntaka* who accompanies Avalokiteśvara and Tārā is indeed Hayagrīva.

It is also appropriate to point out at this stage that in all the images of Hayagrīva which we have so far examined, there is no single set of iconographic characteristics which are inviolably associated with Hayagrīva. Several of the earliest images make the *vinayahasta mudrā*, but then so did the early Yamāntaka and Vajrapuruṣa images. The *vandana mudrā*, which occurs in quite a few Hayagrīva images, is just as consistent in depictions of other *krodha-vighnāntaka*. The club, the hatchet, the noose and the sword have all been seen in more than one example of a Phase One Hayagrīva and in more than one combination. The sword, the noose and the club are equally prominent in the depictions we have discussed of Yamāntaka. And just as we found for Vajrapuruṣa, Hayagrīva seems to have been depicted in both *vīra-* and *vāmana*-Yakṣa form, though the latter certainly predominated.

The evidence so far seems to suggest that with the exception of rare images which include Hayagrīva's horse's head or Yamāntaka's buffalo, most Phase One *krodha-vighnāntaka* images are virtually interchangeable. It is generally only the association with one or another bodhisattva which allows us to identify a specific *krodha-vighnāntaka*. This leads to the conclusion that within certain parameters we must loosen our expectations both for a close correspondence between textual description and actual image, and also for a limited range of appearances for each Phase One *krodha-vighnāntaka*. Taking proper account of his size, relative position (usually the lower left) and more or less aggressive demeanor or attributes, ultimately it is the association with Avalokiteśvara or Tārā which allows us to identify Hayagrīva.

87. Avalokiteśvara with Hayagrīva, Ratnagiri (Orissa), ca. 9th-10th century

2 Middle Period Phase One (ca. 9th-10th c.) South Asian Images of Hayagrīva

Every revolution turns into an evolution if one assembles the preceding storm signals in a pragmatic way. Walter Friedlaender, *Mannerism and Anti-Mannerism*

We have seen that during the eighth and ninth centuries Hayagrīva emerges from the background as a Phase One deity and begins to take on a limited measure of recognizability, at the very least as a member of an identifiable group of *krodha-vighnāntaka*. In addition there are indications that his role, visually and doctrinally, is expanding, since more attention and size is lavished on him *vis-à-vis* the bodhisattva he attends and the other attendants. In the middle period these gains are for the most part maintained, though there is little visible advance. The early images of Hayagrīva often made reference to his formal roots as a Yakṣa, or Yakṣa-derived demi-god. These similarities to Gaṇa and *āyudhapuruṣa* are less overt in the middle period, and he is given hairstyles, for instance, which are more in keeping with his individuality. From the perspective of subsequent imagery, one can find in this middle period the beginnings of a stylization and stereotyping of Hayagrīva's image which culminate in the eleventh and twelfth centuries. In the late ninth and tenth centuries, however, Hayagrīva, as the assistant of Avalokiteśvara and Tārā, maintains his status as the dominant attendant.

2.1 Orissan two-armed Hayagrīva images

There are a number of Orissan images from Ratnagiri and Udayagiri from the late ninth or tenth century which testify to the condition of the *krodha-vighnāntaka* Hayagrīva during this time. There appear to be two forms of Phase One Hayagrīva in these Orissan Avalokiteśvara images: two-armed and four-armed. The first type occurs on a large Avalokiteśvara image (2.43 meters in height), which though presently headless [87], is illustrated by Debala Mitra in more complete form.[25] Mitra and Hock are in agreement that it belongs to the ninth or tenth century.[26]

Hayagrīva [88] seems to have shrunk once again, barely coming to the bodhisattva's knee. He stands to one side of the emerging stem of Avalokiteśvara's lotus, which we have seen associated with a Yakṣa-Hayagrīva. In relationship to Tārā he is still slightly larger in terms of absolute size, but since he stands and she sits, she is proportionately larger. Both are given a lotus pedestal and oval body-nimbus to set them off from the plain background, though Tārā is also provided with a head-nimbus. Hayagrīva has a beard and mustache and thick curls which are bound by a snake into a loose bun on the crown of his head. Snakes also act as ornaments and as a belt for his *dhoti*. His face has the large lips and swollen eyes to go with his distinctly *lambodara*-belly. The *pratyālīḍha* posture is evident as he makes the *vandana mudrā* with his right hand and leans on the handle of a *daṇḍa* that appears to be topped with a skull.

88. Hayagrīva, detail of 87

An image from Udayagiri, now in the Patna Museum, is even larger, having retained its upper portion.[27] It must date also from around the same period, and the Hayagrīva figure closely resembles the two-armed Hayagrīva from Ratnagiri. [88] The same is true for another sculpture at Ratnagiri. Hock, with Mitra, places it in the tenth century.[28] With the latter sculpture in particular, the Tārā on the other side of Avalokiteśvara is actually much larger and takes up more space than Hayagrīva, though in terms of absolute height, he measures 51 cm from the top of his hand, while she is 44 cm.

The nearly identical disposition of iconographic characteristics displayed by these three images (including **88**) is thrown into relief when they are put alongside comparable two-armed images of Hayagrīva from Bihar. [**89**] The Bihar figures are all also *vāmana*-Yakṣa. They make the *vandana mudrā* and lean on upturned *daṇḍas*. The difference is that in the Bihar sculptures, Hayagrīva more frequently is in an informal posture with legs crossed and the *daṇḍa* behind him. With the Orissan images, he adopts a more aggressive posture and the staff is placed in front of his proper left leg. These are small and iconographically meaningless details, but they do indicate that the images in Orissa are becoming increasingly standardized, even down to such small details. Overall, however, in terms of the two-armed form, the ways in which Hayagrīva appears in Bihar and in Orissa are beginning to converge into a single standard.

2.2 Orissan four-armed images of Hayagrīva

89. *Hayagrīva, detail of* 74, *same as* 72

90. *Avalokiteśvara with Hayagrīva, Udayagiri (Orissa), ca.* 10*th century*

The other form of Hayagrīva met with in the middle period in Orissa is the four-armed form. Examples of the four-armed form are equally related to each other and in fact are not far from the two-armed form. They differ from the two-armed form by the addition of the *vinayahasta mudrā* and by a slightly different position of the *daṇḍa*. Perhaps the best preserved of the three is still *in situ* behind the so-called Mahākāla temple, at a little distance from the main *stūpa* of Udayagiri. [**90-91**] Hayagrīva is still discernibly larger than Tārā, stands in *pratyālīḍha*, has long hair loosely bound and makes the *vandana* and *vinayahasta mudrā*. In order to reveal the *daṇḍa* in the lower left hand it was necessary to "excavate" a little more of the base. (Compare **90** and **91**.) Stylistically the work seems to be of a ninth or tenth-century date.

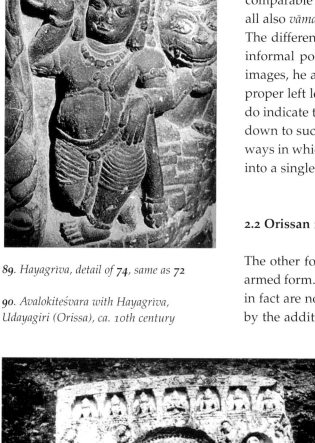

Adding to the importance of this sculpture is the twenty-five-line inscription on the back. It provides some indication of the original purpose and context of the sculpture. The inscription includes the phrase "*Tathāgatādhiṣṭhita dhātugarbha stūpa*," referring to a *stūpa* containing relics set up in that location.[29] The inscription thus links the images directly to the Mahāyāna cult of relics and *stūpa* worship, rather than to exclusively Esoteric Buddhist rituals. This is *prima facie* evidence that Phase One *krodha-vighnāntaka* continue within the Buddhist context marked by open air *stūpa*, *dhāraṇī sūtra*s and the worship of images available to all. No doubt there is considerable overlap in concerns and methods between ninth to tenth century cult Mahāyāna and Esoteric Buddhism, but for Phase One imagery, even long past its early origins, such inscriptions point to cult Mahāyāna, not to mature Esoteric Buddhism.

A second four-armed Avalokiteśvara sculpture from Udayagiri also has a four-armed Hayagrīva in attendance.[30] [**92**] Now in the Patna Museum, it also belongs to the ca. ninth or tenth century. The posture and gestures of its Hayagrīva are similar to the other four-armed Hayagrīva [**91**], but here he is given a narrow crown just above his hair line. He also

91. *Hayagriva, detail of* **90**

92. *Hayagrīva, detail of Avalokiteśvara sculpture, Udayagiri (Orissa), ca. 10th century, Patna Museum*

stands on a lotus which is slightly elevated. He is marginally larger than the beautiful Tārā with whom he is paired. At first glance it seems that he has a small horse's head emerging from his hair, which stands straight up beneath his tiara. A close inspection reveals, however, that it is a cobra hood with the head of the snake wrapping around his hair above the crown. Several snakes ornament the figure. The artist has attempted to give him a ferocious look, a grimace and a deeply furrowed brow.

2.3 Bihar Hayagrīva images with Tārā

Also dating between the ninth and tenth centuries are three Hayagrīva images accompanying Tārā, two from Kurkihar and one probably from Nalanda. The earliest, belonging most likely to the ninth century, is from the ex-Broadley collection, now in the storage chambers of the Indian Museum, Calcutta. **[93-94]** According to the museum staff, it was collected from Nalanda, where Broadley acquired a number of other works,[31] rather than nearby Bihar Shariff or even Kurkihar, which are also possible sites of origin. Although Tārā is rather more robust and flat-footed than slender and graceful, she has a very plastic, active stance which moves her away from the nearly plain background sometimes maintained into the tenth century.[32]

Hayagrīva **[94]** is paired once again with Ekajaṭā (compare **75**), but their relative positions to either side of Tārā are uncharacteristically reversed. Hayagrīva's hair is pulled back away from his face, strapped with a flat band, and then divided into seven spirals, a style which recalls that of the mid-ninth-century Hayagrīva from Nalanda. **[78]** On that sculpture we find a chain hanging above Hayagrīva's head identical to the chain hanging from this Tārā's girdle. **[93]** The slightly later Hayagrīva, however, is more assertive and independent of Tārā. He stands looking up at Tārā, holding what may be a bell in his proper left hand. With his right palm he steadies himself on the handle of a club with a finial. As we have seen, this is a typical attribute and posture for Hayagrīva (compare **80** and **89**), and in conjunction with his attendance of Tārā there is no question about his identity. Lest we receive the impression that here at last is some consistent iconographic characteristic of Hayagrīva, however, it should be remembered that the *daṇḍa* is held in a similar way by Yamāntaka **[55-56, 59]** and Maitreya's wrathful companion. **[48, 50]**

Another Tārā sculpture with Hayagrīva is now in the Norton Simon Museum in Pasadena. **[95-96]** This smooth yet crisply carved piece is stylistically closely related to the ca. tenth century Guneri and

93. *Tārā with Hayagrīva, Bihar, late 9th century, Indian Museum, Calcutta*

94. *Hayagriva, detail of* **93**

95. *Hayagrīva, detail of* **96**

96. Tārā with Hayagrīva, Bihar, late 9th-10th century, Norton Simon Museum

Kurkihar sculptures of Mañjuśrī and Maitreya already discussed.[33] [46, 48, 53] As suggested above, the Kurkihar Mañjuśrī [53] may be slightly earlier, but the Tārā sculpture most resembles it in such small details as the double pearl-band crown, the form of the armlets and the less tapered backdrop.

The Norton Simon Hayagrīva [95] also has points of similarity with the Kurkihar Yamāntaka [53], not only by the axe with its handle up, but notably in the unusual way the hair is parted down the center and then brought back from the forehead. The wavy linear treatment of the hair against the backdrop is characteristic of all of these *krodha-vighnāntaka.* [47-48, 53, 95] What is most unusual about the Norton Simon Hayagrīva [95] is that he is indisputably *vīra*-Yakṣa in body type. His face, too, is small, beardless and delicate, with an inward, almost troubled expression which is a remarkable feature of this workshop or group of sculptors. On the other side of Tārā is a smaller kneeling male figure who holds his hands in *añjali mudrā*. This suggests the figure of Sudhanakumāra, though the book is not visible under his arm.

Hayagrīva stands with his left leg hiked up onto the blade of the hatchet, much like the Hayagrīva of the Hilsa Tārā [77] as well as the Rietberg Hayagrīva. [86] The fact that when he accompanies Tārā Hayagrīva is sometimes *vīra*-Yakṣa and sometimes *vāmana*-Yakṣa in body type fits in with the other evidence that his iconographic characteristics as a Phase One deity were not fixed. It also helps to confirm the identities of the attendants of the Tārā figures discussed above. [82 and 84] Both carry a sword and a noose, but one is *vīra*-Yakṣa and the other *vāmana*-Yakṣa.

It has already been pointed out that when with Avalokiteśvara Hayagrīva sometimes also carries the sword and noose [76, 78], and a *vāmana*-Yakṣa with his foot on the blade of a hatchet sometimes accompanies Avalokiteśvara [86] and Tārā [77]. Now a *vīra*-Yakṣa standing on the hatchet may be added to the list of recognized Hayagrīva images. It seems accurate to say that Hayagrīva is usually depicted as *vāmana*-Yakṣa, but a significant minority of images portrays him as *vīra*-Yakṣa. The sword and noose combination seems to occur with no more frequency than the leg on the hatchet, and there is no consistent pattern of occurrence with either Tārā or Avalokiteśvara to suggest a meaningful combination. All apparently intend to represent Hayagrīva in his roles as personification of *dhāraṇī* and destroyer of obstacles.

A late tenth-century Tārā recorded by the Indian Museum to be from Kurkihar is quite long and narrow. [97-98] Tārā's arms have broken off, and her silhouette has been cut out of the backdrop. The sculpture features a *vāmana*-Yakṣa Hayagrīva

97. *Tārā with Hayagrīva, Kurkihar (Bihar), ca. 10th century Indian Museum, Calcutta*

98. *Hayagrīva, detail of* 97

propping up his leg on an axe, paired once again with Ekajaṭā holding the elephant skin above her head. Hayagrīva wears a short tiger-skin *dhoti* and has snake ornaments. His right hand makes a *vitarka*-like gesture, the thumb holding down the ring finger. His left hand is at his groin, resting on the upturned handle of the axe. His hair is pulled back with curls floating upward behind his left side. Besides the curling mustache, he is given a short ruff-like beard around the edge of his jaw. This manner of facial hair, similar to the treatment found more often in Orissa [**87**, **92**], becomes almost standard for Phase One *krodha-vighnāntaka* in Bihar and Bengal from the tenth century onwards. In fact one can begin to trace an increasing standardization in the images through the twelfth century. There will be much less variety, and postures and gestures will seem more and more familiar, as if the artists had finished working out the type and were content to repeat it with little new insight. Here the type seems to be fully worked out, but has not yet fallen into stylization or irrelevance.

99. Dharmacakra Avalokiteśvara with Hayagrīva, Nalanda (Bihar), late 9th-10th century, Nalanda Museum

100. Hayagrīva, detail of 99

2.4 A transitional Hayagrīva image

Another Avalokiteśvara sculpture with Hayagrīva is also transitional in terms of its treatment of the *krodha-vighnāntaka*. [99-100] There is a certain amount of ambiguity about this example in that it refers back to much earlier Hayagriva images at the same time that it presages the later period, when Hayagrīva is increasingly marginalized. That Hayagrīva is even included at all speaks of the solid niche that he has found in Phase One imagery. The sculpture remains in Nalanda, where it was discovered. Stylistically it resembles the Mañjuśrī from nearby Bihar Shariff now in the Indian Museum in Calcutta. [54] Details of jewelry, the lotus throne and its support are close enough that we may give the Avalokiteśvara a similar date of the first half of the tenth century.

Hayagrīva's position along the central axis directly below Avalokiteśvara making the *dharmacakra mudrā* confers a certain amount of status on him, but he has been reduced to half the size of the standing Tārā and Bhṛikutī to each side of Avalokiteśvara. Moreover, this position recalls both the earlier piece from Nalanda [74] that relegates a very dwarfish, *retardaire* Hayagrīva to the area beneath the throne, where atlantid-Yakṣa are often portrayed between two lions supporting the throne of Buddha or bodhisattva. One such Sumeru pedestal or throne was discovered with the hoard of metalwork at Kurkihar and must date to about this period.[34] Exactly the same placement is given to the *vāmana*-Yakṣa Hayagrīva [100], but he is quite "modern" compared to an earlier Hayagrīva. [74] His hair is pulled back with serpentine coils falling loosely to his left, while he sports the ruff-like beard and mustaches. The staff he leans on and the *vandana mudrā* made with the right hand are both long-standing attributes for Phase One *krodha-vighnāntaka*.

One senses in this image a pivotal change in the fortunes of the Phase One Hayagrīva. Whereas in the formative period of his iconography he was given precedence over female attendants by means of his larger size [70, 74, 82], his placement above them [76], or by replacing them altogether [79, 85, 96], here it seems the trend is being reversed. Like the very first Hayagrīva image discussed, also from Nalanda [65], the female attendants are being emphasized at the expense of Hayagrīva, who is fading into the background to become an almost decorative accoutrement of the lion throne. If visual remains have any value as reflections of religious concerns, it would seem that within the Mahāyāna bodhisattva cult, the *krodha-vighnāntaka* are losing the sharpness of their appeal. They are beginning to be taken for granted.

It speaks well of the artists who were so well versed in their tradition that they could find this way of disengaging Hayagrīva by restoring him, as it were, to the nexus of Yakṣa-related traditions from which his image came. At the same time, it is undeniable that Hayagrīva was still significant enough to include. He still continues to provide a certain liveliness to a hieratic image, something which the mischievousness of the *krodha-vighnāntaka* in its Phase One incarnation was well suited to offer.

101. Hayagrīva, Kurkihar (Bihar), metalwork, ca. 10th century, Patna Museum

2.5 The Kurkihar metalwork Hayagrīva

The final example of a middle period Hayagrīva image is exceptional on a number of accounts. First of all, instead of being carved stone, it is cast metal (gilt copper with silver inlay). [**101-102**] Only 10 centimeters in height, it was discovered in 1930 in the Kurkihar hoard.[35] Second, it would seem to violate the definition proposed for Phase One imagery in that it is an independent piece. It is clearly a secondary figure however, once its non-hieratic posture is taken into account. Surely it was fitted into a metalwork triad or pentad, as an attendant to either Avalokiteśvara or Tārā. As such it is instructive to keep in mind the elaborate Sumeru pedestal also found at Kurkihar mentioned above. Now housed in the same room with the Hayagrīva in the Patna Museum, the pedestal accommodates three levels of iconographic importance and size, such as we find in the type of Avalokiteśvara images we have just been considering. It is tempting to suggest that it was on exactly such a base that the metal Hayagrīva must once have rested, along with Bhṛikutī, Tārā and Sudhanakumāra, surrounding Avalokiteśvara.

102. *Side view of* **101**

The identification of Hayagrīva is widely accepted, but it must be mentioned that in the absence of the main bodhisattva, his identity cannot be absolutely confirmed. If one compares certain Phase One images of Yamāntaka [**55, 60**] it cannot be gainsaid that he is as much a candidate as Hayagrīva. Both Hayagrīva and Yamāntaka figures carry the strange wand with a curling end. In the Kurkihar piece a *makara* joins the handle to the wand's lower half. His similarity to the tenth-century Nalanda Hayagrīva just discussed [**100**] is striking enough to allow us to call him Hayagrīva, with the caveat that it might actually be Yamāntaka. Once again we are reminded of the potential interchangeablity of Phase One *krodha-vighnāntaka* images.

Several conventions for the *krodha-vighnāntaka* which have been brewing crystallize in this carefully made image. One is the serpentine hair. Several images already discussed have had snakes binding the hair, even emerging from the top of the head like this one. A few have also had serpentine curls. The maker of this Hayagrīva takes that metaphor much farther, to the point that it is difficult to distinguish snakes from locks of hair. In the later stage of Phase One *krodha-vighnāntaka* imagery, we will find these serpentine locks to be standard, developing into vertical emanations that are given a new reference as tongues of fire.

A plethora of snakes ornament the Kurkihar Hayagrīva. Serpents wind around both wrists, his upper arms, ankles and neck, while another comprises his *upavīta*. This is not new either, but the insistence with which it is carried out is also often met with in the next phase. The rising mustaches and the rimming beard have already been discussed as a newly consistent feature of the Phase One *krodha-vighnāntaka*.

A final aspect of this image which participates in a new precedent is the emphatically scored third eye. Only a few of the Hayagrīva images so far discussed have a third eye [COLOR PLATE 4, **88, 91**], all incidentally from Orissa, which seems to have been at the forefront of *krodha-vighnāntaka* imagery. Yamāntaka images prior to the late eleventh century [**59**] do not appear with a third eye. However, in the period between the tenth and eleventh centuries, the third eye will often be sculpted or painted onto Hayagrīva's forehead. The exact significance of this is elusive. The eye may reflect influence from *krodha-vighnāntaka* images of Phase Two, which by the tenth century were maturing, or even the beginning of Phase Three. In Phase Two and Three imagery of South Asia the third eye is often present for deities such as Trailokyavijaya and Saṃvara, but still not for Yamāntaka.

To sum up, the *krodha-vighnāntaka* image matured during the middle period of Phase One. By this time it had developed the characteristics which would be maintained into the late period. The middle period was the final period of innovation and variety for the Phase One image. Once the stabilization of *krodha-vighnāntaka* takes place in the tenth century, standardization sets in, with generally deadening effects.

3 Late Phase One (ca. 11th-12th Century) South Asian Images of Hayagrıva

It is strange about everything, it is strange about pictures, a picture may seem extraordinarily strange to you and after some time not only it does not seem strange but it is impossible to find what there was in it that was strange. Gertrude Stein, *Picasso*

The late period of Phase One Hayagrīva images shows no slackening in quantity. Whereas in the early and middle periods we found no samples from the Bengal area (though, admittedly, an investigation in Bangladesh might unearth some), in the later period examples are comparatively plentiful.[36] More than thirty images of Hayagrīva distributed roughly evenly among Bengal, Orissa and Bihar have been identified and studied. By the very nature of the period, it will not be necessary to discuss each one, for they fall into a few types, and representative examples may suffice. We will proceed to examine these types along geographic divisions: first Bihar, then Bengal, and finally Orissa.

3.1 Late Hayagrīva Images from Bihar

103. *Tārā with Hayagrīva, Bihar, early 11th century, Indian Museum, Calcutta*

The Tārā image of the early eleventh century from Bihar and now in the Indian Museum, Calcutta [**103-104**] includes a Hayagrīva image which belongs to the stereotyped form we have seen in the Kurkihar metal Hayagrīva. [**101**] Many of the features already mentioned are brought together here again. The serpentine curls of hair, the tilt of the head, the snake ornaments, the wide open eyes, the smiling mouth, beard, mustaches, even the gestures of the hands bear comparison.

Two other features of note about this image of Hayagrīva is his size relative to Tārā and Ekajaṭā. He is significantly larger than his counterpart and is as large in proportion to Tārā as the "gigantic" Hayagrīva accompanying Avalokiteśvara at Ratnagiri. [**70**] Hayagrīva has had one last burst of growth in this image, but it is his last. From now on the comparative sizes of Hayagrīva and the other attendatns will reverse, Hayagrīva becoming smaller and smaller.

The posture of one leg resting on the axe blade is already quite familiar, particularly when Hayagrīva attends Tārā [**77, 96, 98**], though it also occurs with images of Avalokiteśvara. [**86**] A nearly identical posture is found on a fragment of a sculpture in the storage rooms of the Lucknow Museum, formerly in the Indian Museum, Calcutta.[37] The angle of the leg is somewhat higher in the Lucknow piece, and the handle of the axe is longer. The Lucknow Museum identifies the fragment as Śiva Pratihāra, but comparison with the pieces just mentioned allow us to identify it as Hayagrīva. He stands next to the stem of a lotus, and where the blossom touches the background the stone has been cut away around the silhouette of the missing bodhisattva, just as in **103**. The similarities between the two Hayagrīva images (**104** and the Lucknow Museum fragment) do not stop with the particularized posture, gesture and attributes. A near uniformity is also detectable in the snake ornaments, earrings, tilt of the head and facial expression. There is only a minor difference in the arrangement of the hair. The slightly later Indian Museum Hayagrīva has his hair standing straight up, while the Lucknow Hayagrīva's tumbles towards his left shoulder. But both have distinctly serpentine curls. Even granting that these two sculptures emerged from the same workshop, there is a striking sense that the artists are working from a mental template of the quintessential *krodha-vighnāntaka* image. To judge from the metalwork Hayagriva [**101**], this template seems to be shared by both stone-carvers and bronze-casters.[38]

Clockwise from top left

104. Hayagrīva, detail of 103, same as 63

105. Hayagrīva, fragment with Bhṛikuṭī, Bihar, ca. 11th century, Patna Museum

106. Hayagrīva, detail of 114

107. Hayagrīva, detail of 110

108. Hayagrīva, detail of 109

109. *Avalokiteśvara with Hayagrīva, Nalanda (Bihar), late 11th century, Nalanda Museum*

110. *Avalokiteśvara with Hayagrīva, Rohoi (Bihar), early 12th century, Indian Museum, Calcutta*

111. Avalokiteśvara with Hayagrīva, Bihar or Bengal, late 11th century, Art Institute of Chicago

112. Avalokiteśvara with Hayagrīva, Bihar, late 11th century, Indian Museum, Calcutta

An additional variant within the same basic type occurs in a number of examples throughout the eleventh and early twelfth centuries. One of the highest quality of these is included among a full complement of attendants (including Sūcīmukha beneath the lotus pedestal) to a two-armed Khasarpaṇa Avalokiteśvara. **[108-109]** The sculpture was discovered in Nalanda, where it remains in the Museum. The main figure is so sleek and his posture so mannered as to be positively slinky. Several features, including the high *jaṭāmukuṭa* of the bodhisattva, point to a date in the late eleventh century. Other stylistic indicators are the sculpture's pointed top, the profusion of delicately rendered details and the contradictory sense of excited yet enervated line serving decorative ends.[39]

Hayagrīva stands on the left, in front of a Bhṛikutī almost twice his size. The image-type we have just seen illustrated from the tenth **[101]** and early eleventh centuries **[104]** has been updated slightly, and stylized through exaggeration, but the essential image remains. The serpentine curls stand a little straighter and suggest flames. The odd staff with a curled end which we saw in the Kurkihar metal Hayagrīva is retained, though enlarged. The beard around the edge of the jaw persists in tiny curls, and the mustache twirls. Hayagrīva makes the familiar *vandana mudrā* with his right hand and controls the staff with his left. The snake ornaments are prominent, as is the third eye. A broad grin breaks across the deity's mannered face, revealing his fangs. The expression is slightly manic, slightly comic; one is reminded of Friedlaender's memorable phrase concerning the Mannerist "degeneration of the spiritual into the playful."[40]

There are two nearly identical versions of Hayagrīva, one perhaps slightly earlier in the Nalanda Museum, and another slightly later, in nearby Surajpur village.[41] A much more modest work in the Bodh Gaya Museum, perhaps about the same date, shows a similar Hayagrīva.[42] The pose differs only slightly. Otherwise this Hayagrīva and another fragment in the storage shed of the Patna Museum **[105]** serve to demonstrate that artists are reproducing the type with little variation or innovation.

A third variant among the late Phase One types differs from the standing Hayagrīva with the curling-tipped club **[105, 108]** by its squatting posture. Otherwise this type of Hayagrīva is very similar. A fine early twelfth century example is in the Indian Museum, Calcutta, collected by Broadley in Rohoi.[43] **[107, 110]** Hayagrīva's puffy little body appears just above Avalokiteśvara's left knee, almost engulfed in the details, which are carved with a great variety of depth. None of the factors in the formula are missing; the serpentine curls, beard, mustache, snake ornaments and third eye are all accounted for. Liberties are taken with Hayagrīva's limbs, distortions aimed at squeezing him into as small a space as possible without compromising any of the established features of his stock type. Thus his right arm makes the *vandana mudrā* at an impossible angle, and his left haunch curls conveniently around his abdomen.

A few metalwork images follow this model, including the work in the Art Institute of Chicago **[111, 129]** and one in the British Museum.[44] A similar Hayagrīva crouches in front of Bhṛikutī next to a twelve-armed Avalokiteśvara in the storage chambers of the Indian Museum, Calcutta, while a painted version appears in a manuscript illustration of a two-armed Avalokiteśvara in the Asia Society Gallery.[45] **[114]** More often in this late period, however, Hayagrīva is not given the position next to Avalokiteśvara, but is relegated to a more minor post below the throne. This is the case with two seated two-armed Avalokiteśvara images in the Asia Society Gallery,[46] another in the National Museum, New Delhi,[47] and a fourth in the Indian Museum, Calcutta. **[112-113]** These Hayagrīva figures all conform to the same

113. Hayagrīva, detail of 112

114. Avalokiteśvara with Hayagrīva, manuscript illustration, Bihar, ca. 12th. century, Asia Society, New York

115. Avalokiteśvara with Hayagrīva, Chowrapara (Bengal, now Bangladesh), 11th-12th century, Indian Museum, Calcutta

type. In some cases he is hardly larger than a decorative *cintamani* device which appears immediately next to him, and in others he is about the size of human worshipers or patrons. The difficulty of accommodating extra figures when the bodhisattva is seated with one leg pendent is not responsible, for Hayagrīva is dismissed to the area beneath the lotus pedestal even when Avalokiteśvara is standing. **[112]** Nor is it a matter of quality, for while the sculptor of the latter was certainly less skilled than might be hoped, the quality of the Rohoi sculpture **[110]** and the Asia Society sculpture (see note 46) is superb.

3.2 Late Hayagrīva Images from Bengal

The story is nearly the same in Bengal. I have not found any examples of the subgroup standing with one foot on a hatchet blade, but the other two varieties of the standard type (with *daṇḍa*, standing and squatting) are in evidence. A standing Hayagrīva from Chowrapara in Rajshahi, Bangladesh, now in the Indian Museum, Calcutta, fits the general type, though the right hand holds a lotus bud instead of making the *vandana mudrā*. **[106, 115]** Otherwise, his mustache, beard, wide eyes, snake ornaments and serpentine hair correspond, as well as the gesture of his left hand, leaning on a *daṇḍa* with a curled end.

More often Hayagrīva is in the crouching pose and is much smaller, like a work in New Delhi, where Hayagrīva is below the throne,[48] or the damaged sculpture in the storage rooms of the State Archaeological Museum of West Bengal, where Hayagrīva is on the same level as the seated Avalokiteśvara, at his left knee.[49] Even there, however, Hayagrīva is actually smaller than Sudhanakumāra.

Several other examples may be cited of a small crouching Hayagrīva next to a seated Avalokiteśvara; they vary in quality from crude, to fair, to fine.[50] The most

outstanding is the sculpture from Tapan, West Dinajpur, now in the West Bengal State Archaeological Museum in Calcutta. [**116-117**] The harmonious coordination of its rich vocabulary is impressive. The concentric curving garment folds accentuate the sensual outline of the body and are echoed in the wavering stalks of the lotus flowers at his sides. These features and the cut-out backdrop allow it to be dated to the late eleventh or early twelfth century.[51]

The Hayagrīva image [**117**] is sufficiently detailed and on a sufficiently large scale that one can point to a close comparison with a similarly dated Hayagrīva. [**108**] The hair style is similar, but carries the conceit of flames a bit further by creating a slight point or crest of hair.

In passing, it is necessary to point out that these late images of Hayagrīva from both Bihar and Bengal have a great deal in common with contemporary images of the Bhairava-Śiva and his Buddhistic counterpart, Mahākāla. Two examples of such images are the Bhairava sculptures in the Patna and Indian Museums.[52] [**118-119**] Phase One Hayagrīva, Bhairava and Mahākāla are all wrathful deities, and there seems to be a shared set of characteristics between them, including the *vāmana*-Yakṣa body type and the grinning mask-like bearded face with three eyes, which we have seen on a number of Hayagrīva images. (Compare especially the faces of **108** and **119**.) It may be that in the late period the artists of Phase One Hayagrīva images owe a considerable debt to the artists of Bhairava and Mahākāla, whose cults seem to have flourished in the eleventh and twelfth centuries.

116. *Avalokiteśvara with Hayagrīva, Tapan (Bengal), 12th century, West Bengal State Archaeological Museum, Calcutta*

117. *(above right) Hayagrīva, detail of* **116**

118. *Bhairava, Bihar, 11th-12th century, Patna Museum*

119. *Bhairava, Jalpaigiri (Bengal), ca. 12th century, Indian Museum, Calcutta*

120. *Avalokiteśvara with Hayagrīva in the form of Mahākāla, Bengal, 11th-12th century, West Bengal State Archaeological Museum, Calcutta*

The similarity is demonstrated quite unambiguously by the appearance of Hayagrīva in a crude late work from Bengal. [**120**] Perched above Avalokiteśvara's left knee we find a tiny Hayagrīva in his usual place. He has been given a skull cup, held before his chest in his left hand, and a *karttikā* (flaying knife) in his right. These are among the most distinctive attributes of both Bhairava and Mahākāla, who hold them similarly in front of the chest.

121. *Avalokiteśvara with Hayagrīva, Ratnagiri (Orissa), ca. 11th century*

3.3 Late Hayagrīva Images from Orissa

We turn now to the late Phase One images of Hayagrīva in Orissa. Like the sculptures from Bihar and Bengal, Hayagrīva is once again reduced to a standard type with little in the way of variation. He consistently squats with a *daṇḍa* in hand. The only variation is whether he leans on it with one or two hands or holds it across his chest, and whether he is placed beside Avalokiteśvara's left knee or beneath the lotus pedestal. Four Orissan Avalokiteśvara images of the eleventh or twelfth century may be cited, all with squatting Hayagrīva attendants below the throne. The first, and perhaps the finest, was found at Ratnagiri.[53] [**121, 124**] The *vāmana*-Yakṣa Hayagrīva is closed in beneath the overhanging lotus pedestal. He makes the *vandana mudrā*, saluting the distant bodhisattva, and with his left hand holds a *vajra*-tipped *daṇḍa* across his chest. Unlike contemporary Bihar and Bengal Hayagrīva images, his hair is tied up into a round ball on top of his head. But like them, he has been reduced to a scarcely meaningful element within the composition.

The same may be said for the Hayagrīva beneath Cintāmaṇi Avalokiteśvara, attending the standing bodhisattva who grasps a lotus from a tree producing the *saptaratna*. [**123, 126**] The configuration of Hayagrīva and his attributes [**126**] generally resembles the Ratnagiri Hayagrīva. [**124**] Like the Ayodhya Mañjuśrī with Yamāntaka, with which this sculpture is paired on either side of a Mārīcī image, it may also be dated to the early eleventh century.

122. *Avalokiteśvara with Hayagrīva, Orissa, early 11th century, Indian Museum, Calcutta*

123. *Avalokiteśvara with Hayagrīva, Orissa, early 11th century, Ayodhya Mārīcī Mandir*

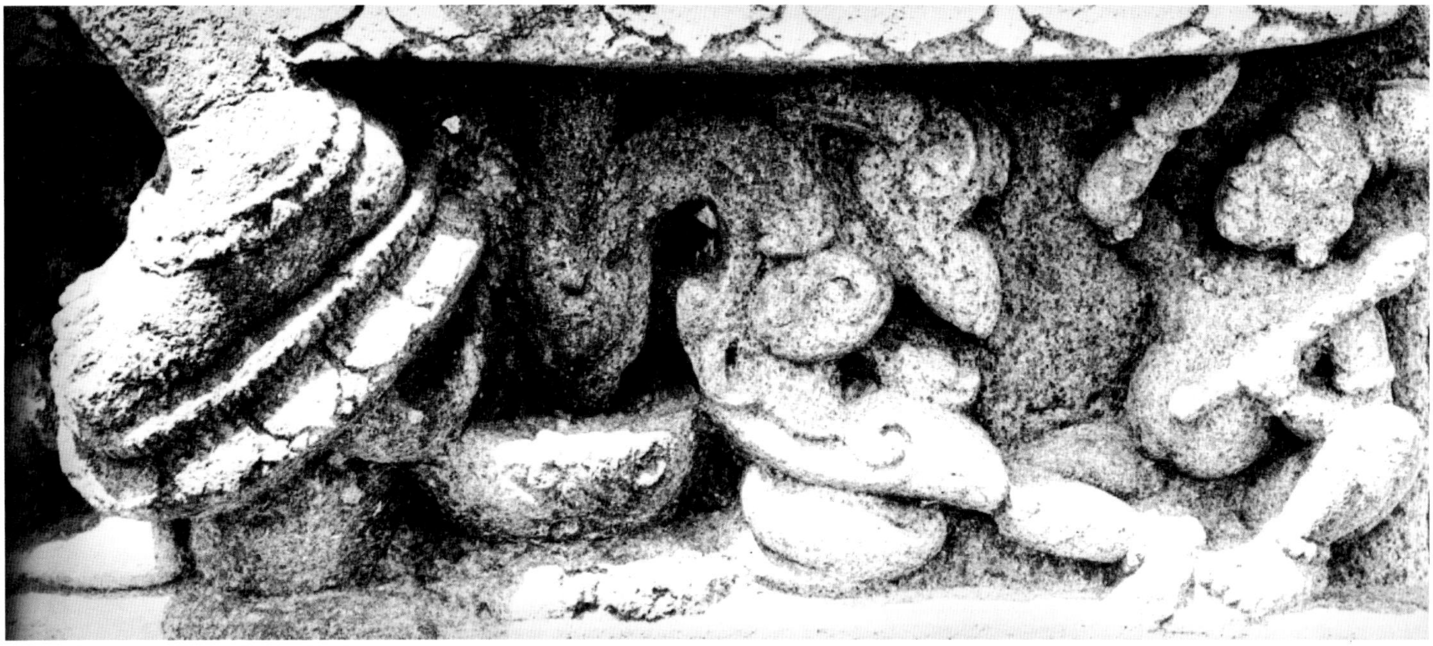

124. Hayagrīva, detail of 121

125. Hayagrīva, detail of 122

126. Hayagrīva, detail of 123

127. (above right) Hayagrīva, detail of Avalokiteśvara sculpture, Orissa, ca. 12th century, Baripada Museum

128. Hayagrīva, detail of Tārā sculpture, Orissa, ca. 12th century, Orissa State Museum, Bhubaneswar

A rather grumpy looking Hayagrīva, seemingly elderly and obese, glares at Avalokiteśvara's gigantic foot in a sculpture at the Indian Museum, Calcutta. [**122, 125**] Not much larger than the worshipers behind him, he leans both hands wearily on a slightly bent *daṇḍa*. Between him and the lower level of the lotus pedestal is a register of the *saptaratna*, a theme which in the late period occurs often in Orissan Buddhist sculpture. The Indian Museum lists its provenance as Ratnagiri, apparently following the conclusion of Ramaprasad Chanda, who actually acquired it at Kendrapara.[54] Other related images are in the Orissa State Museum and Philadelphia Museum of Art.[55]

The inclusion of the *saptaratna* and other narrative motifs in the Kendrapara [**122**] and Philadelphia Avalokiteśvara images signals the rise of what seem to be provincial or folk schools of sculpture in the late period of Orissan Buddhist art. This certainly seems to be the case for an Avalokiteśvara image in the Baripada Museum. [**127**] The stiff-necked, high-crowned Avalokiteśvara is given a large retinue, including the *saptaratna* at the bottom register. Hayagrīva rests both hands on his staff. Bearded and mustachioed, his hair is piled up into a flame shape, which is not, however, flattened like those of Bihar and Bengal.

This Hayagrīva, and another in the Orissa State Museum accompanying another Tārā [**128**], truly represent the frayed end of the Phase One Hayagrīva tradition in eastern India. These images of Hayagrīva deities have submerged once again into the ocean of folk belief from which they emerged five hundred years earlier. The little imp at Tārā's elbow [**128**] bears an eerie resemblance to some of the first Hayagrīva images to be recognized [**67, 71**], the ones which most closely resemble Yakṣa and Gaṇa. On the other hand, the stunted images of the twelfth century have been so reduced that they seem incapable of the spiritual tasks worthy of the "gigantic" Hayagrīva. [COLOR PLATE 4]

129. Hayagrīva, detail of 111

3.4 Late Hayagrīva images: Conclusions

The examination of late Phase One Hayagrīva images as a group leads to the following conclusions, which remarkably, can apply to all three regions covered: Bihar, Bengal and Orissa. The fact of the matter is that most of the late Hayagrīva images have been sapped of vitality, visual interest and iconographic importance. The same cannot be said of Avalokiteśvara or Tārā, for their images continue to be made and revered with lavish care. Hayagrīva has become part of a standard set of accoutrements to these bodhisattva. It is expected that he be there, but it appears that he is there only to complete a set of requirements, not because he is himself of great interest, either to the artists or to those who used these images as the focus of rituals. His image, like that of Yamāntaka, emerged out of the background and was developed with great interest, but now, by the eleventh and twelfth centuries, the very fact that he appears again and again in the same way suggests that his image has become a cliché, and an increasingly tired one, which evoked little in the way of visual or religious interest.

Paul Ricoeur has written about language in a way that makes it irresistible to consider the relevance of the development of the Phase One *krodha-vighnāntaka* image as a parallel form of visual language. "Live metaphors are metaphors of invention," he writes, "within which the response to the discordance in the sentence is a new extension of meaning."[56] This meaningful discordance certainly applies to the *krodha-vighnāntaka* image, which by transgressing the categories of the demonic and the divine, as well as those of Buddhist and chthonic deity, indeed crafted an inventive metaphor. Ricoeur goes on, however:

> *[I]t is certainly true that such inventive metaphors tend to become dead metaphors through repetition. In such cases, the extended meaning becomes part of our lexicon . . .*[57]

Gananath Obeyesekere also discusses the stylization of symbolism, and similarly ties it to a flattening of its meaning:

> *When a symbol is conventionalized it loses its inherent ambiguity . . . . its capacity for leverage and maneuverability.*[58]

The stylization of the *krodha-vighnāntaka* in the late period of Phase One images suggests that as an operative metaphor its power had been deadened through repeated use. The other phases of Esoteric Buddhism had by now capitalized on the *krodha-vighnāntaka*'s expressive content and extracted him from his old context to feature him in new ones. Perhaps this stole some of the visual and doctrinal meaning which surrounded Hayagrīva in the early period of Phase One art. The notion of the icon as a stable image which successfully reflects a certain ideology and resists change most accurately corresponds with the stylized period of repetition of the wrathful theme. This idea of icon is less applicable in the early period of Phase One, characterized by innovation and growth, or for the middle period, when the image maintained its power but continued to transform itself.

Notes to Chapter Six

1 Brandon, *Art and Ritual*, 1-14. The epigraph for this section is from Giuseppe Tucci, "Preliminary report on an archaeological survey in Swat," *East and West* ns 9 (1958): 284.

2 Asher, *Art of Eastern India*, 81. Leoshko identifies the main figure as Amoghapāśa in "Appearance of Amoghapāśa," 132.

3 For Khasarpaṇa, see B. Bhattacharyya, *Indian Buddhist Iconography*, 128-130.

4 Ibid., 129.

5 Ibid., 395, no. 12.

6 Mitra, *Ratnagiri*, 451, pl. CCCXLI.b.

7 Hock, "Buddhist ideology," 77.

8 Hock, however, suggests that **69** dates "slightly later" than **70**. She groups **69** together with another broken torso, an upper one, and relates them stylistically to a fourth work, the bodhisattva of which is indeed thinner, with a more exaggerated posture and an *upavīta* falling in a more stylized manner. The latter does seem later than **70**. Careful examination, however, reveals that the posture of **69** (which again she places later than **70**) is much less swayed, and the *upavita* in fact does not end "in an exaggerated turn to the right" as should her stylistic benchmark. Instead it hangs even more slackly than the *upavita* in **70**. Certainly the bodhisattva's posture of **69** is less emphatic. I believe then that the stylistic chronology of **32, 69** and **70,** which I outlined above, is defensible.

9 B. Bhattacharyya, *Indian Buddhist Iconography*, 130-132.

10 See Pal, *Bronzes of Kashmir*, no. 21, 23, 25, 32, 37. A complex metalwork throne was discovered among the Kurkihar images with an atlantid at the center between two symmetrical pairs of lions. It is in the Patna Museum, #144, and illustrated in Linrothe, "Compassionate Malevolence," figs. 85-86. For the Kurkihar finds, see K.P. Jayaswal, "Metal Images of Kurkihar Monastery," *Journal of the Indian Society of Oriental Art* 2, no. 2 (1934): 70-82.

11 The same is true of a dwarfish Hayagrīva with a large fleshy face, crouching under the lion throne of an Avalokiteśvara image from Nalanda, dating to the ca. 9th c. See Saraswati, *Tantrayana Art*, pl. 55.

12 Various readings of the inscription have been cited by S. Huntington, *"Pāla-Sena,"* 209-210 ("Appendix of Inscribed Dated Sculptures," no. 12).

13 See S. Huntington, *"Pāla-Sena,"* 37; and, Gouriswar Bhattacharya, "A Second Dated Tārā Image of the Reign of Devapāla," *Indian Museum Bulletin* 17 (1982): 21-23.

14 For instance, G. Bhattacharya concludes, "The Hilsa Tārā cannot be called Khadirāvaṇī-Tārā because instead of the prescribed Aśokakānta-Mārīcī she has Hayagrīva as accompanying figure. The *Sādhanamālā* does not describe any Tārā with Hayagrīva." G. Bhattacharya, "A Second Dated Tārā," 23. This seems to me to be another example of an unwise dependence on a single textual source, in this case a relatively late compendium of iconographic descriptions.

15 Saraswati illustrates the piece and identifies it as in the Indian Museum, Calcutta; actually it is in the Nalanda site museum. He also dates it to the ca. 11th c., which seems too late. Saraswati, *Tantrayana Art*, pl. 61, discussed xxix.

16 Tārā with Hayagrīva, Bihar, ca. 9th c., approx 65 cm. Patna Museum no. 11313; Avalokiteśvara with Hayagrīva, Nalanda, ca. 9th c., Nalanda Museum ASI627/68; 4-armed Avalokiteśvara with Hayagrīva, Bodh Gaya, ca. 9th-10th c., on grounds of Mahābodhi temple.

17 For a stylistic analysis of this image, see S. Huntington, *"Pāla-Sena,"* 119. For its provenance, see Asher, "Former Broadley Collection," 107.

18 Contrary to the museum label and records, which indicate Kurkihar as provenance, this Tārā is from Nalanda. See Asher, "Former Broadley Collection," 109. Another Tārā image, unfortunately broken in half, is in the Nalanda site museum and is accompanied by a similar pair of attendants. 12239A/B; ASI negative no. 2236/70, 2237/70.

19 Pal, *Indian Sculpture*, 165. The Huntingtons reject the identification of Ekajaṭā because "The figure does not conform to textual descriptions of Ekajaṭā, who often accompanies Tārā." S. and J. Huntington, *Leaves*, 129, note 1.

20 Meisezahl, "Amoghapāśa: Some Nepalese Representations," 484-485.

21 Van Gulik, *Hayagrīva*, 35-36, pl. VI.

22 For further discussion of this issue, see Linrothe, "Compassionate Malevolence," 210-211.

23 Janice Leoshko, "Buddhist Images from Telhara, a Site in Eastern India," *South Asian Studies* 4 (1988): 89-97.

24 Van Gulik, *Hayagrīva*, 39; B. Bhattacharyya, *Indian Buddhist Iconography*, 146.

25 Mitra, *Ratnagiri*, pl. CCCXL. The epigraph for this section is from Walter Friedlaender, *Mannerism and Anti-Mannerism in Italian Painting* (New York, 1965), 11.

26 Mitra, *Ratnagiri*, 449; Hock, "Buddhist ideology," 70, 79-80.

27 Patna Museum no. Arch 6489, ht. 2.77 m; American Institute of Indian Studies negative AAB 111.15; Patna Museum, *Catalogue of Buddhist Sculptures in the Patna Museum* (Patna, 1957), 84. This is the Udayagiri to the north of Lalitagiri and west of Ratnagiri, not to be confused with the more famous, earlier cave site of Udayagiri and Khandagiri, west of Bhubaneswar.

28 Hock, "Buddhist ideology," 70, 79-82; Mitra, *Ratnagiri*, pl. CCCXXXIV.c and 442. The sculpture was recovered in three fragments, but Mitra illustrates the sculpture in its temporarily reassembled form.

29 The inscription is illustrated in Sahu, *Buddhism in Orissa*, fig. 18, discussed 146. Since the name Padmasambhava appears in the inscription, it has figured in the ongoing debate of the location of Uddiyana. See Linrothe, "Compassionate Malevolvence," 216-217.

30 For a third four-armed Hayagrīva from this period, see Mitra, *Ratnagiri*, 451, pl. CCCXLII.A. This is a fragment of a seated bodhisattva, either Avalokiteśvara or Tārā. Hayagrīva's arms are nearly identical to **91** and **92**, but the stance is slightly different.

31 See Asher, "Former Broadley Collection."

32 Note the Tārā from Bodh Gaya illustrated in S. Huntington, *"Pāla-Sena,"* fig. 105.

33 This work's resemblance to Kurkihar sculptures has also been noted by Janice Leoshko, "Buddhist Art of Northern India," *Asian Art: Selections from the Norton Simon Museum*, ed. Pratapaditya Pal (Pasadena, 1988), 18-19, fig. 16. Leoshko identifies the figure with the hatchet as "a male guardian attendant." One can easily agree with her encomium that this is "one of the most enchanting sculptures of Tārā to survive."

34 This is the Kurkihar metal altar/throne mentioned above. See note 10.

35 For an early report on the Kurkihar hoard, see Jayaswal, "Metal Images of Kurkihar Monastery," 70-83; Hayagrīva is illustrated in Plate XXXVI, there identified as "Bhairava." For a bibliography on this piece, see Ulrich von Schroeder, *Indo-Tibetan Bronzes* (Hong Kong, 1981), 268, no. 62a.

36 Unlike Bihar, where sculpture was produced continuously between the 8th c. and the 11th c., "Bengal's greatest period of artistic activity did not occur until the 11th and 12th centuries." S. Huntington, *"Pāla-Sena,"* 155.

37 Lucknow Museum no. 0.288.

38 Another fragment of a Phase One Hayagrīva that can be added to this group is in the Nalanda Museum, no. 10745, ht. 26 cm; AIIS neg. no. 62-66. He makes the same gesture with his right hand, but holds a *daṇḍa* in his left instead of a hatchet. The posture is also adjusted. He originally stood at the proper right edge of a bodhisattva sculpture. His face, expression, hair, beard etc. all mark him as belonging to the same type.

39 For a stylistic comparison with a work of the same period dated by inscription, see S. Huntington, *"Pāla-Sena,"* 115.

40 Friedlaender, *Mannerism*, 54.

41 The earlier image (ca. 11th c.) is the lower portion of a Khasarpaṇa Avalokiteśvara, retaining only the feet of the bodhisattva, but Tārā, Sudhanakumāra, Bhṛikutī and Hayagrīva remain. Nalanda Museum no. 5668. The later one is illustrated in S. Huntington, *"Pāla-Sena,"* fig. 138.

42 Bodh Gaya Museum no. 41; Linrothe, "Compassionate Malevolence," figs. 95-96.

43 See Asher, "Former Broadley Collection," 108.

44 Indian Museum acc. no. 3795, ht. 76 cm. The date is probably late 10th-early 11th c. British Museum OA 1985.5-11.1.

45 This is part of the same manuscript as that of **60**, but as the Huntingtons point out, it belongs to the second style, probably executed at the time of the re-dedication in the mid-12th c. See S. and J. Huntington, *Leaves*, color illustration 58c (second register, left), discussed 185-189. See also similar Phase One Hayagrīva figures in the "Vredenburg" manuscript in the Victoria and Albert Museum (1S-5-1958, right and IS-8-1958, center).

46 Both are published in The Asia Society, *Handbook of the Mr. and Mrs. John D. Rockefeller 3rd Collection* (New York, 1981), 21-22. **114;** and, S. and J. Huntington, *Leaves*, no. 33, where the provenance and date is corrected.

47 National Museum, New Delhi #66.46.

48 National Museum, New Delhi, #60.1501.

49 West Bengal State Archaeological Museum, Calcutta, #S25.

50 Note the sculpture in storage at the State Archaeological Museum, West Bengal, no. S295, ht. 17 cm.; the Avalokiteśvara in the Museum of the Varendra Research Society, Rajshahi, illustrated in Saraswati, *Tantrayana Art*, no. 60; and the fine Avalokiteśvara from Mahākali, now in the Dacca Museum, illustrated in ibid., no. 59.

51 See S. Huntington, *"Pāla-Sena,"* 181-182.

52 Others are illustrated and discussed in Linrothe, "Compassionate Malevolence," figs. 114-116, 230-231.

53 This piece seems to demonstrate knowledge of stylistic developments in Bihar and Bengal. There are also sculptures from Bengal that seem to have adopted Orissan conventions, like the squared off top of the backdrop. Note the 11th-12th c. sculpture in the Dacca Museum, illustrated in Saraswati, *Tantrayana Art*, no. 58. A tiny Hayagrīva making the *vandana mudrā* squats in front of Bhṛikutī at the bodhisattva's left knee.

54 See Mitra, *Ratnagiri*, 425, note 2; Ramaprasad Chandra, *Exploration in Orissa*, Memoirs of the ASI no. 44 (Calcutta, 1930), 13; pl. VI.6.

55 Orissa State Museum, #AY189, ht. 162 cm. Collected in Baneswaranasi, Cuttack district, it is unfortunately in very poor condition. Stella Kramrisch, *Indian Sculpture in the Philadelphia Museum of Art* (Philadelphia, 1960), 81, plates 12-13.

56 Paul Ricoeur, *Interpretation Theory: Discourse and the Surplus of Meaning* (Fort Worth, 1976), 52.

57 Ricoeur, *Interpretation Theory*, 52.

58 Gananath Obeyesekere, *Medusa's Hair: An Essay on Personal Symbols and Religious Experience* (Chicago, 1981), 51.

7

The Legacy

Images Outside of Eastern India

One would expect that as Buddhism and Buddhist images spread beyond the borders of India, images of Avalokiteśvara with Hayagrīva would also inevitably find their way abroad. After all, they were relatively common in India between the eighth and twelfth centuries. Naturally, however, the transmission of Phase One imagery was conditioned by a number of factors. These include the directness of connections, the timing of the exchange and the type of Buddhism which was most avidly sought by members of the other cultures. Thus Japan had very little in the way of direct links with India, and by the time descriptions or images of Hayagrīva reached there in the eighth century and particularly the ninth century, they mainly belonged to Phase Two. Phase One images of Hayagrīva are virtually unknown in Japan. With some rare exceptions, China is also singularly lacking in Phase One images. This is quite striking considering the importance of Avalokiteśvara and the Mahāyāna cults of the bodhisattva and paradise in Chinese cave sculpture, as well as translations of a number of texts documenting Phase One Hayagrīva thought. However, barring Dunhuang, and excluding sites like Dazu, with its hybrid mixture of folk Buddhism and popular religion, most Chinese cave sculpture predates the ninth century. After that time the influence of Indian imagery in China proper is negligible, and it will be recalled that Hayagrīva becomes part of Avalokiteśvara's standard retinue in eastern India around that time.

The case of Tibet is in some ways the opposite to that of Japan, in that contacts with India were direct and enduring. We are hindered, however, by the lack of surviving early Tibetan imagery, a circumstance usually attributed to the severe persecution of Buddhism in Tibet between 840 and 842,[1] at around the same time as the notorious Huichang suppression in China. By the eleventh and twelfth centuries, when the archaeological record is rich enough to have preserved a number of Hayagrīva images (mostly in Tibet), once again Phase Two images predominate.

There are very few mature Esoteric Buddhist images known from Sri Lanka where Mahāyāna itself was the minority mode of Buddhism. Indeed, "the worship of Avalokiteśvara Bodhisattva was the primary manifestation of Mahāyānism"

130. Hayagrīva, detail of 85*, same as* **86**

131. Hayagrīva, same as **102**

there between the seventh and tenth centuries.[2] The Mahāyāna sites in Sri Lanka have produced at least two Phase One images of Hayagrīva with Avalokiteśvara, and probably more could be turned up.[3] The imagery found there is in line with the development of the Phase One *krodha-vighnāntaka* as examined so far, though the evidence is quite meager, underlining that the Mahāyāna bodhisattva cult was not dependent on "tantric" elements like the wrathful deities.

Southeast Asia would seem to be fertile hunting ground for Phase One imagery. Central Java in particular had well-documented links with Nalanda,[4] the source of many of the sculptures examined above. Moreover, several Phase Two *krodha-vighnāntaka* images survive. Yet except for a few late thirteenth century sculptures originating in east Java, apparently no earlier Phase One *krodha-vighnāntaka* images remain.[5] Thai and Cambodian images of Phase One Hayagrīva appear to be equally rare, despite the "place of honor" of the Avalokiteśvara cult.[6] Later Esoteric Buddhism penetrated the area, and several Phase Two and Three images of *krodha-vighnāntaka* will be cited in subsequent chapters.

Outside India the archaeological record of Phase One *krodha-vighnāntaka* imagery in general is relatively impoverished. Fortunately a few high quality examples exist from Tibet, Central Asia, western China, and Nepal, which demonstrate quite convincingly that Hayagrīva as Avalokiteśvara's attendant was known outside of India. Further, what temporal evidence they do provide works to confirm the broad outlines of the development which we have adumbrated for the Phase One *krodha-vighnāntaka*.

The earliest Phase One image of Hayagrīva from outside of India of which I am aware is in a lovely painted image of a four-armed Avalokiteśvara recovered by Paul Pelliot and now in the Musée Guimet. [COLOR PLATES 5-6] It may be dated to the late eighth or early ninth century.[7] Because of the *pāśa*-noose in Avalokiteśvara's left hand, the bodhisattva is usually identified as Amoghapāśa. He is surrounded by five graceful female attendants, with a sixth figure rather more masculine looking, immediately beneath him.

Hayagrīva, the seventh figure, sits below and to the right of the bodhisattva. The scowling, mustachioed *krodha-vighnāntaka* is four-armed and *vāmana*-Yakṣa, and he holds a lotus, *vajra* and *daṇḍa*. The second left hand is held at the chest, perhaps making the *tarjanī mudrā*. Most interesting is the green horse's head which emerges from the top of his head. This is only the second Hayagrīva so far examined with a literal depiction of this definitive feature which figures in most textual descriptions of Hayagrīva. The only documented Indian example of a Phase One Hayagrīva image with a horse's head is the one accompanying Avalokiteśvara in the Rietberg Museum sculpture, from around the same date. [**130**, **85**]

In fact the Rietberg example is as close as any for an Indian parallel in terms of overall body type and mood of self-contained power. One might point also to the Kurkihar metal Hayagrīva for a similar posture. [**131**] Several Orissan examples depict Hayagrīva four-armed, though none with an arrangement of *āyudha* identical to the Rietberg sculpture. We have seen that the *daṇḍa* is one of the most common of his attributes. The flower which he holds is mentioned in several descriptions of a Hayagrīva attending Amoghapāśa in Bodhiruci's translation of 707 CE,[8] though very few surviving Indian images seem to relate to it. Even if there is no exact Indian prototype, we can tell from Hayagrīva's size relative to Amoghapāśa and to the others in the retinue that he was a deity of some standing and power. That in itself tallies well with the development we have traced, since during the ninth and tenth centuries in Indian Buddhist art the Phase One Hayagrīva was at his height, before the stylizations of the late tenth and eleventh centuries had set in and after the maturation of early attempts to forge an appropriate form out of earlier Yakṣa and Gaṇa imagery.

Situated behind this painting are discernible Indian iconographic features. There are equally evident Indian visual conventions as well. This entrancing painting was recovered from the walled-up "library" at Dunhuang. Stylistically, however, it is not Chinese. Its fine, unmodulated lineament encloses bodies with a much stronger sensuality of soft curves and composed litheness than is found in contemporary Chinese paintings found at Dunhuang. Such details as the oblate (versus circular) nimbi, the wavy line composing the upper eyelid and the transparency of garments set it apart from Chinese painting conventions and link it to Indian art. The possibility of Tibetan intermediation naturally presents itself, particularly since the painting dates from the period of the Tibetan occupation of Dunhuang, between 781 and 847 CE. However, the dearth of contemporary Tibetan art cited above precludes precise attribution either to Tibetan artists working in Dunhuang, or for that matter, to artists working at some other site, from which it was subsequently brought to Dunhuang.[9] A number of paintings were found at Dunhuang with dual Chinese and Tibetan inscriptions, along with others having Tibetan inscriptions alone.[10] Still others have no inscription but are marked by a distinct non-Chinese style. Some of these have similarities with the Guimet painting, though only one is nearly as fine.[11] If, as seems likely, this painting was executed by someone (of whatever ethnic origin) trained in the style most appreciated in Tibet, and if it does reflect high quality Tibetan art of the ninth century, then we can conclude that at this juncture Tibetan art was remarkably transparent, meaning it allowed the contemporary Indian stylistic and iconographic features to pass through it and to predominate.

A final reflection on this painting. It is called a *maṇḍala* by Whitfield, Karmay, Feugère and Heller.[12] There is some justification for a loose definition of this term, in which, as here, deities are arranged in an orderly if not symmetrical fashion, with a coordinated relationship to the larger central deity. However, it is somewhat misleading, since contemporaneously at Dunhuang there were *maṇḍala* in the strict sense of the term, preserving an absolutely symmetrical system of arrangement of deities in the four primary and four subsidiary directions around a central deity. The strictly defined *maṇḍala* reflects Phase Two and Three Esoteric Buddhist concerns. Here we have not a *maṇḍala* but an expanded triadic arrangement. As such it accords perfectly well with the Phase One images of Avalokiteśvara and Hayagrīva which have already been examined in the context of the enduring and widespread cult of the bodhisattva Avalokiteśvara.

The same considerations hold for a related eight-armed eleven-headed Avalokiteśvara recovered by Kozlov from Khara Khoto.[13] Unquestionably there are Tangut stylistic characteristics, but the style derives from painting of eastern India via central Tibet.

Another Phase One Hayagrīva with a horse's head graces the reverse of a Buddha sculpture in Changspa, near Leh in Ladakh, western Tibet. **[132-133]** This sculpture is early enough to qualify for inclusion among the rare images surviving from first diffusion of Buddhism in Tibet. Although in abraded condition, its model in Indian sculpture is clearly pre-tenth century. On the other side is a very svelte-looking Buddha, and some of the smoothness and roundness of form (very different from the Kashmiri idiom which dominates the tenth century) is visible in the bodhisattva. Nevertheless, the awkwardness of the proportions and the slight stiffness betray a provincial western Tibetan reinterptretation of the Indian model. It may be placed in the ninth century, or the tenth century at the latest.

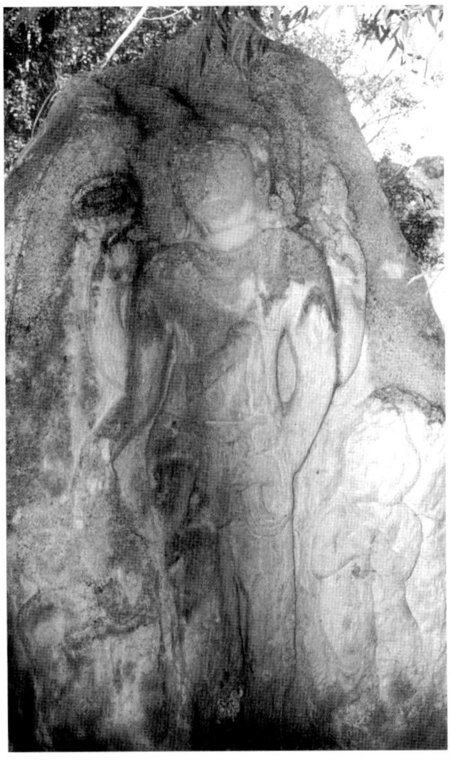

132. *Four-armed Avalokiteśvara with Hayagrīva, Changspa (Ladakh), ca. 9th-10th century*

133. *Hayagrīva detail of* 132

The very tubby, large-headed Hayagrīva leans on the upturned handle of a *daṇḍa*. He is surrounded by a backdrop, possibly of flames. Most significant is the large horse's head which emerges at the crown of his head. [**133**] Both heads turn inward toward the bodhisattva. In terms of the relative proportions, a comparable Indian example would be the Orissan four-armed Avalokiteśvara image. [COLOR PLATE 4] In fact this is the kind of image which must have been the mental model for the sculptor in Ladakh.

A Tibetan image of the Phase One Hayagrīva is preserved in the painting of Amitāyus in the Los Angeles County Museum of Art.[14] [COLOR PLATE 7, **134**] Its late twelfth-century date makes it among the earliest surviving Tibetan hanging paintings.[15] The large Amitāyus figure dominates the composition, but two standing bodhisattva form the essential triad, while monks and adoring bodhisattva form symmetrical groups to either side. In the bottom register are three bodhisattva, Avalokiteśvara, Mañjuśrī and Vajrapāṇi at the center, while on the far proper left is perhaps the blue Vighnāntaka or Acala (mainly Phase Two wrathful deities). As in the Dunhuang painting, Hayagrīva is again in the bottom proper right corner. Instead of squatting, however, he stands in the active *pratyālīḍha*, like some of the images from Orissa. [**92**] He can be identified by the green horse's head emerging from his hair. He brandishes a long *daṇḍa* or staff with his right hand and makes the *tarjanī mudrā* with his left. All in all, it is a much more powerful and aggressive Hayagrīva than most contemporary Phase One images from India. We will see that in Phase Two imagery the wrathful deities take on a much more aggressive demeanor, calling attention to themselves and their power, in contrast to the Phase One *krodha-vighnāntaka*, who salutes the more important figure he attends.

Apparently what we see here is a later Phase Two form imported into a Phase One image. This is, once again, not a *maṇḍala*. It was consecrated to Amitāyus by a specific Tibetan Lama, Chökyi Gyaltsen, on the occasion of his life-attainment ritual.[16] The ritual seems to be related to the Tārā ritual of "initiation into life" designed for the prolongation of life, a ritual which Stephen Beyer has studied. Here too Amitāyus is envisioned:

> *... he has one face, upon his two hands, held in the meditation gesture, he holds a golden flask filled with a stream of the nectar of immortal life.*[17]

Another ritual still practiced by Tibetan Buddhists describes Hayagrīva in just this form, as the patron of the Lotus family over which Amitāyus presides, for the purpose of expelling evil spirits:

> *... his body colored red, having one face and two hands, with his right hand brandishing in the sky a cudgel of khadira wood and his left hand in the threatening gesture upon his breast. His three round eyes gape and stare, his mouth bares four fangs; his eyebrows and beard are red-yellow, blazing like the fire at the end of time; his hair is pale yellow, bristling upward, and on his crest is a green horse head, whinnying. He is adorned with the eight great serpent-kings, his lower garment is a tiger skin, he stands with his right foot drawn in and his left stretched out, in the center of a mass of blazing fire of knowledge.*[18]

134. *Hayagrīva, detail of Amitāyus thangka, Tibet, ca. 12th century, Los Angeles County Museum of Art, detail of* COLOR PLATE 7

The functions of this painting of Amitāyus with Hayagrīva in attendance are not Esoteric Buddhist in the strict sense of the term. Long life and protection are being prayed for here, boons which fit into the realm of traditional cult Mahāyāna. The triadic composition also supports this reading. Hayagrīva performs functions which mesh with Phase One liturgical demands, but his form is that borrowed from Phase Two contexts, which by this time were coeval in Tibet. The same is true of a painted Hayagrīva in an outer chapel of the fifteenth-century Great Stūpa of

135. Hayagrīva, Tibet, copper alloy, ca. 12th century, Zimmerman Family Collection

Gyantse [COLOR PLATES 8-9], and perhaps also for the twelfth-century Zimmerman metalwork [**135**], though here the context is lost. That this aggressive form of Hayagrīva was not a Tibetan invention will be argued in the conclusion of this chapter. Most surviving Tibetan images of Hayagrīva feature the more forcefully wrathful characteristics developed in the second phase, but these are examples of Hayagrīva in Tibetan Phase One contexts.[19] [COLOR PLATES 5-9] They serve to illustrate some of the issues of Hayagrīva's image in Tibet and their complex relationship with Indian traditions.

Stylistically distinct from eastern Indian art, Nepalese sculpture and painting nevertheless were strongly influenced thematically by the Buddhist centers of art in Bihar and Bengal. For our present purposes, it is important to point out that in Nepal, one also finds early wrathful attendants to bodhisattvas. Among these early images are seventh and eighth-century examples of *vāmana*-Yakṣa *krodha-vighnāntaka* attending Vajrapāṇi as personifications of his *vajra*.[20]

Hayagrīva in particular continues to be depicted in paintings and sculptures of Amoghapāśa Avalokiteśvara into the sixteenth century.[21] In images which seem to repeat a standard prototype, Hayagrīva squats with one knee up. His red body is *vāmana*-Yakṣa, and he wears a stylized animal skin *dhoti* and a snake *upavīta*. His serpentine hair stands straight up behind an elaborate bejeweled crown. Atop his head is a small horse's head. His eyes are wide, including the third one, and fangs protrude from his lips. He makes the *vandana mudrā* with the raised right hand, saluting Avalokiteśvara. This Hayagrīva conforms in most of the essentials with the standardized image we found squatting and saluting Avalokiteśvara in tenth, eleventh and twelfth-century Indian Hayagrīva images. [**136**] We can assume that he originally held a small *daṇḍa*. Judging from the paintings, the relationship of Hayagrīva to Bhṛikutī in sixteenth-century Nepal was identical to that which held sway in late period Indian Avalokiteśvara images. Thus Hayagrīva kneels on the level below Amoghapāśa's throne, beneath Bhṛikutī, who hovers at the level of the bodhisattva's torso. She is significantly larger than Hayagrīva.

An inscription on the sixteenth century Leiden painting published by Pott also allows us to learn something of the religious context of such images. It should come as no surprise that the references are not Esoteric Buddhist properly speaking, but rather prayers for earthly benefits of long life, health and wealth. Here is the complete inscription as given by Pott:

> *Hail! In the year 652, in the month of Magha, in the bright half, on the 9th day, a Friday, during the reign of Rāja Pranamalla, the yajñamana Bhiksusri, his wife Jirulaksmi, his son called Kamalasingha, and his wives Basulaksmi and Daralaksmi, having taken this supplication at the foot of Amoghapāśa Lokeśvara, living at the temple of Gosain-Kumara Thakura in the (vihāra) Mahābhuta: that he may live his life without illness, with children and riches, fortune and have an uninterrupted offspring, that he may become old, and receive all the fruits predicted in the sastra.*[22]

136. Hayagrīva, detail of **116**, *same as* **117**

Sixteenth-century Nepalese Hayagrīva images validate two suppositions for us. First, they underscore the power of iconographic orthodoxy by which the standard Hayagrīva image-type, codified in eastern India by the late tenth to eleventh centuries, could still be repeated iconically several hundred years later in Nepal. Second, the inscription of the Leiden painting once again confirms that such images appear in the context of the Mahāyāna bodhisattva cult, which seeks intercession in earthly life, and not in the context of Esoteric Buddhism, where the primary concern is *samyaksambodhi* (absolute enlightenment) in this life. The distinction is that between mundane and supramundane powers, "those concerned with protection or personal benefit of one kind or another in this world, and those concerned with the progress toward enlightenment."[23]

It is necessary to distinguish the two, but not because mature Esoteric Buddhism does not also involve mundane goals as part of its agenda. Certainly it does. However, Phase One images consistently admit to no other interpretation than that of a mundane orientation. Supramundane goals are singularly absent. Phase One imagery has been confined to such a belief system wherever we have inscriptional evidence or a broader iconographic context from which to judge: from the earliest recognized images at Aurangabad and Ellora, to the monastic complexes of Orissa, Bihar and Bengal, to Khara Khoto, Tibet, Java and Nepal. The evidence has been almost univocal that images of *krodha-vighnāntaka* do not necessarily be-token Esoteric Buddhism, any more than do multi-armed images of Avalokiteśvara or *dhāraṇī*. Phase One *krodha-vighnāntaka* images emerged from Mahāyāna, and a strain of Mahāyāna cult images continued to incorporate them, even as they were outgrowing their attendant status.

Conclusions

If one were to chart the course of Phase One *krodha-vighnāntaka* imagery in eastern India between the seventh and twelfth centuries, a lop-sided bell-shaped curve would emerge. It would appear faintly from the late sixth century, rise stiffly in the eighth and ninth centuries, peak in the tenth, and begin to flatten out as it declines again in the eleventh. Such a chart would reflect both the visual and religious interest retained by the *krodha-vighnāntaka* within the context of an enduring "*dhāraṇī*" Mahāyāna. The *mantranaya* practice within Mahāyāna featured the cult of the bodhisattva and borrowed both imagery and practices from Esoteric Buddhism, which in turn was deeply affected by Mahāyāna imagery, vocabulary and deities. Judging by the purposes for which such images were intended (e.g., longevity and rebirth in paradise), it is clear that the Phase One images of *krodha-vighnāntaka* remain for the most part distinct from "pure" Esoteric Buddhism.

The earliest Phase One *krodha-vighnāntaka* were formally dependent on earlier images of Yakṣa and Yakṣa-related demi-gods: the Gaṇa and *āyudhapuruṣa*. A sense of ambiguity, potential malevolence and forced conversion lingers on in the *krodha-vighnāntaka*. Additionally, there was considerable variety in gestures and attitudes, but the *vandana* and *vinayahasta mudrā* are notably frequent. Early artists were not concerned to be either consistent or specific about the individual *krodha-vighnāntaka* deities they represented. At an early stage there was an almost generic quality to the forms (not necessarily the doctrines) of the *krodha-vighnāntaka*, Yamāntaka and Hayagrīva easily substituting for one another.

Middle period references to Yakṣa and Yakṣa-derived forms is less overt. Origins are still an active ingredient, but they are more well-integrated into the total image. The *krodha-vighnāntaka* often seemed to capture the interest of the artist and his co-religionists at the expense of other members of the various bodhisattva entourages. The *krodha-vighnāntaka* build in power and aggression. Iconographic specialization among the members of the group, such as Yamāntaka's buffalo or the tiny horse's head in Hayagrīva's hair, which by this time is evident in their Phase Two incarnations, is only rarely observed.

By the end of the middle period, however, there is a noticeable reduction in the number of ways in which the *krodha-vighnāntaka* is represented. The *vinayahasta mudrā* drops from view. The *vandana mudrā* and the posture of leaning on a short

137. *Avalokiteśvara with Hayagrīva, Nalanda (Bihar), ca. 8th-9th century, same as 73*

staff or club becomes commonplace. By the eleventh century a certain amount of standardization is widely discernible. A template of the generic *krodha-vighnāntaka* seems to have been shared by artists. The result for the *krodha-vighnāntaka* image was a reduction of status, measurable through a literal reduction in size as well as through the standardization of the image-type. Their ability to overawe is atrophied, transformed at times into mere irritability or comic mischievousness.

As a means of bridging the distance to Phase Two images of *krodha-vighnāntaka* belonging to Esoteric Buddhism proper, I would like to examine one last Orissan image. It is a humble piece in ruinous condition, left out in the open on a hill by the remains of a small dressed-stone temple which must once have housed it.[24] It is one of several images standing isolated on the desolate Aragarh hill near Haripur village, south of Bhubaneswar. Despite its abysmal condition, iconographically it is a fine transitional piece, located ideologically between the bodhisattva cult of Mahāyāna and Esoteric Buddhism. The juxtaposition of these two related but divergent modes is apparently unique to this isolated example, a fact which testifies to the otherwise uniform separation of the two.

The work in question is a damaged sculpture of a four-armed Avalokiteśvara, its condition made worse by exposure to the elements. [**138-139**] Like any number of four-armed or six-armed Avalokiteśvara images [**70, 79, 87, 137,** etc.], his upper right hand holds a *mālā*-rosary, and the lower right hand is in *vara mudrā*, the gesture of gift giving. The fact that the right leg is pendant helps to confirm that it is indeed Avalokiteśvara, who often sits in this manner. The upper part of the sculpture is typical of the Phase One Mahāyāna bodhisattva cult imagery to which this section has been devoted.

138. *Seated four-armed Avalokiteśvara, Aragarh Hill (Orissa), ca. late 10th century*

The area beneath the lotus pedestal, however, is most interesting [**139**] and, it would seem, unprecedented in eastern India. It depicts three figures, and all of them belong not to the bodhisattva cult of Mahāyāna, but to Phase Two Esoteric Buddhism. Just above Avalokiteśvara's pendant foot, to its right, is a cross-legged figure making the *bodhyagrī mudrā*: the left hand under the right, its index finger extended and clasped by the fist of the left hand. The *mudrā* is made by only one deity, Mahāvairocana, as in the handsome adorned Buddha Mahāvairocana sculpture at Udayagiri. [**140**] Mahāvairocana, as will be discussed in more detail, is at the center of the paradigmatic Phase Two Esoteric Buddhist *maṇḍala*, the *vajradhātu maṇḍala* of the *STTS* and *SDPS*, and the *garbhadhātu maṇḍala* based on the *Mahāvairocana Sūtra*. While Vairocana is featured in such late Mahāyāna texts as the *Avataṃsaka Sūtra*, he is not depicted in *bodhyagrī mudrā*. It is an exclusively Esoteric Buddhist configuration.

Because of the eroded condition of the sculpture, the middle deity beneath Avalokiteśvara [**139**] is difficult to identify with absolute surety based on the photograph. However, the

139. *Throne beneath Avalokiteśvara (detail of 138)*

140. *Mahāvairocana Buddha, Udayagiri (Orissa), ca. 10th century*

ambiguity evaporates when the piece is examined in person. A bell held at the proper left hip is visible. The object supported in front of the chest by the right hand must be a *vajra*, making this an image of Vajrasattva, comparable to the Vajrasattva from Salempur, Orissa, or the damaged Vajrasattva of the Esoteric Buddhist "Temple Four" at Ratnagiri.[25] Vajrasattva is also one of the banner deities of Esoteric Buddhism, who, as the bodhisattva representative of the *vajrakula,* takes a special place in the *STTS* and is later identified with Vajradhara, the "sixth" Buddha.[26] To find him next to Mahāvairocana is very suggestive of true Esoteric Buddhist ideology. The fact that he is also shown as a subordinate to Avalokiteśvara is unexpected.

While Mahāvairocana and Vajrasattva are sometimes linked in the Esoteric Buddhist texts, there is no reason for them to be attendants to Avalokiteśvara. One could explain the three in terms of the *trikula* (three family) system of early Esoteric Buddhism, in that Mahāvairocana represents the *Tathāgatakula*, Vajrasattva represents the *vajrakula*, and Avalokiteśvara represents the *padmakula*. However, examples of this triadic relationship generally privilege the *Tathāgatakula* by placing his larger figure in the middle. Here it is the representative of the *padmakula* who is largest, while the other two are peripheral. Any way one attempts to interpret the presence of these two deities on the base of an Avalokiteśvara sculpture, one is forced to recognize its uniquely hybrid nature.

The third deity on the base is also the largest. He is two-armed, *vāmana*-Yakṣa, his hair piled onto his head, and he holds up a *vajra*-tipped *daṇḍa* with his proper right hand while making the *tarjanī mudrā* and holding a *pāśa*-noose with the left. The iconography of this figure accompanying Avalokiteśvara, his position and his relative size allow us to identify him as Hayagrīva. The *vajra*-tipped *daṇḍa* is held by at least two Orissan Phase One images of Hayagrīva [**124, 126**], and the noose is also found in Orissan Hayagrīva images [COLOR PLATE 4] as well as in Phase One images from Bihar. [**82, 84**] One even holds it like this one, while making the *tarjanī mudrā*. [**78**]

His active, threatening pose and gestures are far more typical of a Phase Two *krodha-vighnāntaka*, and in that sense fit well with Mahāvairocana and Vajrasattva with whom Hayagrīva is linked on the base. In fact he resembles an Esoteric Buddhist form of Hayagrīva known in Tibet. Van Gulik describes the form:

> *In this form the god ["Hayagrīva with the staff"] has only one head, and two arms. The right hand carries the staff, raised in a threatening attitude. The left hand, bent to the breast, holds the noose [i.e.* tarjanī-pāśa mudrā*]. The colour of the body is red, and from the hair emerges a green horse's head. He wears the tiger-skin, and is adorned with a garland of human heads, and a green snake. Under each foot he crushes an evil spirit.*[27]

This form of Hayagrīva is more generally visible in Phase Two contexts in Tibet, but it also penetrated the Tibetan paintings discussed earlier. [COLOR PLATES 5-9]

The horse's head is not visible in the sculpture [**139**], but as has been discussed, it is extraordinarily rare in Phase One Hayagrīva images in India. The "evil spirit" underfoot suggested by the text is also missing, unless we interpret the tiger on which this Hayagrīva stands as a *vināyaka*-obstacle instead of a *vāhana*-vehicle. The tiger crouches facing Vajrasattva, with his head beneath Hayagrīva's right foot, while its vertical tail snakes up the proper left edge of the sculpture.

The tiger is the vehicle for only one *krodha-vighnāntaka* of which I am aware, Trailokyanasaka.[28] This is a minor figure incorporated within a *krodha-vighnāntaka maṇḍala*, figuring in a commentary on the Phase Two *SDPS* written in the ninth century by Vajravarman, the Sri Lankan master of Anandagarbha. The commentary is only preserved in the Tibetan, but sections of it have been translated, along with the *SDPS* itself, by Tadeusz Skorupski.[29] Obscure as this tiger-riding deity may be, it is perhaps no coincidence that Trailokyanasaka, like Hayagrīva, is the wrathful representative of the *padmakula* and wears the diadem of the Tathāgata of the *padmakula*, Amitābha. Thus there is an iconographic link, however tenuous, between the two wrathful figures, underscoring the fact that a wrathful representative of the *padma* family on a tiger is not totally unprecedented.

The tiger appears on an strikingly anomalous sculpture, beneath a wrathful deity who in other respects falls within an acceptable range of qualifications characteristic of Phase One Hayagrīva. Let us assume, as we must, that the artist was working within the living tradition, knew more than we do about iconographic identities, and was not mad or misinformed. Despite the anomalies, the position of a wrathful deity on the throne beneath Avalokiteśvara is at least in accord with the eastern Indian norm. Most likely the wrathful deity thus associated with Avalokiteśvara is indeed Hayagrīva. The inclusion of the tiger may be explained as the desire on the part of the artist or the patron to imitate on behalf of Hayagrīva the animal mount which was closely associated with Yamāntaka, particularly in Orissa. [**45, 56**] Contrary to the impression one might receive travelling through rural eastern India today, the buffalo of the late tenth century was not a domesticated agricultural beast of burden. Instead the buffalo was considered a powerful, wild and potentially dangerous animal, and thus was suited to be Yamāntaka's *vāhana*-vehicle.[30] The tiger was an equally awesome animal, and it may have been thought, perhaps only locally, that it would serve well as the vehicle for Hayagrīva. This kind of iconographic borrowing from Yamāntaka for the provision of Hayagrīva is paralleled by the textual plundering on the part of devout Japanese adherents to Esoteric Buddhism. Van Gulik has shown how a "description of Hayagrīva sitting on a water-buffalo has been taken from a text that is especially devoted to another Vidyarāja, viz. Yamāntaka."[31] Something of the same nature may have occurred here as well. At any rate we are obliged to identify the figure at least provisionally as Hayagrīva, in spite of the unusual *vāhana*, since it does not contradict the other positive evidence of his identity.

In conclusion, this sculpture [**138**] weds Phase One and Phase Two deities. The upper part is a standard bodhisattva cult figure, the four-armed Avalokiteśvara. The lower part depicts two of the most important deities of Phase Two Esoteric Buddhism, Mahāvairocana and Vajrasattva. It is Hayagrīva, in this ferocious form, who links the two worlds. Hayagrīva is one of the accepted, even expected, attendants to the four-armed Avalokiteśvara in Phase One ideology, yet in his threatening demeanor with *vajra*-tipped *daṇḍa*, *tarjanī mudrā* and *pāśa*-noose, standing on the back of a wild tiger, he is also compatible with Phase Two notions of *krodha-vighnāntaka* as direct and powerful manifestations of the five Tathāgata Buddhas. Phase Two *krodha-vighnāntaka* are not merely the attendants of bodhisattva, but potent, independent deities in their own right. In this unique instance, Hayagrīva plays both roles.

Notes to Chapter Seven

1 "Needless to say, many monuments of the period and virtually all movable works of art vanished. No paintings and only a few metal images survive even to hint at what once existed." John C. Huntington, "Introduction to Tibet and China," in S. and J. Huntington, *Leaves*, 290. This view is gradually being modified. See Roberto Vitali, *Early Temples of Central Tibet* (London, 1990).

2 Diran Kavork Dohanian, *The Mahāyāna Buddhist Sculpture of Ceylon* (New York, 1977), 32. See also von Schroeder, *The Golden Age of Sculpture in Sri Lanka*.

3 Note the 9th c. Hayagrīva with Avalokiteśvara in a niche illustrated in Dohanian, *Mahāyāna Buddhist Sculpture of Ceylon*, fig. 15, 53-55. The photograph is poor but the *krodha-vighnāntaka* seems to follow the pattern of those of northeast India. A 4-armed Avalokiteśvara sculpture from Vijayarama monastery, Anuradhapura of ca. late 9th c. is described with what also must be Hayagrīva: "a small male dwarfish figure raises its arms upward toward the god." Ibid., 55. Also see von Schroeder, *Buddhist Sculptures of Sri Lanka*, 229, fig. 25.

4 See August Johan Bernet Kempers, "The Bronzes of Nalanda and Hindu-Javanese Art," *Bijdragen tot de Taal-, Land-, en Volkenkunde van Nederlandsch-Indie* 90 (1933):1-88.

5 See the group of stone statues attending Amoghapāśa Avalokiteśvara including Hayagrīva, dedicated in the late 13th c. in Candi Jago, illustrated in J.L.A. Brandes, *Beschrijving van de ruïne bij de desa Toempang genaamd Tjandi Djago, in de Residentie Pasoeroean* (The Hague, 1904), plates 1-4; August Johan Bernet Kempers, *Ancient Indonesian Art* (Cambridge, 1959), pls. 253-254, 257; idem, "De Beelden van Tjandi Djago en hun Voor-Indisch Prototype," *Maandblad voor Beeldende Kunsten* 10 (1933): fig. 4; N.J. Krom, *Inleiding tot de Hindoe-Javaansche Kunst*, 3 vols. (The Hague, 1923) 3: pl. 63. Related bronze plaques were made in the late 13th c. See Bernet Kempers, *Ancient Indonesian Art*, 87; idem, "Tjandi Djago," fig. 4; Museum für Indische Kunst, Berlin, *Museum für Indische Kunst, Berlin: Katalog 1976 Ausgestellte Werke* no. 308; and, Marie-Thérèse de Mallmann, "Un point d'iconographie indo-javanaise: Khasarpaṇa et Amoghapāśa," *Artibus Asiae* 11 (1948): 176, fig. 1. J.A. Schoterman compares the 13th c. Hayagrīva with a *sādhana* preserved in Tibetan but cannot understand why the text refers to him as a "dwarf," stating, "a genuine dwarfish Hayagrīva does not exist in Buddhist iconography." His misconception results from his consultation of exclusively literary sources over the visual arts. See J.A. Schoterman, "A Surviving Amoghapāśa sādhana: Its relation to five main statues of Candi Jago," in *Ancient Indonesian Sculpture*, ed. Marijke J. Klokke and Pauline Lusingh Scherleer (Leiden, 1994), 54-77. A related sculpture, dated 1286, is in the National Museum, Jakarta. See F.M. Schnitger, *Hindoe-Oudheden aan de Batang Hari* (Utrecht, 1936), 6-8; de Mallmann, "Un point d'iconographie indo-javanaise," 176-188, fig. 2.

6 Louis Finot, "Lokeçvara en Indochine,"in *Études Asiatique publiées à l'occasion du vingt-cinquième anniversaire de l'École Française d'Extrême-Orient*, Vol. 1 (Paris, 1925), 231.

7 This is the date given by Mme. Nicolas-Vandier et al, *Bannières et Peintures de Touen-Houang Conservées au Musée Guimet*, Mission Paul Pelliot no. 14 (Paris, 1974), 159-162. It has recently been discussed in relation to early rock carvings in Tibet. See Amy Heller, "Eighth- and Ninth-Century Temples and Rock Carvings of Eastern Tibet," in *Tibetan Art: Towards a definition of style*, ed. Jane Casey Singer and Philip Denwood (London: Laurence King, 1997), 86-103.

8 T.20.1092.271a, 302a.

9 The difficulty of assigning stylistic provenance to this painting and others of its type is discussed by Roderick Whitfield, *The Art of Central Asia: The Stein collection in the British Museum*, 3 vols. (Tokyo, 1982-85), 2:21-22. See also Marylin Rhie and Robert Thurman, *Wisdom and Compassion: The Sacred Art of Tibet* (New York, 1991), 122.

10 Heather Karmay, *Early Sino-Tibetan Art* (Warminster, 1975), 8-14; and, Whitfield and Farrer, *Caves of the Thousand Buddhas*, no. 53, 54.

11 An Avalokiteśvara painting on hemp in the British Museum illustrated in Whitfield, *Art of Central Asia*, pl. 2.38. Whitfield notes the style of the two paintings "would seem to indicate the direction that Tibetan art was eventually to take." Ibid., 2:21.

12 Whitfield, *Art of Central Asia*, 2:21; Karmay, *Early Sino-Tibetan Art*, caption to 8, fig. 2; Laure Feugère, "The Pelliot Collection from Dunhuang," *Orientations* 20.3 (1989): 45; Heller, "Eighth- and Ninth-Century Temples," 100. It is also called the "*maṇḍala* d'Amoghapāśa (?)" in Nicolas-Vandier, *Bannieres et peintures de Touen-Houang*, caption to pl. 86.

13 Illustrated in Mikhail Piotrovsky, *Lost Empire of the Silk Road: Buddhist Art of Khara Khoto* (Milan, 1993), no. 12; and in Rhie and Thurman, *Wisdom and Compassion*, no. 128.

14 Pratapaditya Pal, *Art of Tibet* (Los Angeles, 1983), P1, pl. 7.

15 See Jane Casey Singer, "Early Thankas: Eleventh-Thirteenth Centuries," 180-195 in *On the Path to Void: Buddhist Art of the Tibetan Realm*, ed. Pratapaditya Pal (Mumbai: Marg, 1996); idem, "Painting in Central Tibet c. 950-1400," *Artibus Asiae* 54 no. 1/2 (1994): 87-136.

16 Pal, *Art of Tibet*, 134, 259.

17 Beyer, *Cult of Tārā*, 375.

18 Ibid., 351.

19 Another early central Tibetan copy of an eastern Indian image of Avalokiteśvara with Hayagrīva and Sudhanakumāra was published as part of the Essen collection. In the Pāla style, the piece comes from northeast India and is dated to the 11th c., but a Tibetan provenance seems much more likely. Gerd-Wolfgang Essen and Tsering Tashi Thingo, *Die Götter des Himalaya: Buddhistische Kunst Tibets, Die Sammlung Gerd-Wolfgang Essen*, 2 vols. (Munich, 1989), 1:40.

20 See Pal, *Arts of Nepal Part 1*, pl. 14; idem, *Sensuous Immortals*, no. 93.

21 See Pott, "Amoghapāśa from Bhatgaon," 63-65; Pal, "Iconography of Amoghapāśa Lokeśvara," 21; idem, *The Arts of Nepal: Part II, Painting* (Leiden/Köln, 1978), 35, no. 29. See also a closely related painting in the Victoria and Albert Museum, London, in A.W. Macdonald and Anne Vergati Stahl, *Newar Art: Nepalese Art During the Malla Period* (Warminster, 1979), color pl.V, discussed 129. Color photographs of the sculptural Hayagrīva in the Bhaktapur Museum are published in Ernst Waldschmidt and Rose Leonore, *Nepal: Art Treasures from the Himalayas* (London, 1969), no. 55; and Madanjeet Singh, *Himalayan Art* (Greenwich, 1968), 219. For a Nepalese painting (1015 CE) depicting the horse's head, see Saraswati, *Tantrayana Art*, pl. 227.

22 Pott, "Amoghapāśa from Bhatgaon," 64. A Nepalese Amoghapāśa painting, dated 1862 and now in the British Museum, has been studied by R.O. Meisezahl. It carries the same mundane goals: "The purpose of the donation was to bring long life, prosperity or anything connected with temporal welfare to the donor and his family." Meisezahl, "Amoghapāśa: Some Nepalese Representations," 464.

23 Snellgrove, *Indo-Tibetan Buddhism*, 122.

24 For a description of the temple, see D.R. Das, "Semi-Cave Shrines of Orissa," in *Ratna-Chandrikā: Panorama of Oriental Studies (Shri R.C. Arawala Festschrift)*, ed. Devendra Handa and Ashvini Agrawal (New Delhi: Harman Publishing, 1989), 291-304, pls. 36.1-4.

25 Indian Museum, Calcutta, no. A24300/6675; and, Mitra, *Ratnagiri*, pl. CCXL.A.

26 Snellgrove, *Indo-Tibetan Buddhism*, 216ff.

27 Van Gulik, *Hayagrīva*, 35.

28 Except Guru Dorje Grolod, a fierce manifestation of Padmasambhava who stands on a tiger. He is found only in later Tibetan-related contexts. See David Gredzens, *Visions from the Top of the World: The Art of Tibet and the Himalayas* (Minneapolis, 1983), pl. 17; and, Chögyam Trungpa, *Crazy Wisdom* (Boston: Shambhala, 1991), 167-175.

29. Tadeusz Skorupski, *Sarvadurgatipariśodhana Tantra: Elimination of all Evil Destinies* (New Delhi, 1983), 368.

30 For insightful observations on the wild buffalo and the transfer of its experiential meaning into religious iconography, see van den Bosch, "Yama," 45-48.

31 Van Gulik, *Hayagrīva*, 83.

Phase Two

141. *Trailokyavijaya, Mahants compound, Bodh Gaya (Bihar), ca. 10th century, detail of* **7, 162**

8

A New Paradigm

Selon l'ordre des manuscrits nous voyons passer tour à tour, multimanes, polycéphales, ornés d'attributs guerriers, parés d'ornements macabres, et tous en proie aux fureurs de l'amour et de la colère, Caṇḍamahārosaṇa, Heruka ou Hevajra, Saptākṣara, Buddhakapala, Saṃvara, Vajrahūṃkāra, Mahābala, Vajrajvālānalārka, Paramāçva, Bhūtaḍāmara, Vighnāntaka, Mahākāla, et jusqu'à Ganapati: car cette cohue de monstres n'a de bouddhique que le fait de coudoyer des Buddhas et des Bodhisattvas dans un même recueil. Bien qu'ils répondent à une collection de surnoms qui semble avoir été imaginée tout exprès pour vérifier l'adage: quot nomina, tot numina, de tous il y aurait néanmoins une étude à faire, non seulement à l'aide des sādhana qui évoquent, mais encore des tantra spéciaux qui leur sont consacrés.

A. Foucher, *Étude sur l'iconographie Bouddhique de l'inde*

With Phase Two Esoteric Buddhism *krodha-vighnāntaka* move out from under the shadow of a bodhisattva and step into the spotlight. As Foucher notes with a hint of dismay, this unruly throng of wrathful deities has jostled its way into the company of their superiors. Yamāntaka, for instance, who had appeared as one of Mañjuśrī's minions, now appears as a powerful deity in his own right. So too with Hayagrīva. Images of *krodha-vighnāntaka* appear alone, or as part of larger groupings (*maṇḍala*) which are unrelated to a Phase One bodhisattva entourage. The identity of the *krodha-vighnāntaka* class also undergoes transformation. A number of fierce *krodha-vighnāntaka* deities emerge as manifestations of Vajrapāṇi. They replace Vajrapuruṣa, who as an *āyudhapuruṣa* is moored to a subordinate Phase One context. This substitution signals a growth in status for the *krodha-vighnāntaka*, for while in origin they may have been *āyudhapuruṣa* or *dhāraṇīpuruṣa*, now they are much more.

Concomitant with independent depictions of the wrathful deities is the individualization and specialization of their iconographic characteristics. In Phase One we saw that in many cases the *krodha-vighnāntaka* were virtually interchangeable, so that Yamāntaka for instance is sometimes nearly indistinguishable from Hayagrīva. The *krodha-vighnāntaka* were employed to glorify the bodhisattva. Each bodhisattva is distinguished iconographically, but the wrathful attendant need not be. Due to a consistent association in the texts of a particular *krodha-vighnāntaka* with a single bodhisattva (i.e., Hayagrīva with Avalokiteśvara, Yamāntaka with Mañjuśrī) it is often necessary, and possible, to identify the bodhisattva before the wrathful attendant can be named.

The iconography of Phase Two *krodha-vighnāntaka* becomes by contrast more consistently and more obviously defined. Yamāntaka, for example, is routinely given six arms, heads and legs and a buffalo mount. Trailokyavijaya, one of Vajrapāṇi's wrathful manifestations, makes a particular identifying *mudrā*. In these ways the *krodha-vighnāntaka* begin to stand apart from one another by acquiring a stable iconographic profile or "personality."

Iconographic differentiation was the inevitable result of independence. Without a program of identifying marks, recognition of a solitary figure would be impossible. Independent representation brought with it a host of other interrelated considerations as well. The basically hieratic structure of Esoteric Buddhist art requires an unambiguous focus. A subsidiary figure removed from its original context unchanged does not suffice as a central image. The typical Phase One *krodha-vighnāntaka* regards the bodhisattva reverently and salutes him with the *vandana* gesture. Such laterally oriented gestures are inappropriate to a primary image. They create an open or unfinished composition, failing to meet the demand for a complete and self-contained image.

Another new trend is generally evident. The tendency for Phase One *krodha-vighnāntaka* to be two-armed, or at most four-armed, limited efforts to represent infinite power and directed wrath. It is not surprising then that Phase Two *krodha-vighnāntaka* images are inclined to be multi-armed, multi-headed and much more aggressive in stance, gesture and facial expression. Those taken over from Phase One contexts, including Yamāntaka and Hayagrīva, were ferociously transformed.

The visual changes in depictions of the *krodha-vighnāntaka* were embedded in a much broader shift in Esoteric Buddhism. They are overt signs of a fundamental, but in many ways subtle, reorientation of Esoteric Buddhism as a whole. The changes coincide with the emergence of a new type of Esoteric Buddhist text, one in which the change of status of the *krodha-vighnāntaka* is acknowledged. Yet the revaluing of Esoteric Buddhism is far and away much more revolutionary than our topic alone would suggest. The revised treatment of the wrathful deities was but one symptom of change among many. Together the changes constituted the formation of a paradigm out of the earlier unsystematized practices and beliefs. The depth of the change is reflected in the Japanese separation of *zomitsu* ("mixed, or miscellaneous esotericism"), which describes pre-eighth century Chinese Esoteric Buddhism, and *jumitsu* ("pure esotericism"), defined in Phase Two texts. The new Esoteric Buddhist system centers around the cosmic Buddha Mahāvairocana and has as its operative sign the *maṇḍala*. The *dhāraṇi* practices of the bodhisattva cult and the triadic composition that is its quintessential symbol do live on, but the new movement represents a radical advance toward a compelling and unified system. The progression from Phase One to Phase Two is commensurate with Thomas Kuhn's differentiation of a pre-paradigm period (Phase One) and its subsequent paradigm-ordered disciplinary matrix.[1] We must briefly outline the composition of the new system before examining its *krodha-vighnāntaka*.

142. *Mahāvairocana Buddha, Udayagiri (Orissa), ca. 10th century, same as* **140**

The Structure of the New Paradigm

What had formerly mattered was following the sequences of ideas and the whole intellectual mosaic of a Game with rapid attentiveness, practiced memory, and full understanding. But there now arose the demand for a deeper and more spiritual approach. After each symbol conjured up by the director of a Game, each player was required to perform silent, formal meditation on the content, origin, and meaning of this symbol, to call to mind intensively and organically its full purport. . . . In this way the hieroglyphs of the Game were kept from degenerating into mere empty signs.

Hermann Hesse, *The Glass Bead Game*

Leading Tenets

It was probably in the seventh century that the new paradigm first appeared within a narrow but ever-widening circle. Mature Esoteric Buddhism coalesces around the syncretic integrating symbol of the five Tathāgata *maṇḍala*: Mahāvairocana at the center and four other cosmic Buddhas at the primary directions.[2] The nucleus of the *maṇḍala* unifies various elements of earlier Mahāyāna on which the (unknown) formulators drew, as well as new conclusions derived from older propositions. These disparate elements included the Mādhyamika notion of the ultimate emptiness (*śūnyatā*) of all phenomena,[3] as expounded most brilliantly by Nāgārjuna and in the *Prajñāpāramitā* literature. Also essential was the Yogācāra understanding that *saṁsāra* and *nirvāṇa* are not different from each other, but that through praxis what is impure in the mind can be realized as pure. Derived at least in part from this was the new idea that ultimate enlightenment and Buddhahood could be achieved in this very life.[4] Underlying the new Esoteric Buddhism are the notion of the *trikāya*, the three bodies of the Buddha, and the associated idea of a cosmic Buddha, the *dharmakāya*, only just beginning to be represented as an adorned Buddha.

In addition several strands of thought and practice were taken up from the Esoteric Buddhist movement we have identified as Phase One. The use of *mudrā* with *dhāraṇī* is one important such strand. A second is the idea of ordering the pantheon of deities into families, or *kula*, which was expanded from the three to the five family system (*pañcakula*) to accommodate the five Tathāgata *maṇḍala*.[5] Ancient aspects of Indian religion that had surfaced in the early Phase One movement were also integrated into the new paradigm, such as female deities, yogic practices and patterns of thought which equated the macrocosm and the microcosm of the body, the *homa* fire-altar and other magical ritual practices. Last but not least, to the wrathful deities' Phase One functions were added broader responsibilities, and they were also raised considerably in status and prominence.

Welding together disparate elements derived from philosophical, meditational and cultic aspects of Mahāyāna Buddhism was no mean feat. Part of the strength binding the whole was a firmly grasped intention to personally realize the nature of existence and directly experience *saṁsāra* and *nirvāṇa*. The goal of attaining Buddhahood in the present life is to be achieved by uniting the human body, speech and mind with those of the deity and realizing that unity. The Shingon master Kōbō Daishi expressed the ambition:

> *If a Shingon practitioner carefully observes the meaning of this, forming mudrās with the hands, reciting mantras with the mouth, dwelling in samādhi with the mind, then the three secrets bring about the response of empowerment and he quickly attains great enlightenment.*[6]

The fifteenth century Tibetan commentator Kaygrubjay, in a discourse on "Yoga Tantra," echoes Kōbō Daishi:

> *The chief requirement is that the vulgar body, speech, and mind, together with their conduct, be transmuted into the Buddha's Body, Speech, and Mind, together with their Marvelous Action.*[7]

Compared to the motivations and aims of the Phase One movement, Phase Two Esoteric Buddhism was a movement characterized by a higher religious striving.

These aims were carried out through the liturgical ritual, involving consecration, personal meditation and communal performance. The ritual has a regular sequence which varies only slightly. There are one or more stages of preparation, during which the ground (literal or figurative) is prepared by eliminating obstructions and hostile forces. The outer protective border is established and the person of the adept guarded. Confession and purification comes next, along with the realization of *śūnyatā*, and then offerings are made. *Homa* rites may also be performed. The deities of the *maṇḍala* are visualized or "emanated" (*utpatti krama*) and contact is made with them. Empowerment (*adhiṣṭhāna*), union, realization and identification with the deity (*ahamkāra*) and consubstantiation (*utpanna krama*) is then achieved. The special powers or wisdoms associated with each deity are appropriated. Offerings are consecrated and the deities dispersed. A final invocation and dedication of merit for the benefit of all is made.

Though all stages are important, the stage critical to the successful performance of the rite is the visualization of the deities in the *maṇḍala* and an understanding of their symbolism.[8] The visual symbol of the five Tathāgata *maṇḍala* is critical in this regard because it serves excellently to coordinate a vast range of Buddhist teachings. It accommodates all levels of interpretation, from the most abstract philosophical (the five buddhas representing the five kinds of wisdom) to *diesseitig* magic, for the form of the symbol lends itself to amuletic purposes. Besides the five directions (center and primary directions), the five *skandha* are distributed to the Tathāgatas, as well as the five different kinds of wisdom, five different kinds of *samskār*ic binding agents (i.e., the *kleśa*: ignorance, wrath, greed etc.), the five elements, the five sense-organs, and five *cakra* (energy centers) in the body. The list goes on to include colors, *mudrā*, *bīja*, *vāhana* and *kula*, to name just a few, all ordered into a pentad which preserves the essentially mystic combination of unity within multiplicity.[9]

All these ideas are condensed into a five Tathāgata *maṇḍala*.[10] The five Tathāgata also represent in a concentrated form all Buddha throughout the infinite chiliocosm who are mentioned in Mahāyāna *sūtra*s like the *Avataṁsaka sūtra*. As Iyanaga has pointed out, Amoghavajra understood the five Tathāgata to represent the innumerable Buddha of the *dharmakāya* who, as an assembly, take the form of these five. Kōbō Daishi similarly took the five Tathāgata as a defining marker of Esoteric Buddhism, in explicit distinction from the Buddha of the Ten Directions associated with exoteric Buddhism.[11]

The essential Phase Two Esoteric Buddhist *maṇḍala* was conventionally expanded to include the consorts of the four Tathāgata (as emanations of the central deity) at the secondary directions, and four *krodha-vighnāntaka* at the gates to the *maṇḍala*, which was visualized as a kind of cosmic palace.[12] Eight offering deities, generally considered female, were arranged within the *maṇḍala* to symbolize the various offerings made: incense, flowers, perfume, song, and so on. Bodhisattva belonging to the five families were sometimes added.[13] Like the expandable nuclear triad which we saw was the emblematic structure for Mahāyāna and Phase One Esoteric Buddhist imagery, the five Tathāgata *maṇḍala* also lends itself to essential condensation as well as nearly infinite expansion.

The five Tathāgatas additionally may be replaced by their consorts (properly, their Prajñā) or, most interesting to us, by their wrathful manifestations. We will find that there are *krodha maṇḍala* which belong to this paradigm. Far from being merely personifications of either the bodhisattva's attributes or *dhāraṇī*, the new formulation of Esoteric Buddhism allows the *krodha-vighnāntaka* actually to substitute for and represent the five Tathāgata. We will go into more details below, but first we must discuss the textual evidence for where and how this movement emerged.

The power of the new formulation for Buddhists of different camps is apparent in the variety of types of texts in which the new paradigm is found. At around the same time, we find *sūtra* literature (*MVS*), philosophical *Prajñāpāramitā* literature (*Adhyardhaśatikā Prajñāpāramitā*), *maṇḍala* and *sādhana* descriptions, ritual manuals for chanting poetic eulogies (*Mañjuśrīnāmasaṁgīti*), magical-rite literature (*Sarvadurgatipariśodhana* [hereafter, *SDPS*]), and at times *purāṇa*-like mythology in a Buddhist cloak (sections of the *STTS*). All used similar language, metaphors, deities and practices for a common end.[14] The most important early *sūtra* to mark the transition from Phase One to Phase Two is the *Mahāvairocana Sūtra*, featuring Mahāvairocana at the center of the *maṇḍala*. He preaches in response to the questions and comments of Vajrapāṇi "at the vast palace of Vajra-*dharmadhātu*," to a huge celestial audience.[15] A similar audience, setting and group of locutors are found in the *Adhyardhaśatikā Prajñāpāramitā* and the *STTS*, which began to be translated into Chinese at about the same time as the *MVS*, that is, at the end of the first quarter of the eighth century.[16]

In the *sūtra* named for him, Mahāvairocana instructs on very heterogenous matters, which range from observations of great profundity and abstractness[17] to *mudrā* and *mantra* instructions, and general teachings about obtaining *abhiṣeka* initiation from a proper master. Somewhat more unified and consistent in tone and content is the *STTS*. Once again it is Mahāvairocana who preaches before a myriad of bodhisattva and celestial beings.

Both this new spokesperson and the transcendental site are substantial changes from previous *sūtra* literature, even from the early Esoteric Buddhist texts like the *MMK* and the *Mahābala Sūtra*. Generally Mahāyāna literature features Śākyamuni preaching in some earthly location that is historically or traditionally linked to his biography, such as Rajgir, Vaisali or Sravasti. Here instead we have texts preached by the cosmic Buddha Mahāvairocana in settings which "make no claim whatsoever to historicity . . . [and are] revealed by the Lord . . . in a transcendent sphere of existence."[18] Yet the basic *saṁgīti* format of a Buddha preaching to an audience of monks, bodhisattva and other sentient beings is maintained even as the main speaker and locale are transformed. This is significant because Phase Three literature abandons entirely the format of Phase One.

Another identifying characteristic of Phase Two texts is the five Tathāgata *maṇḍala* with Mahāvairocana at the center. Some Phase Two texts, for example the *SDPS*, preserve the older personalities in the introductory sections, but feature Mahāvairocana at the center of the five Tathāgata *maṇḍala*. Primary Phase Two texts like the *MVS* and the *STTS* rely throughout on this core emblem. The later Phase Three Esoteric Buddhist texts which feature Hevajra, Saṃvara and Kalacakra, tend to abandon the *saṁgīti* format for another and substitute Akṣobhya, Vajrasattva or Vajradhara for Mahāvairocana at the center of the five Tathāgata *maṇḍala*. Phase Three *maṇḍala* also tend to surround the central deity with eight female consorts, though the five Tathāgata *maṇḍala* does survive alongside it. Further discussion of the differences between Phase Two and Three texts and images is deferred until the next section.

When and where these Phase Two texts arose is a vexed question.[19] They were in use in both eastern India and Kashmir in the ninth and tenth centuries, and translations into Chinese began in the early eighth century. On the other hand, the sixth-century Gilgit texts do not include five Tathāgata *maṇḍala* or any of the known texts. Therefore a date of the early or mid seventh century for the formation of the *MVS* and the *STTS* seems reasonable.[20]

The preceding must serve as a very general introduction to the intricacies of Phase Two philosophy, practices and origins, as well as a set of its working assumptions.[21] This background allows us to begin to examine the role of the *krodha-vighnāntaka* within the system. Focusing on a few of the Phase Two texts will facilitate the examination. The most important of the texts in terms of recognized impact and widespread acceptance are the *Mahāvairocana Sūtra* and the *STTS*. The two "form the basis of Japanese Tantric Buddhist tradition," while for the Tibetans, the "chief of all Tantras of the Caryā Tantra class is the *Mahāvairocana-ābhisambodhi-tantra*," and "the fundamental one of all the Yoga Tantras is the *Tattvasaṁgraha*."[22] These texts are particularly accessible because their significance within the two living traditions has drawn considerable attention from scholars. We will proceed to examine them for a sense of the *krodha-vighnāntaka* and their new roles. This will be followed by a briefer look at some less foundational texts to show how widespread were the ideas we discover in the *MVS* and the *STTS*. Later on we will investigate the specifics of the iconography of individual *krodha-vighnāntaka*, but first we must orient the *krodha-vighnāntaka* within the new paradigm of Phase Two.

Notes to Chapter Eight

1 See Kuhn, *Scientific Revolutions*. The chapter epigraph comes from Alfred Foucher, *Étude sur l'iconographie Bouddhique de l'inde, d'après des textes inédits* (Paris, 1905), 61.

2 The standard arrangement has at center Mahāvairocana; to the east Akṣobhya; the south Ratnasambhava; the west Amitāyus; and the north Amoghasiddhi. Names and positions sometimes vary. The *Mahāvairocana-Sūtra* arrangement has at center Mahāvairocana; to the east Ratnaketu Tathāgata; the south Samkusumita-rāja Tathāgata; the west Amitāyus; and the north Divya-dundubhi-meghanirghoṣa Tathāgata. See Tajima, "Les Deux Grands Maṇḍalas," 65. The section epigraph is from Hermann Hesse, *The Glass Bead Game (Magister Ludi)*, trans. Richard and Clara Winston (New York, 1969), 38-39.

3 "All the many phenomena arising from the mind, they are all empty like this (i.e. like a magician's illusion)." (*MVS*) T.18.848.41a.

4 "Despite seeking it for innumerable *kalpa*s while performing austerities, it will not be attained. But all bodhisattva who cultivate the practices of *dhāraṇī* will in this very life attain it [*samyaksambodhi*]." (*MVS*) T.18.848.19b; Yamamoto, 76. I am indebted to the English translation of Yamamoto. It allows English readers to rapidly acquire an overall sense of the text, but the translation presents problems of interpretation beyond those of awkward English. Therefore, in most passages of the *MVS* included here, I have translated directly from the Chinese text and cited both the Chinese text and Yamamoto's translation. Also see an abstract of the *MVS* by Robert Duquenne, "On Realizing Buddhahood in One's Body," *Transactions of the International Conference of Orientalists in Japan* 26 (1981): 148-149.

5 For deity "families" in Esoteric Buddhism, see Alex Wayman, "Totemic Beliefs in the Buddhist Tantras," *History of Religions* 1.1 (1961): 81-94.

6 Quoted in Taikō Yamasaki, *Shingon: Japanese Esoteric Buddhism*, trans. Richard and Cynthia Peterson (Boston, 1988), 107.

7 Lessing and Wayman, *Mkhas-grub-rje's*, 241.

8 In Saunders's conception the adept enters and interiorizes the iconography of the deity, an activity that is more than "simply looking at a given statue and being aware of its symbolism." It is neither "imagining" nor "passively receiving," but "a quickening of one's inner forces in concert with given cosmic forces." E. Dale Saunders, "Some Tantric Techniques," in *Studies of Esoteric Buddhism and Tantrism* (Koyasan, 1965), 169. The same point is made by Shotaro Iida, who states that "vision is never simply a picture or an image; it is always accompanied by strong emotion and deep understanding." Shotaro Iida, "Toward a Second Look at Visual Mode in Buddhist Tradition," in *Facets of Buddhism* (Delhi, 1991), 44.

9 See the extended discussion of the symbolism of the five Tathāgata in Giuseppe Tucci, *The Temples of Western Tibet and Their Artistic Symbolism: The Monasteries of Spiti and Kunavar (Indo-Tibetica III.1)*, trans. Uma Marina Vesci et al and ed. Lokesh Chandra (New Delhi, 1988), 145-159.

10 For an important treatise on the definition, structure and symbolism of the Phase Two *maṇḍala* as understood by an 8th c. Esoteric Buddhist master, see Eberto Lo Bue, "The Dharmamaṇḍala-Sūtra by Buddhaguhya," in *Orientalia Iosephi Tucci Memoriae Dicata Serie Orientale Roma* no. 56 (Rome 1987) 2: 787-818. Buddhaguhya understood the *maṇḍala* as a cosmic "royal residence" on Mt. Sumeru for the five Tathāgata. Every aspect of this citadel, its domes, the gateways, their beams, posts, capitals, etc. has symbolic meaning. Buddhaguhya's interpretation was directly rooted in the primary Phase Two texts.

11 Iyanaga, "Récits de la Soumission," 660-661, note 8.

12 Alex Wayman, "Contributions on the Symbolism of the Maṇḍala-Palace," in *Études Tibétaines dédiées à la mémoire de Marcelle Lalou* (Paris, 1971), 557-566.

13 See Snellgrove, *Indo-Tibetan Buddhism*, 209-213.

14 See Edward Conze, "The *Adhyardhaśatikā Prajñāpāramitā*," in *Studies of Esoteric Buddhism and Tantrism* (Koyasan, 1965), 101-115; idem, "Tantric Prajñāpāramitā Texts," 101-102, 107-108; and, Ronald M. Davidson, "The *Litany of Names of Mañjuśrī*: Text and Translation of the *Mañjuśrīnāmasaṁgīti*," in *Tantric and Taoist Studies in Honour of R.A. Stein*, ed. Michel Strickmann (Brussels, 1981), 1-69. This is a Phase Two text which states it is a section of the *Māyājāla* and which Davidson has shown to be derived ultimately from the *STTS*. "*Litany of Names of Mañjuśrī*," 2-4. It seems to have actually been better known among Buddhists than the *MMK*. It was translated into Chinese in the 12th c. (T.18.1188) and twice in the early 14th c. by a Tibetan (T.18.1190) and a disciple of Phagpa, who may have been a Tangut (T.18.1189). Also see Skorupski, *Sarvadurgatipariśodhana*.

15 T.18.848. *Mahāvairocana-ābhisambhodhivikurvitādhiṣṭhānā-vaipulya sūtra*, translated by Śubhakarasiṁha and Yixing ca. 724 CE. For an annotated discussion of the Chinese translation and Sino-Japanese commentarial tradition, see Iyanaga, "Récits de la Soumission," 649-655; Yamamoto, 1; and, Alex Wayman and R. Tajima, *The Enlightenment of Vairocana* (Delhi: Motilal Banarsidass, 1992).

16 For the *STTS*, see T.18.865, 866, 882. The edited Sanskrit text is found in Isshi Yamada, *Sarvatathāgatatattvasaṁgraha* (New Delhi, 1981); and a facsimile of a 10th c. Sanskrit copy in Lokesh Chandra and David L. Snellgrove, eds., *Sarva-tathāgata-tattva-saṅgraha* (New Delhi, 1981).

17 Yamamoto, 3.

18 Snellgrove, *Buddhist Himalaya*, 55. For an analysis of these two types of texts which is similar to my own, though framed as the difference between "Miscellaneous Esoteric Buddhism" and "Pure Esotericism," see Yukei Matsunaga, "Tantric Buddhism and Shingon Buddhism," *The Eastern Buddhist* 2.2 (1969): 5-7.

19 See Linrothe, "Compassionate Malevolence," 267-270.

20 "Tantra texts in this sense cannot be proved to have existed before the 7th century, though some of the elements constituting the Tantras may have existed before that time." Moriz Winternitz, "Notes on the *Guhyasamāja-Tantra* and the Age of the Tantras," *The Indian Historical Quarterly* 9 (1933): 8. Y. Matsunaga and others accept a date of the mid-7th c. for the *MVS*, and the end of the 7th c. for the truncated form of the *STTS*. See Y. Matsunaga, "Tantric Buddhism," 10-11; idem "Indian Esoteric Buddhism as Studied in Japan," in *Studies of Esoteric Buddhism and Tantrism* (Koyasan, 1965), 235, 237. Other references for these dates are found in Charles Willemen, *The Chinese Hevajratantra*, 12-13, notes 15,16. Iyanaga concludes that the *terminus a quo* for the *STTS* is the early 7th c. and its *terminus ad quem* is Śubhakarasiṁha's arrival in China, i.e., 716 CE. Iyanaga, "Récits de la Soumission," 727.

21 My Phase Two has much in common with the Tibetan text classification category of "Yoga-tantra," which many scholars use to define a type of Esoteric Buddhist practice. Phase Two also largely corresponds to the type of Esoteric Buddhism accepted in Japan and practiced as Shingon ("True Word"), eliminating the developments largely creditable to Kōbō Daishi, Saichō, and the important masters working in China. With this in mind, a broader overview and more detail can be derived from a number of excellent studies on Esoteric Buddhism. These include Giuseppe Tucci, "The Religious Ideas: Vajrayāna," in *Tibetan Painted Scrolls*, 1:209-249; Snellgrove's *Buddhist Himalaya*, which remains a trustworthy guide 35 years after its publication; his more recent *Indo-Tibetan Buddhism*; Wayman's "Introduction to Buddhist Tantrism," in *Yoga of the Guhya-samājatantra*; Dasgupta's *An Introduction to Tantric Buddhism*; and Yamasaki's *Shingon: Japanese Esoteric Buddhism*, all of which already have been cited.

22 Japanese: Minoru, *Shingon Buddhism*, 18; Tibetan: Lessing and Wayman, *Mkhas-grub-rje's*, 205, 215.

9

New Texts, New Functions

Now it seems possible . . . to ascribe to the 'terrifying' deities a function agreeing with their actual character. In this way it becomes clear how and why their more important task is the furtherance of the believers' striving after supreme understanding, whereas their character as 'guardians of the doctrine' is relegated to the status of a secondary explanation.

P. H. Pott, *Yoga and Yantra*

1 Mahavairocana-Sutra

In Yixing and Śubhakarasiṁha's 724 CE translation of the *Mahāvairocana-Sūtra* (*MVS*, T.18.848), only three *krodha-vighnāntaka* are singled out for special attention: Acala, Trailokyavijaya and Hayagrīva. Hayagrīva alone is familiar from Phase One contexts. The other two seem to be new. Hayagrīva is not as important in the *MVS* as the other two and is not mentioned as often. When he is named, it is as a member of Avalokiteśvara's *parivāra*-entourage, along with Tārā, Bhṛikutī and Pāṇḍaravāsinī. It is clear that his earlier presence in Phase One contexts has been maintained but not transformed. He is described as follows:

> *The Vidyārāja who holds great power, he is the color of the morning sun, adorned with a white lotus, encircled with flames. He roars frightfully, his fangs protruding. His talons are sharp and his hair is a lion's mane. This is Hayagrīva.*[1]

Aside from this description, which contains nothing new, as well as the register of his *dhāraṇī* and an occasional entry in lists of Avalokiteśvara's entourage, very little is said about Hayagrīva regarding his capacities or functions. The text devotes a markedly greater amount of attention to Acala and Trailokyavijaya.

1.1 Acala

Acala is mentioned in conjunction with Trailokyavijaya on a number of occasions in the *MVS*. Several duties are assigned to both or to either of them. Nevertheless,

143. *Acala, eastern India, metalwork, ca. 11th century, author's collection*

they maintain enough individual autonomy to justify treating them separately here, after pointing out that there is a significant overlap.

The task of *bandhāya-siman* is usually the first step in the Esoteric Buddhist ritual procedure.[2] The exercise secures the boundaries and purifies the grounds where the *maṇḍala* will be constructed and rituals will take place. It is an important preliminary stage which ensures that the rite will not be contaminated by impure objects and actions. It also protects the adept who is about to unleash potentially overpowering spiritual forces. Acala is called upon for this critical task of "holding ground"[3] to ensure the adept is not besieged when most vulnerable by impure outside forces, demons or Māra's hordes. Acala's power to maintain sacred ground may account for his distinctive posture in South Asian images, in which he literally puts his knee to the ground. **[143]**

The previous section cited passages of Phase One texts in which the *krodha-vighnāntaka* are called upon to perform duties similar to those of Acala. Phase Two texts depart significantly from the nature of Phase One by advancing the tasks out of the realm of magic into the realm of spiritual, or psychological, endeavor. More precisely, the magical and the spiritual are allowed to co-exist. The *MVS* offers an expressly inner interpretation of these "outer" (even if invisible) attacks of demons, impurities and obstacles. Chapter Three of the *MVS*, entitled "Cessation of Hindrances," equates present obstacles and past actions (i.e., *karmic* debt), and the role of Acala in eliminating both is set forth by Mahāvairocana:

> *Obstacles derive from one's own mind, following from past parsimonious actions. In order to rid oneself of the causes, meditate on the bodhicitta, eliminating false distinctions arising from one's own thoughts. Recall and hold the thought of enlightenment (bodhicitta), and the adept will leave behind the whole past. Often one should think of Acala Mahāsattva, and, making his secret mudrā, one can do away with all obstructions.*[4]

Later in the chapter Mahāvairocana makes clear that the image of Acala is called up to destroy one's own *karmic* obstacles by saying:

> *Next I should explain how to put a stop to all obstructions. Meditate on the dhāraṇī of great fierceness, that of Acala-Mahābala. Reside (one's mind) in his original maṇḍala. It is as if the adept himself was in the center or else sees this image [of Acala] . . . these obstacles will be destroyed; having been stopped they will not be produced.*[5]

Further on, in Chapter Eleven, "The *Guhya*-secret Maṇḍala," preparing the ground for the *maṇḍala* (in other words, clearing away stones, gravel, bone and other detritus) is equated metaphorically with purifying the mind.[6] The same verbal pun on "ground" seems to be preserved in Sanskrit, Chinese and English, for the earth-ground in Sanskrit is *bhūmi*, while the mental-ground is *citta-bhūmi*. Into the crucial implication of the inner nature of the *maṇḍala*-ritual process, the *krodha-vighnāntaka* are inserted.[7]

The inner aspect is essential to keep in mind whenever Acala, Trailokyavijaya, or any other of the Phase Two *krodha-vighnāntaka* are mentioned. Phase Two ideology always provides an inner explanation for outer actions.[8] To visualize Acala and to perform his *mudrā* and *dhāraṇī* is tantamount, not just to keeping malevolent demons at bay, but to purifying one's inner state. The *MVS* states directly that Acala's ritual is effective in "averting all obstacles which rise out of oneself."[9] This is not to say that the demons which most of us might now reject as superstitious projections are not taken to be real by practitioners. But it does demonstrate that they have another dimension, and that the *krodha-vighnāntaka* themselves become in this sense symbols for the elimination of the practitioner's inner obstacles to enlightenment.

This "inner," "secret," or metaphorical meaning is not merely a modern projection. Iyanaga has focused attention on portions of the early eighth-century commentary on the *MVS* by Yixing, based on Śubhakarasiṁha's teachings. They substantiate our appeal to interpret the actions of the *krodha-vighnāntaka* in destroying obstacles as metaphors for the internal yogic processes employed to gain enlightenment. The following passage comments on portions of the *MVS* dealing with the elimination of all obstructions by Acala. The commentary describes in detail a rite in which the adept draws a picture of the obstruction inside a triangular altar. Acala is within the altar, and the practitioner visualizes his own body as that of Acala, who stamps his foot on the head of the image of the obstruction, which will then take rapid flight. If it does not, the demon will be cut off from its life-force. The commentary interprets this drama for us:

> *There is a secret sense to this: that which is called the Obstruction, are those dharma such as Avarice and Desire which are produced in the mind: it is these which cause all sorts of Obstruction to the practitioner. The Vidyārāja Acala acting here is the Great Mind of Enlightenment, Omniscient Wisdom: it is necessary to realize that this Mind is a great force with a powerful ferocity; it is capable of destroying for ever the faults that remain. It cuts off [the Obstructions] for ever, that is, they are put to death.*[10]

In other passages of the *MVS*, Acala is described as "the great obstacle smasher," whose *dhāraṇī* is revealed by Mahāvairocana, dwelling in *samādhi*, in order to put a stop to all obstructions. Acala is relied on to eliminate stains and to protect the body. The *mudrā* representing Acala's wisdom sword is used to eliminate obstacles and to purify offerings. Rotating the *mudrā* to the right eliminates impurities, to the left removes obstacles. These aims of protection, purification and the removal of obstacles are extended in the case of Acala to the sacralization of mundane activities such as eating and bathing.[11] As Jishu Oda explains:

> *[Acala] guards and protects the practiser at all times and bestows on him long life, recovering from him, as offering, food that is left over. He is the god who completes the bodhi of the practiser. His partaking of the food which is left over signifies the extinction of all defilements.*[12]

One other point is worth noting at this stage. Acala's *dhāraṇī*, which are given in more than one passage of the *MVS*, use his alternate name, Caṇḍa Mahārosaṇa, "The Fierce and Greatly Wrathful One."[13] This provides a significant link with the later Phase Three transformation of Acala, where he is primarily known as Caṇḍamahārosaṇa. In this early Phase Two text the epithet is embedded in his *dhāraṇī* and is probably descriptive rather than titular. But it will grow to signify a deity whose importance is central and at the heart of his own *maṇḍala* and Esoteric Buddhist text, the *Caṇḍamahāroṣaṇa Tantra*.[14]

In the *MVS* Acala is described in the main *maṇḍala* of Chapter Two:

> *Below the Lord of Mantra [Mahāvairocana], in the nirṛti (south-west) position is Acala, servant of the Tathāgata. He holds a sword of discrimination and a pāśa-noose. His hair falls from the top of his head onto his left shoulder. He has one eye which squints intently. His awe-inspiring and wrathful body emanates flames. He sits serenely on a round rock. His forehead is marked by [frown] lines like waves on the sea, but his form is that of a completely filled youth; this is he who is filled with prajñā.*[15]

Although we will be unable to pursue this topic further here, Chinese and Japanese images of Acala resemble this description, though South Asian images **[143]** consistently deploy a different pose.[16]

1.2 Trailokyavijaya

As already mentioned, Trailokyavijaya appears together with Acala in a number of passages of the *MVS*. In one place he is listed after Acala, as an alternate choice for securing the ground (literal and metaphorical) of the *maṇḍala*.[17] Another section suggests a division of responsibilities, relying on Acala to eliminate impurities and protect the body, while Trailokyavijaya secures the boundaries of the *maṇḍala*.[18] Trailokyavijaya's *dhāraṇī* is also recited in order to sacralize the water used in initiation and, along with Acala's, to assure purification by means of bathing.[19] Another equation with Acala is made when Trailokyavijaya is likewise called one "who smashes the great obstacle-makers," though this may be an epithet for all members of the class.[20]

The standard Genzu *garbhadhātu maṇḍala* of Japan, is based on a combination of three sources: the *MVS*, the commentary written down by Yixing according to Śubhakarasiṁha's teaching, and oral traditions.[21] In it Trailokyavijaya figures three times. He appears in the *vidyādhara* quarter as Vajrahūṃkāra and Trailokyavijaya, and once in the Vajrapāṇi quarter as Candratilaka.[22] This seems to have been accurately forecast in the *MVS*, when in the course of describing the Guhya-*maṇḍala* Mahāvairocana explains that Trailokyavijaya dwells in three stations.[23]

However, only two of the three forms of Trailokyavijaya actually found in the *maṇḍala* are spelled out in the *MVS*. Candratilaka is described as the form of Trailokyavijaya who accompanies Vajrapāṇi:

> *Below Vajrapāṇi is the krodha Trailokyavijaya, who smashes all great obstacles, called Candratilaka. Three eyes and four fangs protrude, in color he is like a summer storm cloud. Laughing out A TA TA, he is adorned with diamonds and jewels. Because he assists and protects all sentient beings, he is surrounded by uncountable beings. He has a hundred thousand hands, wielding various āyudha.*[24]

Twice Trailokyavijaya is described in the text, placed in the corner opposite Acala. In both instances, Trailokyavijaya's only prominent attribute is the *vajra*:

> *Next in the Vayu corner (northwest) again paint the krodha deity, so-called Trailokyavijaya. Awesomely surrounded by flames, with a gem-encrusted crown, holding the vajra, he is unconcerned for his own body and life, but only requests and receives the [Buddhist/Mahāvairocana's] teachings.*[25]

> *In the northwest corner is Trailokyavijaya, who smashes the great obstacle-makers. Above there is an aura of flames. He has great power and awe-inspiring wrath like Yama. He is dark in color and is terrifying in the extreme. His hands twirl a vajra.*[26]

1.3 The vidyādhara section of the maṇḍala

Acala and Trailokyavijaya are placed at either end of the "mansion" of the *vidyādhara* in the *maṇḍala*, in accord with the description given by the *MVS*.[27] This area of the *maṇḍala* is located immediately below (i.e., to the west of) the central section with the five Tathāgata and is considered to be part of this central section.[28] The *MVS* specifies here only these two *krodha-vighnāntaka*, but instructs its readers to envision the empty space as filled with innumerable and varying *vajra*-holders. To represent the rest of these wisdom-holders, the standard form of the *maṇḍala* transmitted to Japan adds Yamāntaka and a second form of Trailokyavijaya (Vajrahūṃkāra) along with the female bodhisattva Prajñāpāramitā.[29] The Tibetan tradition, as represented by the

Ngor collection, follows the *MVS* literally by including only Acala and Trailokyavijaya.[30]

According to the exegetical tradition as transcribed by Snodgrass:

The [vidyādhara] mansion belongs to the Buddha section. It represents the path of the undivided (mukendō), in which the passions are completely cut away and Right Wisdom is manifested; it represents Mahāvairocana's "virtue of severance" (dantoku), his virtue of severing the passions, delusions and karma. The Mansion brings together the wrathful figures who obey the command of the Tathāgata by directing their fury against the beings who are unamenable to less violent forms of influence and who use anger to destroy the obstacles to Awakening. . . . Acalanatha and Trailokyavijaya represent the beginning and completion of the virtue of severance.[31]

Enough evidence has already been presented to spell out a major shift in the status and function of the *krodha-vighnāntaka* as they are described in Phase One texts. They are no longer merely sent by bodhisattva to gather together and to intimidate the recalcitrant beings of the universe and protect the human aspirants. Now they are intimately involved in the primary task of Esoteric Buddhism: the transformation of the passions and ignorance into compassion and wisdom. The command of the *krodha-vighnāntaka* is given not just to the bodhisattva, as it was in Phase One texts and imagery, but also to the Buddha. The *krodha-vighnāntaka* remain associated with bodhisattva in the *MVS* in so far as Hayagrīva remains within the Avalokiteśvara section (*padmakula*) and Candratilaka-Trailokyavijaya is in the Vajrapāṇi section (*vajrakula*). But both are also now brought into the central section (*Tathāgathakula*), where they personify the symbolic attributes of the Tathāgatas themselves.

2 Sarvatathagata-tattvasamgraha

The title of the *STTS* has been rendered into English as the "Compendium of Truth of all the Buddhas."[32] This name is actually found only as part of the title of the fifth and last section. The first four parts refer to themselves as *kalpa-rāja* and set down ritual prescriptions. The fifth and final part "assumes a knowledge of the actual rituals and represents a 'thread of discourse' conducted by Buddha (still understood as Vairocana) and the Bodhisattvas who lead the various Buddha-families."[33] The *STTS* was understood, in East Asia as well as Tibet, as forming one section of a vast cycle of texts known as the *Vajraśekhara*.[34]

Vajrabodhi translated into Chinese portions of the text in 723 CE (T.18.866). Amoghavajra translated the first part (Chapters 1-5) into Chinese in 753 CE (T.18.865), but the entire text in five sections and twenty-six chapters was not translated into Chinese until Dānapāla finished it between 1012 and 1015 CE.[35] The Japanese did not acquire the entire *STTS* until the late eleventh century,[36] but even before that they were aware of more of the contents than merely the first section. This is easily demonstrated by the fact that in the Shingon Vajradhātu *maṇḍala* five of the nine separate *maṇḍala* derive from the first section of the *STTS*, and the last two *maṇḍala*, the Trailokyavijaya and Trailokyavijaya Samaya *maṇḍala*, belong to the second part of the *STTS*. (The precise origin of the remaining Naya *maṇḍala* is unknown.) Moreover, Amoghavajra translated short treatises on individual deities which seem to derive either from later sections of the *STTS* or from the *Vajraśekhara*, and he summarized the contents of the first four sections of the *STTS* in another text.[37] Iyanaga has also convincingly argued that Yixing and Śubhakarasiṁha (or whoever wrote the commentary T.39.1796) had at their disposal "un text assez développé de la Deuxième Section de [*STTS*], déjà proche de la recension qu'a traduite plus tard à Shih-hu [Dānapāla]."[38]

The *STTS* was re-translated into Tibetan by Rinchen Zangpo and Śraddhakāravarma in the eleventh century. The Tibetan, Sanskrit and Dānapāla versions of the *STTS* are in basic agreement.[39] The fact that it was translated into both Tibetan and Chinese around the beginning of the eleventh century testifies to the continuing importance of this text. The translators into Tibetan would have had the benefit of Buddhaguhya's mid-eighth-century commentary and two more written in the ca. tenth century by Śākyamitra and Ānandagarbha.[40]

The *STTS* is a marvelously rich and intricately orchestrated text. Snellgrove worked on this text for a considerable period and included translations of extended passages in several of his works.[41] The most helpful is his lucid and detailed résumé of the contents of the entire text.[42] Tucci, Iyanaga, and Davidson[43] have also dealt with passages from the second section concerning the subjugation of Maheśvara by Vajrapāṇi-Trailokyavijaya. Thus a considerable amount of material has already been sorted out by these eminent scholars. While I have read the relevant chapters of section two in Dānapāla's Chinese version, as well as some of the minor related texts translated into Chinese, I depend significantly on the work of others for my understanding of the *STTS*.

Although Mahāvairocana, together with the other four Tathāgatas, does much of the preaching, Vajrapāṇi is actually the main protagonist throughout the first two sections (Chapters 1-14) and the fifth (Chapters 23-26). Since these chapters constitute seven-ninths of the total text, we may follow Snellgrove by nominating Vajrapāṇi as the "dominating influence."[44] In the *STTS* Vajrapāṇi is also known as Samantabhadra, Vajrasattva, Vajradhara, Vajrahūṃkāra and Trailokyavijaya.

The quintessential Phase Two *maṇḍala* is made up of thirty-seven deities, a structure utilized in all twenty-four *maṇḍala* discussed in the four sections of the *STTS* devoted to the Tathāgata, *vajra*, *padma* and *ratna/karmakula* respectively.[45] The thirty-seven deities can be divided into three types: Buddha, bodhisattva and subsidiary deities. Phase One ideology limited the *krodha-vighnāntaka* to the latter category. In the *STTS* their field of action is expanded to include the bodhisattva as well. The innermost section of the *maṇḍala*, consisting of the five Tathāgatas with Sarvavid Mahāvairocana in the center, remains the exclusive domain of the Buddhas. Surrounding the four Tathāgatas of the primary directions are sixteen bodhisattva, who are divided into four groups. The first is Vajrapāṇi, inseparable from his *krodha-vighnāntaka* form. Others like Mahātejah, destroyer of ignorance, might be included as a wrathful deity, but there is surely no doubt about the inclusion of the fifteenth member, known as both Vajracaṇḍa (Diamond-fierce) and Vajrayakṣa. The text describes his coming into being:

> *Vajradhara becomes a multiplicity of fanged weapons emerging from the hearts of All the Tathāgatas and these become a single one on Vairocana's hand.*

The weapon turns into Vajracaṇḍa, who says:

> *I am the great expedient of the compassionate Buddhas, in that while being gentle they act with fierceness for the benefit of living beings. . . . This is the means of subduing all the enemies of all the Buddhas, a harsh vajra-armour with fangs, an expedient of the compassionate ones.*[46]

The passage demonstrates that like Acala, Yamāntaka and Trailokyavijaya in the *vidyādhara* section of the *MVS*'s *maṇḍala*, these *krodha-vighnāntaka* are now of equal rank to the bodhisattva as personifications of the qualities of the Tathāgata. It is also of considerable interest that Vajracaṇḍa's origin recalls that of Vajrapuruṣa and other Phase One *krodha-vighnāntaka*. Born from a weapon held in Vairocana's hand, the *krodha-vighnāntaka* Vajracandra takes his place in a long line of Esoteric Buddhist *āyudhapuruṣa*.

After the sixteen bodhisattva are generated in the ritual and the *maṇḍala*, the subsidiary deities come forth. First are the four goddesses, consorts of the Tathāgata, representing four *pāramitā* (perfections) and corresponding to the four families (the *ratna* and *karmakula* are conflated at times in the *STTS*, though the five Tathāgata system is maintained). There are no wrathful types among them, nor among the eight subsidiary goddesses who represent the offerings made in the rituals.[47] But the four deities next to appear, who are on par with the goddesses, are all *krodha-vighnāntaka*. These are the four guardians of the gateways, Vajraṅkuśa (Diamond-hook), Vajrapāśa (Diamond-noose), Vajrasphoṭa (Diamond-burst, carrying a chain) and Vajrāveśa/ghaṇṭa (Diamond-enchanter/bell). These *krodha-vighnāntaka* carry on the Phase One tradition of protection. Snellgrove notes that sometimes Hayagrīva replaces Vajraṅkuśa in *maṇḍala* dealing with the *padmakula* to which Hayagriva and Avalokiteśvara belong.[48]

After having studied images of Phase One *krodha-vighnāntaka* and examined the powers credited to them in earlier texts, it is possible to understand the benefits which the *STTS* attributes to union with the four gate-guardians. The practitioner gains unlimited spatial access and the ability to coerce expertly and cast spells everywhere.[49] These are mundane (*laukika*) goals indeed, especially when compared with the goal of union with the five Tathāgata (Buddhahood) or with Vajrapāṇi (as Vajrasattva). Yet these mundane goals are largely the very ones facilitated by Hayagrīva and Yamāntaka in Phase One texts. Being themselves hypostases of Vedic personages, both were singled out as having access to all areas of the universe, and they could coerce and bind recalcitrant beings. The formulators of the new paradigm, versed in the older texts and participating in a similar *Weltanschauung*, maintained the *krodha-vighnāntaka* as guardian deities of relatively minor importance.

However, in accord with the more spiritual outlook of Phase Two texts, the formulators gave these tasks a metaphorical gloss. The four gate guardians are not merely protective deities. They "represent the four stages of introducing the divinities into the *maṇḍala*." Snellgrove explains:

> *Vajraṅkuśa (Vajra-Hook) summons them; Vajrapāśa (Vajra-Noose) draws them in; Vajrasphoṭa (Vajra-Fetter) binds them and Vajrāveśa (Vajra-Penetration) alias Vajra-ghaṇṭa (Vajra-Bell) completes the pervasion of the maṇḍala by wisdom. This fourfold process is clearly defined in . . . [the STTS where] . . . it is said that "all the Great Beings, the buddhas and the others, are summoned, drawn in, bound, so entering his power."*[50]

The creators of the *STTS* saw the peculiar aptness of the wrathful image for more advanced, supramundane (*lokottara*) tasks as well. Even as they penetrate the ranks of the bodhisattva (as Vajrapāṇi and Vajracanda) and their mythological powers are spiritually reconfigured, the *krodha-vighnāntaka* are catapulted to greater status. In section two of the *STTS* the *krodha-vighnāntaka* are featured at the very center of the *maṇḍala*, replacing, or displacing, the Tathāgata.

Five chapters of section two (Chapters 6-10) are devoted to the Trailokyavijaya *maṇḍala* and its permutations (*guhyā*, *samaya*, *karma* and *caturmudrā*), while the other four chapters (Chapters 11-14) are concerned with the Trailokya-cakra *maṇḍala* and its variations.[51] In all these *maṇḍala*, Vajrapāṇi presides in the form of Trailokyavijaya. Other *maṇḍala* have Trailokyavijaya surrounded by the sixteen bodhisattva, all of whom are wrathful. In still others Trailokyavijaya is surrounded by Hindu deities he has converted. In the course of the text, Vajrapāṇi-Trailokyavijaya is actually referred to as "the Lord of All the Tathāgatas,"[52] an astounding epithet, unthinkable in Phase One contexts.

The Trailokyavijaya *maṇḍala* presents him twice, once at the center, replacing Sarvavid Mahāvairocana, and again as the primary deity of the eastern quarter, representing Akṣobhya Buddha and the *vajrakula*. Snellgrove remarks:

> *It is scarcely necessary to observe at this stage that Vajrapāṇi[-Trailokyavijaya] may appear as the equal of Vairocana (the various eulogies make this quite clear), as the chief divinity in his own right, as in the present case, as well as being presiding Bodhisattva of the eastern quarter.*[53]

The specific symbolism of Trailokyavijaya's triumph over Hindu divinities and its meaning as a metaphor for victory over the illusion of self will be discussed later. Here it suffices to perceive him as representative of the class of *krodha-vighnāntaka* as a whole and to emphasize the new distinction bestowed on them by the *STTS*.

3 The Adhyardhasatika Prajñaparamita

The *Adhyardhaśatikā Prajñāpāramitā* has begun to receive the attention it deserves. It has been studied and translated into English by Edward Conze, the authoritative scholar of Prajñāpāramitā literature. Recently Ian Astley-Kristensen has given an annotated translation and dealt comprehensively with the Japanese secondary literature surrounding this important Phase Two text.[54] Conze's translation is based on his examination of the edited Sanskrit and Tibetan texts, as well as Leumann's German translation of the Khotanese version. Though Conze was aware of the six Chinese translations, he did not employ them. The latter range in date from Xuanzang's translation of 660 CE to Dharmabhadra's translation of ca. 1000 CE. I have closely examined only one of the six, Amoghavajra's (T.8.243), translated before 774 CE. According to K. Yu, and confirmed by Astley-Kristensen's work, this text had an important influence on Amoghavajra, as it was his ultimate source for the Esoteric Buddhist *mahāsukha* (great bliss) theories.[55] It is also the version most often read and daily chanted by Japanese Esoteric Buddhists.[56]

The text features Mahāvairocana dwelling in the *kamadhātu* (desire-realm) Paranirmitavaśavartin paradise, preaching along with other Tathāgatas to the great bodhisattva. Chief among these, and the most prominent personage in the text after Mahāvairocana, is Vajrapāṇi. Moreover, it is clear that Vajrapāṇi's wrathful form of Trailokyavijaya is intended. At one point he is described as follows:

> *At this time, Vajrapāṇi Mahāsattva, desiring to more deeply demonstrate the teaching, made the trailokyavijaya mudrā . . . he smiled and frowned angrily, manifesting his sharp fangs. Standing in the posture of subjugating, he spoke this Vajrahūṃkāra hṛdaya HŪṀ.*[57]

The object of the entire text seems to be to demonstrate the effectiveness of the Esoteric Buddhist path to "supreme enlightenment" and its identity with Prajñāpāramitā notions of the ultimate "sameness" of all things and emptiness of all the *dharmas*. As in the *STTS*, one finds here that the five family system is compacted to four.[58] One of the most imporant of the four is the "*dharma*-gate of wrath" or, as Conze translated it, of "frenzy." The bodhisattva "Smashing All Māras" (Sarvamārapramardin) teaches the method of adopting the form of Vajrayakṣa, a *krodha-vighnāntaka* featured in the *STTS* as one of the sixteen bodhisattva of its *maṇḍala*. He holds the Vajra-fang, terrifying all the Tathāgata, and speaks the Vajrakrodha *hṛdaya* of great laughter, *HA*.[59]

This *Prajñāpāramitā* text demonstrates that the new integration of the *krodha-vighnāntaka* into the inner circle of Esoteric Buddhist literature and praxis is not an isolated phenomenon. Vajrapāṇi-Trailokyavijaya and Vajrayakṣa play important roles in the *Adhyardhaśatikā Prajñāpāramitā*, just as they did in the *STTS*. By contrast, in the *Svalpākṣarā Prajñāpāramitā Sūtra* (T.8.258, considered "Tantric" by some because of its emphasis on *dhāraṇī*[60]) Śākyamuni recites the *dhāraṇī* for Avalokiteśvara, and no *krodha-vighnāntaka* are mentioned. The elevated treatment of *krodha-vighnāntaka* is one characteristic of these texts which sets them apart from Phase One texts. Other differences include the use of the five Tathāgata *maṇḍala*, substitution of Mahāvairocana for Śākyamuni, the types of initiations detailed and a stress on supramundane accomplishments.[61] But the status of the *krodha-vighnāntaka* is an indicator at least as telling and can be used more than it has in the past as a means of revealing affinity among texts which are structurally and formally as different as the *MVS*, the *STTS* and the *Adhyardhaśatikā Prajñāpāramitā*.

4 The Sarvadurgatiparisodhana Tantra

One should perhaps begin, rather than end, a survey of the *krodha-vighnāntaka* within Phase Two texts with the *SDPS*, since in some ways it illustrates the transition between Phases One and Two. Its introductory section seems to be its earliest, not only because it adheres to the characteristics of Mahāyāna *saṁgiti* literature with little or nothing Esoteric about it, but also because a version of it appears to have been translated into Chinese as early as 670 CE as the *Sarvadurgatipariśodhana-ushṇīshavijayā-dhāraṇī Sūtra*.[62] Sometime after the early recension had been transmitted to China, it was revised and fitted with *dhāraṇī*, deity and *maṇḍala* more in keeping with Phase Two Esoteric Buddhist interests. In this form it was translated into Tibetan at the end of the eighth century CE by Śāntigarbha (Indian) and Jayarakṣita (Tibetan), and three commentaries on it were written in India in the eighth and ninth centuries. Its importance continued in Tibetan Buddhism, as we see from the fact that Rinchen Zangpo studied it and translated two related texts in the eleventh century.[63]

Despite the presence of *dhāraṇī* and *maṇḍala*, Phase One qualities, most evident in the introductory section, seem to pervade the *SDPS*.[64] Unlike the *MVS* and *STTS*, which give enlightenment pride of place, the *SDPS* is oriented toward mundane accomplishments: preliminary and worldly benefits. As Skorupski explains in his preface, "The whole teaching is geared towards procuring a better rebirth for the dead and a better life for those who are living."[65] It is as if advanced tools and methods are borrowed and retro-fitted onto an earlier text with a narrower agenda. The seams and the joins are legible.

Here it will suffice to leave the *SDPS* by noting that Vajrapāṇi, particularly in the form of Trailokyavijaya, plays a prominent role in the text.[66] He is at the center of a number of *maṇḍalas*, and he performs the tasks belonging to Acala and Trailokyavijaya in the *MVS* and the *STTS*. The *SDPS* often states that the principal defining task of the *krodha-vighnāntaka* is to eliminate obstacles to enlightenment. Some are exterior obstacles, such as the evil influences of the eight planets; others are internal obstructions, such as the sins of past lives. A more developed understanding of the obstacles, most clearly articulated in the *MVS* and *STTS*, is already apparent in the *SDPS*: obstructions are inner enemies who disappear with the attainment of enlightened wisdom. These two approaches to the *krodha-vighnāntaka* encapsulate the differences between Phase One and Phase Two ideology. In both the *krodha-vighnāntaka* excel in their appointed tasks.

Notes to Chapter Nine

1 T.18.848.7a; Yamamoto, 21. The epigraph for this section is from P. H. Pott, *Yoga and Yantra: Their Interrelation and their Significance for Indian Archaeology*, trans. Rodney Needham (The Hague, 1966), 140.

2 See Snodgrass, *Matrix and Diamond World*, 60-66, 154-155.

3 T.18.848.5a; Yamamoto, 16.

4 T.18.848.13b; Yamamoto, 41.

5 T.18.848.13c; Yamamoto, 41.

6 Snodgrass quotes Yixing/Śubhakarasiṁha's commentary on the *MVS* to the effect that "pebbles, for example, represent the false tenet that a self exists and lack of faith in the Right Dharma." Snodgrass, *Matrix and Diamond World*, 155.

7 T.18.848.32b; Yamamoto, 129-130. The same chapter also describes *homa* rites as "inner and outer." T.18.848.32c;Yamamoto, 130-131.

8 Tsongkhapa's chief disciple Kaygrubjay (1385-1438) divides Esoteric Buddhist texts into those concerned with "outer action" (*bāhya-kriyā*) and "inner yoga" (*adhyatma-yoga*). The Tibetan textual classification of Caryā Tantra, to which the *MVS* traditionally belongs, consists of texts "expressed for subduing the candidates who delight in practicing *outer action* and *inner yoga* in equal measure." Yoga Tantra, to which the *STTS* traditionally belongs, consist of teachings for adepts "who delight in the *yoga of inner samādhi*." Lessing and Wayman, *Mkhas-grub-rje's*, 219 (emphasis in original).

9 T.18.848.49b; Yamamoto, 188.

10 Iyanaga, "La Soumission de Maheśvara," 690 (my translation from the French after consulting the Chinese). The passage quoted is from T.39.1796.679b.

11 T.18.848.15b, 48c, 47c, 49a, 54a-b; Yamamoto, 54, 185, 183, 197, 198. Water sacralized through Acala's *mudrā* and *dhāraṇī* is then sprinkled on offerings in order to purify them. T.18.848.50a-b; Yamamoto, 187.

12 Jishu Oda, "Acalagra Vidyārāja," *Encyclopaedia of Buddhism, Fascicle: Acala-Akankheyya Sutta*, ed. G.P. Malalasekera (Colombo, 1963), 155. Elsewhere the author states that "[Acala] himself is given remnants of food, and by partaking of them, Acalagra [sic] manifests the non-duality of purity and impurity." Ibid., 160.

13 T.18.848.15b/Yamamoto, 54; T.18.848.48c/Yamamoto, 185; T.18.848.54a /Yamamoto, 197. The epithet also appears in the *dhāraṇī* of Vajrapāṇi and of Vajrasattva. Yamamoto, 46, no. 33 and 113, no. 216; and ibid., 186, no. 275.

14 George, *Caṇḍamahāroṣaṇa Tantra*.

15 T.18.848.7b; Yamamoto, 22. In other *maṇḍala* descriptions of the text, Acala has a similar appearance. See T.18.848.23b; Yamamoto, 88.

16 See Rob Linrothe, "Provincial or Providential: Reassessment of an Esoteric Buddhist 'Treasure'," *Monumenta Serica* 37 (1986-87): 197-225.

17 T.18.848.5a; Yamamoto, 16.

18 T.18.848.48c; Yamamoto, 185.

19 T.18.848.15b/Yamamoto, 54; T.18.848.6b/Yamamoto, 20; T.18.848.54b /Yamamoto, 198.

20 T.18.848.23b; Yamamoto, 88.

21 T.39.1796. For issues of modern scholarship related to this commentary, see the bibliographic comments in Iyanaga, "Récits de la Soumission," 650-651. For the model of mixed textual and oral instructions in the formation of the Genzu *garbhadhātu maṇḍala*, see Chikyō Yamamoto, *Introduction to the Maṇḍala* (Kyoto, 1980), 5-15; and, Snodgrass, *Matrix and Diamond World*, 171-182ff.

22 See Snodgrass, *Matrix and Diamond World*, 275-279 and 314-316 (where Candratilaka's name is explained variously according to East Asian and Tibetan exegetical traditions). The former considers it as "Moon Spot," relating to the Buddha's *urna* which "radiates a light that burns away all hindrances." The Tibetans translate *tilaka* as "Lord" and so interpret the name as "Moon Lord," explaining that by conquering the passions he has attained a moon-like purity.

23 T.18.848.34c; Yamamoto, 135.

24 T.18.848.7b; Yamamoto, 22.

25 Ibid.

26 T.18.848.23b; Yamamoto, 88.

27 T.18.848.7b; Yamamoto, 22.

28 Snodgrass, *Matrix and Diamond World*, 165, 201-206. Normally *maṇḍalas* configure west at the top. The *maṇḍala* based on the *MVS*, however, places west at the bottom. This is true in Japan as well as in Tibet. For instance, west is at the bottom in the 122-deity "Ābhisambodhi Vairocana *maṇḍala*" that is part of a set of 139 paintings made in the 19th c. at Ngor monastery in Tibet. It closely follows the text's description, more so than the Japanese version, which reflects the impact of exegetical literature. See Ngor Thar rtse mkhan po, *Tibetan Maṇḍalas: The Ngor Collection*, 2. vols. (Tokyo, 1983), no. 20.

29 See Tajima, "Les Deux Grands Maṇḍalas," 84-86; Snodgrass, *Matrix and Diamond World*, 269-283. The personified Prajñāpāramitā is a "wisdom holder" (*vidyādhara*), but not a *vidyarajñī* or a *krodha-vighnāntaka* like the other members of this section. Edward Conze, "The Iconography of the Prajñāpāramitā," in *Thirty Years of Buddhist Studies, Selected Essays* (Columbia, 1968), 258-260.

30 Ngor Thar rtse mkhan po, *Tibetan Maṇḍalas*, no. 20.

31 Snodgrass, *Matrix and Diamond World*, 269-270.

32 Snellgrove, "Introduction," 6. Snellgrove renders it as the "Symposium of Truth of All the Buddhas," in *Indo-Tibetan Buddhism*, 120.

33 Snellgrove, "Introduction," 9.

34 See the discussion in Iyanaga, "Récits de la Soumission," 638, note 2, 647-648. In Amoghavajra's important text explaining the 18 Māyājāla assemblies (i.e., 18 separate texts) of the *Vajraśekhara* (T.18.869), he states that the *STTS* formed the first of them. It is sometimes conjectured that the *Vajraśekhara* of 100,000 verses never actually existed. Ibid., 647. For a contrary opinion, see Kenneth W. Eastman, "The Eighteen Tantras of the Tattvasaṁgraha/Māyājāla," (Summary Report), *Transactions of the International Conference of Orientalists in Japan* 26 (1981): 95-96. Eastman identifies the texts with a Tibetan Nyingma collection known as the "Eighteen Tantras of the Māyājāla Class."

35 T.18.882. For this and the earlier partial versions, see the bibliographic commentary in Iyanaga, "Récits de la Soumission," 638 note 2, 656 -657.

36 Iyanaga, "Récits de la Soumission," 657. Dānapāla's full translation of the *STTS* was among the texts sent to Japan in 1073 by Jōjin.

37 Lessing and Wayman, *Mkhas-grub-rje's*, 145. For an example of short relating to the *STTS* translated by Amoghavajra, see T.21.1209 (*Njo* 1389 *KBC* 1380), the title of which Lokesh Chandra has reconstructed as follows: "Trailokyavijaya-sādhana-vidhi-atiguhya-dvāra from the Vajraśekhara-tantra." For Amoghavajra's summary, see T.18.869; Bunyiu Nanjio, *A Catalogue of the Buddhist Tripitaka, with additions and corrections by Lokesh Chandra* (New Delhi, 1980), 21 no., 1389; Tajima, "Les Deux Grands Maṇḍalas," 145-149; and, Iyanaga, "Récits de la Soumission," 659-664.

38 Iyanaga, "Récits de la Soumission," 705-706.

39 *Zhiyuan Fabao kantong zong lu*, fasc. 6, fol. 3b, after *Njo* 1017, 224. There are variations. For instance, certain verses in the Sanskrit are translated as prose. See Shinten Sakai and Shindo Shiraishi, "Two *ślokas* in the Sanskrit Text of Tattva-saṁgraha-tantra, Chapter of (Vidyārāja) Trailokyavijaya, with a Commentary and Indices," *Indogaku bukkyōgaku kenkyū* VII.2 (1959): 722-728. There are also small discrepancies due to the Chinese official translation methods. Sakai and Shiraishi note of one such passage, "this is a liberal translation refined by [Dānapāla's] collaborators, as it is usual in the Chinese translation by Imperial Order." Ibid., 727. Kiyota compares the Chinese translations and a Sanskrit manuscript discovered by Tucci and finds there is general agreement with only minor variations and errors. Jakuun Kiyota, "Kongōchokyō no Bon-Kan taishō ni tshuite" (Comparison between the Sanskrit and Chinese texts of the Tattvasamgraha), *Indogaku bukkyōgaku kenkyū* 4, no. 1 (1956): 89-92. For a discussion and some examples, see K.W. Lim, "Studies in Later Buddhist Iconography," *Bijdragen Tot de Taal-, Land- en Volkenkunde van Nederlandsch-Indie* 120 (1964): 331-332.

40 Lessing and Wayman, *Mkhas-grub-rje's*, 24-25, note 13. The commentaries have a considerable part in Kaygrubjay's explication of the *STTS* as the fundamental work of the Yoga Tantra class. Ibid., 24-35, 215-249.

41 Snellgrove, *Buddhist Himalaya*, 69-73; retranslated in idem, *Indo-Tibetan Buddhism*, 215-220; ibid., 136-140, *passim*. Also see idem, "Divine Kingship," 204ff, esp. 208-211.

42 Snellgrove, "Introduction," 5-67.

43 Giuseppe Tucci, *Stūpa: art, architectonics and symbolism (Indo-Tibetica I)*, trans. Uma Marina Vesci and ed. Lokesh Chandra (New Delhi, 1988), 140-145; Iyanaga "Récits de la soumission," 633 -745; and, Ronald M. Davidson, "Reflections on the Maheśvara Subjugation Myth: Indic Materials, Sa-skya-pa Apologetics, and the Birth of Heruka," *JIABS* 14, no. 2 (1991): 197-235.

44 Snellgrove, "Introduction," 35.

45 The same essential *maṇḍala* is at the heart of all those in the *SDPS* cycle as well. Tucci describes iconographically all 37 deities, along with some variants, for both the *STTS* and the *SDPS*, in a study of Indian and Tibetan sources of the Sarvavid Mahāvairocana *maṇḍala* as depicted in sculpture at Tabo, western Tibet. Tucci, *Spiti and Kunavar*, 32-72; and, Deborah E. Klimburg-Salter, *Tabo A Lamp for the Kingdom: Early Indo-Tibetan Buddhist Art in the Western Himalaya* (New York, 1997).

46 Snellgrove, "Introduction," 24.

47 In the *SDPS* the eight offering goddesses are also equated with the eight *pāramitā*. Skorupski, *Sarvadurgatipariśodhana*, 8, note 11.

48 Snellgrove, "Introduction," 31.

49 Ibid., 34.

50 Snellgrove, *Indo-Tibetan Buddhism*, 222-223. The *SDPS*, which shares this *maṇḍala*, also states of the gate guardians, "Then by means of Vajrāṁkuśa [sic] and (the three) others he summons (the divinities), leads them (into their places), binds them and subdues them." Skorupski, *Sarvadurgatipariśodhana*, 20.

51 Snellgrove, "Introduction," 39-51.

52 Ibid., 39.

53 Ibid., 42.

54 Conze, "*Adhyardhaśatikā Prajñāpāramitā*," 101-115. The text is also discussed by Conze, "Tantric Prajñāpāramitā Texts," 100-122; the six Chinese translations are listed in ibid., 107-108. Also see Ian Astley-Kristensen, *The Rishukyō: The Sino-Japanese Tantric Prajñāpāramitā in 150 Verses (Amoghavajra's Version)*, Buddhica Britannica Series Continua III (Tring: The Institute of Buddhist Studies, 1991).

55 K. Yu, "Amoghavajra (2)," *Encyclopaedia of Buddhism, Fascicle: Akankheyya Sutta-Anabhirati*, ed. G.P. Malalasekera (Colombo, 1964), 486. The concept of *mahāsukha* is indeed found in this text. Conze's section XIV reads, "The supreme Success of the great Passion on the part of the great Bodhisattvas leads to the supreme Success of the Great Bliss (of all the Tathāgatas); the supreme Success of the Great Bliss on the part of the great Bodhisattvas leads to their supreme Success in winning the great enlightenment of all the Tathāgatas." Conze, "*Adhyardhaśatikā Prajñāpāramitā*," 112.

56 Y. Matsunaga, "Indian Esoteric Buddhism as Studied in Japan," 238; Wayne Gelfman, "Kukai's Interpretation of the *Rishukyō*," *Transactions of the International Conference of Orientalists in Japan* 23 (1978): 103-104. The versions of the text are treated in considerable detail in Shoun Toganoo, *Rishukyō no kenkyū* (Researches on the Nayasūtra) (Koyasan, 1930); abstract by Paul Demiéville, *Bibliographie bouddhique* 4-5 (1931-33): 96-98.

57 T.8.243.784c. Compare Conze, "*Adhyardhaśatikā Prajñāpāramitā*," 105; and, Astley-Kristensen, *The Rishukyō*, 136.

58 Conze, "*Adhyardhaśatikā Prajñāpāramitā*," 110, section 12.

59 T.8.423.785b; Conze, "*Adhyardhaśatikā Prajñāpāramitā*," 109; Astley-Kristensen, *The Rishukyō*, 153. Conze has "the Laughter of Vajrabhairava in his shape as the Adamantine Yakṣa and the Seal of the Adamantine Eye-tooth." Vajrabhairava, the name of a later deity, is misleading in this context and does not occur in the Chinese text, which names Vajrakrodha, though the literal meanings are related. Astley-Kristensen has, "Holding the emblem of Vajrayakṣa and baring the Thunderbolt fang, he instilled fear into all the Tathāgatas and expounded the essence of the great laugh of Thunderbold Wrath: *hah*."

60 It is discussed as such in Conze, "Tantric Prajñāpāramitā Texts," 113-115; and translated in Charles Willemen, "A Tantric 'Heart-Sūtra'," *Samādhi: Cahiers d'Études Bouddhiques* 7.1 (1973): 2-11.

61 For the characterizations of Esoteric Buddhism as "miscellaneous" vs. "pure," see Y. Matsunaga, "Tantric Buddhism," 6-7. J.W. de Jong has researched and reviewed several studies of the *Sang Hyang Kamahayanan Mantranaya* manuscript of 42 Sanskrit verses with an Old Javanese commentary discovered in Bali. Its focus is initiation rites. The last 17 verses were taken from the *Adhyardhaśatikā Prajñāpāramitā*, while 15 come from the second chapter of the *MVS*. It is likely that this text was put together in India and then transmitted to Java. At any rate it shows how Phase Two texts have enough in common for portions to be stitched together. See J.W. de Jong, "Notes on the sources and the text of the Sang Hyang Kamahayanan Mantranaya," in *Buddhist Studies*, ed. Gregory Schopen (Berkeley, 1979), 619-636.

62 T.19.968 (Njo 349 KBC 319), translated by Du Xingkai.

63 Tucci, *Rin-chen-bzan-po and the Renaissance of Buddhism in Tibet Around the Millenium* (Indo-Tibetica II) (New Delhi: Aditya Prakashan, 1988), 35, 47, nos. 76, 77.

64 One sign of the mixed or transitional character of the *SDPS* is the inclusion of instructions which clearlyshare the 2-dimensional triadic structure of Phase One texts and imagery. While most of chapters Two and Three refer to a 3-dimensional *maṇḍala* structure proper to Phase Two ideology, in a section on painting an image in Chapter Three we find a distinctly triadic structure, linking (in ascending order) Trailokyavijaya, Vajrapāṇi and Śākyamuni on the left side of Mahāvairocana, and Hayagriva, Avalokiteśvara and Sarvadurgatipariśodhanaraja on the right.

65 Skorupski, *Sarvadurgatipariśodhana*, vii.

66 For a more detailed analysis of the *krodha-vighnāntaka* as they are treated in the *SDPS*, see Linrothe, "Compassionate Malevolence," 615-618.

144. Yamāntaka, Mahants compound, Bodh Gaya (Bihar), ca. 10th century

10

Yamantaka Imagery

En somme, la question: quelle est la nature des cinq krodha: Navabhava, Yamāmāra, etc.? revient sans doute à demander quelle était primitivement la nature de Yamāntaka.
Jean Przyluski, "Le Bouddhisme Tantrique à Bali"

There is considerable precedent and utility in beginning with Yamāntaka. Yamāntaka is named first of ten *krodha-vighnāntaka* listed by Mahāvairocana in a Phase Two text translated into Chinese in the late tenth century.[1] As the epigraph illustrates, Przyluski also felt Yamāntaka was primary among all the *krodha-vighnāntaka*.

Another reason why an examination of Yamāntaka is an appropriate beginning here is that there is a great deal of continuity in his iconography across Phase One to Phase Two. Unlike Acala and Trailokyavijaya, who have the highest profiles in the Phase Two texts, Yamāntaka is not introduced with Phase Two. His prominence as a Phase One *krodha-vighnāntaka* is reconceived to fit the new paradigm. A significant aspect of the revised conception concerns the dynamic between Mañjuśrī and Yamāntaka. Their relationship in the Phase One *MMK* is that of a powerful but inferior attendant and his presiding master; by the writing of the Phase Two *Mañjuśrīnāmasaṃgīti* Mañjuśrī *is* Yamāntaka, just as he is Mahāvairocana and Vajrasattva.[2]

Yet while Yamāntaka's name, his basic identity and iconographic association with the buffalo are maintained, in other ways Yamāntaka's image is radically transformed to express the changes in the role and status of the Phase Two *krodha-vighnāntaka*. The most obvious change is independence: Yamāntaka images begin to appear without solely being linked to an image of Mañjuśrī, or any other dominating figure.

1 The Bodh Gaya Yamantaka

At some point in the seventeenth or eighteenth century, a group of Hindu Shaiva *sannyāsī* moved to the Bodh Gaya area and began to lay claim to the vast holdings of agricultural land and village property which they still control. The Mahābodhi temple, which then lay in ruins, was within the precincts of the area they held, and they began to move heavy stone Buddhist sculptures from the Mahābodhi temple

145. *Trailokyavijaya (left) and Yamāntaka, Mahants compound, Bodh Gaya (Bihar), ca. 10th century*

down to the walled monastery and cattle compound which the successive Mahants and their followers built for themselves closer to the Nairañjana (now called the Lilajan) river. The process of appropriation was stimulated, if not initiated, in the early nineteenth century by the glimmerings of interest in the Mahābodhi temple on the part of outsiders, with the visits of the King of Burma in 1811 and the proto-archaeologist Buchanan Hamilton in 1812. Some objects which were noted by that scholar at the temple site are now found in the Mahants compound.[3]

Among the objects taken by the Mahants at a date prior to Buchanan Hamilton's visit is a large stone sculpture of Yamāntaka. [**145** right, **144**, **147**] It now stands in a tiny shed, sunk into the ground and cemented into the walls. The backdrop is severely damaged, the proper left side and top completely broken off. Drawings published in 1838 and 1878 of this figure show that the bull stood on an elaborate base decorated with pairs of elephants and horses and a Yakṣa-atlantid.[4] This base is now either broken off or obscured beneath the present level of the floor. When I visited the sculpture in 1989 and 1990, I cleaned off layers of loose dirt, dust, and rodent and bird droppings. A priest still comes relatively regularly to refresh the vermillion paste rubbed on the forehead, and a flower is left occasionally. Visitors to the temple seeking Buddhist sculpture are steered away from the shed to the open corridor at the rear of the compound, where a large group of Buddhist sculp-

146. *Yamāntaka, detail of* **46** *, same as* **47**

147. *Yamāntaka, detail of* **144**

tures taken from the Mahābodhi temple (including **50** and **52**) are interspersed among the small temples built to commemorate each deceased Mahanta. I was informed that because of the wrathful nature of the Yamāntaka sculpture and the closely-related Trailokyavijaya adjacent to it [**145**], these are kept out of open view.

Yamāntaka is of the *vāmana*-Yakṣa type. He is *lambodara*, his belly hanging over the belt of his *dhoti*. Around his hips is a lion skin, its maned head on Yamāntaka's left thigh, and two of its limbs are knotted together between his legs. He wears a full complement of jewelry at the wrists, upper arms, neck and ankles. Instead of an *upavīta*, he wears a long garland, in which heads alternate with medallions.

Yamāntaka's head is large and his central face full. A short-cropped beard lines his jaw, and mustaches are seen on some of his six faces. Two faces are on the proper right of the central face and three on the proper left, though the third is almost completely broken off. None have the third eye. In the headdress above the main head is an image of Akṣobhya Buddha. Yamāntaka's hair, which bears a low crown, is pulled back away from the forehead and then splays out behind him in a circular fashion, recalling the Guneri Yamāntaka figure from between the ninth and tenth centuries. [**146**] A few tightly curled strands fall onto the shoulder.

Six-armed, he holds a sword above his head with the upper proper right hand. The middle right holds up a *vajra*, while the third holds the *daṇḍa*-club, which is a common *āyudha* for Yamāntaka images of all phases. His left arms are broken off, two at the elbow, though the hand of the third remains at the chest. No doubt it once made the *tarjanī mudrā* and held a *pāśa*-noose, one *vajra*-tipped end of which hangs down along his belly.

There are other six-armed deities, and fewer six-headed ones, but Yamāntaka's special Phase Two iconographic characteristic is the presence of six legs standing on the buffalo. The buffalo under Yamāntaka's feet has been discussed already in relation to two Phase One images from Orissa [**44**, **56**], but six legs do not appear in Phase One images of Yamāntaka as attendant to Mañjuśrī. In keeping with the new emphasis on more profound aims in Phase Two Esoteric Buddhism in general and a deeper symbolism attached to the *krodha-vighnāntaka* in particular, the number six is invested with symbolic meaning. For example, Duquenne has pointed out that in Amoghavajra's eighth-century translation of a Yamāntaka ritual text, the deity has six feet because he purifies the six Destinations (*gati*), six heads because he accomplishes the six Perfections (*pāramitā*) and six arms because he realizes the six Powers of Meditation (*abhijñā*).[5]

Phase Two texts describing Yamāntaka, such as the *Māyājāla Mahātantra*, mention not only the six legs, arms and heads and the buffalo underfoot, but other specific details as well. These include the image of Akṣobhya in his headdress, the fact that his stature is short but his belly is big, and the sword and the *vajra* in the right hands. It describes an arrow instead of a *daṇḍa* in the other right hand, but the noose and the *tarjanī mudrā* are specified in the left. According to this text, the hands which are broken off in the Mahants compound image should have carried the *Prajñāpāramitā* text and a bow,[6] but the Bodh Gaya image may very well have been at variance with the text.

In this instance, the buffalo is facing toward's Yamāntaka's right, and the deity's right feet are on the buffalo's head. The buffalo has a saddle-cloth on its back and a bell tied under its neck. Presumably these indicate that the dangerous wildness which the buffalo represents has been subjugated and tamed. The aggressive *pratyālīḍha* posture emphasizes the active aspects of the image.

Janice Leoshko has discussed this "impressive" work. She writes that the artist "has effectively sculpted the powerful form of Yamari's [i.e., Yamāntaka's] corpulent body which symbolizes his fierce strength."[7] While images of Yamāntaka and Trailokyavijaya are not quite as rare as she suggests, Leoshko is correct in observing that the significance of this Yamāntaka sculpture is enhanced by its imposing dimensions.[8] The present proximity of the Trailokyavijaya sculpture and the details of workmanship the two works share certainly suggest they are components of a complex three-dimensional arrangement, now dismantled. Originally they may have stood alongside others, notably a related Chunda image, a grouping described in the Vidyadhara quarter of the *MVS*. Alternatively, they may have been placed as gate guardians to a *vajradhātu maṇḍala*, or represented the five Tathāgata in a *krodha maṇḍala*, as do the deities described in the *STTS* and *SDPS*. However, without more of a context, any such reconstruction must remain inconclusive.

2 The Nalanda Yamantaka

Speculation on the original arrangement of sculptures is even harder to resist for a much smaller, but still fine, stone Yamāntaka recovered at Nalanda. [**148**] It belongs to a large group of images from Nalanda of similar size and style with pierced backdrops, which includes a four-headed Sarvavid Mahāvairocana figure making the *bodhyagrī mudrā*.[9] It is tempting to imagine it as part of an *STTS maṇḍala*, but unfortunately the intact contexts of the three-dimensional *maṇḍala* from Nganjuk (eastern Java), Tabo and Tsaparang (western Tibet) are lacking here.[10] Without a reliable context, we must continue to examine each work individually.

The Nalanda Yamāntaka was found in 1920-21 at the monastery site 1A.[11] An inscription on the back recites the standard Buddhist creed, and according to the excavators it is written in "correct" Sanskrit of around the ninth century. However, the ca. tenth-century date of the Bodh Gaya Yamāntaka seems to suit this work as well, so one compromises at ca. ninth to tenth century.

Iconographically there are numerous features in common with the Bodh Gaya Yamāntaka as well. First of all there are of course six arms, legs and heads. The faces are distributed three to the proper right of the central head and two to the left, the exact reverse of the Bodh Gaya sculpture. The *pratyālīḍha* posture is the same, as is the Akṣobhya in the headdress. Four of the arms and *āyudha* are comparable to those of the larger damaged Yamāntaka in the Mahants compound. The sword held overhead, the *tarjanī mudrā* at the chest, the *vajra* held in the middle right hand are all identical. The lower right hand is nearly the same, except the *daṇḍa* has been exchanged for a hammer (visible from the side). The other two left hands of the Nalanda piece, missing on the Bodh Gaya sculpture, hold a severed head by the hair (Yama's? Māra's?) in the upper and a skull cup in the lower.

There are a few minor differences. The Nalanda Yamāntaka wears a garland of skulls rather than heads, though a few heads are intermixed. The beard is much longer at the chin. Also, the buffalo faces the other way, has a bridle through its nose and a bell around its neck, though it wears no saddle blanket. One can also point to the fact that snake ornaments are much more prominent on this Yamāntaka, in his hair, around his upper arms, his neck, waist and ankles.

It is necessary to affirm conclusively that this Yamāntaka is depicted with six legs, since Leoshko writes that it has only two legs.[12] In the mistaken belief that it is a two-legged image, she argues that the Bodh Gaya Yamāntaka is unique. Seen from photographs taken straight on, it does appear that the Nalanda Yamāntaka is two-legged. However examination of the work itself in the Nalanda Museum, or of the American Institute of Indian Studies photograph of the rear **[149]**, dispels any doubt: this Yamāntaka has six legs.[13]

148. *Yamāntaka, Nalanda (Bihar), ca. 10th century, Nalanda Museum, same as 8*

Certain details lead one to consider the possibility that these two Yamāntaka sculptures, an image of Trailokyavijaya that is part of a later discussion and a few other works may have been made at the same workshop.[14] In particular, the hilt of the sword, with a button at the base, three or four indentations on the part facing out below the hand, and the ogee-shaped part above the hand correspond precisely to the form found on the swords held by the Yamāntaka and Trailokyavijaya in the Mahants compound. **[145]** Still the enormous difference in scale and a possible slight difference in age (the Nalanda piece being the earliest of the three) makes it difficult to be sure.

149. Yamāntaka, rear view of **148**

The two Yamāntaka sculptures from Bihar nevertheless demonstrate that there was a demand in the tenth century for widely varying sizes of this Phase Two deity. The Mahants compound Yamāntaka is large enough to be the central image of a small shrine, or to have been fit into a set within a larger shrine. The scale of the Nalanda Yamāntaka suggests it was a nun's or a monk's tutelary *yidam*, or *ishta-devata* (personal deity) on a private altar. The sculpture also may have been fitted into a transportable three-dimensional *maṇḍala* of a manageable scale.

The similarity of iconographic features between the two images and the description found in the *Māyājāla Mahātantra* quoted above suggest that there was a set of standard characteristics for the image of Phase Two Yamāntaka, at least in Bihar, but there was also room for variations as well. Among the standard features are the six arms, legs and heads, the *vāmana*-Yakṣa body type, *pratyālīḍha*, the sword and *vajra* in the right hands, the *tarjani-pāśa mudrā* made with the left and Akṣobhya in the headdress. The objects carried by the other hands seem to have varied. Several of these characteristics will be found outside the Bihar region as well.

3 The Orissan Yamantaka of Kuruma

150. Yamāntaka, Kuruma village (Orissa), ca. 9th-10th century

An Orissan image of Yamāntaka [**150-151**] may be slightly earlier than the two in Bihar. It now stands in a small brick shed, along with an adorned Akṣobhya and an Avalokiteśvara, at Kuruma village, eight kilometers northeast of Konarak. The site of Kuruma was excavated in 1974-1977 by P.K. Ray, B.K Rath and B.B. Barik, who unearthed a small Buddhist monastery there.[15] Villagers have continued to discover seals and other objects in the surrounding fields, which have been collected and kept in safe-keeping at the village school. Based on these objects and ones found in the course of excavation, P.K. Ray believes the monastery was occupied during the ninth and tenth centuries, dates which provide an acceptable range for the sculpture found there as well.

The sculpture was recovered from a tank nearby, known to local people as the "Yamadharma tank." Despite the fact that some have identified the figure as Heruka,[16] the Hindu ritualist in charge of the shrine and its keys informed me that he (shrewdly) recognizes it as Yama, and it is worshipped as such. The piece is damaged, and the greyish pitted stone is very weathered. It is also something of an iconographic anomaly. Only three heads are visible, instead of the normal six, and only two legs trample on the back of the buffalo. Rather than six arms, this image seems to have had eight. Several of those eight hands, however, held *āyudha* in the customary ways. Thus we have both the sword and the *daṇḍa* held in upper right hands, and a noose held in one of the left hands. The *vajra* is held in a hand broken off from the main body, which fits into the proper right side and was recovered separately from the tank. The other left hands hold a head (as does the Nalanda Yamāntaka) a hatchet and a staff held against the body. The bottom of the staff rests on the buffalo's neck and has a *vajra* finial above a skull.

Although some major differences are apparent from comparison with Yamāntaka images of Bihar, the identity of the Kuruma sculpture is not in doubt. The buffalo argues most convincingly for Yamāntaka. Generally the sculpture fits into the Phase Two Yamāntaka type, since he is *vāmana*-Yakṣa, wears snake ornaments, stands in a slight *ālīḍha*, has grotesque facial features, sports mustaches and has a very aggressive demeanor. Moreover, the sword, *daṇḍa* and *vajra* held aloft in right hands, and the noose and head in the left hands, are shared by Bihar examples. Too many attributes coincide to be purely adventitious.

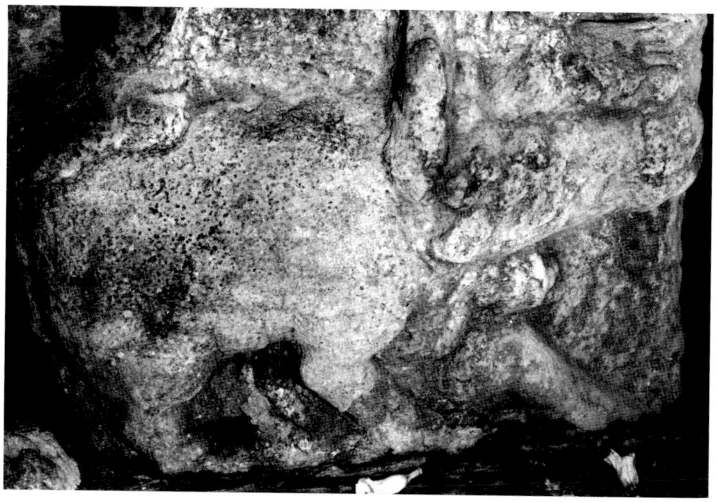
151. *Yamāntaka's buffalo, detail of* 150

Despite its wracked condition, this is a very important sculpture, for it suggests that Phase Two practices and texts were known, if not prevailing, in Kuruma. The suspicion seems to be confirmed also by the recovery from the tank of an over life-size adorned Buddha (now in the same shrine), but once again the lack of a fuller context frustrates any attempt to suggest a more specific cycle within Phase Two Buddhism. We must sacrifice appreciation of a considerable part of the original significance of the Kuruma Yamāntaka. As Tucci points out:

> *. . . an image thus isolated is often an abstraction, i.e. it loses its value as a symbol and loses that ideal connection that inserts it in given religious experiences.*[17]

Nevertheless, the Kuruma sculpture documents the presence of independent images of Yamāntaka in Orissa at about the same time as the ones from Bodh Gaya and Nalanda.

4 A twelfth-century Nepalese manuscript illumination

It is generally accepted, even by those who agree on little else, that Pāla and Nepalese painting are closely related.[18] For this reason, it may be acceptable to present a Nepalese manuscript illumination of Yamāntaka [**152**] as indicative of the standard Yamāntaka image of the twelfth century, both for the Indian centers in Bihar and for those in the Kathmandu valley. The illumination illustrates part of the Sanskrit *Paramārthanāmasaṁgīti*, a litany of the names of Buddha. The British Library, where it is preserved, dates it to 1184 CE.[19] The three other illustrations depict a teaching Buddha in a shrine, Mahāvairocana making the *bodhyagrī mudrā* against a *visvavajra* with eight spokes, and Nāmasamgīti bodhisattva, the personification of the text. The illustration of Mahāvairocana, the central deity of the essential Phase Two *maṇḍala*, underscores that this form of Yamāntaka (trampling on a buffalo, making the *tarjanī mudrā*, with six legs and heads, a sword etc.) is especially associated with Phase Two Esoteric Buddhism.

The painted Yamāntaka [**152**] has six heads and six legs, like the two ca. tenth-century Yamāntaka images from Bihar. [**144, 148**] The anomalous eight arms found on the Orissan sculpture [**150**] are also reproduced in the painting. The large *vāmana*-Yakṣa body in *pratyālīḍha* is painted blue, and he tramples on the buffalo. Snake ornaments and a tiger-skin apron adorn his imposing figure, and he carries the sword in an upper right hand and makes the *tarjanī mudrā* with the front left. This particular constellation of *āyudha* seems to be a regular feature of Phase Two Yamāntaka images, since it occurs on each we have met with so far. A slender *daṇḍa* is carried in another right hand. The remaining *āyudha* are innovations. A wheel, a hatchet and an *aṅkuśa*-hook are distributed to left and right hands. Most striking is the drawn bow, apparently aiming an arrow to his proper left.

The artist appears to have been sensitive to the perspectival limitations of the two-dimensional medium, for certain adjustments have been made to Yamāntaka's standard image to accommodate iconographic clarity. Lest any of the six legs be invisible in the painted image, they do not all make *pratyālīḍha*, as they do in the Bodh Gaya and Nalanda Yamāntaka. Only the outer pair actually stands in contact with the buffalo. One pair is loosely crossed and hangs below a more tightly

152. *Yamāntaka, Nepal, manuscript painting, late 12th century, British Library*

crossed pair, making Yamāntaka look as if he were simultaneously sitting and standing. The six heads are also rearranged for the sake of visibility. There are two on each side of the central head, and the sixth is set on top of these five. Thus all requisite features can be seen in the painting.

5 Observations

Phase Two images of Yamāntaka from eastern India are relatively scarce. The earliest are also comparatively late, since they postdate the seventh and eighth centuries, when we know the texts were being formulated and promulgated. The reason for this may be imputed to historical accident. Other and earlier images simply may have not survived, or they may not have been discovered or recognized. But this is likely to be only part of the answer. The three sculpted images from the ninth and tenth centuries are all associated with a monastic context. It may be that practitioners who utilized Phase Two texts in established monasteries with distinguished traditions in other forms of Buddhism were not immediately influential enough, or were not of sufficient numbers at those sites to justify large scale sculpted images. The creation of the two nearly life-size Yamāntaka required the mobilization of considerable resources and support. Since we find a small cluster of Yamāntaka images during the ninth and tenth centuries, it seems likely that it was only then that Phase Two Esoteric Buddhism had become fully established in an institutional sense. This conclusion will also be supported by evidence provided by the occurrence of other Phase Two *krodha-vighnāntaka* images.

It is unwise to generalize on the iconographic characteristics of Yamāntaka in eastern India from so limited a sample. When iconography is confirmed by textual descriptions, we are on firmer ground. On the basis of textual evidence, we can identify a core set of characteristics. The buffalo is a consistent but not invariable component of the standard image. The sword and *tarjanī mudrā* are somewhat more regular in appearance, while the *daṇḍa* is frequent. Finally, though the texts' prescription of six heads, arms and legs is contradicted by the two eight-armed examples we have mentioned, we may say that all the images of Yamāntaka from eastern India depict him in the *vāmana*-Yakṣa form.

6 The early temples of western Tibet

Before leaving the topic of Yamāntaka, it will be useful to consider the expansion of Kashmiri Phase Two Esoteric Buddhism into western Tibet. Examination of the Kashmiri movement provides the opportunity to survey images which are clearly based on prototypes similar to eastern Indian Yamāntaka images. Despite obvious connections to Indian images, however, western Tibetan images retain much more of their original contexts.

The earliest paintings and sculptures at temples in Ladakh and Zangskar such as Alchi, Sumda and Mangyu, along with Tabo in Spiti, belong to Phase Two Esoteric Buddhism and feature the five Tathāgata *maṇḍala* with Sarvavid Mahāvairocana at the center, as described in the *STTS* and *SDPS*.[20] These works of art reflect Kashmiri stylistic traits, and the temples are associated with followers of Rinchen Zangpo, who at one time studied in Kashmir.[21] In fact it was Rinchen Zangpo who introduced or reintroduced the *STTS* and *SDPS* into western Tibet, and it was he who translated the latest version of the *STTS*, the *Tattvalokakari* (Anandagarbha's influential commentary on the *STTS*) and at least two commentaries on the *SDPS*.[22] Despite his conversion to Phase Three teachings when he was in his mid-eighties (he lived to be 98), the momentum of the great monk's early work with Phase Two ideology, texts and images continued to dominate many sites in western Tibet until well into the twelfth century. Fortunately, some of these (Phase Two) western Tibetan temples were not repainted when later schools took over and redecorated western Tibetan temples according to Phase Three ideology and artistic style.[23]

Roger Goepper places the founding of the Sumtsek, one of the most important buildings at Alchi, to the decades immediately following 1200 CE.[24] Recently discovered inscriptions on portraits of patriarchs (monks and *mahāsiddha*) on the third story of the Sumtsek place paintings within the Drigungpa lineage of the Kagyüpa order.[25] Since the early paintings at Sumda and Mangyu, as well as those at the Dukhang at Alchi, resemble those of the Sumtsek in style, theme and content, it is possible to accept a date for the group as roughly between the twelfth and early thirteenth centuries.

6.1 Western Tibetan Yamāntaka images in maṇḍala

Yamāntaka is included in at least one of the *maṇḍala* paintings of the Dukhang at Alchi. Given his long-standing connection with Mañjuśrī, it is not surprising that Yamāntaka is found in a *maṇḍala* which features Mañjuśrī as "Lord of the Elemental Sphere," the *dharmadhātu vagisvara maṇḍala*. This *maṇḍala* is derived from an early tenth-century commentary on the *Mañjuśrīnāmasamgīti* that delineated a new ritual structure.[26] Like the *Mañjuśrīnāmasamgīti* itself, the *maṇḍala* is closely related to the basic structure of the *STTS vajradhātu maṇḍala* and features most of the same personages. It is not anomalous then for it to be found mixed with *maṇḍala* which derive more directly from the *STTS*.

The Alchi Dukhang painting is the second *maṇḍala* on the left hand wall as one enters.[27] The gatekeeper at the bottom of the *maṇḍala* is Yamāntaka with six arms, heads and legs. He stands on a buffalo and holds a sword, arrow and *aṅkuśa*-hook in the right hands. One left hand makes the *tarjanī pāśa mudrā*, while the other two carry a *vajra* or *vajra*-handled bell and bow.

Sumda, a grueling day and a half walk from Alchi over the Stakpsi La pass, possesses a monastery with *maṇḍala* of the same period and style as the early ones at Alchi.[28] On the left hand wall as one enters there is again the Mañjuśrī *dharma-dhātu vagisvara maṇḍala*, and one finds Yamāntaka in the identical position holding identical attributes.[29] Unfortunately, the image is very damaged, but he seems to be standing on a buffalo.

6.2 The Sumtsek Yamāntaka

In the Sumtsek there is a painting of Yamāntaka on the second floor. [COLOR PLATE 10] Sometimes mistaken for Mahākāla, it is clearly Yamāntaka. The six legs, six arms and six heads are arranged in two tiers, as in early East Asian images. He stands in *pratyālīḍha* on the back of a buffalo, holds the sword in a raised right hand, makes *tarjanī-pāśa mudrā* with a left, and holds an arrow and a long-handled *aṅkuśa*-hook in right hands. The bow and a *vajra*-handled bell are held in the remaining left hands. This image is nearly identical to those in the *maṇḍala* in the Dukhang at Alchi and at Sumda, though on a much larger scale, and its identification as Yamāntaka is beyond doubt.

The placement of Yamāntaka above the door of the second floor is meaningful. Like Mahākāla, who is painted above the first floor entrance, Yamāntaka functions here as a gate keeper. Mahākāla is a Dharmarājā, a great protector, and a tutelary deity, especially in Tibet. Important as these roles are, he is generally invoked for the kind of *abhicaraka* rites which we saw associated with Yamāntaka in Phase One contexts. This association is emphasized in the first floor image of Mahākāla, for as Goepper points out, he stands on a skull-lined triangular *homa*-altar. In fact Mahākāla remains primarily a prophylactic deity, preventing malevolent forces from entering the sanctuary. Yamāntaka retains this apotropaic role, which he plays in both Phase One and Phase Two contexts, but Phase Two ideology raises the status of the *krodha-vighnāntaka* above the Dharmarājās. They play roles which are defensive *and* active in aiding the transformation of the adept into a Buddha. As a result Yamāntaka is placed literally above Mahākāla in the Sumtsek.[30]

6.3 The Yamāntaka inside the stūpa at Mangyu

A half-day's easy walk from Alchi, staying on the south side of the Indus river and turning south at Gira village, brings one to Mangyu, a small village perched on high bluffs above a tributary.[31] In the middle of the village are old monastic buildings. To the right and left of the old temples are two large stucco bodhisattva figures, which recall those of Alchi's Sumtsek, though they are not in as good condition. One is four-armed and has vignettes of the Buddha's life or Mahāsiddhas painted on the *dhoti*, while the other is two-armed, makes *abhaya mudrā* and holds a vase. On the back walls are extremely faded murals, but to the proper left of one figure a large eight-armed Mañjuśrī is discernible, and just below him is Yamāntaka, in the same form as already met with at Alchi and Sumda. Inside the

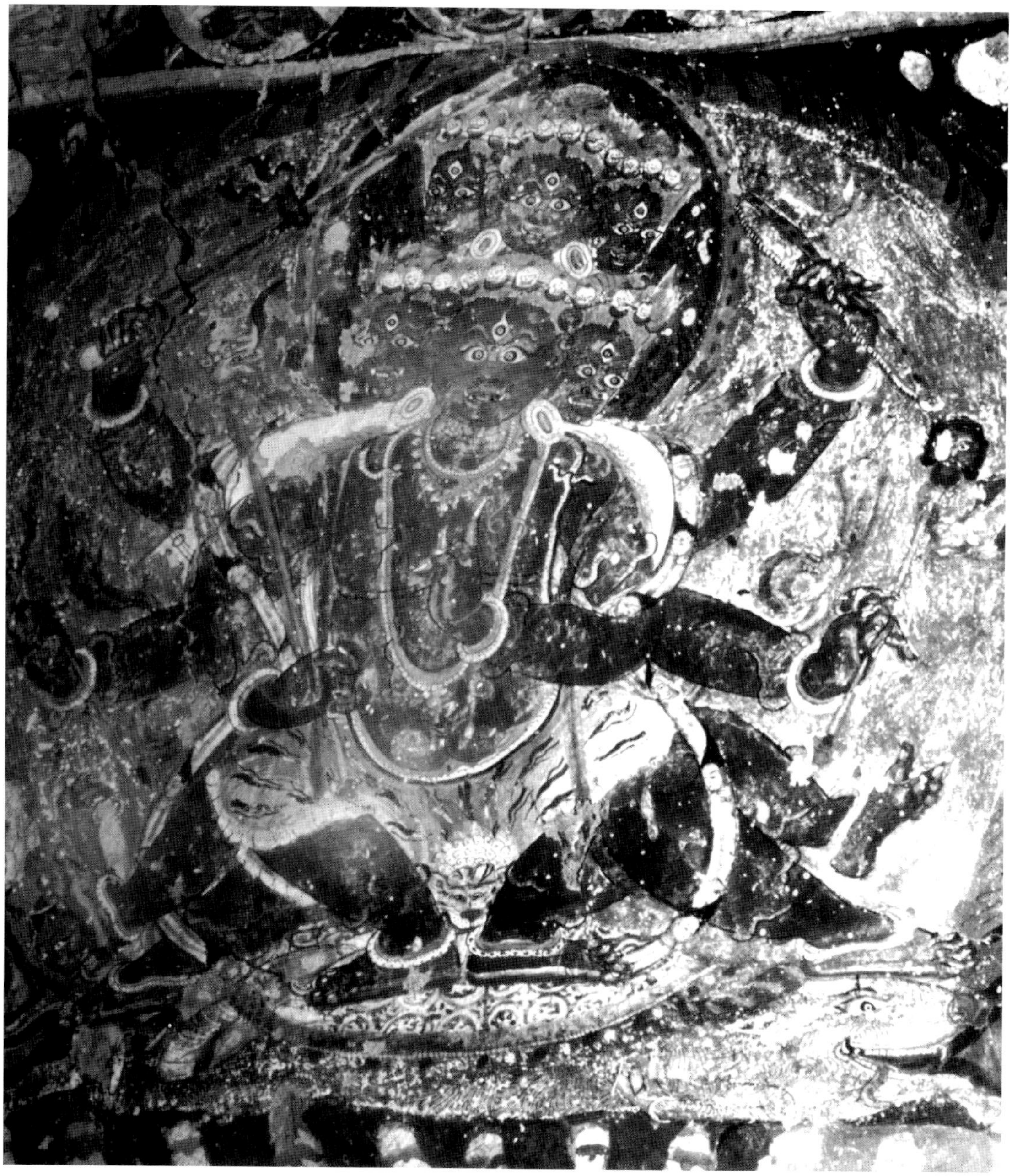

153. Yamāntaka, Mangyu stūpa (Ladakh), wall painting, ca. late 12th-early 13th century

two larger rooms are *maṇḍala* of the same date, style and iconography as those of Alchi and Sumda, but the paintings at Mangyu have not fared as well.

Above the village is a line of *chörten* or *stūpa*. The one closest to the village is a *chörten* which one can enter. Inside on the upper walls leading to a ceiling with a lantern roof are exquisite paintings in much better condition than the ones in the main monastery of the village. In terms of delicacy, modeling and detail they rival the best painting of the Dukhang, if not the Sumtsek of Alchi. They are obviously done in the same tradition as Alchi. The robes of the Buddhas and the *dhoti*s of the bodhisattva exhibit finely-rendered "Sassanian" style textile patterns with interlocking geometric designs and repeated medallions containing griffins, as found too in the Sumtsek. There is also a similar treatment of faces and bodies.

The center of each wall has stucco sculptures above the ground level which are late replacements. To either side of each sculpture is a vertical rectangular panel containing mural paintings. On the entrance wall a standing Mañjuśrī is on one side and a standing Prajñāpāramitā is on the other; opposite the entrance wall there is a standing eleven-headed Avalokiteśvara and a standing green Tārā. The two other walls contain six images of Tathāgata and two of the *krodha-vighnāntaka* Yamāntaka and Hayagrīva. There are two images of Mahāvairocana, one as an unadorned Śākyamuni seated above the adorned Akṣobhya, and the other as an adorned Sarvavid Mahāvairocana, seated above Amoghasiddhi. Hayagrīva stands above the seated Amitayus, and finally Yamāntaka stands above Ratnasambhava. [153] Yamāntaka is iconographically identical to the Sumtsek Yamāntaka [COLOR PLATE 10] and to the other western Tibetan Yamāntaka discussed so far.

It is necessary briefly to point out a few pertinent aspects of the Mangyu *stūpa*. The four types of deities depicted on the walls, Buddha, bodhisattva, female deity and *krodha-vighnāntaka*, form a kind of truncated five Tathāgata *maṇḍala*, dismantled and reassembled to fit the special physical requirements of the site. Typically the fully-formed Phase Two *krodha-vighnāntaka* is shown as an independent image but fit into a larger composition. He is not placed in particular association with the bodhisattva he accompanied in Phase One images; at Mangyu, Yamāntaka in fact abuts the eleven-headed Avalokiteśvara, and Hayagrīva is next to Prajñāpāramitā. The wrathful deities are placed in direct relationship with the five Tathāgata, who form the nuclear structure of the Phase Two paradigm. It should not pass without comment that the two *krodha-vighnāntaka* are placed above the Buddha with whom they are paired, at the same level as the two forms of Mahāvairocana (*nirmanakaya* Śākyamuni and *dharmakaya* Sarvavid). This is another graphic indication of the increased status of the Phase Two *krodha-vighnāntaka* compared to their Phase One counterparts.

6.4 The western Tibetan Yamāntaka type

More so than the eastern Indian or East Asian Yamāntaka, the western Tibetan Yamāntaka images are remarkably uniform. There is little or no variation in attributes, *vāmana*-Yakṣa body-type, posture, or the number and arrangement of heads. The main detectable difference when comparing the Sumtsek and Mangyu Yamāntaka images [COLOR PLATE 10, 153] is that in the former the buffalo faces to Yamāntaka's proper right and in the latter to his left, a discrepancy which probably has little significance. (In most of the Indian images, the buffalo faces to his left, but in the Bodh Gaya image, to the right.) The uniformity of western Tibetan images is not affected by major differences in scale or context. The large semi-independent images in the Sumtsek and the Mangyu *chörten* are identical to small images inside the *maṇḍala* at Sumda and in the Dukhang at Alchi. It is possible to attribute the near uniformity to the dominance of a single Kashmiri-influenced painting tradition in western Tibet, operating at nearby sites within a limited period of time.

By comparison, surviving images in eastern India are considerably more varied. A number of characteristics have carried over to the early western Tibetan Yamāntaka type, notably the buffalo and consistent number of six heads, arms and legs. At the same time in eastern India there seems to be a minor alternate tradition of eight arms, represented by the Nepalese manuscript [152] and the Kuruma sculpture. [150] The sword and *tarjanī mudrā* are shared by all eastern Indian examples, but only the Nepalese painting, approximately contemporary with western Tibetan images, includes the bow and arrow as well. The painted Yamāntaka is beardless too, though the arrangement of the heads differs from the sculpture. One could say that the later the eastern Indian image, the closer it matches specific details of the Tibetan type.

It must be recalled, however, that stylistic and iconographic evidence points to Kashmir and not to eastern India as the immediate source for the western Tibetan images. Rinchen Zangpo brought the Sarvavid Mahāvairocana *maṇḍala* cycles in particular, and Phase Two Esoteric Buddhism in general, back with him from Kashmir in the eleventh century. But if Goepper is right that Kashmiri artists played an important role in the creation of the Alchi paintings, then we must presume the continued survival of these traditions in Kashmir for at least a century more.

The western Tibetan Yamāntaka are the latest images in South Asia to survive in the full context of a Phase Two cycle. Eastern Indian Esoteric Buddhism by this time had embraced its third phase and was struggling against the invasion of the Muslim army of Bhaktiar Khalji. Kashmir avoided Muslim occupation for another century, but as far as Buddhism is concerned, the twelfth was the beginning of "les siècles de déclin."[32]

What should we expect to see in later central Tibetan images of Yamāntaka? A full understanding of the situation in central Tibet will have to wait upon an exploration of the third phase of Esoteric Buddhism in eastern India. By the time Esoteric Buddhism was securely transplanted to Tibet, sometime during the thirteenth or fourteenth century, all three phases had emerged in eastern India, and so were imported together into Tibet from eastern India and from Nepal. Phase Two forms of Yamāntaka survive alongside the more important Phase Three forms, such as Yamāntaka-Vajrabhairava and Yamāri. Phase Two *krodha-vighnāntaka* are not accorded as high a status as the Phase Three forms. In the Great Stupa of Gyantse, for example, the Phase Two Yamāntaka finds a place in a set of wrathful protectors of the ten directions, along with Trailokyavijaya and Vighnāntaka. [COLOR PLATES 11-12] They are painted in a vestibule on the fourth level, below the upper *harmikā*, where the Phase Three Vajrabhairava is found.[33] Images of Phase Two Yamāntaka continue to be made in Tibet through the twentieth century. They are included in Phase Three *maṇḍala* of Raktayamāri, or even made as the central figures of independent images.[34] I have confined the present study to the earlier stages of Tibetan representation of *krodha-vighnāntaka*, since they are most closely tied to their Indian prototypes. No doubt later Tibetan Yamāntaka images are deserving of a more detailed study.

We have now followed the career of a *krodha-vighnāntaka* who appears early in Phase One and then is redefined in Phase Two. We have seen that Yamāntaka is of considerable importance as a Phase Two deity in South Asia. Other Phase Two deities, however, are equally, if not more important. Acala and Bhūtaḍāmara are deserving of more attention than we can afford here. The remainder of this section will take up a previously unseen deity, who is closely identified with Phase Two ideology: Trailokyavijaya.

Notes to Chapter Ten

1 T.18.891.583b (Njo 1061; KBC 1210). This text was translated by Dharmabhadra between 989-999 CE. Titled the *Māyājāla mahāyoga tantra daśakrodha vidyārāja mahāvidyā dhyāna kalpa sūtra*, it is a ritual and an "explanatory" text for the *Māyājāla Mahātantra* (T.18.890), which also names Yamāntaka first in its list (T.18.890.566a). The epigraph for this chapter comes from Jean Przyluski, "Le Bouddhisme Tantrique à Bali, d'après une publication récente," *Journal Asiatique* 218 (1931): 161.

2 T.20.1188.816a-b; T.20.1189.821a-822b; T.90.1190.828a-b. See the English translation of verses 62-71 in Davidson, "*Litany of Names of Mañjuśrī*," 26-27.

3 For a fascinating account of the Mahābodhi temple's history since the 17th c. and the activities of the Mahants to preserve their control in the 20th c., see Dipak K. Barua, *Buddha Gaya Temple: Its History*, 2nd ed. (Buddha Gaya, 1981), 72-129.

4 Francis Buchanan and R. M. Martin, *The History, Antiquities, Topography, and Statistics of Eastern India* (London, 1938), pl. IX.9; Rajendralala Mitra, *Buddha Gaya: The Great Buddhist Temple, the Hermitage of Śākya Muni* (Calcutta 1878; reprint, Delhi, 1972), pl. XXX, fig. 4. In both drawings the backdrop appears unbroken and the sword is whole, and the piece is located at the Mahants compound. R. Mitra identified the image as "apparently that of a Bhairava, a class of demoniacal attendants of Mahādeva." *Buddha Gaya*, 139. An unattributed, scathing review of Mitra's work is found in the *Indian Antiquary* 9 (1890): 113-116, 142-144.

5 T.21.1214.74c. Compare Duquenne, "Daiitoku Myōō," 662.

6 T.18.890.566a and T.18.891.583b-c, both translated by the Kashmiri monk Dharmabhadra, who received this name in 987.

7 Janice Leoshko, "Buddhist Sculptures from Bodhgaya," in *Bodhgaya, the site of enlightenment*, ed. J. Leoshko (Bombay, 1988), 50; idem, "Pilgrimage and the evidence of Bodhgaya's images" in *Function and Meaning in Buddhist Art*, ed. K.R. van Kooij and H. van der Veere (Groningen: Egbert Forsten, 1995), 45-57.

8 "I know of no other image from Bihar or Bengal depicting this particular form." Such images "seldom appeared anywhere in Bihar and Bengal." Leoshko, "Buddhist Sculptures from Bodhgaya," 50.

9 Nalanda Museum no. 00015.

10 For Nganjuk, see Jan Fontein, *The Sculpture of Indonesia* (New York, 1990), 223-233; Lokesh Chandra, "Identification of the Nañjuk Bronzes" and "The Bronze-find of Nañjuk," in *Cultural Horizons of India* Volume IV (New Delhi: Aditya Prakashan, 1995), 97-120. For Tabo and Tsaparang, see Tucci, *Spiti and Kunavar*; and, idem, *The Temples of Western Tibet and their Artistic Symbolism: Tsaparang (Indo-Tibetica III.2)*, trans. Uma Marina Vesci, ed. Lokesh Chandra (New Delhi, 1989).

11 ASI, *Annual Report 1920-21*, 39, 48 no. 17; Hirananda Sastri, *Nalanda and Its Epigraphic Material*, Memoirs of the Archaeological Survey of India no. 66 (Delhi, 1942), 118. Also discussed in Debjani Paul, *The Art of Nālandā: Development of Buddhist Sculpture AD 600-1200* (New Delhi, 1995), where it is dated "no later than the 11th century."

12 Leoshko, "Buddhist Sculptures from Bodhgaya," 50.

13 AIIS Negative no. 63-1.

14 These include the Trailokyavijaya **[162-164]** from Bodh Gaya; the Mārīcī sculpture in the field between Nalanda and the adjacent village of Bargaon; the 18-armed Chunda now cemented onto the outside of the Mahants compound wall, facing the river in an open chamber; and the Andhakāsurvadhamūrti on the porch of the Konch village *mandir* **[165-166]**, also discussed below in relation to the Mahants compound Trailokyavijaya.

15 P.K. Ray, "Kuruma, an Ancient Buddhist Site," *The Orissa Historical Research Journal* 24-26 (1980): 93-96.

16 See R.P. Mohapatra, *Archaeology in Orissa (Sites and Monuments)*, 2 vols. (Delhi, 1986), 1:144.

17 Giuseppe Tucci, *Gyantse and Its Monasteries: Part 1, General description of the Temples (Indo-Tibetica IV.1)*, trans. Uma Marina Vesci, ed. Lokesh Chandra (New Delhi, 1989), 9.

18 "Between the years 1000 and 1300 manuscripts were also illustrated in the Buddhist monasteries of Eastern India. A number of these have survived, and they clearly indicate that the Indian and the Nepali styles of illuminations belong essentially to the same fundamental tradition." Pal, *The Arts of Nepal*, Part II, 41. "It is the painted manuscript illustrations that display the most dramatic Pāla influences. Sometime around 1100 or slightly later a Pāla stylistic convention literally overwhelmed the Nepali convention in manuscript painting." S. and J. Huntington, *Leaves*, 258. The complex circumstances surrounding the creation of eastern Indian and Nepali (i.e., Katmandu valley) illuminated manuscripts, in which, for example, texts written in Nepali script are illuminated in Bihar figural style, and vice versa, are described in Losty, "Bengal, Bihar, Nepal?," 86-96, 140-149.

19 OR 13971B; W. Zwalf, *Buddhism: Art and Faith* (New York, 1985), 130.

20 On these temples, see Snellgrove and Skorupski, *Cultural Heritage of Ladakh*; and, Tucci, *Spiti and Kunavar*.

21 Pal, "Kashmir and the Tibetan Connection," 68-72. For a survey of some of the western Tibetan monasteries associated with Rinchen Zangpo's followers, see Romi Khosla, *Buddhist Monasteries in the Western Himalaya* (Kathmandu, 1979), 29-72. For Rinchen Zangpo, see Tucci, *Rin-chen-bzan-po*; and, Snellgrove and Skorupski, "Biography of Rinchen bZang-po," in *Cultural Heritage of Ladakh*, 2:83-116.

22 Tucci, *Rin-chen-bzan-po*, 31, 40 no. 6, 46 no. 64, 47 nos. 76, 77.

23 Snellgrove, *Indo-Tibetan Buddhism*, 485-486.

24 Goepper, "Clues for a Dating," 160; and, idem, *Alchi, Ladakh's Hidden Buddhist Sanctuary*. Though the date still remains controversial, a 12th c. date is more likely than a mid- to late 11th c. date, suggested by a previous belief that the Sumtsek was nearly contemporary to Rinchen Zangpo. See Deborah E. Klimburg-Salter, "Reformation and Renaissance: A Study of Indo-Tibetan Monasteries in the Eleventh Century," in *Orientalia Iosephi Tucci Memoriae Dicata* (Rome, 1987), 693.

25 The last 2 of the 9 patriarchs are the Kagyüpa hierarch Phakmo Drupa (1110-1170 CE) and the founder of the Drigungpa order, Jigten Gompa (1134-1217 CE). Both are discussed in Luciano Petech, "The 'Bri-gun-pa Sect in Western Tibet and Ladakh," in *Proceedings of the Csoma de Körös Memorial Symposium* (Budapest, 1978), 313-325.

26 Davidson, "*Litany of Names of Mañjuśrī*," 12.

27 Described in Snellgrove and Skorupski, *Cultural Heritage of Ladakh*, 1: 38-39. Parts of this *maṇḍala* (unfortunately none of Yamāntaka) are illustrated in Pal, *Buddhist Paradise*, D14-D18; and, Charles Genoud, *Buddhist Wall-painting of Ladakh* (Geneva, 1982), Alchi no. 7.

28 Snellgrove and Skorupski, *Cultural Heritage of Ladakh*, 2: 61-69.

29 Ibid., 2: 64-70, where the *maṇḍala* is described in detail, including Yamāntaka.

30 For the role of Yamāntaka within the overall context of the Sumtsek, see Rob Linrothe, "Mapping the Iconographic Programme of the Sumtsek," in Goepper, *Alchi, Ladakh's Hidden Sanctuary*, 269-272.

31 See Khosla, *Buddhist Monasteries*, 71-72; Snellgrove and Skorupski, *Cultural Heritage of Ladakh*, 1:22; Genoud, *Buddhist Wall-Painting*, 57-58; Rob Linrothe, "The Murals of Mangyu: A Distillation of Mature Esoteric Buddhist Iconography," *Orientations* 25, no. 11 (1994): 92-102.

32 Naudou, *Bouddhistes Kasmiriens*, title of Chapter Seven.

33 Franco Ricca and Eberto Lo Bue, *The Great Stupa of Gyantse: A Complete Tibetan Pantheon of the Fifteenth Century* (London, 1993), pls. 52, 49.

34 Note the bottom proper left hand corner of a 14th c. Raktayamāri *maṇḍala* in the Zimmerman Family collection, illustrated in Rhie and Thurman, *Wisdom and Compassion*, no. 75. As a central figure, see the 19th c. black-ground painting of Yamāntaka from the Joseph Heil collection, illustrated in Eleanor Olson, *Tantric Buddhist Art* (New York, 1974), no. 53 (cover illustration in color).

154. Trailokyavijaya in Vajradhātu maṇḍala, Alchi Dukhang (Ladakh), wall painting, ca. 12th century

11

Introduction to Trailokyavijaya

Oh, how great the upāya which rightly subdues;
of all upāya it is the greatest.
If through this upāya applied to transform sentient beings,
I manifest the krodha form, there are no [evil] effects of contamination.

Oh, how great the peerless mind of enlightenment (anuttara
bodhicitta), universally good, pure by nature.
If I cause sentient beings to submit, that krodha is born of a mystic love.

Stanzas spoken by Vajrapāṇi-Trailokyavijaya in the *STTS*

It is no exaggeration that Vajrapāṇi is "by far the most interesting divine being throughout the whole history of Buddhism."[1] Among his transformations, his incarnation as Trailokyavijaya is certainly one of the most fascinating and tightly packed, touching as it does on a number of key issues in the history of art and religion. At the core of these issues is the expression of the essential teachings of Esoteric Buddhism. The central metaphor is the *dompteur-dompté* relationship, which is not in itself confined to Esoteric Buddhism, but originates in the conquering of Māra by Śākyamuni.[2] Esoteric Buddhism appropriated this trope and used the *krodha-vighnāntaka* to express it. Yamāntaka, for instance, vanquishes Yama, and Bhūtaḍāmara tramples on Śiva-Aparājitā, the Lord of Demons. Trailokyavijaya extends and refines the *dompteur-dompté* relationship by conquering not deities associated with the underworld, but the Lord of the Three Worlds above them, Śiva-Maheśvara.

In the process of expressing the new paradigm, Esoteric Buddhist authors and artists renew this metaphor by permeating it with the peculiarly mystical principle of inversion.[3] One of the obvious ways this principle works is as the very notion of compassionate malevolence, of a terrible demonic violence lovingly applied, which is the essence of the *krodha-vighnāntaka*. At a deeper level the inversion penetrates the valence of conqueror-conquered, for their separate identities become transformed, exchanged, confused, and obliterated.

To a certain extent these issues are expressed in the relevant texts, some of which we have already mentioned (e.g., the *STTS* and the *SDPS*). Yet texts tend to remain in the realm of "pure" doctrine, making it too easy to ignore the historical reality necessarily affecting the creation of doctrine and its expression. Visual images make it more difficult to remain on the level of abstraction. Images are created by artists who, consciously or unconsciously, rely on historical precedents and contemporary innovations to dictate forms. The artist's world is rarely, or never, isolated and purely ideational; the form taken by a work of art refers unavoidably and directly to its historically conditioned material context. Only through a close reading of visual expressions of Trailokyavijaya will the Esoteric Buddhist message be perceived. The images are at least as potent as the dramas and descriptions found in texts. Ultimately texts and images are mutually comprehensible.

Together the two sources allow us to unite an understanding of the determining factors, historical and doctrinal. The primary historical issue which has been raised concerning Trailokyavijaya is the competitive relationship between Hinduism and Buddhism evoked by his image. Doctrinally, Trailokyavijaya has served to symbolize the adamant struggle toward enlightenment by conquering the *kleśa* which obstruct the realization of *samyaksambodhi*. In images of Trailokyavijaya history and doctrine, the mundane and the supramundane, coalesce.

1 Conquering the Three Worlds

Trailokyavijaya literally means "Conqueror of the Three Worlds." What are the three worlds? The three-fold world is an ancient conception of the cosmos. Vedic cosmology designates heaven, the ether and earth. In later Purānic thought the three become heaven, earth and the underworld, or hell.[4] The latter conception of the cosmos is particularly widespread, if not pan-Asian.[5]

For Buddhists there is yet another prominent interpretation of the three worlds. Stutterheim and Heine-Geldern first recognized the system as the basic structural arrangement of the temple at Borobudur: the worlds of desire, form, and formlessness.[6] The three worlds of heaven, earth and underworld all belong to the first two worlds of the Buddhist system. An extended quotation from Adrian Snodgrass's description of Buddhist cosmology is helpful for a fuller understanding of Trailokyavijaya's name and symbolism:

> *The Buddhist cosmos is divided into three worlds (trai-dhātuka, trai-lokya): the World of Desire (kāma-loka), the World of Form (rūpa-loka), and the Formless World (arūpa-loka). Together they make up the totality of the states of existence wherein deluded beings transmigrate in a succession of births and deaths, determined by the inexorable laws of causality. The World of Desire includes all those planes of existence where the inhabitants are subject to sensual cravings, those in which food, sexuality and sleep exist, ranging from the lowest hells through the six migratory realms to the six Heavens of Desire.*
>
> *The lowest of the six Heavens of Desire is the Heaven of the Four Celestial Kings (catur-mahā-rāja-kāyika), that is, the heaven of the Regents of the Four Directions, located on the sides of Mt. Meru. On the summit of Meru is the Heaven of the 33 Gods (trāyastriṃśa), ruled by Indra. These two heavens are called the Heavens of the Earth-Dwelling Gods (Jap. jigoten). Above them are the four Heavens of the Sky-Dwelling Gods: the Heaven of Time (yama); the Heaven of Contentment (tuṣita), where the future Buddha, the Bodhisattva Maitreya, resides; the Heaven of Joyful Transformations (nirmāṇa-rati); and the Heaven of Free Transformations by Others (para-nirmitavaśa-vartin).*
>
> *Above the six heavens of the World of Desire are the heavens of the World of Form. The beings dwelling in these heavens are no longer subject to desires or passions, but nevertheless still*

> *possess forms of an ethereal nature. . . . An ascent through these heavens is a passage to ever more refined and rarefied levels of consciousness and a withdrawal of consciousness towards its Centre. The World of Form comprises eighteen levels . . . the uppermost of these is the Heaven of the Final Limit of Form (akaniṣṭha), which is the heaven of the Non-Returners (anāgāmin).*
>
> *Beyond the Heaven of the Final Limit of Form is the third of the Buddhist Worlds, the Formless World (arūpa-loka), which includes those states of manifestation that do not possess any vestige of form but are nevertheless relative in that they are still subject to the workings of causation.*[7]

This discussion of the three worlds and of the Akaniṣṭha Heaven is of greater relevance for Trailokyavijaya than it might at first appear. Not only is the name Trailokyavijaya meaningful in this regard, but also the fact that he tramples Maheśvara. How are they connected? Akaniṣṭha is the highest realm attainable by sentient beings, men or gods, and is located at the uppermost limit of the *rūpa-loka*. According to the *STTS*, Akaniṣṭha is the site of the ultimate enlightenment of Śākyamuni.[8] Kaygrubjay summarizes the position of the *STTS* and that of three eastern Indian commentaries when he states that while Śākyamuni's maturation body (*vipākakāya*) remained at Bodh Gaya, "the mental body (*manomayakāya*) of the Bodhisattva Sarvārthasiddha proceeded to the Akaniṣṭha heaven," where the Buddhas of the ten directions initiated him into the five Abhisaṃbodhi. Following his initiation, he became Mahāvairocana and "proceeded to the summit of Mt. Sumeru and pronounced the Yoga Tantras," the fundamental "Yoga Tantra" being the *STTS*.[9]

In Buddhist cosmology Akaniṣṭha is ruled by Maheśvara from his radiant Palace.[10] Thus Trailokyavijaya's name implies mastery over all that lives in the three realms, a supremacy expressed visually by his subjugation of the Lord of the highest heaven, Maheśvara. Maheśvara is limited to the two lower realms of desire and of form. Although enlightenment takes place in Maheśvara's realm, it is not directed by him. The only exit from the realms he rules is through absolute enlightenment, which requires acceptance of the truth of the Buddhist path. The conflict created by Maheśvara's exalted but still limited ontological status is at the heart of the struggle in the second section of the *STTS*.

2 Conquering the Triple City and the Demon Brothers

Before we give a condensed version of the *STTS* narrative describing Maheśvara's submission to Trailokyavijaya, it is worthwhile to consider an analogous name in Brahmanical Hinduism. While Trailokyavijaya is the Conqueror of the Triple World, one of Śiva-Maheśvara's names is Tripurāntaka (-mūrti), the Destroyer of the Triple City. The story behind it is "one of the great myths of Śiva," with its roots in the Brāhmanas.[11]

There are a number of versions of this myth, but the basic story involves a group of demons who acquire several boons from Brahma through great asceticism. They are allowed to establish the Tripura, three cities of gold, silver and iron. The demons grow in power and harass men and gods, but because they perform sacrifices to Śiva, he declines to destroy them. According to some versions, in order to manipulate Śiva to destroy them, the gods trick the demons into becoming Buddhists. Viṣṇu produces the heretical *avatāra* of the Buddha, who beguiles the demons from worship of Śiva. They no longer slaughter animals for the requisite sacrifices. After various provocations, Śiva is induced to destroy the demons, using an arrow of which "Viṣṇu was made the point, Soma the head, and Agni the shaft of the arrow. Earth was the chariot."[12]

With Brahma as charioteer, Śiva shoots the fire-arrow, engulfing Tripura with flames and driving the demons from the three worlds. Śiva then chooses a boon as a reward: "Let me be overlord of the animals."[13] In an eighth-century stone carving [**155**], Śiva-Tripurāntaka is six-armed, and he stands in *ālīḍha* as he shoots an arrow at the triple cities which are stacked like boxes, one on top of the other. One city seems to come tumbling down. The four-headed Brahma can be identified as the charioteer.

The myth can be interpreted in a number of ways. On one level, the myth reminds Hindus that Śiva is the ultimate destroyer of the Three Worlds. In this case, Śiva as Lord of the Universe and on behalf of the other gods slays the demons, whose leaders were Pride, Anger, Shameful Behavior and Delusion, all dwelling in man. The flaming arrow Śiva aims is homologized with the *upasad* rites performed with Agni as agent.[14] In this sense, the "unlawful and unruly elements of life" are being brought under control through the socializing power of Vedic ritual, and Tripurāntaka is the "manifestation of the god's power utilized to uproot those who violate the established order of life."[15]

155. *Tripurāntaka, Pattadakal (Karnataka), ca. 8th century, National Museum, New Delhi*

It is difficult precisely to locate the temporal origin of these myths. Goswami places the earliest Tripurāntaka images between the sixth and seventh centuries, but he proposes, "the story of the destruction of the Tripuras by Śiva dates back to the period of the Brahmanas."[16] Doniger suggests certain Vaishnavite elements enfolded into the myths, such as Viṣṇu as Buddha-*avatāra*, who first deludes the demons and then manifests Kalki-*avatāra* to destroy them, "presuppose a political situation in the pre-Gupta period (precisely when the myth of the Buddha *avatāra* first appears), when orthodox Brahmins were fighting a desperate battle of two fronts, against foreign invaders and a thriving Buddhist community at home."[17] It is not unreasonable to assume that by the seventh century, when the *STTS* was being created, the Tripurāntaka myth was already established.

The parallels between the names Trailokyavijaya ("Conqueror of the Three Worlds") and Tripurāntaka ("Destroyer of the Three [Demon] Cities") should be clear. Other formal and iconographic parallels exist between Trailokyavijaya and Śiva. Trailokyavijaya invariably holds the bow and arrow and stands in *pratyālīḍha*, two elements of the ca. eighth-century Tripurāntaka image from Pattadakal.[18] [**155**] Most tellingly, Trailokyavijaya stands on Maheśvara-Śiva, Lord of the Universe, as if to supplant the Shaivite rituals with Buddhist methods of enlightenment in destroying the demons of Pride, Anger and Delusion. Moreover, he demonizes Śiva himself. Given the unorthodox, caste-violating character of Esoteric Buddhism, inner mystic features are emphasized at the expense of Hindu socially-directed ones.

Could these characteristics imply that the formulators of Trailokyavijaya, presumably the creators of the *STTS*, drew on earlier Shaivite myths and forms in shaping the character and form of

Trailokyavijaya? There is another strong indication given by the text that this is exactly what they did.

At the start of the second part of the *STTS*, which begins with the sixth chapter, Mahāvairocana has descended from Akaniṣṭha heaven to preach on the summit of Sumeru. He enters a *samādhi* called the *sarvatathāgata mahākrodha vajra-samaya vajra-adhiṣṭhāna samādhi* (the All-Tathāgata Great Wrathful *vajra*-pledge *vajra*-empowerment *samādhi*) and pronounces Trailokyavijaya's secret *dhāraṇī*:

> *Oṃ Śumbha, Niśumbha hūṃ gṛhṇa gṛhṇa hūṃ gṛhṇāpaya hūṃ ānaya ho bhagavan vajra hūṃ phaṭ.*[19]
>
> *(Oṃ Śumbha, Niśumbha! hūṃ, seize, seize, hūṃ, go and seize! Make them come, O Vajra Bhagavan hūṃ phaṭ.)*

Besides continuity with the kinds of commands and tasks given to Phase One *krodha-vighnāntaka* discussed in a previous chapter, what is remarkable here are the names Śumbha and Niśumbha. These names are so closely associated with Trailokyavijaya that he is sometimes known as the "Śumbharāja" or "Śumbha Vidyārāja."[20] But the pair has an earlier and more primary referent.

Śumbha and Niśumbha are two mighty demons, enemies of the gods, who were ultimately defeated by Devī-Pārvatī, the consort of Śiva, also known as Durga.[21] The story of Śumbha and his younger brother Niśumbha is recounted in the *Devī-Māhātmya*, which was incorporated into the *Mārkaṇḍeya Purāṇa* before the seventh century. *The Devī-Māhātmya* remained a popular text, and because it was sometimes illustrated, depictions of Pārvatī slaying Śumbha and Niśumbha survive.[22]

Having driven off all the gods who sing the praises of Pārvatī in order to win her over, Śumbha and Niśumbha receive reports of the beauty of Devī's emanation Kauśikī. Kauśikī replies to the demon-brothers' offers of marriage by vowing to marry only him who wins her in combat. When Śumbha's demon lieutenants are killed off in preliminary skirmishes, he sends two extraordinary demons, Chaṇḍa and Muṇḍa, to fight the goddess. From her forehead Kālī emerges with a sword and a noose. Kālī attacks and beheads Chaṇḍa and Muṇḍa and is rewarded by Pārvatī with the new name Chāmuṇḍā. Now Śumbha and Niśumbha lead their demon army themselves, ignoring a message carried by Śiva to release the gods and return their property. On the side of the demons is Raktabīja ("Red seed"), who had won a boon that from any drop of blood which fell from a wound another demon would spring. The demons' defeat is conclusive when Kālī/Chāmuṇḍā drinks up Raktabīja's blood before it falls to earth. Soon Śumbha and Niśumbha are also killed.

Trailokyavijaya's *dhāraṇī* reprises this myth, but for what reason, and in what way? With Śiva and his consort underfoot, Trailokyavijaya is hardly taking the side of the gods. Instead he calls on these demon-enemies of Śiva's consort to compel Maheśvara to appear, however unwilling he may be, just the way Phase One bodhisattva call on their attendant *krodha-vighnāntaka* for similar tasks. In the *STTS*, the two myths of Tripurāntaka and Devī are inverted, their victories reversed. The winners of the Hindu myths are the very ones who are trampled down, while the demons seem to be defended. Iyanaga thus calls Trailokyavijaya a Buddhist "*travestissement*" of Śumbha, who is subjugated by Śiva's consort.[23]

We may take it as established then that the account of Trailokyavijaya's subjugation of Maheśvara in the *STTS* is conditioned to a certain extent by earlier Hindu

Purāṇic and Shaivite elements. Before we can fully understand the significance of this, we need to examine more material. Let us turn now to a summary of the account found in the *STTS*.

3 Conquering Mahesvara in the *STTS*

The drama of Maheśvara's forced surrender to Trailokyavijaya is recounted most fully in the second section of the *STTS*. Sanskrit, Tibetan and Chinese versions of this account have been studied and at least partially translated or summarized in western languages by a number of scholars.[24] The primary account, in the *STTS*, was not translated into Chinese until between 1012 and 1015, while the Tibetan version was translated by Rinchen Zangpo (958-1055 CE), assisted by Śraddhakāravarma.[25] However, in the eighth century a somewhat truncated but still extensive and completely faithful account was given by Amoghavajra in his "Synopsis of the Eighteen Assemblies of the *Vajraśekhara*."[26] A related version, containing a few more details, also explicitly bases itself on the *Vajraśekhara* and is found in Amoghavajra's ritual for longevity.[27]

The main action takes up several dense pages of Chinese text, and is too long to translate literally here.[28] The passage itself has attracted several scholars for its considerable literary and dramatic interest, but other summarizations have sometimes omitted the most interesting passages for our purposes. What follows is a combined detailed summary and translation.

3.1. The drama of Maheśvara's submission: pride before a fall

Invited by all the Tathāgata to bring forth his own *kula*, Vajrapāṇi declines, because he is disturbed by Maheśvara and his evil cohorts: "If all the Tathāgata are unable to subjugate them, how can I control them?"[29] Mahāvairocana's entry into *samādhi* transports the Buddhist entourage to Sumeru, where more *samādhi* are achieved. Mahāvairocana produces from his heart the wrathful form of Vajrapāṇi (Trailokyavijaya) by means of *mantra* and *dhāraṇi*. "His eyebrows tremble with rage, with a frowning face, and protruding fangs, he has a great *krodha* appearance. He holds the *vajra*, *aṅkuśa*-hook, sharp sword, *pāśa*-noose and other *āyudha*."[30] Vajrapāṇi-Trailokyavijaya then utters the first of the two stanzas given at the start of this chapter and the second after entering Mahāvairocana's heart.[31] Upon Vajrapāṇi-Trailokyavijaya's emergence, Mahāvairocana utters the "hook" *dhāraṇi*, which assembles all the beings of the world around Sumeru.

Vajrapāṇi-Trailokyavijaya fingers his *vajra* and tells the assembly that, because they are now in the presence of the five Tathāgata, they should act in accordance with his orders. Maheśvara snaps, "What are you ordering me to do?"[32] Vajrapāṇi replies that he should take refuge in the Three Jewels, which will result in wisdom's wisdom. Maheśvara puffs himself up and manifests his wrathful form, saying:

> *You, Vajrapāṇi, are [merely] King of the Great Yakṣa. I am the paramount Lord of the Three Worlds. I create or destroy all classes of beings. I am self-existent, devatideva mahādeva (the great god of gods). And yet you order me to act as you, a Yakṣa King, would wish?*[33]

Vajrapāṇi-Trailokyavijaya, still fingering his *vajra*, calls him a wicked being who causes much harm and orders him quickly to enter the *maṇḍala* and obey the teachings. Maheśvara turns to Mahāvairocana and asks how it is possible that this "great gentleman" sees fit to command him. Mahāvairocana tells Maheśvara that he ought to listen lest he provoke Vajrapāṇi-Trailokyavijaya's angry form. "Don't make his *vajra* emit light! It will consume the Triloka!"[34]

Maheśvara laughs wickedly and manifests his own evil form, bringing forth his legions. He says, "Vajrapāṇi, I am the only Master of the Three Worlds. You should act on the basis of my teachings!" Vajrapāṇi-Trailokyavijaya fingers his *vajra* and gently laughs. "You stinking demon,[35] you eat the charred flesh of cremated corpses, your bed and clothes are disgusting remains," he replies. "Acting like this, how will you receive my teachings?"

Maheśvara assumes his Mahākrodha (Great Wrathful) form and says, "So it's like this, is it? I'll act according to my own inclinations." Vajrapāṇi-Trailokyavijaya appeals to Mahāvairocana:

> *Bhagavan, this Great Maheśvara relies on his own knowledge and power, his high position matching his pride in himself. He won't submit to the teachings of the pure dharma of all the Tathāgata. How can I let him get away with this?*

Mahāvairocana produces another *dhāraṇī*, which again mentions Niśumbha (*Oṃ* Niśumbha *vajra hūṃ phaṭ*[36]) and Vajrapāṇi-Trailokyavijaya speaks his own *hṛdaya* (*hūṃ*). At this all the gods are thrown into great suffering and they appeal to Vajrapāṇi. Maheśvara falls to the ground, loses consciousness and is about to die. Mahāvairocana tells Vajrapāṇi not to let them die. Vajrapāṇi commands Maheśvara and the others to take refuge in the Three Jewels and obey orders. Maheśvara asks, "If I take refuge in the Three Jewels, whose orders will I have to take? That's my question." Mahāvairocana tells him:

> *You should now know that this [i.e., Vajrapāṇi-Trailokyavijaya] is the Supreme Lord of All Tathāgata, the Father of All Tathāgata, who performs the will of All Tathāgata, the highest son of All Tathāgata, the all-virtuous Samantabhadra Vajrapāṇi Mahāsattva Bodhisattva. In order to transform all sentient beings he has received the Mahākrodharāja abhiṣeka-consecration. Why? This is because of you and yours who are so evil not even all the Tathāgata can tranquilize you. Because of this Vajrapāṇi commands all evil beings to be transformed and established in the samaya.*

Maheśvara replies to Mahāvairocana Buddha, "Bhagavan, I can't hold on to my life any longer. I'm willing to receive your teachings. If it's you who teaches me, I will accept and obey." The Buddha tells him, "If you can take refuge in Vajrapāṇi he can truly save you. And only he can save you."[37] The assembled gods plead in unison with Vajrapāṇi to save them. Vajrapāṇi again threatens to incinerate them with the flame of the *vajra* if they don't accept the teachings and revert to harming sentient beings. He defends his threat as in accordance with the will of all the Tathāgata. Setting Maheśvara aside, he consoles all the other *deva*, and by means of a *dhāraṇī* fills them with such joy that their hair stands on end. They are finally able to stand up on their own.

Mahāvairocana asks Vajrapāṇi why Maheśvara has not stood with the others. Is he dead? Vajrapāṇi speaks the *mantra* of restoring life, *vajrāyuh*.[38] Maheśvara wants to arise, but he exhausts his strength in the unsuccessful attempt. He asks Mahāvairocana, "Bhagavan, who is my master now?" The Buddha answers, "It is not I. It is by Vajrapāṇi that you are to be taught. Are you now unwilling to be taught and act as you should?" Maheśvara answers, "Bhagavan, if you are not my master, who will be able to protect all [of us] evil beings?" Mahāvairocana replies, "Vajrapāṇi can, but not I."

"How can this be?" Maheśvara asks. The Buddha says, "Because Vajrapāṇi is the Supreme Lord of All Tathāgata." Maheśvara pleads, "I don't understand what the Buddha means. The [five] Tathāgata Buddha are masters of the Triloka. So how can you say Vajrapāṇi is Supreme? I just really don't understand."[39]

At this point Vajrapāṇi-Trailokyavijaya once again steps in and admonishes Maheśvara, "You evil being! Why don't you obey my instructions?" Maheśvara, hearing Vajrapāṇi speak to him this way, once again produces his angry, fierce appearance and swears, "I'd rather die -- never will I accept your teachings!"

Vajrapāṇi-Trailokyavijaya manifests the Supreme Angry form and utters the *dhāraṇī*: *Oṃ pādākarṣaṇa vajra hūṃ*.[40] Mahāvairocana lifts his foot and from it there comes a *krodha-vighnāntaka* who encircles him, all in flames, frowning, with protruding teeth and a large terrifying head. He places himself before Mahāvairocana and asks for instructions. Then Vajrapāṇi-Trailokyavijaya, in order to purify Maheśvara, recites this *dhāraṇī*: *Oṃ pādākarṣakarṣaya sarva-vajra-dha . . . vajra hūṃ*.[41]

At the sound of the *dhāraṇī*, Maheśvara and Umādevā fall flat on their backs, their feet high in the air, exposing their disgusting nakedness. All the onlookers laugh at the spectacle. Summoned by the *krodha* deity who had emerged from the foot, all the gods stand at attention before Vajrapāṇi-Trailokyavijaya. He asks Mahāvairocana, "Bhagavan, these incredibly evil Rāja and Rāni, how should they be stopped?"[42]

Mahāvairocana pronounces another *dhāraṇī* as Vajrapāṇi-Trailokyavijaya tramples Maheśvara with his left foot and steps on Umādevā's breasts with his right. He speaks another *dhāraṇī*, which compels Maheśvara to clench his hands into one thousand fists and strike his thousand faces. Outside the pavilion where the spectacle takes place, the assembled *deva* cry with one great voice, "Today our Lord Maheśvara has been conquered by Vajrapāṇi!"

3.2. The drama of Maheśvara's submission: resurrection

Out of his great compassion for Maheśvara, Mahāvairocana speaks the *dhāraṇī* of the goodness of all the Buddhas, drawing Maheśvara immediately into *samādhi*, where his pain eases. Contact with Vajrapāṇi-Trailokyavijaya's foot then confers upon Maheśvara peerless powers, marvelous consecrations, *samādhi*, the ability to expound and other extraordinary boons. Having fully entered the gate of *samādhi*, Maheśvara's body emerges from beneath Vajrapāṇi's foot. Far past the earth, traversing as many worlds as thirty-two times the number of sands of the Ganges river, Maheśvara arrives at a world called Bhasmācchanna (Shelter of Ashes), where he is reborn as the Buddha Tathāgata Bhasmeśvara-nirghoṣa (Soundless Lord of Ashes).[43] Maheśvara then reappears at Sumeru and exclaims in a verse his new respect and understanding of the peerless Buddhist wisdom.

The Chinese apparently varies here from the Sanskrit, for while the first part of the verse agrees with the translation given by Snellgrove, the second part is completely different. Here we follow Snellgrove's translation for Maheśvara's speech:

> *Oho! the peerless wisdom of all the Buddhas! Falling at the feet of a yakṣa, one is established in nirvāṇa!*[44]

Vajrapāṇi-Trailokyavijaya then brings all the gods, including Maheśvara and Umā, into the *maṇḍala* of all the Tathāgata's Vajra Pledge, and instructs them in the *mudrā*, *dhāraṇī* and the vows they must pledge. They all receive new "Vajra" names.[45] Thus is Vajrapāṇi's *maṇḍala* formed.

The pictorial Trailokyavijaya *maṇḍala* is described further on in the chapter.[46] It is to resemble the *vajradhātu maṇḍala*, which is detailed in the first section of the *STTS*. We will pass over all the instructions for creating the *maṇḍala* and isolate the description of the central deity:

> *In the center paint Mahāsattva, that is, Vajrapāṇi. He is on a great blue lotus. He appears grandly as Vajrahūṃkāra.*[47] *His fangs protrude, he is very fierce and angry, and with an angry yet gleeful laugh and eyes. He holds up a vajra, marvelous in appearance. He has fiery hair and a nimbus of light. His left foot is lifted in an awe-inspiring stride, trampling on Maheśvara. His right foot should be painted this way, planted on Umādevī's breasts.*[48]

3.3. The drama of Maheśvara's submission: findings

From this account in the *STTS* four important points of relevance to the investigation of the position and function of wrathful deities in Phase Two Esoteric Buddhism may be drawn: 1) the glorification of Trailokyavijaya in the text; 2) the nature and character of Maheśvara's resistance; 3) Maheśvara's rebirth; and 4) the question of Vajrapāṇi-Trailokyavijaya's iconographic image.

In terms of Vajrapāṇi-Trailokyavijaya's status in the text, there is an interesting tension between highest and lowest. On the one hand, Maheśvara derides him as a mere Yakṣarāja. This accurately reflects Vajrapāṇi's historical antecedents in considerably earlier Buddhist literature and art. In the context of the *STTS* it is an outright insult. On the other hand, Mahāvairocana calls him the Lord of all the Tathāgata, both their father and their eldest son. Maheśvara, with us, asks, "How can this be?" Mahāvairocana is not given a chance to directly answer this question, for at this point Vajrapāṇi-Trailokyavijaya conveniently interrupts the conversation with another threat. So we too are left without an explicit doctrinal justification for the paramount functional distinction of a "lowly Yakṣa" and *krodha-vighnāntaka*. Mahāvairocana is allowed to reiterate that Trailokyavijaya is specially commissioned and equipped to perform those necessary tasks the Tathāgata cannot perform *with only peaceful means*. Nevertheless, Vajrapāṇi-Trailokyavijaya is extraordinarily esteemed. This degree of prominence would be unthinkable in a Phase One Esoteric Buddhist context. Even in its Phase Two context it is somewhat contrarily presented; after all, Vajrapāṇi-Trailokyavijaya himself says he merely executes the Tathāgata's orders. It is only in Phase Three contexts where the *krodha-vighnāntaka* fully realize their position of unambivalent dominance.

To compound the ambiguity of Vajrapāṇi-Trailokyavijaya's position, Maheśvara reacts immediatedly and vociferously against taking orders. He consistently resents being ordered by anyone, but particularly by someone he considers his inferior. He is willing to submit to Mahāvairocana, but to obey Vajrapāṇi-Trailokyavijaya is beneath his exalted position. The authors have framed his reactions as an archetypal instance of arrogance, pride and egoism. "I am the Lord of the Three Worlds, yet you presume to order me?" The text explicitly mentions his pride when Vajrapāṇi-Trailokyavijaya comments to Mahāvairocana that Maheśvara's pride matches his high position -- high indeed, having reached the overlordship of the highest heaven in the worlds of form.

As far as the text is concerned, Maheśvara's "wickedness" consists of his wrongful pride. He marshals his wrathful form and legions not reflexively but as a response to what he considers an insult to his dignity. His tenacity is admirable. Crippled and exhausted, unable to get up, he grimly vows, "I'd rather die" than submit to force. It is true that the text makes reference to his evil behavior outside the theater of the described action. Vajrapāṇi-Trailokyavijaya calls him an eater of cremated human flesh, an inhabitant of cemeteries who dresses in shrouds and ornaments himself with bits of bone. This is a clear reference to Shaivite sacrifices and customs.[49] But these trespasses Mahāvairocana would have been willing to forgive at the start had Maheśvara peacefully submitted. It was his intransigence, fed by ego, which required the intervention of Vajrapāṇi-Trailokyavijaya.

The punishment that is inflicted on Maheśvara just before he undergoes death and rebirth is another indication that the authors of the text intended to highlight pride, arrogance and self-centeredness as the principal obstacles in Maheśvara's behavior. He and his consort are made to suffer what the prideful fear most: humiliation. They are thrown on their backs, legs in the air, their nakedness revealed. In this degraded state, they are the objects of derision for their former minions and the entire assembly. Only then, in his "dark night of the soul," is Maheśvara's elemental *viśvarūpa* form revealed repentant. One thousand fists batter one thousand faces as Maheśvara surrenders.

From a close reading of the text and an analysis of its themes, it is obvious that pride, disgrace and redemptive transformation are the essence of the drama. Elsewhere I have discussed previous interpretations of Trailokyavijaya's humiliation of Maheśvara, which focus on sectarian rivalry between Hinduism and Buddhism.[50] The present reading does not preclude these interpretations. I believe, however, that it is not Śiva, or Shaivism, bearing the insult but at worst the pride lodged in the ontological position of "Lord of the Universe." Maheśvara is chosen primarily for his intelligibility as a symbol of pride, not for sectarian reasons.

We should also note that Maheśvara is not destroyed but transformed. Iyanaga has researched in detail the role of Maheśvara in Esoteric Buddhist texts. He finds that as the Master of the Three Worlds Maheśvara is still within the mundane plane but the closest of all beings to the Supramundane. As such he is the "Souverain dans l'Inscience."[51] Through contact, however unwilling, with Vajrapāṇi-Trailokyavijaya's foot, he is reborn as a Tathāgata in another world, re-enters a transformed body, is renamed and newly consecrated in wisdom. He pledges to be benevolent to sentient beings and to subdue evil ones.

We see then that the humiliation of Maheśvara is not malicious but productive. The object is not to eliminate his characteristic pride, but to transform it, to harness it and bring it to bear on Esoteric Buddhist ambitions. In the practice of Esoteric Buddhism there are two kinds of pride, one based on ignorance and one on wisdom. As a result of what is known in Tibet as "deity Yoga" Tsongkhapa instructs, "one should increasingly gain the ability to cut off one's ordinary ego through (1) [visualizing] the vivid appearance of the deity, and (2) [taking on] the ego of the deity."[52] The "special ego" is generated through identification with the deity. Kaygrubjay explains it with this example:

> *Then, muttering "Vajrasattva," one imagines in back of Vairocana a sun halo; and muttering "Vajrasattva samayas tvam ahaṃ" ('O Vajrasattva, you the symbol am I'), one brings about the 'pride' (garva) in oneself that oneself and the Knowledge Being are non-dual."*[53]

Once the "divine ego" is stabilized, the "ordinary ego" based on a false or ignorant conception of reality, falls away. Analogously, Maheśvara's pride is stabilized in his new wisdom, and no longer in the elevated, but ultimately illusory and transitory, position he previously occupied.

This essentially mystic process of transformation, using venom (humiliation) as a antidote to poison (pride), occurs time and again in Esoteric Buddhist texts. We cannot hope to understand it but merely to take notice of it here.[54] Based on his analysis of episodes in which forms of Śiva are trampled, R.A. Stein concludes:

> *Contrairement à ce qu'on a souvent dit, les divinités indiennes ne sont pas simplement placées à un rang inférieur pour marquer la supériorité du bouddhisme. Ce qui intéresse les tantristes, c'est la consubstantialité du "mal" (etc.) et du "bien," du "mondain" et du "supramondain," ou la transmutation de l'un en l'autre.*[55]

Finally, we must account for Trailokyavijaya's iconographic descriptions in the text. They are not as explicit as one might wish. At the very beginning of the second section devoted to Trailokyavijaya, we find the following description:

> *His eyebrows tremble with rage, with a frowning face, and protruding fangs, he has a great krodha appearance. He holds the vajra, aṅkuśa-hook, sharp sword, pāśa-noose and other āyudha.*

Besides generalized wrathfulness, the passage tells us that he must be more than four-armed, since four *āyudha* are specified and others are mentioned but left unspecified. We are told more than once that Vajrapāṇi-Trailokyavijaya's left foot tramples Maheśvara and his right foot tramples on Umādevā, or more precisely, on her breasts. In the passage describing the *maṇḍala*, the *pratyālīḍha* posture seems to be implied. Otherwise only the *vajra* is mentioned. This is not a thorough or detailed description of Trailokyavijaya, and the *SDPS* is not much more forthcoming. Generally it says of the *maṇḍala* painter, "In the center he draws the Lord Vajrapāṇi having the form of Trailokyavijaya."[56] In the *MVS* Trailokyavijaya, Vajrahūṃkāra and Trailokyavijaya-Candratilaka are also variously described, though usually they are said to hold the *vajra*. Apparently at the time these texts were composed, around the seventh century, the iconography of Trailokyavijaya was not yet firmly established.

Fortunately, there are a number of other texts, some translated in the eighth century before the majority of surviving bronze, stone and painted images were made, which give a fuller treatment to Trailokyavijaya's visual appearance. It is to them that we now turn.

4 Iconographic Information from Other Texts

The *Vajrāyuh dhāraṇī adhyāya kalpa* (T.20.1133, 1134A,B) also contains an account of Maheśvara's submission to Trailokyavijaya. Though the text is credited to Amoghavajra, Iyanaga accepts its three recensions more generally as belonging to the "school of Amoghavajra."[57] However, it seems likely that we can rely on its attribution to Amoghavajra himself, since the title appears in a list of more than seventy of his translations included in a memorial sent to the emperor Daizong on his birthday in 771 CE requesting that they be entered into the imperial catalogue.[58] Thus the work was translated around mid-century. It provides us with two crucial details. All three recensions are nearly identical to the following passage:

> *Then Bhagavan [Mahāvairocana] entered krodha samādhi. At his heart there was manifested the five pointed vajra of mahābodhicitta [the great thought of enlightenment]. From this there emerged Trailokyavijaya Vajrabodhisattva, with four heads and eight arms, awesome, giving off such great effulgence he was difficult to look at.*[59]

A text credited to Yixing (683-727 CE) also describes Trailokyavijaya as four-headed and eight-armed.[60] The adept is to visualize Trailokyavijaya with four wrathful heads and eight arms. Each hand holds an unspecified *āyudha*. His left foot is on Maheśvara and his right on Umā. If this is indeed a translation of Yixing, then this specific image was known by the first quarter of the eighth century.

Certainly by the mid-eighth century Trailokyavijaya's description was standardized. This is again confirmed by one of Amoghavajra's translations, in an explanatory ritual text, possibly written down ca. 765 CE by his disciple, concerning the *Sūtra of Benevolent Kings*.[61] Amoghavajra briefly discusses Trailokyavijaya and his iconography in relation to the set of five *krodha-vighnāntaka*. He specifies a connection with the *Vajraśekhara* cycle and observes that Vajrapāṇi's "Commanding Sphere" manifestation (Trailokyavijaya) can extinguish the ego and the subtlest of *karma*. "The wrathful Trailokyavijaya is four headed, eight armed, smashing Lord Maheśvara and his demon legion, who would invade and injure the True Dharma."[62]

Still another of Amoghavajra's texts gives us the fullest description of Trailokyavijaya.[63] A short text which again is referred to as a section of the *Vajraśekhara*, it is devoted to Trailokyavijaya alone. Lokesh Chandra reconstructs the Sanskrit title as follows: *Trailokyavijaya sādhana vidhi atiguhya dvāra from the Vajraśekhara-tantra*.[64] This text derives its sterling pedigree from the inclusion of its title in a list of texts brought back to Japan by Kōbō Daishi in 806 CE[65] and in the complete list of Amoghavajra's translations found in Yuanzhao's *Zhenyuan xinding shijiao mulu* (T.55.2157.879-881). Since this was compiled in 800 CE, and the title does not appear in the memorial of 771 CE, the translation must have been finished by Amoghavajra between 22 November 771 CE, when the memorial was submitted, and his death on 28 July 774 CE. One passage reads as follows:

> *Samantabhadra Vajrapāṇi, in order to transform everything, manifests the body of [Vajra-] Hūṃkāra, who utterly destroys the poisons (kleśa) in the three worlds, establishing bodhi in its place. This is the great and profound mystery, Trailokyavijaya.*[66]

In the ritual the adept performs the "self-generation" by visualizing Vajrapāṇi-Trailokyavijaya. The visualization begins with a *vajra* transformed into Vajrahūṃkāra, with whom the adept identifies. Having received the five *abhiṣeka*-initiations and recited the 108 names, one enters into total union with the deity. Then:

> *Stepping from right to left (i.e. pratyālīḍha), pacify that rude and insolent one, Maheśvara, Kāmarāja (King of Lust) by striking him to the ground. Fix the left foot on his head while the right tramples the breasts of his consort Umā. Their selfishness and rudeness will be cut off by means of this foot to the head. In the world of ashes (Bhasmācchanna) he will become a Buddha, and will remain in the samaya-pledge.*[67]

At the end of the text we find the following description of Trailokyavijaya:

> *Make the "two-wing mudrā" at the level of the heart (i.e. hands in front, little fingers entwined); the right hands hold a vajra with five points, the others like this: an arrow and a sword are held. The upper left hand holds a hook with a vajra-finial (?), then a bow and then a pāśa-noose, all held by outstretched arms. Of the four faces, the central one is dark (blue), the right one yellow, the left one green, and the rear head is red and very wrathful. Maheśvara and consort form his "throne" as described before. Vajrahūṃkāra -- [his image] is made with these lakṣana (auspicious marks).*[68]

This specific and detailed description does not in any way contradict the generalized one found in the *STTS*. Between the descriptions found in the *MVS* and those in the *STTS* cycle, we have found two forms of Trailokyavijaya in texts current in the eighth century. One is a two-armed form in which the raised *vajra* is most prominent. The second is the eight-armed form characterized by the "two-wing" *mudrā* (i.e., the *trailokyavijaya mudrā*), the *vajra*, arrow and sword in right hands, and the bow, *aṅkuśa*-hook and *pāśa*-noose in the left. In the latter he stands in *pratyālīḍha* on Maheśvara and Umādevā with the proper left and right feet respectively.

The combination of specific descriptions and parallel functions in accord with those found in the *STTS* makes it clear that the four-headed, eight-armed Trailokya-vijaya standing in *pratyālīḍha* on Maheśvara and Umādevā is the hero of the second section of the *STTS*. It is important to clarify this, because the text itself nearly always calls him Vajrapāṇi, despite the fact that Trailokyavijaya is the name of the entire section and the *maṇḍala*. Iyanaga has noted this anomaly in the text, and he cites different textual evidence to demonstrate that Trailokyavijaya was understood as the form of Vajrapāṇi who subjugates Maheśvara.[69] Moreover, where the text outlines the Trailokyavijaya *maṇḍala*, Vajrapāṇi is described as appearing as Vajrahūṃkāra, a well-established variant of Trailokyavijaya.[70]

The late seventh and eighth-century texts do not distinguish between Vajrahūṃkāra and Trailokyavijaya. Both names are used interchangeably to refer to the form of Vajrapāṇi who conquers Maheśvara and Umādevā. This is complicated by the fact that two standard visual forms, the two-armed and eight-armed forms, are known to South, East and Southeast Asian Esoteric Buddhism. During the early period both are recognized as variants of the same deity. We have just seen that Vajrahūṃkāra is used as the name of the eight-armed deity, and that a text using Trailokyavijaya in its title (T.21.1209) still uses Vajrahūṃkāra as an epithet. But in the late anthologies of *sādhana*, the *Sādhanamālā* and *Sādhana samuccaya*, the name Vajrahūṃkāra designates the two-armed form, and Trailokyavijaya the eight-armed form.[71] The *Sādhanamālā* was most likely compiled in the twelfth century,[72] more than a century after Trailokyavijaya's period of florescence in eastern India, as evidenced by the circulation of texts like the *STTS* (ca. late seventh through eleventh centuries) and extant images (ca. ninth and tenth centuries). The assignment of different names to the two forms, though convenient, is not supported by the texts from which the *sādhana* were culled, adapted and anthologized. Therefore we will follow the more authoritative example of the full texts and not that of the late iconographic digests by using both names for both forms.

Having investigated Trailokyavijaya's names, appearance and intrinsic meaning as derivable from a survey of some of the more important texts dealing with him, we can turn now to the surviving images themselves. As we do so, we need to keep in mind the deep structural relationship between Trailokyavijaya and Śiva in terms of Trailokyavijaya's name, function, activity and description. Although we have uncovered these issues through the textual part of our analysis, we will find that they orbit around the pictorial representations of Trailokyavijaya as well. Only after examining both in conjunction can we attempt to synthesize Trailokyavijaya's iconologic value.

Notes to Chapter Eleven

1 Snellgrove, *Indo-Tibetan Buddhism*, 134. The epigraph for this chapter comes from T.18.882.370b and 370c.

2 In the ca. 2nd c. Sarvastivadin *Aśokāvadāna* the monk Upagupta subjugates and then converts Māra. See John S. Strong, *The Legend of King Aśoka: A Study and Translation of the Aśokāvadāna* (Princeton, 1983), 185-198. This is an interesting mediating step between Early Buddhism and the *krodha-vighnāntaka*. Several parallels can be made, including the forced conversion through the power of compassion, the vow Māra makes in some versions to become a Buddha, as well as his temporary metamorphosis into the form of the Buddha for Upagupta. See also Lowell W. Bloss, "The Taming of Māra: Witnessing to the Buddha's Virtues," *History of Religions* 18.2 (1978): 156-176.

3 Iyanaga stresses that this "inversion des valeurs . . . est une caractéristique extrêmement importante du bouddhisme ésotérique." Iyanaga, "Recits de la Soumission," 733. R.A. Stein's structuralist analysis of the Trailokyavijaya-Maheśvara and related myths features inversion and "renversement." R.A. Stein, "Recherches autour du récit de Rudra (Tibet)," *Annuaire du Collège de France* 74 (1974): 508-517; and idem, "Problèmes de mythologie et de rituel tantriques (Tibet)," *Annuaire du Collège de France* 73 (1973): 463-470.

4 Wendy Doniger O'Flaherty, *The Origins of Evil in Hindu Mythology* (Berkeley, 1976), 180.

5 See Schuyler V.R. Cammann, "Religious Symbolism in Persian Art," *History of Religions* 15 (1976): 204; and, idem, "Symbolic Meanings in Oriental Rug Patterns," *Textile Museum Journal* 3 (1972): 24-25.

6 See Luis O. Gómez and Hiram W. Woodward, Jr., "Introduction," in *Barabudur: History and Significance of a Buddhist Monument* (Berkeley, 1981), 9; and Marea A. Johnstone, *Borobudur: An Analysis of the Gallery 1 Reliefs*, Pelita Borobudur Series C no. 3 (Borobudur, 1981), 3. Stutterheim's identification, which has been generally accepted, is criticized in Luis O. Gómez, "Observations of the Role of the *Gandavyuha* in the Design of Barabudur," in *Barabudur: History and Significance of a Buddhist Monument*, 180-181.

7 Adrian Snodgrass, *The Symbolism of the Stūpa* (Ithaca, 1985), 329-330 (including full references).

8 Snodgrass quotes Śubhakarasiṁha to the effect that Akaniṣṭha is "the place where Buddhas have attained Awakening since ancient times." *Symbolism of the Stūpa*, 335

9 Lessing and Wayman, *Mkhas-grub-rje's*, 27.

10 Snodgrass, *Symbolism of the Stūpa*, 335, 340.

11 O'Flaherty, *Origins of Evil*, 180-189, 198-211. Versions of the myth are also recounted in Stella Kramrisch, *The Presence of Śiva* (Princeton, 1981), 405-421; Niranjan Goswami, "A Study of the Ugra-Mūrtis of Śiva" (Ph.D. dissertation, University of Pennsylvania, 1972), 76-83; and, Arya Ramchandra Tiwari, "Rare Image of the Tripurāntaka in the Watson Museum, Rajkot," *Bulletin of the Baroda Museum* 28 (1978-79): 221-234.

12 Goswami, "Ugra-Mūrtis of Śiva," 78.

13 Kramrisch, *Presence of Śiva*, 405.

14 Ibid., 415.

15 Goswami, "Ugra-Mūrtis of Śiva," 74, 76. Another interpretation of the Tripurāntaka myth stressing the death and rebirth of the year-cycle is given in G.P. Upadhyay, "Reappraisal of the Myth of Tripurādahana," *Journal of Indian History* 54 (1976): 539-546. Later the Tripurā is reconfigured as a Hindu tantric goddess with strong inner yoga symbolism. See Douglas Renfrew Brooks, *The Secret of the Three Cities: An Introduction to Hindu Śākta Tantrism* (Chicago, 1990).

16 Goswami, "Ugra-Mūrtis of Śiva," 44.

17 O'Flaherty, *Origins of Evil*, 200.

18 Also see Kramrisch, *Presence of Śiva*, pl. 31, for the Ellora Kailasa image of Tripurāntaka; Stella Kramrisch, *Manifestations of Śiva* (Philadelphia, 1981), no. 40; and, Goswami, "Ugra-Mūrtis of Śiva," figs. 1-7.

19 T.18.882.370b-c. I follow Iyanaga's reconstruction of the Sanskrit *dhāraṇī*. Iyanaga "Récits de la Soumission," 668. For the translation, see Ibid., note 44; and, Snodgrass, *Matrix and Diamond World*, 723. Snellgrove seems to interpret the names Śumbha and Niśumbha in Vajrapāṇi-Trailokyavijaya's *dhāraṇī* as names of Śiva. Snellgrove, *Indo-Tibetan Buddhism*, 141-142, note 50. Snellgrove's translation of another *dhāraṇī* from the same section of the *STTS* which mentions Śumbha and Niśumbha is difficult to square with the belief that these are names of Śiva: "O vajra-action, most excellent, bear in mind the pledge of Vajradhara. Śumbha niśumbha -- coerce, induce, prevail, bind, hold to the pledge, affect all actions for me, O Vajrasattva." Ibid., 142.

20 See the Phase Two Mañjuvajra or Dharmadhātu Vāgiśvara Mañjuśrī *maṇḍala* in Snellgrove and Skorupski, *Cultural Heritage of Ladakh*, 2:64-68; B. Bhattacharyya, *Niṣpannayogāvali*, 58-60. On this epithet of Trailokyavijaya, see Iyanaga, "Récits de la Soumission," 668, note 44. Snodgrass points out that the *Susiddhikara sūtra* (T.18.893) refers to Trailokyavijaya as Śumbharāja in *Matrix and Diamond World*, 278.

21 Devī defeats them in the wrathful form of Kālarātri, who "is regarded as the creative force of Viṣṇu," but when "Kālarātri is required to annihilate the demoniac forces in the universe she has to imbibe in herself the qualities of Pārvatī," that is, the consort of Śiva. Shyam Kishore Lal, *Female Divinities in Hindu Mythology and Ritual* (Puna, 1980), 147-148.

22 Marie-Thérèse de Mallmann, "Un manuscrit illustré du Devī-Māhātmya," *Arts Asiatiques* 2 (1955): 178. For a 14th c. Nepalese manuscript in the Bharat Kala Bhavan, Benares, see Pal, *Arts of Nepal: Part II*, fig. 58. For an 18th c. manuscript in the Musée Guimet, see Marie-Thérèse de Mallmann, "Un manuscrit illustré," esp. figs. 8, 17-18.

23 Iyanaga "Récits de la Soumission," 668, note 44.

24 Tucci, *Stūpa*, 140-145; R.A. Stein, "Recherches autour du récit de Rudra," 512-514; Snellgrove, *Indo-Tibetan Buddhism*, 136-140; idem, "Introduction," 39-48; Iyanaga "Récits de la soumission," 668-682; Davidson, "Reflections," 200-202. It is striking that with the exception of the earliest of these authors (Giuseppe Tucci) none of these keen scholars have utilized, or drawn attention to, the many images of Trailokyavijaya.

25 Ui Hakuju et al, *A Complete Catalogue of the Tibetan Buddhist Canons (*bka'-'gyur *and* bstan-'gyur*)* (Sendai, 1934), no. 479. Amy Heller informs me that commentaries of the *STTS* were translated into Tibetan in the mid-eighth century, and a version of the text itself was translated by the late eighth. Personal communication.

26 T.18.869.285a-b. This is dealt with by Iyanaga, "Récits de la Soumission," 659-664. Snodgrass points out that according to the *Zhenyuan xinding shijia mulu* by Yuanzhao (T.55.2157; KBC 1401) dated 800 CE, Amoghavajra received the complete *Vajraśekhara Sūtra* in 18 assemblies and 100,000 stanzas from King Śilamegha in 742 CE during his *sūtra-* and *abhiṣeka*-collection trip in Sri Lanka. The "Synopsis" would have been based on this. *Matrix and Diamond World*, 559.

27 *Vajrāyuh dhāraṇī adhyāya kalpa*, T.20.1133, 1134A,B (Njo 1391, KBC 1319). Iyanaga, who translates sections of this text into French and has compared it closely to the "Synopsis," bravely concludes that Amoghavajra must have read it just before writing the "Synopsis." Iyanaga, "Récits de la Soumission," 664.

28 T.18.882.369b-373b.

29 T.18.882.370a.

30 T.18.882.370b.

31 T.18.882.370b-c.

32 T.18.882.370c.

33 T.18.883.371a.

34 Ibid.

35 *Kaṭapūtana*, meaning *preta* of the lower regions.

36 T.18.882.371b. I have followed the Sanskrit in Tucci, *Stūpa*, 141; Snellgrove *Indo-Tibetan Buddhism*, 137; Snellgrove, "Introduction," . 41; and, Iyanaga,"Récits de la soumission," 670.

37 T.18.882.371c.

38 T.18.882.371c. This life-restoring *mantra* is at the center of Amoghavajra's ritual mentioned above. (See Note 27.)

39 T.18.882.372a.

40 Ibid. Sanskrit after Tucci, *Stūpa*, 144; and, Iyanaga "Récits de la soumission," 673. Possibly, "*Oṃ*, drawn-from-the-foot, *vajra hūṃ*."

41 T.18.882.372a. Sanskrit after Tucci, *Stūpa*, 144.

42 T.18.882.372b.

43 Ibid. Sanskrit after Tucci, *Stūpa*, 145; and, Iyanaga, "Récits de la soumission," 675. Snellgrove has "Bhasmacchatra (Umbrella of Ashes)." *Indo-Tibetan Buddhism*, 138.

44 Snellgrove, *Indo-Tibetan Buddhism*,138. However, a similar *gātha* is spoken by Maheśvara during a retelling of the events (as part of Chapter 11 detailing the Trailokyavijaya-*cakra-maṇḍala* cycle). T.18.882.389c.

45 T.18.882.372c-373a.

46 T.18.882.376a-381a.

47 Vajrahūṃkāra is the standard epithet of Trailokyavijaya, and many texts use the two interchangeably. See Snodgrass, *Matrix and Diamond World*, 275-277.

48 T.18.882.376c. This appears in 7-character verse format, but I have translated it as prose.

49 For an example of corpse rituals performed in a cremation ground, see David N. Lorenzen, *The Kāpālikas and Kālāmukhas, Two Lost Saivite Sects* (New Delhi, 1972); 63. For the use of ashes and bones as ornaments, see ibid., 2-3.

50 Linrothe, "Beyond Sectarianism," 17 -25.

51 Iyanaga "Récits de la soumission," 741. See also Iyanaga Nobumi, "Daijizaiten," *Hōbōgirin* 6 (1983): 713-765.

52 As translated by Beyer, *Cult of Tārā*, 77.

53 Lessing and Wayman, *Mkhas-grub-rje's*, 243.

54 "As a washerman makes a dirty cloth clean with some matter which itself is dirty, as a man infected with poison is sometimes cured of it by poison itself or as some water accidentally gone into ones ears is taken out by the help of some additional water itself, so, the writer wants to assert, one can get rid of *rāga* and *kāma* by those *rāgas* and *kāmas* themselves, which become the cause of bondage only when they are resorted to by the foolish, but not by the wise in whose case they are actually the cause of emancipation." Prabhubhai Patel, "Cittaviśuddhiprakaranam of Āryadeva," *Indian Historical Quarterly* 9 (1933): 720.

55 R.A. Stein, "Problèmes de mythologie," 46.

56 Skorupski, *Sarvadurgatipariśodhana*, 55 (emphasis in original). For similar passages, see ibid., 59, note 52, 60. Vajravarman's commentary mentions an unusual 4-armed form of "Jñānadeva Trailokyavijaya" in a *homa* ritual: white, holding a *vajra*, noose and lotus and making *tarjanī mudrā*, he tramples on the sins of the person performing the ritual. Ibid., 84, note 28.

57 T.20.1133 is attributed to Vajrabodhi and Amoghavajra, while T.20.1134A, B are attributed to Amoghavajra alone. Iyanaga, "Récits de la soumission," 664, note 22. Iyanaga takes a very critical attitude toward the integrity of Amoghavajra as translator. (He is far from alone in this; Michel Strickmann considers that "most of the seventy-five-odd tantric texts attributed to Amoghavajra as translator" are not translations, "but rather works composed in China, and directly in Chinese." Michel Strickmann, "Heralds of Maitreya," unpublished paper at the Princeton Conference on Maitreya Studies 1- 3 May 1983, 22.) Iyanaga suggests that "apart from a few texts of Śubhakarasiṁha of which the authenticity seems assured, many of the 'translations' of Vajrabodhi, and the immense majority of those of Amoghavajra were composed in China. . . . In general it is the translations dating to the second half of the Tang (from the time of Amoghavajra) which are the most doubtful." Ibid., 640-641. Nevertheless, Iyanaga relies on these very texts for most of his analysis. It may well be that many of the ritual texts were compiled in China, but the more closely they are compared to texts and archaeological remains from eastern India, Southeast Asia and the Himalayan region, the more convincing they become as evidence that Amoghavajra was deeply learned in "authentic" Sanskrit traditions.

58 This memorial is included in the *Daizongchao zeng sikong dabian zheng guangzhi sanzang heshang biaozhi ji* (T.52.2120), a collection of memorials and their responses of Amoghavajra assembled at the end of the 8th c. by his disciple Yuanzhao. The memorial is translated in Orlando, "Tantric Buddhist Patriarch Amoghavajra," 67-71. The list of titles is not translated there, but is found in T.52.2120.839a-840a. The *Vajrāyuḥ dhāraṇī adhyāya kalpa* is found at T.52.2120.839b.

59 T.20.1133.575b; 1134A.576a; 1134B.577c (emphasis added).

60 T.19.981.411b-c. This text is accepted by Mochizuki as having been translated by Yixing. Mochizuki Shinkō with Tsukamoto Zenryū, *Bukkyō daijiten*, 4th ed. (Tokyo 1958-1963) 1:129c.

61 T.19.994. This text is probably the ritual text on the *Sūtra of Benevolent Kings*, which appears in Amoghavajra's memorial list of 771 CE, though in the list the title has been shortened. T.52.2120.840a.

62 T.19.992.514b-c.

63 T.21.1209 (Njo 1389, KBC 1380). T.21.1210 is another short ritual text on Trailokyavijaya, also credited to Amoghavajra. It is found only in Japan and is an *abhicāraka* text with many *homa* rituals for various purposes. It may be a Japanese compilation.

64 Nanjio, *Catalogue*, 21, no. 1389.

65 Kūkai, *Kōbō daishi zenshū*, 7 vols. (Kyoto, 1965), 1: 81.

66 T.21.1209.39c. This and following passages are expressed in 5-character verse form, but I have rendered them in prose.

67 T.21.1209.40b.

68 T.21.1209.41a.

69 Iyanaga, "Récits de la soumission," 725-727, note 5. I find it remarkable that this truly learned scholar, for whom I have the profoundest respect, did not use the iconographic evidence of descriptions contained in the text he studied so well.

70 T.18.882.376c. Debala Mitra gives other examples of Vajrahūṃkāra used as an epithet of Trailokyavijaya in *Achutrajpur*, 90.

71 Both are given in truncated form in B. Bhattacharyya, *Indian Buddhist Iconography*, 181-182, 184-185. For a slightly fuller Sanskrit text and French translation, see Foucher, *Étude sur l'iconographie Bouddhique*, 58-60.

72 B. Bhattacharyya, *Indian Buddhist Iconography*, 385.

156. *Two-armed Trailokyavijaya, Nalanda (Bihar), ca. late 8th-9th century, National Museum, New Delhi*

12

Trailokyavijaya: Images

Trailokyavijaya is one of the premier Phase Two *krodha-vighnāntaka*, and a number of eastern Indian Trailokyavijaya images bear examination. The images furnish strong evidence for the status of the *krodha-vighnāntaka* as independent of Buddha or bodhisattva in the second phase of Esoteric Buddhism. In terms of both size and expression, several are by any standard extremely powerful images. Their skillful execution reflects the care and attention elicited by Trailokyavijaya's importance. Representations of Trailokyavijaya are consistently *vīra*-Yakṣa, the type that conveys the heroic tasks of the warrior perhaps better than the *vāmana*-Yakṣa type, which was retained mainly for reformulated Phase One *krodha-vighnāntaka* such as Yamāntaka and Hayagrīva.

If eastern Indian Trailokyavijaya images are consistently of the *vīra*-Yakṣa body-type, they can otherwise be split into two types: two-armed and eight-armed. The earliest surviving eastern Indian Trailokyavijaya image happens to be two-armed, but around the tenth century both types are found contemporaneously. If we endorse a commonsense model of simplicity evolving into complexity, it is tempting to imagine that the two-armed form of Vajrapāṇi-Trailokyavijya was succeeded first by a related four-armed form, known as Bhūtaḍāmara,[1] and finally by the eight-armed Trailokyavijaya. But too few images have survived to demonstrate this or any other developmental scenario. Textual evidence suggests both two-armed and eight-armed forms equally represent Trailokyavijaya-Vajrahūṃkāra, and there is no absolute proof that one developed earlier than the other.

1 Two-armed stone Trailokyavijaya from Nalanda

A stone sculpture from Nalanda conforms to all identified Trailokyavijaya images in that he is *vīra*-Yakṣa. [**156**] He stands in a rather angular *pratyālīḍha*, making his principal *mudrā* in front of his chest, little fingers intertwined. In his crown are three tiny images of seated Tathāgata in *dhyāna mudrā*. His other adornments include upper arm bands, bracelets, a jeweled girdle, necklace, earrings and an *upavita*. His scarf winds around his arm and shoulder in a complicated manner, ending in swallow-tails.

Trailokyavijaya stands on Maheśvara and Umādevā, as the texts describe. Maheśvara-Śiva is two-armed and twisted around ignominiously, with his buttocks in the air, recalling the *STTS* account of his humiliation. Trailokyavijaya's right foot is placed on Umā's breasts. She rests on top of Maheśvara's left leg. Unlike Trailokyavijaya, Maheśvara has an incised third eye.

Though deeply cut and nearly free-standing, Trailokyavijaya stands against a backdrop on which there are nine spurts of flame. The flame motifs are suggestive of passages in some of the texts already cited. For instance, the *Vajrāyuh dhāraṇī adhyāya kalpa* describes Trailokyavijaya as emitting almost blinding light, and in the *STTS* the light from his *vajra* is capable of consuming the Triloka in flames.

At the top of the backdrop, just to the proper right of Trailokyavijaya's crown, is an obscured Sanskrit letter. On the rounded back of the highly polished black stone is a legible donative inscription.[2] The piece was discovered at Nalanda Monastery Site 1A. The date is a matter of conjecture. Saraswati published this image as "Bihar (?) c. 11th century."[3] The sculpture indeed originated in Bihar, where Nalanda is located, but an eleventh century date is far too late. In fact, one of the most stylistically comparable works is the eighth-century Phase One masterpiece depicting Hayagrīva attending Avalokiteśvara, also from Nalanda. **[157]**

157. *Twelve-armed Avalokiteśvara with Hayagrīva, Nalanda (Bihar), ca. 8th century, Nalanda Museum, same as* 65

Despite the vast disparity in scale, the two sculptures share several stylistic elements. The shape of Trailokyavijaya's backdrop, for instance, echoes those of the seated Buddha at the upper register of the Avalokiteśvara piece. Also comparable are the heavy, bulging eyes, the sensual mouths and the U-shaped indentations on the knees. The form of the garment-end between Trailokyavijaya's legs resembles the diagonal trails of fabric gathered at Avalokiteśvara's proper left side. Trailokyavijaya's eyebrows are connected by the same hooked semi-circle over the bridge of the nose as are Avalokiteśvara's, and Umādevā wears the narrow breast-band not found on later images but prominent on some of the female figures in the larger sculpture. The much larger scale and greater artistic mastery of the Avalokiteśvara image make the ornamental details of the Trailokyavijaya seem cruder, but the two crowns and the medallions on the necklaces are generally related. There is also a similar treatment to the garment folds in the scarves, though Trailokyavijaya's has a stepped wedge-shaped fold, more deeply cut and less regular.

On the basis of these similarities, the Nalanda Trailokyavijaya **[156]** may be placed in the late eighth or ninth century. As such it is probably the earliest extant Trailokyavijaya image from eastern India.

2 The Achutrajpur Trailokyavijaya

In June of 1963, at a village called Achutrajpur on the outskirts of Banpur, south of Puri in southeastern Orissa, the grounds around a high school were being leveled. A gold-plated water-pot was uncovered, and then, two days later, a large hoard of metal images was found inside three earthen pots. Seventy-five of the ninety-five metal images recovered from the site are Buddhist, and an additional twenty metal *stūpas* were also found. The remaining metal figures are Jain, Hindu or undetermined. These Buddhist sculptures and a few stone fragments with Buddhist inscriptions testify that the site was most likely a Buddhist monastery. Brick walls were found, but in order to preserve the school built over them in 1930, the site has

158.*Two-armed Trailokyavijaya, Achutrajpur (Orissa), metalwork, ca. 10th century, Orissa State Museum, Bhubaneswar, same as 3*

159. *Tripurāntaka, same as 155*

not been excavated. Based on her on-site inspection within a month of the discovery, Mitra suggests that the hoard "might have been stored in one of the cells of the monastery."[4]

One of the largest metalwork images (47.1 cms. in height) was found alongside the earthen pots. It depicts the two-armed Trailokyavijaya, making his name-sake *mudrā* while also grasping a *vajra* and bell in the two hands. [**158**] Shyam Sundar Pattnaik implies that based on paleographic evidence the date of this piece falls between the ninth and tenth centuries. Debala Mitra suggests it "may perhaps be dated in the second half of the tenth century AD."[5] A date of ca. tenth century is accepted here.

Trailokyavijaya has a high crown in which appear four of the five Tathāgata Buddha (Amitābha is rendered invisible by the backdrop). Trailokyavijaya wears a fearsome grimace, his fangs projecting out of his mouth, with furrowed brow and bulging silver-inlaid eyes. The pupils are notched as if once inlaid. He stands in an exaggerated *pratyālīḍha* against a circular backdrop bordered by small flames that enclose larger flame motifs, recalling the Nalanda backdrop. Underfoot we find an eight-armed Maheśvara and a four-armed Umādevā.

This is the most elaborate version of Maheśvara in known images of Trailokyavijaya and is deserving of close attention here. The naked Maheśvara lies on his back. There are a cobra and a crescent moon in his hair, two attributes characteristic of forms of Śiva. Two more distinctive attributes of Śiva are his third eye (Trailokyavijaya has none) and garland of skulls. His nakedness and gestures poignantly convey the message of humiliation and subjugation found in the *STTS* text. His arms are spread out, palms up, as if to surrender. One pair of Umādevā's arms are similarly arranged, but her second right hand touches Trailokyavijaya's foot almost tenderly. The gesture is found consistently on Trailokyavijaya images of both eastern India and Japan. On the platform beside her are a sword and *triśūla*, while scattered about Maheśvara are a *pāśa*-noose, arrows, a bow with a broken string, a bell, another *triśūla*, a *ḍamaru*-drum between his feet and a sword or hatchet at his back.

These *āyudha* are all proper to Śiva in various forms. The bow and arrows particularly remind us in this context of Tripurāntaka [**159**], but they remind us as well of the description of the *āyudha* held by the eight-armed Trailokyavijaya as given in the Amoghavajra text mentioned above.[6] The bow and arrow, the *pāśa* and the sword all correspond to the text's catalogue. Only the *ḍamaru* and the *triśūla* are not taken up by Trailokyavijaya, but we will discover that images of the *krodhavighnāntaka* sometimes include at least the *triśūla*. It is almost as if we have here a visual depiction of an eight-armed Maheśvara surrendering his weapons (or, more to the point, his powers) to Trailokyavijaya. Having conquered the eight-armed Śiva, Trailokyavijaya is about to be transformed into his eight-armed form, which will enable him to pick up the weapons and wield them for Buddhist purposes. We will return to this interpretation once other images have provided additional support.

160. *Trailokyavijaya, Nalanda (Bihar), metalwork, ca. 10th century, Patna Museum*

3 Metal eight-armed Trailokyavijaya from Nalanda

Among a hoard of seventy-five metal and stone images found at monastery site 9 at Nalanda in 1932-33 was a twenty-five centimeter Trailokyavijaya. [**160-161**] Now in the Patna Museum, the figure is solid cast in one piece of bronze, with silver inlaid eyes. Once again the piece has been variously dated. In the Patna Museum catalog of 1965 we find a date of seventh century CE, while an earlier catalogue of 1957 was closer to the mark in assigning a tenth-century date.[7] Here we will follow von Schroeder's date of 850-950 CE.[8]

Like the Orissan Trailokyavijaya [**158**], this one holds the *vajra* and *ghaṇṭa*-bell in the right and left hands respectively, even as they intertwine the little fingers in *trailokyavijaya mudrā*. The other attributes are almost entirely lost. There is the end of a weapon handle or short staff in the middle left hand. A *vajra*-tipped *pāśa* also remains in the lower left hand. As befitting a manifestation of Vajrapāṇi and a member of the *vajrakula*, his throne is supported by elephants otherwise associated with Akṣobhya, the Tathāgata Buddha of the *vajrakula*. Since this is a free-standing image, we can confirm that the eight-armed Trailokyavijaya is indeed four-headed, as the photograph from the rear demonstrates. [**161**]

Maheśvara and Umādevā are both two-armed, and their postures mimic one another. Their ankles are crossed, and each places one hand at a hip. Maheśvara's left leg rests on top of Umādevā's. A *triśūla*-tipped staff lays at Maheśvara's left side, and his right hand holds what appears to be a *karttikā*-chopper.

Another notable aspect of this bronze image is the large garland or *vanamālā* hanging around Trailokyavijaya's neck and down between his knees. The garland is strung with tiny Buddha images, each an individually rendered plaque. They are too small and indistinct to make out the *mudrā* of each Buddha, but all seem to be making standard gestures of meditation. In light of what we learned in the *STTS* about the subjugation, conversion and rebirth of Maheś-vara, it is tempting to see this garland as the counterpart of the garland of skulls with which Śiva-Maheśvara is associated generally. The Orissan eight-armed Maheśvara [**158**] wears the garland of skulls. Just as one imagines that the eight-armed Trailokya-vijaya has picked up Śiva's abandoned *āyudha* so as to wield them in the service of Buddhism, so too the garland of skulls undergoes a Buddhist metamorphosis. The structural inversion is visible only in art, though it has a basis in a deep understanding of the teachings verbally expressed in the literature.

161. *Rear view of* **160**

4 Stone Trailokyavijaya from Bodh Gaya

The most important eastern Indian Trailokyavijaya image to survive, and arguably the most important extant eastern Indian Phase Two *krodha-vighnāntaka* image, is the nearly life-size stone sculpture of Trailokyavijaya now in the sculpture shed of the Mahants compound, Bodh Gaya.[9] [**145** left, **162-164**] It depicts a handsome *vīra*-Yakṣa, eight-armed Trailokyavijaya in *pratyālīḍha* trampling Maheśvara and Umādevā. An inscription, *"paindapātika-vi(r)yendrabhadrasya,"* indicates that the sculpture was a gift of a Buddhist monk named Viryendrabhadra.[10] There seems to be general agreement that this is a tenth-century work. Leoshko places it there, while Susan Huntington specifies a mid-tenth-century date.[11]

The jewelry is evenly distributed on the main figure, providing densely ornamented contrasts to the smooth tubular limbs. An elegant pattern is formed at the waist and between the legs of Trailokyavijaya by the *vanamālā*, a thinner *upavita* and a series of belts. Three ends curl from a central clasp, the two outer ones given bell finials. The entire sequence is enclosed by the triangular drape of his *dhoti*-skirt. Along the thighs the *dhoti* is inscribed with an evenly-spaced linear pattern of incised garment folds. The vigor of the active posture and gestures is contained by the still, inner-directed gaze and sinuous sway of Trailokyavijaya. The overall effect of the sculpture is one of power, langour and detachment.

A clue to the value of iconographic precision is found in the arrangment of the heads. In order that there be no mistaking that it is a four-headed deity, the artist has sacrificed symmetry and moved the fourth head from the back, where it would have been invisible and uncarvable, to the right side. Thus there are two heads on the right, one on the left and one in the center. [**164**] The central face is damaged, and it is difficult to determine if it had a third eye, as have the other three heads, but it seems not. In the crown of the central head there is an image of Mahāvairocana in front and Amitāyus on the right side. The left side of the crown is damaged. Long tendrils of hair fall down onto both shoulders from beneath the crown.

The condition of this image is sufficient for identification of all the attributes. Trailokyavijaya has eight arms, the two central hands distinguished from the other six by having two wrist bracelets instead of one. They make the *trailokyavijaya mudrā* and hold the *vajra* and the *ghaṇṭa*-bell. The upper proper right hand swings a sword overhead; the middle hand holds a long handled *aṅkuśa*-hook [**164**]; the lower right plucks an arrow out of a quiver.[12][**162**] The left hands hold a wheel, a bow and a *pāśa*. We find once again a *vanamālā* of Buddha images, all in *dhyāna mudrā*, joined at the bottom by a central medallion.

Maheśvara and Umādevā are both two-armed. A short inscription beneath Maheśvara reads "Bhūta" (demon) and under Umādevā "Bhūti" (demoness).[13] Their legs are intertwined in a somewhat suggestive manner. [**163**] Śiva-Maheśvara's long hair, piled up into a *jaṭāmukuṭa*, is starting to unfurl and spill onto the pedestal behind his head. He holds a *daṇḍa* in his proper left hand and gestures upward as if in the *vandana mudrā* of submission with his right. With her right hand, Umādevā rather tenderly cups Trailokyavijaya's right foot, which presses on her breasts. Her left hand rests on her knee. It is curious to note that in the Orissan bronze [**158**], a two-armed Trailokyavijaya tramples an eight-armed Maheśvara, while in the Nalanda bronze [**160**] and the Bodh Gaya stone sculpture [**162**], an eight-armed Trailokyavijaya tramples a two-armed Maheśvara.

Hardly twenty-five miles northwest of Bodh Gaya, where the Trailokya-vijaya now in the Mahants compound stands, there is a Śiva sculpture which focuses visually the intertwined iconography of Trailokyavijaya and Śiva already hinted at in

162. *Trailokyavijaya, Mahants compound, Bodh Gaya (Bihar), ca. 10th century, same as* **7, 141**

163. *Detail of* **162**

the texts discussed. This is a fine Andhakārimūrti-Śiva sculpture set up on the porch of the Konch Mandir.[14] [**165-166**] The overall form-feeling and the details of jewelry, ornamentation and *āyudha* indicate a more than generic similarity. This manifestation of Śiva closely resembles not only the Śiva-Maheśvara under Trailokyavijaya's left foot, but in many ways Trailokyavijaya himself.

A few decorative details along with formal values establish the common style of the two. The precise form of the broad necklace, the narrower garland, the upper arm bands and the sword (shape, hilt, decoration) are roughly identical. The necklace, in fact, corresponds exactly to that worn by the trampled Maheśvara. [**163-164, 166**] So too the distinctive earrings, adorning both Trailokyavijaya and Maheśvara in the Mahants compound sculpture [**163-164**] and Śiva in Konch village. [**166**] Śiva's hairdo in both instances is the same, though in the Buddhist sculpture [**163**] it is beginning to unfurl. The thrust of three-dimensionality from the flat backdrop in both sculptures is revealing of a similar origin, as are the proportions of the main figures in relation to the backdrops and the feeling of internalized languid power. Perhaps most telling is the splayed outlay of bell-tipped belt-ends dangling from a central volute between the thighs of both the Konch Śiva and the Mahants compound Trailokyavijaya. Many more details and technical features could be pointed out, including an approximately equal size, but there is already enough to conclude they were made at about the same time (ca. tenth century) and that they come from the same immediate milieu, if not from the same workshop.

Those born into that milieu would be able to recognize Śiva underneath Trailokyavijaya's foot. Not only would the hair, jewelry and costume appear similar, but also the one visible *āyudha* which Maheśvara carries in his right hand, the *daṇḍa*. [**163, 166**] They might also pause at the main figure of Trailokyavijaya [**162**] and wonder for a moment at its similarity to Andhakārimūrti. [**166**] Both are eight-armed, both hold a sword in the upper right hand, their poses are mirror-images (*ālīḍha* and *pratyālīḍha*) and both trample demons. Where Śiva-Andhakārimūrti wears a *vanamālā* studded with skulls, Trailokyavijaya wears one made up of plaques of the Buddha. The wheel which Trailokyavijaya holds in the upper left hand is also identified with Andhakārimūrti, though it does not appear in the Konch image.[15] Finally, as already discussed, the bow and arrow which Trailokyavijaya holds in left and right hands respectively, are closely associated with another wrathful form of Śiva, Tripurāntaka. [**155**]

164. *Trailokyavijaya, detail of* **162**

A blaze of refractions between the two myths of Andhakārimūrti's defeat of the demon Andhaka and Trailokyavijaya's subjugation of Maheśvara flash between the two images. Andhakārimūrti carries a skull cup to catch every drop of Andhaka's blood before it spawns another Andhaka. The wrathful female, Yogeśvarī (located above the head of the demon on Andhakārimūrti's left in **166**), must drink up the blood from the skull cup before Andhaka can be defeated. The necessity is mirrored in the *Devī-Māhātmya* when Kālarātri must drink up the blood of Śumbha's warrior, Raktabīja. Śumbha, it will be recalled, has now become Trailokyavijaya's minion and features in his *dhāraṇī*. Moroever, Andhaka is described in terms which remind us of those used for Maheśvara in the *STTS*. Goswami describes him thus:

> *[Andhaka] the invincible ruler thoroughly enjoyed the three worlds, which increased his arrogance and blinded him by pride. [By lusting after Śiva's consort] he unknowingly invited his own destruction. . . . Śiva defeated him, pierced his heart and transfixed him with his trident. He was then held aloft in the sky like a banner staff. The Asura king, however, did not die even after this. He praised Śiva and was made the chieftain of the Śivagaṇas.*[16]

This sounds strikingly like the *STTS* account, which tells of Maheśvara, blinded by pride and finally conquered by Trailokyavijaya's *vajra* (in a sense, the Buddhist equivalent of the *triśūla*), but even then not exterminated. He flies through the universe, is reborn as a Tathāgata, returns to the assembly singing the virtues of Trailokyavijaya and becomes one of the chief protectors of beings. The main adaptation is that in the Buddhist version, Trailokyavijaya has taken over the role of Śiva, and Śiva is assigned a role as the symbol of pride and ignorance.

Visually the parallels move in the same direction of multiple identity and inversion: Maheśvara tramples, and is trampled by Trailokyavijaya, and both seem to be forms of Śiva. In Buddhist terms, this means both *dompteur* and *dompté* are forms of the deluded, contingent self, before and after enlightenment. The Mahants compound Trailokyavijaya is a visible expression of the inner process of self-transformation. It is not an image of a "god" meant to inspire prostration and worship

165. *Andhakārimūrti, detail of* **166**

of its powers, but a symbol of the processes of purification and regeneration undertaken by Phase Two Esoteric Buddhist practitioners.

In order to embody these processes graphically, the artists seem to have consciously refered to Shaivite imagery. We must postulate the priority of Śiva imagery since Buddhist texts and sculptures refer to Shaivite forms, and not vice versa. Images such as the Mahants compound Trailokyavijaya were intended for an audience of initiated practitioners. These observer-participants would have been familiar with Śumbha and Niśumbha. They could understand the connotation of the name Trailokyavijaya, and they would recognize Śiva in Trailokyavijaya as much as in Maheśvara underfoot. Iconographic references to Shaivite imagery, and even to specific images of Śiva, are the visual counterparts of the cross-referenced layering of myths in the texts. By creating an image of Trailokyavijaya which emanated a shadow image of Śiva in the minds of the viewers, the artists transcended sectarian animosity. For it is a transformed echo image of Śiva who tramples Maheśvara underfoot. The net effect is a subtle and tightly packed symbolic form.[17]

This is the product of a highly sophisticated art form, integrating artistic conventions with intellectual, emotional and deep psychological insights directed to Buddhist purposes. The Bodh Gaya Trailokyavijaya is in this regard one of the most powerful and successful images of eastern Indian Esoteric Buddhism. Through its relations with other images, myths and texts, the deep structure of Trailokyavijaya is revealed. Though derived immediately from the Mahants compound image, this interpretation may be extended to the other Trailokyavijaya images which survive and, to the extent that it is applicable, to Phase Two *krodha-vighnāntaka* in general.

5 Stone Trailokyavijaya fragment from Nalanda

We can apply the insight gained from the study of the texts and of the Bodh Gaya Trailokyavijaya to a stone fragment recovered at Nalanda and still in the site museum there. [**167-169**] It is also datable to the ca. tenth century. The sculpture is

166. *Andhakārimūrti (Śiva), Konch (Bihar), ca. 10th century*

presumably a product of the Nalanda school, distinct from the Gaya/Bodh Gaya works found at the Mahants compound and in Konch. However, all three belong to the same regional style.

The upper half of the sculpture has not been recovered. The lower half itself was recovered in at least two pieces. A photograph taken prior to repair shows it lacking a triangular wedge demarcated by Trailokyavijaya's proper left leg.[18] The piece has now been reattached.

Only Trailokyavijaya's lower right hand is visible, plucking an arrow out of a quiver [**167**], just as in the Mahants compound sculpture. [**162**] Another visible *āyudha,* the *vajra*-tipped *pāśa*-noose, was once held in the lower left hand and again corresponds to the Bodh Gaya piece. The distinctive *vanamālā* of Buddha images is also present. Each of the fifteen Buddha images is rendered clearly enough to see that, unlike the Bodh Gaya image, not all make the *dhyāna mudrā.*[19] Trailokyavijaya stands in *pratyālīḍha,* trampling a two-armed Maheśvara, who is laid out on his back holding a *triśūla* and a *vajra,* and Umādevā, who holds the same implements. A skull joins the handle to the trident of the *triśūla.* Śiva smiles beneficently, as if to suggest his reawakening with a transformed attitude of willing surrender. Maheśvara and Umādevā intertwine their ankles, somewhat similar to the Nalanda bronze [**160**], a piece which dates to the same period and features nearly identical pricked floral roundels on the *dhotis*.

Despite the severe loss of much of the sculpture, these attributes are enough to identify the main figure unquestionably as Trailokyavijaya. The sculpture's size indicates that it was a relatively major piece, and thus we know that during the tenth century, at Nalanda as well as at Bodh Gaya, Trailokyavijaya was not a deity of minor importance. His status required more than small votive pieces [**156**] or even medium sized bronzes. [**158** and **160**]

167. *Trailokyavijaya fragment, Nalanda (Bihar), ca. 10th century, Nalanda Museum*

The Nalanda fragment contributes even more exciting information. Emerging out of the flaming backdrop, in low relief, are two shadowy figures. Both have two arms and long wavy hair pulled up into a loose bun. Each carries a shield and either a *daṇḍa*-club or a sword. Only the upper torso of each is visible, naked but for a necklace. One is poised over Umādevā's thighs [**168**], the other over Maheś-vara's head. [**169**] These two figures closely resemble contemporary Phase One *krodha-vighnāntaka*, such as those we found accompanying bodhisattva. One could compare the hair style, for instance, to that of Hayagrīva. [**95**] Who are these beings?

They can only be Śumbha and his brother Niśumbha. Invoked by Trailokya-vijaya's *dhāraṇī*, the two demons appear out of the flames to battle once again their old nemeses, the tricksters whom they once worshipped, and who then betrayed and defeated them.[20] Under Trailokyavijaya's aegis , they now return to harrass the

168. *(below right) Śumbha or Niśumbha, detail of* **167**

169. *Śumbha or Niśumbha, detail of* **167**

fallen symbols of pride, lust, and anger. This is the only known depiction of these figures in a Trailokyavijaya composition. There are no obvious alternatives, though I am not aware of any instance in modern scholarship where they have been identified as Śumbha and Niśumbha.

In the light of all we have learned about the nexus of meaning surrounding Trailokyavijaya, this identification seems to fit most easily. It is also a fine marker in the overall development of *krodha-vighnāntaka* imagery. We have here an instance where Trailokyavijaya, a Phase Two wrathful figure, is himself attended by *krodha-vighnāntaka*. Their classification as Phase One deities is determined by their subsidiary status and their participation in the general scope of Phase One iconography. Conforming to the conventions we identified in Chapter Three, they are typical two-armed, *vāmana*-Yakṣa and small in stature compared to the dominant figure. What we know of their identities from the texts also fits with the early development of Phase One *krodha-vighnāntaka*. As are the earliest such figures, Śumbha and Niśumbha are converted demons, Yakṣa and Asura. That Trailokyavijaya utilizes such attendants demonstrates the overall rising status of *krodha-vighnāntaka* within the historical framework I am proposing. The texts have proved valuable for making sense of the images. The images in turn demonstrate the truth that "Myth is tied to form, and art is the expression of a mythic conception of the world."[21]

6 Western Tibetan Images of Trailokyavijaya

We have already had occasion to introduce the historical context of Esoteric Buddhism in western Tibet and to explore aspects of the Phase Two Esoteric Buddhist art at Alchi, Sumda and Mangyu. It is therefore necessary only briefly to discuss the three types of situations in which one finds Trailokyavijaya images. All three are *maṇḍala* of the five Tathāgata variety. Two are variations of *STTS maṇḍala*, while the third is a Mañjuśrī *maṇḍala*. Both eight- and two-armed forms appear, and Trailokyavijaya's status in the *maṇḍala* varies from primary to secondary, or even tertiary. They provide a number of parallels with surviving eastern Indian images. At the same time the image-type stands outside the eastern Indian tradition in that Trailokyavijaya is consistently depicted as *vāmana*-Yakṣa, instead of the more usual *vīra*-Yakṣa. Furthermore, in the four-headed eight-armed images, the fourth head is generally placed atop the other three. All in all, the western Tibet images are extremely valuable for this study because they provide images which are fully contextualized within the Esoteric Buddhist system.

6.1 The Sarvavid Mahāvairocana krodha maṇḍala

The first *maṇḍala* on the left hand (south) wall as one enters the Dukhang at Alchi is a huge five Tathāgata *maṇḍala*. It has been well published.[22] Pal, Snellgrove and Skorupski identify it as a *vajradhātu maṇḍala*. They agree that at the center is a white four-headed, two-armed Sarvavid Mahāvairocana Tathāgata. Pal notes that the other four Tathāgata are each represented by an "[a]ngry manifestation," but he does not identify them individually. Snellgrove and Skorupski observe:

> *Special attention is given to Akṣobhya in the east, who alone in this set of major manifestations [is] four-headed and eight-armed. The other Buddha-manifestations are one-headed and two-armed.*[23]

170. Trailokyavijaya in eastern quadrant of vajradhātu maṇḍala (detail), Alchi Dukhang (Ladakh) wall painting, ca. 12th century, same as **154**

Despite taking special note of the eight-armed figure in the eastern quadrant, the two scholars do not name the wrathful deity, who is clearly Trailokyavijaya.[24] **[170]** He stands in *pratyālīḍha* on Maheśvara and Umādevā, each under the appropriate foot. The *lambodara* Trailokyavijaya carries the sword, arrow and hook in the proper right hands, the bow, *tarjanī mudrā* and a noose in the proper left. These features leave no doubt that the artists at Alchi were following textual and/or artistic models and traditions which derived from eastern India.[25]

This *maṇḍala* closely relates to the *maṇḍala* described in the *STTS*. There too the four-headed Mahāvairocana sits in the center of the five Tathāgata *maṇḍala*, but in the Alchi Dukhang painting the other Tathāgata also appear in their *krodha-vighnāntaka* manifestations. The importance of this *maṇḍala*, and the others to be described shortly, cannot be overestimated. It visually equates the *krodha-vighnāntaka* with the Tathāgata, in the same way that the *STTS* itself calls Trailokyavijaya "Supreme Lord of the Tathāgata."

6.2 The Trailokyavijaya maṇḍala

A Trailokyavijaya *maṇḍala* not commented on by Snellgrove-Skorupski or Pal is preserved above Mahākāla on the inside of the entrance wall of the Dukhang of Alchi.[26] **[171]** It follows very closely the description in the second section of the *STTS*.[27] A number of details also correspond to the structure of the eighth and ninth *maṇḍala* in the *vajradhātu maṇḍala* as preserved in Japan.[28] In the center is the blue two-armed Trailokyavijaya making his namesake *mudrā*, and at the four primary directions are two-armed *krodha-vighnāntaka*. This leads us to believe that the *krodha maṇḍala* with all five Tathāgata represented by their wrathful forms existed in the eastern Indian tradition (though none survive), a contention which is further confirmed by a textual reference in the Sanskrit *Sang hyang Nagabayusūtra*, a text discovered in Bali.[29]

171. *Trailokyavijaya maṇḍala, Alchi Dukhang (Ladakh), wall painting, ca. 12th century*

We have discovered that Trailokyavijaya plays two different roles in the same Phase Two setting of the Dukhang at Alchi. [170-171] First he is given special attention in the Sarvavid Mahāvairocana *vajradhātu maṇḍala*, being the only one of four *krodha-vighnāntaka* individualized by his full eight-armed form. He is honored as well at the center of his own *maṇḍala* in his two-armed form. Trailokyavijaya occurs a third time in the same room, however, as a comparatively minor figure.

6.3 Trailokyavijaya in the Mañjuśrī dharmadhātu maṇḍala

The second *maṇḍala* on the south wall of the Dukhang at Alchi is the Vāgishvara Mañjuśrī *dharmadhātu maṇḍala*.[30] Unfortunately none of the published photographs includes the whole painting. Thus the Trailokyavijaya in the lower proper left corner of the outer square has not been published in detail.[31] [172]

Trailokyavijaya is blue and tramples in *pratyālīḍha* on Maheśvara and Umādevā. The positions of the latter are reversed. Trailokyavijaya is once again *vāmana*-Yakṣa, and he makes the *trailokyavijaya mudrā* while holding the bell and *vajra*. His right hands hold the sword, an arrow and the *aṅkuśa*-hook. His left holds the bow, a noose and a *vajra*. These *āyudha* are quite standard. Rather unusual is the Buddha head which rises from his crown. While small seated Buddha images are found in the crowns of eastern Indian images [158, 160, 162] and in East Asian ones

172. *Trailokyavijaya, Vāgishvara Mañjuśrī dharmadhātu maṇḍala (detail), Alchi Dukhang (Ladakh), wall painting, ca. 12th century*

173. *Trailokyavijaya, Vāgishvara Mañjuśrī dharmadhātu maṇḍala (detail), Sumda (Ladakh), wall painting, ca. 12th century*

as well,[32] only a central Javanese metalwork Trailokyavijaya now in Leiden offers a parallel for the head alone.[33]

At Sumda the same Vāgishvara Mañjuśrī *dharmadhātu maṇḍala* is found in nearly the identical position as in the Dukhang at Alchi. Trailokyavijaya appears again in the northeast corner. [173] Iconographically the Sumda image is nearly identical to the one in Alchi, except that the top head is Trailokyavijaya's fourth, rather than a fifth Buddha head. Both Trailokyavijaya are included in this Phase Two *maṇḍala* as part of a set of wrathful deities which also includes Yamānataka. In terms of the overall theme, Trailokyavijaya plays a relatively modest role. This is true particularly when compared to the two other *maṇḍala* in Alchi's Dukhang, where Trailokyavijaya plays prominent roles.

All of Trailokyavijaya's appearances at Alchi and Sumda of which we have made note are confined to Phase Two contexts. Even when Trailokyavijaya's role is tertiary, he is one of a group of four or ten *krodha-vighnāntaka* and not a component of a Phase One triadic structure. His relatively minor role in the Mañjuśrī *maṇḍala* is nonetheless a reminder of the lesser status and function of earlier *krodha-vighnāntaka*. In the same space the Phase Two status of the *krodha-vighnāntaka* is asserted by Trailokyavijaya's pivotal role in the Sarvavid Mahāvairocana *maṇḍala* [170] and the presence of his own *maṇḍala*. [171] The coincidence of Phase One and Phase Two style images of Trailokyavijaya in western Tibet is a forceful illustration of the evolution of Esoteric Buddhism and the growth of the *krodha-vighnāntaka* within that system. Like a bamboo, new growth does not discard the old, but uses it as a foundation for higher aspirations.

7 Trailokyavijaya in later Tibetan art

Trailokyavijaya nearly disappears with the advent of Phase Three Esoteric Buddhism. Or perhaps more accurately, he is transformed into a Phase Three *krodha-*

vighnāntaka. Despite his importance to Phase Two Esoteric Buddhism, there are relatively few central Tibetan images of Trailokyavijaya. It is not difficult to account for his loss of importance. By the thirteenth century, Esoteric Buddhism in eastern India was predominantly Phase Three, and it was this mode that was transplanted to Tibet as well. In Phase Three Trailokyavijaya is often relegated to the type of relatively minor protective role in a set of *krodha-vighnāntaka* we saw in the Mañjuśrī *maṇḍala* discussed above.

However, since Phase Three Esoteric Buddhism promoted the newest paradigm without completely negating earlier phases, Trailokyavijaya remains a part of the vast inclusive pantheons of Tibetan and Tibeto-Chinese Buddhism.[34] Thus in the Ngor *maṇḍala* collection Trailokyavijaya appears in the Tibetan versions of the 122-deity Ābhisambodhi Vairocana *maṇḍala* based on the *MVS*, and in the 1037-deity Trailokyavijaya *maṇḍala* based on the second section of the *STTS*.[35] Trailokyavijaya also appears there in a number of other *maṇḍala* based on the *SDPS*.[36]

At the Great Stūpa of Gyantse eight-armed [COLOR PLATE 12] and two-armed forms of Trailokyavijaya are found on the first, third and fourth of eight levels, but he is absent at the uppermost level, which is reserved for Phase Three *krodha-vighnāntaka*.[37] A graphic sign of the reduced status of Trailokyavijaya, and that of Phase Two teachings in general, is his transformation at Gyantse into a *vamāna*-Yakṣa form. All major Phase Three *krodha-vighnāntaka,* with the exception of Vajrabhairava, are *vīra*-Yakṣa in body type. Phase Two wrathful deities incorporated into the Tibetan systems were changed into lesser status *dharmapāla*-type deities with *lambodara* bellies, even when, as is the case with Trailokyavijaya, they were never represented in anything but the heroic-warrior form in India. A similar process was applied to Phase Two Acala in his various forms. In Indian contexts and in the very earliest Tibetan art he is slim. [COLOR PLATE 1] By the fourteenth century he too is made to conform to the *vāmana*-Yakṣa form. [COLOR PLATE 2] Vajrabhairava proves an exception as the only Phase Three wrathful *yidam* with a large-body form. He is a Phase Three reincarnation of Yamāntaka, whose Phase Two Indian counterpart is also invariably *vamāna*. **[144, 147-150]**

Other notable Trailokyavijaya images include the Nepalese fifteenth-century two-armed form in the Trailokyavijaya *maṇḍala* at the Jampa Lhakhang of Lo Mönthang.[38] Late Tibeto-Chinese pantheons incorporate several forms of Trailokyavijaya, sometimes labelled Vajrahūṃkāra, alone and with consort, two-armed and eight-armed.[39] Tibeto-Chinese images continue the Tibetan tendency to depict him in *vāmana*-Yakṣa form.

Trailokyavijaya had a long and distinguished career within Phase Two Esoteric Buddhism. If one considers all the areas to which he was carried, he is probably the most important, if not the most often represented, Phase Two *krodha-vighnāntaka*. It is this which has justified our extended treatment of him at the expense of other important Phase Two *krodha-vighnāntaka*.[40] He clearly embodies the important principle of transforming inner obstacles. As this idea came to the fore of Phase Two Esoteric Buddhism, he was catapulted into the ranks of bodhisattva and Buddha. The momentum carried over into Phase Three, which transformed him into Saṃvara. This transformation of Trailokyavijaya will be explored in our study of Phase Three.

Notes to Chapter Twelve

1 For Bhūtaḍāmara, see Linrothe, "Compassionate Malevolence," Appendix 5.

2 "Ākāśalakshaṇam sarvva[m*] Ākāśam ch=āpy=alakshanam [*] Ākāśa-samātā-yōgāt-sarvvāgra-samatā sphuṭāḥ (ṭa) [*];" the bottom reads, "Udyabhadrasya," "the gift of Udayabhadra." H. Sastri, *Nālandā*, 113, no. 108:

3 Saraswati, *Tantrayana Art*, 64, no. 178.

4 Mitra, *Achutrajpur*, 2. Also see Kunja Behari Tripathy, "Banpur Copper-plate Inscription of Somavaṁśi Indraratha," *Journal of the Asiatic Society* 8.4 (1966): 271-276.

5 Mitra, *Achutrajpur*, 86. Mitra argues that this is Vajrahūṃkāra and not Trailokyavijaya, a distinction which, as just discussed, cannot be sustained. Also see Shyam Sundar Pattnaik, "Trailokya Vijaya Images from the Banpur Bronzes," *The Orissa Historical Research Journal* 16.1-2 (1967): 82-83.

6 T.21.1209.41a.

7 Patna Museum, *Patna Museum Catalogue of Antiquities*, ed. Parmeshwari Lal Gupta (Patna, 1965), 120-121; and, Patna Museum, *Catalogue of Buddhist Sculptures*, 62.

8 Von Schroeder, *Indo-Tibetan Bronzes*, 262, no. 59B.

9 Discussion of the location of this sculpture in the Mahants compound has already been made with reference to the Phase Two Yamāntaka sculpture. Drawings of this sculpture were published as early as 1838 and 1878. See Buchanan and Martin, *History, Antiquities, Topography*, pl. IX.2, captioned "Image on the south-east side of the Sannyāsis house at Bodhgaya;" and, R. Mitra, *Buddha Gaya*, pl. XXVI.2, captioned "Bhairava from Math." Neither drawing depicts the damage to the face or to the top which it has subsequently (?) sustained. The damage had occured by 1905 when a photograph appeared in Foucher, *Étude sur l'iconographie Bouddhique*, fig. 4, 59, captioned, "Trailokyavijaya (Couvent brahmanique de Bodh-Gayâ. Hauteur 1 m. 60)."

10 Debala Mitra, personal communication, 25 May 1990. Also see *Indian Antiquary*, 116.

11 Leoshko, "Buddhist Sculptures from Bodhgaya," 55 (caption to Figure 11); S. Huntington, "*Pāla-Sena*," 101. Leoshko somewhat quizzically associates the Trailokyavijaya figure with Mañjuśrī in "Pilgrimage and the evidence of Bodhgaya's images," 48-50.

12 This *āyudha* has baffled more than one observer. Rajendralala Mitra, for example, describes it as a "closed umbrella. . . . a curious article, and I have nowhere else seen a counterpart of it." R. Mitra, *Buddha Gaya*, 139.

13 Debala Mitra, personal communication, February 1990. Also see *Indian Antiquary*, 115-116.

14 Andhakārimūrti is also known as Andhakāsuravadhamūrti, meaning, "Manifestation [of Śiva who] Slays the Asura named Andhaka." However, as Goswami points out, in some versions of the myth Andhaka is not killed but merely defeated and made the chief of Śiva-gaṇas. Goswami, "Ugra-Mūrtis of Śiva," 100. Thus Goswami prefers Andhakārimūrti, meaning "enemy of the Asura Andhaka." Monier-Williams, *Sanskrit-English Dictionary*, 45. For the myth of Andhakārimūrti, see Goswami, "Urga-Mūrtis of Śiva," 98-104; Kramrisch, *Manifestations of Śiva*, no. 42; and, O'Flaherty, *Origins of Evil*, 361-362. On the Konch *mandir* and nearby sculptures, see D.R. Patil, *The Antiquarian Remains in Bihar* (Patna, 1963), 213-215; A. Cunningham and H.B.W. Garrick, *Report of tours in North and South Bihar in 1880-81* ASI no. 16 (Calcutta, 1883) 52-59; J.D. Beglar, *Report of A Tour Through the Bengal Provinces . . . in 1872-73* ASI no. 7 (Calcutta, 1878), 54-61; Buchanan and Martin, *History, Antiquities, Topography*, 66-67 (includes drawings of the Konch *mandir* and the Andhakārimūrti-Śiva sculpture [Pl. VII.2]); and, Francis Buchanan, *Journal of Francis Buchanan (Afterwards Hamilton) Kept During the Survey of the Districts of Patna and Gaya in 1811-1812*, ed. V.H. Jackson (Patna, 1925), 37-38.

15 "In fact in the Andhakāri episode, it is said that Śiva created the famous Sudarśana Cakra[-wheel], with which he eventually killed Andhakāsura." Goswami, "Ugra-Mūrtis of Śiva," 20, note 54.

16 Ibid., 99-100.

17 This conclusion, which I draw from all available textual and visual evidence, is the premise from which Iyanaga begins his analysis using textual sources alone: "L'examen de ces sources permet de poser une prémisse qui paraît assez certaine: c'est qu'il semble bien que les éléments de ce récit *représentent* chacun un contenu abstrait -- ils peuvent donc être traités comme des symboles ou des allégories." Iyanaga, "Récits de la soumission," 732 (emphasis in original). The conclusions I draw regarding the contents of the symbolism, however, are quite similar, at least to the extent he argues: "il ne peut y avoir aucune opposition réelle entre le bouddhisme et d'autres systèmes religieux . . . D'ailleurs, cette lutte elle-même est fictive, car elle oppose deux plans, le Mondain et le Supramondain, qui, logiquement, ne peuvent être opposés," and that there is "un rapport de projection analogue entre Maheśvara et son dompteur [Trailokyavijaya] . . . . Tout ce drame cosmique -- et, tout à la fois, ontologique et théologique -- est donc une représentation, obtenue grâce au Moyen salvifique, de la Réalité absolue, dont le caractère indicible est marqué par une succession d'inversions paradoxales de valeurs, qui suppriment toutes les oppositions." Ibid., 737-738; 739-740.

18 AIIS negative no. 65-42. The repair is visible cutting through the figure in low relief of **169**.

19 There are five different *mudrā* combinations among them (corresponding to the five Tathāgata), but they are not equally distributed, nor are they repeated in a discernible pattern. Five make the full *dhyāna mudrā* (Amitāyus), three the *bhūmisparśa* with the left hand in *dhyāna* (Akṣobhya), three the *abhaya* with *varada* (Ratnasambhava?), three the *bhūmisparśa* with the left hand holding the garment at the shoulder (Amoghasiddhi?), and one the *bodhyagrī* (Mahāvairocana).

20 See the discussion above, including their parts in the *Devī-Māhātmya*.

21 Argan, "Ideology and Iconology," 16.

22 Snellgrove and Skorupski, *Cultural Heritage of Ladakh*, 1: 38, fig. 19; Pal, *Buddhist Paradise*, D5-D13; Genoud, *Buddhist Wall-painting*, Alchi no. 12.

23 Snellgrove and Skorupski, *Cultural Heritage of Ladakh*, 1: 38.

24 Pal, *Buddhist Paradise*, D6, captioned, "Angry manifestation of Akshobhya."

25 In the main shrine room of Mangyu there is a *vajradhātu maṇḍala* which appears to be of the Sarvavid Mahāvairocana type like the Alchi Dukhang painting. It is likewise on the left hand wall as one enters, close to the entrance. Unfortunately much of the *maṇḍala* at Mangyu is obscured by paintings hung from the ceiling. However, the eastern position (directly below the center) is occupied by a 2-armed Trailokyavijaya making the *vajrahūṃkāra mudrā* with *vajra* and bell, instead of the 8-armed form.

26 It was published and properly identified in Genoud, *Buddhist Wall-painting*, Alchi no. 6, 50 captioned, "Maṇḍala of Trailokyavijaya, the Conqueror of the Triple World . . . The principal figure is blue. His right leg is drawn in and the left is extended. He wears a tiger-skin loincloth. In the four angles of the inner square are four goddesses and in the angles of the outer square, the four offering goddesses." Also published in Yukei Matsunaga and Kei Kato, *Maṇḍala: Buddhist Art of Western Tibet*, 2 vols. (Tokyo, 1981), 1: no. 35.

27 T.18.882.376c-377c.

28 Snodgrass, *Matrix and Diamond World*, 716-727. As Snodgrass notes, the Genzu *vajradhātu maṇḍala* does not follow the *STTS* to the letter in this section. Of course it will be recalled that the full translation of the second part of the *STTS* was not available in the 8th and 9th centuries when the East Asian *vajradhātu maṇḍala* was codified. To a degree, the eighth and ninth (Trailokyavijaya) sections of the East Asian *vajradhātu maṇḍala* more closely resemble the Sarvavid Mahāvairocana *krodha maṇḍala* on the south wall of the Dukhang, in that the central Mahāvairocana makes the *bodhyagrī mudrā*, and Trailokyavijaya is shown 8-armed and in the eastern quarter. Ishimoto Yashuhiro, *Kyōō-gokokuji zō den Shingon'in ryōkai mandara* (Tokyo, 1977), no. 2-18.

29 Sylvain Lévi, ed., *Sanskrit Texts from Bali*, Gaekwad's Oriental Series no. 68 (Baroda, 1933); F.D.K. Bosch, "Buddhistische Gegevens uit Balische Handscriften," *Mededelingen der Kon. Nederl. Akad. van Wetenschappen* 68B.3 (1929): 43-77; English translation in *Selected Studies in Indonesian Archaeology* (The Hague 1961), 109-133; Przyluski, "Bouddhisme Tantrique à Bali," 160-161; Lim, "Later Buddhist Iconography," 327-341. Also see the discussion of this text and others referring to *krodha-vighnāntaka maṇḍala* in Linrothe, "Compassionate Malevolence," 305-310.

30 Genoud, *Buddhist Wall-painting*, Alchi no. 7; Pal, *Buddhist Paradise*, D14-18. The relationship of this *maṇḍala* to the structure of the *STTS* and its Phase Two nature was discussed earlier in relation to Yamāntaka's appearance in it.

31 Jaro Poncar was kind enough to send me a few photographs taken at my request in July, 1990.

32 Cheng, "Tang tiejin," 61-63. The Trailokyavijaya image is illustrated in color in Nara National Museum, *The Grand Exhibition of Silk Road Civilizations Vol Three: The Route of Buddhist Art* (Nara, 1988), no. 75. For East Asian Trailokyavijaya, see Linrothe, "Compassionate Malevo-lence," 380-414.

33 Tibor Bodrogi, *Art of Indonesia* (Greenwich, 1972), 130, pl. 98, captioned, "Java. Wajrapani [sic] as Dharmapala. A four-faced figure. Height 17 cm. Rijksmuseum voor Volkenkunde, Leiden, No. 1403/1760." Also published in C.M. Pleyte, "Bijdrage tot de kennis van het Mahāyāna op Java," *Bijdragen tot de Taal-, Land- en Volkenkunde* 52 (1901): figs. 3-4; 54 (1902): fig. 1. A description, which mentions the silver inlay of the eyes as well as two earlier Dutch publications that refer to the piece, appears in A.C. Tobi, "De Buddhistische Bronzen in het Museum te Leiden," *Oudheidkundig Verslag* (1930): 191. For this and other Southeast Asian Trailokyavijaya images, see Linrothe, "Compassionate Malevolence," 414-426.

34 For example, that of the Zhangjia Hutukhtu. See Sushama Lohia, *Lalitavajra's Manual of Buddhist Iconography* (New Delhi: Aditya Prakashan, 1994), no. 222.

35 Ngor Thar rtse mKhan po, *Tibetan Maṇḍalas*, nos. 20, 23. The latter is nearly identical to the Sarvavid Mahāvairocana *maṇḍala* represented at Alchi, but is called here the Trailokyavijaya *maṇḍala*. Trailokyavijaya is represented in 8-armed, 4-headed form in the eastern direction, immediately below Mahāvairocana.

36 Ngor Thar rtse mKhan po, *Tibetan Maṇḍalas*, nos. 35, 37 and 38.

37 Giuseppe Tucci, *Gyantse and Its Monasteries: Part 2, Inscriptions, Texts and Translations (Indo-Tibetica IV.2)*, trans. Uma Marina Vesci, ed. Lokesh Chandra (New Delhi, 1989), 262-263; idem, *Gyantse and Its Monasteries: Part 3, Plates (Indo-Tibetica IV.3)*, trans. Uma Marina Vesci, ed. Lokesh Chandra (New Delhi, 1989), figs. 190, 264, 340. Also see Ricca and Lo Bue, *The Great Stūpa of Gyantse*, 244, 280-281, 300, pls. 157-158.

38 Keith Dowman, "The Maṇḍalas of the Lo Jampa Lhakhang," in *Tibetan Art: Towards a definition of style*, ed. Jane Casey Singer and Philip Denwood (London: Laurence King, 1997), 186-195.

39 Walter Eugene Clark, *Two Lamaistic Pantheons* (Cambridge, 1937), A: 2A34, 4B30, 4M7; B: 56, 343, 359. Trailokyavijaya is also featured in a unique 18th c. series of paintings produced "by order of a Lamaist teacher for the sake of his Chinese pupil" and acquired in the imperial monastery of Jehol in 1923. See Tsering Tashi Thingo, *Leidraad Bij de Meditatie Over de Sarvavid-Vairocana-Maṇḍala* (Antwerp, 1980), 37, fig. 13.

40 Justice has not been done here to Phase Two forms of Hayagrīva, nor to the Phase One or Two forms of Acala, not to speak of other *krodha-vighnāntaka*. Trailokyavijaya and Yamāntaka provide models for the development of a new Phase Two wrathful deity and for the transformation of an older one, respectively. The other Phase Two *krodha-vighnāntaka* for the most part follow one of these two patterns.

13
Findings

Les tantra formulent clairement le principe qu'il ne s'agit pas de tuer (bsad) le démon ou l'ennemi, mais de le libérer (bsgral) par compassion en donnant au corps aussi bien qu'à "l'esprit" (vijñāna) la qualité de vajra.

Rolf A. Stein, "Problèmes de mythologie et de rituel tântriques"

After having explored the function and form of Yamāntaka in Phase One contexts, we saw how Phase Two Esoteric Buddhism utilized a number of Yamāntaka's iconographic characteristics and reshaped his function to reflect the values of the new paradigm. Since Trailokyavijaya came into being with Phase Two Esoteric Buddhism, we did not have the opportunity to watch the transformation of his form and meaning, though we were still able to mine the complementary sources of texts and images to develop a picture of his deep structure. This involved many aspects shared by the class of Phase Two *krodha-vighnāntaka* as a whole, notably the transformation of the inner obstacles to enlightenment such as egoism, lust, anger and ignorance. In the process we were reminded through analysis of both texts and images that this inner transformation process was psychologically sophisticated, in that it featured complex inversions, transfers of identity, death and transformative rebirth.

It becomes increasingly clear that the essential metaphor behind the *krodha-vighnāntaka* is that of the *dompteur-dompté* relationship. In Phase Two Esoteric Buddhism the two elements comprise an indissoluble binary, in which the conquered is nothing less than the conqueror in a pre-enlightened state, and the conqueror is nothing more than the vanquished transformed. The *dompté* is recreated in the image of his conqueror. For example, Maheśvara's new name after *abhiṣekha* is "Krodhavajra."[1] More obvious visually, the *dompté* determines the identity of the *dompteur*, reproducing his iconographic attributes, epithets and character. This is as true for Yamāntaka and Yama as it is for Trailokyavijaya and Maheśvara. The second aspect of the deep-structure relationship is less apparent in some of the other *krodha-vighnāntaka*, though with Mahābala (who subdues Māra), Bhūtaḍāmara (who dominates Aparājitā-Śiva) and Acala and Vighnāntaka (who are both depicted dominating "obstruction" itself, in the form of Ganeśa or Vināyaka), the destruction of obstacles is clearly their *raison d'etre*.

Yamāntaka's battle with Yama, which began in Phase One Esoteric Buddhism, prefigures the epic struggle between Trailokyavijaya and Maheśvara in Phase Two. Once elaborated in the *STTS*, Trailokyavijaya's struggle became paradigmatic. The account of Trailokyavijaya's subjugation of Maheśvara was the model for several other accounts, including those of Acala, Hayagrīva, Ucchushma and Yamāntaka. The paradigm defined by Trailokyavijaya's transformation struggle can be seen as the clarified essence beneath the angry surface of every other *krodha-vighnāntaka*.

As early as the eighth century, in their commentary to the *MVS* (T.39.1796), Yixing and Śubhakarasiṁha retell the story of the subjugation of Maheśvara, substituting Acala for Trailokyavijaya.[2] Because of his prideful spirit, Maheśvara refuses to respond to Mahāvairocana's call to assembly. Acala produces Ucchushma, who is to swallow all of the filth which Maheśvara produces as defense. Maheśvara mocks Ucchushma as a species of Yakṣa. Mahāvairocana orders Acala to force him into submission, so Acala presses his left foot to the half-moon on Maheśvara's head and his right to Umādevā's. The results are the same as in the *STTS*: Maheśvara "dies," but only to be reborn converted. Yixing explains the inner meaning of the episode:

> *"Eat all the impurities" signifies that one has swallowed the impure dharmas and the karmic residue of the acts of evil and passions. "His life ended," this signifies that all the dharma of his mind-heart are cut forever. Having entered into the Nature of dharma without production, one is able to obtain the Prophecy of all the Buddha. So this doesn't mean he was really killed.*[3]

As Iyanaga points out, regardless of the source of Śubhakarasiṁha-Yixing's version and the substitution of Acala for Trailokyavijaya, the interpretation they make of the events is of great interest.[4] It allows us to confirm beyond doubt that the Phase Two masters considered the obstacles to be symbolic of inner impurities which had to be cleansed, mastered or transformed. Śubhakarasiṁha's credentials, including a period of study at Nalanda, suggest that this interpretation was not merely a secondary gloss put on it by later Tibetans or Japanese but intrinsic to the original eastern Indian texts.

Acala was not the only *krodha-vighnāntaka* inserted into the account of Trailokyavijaya's triumph over a form of Śiva. Chang Chen Chi has translated into English a Tibetan *terma* and initiation text which quotes an account of the Green Hayagrīva's encounter with Śiva.[5] Hayagrīva must deal with a frightful demon named "Prideful-actor Multitude-conjurer." This is actually Śiva-Rudra.[6] Śiva refuses to submit to Amitāyus, or to Hayagrīva, and brings misery to the people. Hayagrīva then plunges into the chest of Śiva, cutting him to pieces. "After the extinction of the demon, his demon-body became the abode of Hayagrīva. Then he was bound by the Precepts and became known as Mahāgāla [sic], the Guardian of the Dharma."[7]

R.A. Stein has discovered and explicated a number of other late Tibetan texts, which are most interesting in their additions, complications and substitutions to the nucleus of the *dompteur / dompté* account. He and Matthew Kapstein discuss Tibetan versions in which Hayagrīva and Ucchushma subdue Rudra (i.e., Śiva) and Yamāntaka subdues Yama.[8] The debt owed to the *STTS* is clear from the way some of the texts slip back and forth between Vajrapāṇi-Trailokyavijaya and the other *krodha-vighnāntaka*. In one version Vajrapāṇi draws Ucchushma from his anus. Ucchushma goes to Śiva-Rudra's palace while he is absent and, assuming the form of Rudra, has intercourse ("consecration") with the Queen of Desire, Rudra's consort. From this union comes a son, Vajrakumāra Ucchushma. It is this son who will ultimately murder ("liberate") the father Rudra. In some versions Vajrakumāra is a *phurbu* (*vajra*-handled dagger), and he kills Śiva by penetrating him in the anus and exiting at the upper part of the forehead. The culmination is that Śiva is resuscitated and attains a place for himself and for his followers in the *maṇḍala*.[9]

The "son" of Vajrapāṇi takes on the form of Śiva to make love with Śiva's wife, re-producing himself as a son who then murders Śiva! This is a tangled yet nonetheless transparent reinforcement of the underlying identity between *dompteur-dompté*. The inevitable oedipal connotations are not without parallel; Jean Filliozat has noted similar tendencies in a Phase Three text on Acala.[10] But one must not forget that these were not merely myths to be read or heard, passed on and contemplated, but were integrated into ritual procedure and practice. The adept is to "visualize" and to become Trailokyavijaya, Acala, Hayagrīva or Ucchusma, and to participate in the subjugation of the self.

At times the process is even publicly enacted. P.H. Pott has shown how annual costumed dances performed in Tibetan monasteries, which ostensibly reenact the destruction of the wicked anti-Buddhist King Lang Darma (r. 836-842 CE), are "far beyond that of giving a dramatic expression of a historical event." Actually they mark "a symbolic expression of the destruction of the ego, which is necessary to attain the highest insight." The eight Śiva-Bhairavas portrayed in the drama, who are those surrounding Trailokyavijaya in the *SDPS maṇḍala*, "are no more [i.e., no longer] terrifying, but assistants on the way leading towards salvation."[11]

Generally, however, the rituals are performed internally, through meditation, visualization and identification. The idea of identification with the visualized deity (*ahamkāra*) is an important one and has already been mentioned several times. The practice is by no means confined to identification with wrathful deities. Yet identification with Yamāntaka provides a prime example of the almost confounding circularity of identity. The adept assumes the identity of Yamāntaka who has himself taken on the appearance of Yama in order to destroy the latter. Rolf Stein explains the practice as follows:

> *The adept becomes Yamāntaka who carries in himself Mañjuśrī, Hayagrīva and Vajrapāṇi, that is to say, the "Dompteurs" who figure in the parallel accounts. He receives the consecration (abhiṣeka) in the form of water which penetrates through the forehead, purifies his body and is excreted upwards where it becomes Akṣobhya as a head ornament.*[12]

The three heads of the demon are said to represent jealousy, pride, and stupidity, the top of the body as hatred and the bottom as desire-passion. These constitute the five poisons (*kleśa*). In other rituals the *kleśa* are transformed into *amṛit* by cooking. This cooking seems to be only a prelude to digestion: the demon is swallowed, remains in the stomach where he suffers, and is excreted.[13]

The end result in all the rituals and in the interpretation of the works of art which represent these *krodha-vighnāntaka* is the same. The external demons who take the form of Śiva are subjugated, "digested," "murdered" and finally reborn as supporters of the Buddhist teachings. The stages seem to represent the processes of inner yoga by which the *kleśa* are purified. While there is significant overlap with Phase One ideology, at least in the exteriorization of demon-obstacles, I have tried to show that the interpretation of the obstacles as spiritual or internal to the self is more characteristic of Phase Two Esoteric Buddhism.

In addition to the ideological change between the two phases are concomitant changes in the appearance of the *krodha-vighnāntaka*. The most notable of these changes are independent representations, more specialized and individualized iconographic characteristics, more arms and heads to suggest extraordinary powers, and a preference for the more heroic *vīra*-Yakṣa form instead of the more grotesque *vāmana*-Yakṣa form. There are exceptions to each of these tendencies, but generally they stand up to detailed examination. The characteristics of the *krodha-vighnāntaka* group as a whole can be tied to the general shift in their status. As independent, individualized, heroic and powerful deities they are better able to express the idea of the compassionate destruction of inner obstacles. It was this idea which became an increasingly essential metaphor with the Esoteric Buddhist system. In the next section we can follow its rise to an apex.

In concluding this chapter, it is appropriate to mention the temporal gap between when we know the texts must have been written in eastern India and the period of the earliest Phase Two *krodha-vighnāntaka* images. Texts like the *MVS* and *STTS* begin to be translated into Chinese and Tibetan in the early eighth century, so they must have been available in the seventh century in eastern India. But one does not find surviving images in stone or metal in India until the late eighth or ninth centuries. This may be due in part to the fact that the images may first have been committed to two dimensional media, such as illuminated manuscripts or cloth paintings, and paintings do not survive from so early a period. Another explanation may be that there is a lag between the time ideas are exchanged among a small group of people interested in propagating those ideas and the time when there is sufficient interest and knowledge to represent those ideas in non-perishable media. This serves as something of a caution in dating cultural phenomena. If a discrepancy of as much as one hundred and fifty years remains between the time we know a text existed and the time it is represented in art, how meaningful is it to date an intellectual or religious movement from the moment of the existence of such a text? It seems that the existence of art pertaining to a movement indicates a wider circulation of the ideas expressed in texts and might serve as at least as accurate a measure of the importance or influence of a school of thought. We will continue to track this discrepancy as we follow the transformations of the *krodha-vighnāntaka* in Phase Three Esoteric Buddhism.

Notes to Chapter Thirteen

1 Iyanaga, "Récits de la soumission," 677. The epigraph for this chapter comes from R. A. Stein, "Problèmes de mythologie et de rituel tantriques," 468.

2 See the study of this commentary in ibid., 682-723.

3 Ibid., 700-701 (adapted from the French).

4 Ibid., 708.

5 Chang, *Esoteric Teachings of the Tibetan Tantra*, 60-81.

6 Ibid., 62 has "Matram Rutras," clearly meant as Rudra.

7 Ibid., 63. Mahāgāla also must be an error for Mahākāla.

8 R. A. Stein, "Problèmes de mythologie et de rituel tantriques," 463-470; idem, "Recherches autour du récit de Rudra," 508-517; idem, "La soumission de Rudra et autres contes Tantriques," *Journal Asiatique* 283 no. 1 (1995): 121-160; Matthew Kapstein, "Samantabhadra and Rudra: Innate Enlightenment and Radical Evil in Rnying-ma-pa-Buddhism," in *Discourse and Practice*, ed. Frank Reynolds and David Tracy (Albany: SUNY, 1992), 51-82. Davidson has studied a similar transformation of Maheśvara and Heruka in "Reflections," discussed below.

9 Various versions of these accounts unraveled by Stein in the previously cited articles are much more explicit in terms of sexual and violent "metaphors" than other Phase Two texts, and in this way exhibit Phase Three characteristics. They survive only in Tibetan but are clearly transformations of earlier accounts, such as the *STTS*.

10 Jean Filliozat, "Le Complexe d'oedipe dans un tantra Bouddhique," in *Études Tibétaines dédiées à la mémoire de Marcelle Lalou* (Paris, 1971), 142-148.

11 P.H. Pott, "Some Remarks on the 'Terrific Deities' in Tibetan 'Devil Dances'," in *Studies of Esoteric Buddhism and Tantrism* (Koyasan, 1965), 277.

12 R. A. Stein, "Recherches autour du récit de Rudra," 510 (my translation from the French).

13 R. A. Stein, "Recherches autour du récit de Rudra," 510-511. The digestion of inner obstacles is maintained in Bengali Tantric goat sacrifices to Kālī at the Kālīghat temple in Calcutta. See Suchitra Samanta, "Transformation and Alimentation: An Interpretation of Sacrificial Blood Offerings (Balidan) to the Śakti Goddess Kālī," paper presented at the 20th Annual Conference on South Asia, Madison, Wisconsin, 1 November 1991.

Phase Three

174. Hevajra with consort, Saspol cave (Ladakh), wall painting, ca. 14th century

14
Esoteric Buddhism Recast

[O]n admire que la recherche de l'horrible pour l'horrible et de l'absurde pour l'absurde ait pu être poussée aussi loin.
Louis de La Vallée Poussin, *Bouddhisme: Opinions sur l'histoire*

Beginning in the late tenth or early eleventh century we find a new set of *krodha-vighnāntaka* in sculpture and painting. Initially it may be difficult to recognize Phase Three deities as innovative, so closely do they resemble Phase Two *krodha-vighnāntaka*. Generally of the *vīra*-Yakṣa body type, the new wrathful figures stand in aggressive poses and wield one or more of familiar classes of weapons, trophies or emblems. There are two-armed and multi-armed examples, and frequently Phase Three *krodha-vighnāntaka* trample prostrate figures representing obstacles to enlightenment. Perhaps most importantly, the independence which emphatically distinguished Phase One from Phase Two is strengthened in Phase Three. The Phase Three *krodha-vighnāntaka* shed completely any lingering impressions of being either tertiary protective deities or secondary subordinates of moderate importance. The bodhisattva who were compositionally and ideologically the superiors of Phase One *krodha-vighnāntaka* withdraw from center stage, as do Buddhas like Mahāvairocana who were their mentors in Phase Two. The Phase Three *krodha-vighnāntaka* are honored at the heart of the altar, shrine, temple, *maṇḍala* and ritual, where they are themselves attended by subsidiary deities. The male wrathful deity's frequent companion is his female consort, who is either embraced or arranged with three to eight others around the central male.

The Phase Two *krodha-vighnāntaka* is admittedly known at the center of a *krodha-maṇḍala* in art and in rituals. **[171]** Phase Three male *krodha-vighnāntaka* appear much more frequently in this exalted format. Their privileged status is the culmination of the pattern of growth we have followed from Phase One. The Phase Three *krodha-vighnāntaka* is identified as a primary manifestation of the "sixth" Tathāgata, an entity encompassing and elevated above the conventional five Tathāgata set. Phase Three Esoteric Buddhism is dominated by the *krodha-vighnāntaka* in a way which was unimagined by Phase One Esoteric Buddhism and unrealized by Phase Two.

Comparisons of iconographic traits in works of art with inscriptions and textual descriptions establish the identities of the Phase Three *krodha-vighnāntaka*. They constitute a distinct group, though a few are explicitly related to the iconography of earlier deities. Yamāntaka is transformed by the changing interests of Phase Three from the six-armed, -headed, -legged deity of Phase Two into a thirty-four armed *krodha-vighnāntaka*, renamed Vajrabhairava. Acala's inventory of attributes remains basically intact, but his context, powers and consorts are radically transformed, effecting his reconsecration as Caṇḍamahāroṣaṇa. Other members of the set seem to be formal metamorphoses of Trailokyavijaya, but for the most part these are names and deities unique to Phase Three: Heruka, Hevajra, Saṃvara, Yamāri, Guhyasamāja and Kālacakra. Remarkably the major texts of Phase Three Esoteric Buddhism which feature these new *krodha-vighnāntaka* also take their names as titles.

Phase Three Esoteric Buddhism, the last stage of a complex evolution in India, came to be the primary form practiced in Tibet, since the Tibetans did not fully assimilate Indian Buddhism until the eleventh and twelfth centuries. The most important of the *krodha-vighnāntaka* found in Tibet represent Phase Three. It was no doubt the Phase Three *krodha-vighnāntaka* Sir John Marshall intended when he referred disparagingly to "those monstrous idols which throng the lamaic temples today."[1] Phase Three *krodha-vighnāntaka*, especially Heruka and Hevajra, appear after the eleventh century in Southeast Asia as well, in Java and in Thai and Khmer contexts. They do not reach Tang China, nor is there any indication that such images were ever transmitted to Japan. In China proper Phase Three *krodha-vighnāntaka* are found only during the periods of Tibetan sponsored Buddhism, that is, in the Yuan, Ming and Qing periods.

It will not be possible here to follow the careers of all the Phase Three *krodha-vighnāntaka*. Only the images of Heruka, Hevajra and Saṃvara will be examined, and we will concentrate on the earliest period of their depiction. The first topic to be covered is the Esoteric Buddhist context in which the *krodha-vighnāntaka* were featured, including a treatment of their iconologic significance. Subsequently we will study the early images.

1 The Structure of Phase Three Esoteric Buddhism

The model of Phase Three I propose is basically contiguous with the teachings found in texts belonging to the fourth category of the four-part Tibetan classification system, those of *anuttara yoga* (Supreme Yoga).[2] I have chosen to designate late Esoteric Buddhism as "Phase Three," rather than to borrow the term *anuttara yoga* from a somewhat problematic textual classification system, for two reasons.[3] First of all, Phase Three Esoteric Buddhism is not constituted exclusively by texts; secondly, the term Phase Three distinguishes the period from Phases One and Two without denying its links to those earlier stages.

In order to establish immediately the constitutive importance of *krodha-vighnāntaka* for Phase Three, it is important to have a general idea of the deities and texts considered essential by modern scholars and by representatives of the living (Tibetan) system as well. There are a number of different sub-classifications of texts within the Tibetan system of the *anuttara yoga* class. The details need not detain us here, though the ones heading the lists are the very ones dominated by *krodha-vighnāntaka*. Following the system explicated by Kaygrubjay, the *anuttara yoga tantra* class is divided into two categories, "Father Tantra" and "Mother

Tantra."[4] Among the most important Father Tantra are the *Guhyasamāja*, the texts of the red and black Yamāri, and of Mother Tantra are emphasized the *Saṃvara*, *Hevajra*, and *Kālacakra tantras*. The modern scholar Shiníchi Tsuda takes these same texts as "the basis of the seemingly abominable, heretical cult of cemetery (*śmaśāna*)."[5]

David Snellgrove defines texts of the *anuttara yoga* (Phase Three) class as those:

> *which claimed to give supreme realization here and now, involving the psycho-physical reintegration of personality through sexual symbolism. The two most important cycles are those of Guhyasamāja and Hevajra.*[6]

Giuseppe Tucci also deals with Phase Three texts and their classification. Following Tibetan systems criticized by Kaygrubjay, Tucci writes:

> *. . . Anuttaratantras are of three kinds; a) Tantras based on the means (upāyatantra) like the Guhyasamāja . . . b) Tantras based on gnosis (prajñāt) like bDe mc'og [Saṃvara] or Heruka or Hevajra . . . [c)] Tantras centering on non-duality (advayat) like the Kālacakra.*

Tucci further observes:

> *Nearly all the Tantras of the Anuttara class centre round the symbol of Akṣobhya or of his hypostases: Heruka, Hevajra, Guhyasamāja.*[7]

The various Tibetan classification systems differ slightly from one another.[8] There is little disagreement, however, among the traditional Tibetan systems or among modern scholars, as to which texts belong to this class as a whole, and which are the most important: those spoken by and featuring wrathful deities such as Heruka, Hevajra, Saṃvara, Guhyasamāja and Kālacakra. Phase Three Esoteric Buddhism brings the *krodha-vighnāntaka* to their ultimate apotheosis.

1.1 Traits Shared with Phase Two

Phase Three Esoteric Buddhism has attracted the most scholarly attention, largely due to the extremity of its ritual practices, which "impress[es] itself all too readily upon the reader."[9] Polarity symbolism and sexual practices are discussed graphically in its texts and displayed in its images. Accordingly, female deities play a much more prominent role. There are also many scatological references to the ritual consumption of urine, feces, menses, semen and blood, of human and animal meat, intoxicating beverages, and to acts of incest and various sexual activities. Too much ink has been spilled on interpreting, apologizing for or condemning these passages to require any more comment. For my purposes, even where these overt references are not fully understood, they still act as unmistakable markers of a new Esoteric Buddhist dispensation, which inspired a new set of images.

We must not forget, however, the likenesses between Phases Two and Three. The intention of their practices is to provoke supreme enlightenment in this body through psycho-physical means. Visualization (*bhavana*) and identification (*ahamkāra*), among other practices, are common to both. The sexual symbolism latent in Phase Two contexts is overt in Phase Three. Before examining the unique characteristics of Phase Three Esoteric Buddhism, we will briefly survey continuities with the earlier paradigm in an effort to demonstrate that the conceptual roots of Phase Three *krodha-vighnāntaka* grow out of the earlier Esoteric Buddhist movements we have followed so far.

Philosophical Orientation

Phase Three Esoteric Buddhism, like Phase Two, emphasizes praxis. The bias is so highly pronounced in the later stage as to make it difficult to discern its theoretical basis. The *Saṁvarodaya Tantra* (*ST*), one of the important Phase Three texts, is quite arrogant towards those taking an intellectual, non-experiential approach. Explaining its methods, the text interjects bluntly, "Dialecticians do not understand it."[10] Lakṣmīnkarādevī asks, "What is the use of much talk?"[11] Saraha claims, "The whole world is confused by schools of thought," and continues, "Those who recite commentaries do not know how to cleanse the world." He satirizes claims to erudition:

> *All these pandits expound the treatises,/But the Buddha who resides within the body is not known./. . . But they shamelessly say: "We are pandits."*[12]

Provocations like these have led many distinguished scholars to comment on the dearth of philosophical treatments in the texts themselves. Louis de La Vallée Poussin writes:

> *The Tantras are not rich in dogmatic expositions or discussion. For the masters as for the adepts of magic, the chief business is the description of the Maṇḍalas, the panegyric of the Siddhis, the drawing up of pharmaceutical recipes and dhāraṇīs. Only a small space is accorded to theory.*[13]

In a similar vein, Étienne Lamotte comments that "contrary to appearances, in Vajrayāna, philosophical speculation plays only a subordinate role."[14]

Yet it is still possible to find a theoretical thread running through Phase Three texts. Scholars such as Giuseppe Tucci and David Snellgrove, as well as Herbert Guenther, have pioneered the way by commenting on passages which reveal a conceptual substratum.[15] Their studies indicate that both Phase Two and Phase Three are rooted in the Mādhyamika philosophy, which accepts that *saṁsāra* is not ultimately different than *nirvāṇa*. Enlightenment remains the goal, and can be attained in this life, in the human body.[16] Saraha says:

> *As is Nirvāṇa, so is Saṁsāra./ Do not think there is any distinction./ Yet it possesses no single nature,/ For I know it as quite pure.*[17]

Liberation is a matter of destroying the ignorance that prevents *realizing* that *saṁsāra* is not ultimately different from *nirvāṇa*. Both the Sanskrit and Chinese versions of the *Hevajra Tantra* (*HT*) state the task:

> *The purified condition of all things whatsoever is known as the very truth itself. Proceeding from this we now speak of the purification power of the divinities . . . The six faculties of sense, their six spheres of operation, the five skandhas and the five elements are pure in essence, but they are obscured by the molestations of ignorance.*[18]

Elsewhere the *HT* states:

> *All beings are buddhas, but this is obscured by accidental defilement. When this is removed, they are buddhas at once, of this there is no doubt.*[19]

Saraha puts it this way:

> *The nature of the sky is originally clear,/ But by gazing and gazing the sight becomes obscured./ Then when the sky appears deformed in this way,/ The fool does not know that the fault's in his own mind.// Through fault of pride he does not see truth,/ And therefore like a demon he maligns all ways. The whole world is confused by schools of thought,/ And no one perceives his true nature.*[20]

The central task of removing defilement is performed by the ritual visualization of and identification with Phase Three *krodha-vighnāntaka*, who wield compassion ruthlessly to destroy the impurities caused by ignorance. Obviously their duties do not differ fundamentally from those performed by *krodha-vighnāntaka* of earlier phases, but the significance of their activities continues to be elevated. Two conjoined movements characterize the passage from Phase One to Phase Three. One steadily shifts the functions of the *krodha-vighnāntaka* to central importance; the second increasingly links iconographic forms to symbolic rather than literal functions. The Phase One objectification of obstacles as demons has steadily given ground. It can still be found, but the inner significance is not left to later commentators. For instance, the symbolic nature of Hevajra and his troupe, as well as their spheres of influence, is mapped out in the *HT* text:

> *The purificatory significance of the sixteen arms [of Hevajra] is the sixteen kinds of voidness. The four legs signify the crushing of the four Māras, The faces the eight releases, The eyes the three adamantine ones . . .*

In the same passage Nairātmyā is associated with overcoming wrath, Vajrayoginī with passion, Vajraḍākinī with envy, Gaurī with malignity and Vajrā with delusion, each of the five inner poisons.[21] These associations with traditional Buddhist categories demonstrate Phase Three's continuities with earlier Esoteric Buddhism.

Visualization and Identification

The *krodha-vighnāntaka* symbolize the process of destroying the obstacles which prevent the realization that *saṁsāra* is not different at the absolute level from *nirvāṇa*. The practice advocated is still that of visualization (*bhavana*) and identification (*ahaṁkāra*) with the deity, internalized meditative rituals that were part of Phase Two Esoteric Buddhism.[22] The deities visualized, however, are peculiar to Phase Three. The continuities and the innovations are made apparent in the following passages of Phase Three texts. The *HT* evokes a unifying vision of Hevajra:

> *Forms like to his in brilliance shoot forth and cover the expanse of the sky. Drawing them together he induces them into his own heart, and the yogin becomes the Wrathful One himself.*[23]

The *ST* directs the yogin:

> *. . . [to] imagine himself to be in the state of Heruka (herukatva) which consists of prajñā (wisdom) and upāya.*[24]

Likewise the *Caṇḍamahāroṣaṇa Tantra* (hereafter, *CMT*) teaches:

> *'I am Buddha, and the Perfected One, Immoveable, she [the yogin's consort] is cherished Prajñāpāramitā,' thus the wise person should meditate with fixed thought.*[25]

This brief sampling of Phase Three texts demonstrates the indisputable primacy of the wrathful deities in Phase Three Esoteric Buddhism. They are the masters of the texts, the objects of visualization and identification, and union with these *krodha-vighnāntaka* is now essential to enlightenment.

The Maṇḍala

The fundamental structure of Phase One Esoteric Buddhism was a triadic nuclear arrangement. Phase Two introduced the pentadic *maṇḍala* structure, which Phase Three retains with some modifications. The most important modification for our purposes is that the *krodha-vighnāntaka* is much more frequently the central deity. The occasional occurrence of a nine-member *maṇḍala* in place of a five-member one does not disrupt the deity's central position. The *HT*, for example, describes a nine-part *maṇḍala* as having Hevajra at the center and his eight yogin-consorts arranged at the cardinal and intermediate points.[26] Most of the *HT* adheres to the fivefold system of the *maṇḍala*, as do other Phase Three texts featuring the *krodha-vighnāntaka* Saṃvara and Caṇḍamahāroṣaṇa at the center of their main *maṇḍala*.[27] A description of a *samaya maṇḍala* (comprised of symbols instead of figures) in the *CMT* precedes that of a five-part *maṇḍala*. The four primary directions bear four forms of Caṇḍamahāroṣaṇa distinguished by the conventional colors of Phase Two *maṇḍala*, with the exception that the eastern figure is white instead of blue.[28] At the intermediate directions are their respective consorts. One is to paint the dark blue Caṇḍamahāroṣaṇa embraced by his consort in the center.[29] Clearly the *maṇḍala* continues to function integratively in Phase Three Esoteric Buddhism.

The Five Tathāgata: Continuities

The five Tathāgata are maintained by Phase Three Esoteric Buddhism. The *Guhyasamāja Tantra* (hereafter *GST*), one of the earliest Phase Three texts, names the five "Vajra Tathāgata" at the beginning of its first chapter: Akṣobhya, Vairocana, Ratnaketu, Amitābha and Amoghasiddhi.[30] An extended treatment of the five Tathāgata is found in another Phase Three commentary of around the eleventh century by Advayavajra.[31] The *HT* also names the five Tathāgata and equates them with the *kleśa* each overcomes:

> *Vairocana is deemed to be delusion . . . wrath is Akṣobhya . . . passion is Amitābha . . . envy is Amoghasiddhi . . . malignity is Ratnasambhava. Thought is one but consists in this five-fold form.*[32]

Clearly the character of the Tathāgata and the corresponding *pañcakula* system of organization is retained by Phase Three. "Vajra, Padma, Karma, Tathāgata, Ratna; these are known as the Five Families supreme."[33]

The Five Tathāgata: A formalized system of order

The five Tathāgata, inseparable from the *pañcakula*, is the ordering principle of the Phase Two *maṇḍala*, a model to which Phase Three introduces several changes. The Tathāgata are of interest, not individually, but as a single entity representing the fivefold *maṇḍala*. To be sure, as Tucci points out:

> *in every tantric liturgy, it does not matter which cycle is followed, the invocation and meditation on the five Buddhas is necessary and a preliminary element of every rite.*[34]

Yet rather than serving to valorize the Tathāgata, their necessary invocation at the start of every rite formalizes and dulls their potency. The fivefold system becomes almost a mnemonic device, and other deities, especially the wrathful and female, supplant the Tathāgata's positions and functions. For example, the *HT* names five *yoginī* (female consorts) as the representatives of the families.[35] The *yoginī* participate in the narration of the text, while the voices of the Tathāgata are absent. Five Tathāgata of the *ST* are listed similarly in association with various substances which play a much greater role in the yogic practices and rituals of Phase Three than do the Tathāgata themselves.[36]

The Five Tathāgata: Forms of Heruka

Phase Three Esoteric Buddhism considers the five Tathāgata forms of the *krodha-vighnāntaka* Heruka, a kind of sixth Buddha we will investigate further on. The simultaneous preservation and alteration of the five Tathāgata system is manifest in the following passage from the *HT*:

> *Then you will be consecrated by those buddhas who have all assumed the form of Heruka, with the five vessels which symbolize the Five Tathāgatas and which contain the five ambrosias.*[37]

The yogin-practitioner is to identify with Heruka. This marks a significant conceptual change from earlier practice, represented by the *STTS*, in which one was consecrated in order to realize one's identity with the Tathāgata: "*Om yathā sarvatathāgatas tathāham.*"[38]

The Five Tathāgata: Akṣobhya in the center

The repositioning of symbolic colors encountered in the *CMT* is equivalent to the privileging of Akṣobhya over Mahāvairocana. Blue Akṣobhya is consistently found at the center, where white Mahāvairocana once presided. Already the earliest Phase Three text, the *GST*, features Akṣobhya at the center of the Guhyasamāja *maṇḍala*, while Vairocana is shifted to the east.[39] This is a meaningful change, as it is directly connected to the rise in status of the *krodha-vighnāntaka*. It signifies that the paramount deity is no longer Mahāvairocana, who represents the *tathāgatakula*, but Akṣobhya, chief of the *vajrakula*. At one point the *HT* says simply, "Akṣobhya's family . . . is the highest."[40]

> *But these six or five families are comprised in one, that one family which has mind as its Lord and consists in the wrath of Akṣobhya. Such is the adamantine power of wrath.*[41]

The *vajra* is a symbol of wisdom and of the forceful methods employed to overcome resistance, which are in contrast to gentler methods represented by the *padmakula* (lotus family). The *vajrakula* is also the family of the *krodha-vighnāntaka*, now recognized as the paramount family.

Thus the new phase of Esoteric Buddhism preserves the five family system, with the crucial difference that Akṣobhya inhabits the center, displacing Mahāvairocana to the eastern direction. The wrathful representatives of Akṣobhya (Saṃvara, Hevajra, Heruka, Caṇḍamahāroṣaṇa, among others) are featured at the center more frequently than they were under the Phase Two system.

Phase Two krodha-vighnāntaka Roles in Phase Three

Despite their rise in status, the Phase Three *krodha-vighnāntaka* are not fundamentally different in character, form or function from those of Phase Two. The names of the new deities refer to characteristics not unlike those of earlier wrathful deities. For instance, the thirteenth chapter of the *CMT* explains the derivation of its namesake wrathful deity, Caṇḍamahāroṣaṇa, in terms which are quite familiar:

> *Caṇḍa means one who is very violent (tīvratara) and he is said to be very wrathful (mahāroṣaṇa). He is known as being wrathful (roṣaṇa) because he devastates all evil ones (māra) with his anger (krodha).*[42]

The same kinds of tasks are assigned *krodha-vighnāntaka* in ritual practices as were given them in the *MVS* and *STTS*. Generally, the same purification and protective rites take place at the beginning of meditation and painting rituals, and for these the wrathful deities are still evoked. Tucci explains these functions in relation to the Saṃvara temple at Tsaparang, a fifteenth-century western Tibetan Phase Three structure that houses a set of mural paintings. The *krodha-vighnāntaka* there, he writes:

> *form the 'circle of defence' (rakṣā-cakra, srun-bahi-hkhor-lo) and . . . protect the rite, the beatitude and the power deriving from them, from the assaults of contrary forces, not only the external ones but especially the internal ones; that is to say, those passions, those desires and those inclinations, which, coming out from the psychic background frustrate or pollute the aura of purity or of sanctity promoted by the ceremony.*[43]

The *krodha-vighnāntaka* are conceived as being able to destroy all obstacles to enlightenment, obstacles which are personified as demons, but understood symbolically. To perform their tasks they use the same tools as their predecessors, primarily their own *dhāraṇī*. The *dhāraṇī* are of a character identical to those encountered in Phases One and Two, though they are wielded in a slightly different way. Rather than being bestowed on the wrathful deity by bodhisattva or Buddha, or recited upon a superior's command, the *dhāraṇī* are uttered by the chief *krodha-vighnāntaka* of the text itself. The fifth chapter of the *CMT* begins with Caṇḍamahāroṣaṇa entering the *samadhi* entitled "The Vanquishing of All Demons," from which he speaks the *dhāraṇī*. His primary *dhāraṇī* are typically threatening, composed of the same locutions as *dhāraṇī* of Phases One and Two: "kill, kill, slay, slay all Ḍākinīs, demons, ghosts and evil spirits."[44] Another *dhāraṇī* translation is worth noting:

> *Om homage to Lord, Reverend Caṇḍamahāroṣaṇa, the frightener of gods, titans and men, the destroyer of the strength of all demons . . . destroy, destroy all my obstacles, remove the four demons, frighten, frighten, confuse, confuse.*[45]

In this case the main deity is called on for generalized protective and purificatory functions. Other texts seem to remain very close to the pattern of Phase Two rituals. The focus of the entire ritual is adjusted to accommodate the new main deity, but the older processes within the ritual are continued with little modification. Thus, at the same time that the most important activities are performed by Phase Three *krodha-vighnāntaka* deities, Phase Two wrathful deities are admitted into the Phase Three *maṇḍala* as subordinate guardians, and are called on for protection and purification. For instance, we find that Vajrahūṃkāra-Trailokyavijaya, Mahābala and Hayagrīva are included in the second enclosure of the Saṃvara *maṇḍala*.[46] And in one of the latest Phase Three systems of India, the Kālacakra tradition, the *krodhāvesā* ritual evokes a wrathful form of Vajrapāṇi:

The disciple possessed by the wrathful deity frightens [his] mischievous powers and breaks the unconscious ties present within him and surrounding him, which might otherwise be an unsurmountable hindrance to the mystic realization. This effect is mythically signified by the Māras' destruction.[47]

Much of the earlier system found in the *STTS* is maintained by the *GST*, including the *maṇḍala*-creation ritual. As in the *MVS* and the *STTS*, Trailokyavijaya is evoked for the *bandhaya-sīman* section of the rite, when the colored threads which bind the arena of the *maṇḍala* are tied:

One should proceed to the laying down of the threads, envisaging oneself [the master] as Vairocana and the neophyte as Vajrasattva or he is known as Amṛtavajra (Elixir-Vajra) of adamantine brilliance. One should lay the adamantine thread of the Great Kings, the Five Buddhas. . . . As for the application of the color with its twenty-five distinctions, this is the secret of all adamantine ones, the highest enlightenment. In the case of all these mantra(-divinitie)s one evokes Vajra-HŪṂ-kara (a fierce form of Vajrapāṇi [i.e., Trailokyavijaya]) evoking this divine sacrament, bodily and vocally, in the five sections (of the maṇḍala).[48]

The continuities with Phase Two Esoteric Buddhism are quite marked, particularly in the last textual examples. Extracting the passages from their overall context and grouping them arbitrarily, however, may make the continuities seem much more pronounced than they actually are. We need to balance the view by examining characteristic structures of Phase Three Esoteric Buddhist ideology which represent new developments. In some cases the new features are radically different and much more important to the movement as a whole than are aspects with precedents in Phases One and Two.

1.2 Traits Unique to Phase Three

Phase Three Esoteric Buddhism participates in the discourse of Mahāyāna Buddhism while specifically locating itself within the Esoteric Buddhist movement. As we have just seen, it builds on a number of shared assumptions, notably the equivalence of *saṁsāra* and *nirvāṇa*, and the efficacy of meditation rituals. These characteristics can be attributed to the monastic practitioners and formulators working in the same milieu which produced Phase Two Esoteric Buddhism. But while these aspects serve as a foundation for Phase Three, to a certain extent they tend to regress into the background in favor of unique practices, conceptualizations and imagery. The unprecedented aspects appear to derive from meditating yogins, a source outside the monasteries and Buddhist universities. A distinctive style is strikingly evident from the very first lines of major Phase Three texts.

The New Texts: Format, Interlocutors, Setting and Language

The first lines of the *HT*, *GST* and *CMT* are slight variations of the following:

Thus have I heard: at one time the Lord reposed in the vagina of the Lady of the Vajra-sphere — the heart of the Body, Speech and Mind of all Buddhas.[49]

Other passages of the text make the intended meaning unambiguous. A passage of the *HT* reads:

Placing the liṅga in the bhaga and kissing her again and again, so producing the experience of Great Bliss, the Adamantine One talked about . . .[50]

The sexual references which are immediately encountered in a Phase Three text are a prominent characteristic of Phase Three literary and visual expressions. We will have occasion later in this chapter to examine their psychophysical basis in yogic practice and their philosophical ramifications. For now it is instructive to note the comparisons and contrasts with the Phase Two texts.

In Chapter Eight we discussed the typical Phase Two text format and the ways in which it differs from Mahāyāna texts and related Phase One texts. To briefly summarize, Phase One texts feature Śākyamuni as the main speaker answering questions put to him by bodhisattva in an earthly or celestial setting. In Phase Two texts, such as the *MVS* and *STTS*, it is Mahāvairocana who reveals the new teachings, usually to or through Vajrapāṇi, at Mt Sumeru or another cosmic setting. For the sake of comparison, one can contrast the beginning of the *MVS*:

> *Thus have I heard: At one time the Bhagavan dwelled in the palace of the boundless Vajradharmadhātu, [the realm of] the Tathāgata's adhiṣṭhāna body. All the Vajradhara were assembled . . .*[51]

And the *STTS*:

> *Thus have I heard at one time. The Reverend Lord . . . Vairocana of great compassion . . . dwelt in the palace of the king of the deities of the uppermost stratum of the region of forms resided in by all the Tathāgatas . . . . together with ninety-nine kotis of bodhisattvas.*[52]

Phase Three texts transform this format significantly. Snellgrove explains:

> *[T]he Lord (Bhagavān) is no longer Śākyamuni in any of his recognizable hypostases [viz. Mahāvairocana], but a fearful being with the name of Saṃ[v]ara, Vajraḍāka, Heruka, Hevajra or Caṇḍamahāroṣaṇa.*[53]

Thus "the Adamantine One" of the *HT* and "the Lord" of the *ST* and *CMT* do not refer to Śākyamuni or one of the five Tathāgata, but to a *krodha-vighnāntaka* who is the main deity of the text. The Adamantine One/Hevajra begins his text speaking with Vajragarbha ("womb of the *vajra*"), and later responds to the questions of his consort Nairātmyā and the *yoginī*.[54] At the beginning of the *CMT*, it is Vajrasattva who resides in the *bhaga* of the Mistress of the Vajra Realm. He then enters the *samādhi* of Krishna-Acala (Blue-Caṇḍamahāroṣaṇa), and by the end of the chapter the "Lord" (Vajrasattva) is addressed as Krishna-Acala. The rest of the text is spoken by Krishna-Acala from the "firm embrace" of his consort, Dveṣavajri (Anger/Hatred-*vajrī*, also called Prajñāpāramitā), in response to her inquiries. The reverse is true of Chapter Eight, however, in which she narrates in reply to his questions.[55]

A wrathful deity answering the questions of his consort while in her embrace — a more striking contrast with the narrative format of Phase One and Two texts could hardly be conceived. The "setting" is not Rajagrha, Sumeru, Akaniṣṭha, or Sukhāvatī, but the *bhaga* of the consort. Snellgrove is quick to point out that "what is here suggested is the union of the practicing yogin with the absolute state of buddhahood."[56] Commentators in Sanskrit and Tibetan explain the symbolism of the verse in various ways.[57] However the sexual content of Phase Three texts is understood, its ubiquity is undeniable. The prevalence of the *krodha-vighnāntaka* and the endorsement of sexual yoga are the foremost qualities that set Phase Three writings apart from earlier Esoteric Buddhist texts. Even if the unabashedly sexual intent of the practices can be shown to be either purely symbolic, and thus in harmony with the ideals of Phase Two Esoteric Buddhism, or an explicit expression of secret ideals held but not expressed in Phase Two Esoteric Buddhism, the form remains unique to Phase Three texts. As such it dramatically announces a separate modality of Esoteric Buddhism.

An additional note on the texts themselves: the *STTS* and *MVS* are in the same type of Sanskrit language as the standard Mahāyāna texts. By contrast, the language of Phase Three texts is often "written in clumsy, often seemingly ungrammatical Buddhist Sanskrit, as though it were a sanscritization of a local dialect."[58] This lends credence to Snellgrove's view that Phase Three texts represent a hybrid of monastic and yogic priorities evolved largely outside the monastic community of Phase Two. Linguistic eccentricities may also indicate the texts' later date of origin. The position adopted here is that Phase Three texts arose in eastern India (Bihar, Bengal and Orissa) no earlier than the eighth century, after Phase Two texts were well established. The texts generated commentaries in eastern India during the ninth through the eleventh centuries and inspired eastern Indian art in the eleventh and twelfth. The complex issues of date and place of origin will be deferred to the end of this section after we first introduce more of the characteristics of Phase Three Esoteric Buddhism.

For laymen as much as monks, women as well as men

Extensive sections of the Phase Three texts are addressed to a non-monastic audience. The *ST*, for example, assures that a ritual participant may be "a layman or a novice, (even) a mendicant (of exoteric sects)." The practitioner is to "give up his wealth, his wife and likewise (his own) life as offering; getting rid of these three ties, he should always be a practiser of the practice."[59] While these tenets seem to advocate renunciation, the *ST* does not suggest the new practitioner take the tonsure. Furthermore, the text solicits among married householders. Unlike monks, adepts are reported in the *HT* as wearing long hair and tiger-skins instead of robes. Saraha says:

> *Without meditating, without renouncing the world,/ One may stay at home in the company of one's wife. Can that be called perfect knowledge, Saraha says,/ If one is not released while enjoying the pleasures of sense?*[60]

Obviously these lines describe yogins, not monks. Were the novice a monk or nun, his or her practice would rapidly violate monastic precepts. Open practice would lead to expulsion from the monastery. Many of the rites include drinking alcohol, eating flesh, dancing and coition. The *GST* recommends rituals which involve consuming the flesh of humans, elephants, horses, dogs and cows, as well as feces and urine.[61] Benoytosh Bhattacharyya characterizes the *GST* as follows:

> *[It] definitely asks its followers to disregard all social laws which to a Yogi have the least importance. "You should freely immolate animals, utter any number of falsehoods without ceremony, take things which do not belong to you, and even commit adultery."*[62]

Assuming the text intends to be taken literally, any monk performing the following rite prescribed by the *CMT* would violate several different precepts at once:

> *After washing the Lotus with the tongue, he should have Wisdom [i.e., the yogin's consort] stand up and he should kiss her. And, after hugging her, he should eat meat and fish. He should drink milk or wine, in order to increase his desire. After his fatigue has decreased, he should desire with pleasure, etc. And, in the foregoing manner, the couple should begin again with each other.*[63]

There are indications in later Tibetan records that monks who engaged in these unorthodox methods were ejected from eastern Indian monasteries. When Atīśa was "provost-sergeant" of Vikramaśila monastery in the Antichak area of modern eastern Bihar, an ordained Buddhist monk became a disciple of Nāropa, who was an important Mahāsiddha in the Kālacakra tradition. The monk was discovered with a quantity of wine which he alleged he acquired in order to present to a Buddhist yogin "whom he intended to consult on certain matters." The monastic community decided to expel him, and Atīśa carried out the order. Atīśa later regretted doing so, and as penance he went to Tibet to teach.[64] Although this story is likely apocryphal, it betrays at least a hint of the antagonism between traditional monks and the extremist practitioners of Phase Three. The practitioners of Early Buddhism must have been particularly offended by Phase Three practices and imagery. A similar incident is reported by the seventeenth century Tibetan historian, Tāranātha. He writes that in Bodh Gaya a silver statue of Heruka was intentionally destroyed by Sinhalese monks.[65] And in the late tenth century, the royal monk of Guge, Yeshe Ö, "banned the practitioners of whatever was heretical, such as liberation through sexual union, meditations on corpses."[66] The practices had obviously already begun to enter western Tibet.

Much Phase Three imagery and some yogic practices involve women. This alone suggests a more active role for women in Esoteric Buddhism than has until recently been accepted.[67] The *CMT* takes the involvement of women quite a bit further, in that it alternates instructions given to male disciples with those directed at female practitioners. Significant portions of the text, notably Chapter Eight, are narrated by Caṇḍamahārоṣaṇa's consort. There she answers his queries, instead of the reverse. Thus we see it is not the case that the consort instructs only female practitioners, leaving male initiates to Caṇḍamahāroṣaṇa. Prajñāpāramitā describes the manner in which the yogin should honor her, so she directs the male practitioners as well.[68]

The female companion to the yogin was considered a necessary component of enlightenment practice. Shiníchi Tsuda calls the yogin "the new matrix of Enlightenment" and describes how the consorts of the *krodha-vighnāntaka* replace the Tathāgata at the core of the Phase Three *maṇḍala*.[69] The *CMT* praises women in the highest terms:

> *Women are heaven; women are Dharma; and women are the highest penance. Women are Buddha; women are the Saṁgha; and women are the Perfection of Wisdom.*[70]

Several of the semi-historical yogins who championed Phase Three practices, known as the Mahāsiddhas, were women.[71] They too were links in the chain of transmission, who could receive teachings from male or female masters and pass them on to both male and female disciples.[72] The relative equality of women in religious practice is another unique feature of Phase Three ideology.

Polarity Symbolism

The act of union is a highly charged symbol in Phase Three Esoteric Buddhism. It may be ritually performed with a living consort, between couples or among groups of yogins, or take place internally as part of solitary meditation symbolically joining the principles of compassion and wisdom. The symbolism is spelled out unmistakably in the texts. The blissful union of male and female expresses the union (*maithuna*) of two important Buddhist notions, wisdom and compassion. Saraha sings:

> *That blissful delight that consists between lotus and* vajra*,/ Who does not rejoice there? In the Triple world whose hopes does it fail to fulfil?// This moment may be the bliss of Means or of both (Wisdom and Means).*[73]

The two values of wisdom (*prajñā*, considered to be female, and equated with the *padma*-lotus) and means (*upāya*, considered to be male, here equated with the *vajra* and *karuṇa*-compassion)[74] are by no means unique to Esoteric Buddhism, but are fundamental to Mahāyāna as a whole. They are promoted in Phase Two Esoteric Buddhism as well, although as we will see, there the sexual associations are latent at most.

Even the name of the *krodha-vighnāntaka* Hevajra is considered to encapsulate this notion of "two-in-one" (*yuganaddha*) union. *He* refers to compassion, and *vajra* to wisdom; *mahāsukha* (great bliss) expresses the union, which is nothing other than the experience of absolute reality or enlightenment.[75] The *ST* explains the experience this way:

> *The pleasure (caused by the) ardent, undivided (union) of the two is nothing but the great pleasure (mahāsukha); distinction between prajñā-wisdom and karuṇa (compassion) is like (that between) a lamp and (its) light. These two are of (one) undivided essence; they appear in the form of one mind. It is caused by the union of prajñā-wisdom and upāya (means); and it effects the complete enlightenment.*[76]

Often the two elements of the polarity are said to result in bliss. Thus the verse inspired by the thirtieth syllable of the first line of the *GST* reads:

> *Knowing the portions of the three knowledges, through union of thunderbolt and lotus [vajrapadmasamāyogā], the defiled and the undefiled intelligence would dwell therein with bliss for ever.*[77]

Snellgrove considers the "two-in-one" conception of enlightenment to be one of the essential qualities of late Esoteric Buddhism. He sees it, in a sense, as a semi-transparent layer placed on top of the earlier fivefold system of Buddhahood on which Phase Two Esoteric Buddhism was founded:

> *. . . the tantras of the Supreme Yoga class accept this fivefold arrangement in a general way, but it has ceased to be particularly relevant to their changed patterns of thought. . . . [T]he favored expression now is twofold, for the absolute is the union of the two.*[78]

Snellgrove and other scholars have maintained that the blatant sexual content in Phase Three texts is also a theme of Phase Two texts such as the *STTS*.[79] Rolf Stein is satisfied that in the eighth century the sexual references and, to a lesser extent, the sexual practices were known in China as intimately as they were in India and later on in Tibet. Nevertheless, Stein reasons that East Asian Buddhists probably did not enact the graphic rituals suggested by texts because the oral instruction of a master was missing.[80] One can find sexual symbolism in the Japanese Esoteric Buddhist tradition of the "Five Secrets *maṇḍala*." According to Amoghavajra's translation of the *Prajñāpāramitā* in 150 Verses, Vajrasattva is surrounded by Desire Vajra, Touch Vajra, Love Vajra and Vajra Pride.[81]

Certainly it can be shown that in the *STTS* there were already sexual connotations to the metaphor of the union between the *vajra* and the *padma* or *bhaga*. In the twenty-fourth chapter (not translated into Chinese until the early eleventh century), one finds the following passage:

> *This is the Secret Tantra of the Pledge-Perfection of the Tathāgata Family: Gratification should not be despised. One should gratify all women. Holding to this Secret Pledge of the*

> *Adamantine One (vajrin), one succeeds. So said the Lord Vairocana . . . . This is the Secret Tantra of the Pledge-Perfection of the Gem Family: First fixing the Vajra-Gem in union with the Vajra-Womb* (alternative meaning: *in deep meditation on Vajragarbha) and seizing the possessions of evil folk, this Pledge bestows perfection.*[82]

The passage is admittedly as provocative as Phase Three texts. It is notable, however, that this most overt sexual reference is visibly flagged as secret, buried mysteriously in one of the final chapters in such a way to be still open to non-literal interpretation.

Lo Bue also proposes that in Buddhaguhya's Phase Two *Dharmamaṇḍala Sūtra* "there are already suggestions of the sexual symbolism of later Vajrayāna schools in the reference to the union of *vajra* and lotus as defined in the 'secret' type of *maṇḍala*."[83] Lo Bue goes further than suggesting that the "secret" *maṇḍala* implies "the union of *vajra* and lotus":

> *References to yab-yum (Tib. for 'father-mother') with specific reference to male and female deities are found in vv. 148-50, and also in connection with a fivefold scheme (vv. 209 and 211).*

Let us examine these verses closely. First verses 148-50:

> *In the maṇḍalas provided with female consorts/the females look towards their male partners from the left./ When there are pairs of male and female gate-keepers,/ the males are on the right and the females on the left.*

Verses 208-211:

> *(The five elements,) space, air, fire, water and earth,/ are indicated by the five female consorts, corresponding to Mount Meru, with/ the (seven) smaller mountain (ranges and) the (four) continents with the (eight) smaller continents,/while the palace with its pinnacles, fit for a universal monarch, is indicated by the male consorts.*[84]

None of these compare with the extremely open sexuality featured in Phase Three texts. The contrast in the degree of explicitness of Phase Three writings is apparent in the following excerpt from the *CMT*. Compared to many examples, Buddhist concerns are actually cast in relatively high relief here, while graphic sexuality is minimized:

> *In a pleasing place where there are no disturbances, in secret, he should take a woman who has desire. [The yogin says:] 'I am Buddha, and the Perfect One, Immoveable, she [the yogin's consort] is cherished Prajñāpāramitā,' thus the wise person should meditate with fixed thought, each one having his respective [divine] form. . . . [H]e should meditate ardently — the two coupled with each other.*[85]

Passages of even this relatively low level of suggestiveness are not to be found in the *STTS* or the *MVS*.[86] Compared with excerpts of the *CMT*, *HT* and *ST*, the Phase Two passages seem perfectly orthodox. To concede that eighth-century masters of Phase Two Esoteric Buddhism understood the description of sexual acts as metaphors for wisdom and compassion does not diminish the significance of the radically increased prominence of *yuganaddha* imagery in Phase Three texts.

Sexual Yoga

Yuganaddha would appear to be more than the allegorical linking of two principles in ritual, however apt the metaphor is for more abstract levels of understanding.[87]

Snellgrove has placed sexual yoga practice into an Indic context, citing a passage by the fifth-century Asaṅga as a precedent.[88] The issue is endlessly problematic and will remain controversial.[89] Real understanding requires initiation, as the texts themselves repeatedly assert. Initiates who possess firsthand knowledge of Esoteric Buddhist practice are bound by a vow of secrecy, and any who claim to explain the methods despite the vow are dubious sources. Nonetheless, only the most unabashed apologist would deny that sexual yoga was advocated and performed literally, ritually or in meditation by post-eighth-century Phase Three practitioners.[90]

Guides to sexual yoga are relatively plentiful. Nāropa's commentary on the *Kālacakra Tantra* is among the most manifestly sexual.[91] The ca. twelfth-century *Caryāgīti* elliptically celebrates the enlightenment achieved through this type of practice.[92] In the *GST* "stress is laid again and again on the necessity of having Śaktis [sic] for the purpose of Yaugic [sic] practices."[93] None of the written sources, however, were meant to be used without the accompanying oral instructions of a master.

I do not presume to explain the practice as it was performed, nor do I claim to be able to penetrate the many layers of intentional obfuscation which are evident in the texts and images. Here I merely point out that Phase Three texts do occasionally advance justifications for sexual yoga and other acts which violate traditional codes of Buddhist conduct, but which they nonetheless espouse. The *CMT* instructs:

> *By following lust, merit is obtained; from aversion demerit accrues. There is no greater evil than aversion, no greater merit than pleasure.*[94]

> *Just as when manure is applied, a tree becomes abundantly fruitful, so does a person have the true fruits of pleasure by eating unclean things . . . Never should the practitioner think in terms of "edible" or "inedible," "to be done" or "not to be done," "suitable for love-making" or "not suitable for love-making" . . . the yogi should remain with a composed mind, the embodiment of Innate Bliss alone.*[95]

Inner Yoga

Inner yoga is much more developed in Phase Three Esoteric Buddhism. It too participates in polarity symbolism. There are references throughout the texts and commentaries to a psycho-physical system which has its parallels in non-Buddhist yoga as well. There are three main nerve channels (*nādi*) along the spine connected to the "winds" of the breath. The central channel is called the *avadhūtī* (*sushumnā* in Brahmanical yoga) and is closed off in the uninitiated. The *upāya* (male) channel is the *rasanā* (or *piṇgalā*) and the *prajñā* (female) channel is the *lalanā* (or *iḍā*). The three channels penetrate four (seven in the Brahmanical yoga system) *cakra*, or energy centers, in the lower region, heart, throat and the top of the head.

Bodhicitta is the "seed" formed when the two "breaths" are united at the lower channel. The concept is the equivalent of both the union of *prajñā* and *upāya*, and sexual union, which produces *śukra* (the mixture of semen with menses/ovum).[96] Tucci has described *bodhicitta* at a philosophical level as:

> *the thought of illumination understood as cause and effect at the same time; that is, not only as initial motive of the long career towards liberation, but as synonymous both with the eternal background of things and with the germinal essence of the all.*[97]

Per Kværne suggests that the *bodhicitta* was regarded from two points of view, the relative (*samvṛti-satya*) and the Absolute (*paramārtha-satya*). The transition between these two planes of truth is a "dialectical process which aims at uniting both planes of being."[98] In contrast to the orthodox Mahāyāna method of gradual purification of the mind through meditation, yogic methods swiftly raise the *bodhicitta* upward along the *avadhūtī* through the psychic centers of the body.

In the terminology of inner yoga, *bodhicitta* is formed by the union of the flows in the two outer channels, when the "winds" are locked. This produces relative *sukha* (pleasure), likened to sexual pleasure. The union causes the central nerve channel to open, and the *bodhicitta* rises, fired by the inner *yoginī* called Caṇḍālī or Ḍombī (Kuṇḍaliṇī, the serpent goddess in Brahmanical yoga). Passing through the *cakra*s, *bodhicitta* ultimately melts the moon at the summit of the head, releasing bliss downwards into the body. This bliss is *mahāsukha* (great bliss).[99]

The Inner Maṇḍala

The yogin vizualizes the human body as a series of channels through which the *amrit* (elixir) of enlightenment can flow, reflecting another notion of the human body as a *maṇḍala*. The power which the *dhāraṇī* has on the outer world resonates also within the body. Phase Three conceptualizes the four *cakra* as equivalents of the traditional three Buddha bodies of Mahāyāna (*nirmaṇakāya*, *sambhogakāya* and *dharmakāya*), along with a fourth, called the *mahāsukhakāya*. As in a *maṇḍala*, all the Buddhas and deities are located inside the human body. The *maṇḍala* is both the metaphysical expression of the inter-penetration of *prajñā* and *upāya* and the human body itself.[100]

Yogic theory correlates the universe with the human body as equivalent fields of enlightenment. Individual parts of the body are further correlated with geographical places, abstract joys, sounds, and material elements. Tsuda describes this process of identifying the physical body with the world in the *ST*:

> *There is the tendency to identify the universal with the individual, the cosmic or global with the internal or corporeal, or the ultra-sensory with the sensory through the medium of structural or qualitative similarity. . . . [I]t is the fundamental postulate or belief in the unconditional identity of the ultimate reality and the individual existence.*[101]

Secret meeting places for yogins, known as *pītha*, were the most common geographic projections. Pilgrimages to hallowed *pītha* could be actual journeys culminating in the performance of the rites, or they could be internal meditative sojourns through the yogin's own body. *Pītha* were identifiable places, such as Jalandhara and Odiyana, and not simply idealized locations, but they were also symbolically equated with the ten or twelve stages (*bhūmi*) of the bodhisattva path.[102]

The *ḍākinī* and their male consorts were associated with twenty-four *pītha*, which were in turn connected to the *nāḍī*-channels flowing through parts of the human body. In this way, a human body was constructed as a *maṇḍala*. Each of the twenty-four *pītha* is assigned a presiding deity, who together preside over "the body of the mystic . . . [and have] dominion of the earth."[103]

The Śmaśāna (Cemetery) Cult of "Tantric Feasts"

Cemeteries often served as actual *pītha* sites, where yogins met for secret rites involving consumption of illicit substances, singing of mystic songs (*dohā*), and performance of sexual ceremonies. The texts devote considerable space to explanations of the acts performed and the secret signs by which the wandering yogins might recognize each other in order to communicate silently the places and times of the rites.[104] Extended descriptions of these secret circles in both non-Buddhist and Esoteric Buddhist contexts is readily available in a number of sources and need not detain us here.[105] It should be noted that some scholars deny that any of these rituals took place by arguing that all references in the texts to such practices are actually veiled references to inner yoga and have been misunderstood.[106]

Cemeteries were historically sites for meditation in Buddhism. They provided necessary isolation and an ideal environment for contemplation on the mortality of flesh and bone. During Phase Three cemeteries become locales of power. In listing the cemeteries, the texts associate eight great cemeteries to the senses, sensations and the eight directions.[107] Evidently the cult of the cemetery and its corollary rituals are subjects unique to Phase Three texts.

Consecrations

To the initiations and consecrations required by Phase Two Esoteric Buddhism were added unprecedented Phase Three rites. Naturally the new consecrations correspond to the new practices of inner yoga and polarity symbolism. The specialized topic of consecration touches upon our subject to the extent that the deity-yoga initiations were introductions to the primary *krodha-vighnāntaka* and in that the emphasis on these special rites helps to confirm Phase Three as a distinct form of Esoteric Buddhism. A number of treatises on this topic are available.[108]

Heruka: The Sixth Buddha

For Phase Two Esoteric Buddhism there is no sixth Tathāgata. Mahāvairocana, the central Tathāgata of the *STTS*, unified the five Tathāgata.[109] Phase Three, by contrast, considers a sixth Buddha to be the supreme unifier, usually called either Vajrasattva or Vajradhara.[110] He is simultaneously the integrative sum of the five Tathāgata and the source from which they emanate.

This new expansion of the five Tathāgata is of considerable significance for our subject, because the "Ādibuddha" or Supreme Buddha is described as identical to the presiding *krodha-vighnāntaka* of core Phase Three texts.[111] Thus in the Saṃvara cycle, the sixth Tathāgata is Heruka-Saṃvara as the integrated sum of the group, "the whole constituting the revered and glorious Heruka."[112] In the Kālacakra tradition, the *krodha-vighnāntaka* Kālacakra is the Ādibuddha.[113] Tsuda explains the conflation of identities in this way:

> *The one and only god Hevajra who is sexually united with the group of five yoginīs is nothing other than the dharmakāya (the body of the ultimate reality) of Vairocana who is himself the aggregate of the five families . . . A buddha in the dharmakāya form, constituting both the whole of the maṇḍala and the centre of the maṇḍala, as was referred to in the [MVS] and the [STTS] in idea only, actually appeared on the earth as the demonic God Heruka, alias Hevajra.*[114]

And Snellgrove describes it as follows:

> *All these divinities [Guhyasamāja, Hevajra, Caṇḍamahāroṣaṇa, Saṃvara, Kālacakra] may be conventionally identified as horrific forms of Akṣobhya as the central one of the Five Buddhas or equally well as manifestations of a sixth supreme Buddha, whether known as Primary Buddha (Ādibuddha) or Great Vairocana or Vajra-Being (Vajrasattva) or whatever title may be used.*[115]

Krodha-vighnāntaka as Central To Phase Three: Heruka

The sixth Buddha brought Phase Three Esoteric Buddhism perilously close to the notion of a supreme godhead. Such a monist or pantheist conception is anathema to Buddhism, and laid Phase Three Buddhism open to charges of being Hinduism in disguise.[116] The absolute deity is named Heruka, and the major Phase Three *krodha-vighnāntaka* are considered to be various emanations of the meta-reality he collectively represents. The *Herukābhyudaya* describes the exaltation:

> *[H]eruka evolves himself as the phenomenal world; he is the supreme sarvajñajñāna. He is the essence of (all) living beings; he is all the buddhas; he is Vajrasattva, the supreme pleasure.*[117]

The *HT* speaks in no less exalted terms of Heruka-Hevajra, when Hevajra reveals himself to Vajragarbha.

> *I am existence, I am not existence, I am the Enlightened One . . . I dwell in Sukhāvati*[118] *in the bhaga of the Vajra-maiden, in the casket of Buddha-gems with the form of the letter E . . . I am the goal, and I am the trainer. . . . My nature is that of Innate Joy and I come at the end of the Joy that is Perfect . . .*[119]

Likewise in the *CMT* Caṇḍamahāroṣaṇa is envisioned as the yogin recites, "I am Buddha, and the Perfected One, Immoveable [i.e., Acala]."[120] And the *HT* refers to Hevajra as "the Lord, the saviour of the world."[121]

The pinnacle attained by the *krodha-vighnāntaka* in Phase Three ideology is projected onto complexes which represent the entire system by graphic means. The primary such symbolic form which depicts the Phase Three ideology as a totality is the *maṇḍala*, whether two-dimensional or architectural. Phase Three Esoteric Buddhists asserted the supremacy of the *krodha-vighnāntaka* by placing them at the center of the *maṇḍala*. The *maṇḍala* of Heruka, Hevajra, Saṃvara and Kālacakra are relatively common in texts and visual art. Attempts have also been made to unify the system on a vast scale. The Great Stūpa of Gyantse, with its seventy-five shrine areas, is probably the most prodigious example to survive, depicting "practically the whole pantheon of Indo-Tibetan religion up to the time of its construction during the first half of the 15th century."[122] Dominating the walls of the uppermost storey, in the *harmikā*, are Kālacakra, Hevajra, Heruka and Cakrasaṃvara. [COLOR PLATES 14, 16] Though more than 27,000 deities precede the *krodha-vighnāntaka* on the lower levels, they are surmounted by only a statue of the Ādibuddha, Vajradhara, who is but a symbol of their essence in undifferentiated form.[123]

The *krodha-vighnāntaka* have arrived at an extremely elevated status. No higher is possible in Esoteric Buddhism. Yet the functions of the wrathful deity have altered very little from the time they were lowly Yakṣa converts enlisted to control their recalcitrant brethren in Phase One.[124] As we will see later in this section, the Phase Three *krodha-vighnāntaka* are also formally very close to Phase Two *krodha-vighnāntaka*. Form and function have not changed as much as the increased status and importance of the tasks they continue to perform and the position of their images within the shrine.

1.3 Geographic Provenance

Phase Three ideology is usually considered to have developed in one of three areas. There is general agreement that eastern India (Bengal, Bihar and Orissa) played perhaps the largest role. The prominence of yogic elements in the system supports the hypothesis that eastern India made a formative contribution, for the southern slopes of the Himalayas and sites along the eastern Ganges were havens for yogis. The Buddhist Mahāsiddhas and adepts who espoused the new texts are also associated with eastern India.[125] Kashmir is mentioned secondarily as a place of origin. It is possible to confirm this general provenance on the basis of the areas which played a role in the transmission of Esoteric Buddhism to Tibet. Snellgrove points out:

> *[T]he later yoginī-tantras, of which the Hevajra is the chief example were probably formulated in central India under the influence of Shaivite beliefs. It is significant that during the later spread of Buddhism into Tibet (tenth century onwards), these texts and practices were introduced mainly through Nepal, where Akṣobhya is still the foremost of the buddhas, and where his tantric manifestations, Hevajra and Saṃvara, still receive the worship due to them in the inner sanctums of the vihāras. By contrast the tantras that were introduced from Kashmir by [Rinchen Zangpo] and his assistants, were generally of the yoga-class.*[126]

Snellgrove agrees with Tucci's conviction that a number of Phase Three texts belong to India's northwest, in particular Swat.[127] However, only indirect evidence supports Swat as a source of Phase Three texts and practice. A third area sometimes suggested is South India.[128]

It appears overall that these texts and practices originated in and were most intensely championed by Buddhist monasteries in eastern India. The majority of surviving Indian Phase Three sculpted and painted images were made in eastern India. Phase Two, to which Phase Three owes so much, also flourished in monastic centers there. Both movements spread over a wide portion of India, including the west, south and north. Nepal and Tibet proved to be the most receptive of Phase Three teachings. The teachings continued to thrive and develop in both regions after Buddhism disappeared in eastern India. Textual, inscriptional and archaeological evidence seems to speak with a single voice in support of this historical outline.

1.4 Temporal Provenance

Assigning a date of origin to Phase Three Esoteric Buddhism has generated more controversy than locating its place of origin. The question is problematic because it requires knowledge of the time of emergence and the exact relationship of Phase Three texts to Phase Two writings. Examining theories which attribute characteristics shared by Phase Two and Phase Three and those unique to Phase Three to two different milieus in eastern India may facilitate a solution.

Relative Developmental Sequence

Our analysis of Phase Three characteristics as found in the major texts reveal a mixture of two strains. Phase Two practices and structures provide a fundamental basis in the first, but the second strain is manifestly outside the purview of Phase Two

Esoteric Buddhism. Phase Three amalgamated the two components so successfully that they can only be artificially separated. As fully developed Phase Two supplied formative elements to Phase Three, which appropriated and modified them, Phase Three must have evolved after Phase Two had matured.

Several authors have devised models of the development of Esoteric Buddhism. Shiníchi Tsuda creates a credible diachronic model, in which the kind of practice advocated by the *MVS* is gradually supplanted by that of the *STTS*. The *STTS* is itself succeeded by the *anuttara yoga* texts which are representative of Phase Three. According to Tsuda a dialectical process resulted in a decline in Buddhist content and a consequent "lack of religious substantiality." Tsuda specifically points to the non-Buddhist origins and character of the "cult of cemetery . . . a diabolical cult of Bhairava."[129] Tsuda feels Buddhists adopted this aspect Phase Three Esoteric Buddhist practice at the expense of their Buddhist identity.

Snellgrove instead stresses continuities between "later Tantrism" and the earlier ideology espoused in *STTS*. While recognizing the unique characteristics of Phase Three texts and practice, Snellgrove does not set them apart as essentially different from Phase Two, nor does he find them to be of a diminished Buddhist orientation. He acknowledges the contribution of yogins outside the orthodox Buddhist monastic community, who in his eyes were "no more Hindu than Buddhist."[130] However, he feels that ultimately the *anuttara yoga* texts:

> *offer in effect nothing higher [than those of yoga tantra, i.e., Phase Two]; they merely provide the same teachings in the more outspoken and deliberately scandalous language and in the unorthodox terminology, which one might well expect of wandering tantric yogins, who claim to have no allegiance anywhere except to their own revered teacher.*[131]

Snellgrove seems to propose a synchronic relationship between Phases Two and Three. He suggests that they evolved contemporaneously as slightly different modalities of the same system. Disparities are attributed to social milieu, rather than to the temporal priority of one or the other. Phase Two evolved within the Buddhist monasteries among monks, and Phase Three came into being among wandering yogins who congregated at the *pitha*. Snellgrove suggests as much when he writes:

> *It would seem that tantric Buddhism took shape simultaneously in both settings, those that were strictly Buddhist but which willingly accepted the new theories of meditational and yogic practice, and those that were primarily interested in the yogic practices . . . It is likely that the teachings recorded in properly Buddhist settings were the first to gain more general acceptance.*[132]

The more conservative tenor of Phase Two texts would explain why they were transmitted by monks to China in the seventh, eighth and ninth centuries, while the Phase Three texts remained secret and alien to the monastic community. Only in the tenth century did texts such as the *HT* and *GST* arrive in China, at which time they still had little or no influence.

Although Snellgrove has provided the most sophisticated and compelling model for the development to date, his scenario is not beyond criticism. The identification of two groups, one located within Buddhist discourse and another without, is certainly tenable. It may be that some yogins were practicing the methods advocated by the *anuttara yoga* texts as early as the seventh century, when Phase Two texts were being codified. But the synthesis of the monastic and the inner yogic strains, which consisted of teachings generated by non-monastic practitioners and cloaked in Phase Two discourse,[133] logically could not have taken place until Phase

Two had fully developed (late seventh century). Phase Three texts which have one or more Phase Two texts as their foundation freely betray their sources. The *HT*, for instance, begins to describe the Hevajra *maṇḍala*, but abruptly breaks off:

> *But why say more? The maṇḍala-ritual should be performed as it is given in the Tattvasaṃgraha [i.e., STTS].*[134]

Davidson shows that the *samādhi* chapter of the *Māyājāla tantra*, the third chapter of the *GST* and the *Mañjuśrī nāmasaṃgīti* together share a common inspiration in the *STTS*.[135] If the two movements were truly contemporaneous one would expect to find the important Phase Three deities or texts similarly mentioned in Phase Two texts. As this is not the case, it is hard to accept that the two modalities were perfectly coeval.

I find a partially overlapping relationship is most reasonable not only for their respective periods of acceptance, but also for the time of origin. In order to maintain that Phase Three texts existed as early as those of Phase Two (perhaps merely kept underground longer[136]) the testimony of artistic remains must be disregarded. Images with Phase Three themes are found in the same monasteries which earlier produced Phase Two sculptures. We find images of Heruka at Sarnath, Nalanda, Ratnagiri and Somapura, and Saṃvara at Vikramaśīla and Ratnagiri from the eleventh and twelfth centuries. Phase Three was clearly not rejected in the monasteries of eastern India.

The Dates of the Texts

Before concluding with a specific hypothesis on the absolute dating of the origins of the Phase Three movement, let us consider some of the dates established by scholars for the texts we have designated Phase Three.

a. The Guhyasamāja Tantra

The *GST* is generally agreed to be the earliest Phase Three text. Its content is closely related to the earlier ritual structure, but its emphases mark the *GST* as transitional. Its date is a critical clue to the date of the Phase Three movement as a whole. Because it has been accepted as the earliest text of its type, it has been used as the linchpin in devising a chronology. Reginald Ray believes:

> *Tantric Buddhism arose and developed into its classical form sometime. . . [between] the Second Century BC and the appearance of the Guhyasamāja Tantra in the Third Century AD or slightly later.*[137]

Ray reasons that the consistency of the style of the *GST* required a considerable period of development. One cannot argue with his reasoning that the *GST* could not have appeared fully-formed without a long period of development. Although Ray's observations are sound, I believe the third century is too early a date for the *GST*.

Ray is not alone in suggesting so early a date for the *GST*. Benoytosh Bhattacharyya concludes from the evidence of much later Tibetan sources that the *GST* was written by Asaṅga in the third century. Acknowledging that no references to the *GST* are found in the voluminous early Mahāyāna literature, Bhattacharyya suggests:

> *the Tantra was kept secret among the professors and the doctrines inculcated therein were confined to a few adepts for three hundred years until Buddhist Tantras of the Yoga and Yogatantras classes obtained publicity during the time of the Siddhācāryyas mainly through their mystic songs, preaching and works.*[138]

Moriz Winternitz criticizes the attribution of the *GST* to Asaṅga, which is the sole foundation of Bhattacharyya's argument for a third-century date. Without specifying a date, Winternitz rightly points out that "Tantric texts in this sense cannot be proved to have existed before the 7th century, though some of the elements constituting the Tantras may have existed before that time."[139] David Snellgrove also doubts a fourth-century date, accepting instead the sixth or seventh century.[140]

Despite the knowledge that a commentary on the *GST* was composed between the eighth and twelfth centuries and his rejection of Asaṅga as the text's author, Alex Wayman continues to support an early date. "[O]n a purely tentative basis, [I] ascribe the *Guhyasamājatantra* to the fourth century, AD."[141]

Others have argued against so early a date. Ronald Davidson takes both Bhattacharyya and Wayman to task for the "very unhistorical methods" they employ in their dating of the *GST*.[142] Wayman's grounds are involved and complex, but they have been adequately treated by Yukei Matsunaga.[143] According to Matsunaga, the *GST* was in its formative stages in the first half of the eighth century and was not complete until the latter half of that century.[144] The date of the Chinese and Tibetan translations offer no definitive evidence, but it is not insignificant that both are later than the primary Phase Two texts; the Chinese translation (T.18.885) was finished in 1002 CE by Dānapāla, about the same time as Śraddhakāravarma and Rinchen Zangpo's Tibetan translation.[145] Nyingma traditions contrarily claim that the *GST* was translated by Vimalamitra and Peltseg in the third quarter of the eighth century.[146]

The debate is alternatively enriched and confused by the varying opinions of scholars, but I find the most credible historical evidence weighs toward the mid- to late eighth century. The *STTS*, a Phase Two text which strongly colored the development of Phase Three texts like the *GST*, was a product of the mid-seventh century. A date of the late eighth century for the *GST*, the earliest Phase Three text, would allow for a requisite period of borrowing and modification. The eighth century is therefore accepted here as the most appropriate conclusion.

Ray's relative chronology must be shifted considerably forward. The period of development which he felt must have preceded the formulation of the *GST* began in the sixth and seventh centuries with Phase One texts like the *MMK*. The evolution continues in the seventh and eighth centuries with the Phase Two texts, and then, in the late eighth, produces the *GST* as one of the earliest Phase Three texts. Other Phase Three texts provide evidence of a contemporary or later origin.

b. The Hevajra Tantra

One of the internal clues which establish a *terminus a quo* for the *HT* is the passage already cited, in which the *HT* acknowledges the mid-seventh century *STTS* as its authority on *maṇḍala* ritual. It is generally accepted that the *HT* was "brought to light" at the end of the eighth century by Kamapala and Padmavajra/Saroruha,[147] an assumption based to a large extent on considerably later Tibetan evidence. Snellgrove's dating of the text to the late eighth century is based on the time of the active period of Kāṇha, who wrote an early commentary. In his study of the *HT* Snellgrove observes that Kāṇha "is stated by Tāranātha to have been a contemporary of King

Devapāla, who ruled in the first half of the ninth century."[148] More recently Snellgrove has acknowledged that "Kāṇha's commentary on the Hevajra Tantra, which I dated hesitatingly to the ninth century . . . may well be later . . ."[149]

The *HT* may belong to the early ninth century. A number of its commentaries were written between the ninth and eleventh centuries, including one by Nāropa (1016-1100 CE), master of Marpa (1012-1097 CE).[150] The translations into Tibetan and Chinese once again belong to a later period. Willemen notes that the Chinese text (T.18.892), translated by Dharmapāla between 1054 and 1055 CE, "is a little more recent than the Tibetan version which dates back to the middle of the eleventh century."[151] The *HT* was translated into Tibetan by Drogmi (992-1072 CE), who had studied the text at Vikramaśila.[152] The *HT* is almost certainly a late eighth or early ninth-century text.

c. Dates of other Phase Three texts

I believe Shiníchi Tsuda to be correct when he places the *Saṁvarodaya Tantra (ST)* slightly later than the *HT*. Given its relative relationship to the *HT*, Tsuda's conclusion that it "cannot be earlier than the late eighth century"[153] seems appropriate. The *ST* never entered the Chinese Buddhist canon, and was probably never translated into Chinese. By the time of the text's influence China had little interest in Phase Three Esoteric Buddhism.

The dates usually given for the *Kālacakra Tantra* are relatively specific: between 1027 and 1087 CE.[154] Nāropa, the eleventh-century Mahāsiddha from Bengal, is credited with having written a commentary on it, so it must have been in existence before his death in 1100 CE.[155] One passage of the text has been interpreted as making reference to Muslim armies; if this reading is accurate, the text is likely to have been written (or revised) after the very late tenth-century raids of Mahmud of Ghazni (971-1030 CE).[156]

The *CMT* has been situated by Christopher George in the broad range of 1100 and 1297 CE.[157] R.A. Stein narrows the range by pointing out that the *CMT* was translated into Tibetan at the end of the twelfth century.[158] Therefore a twelfth-century date for the *CMT* seems reasonable.

1.5 Conclusions

It has already been suggested that the combination of non-monastic yogic teachings with monastic Phase Two Esoteric Buddhism gave rise to Phase Three Buddhism. Whether the genesis took place within or without the monastery walls, the new teachings eventually penetrated the monasteries of eastern India. We have looked to the dates of texts to help determine the emergence of Phase Three ideology. The chronological evidence from Phase Three texts relates to the very end of the eighth or beginning of the ninth century through the twelfth century. It should be recalled, however, that these dates apply to the completion of manuscripts which probably circulated in very narrow circles. We must once again caution against confusing the origin of texts with their period of substantial influence.

The evidence of extant images suggests that early Phase Three texts (*HT*, *ST*) did not inspire much art before the late tenth or eleventh century, and the *Kālacakra Tantra* had little impact in India at all. It seems reasonable to hypothesize that the synthesis of the Phase Two and yogic strains took place during the eighth and ninth centuries. These texts and practices were subsequently introduced to the monasteries in the tenth century, and gradually they acquired enough of a following that resources — monastic, personal, royal or other — were devoted to the creation of large and small-scale images.

Snellgrove has most clearly grasped the process of development and the problems of relying on texts for chronology. He summarizes for us:

> *[T]he whole question of datings remains open to speculation and consequent disagreement. For the history of Buddhism in India what is important is not so much the dates of the earliest versions of texts which are only known to us in later versions, but the effects that such texts had on Buddhist beliefs and practices once they went into wider circulation . . .*[159]

Sculpted and painted images of the *krodha-vighnāntaka* are the unique effects of ideas that have achieved "wider circulation." Examining representations of the three primary Phase Three *krodha-vighnāntaka*, Heruka, Hevajra and Saṃvara, will assist us in gauging the temporal and ideational origins of the final stage of mature Esoteric Buddhism.

Notes to Chapter 14

1 Sir John Marshall and Alfred Foucher, *The Monuments of Sañchi*, 3 vols. (London, 1940), 255. The epigraph for this chapter comes from Louis de La Vallée Poussin, *Bouddhisme: Opinions sur l'histoire de la dogmatique* (Paris, 1909), 405.

2 As expounded by Tsongkhapa and other Tibetan scholastics and discussed further in the Afterword. Tsongkhapa, *Tantra in Tibet: The Great Exposition of Secret Mantra*, trans. and ed. Jeffrey Hopkins (London, 1977), 151-164, *passim*; Lessing and Wayman, *Mkhas-grub-rje's*; Tucci, *Tibetan Painted Scrolls*, 220-226.

3 Another way to differentiate this mode of Esoteric Buddhism from Phase Two would have been to follow Hajime Nakamura by using "The Final Stage" for Phase Three, and "Systematization" for Phase Two. Nakamura, *Indian Buddhism*, 321, 331.

4 Lessing and Wayman, *Mkhas-grub-rje's*, 250-269.

5 Tsuda, "Critical Tantrism," 172.

6 Snellgrove, *Buddhist Himalaya*, 202-203.

7 Tucci, *Tibetan Painted Scrolls*, 221.

8 Alex Wayman, "Received Teachings of Tibet and Analysis of the Tantric Canon," in *The Buddhist Tantras: Light on Indo-Tibetan Esotericism* (New York, 1973), 225-239.

9 Snellgrove, *Hevajra Tantra*, 1:11.

10 Tsuda, *Saṁvarodaya-tantra*, 259, VI.10.

11 Malati Shendge, *Advayasiddhi, Edited with an Introduction*, (Baroda, 1964), 29.

12 Translated from the *Dohākosha* by David Snellgrove, in Edward Conze et al, *Buddhist Texts Through the Ages* (New York, 1954), 229, no. 35, 231 no. 51 and 233, no. 68.

13 Louis de la Vallée Poussin, "The Buddhist 'Wheel of Life' from a New Source," *Journal of the Royal Asiatic Society* (1897): 464.

14 Lamotte, "Vajrapāṇi en Inde," 155.

15 See Herbert V. Guenther, *The Tantric View of Life* (Berkeley/London, 1972); and, idem, *The Life and Teaching of Nāropa: Translated from the original Tibetan with a Philosophical Commentary based on the Oral Transmission* (Oxford, 1963).

16 For a discussion of the human body as the medium in which enlightenment is to be obtained, see Tsuda, *Saṁvarodaya-tantra*, 50.

17 *Dohākosha*, trans. Snellgrove in Conze et al, *Buddhist Texts Through the Ages*, 238, no. 102.

18 Snellgrove, *Hevajra Tantra*, 1:78-79, I.ix.1-2; Willemen, *Chinese Hevajratantra*, 69.

19 Snellgrove, *Hevajra Tantra*, 1:107, II.iv.69.

20 *Dohākosha*, trans. Snellgrove in Conze et al, *Buddhist Texts Through the Ages*, 229 no. 34-35.

21 Snellgrove, *Hevajra Tantra*, 1:80, I.ix.15-18; Willemen, *Chinese Hevajratantra*, 71.

22 See the discussion of visualization and identification in "The Practice of Concentration," Snellgrove, *Hevajra Tantra*, 1:32-33.

23 Snellgrove, *Hevajra Tantra*, 1:58, I.iii.11. Similarly, the *HT* also teaches, "at all times remain consubstantiated with the divinity." Ibid., 1:60, I.iv.3; Willemen, *Chinese Hevajratantra*, 51.

24 Tsuda, *Saṁvarodaya-Tantra*, 52.

25 George, *Caṇḍamahāroṣaṇa Tantra*, 67.

26 Snellgrove, *Hevajra Tantra*, 1:127, diagram II. For an extended study of the *HT maṇḍala*, see Ray, "*Maṇḍala* Symbolism," 243-329.

27 For instance, Chapters 13 and 17 of the *ST*. Tsuda, *Saṁvarodaya-tantra*, 283-286, 287-293. See also the discussion of Saṃvara and related *maṇḍala* in Martin Michael Kalff, "Selected Chapters from the Abhidhānottara-Tantra: The Union of Female and Male Deities," (Ph.D. dissertation, Columbia University, 1979), 23-66.

28 Phase Two Esoteric Buddhism frequently associates white with the center (with Mahāvairocana Tathāgata and the *tathāgatakula*); blue with east (Akṣobhya and *vajrakula*); yellow with south (Ratnasambhava and *ratnakula*); red with west (Amitābha and *padmakula*); and green with north (Amoghasiddhi and *karmakula*).

29 George, *Caṇḍamahāroṣaṇa Tantra*, 49-50.

30 The first chapter of the *GST* is translated in Tucci, *Theory and Practice*, 98-104. See also, B. Bhattacharyya, *Guhyasamāja Tantra*.

31 See Advayavajra, *Advayavajrasaṁgraha*, ed. H. Sastri, Gaekwad's Oriental Series no. 40 (Baroda, 1927). The relevant section is translated by Snellgrove in *Buddhist Texts Through the Ages*, 249-252.

32 Snellgrove, *Hevajra Tantra*, 1:93, II.ii.53-58; see also 118-119, II.xi.3-9, where the colors and symbols for the five families are given.

33 Snellgrove, *Hevajra Tantra*, 1:61, I.v.5; Willemen, *Chinese Hevajratantra*, 52.

34 Tucci, *Tsaparang*, 63.

35 On this topic, see also Tsuda, "Critical Tantrism," 173-174, 208-210.

36 Tsuda, *Saṁvarodaya-tantra*, 241-242.

37 Snellgrove, *Hevajra Tantra*, 1:59, I.iv.2; Willemen, *Chinese Hevajratantra*, 51.

38 "*OM*, As all the Tathāgata are, so am I." Tsuda, "Critical Tantrism," 202.

39 This *maṇḍala* is graphed and explained in Wayman, *Guhyasamājatantra*, 122-126.

40 Snellgrove, *Hevajra Tantra*, 1:119, II.xi.3.

41 Ibid., 1:109, II.iv.103.

42 George, *Caṇḍamahāroṣaṇa Tantra*, 44, note 1.

43 Tucci, *Tsaparang*, 64.

44 George, *Caṇḍamahāroṣaṇa Tantra*, 64.

45 Ibid., 65.

46 This *maṇḍala* is graphed and explained in Tsuda, "Critical Tantrism," 224-228.

47 Carelli, *Sekoddeśatikā*, 29.

48 Snellgrove, *Indo-Tibetan Buddhism*, 274.

49 After the translation in Snellgrove, *Indo-Tibetan Buddhism*, 152. For the *HT*, see Snellgrove, *The Hevajra Tantra*, 1:47; for the *CMT*, see George, *Caṇḍamahāroṣaṇa Tantra*, 44; for the *GST*, see Tucci, *Theory and Practice*, 98; and, Wayman, *Guhyasamājatantra*, 108. The 40 Sanskrit syllables in this verse were each taken as the "seed" for 40 verses, on which a lengthy commentarial tradition was based. Wayman, *Guhyasamājatantra*, 181-331.

50 Snellgrove, *Indo-Tibetan Buddhism*, 160. *Bhaga* means happiness, welfare, loveliness, amorous pleasure and the *pudendum muliebre*. Monier-Williams, *Sanskrit-English Dictionary*, 743. Here the last meaning is intended and the others connoted.

51 Minoru Kiyota, *Tantric Concept of Bodhicitta: A Buddhist Experiential Philosophy* (Madison, 1982), 56.

52 Tsuda, "Critical Tantrism," 197.

53 Snellgrove, *Indo-Tibetan Buddhism*, 153.

54 Snellgrove, *The Hevajra Tantra*, 1:II.iii.31; II.iv.65; with Nairātmyā, II.iv.89.

55 George, *Caṇḍamahāroṣaṇa Tantra*, 18, 44-47; 65,VI.1; 80,VII.32.

56 Snellgrove, *Indo-Tibetan Buddhism*, 152. This is not to suggest that Snellgrove believes all such references to sexual union are purely symbolic: "when modern apologists use the term 'symbolic' as though to suggest that the external practices were never taken in any literal sense, they mislead us." Ibid., 160.

57 For example, Indrabhūti explains the reference to the Lord "dwelling in those *bhagas* of the diamond ladies of the heart" as "belonging to the Body, Speech, and Mind of all the Tathāgatas, where the diamond ladies are precisely the heart knowledge, because of the self-existence of non-dual insight, and where the *bhaga* is precisely the same, because of destroying all defilement." Wayman, *Guhyasamājatantra*, 109. Candrakirti comments on the *GST* verse, "With union of the two organs one should contemplate an image of the Buddha," by saying, "The *bhaga* is supreme truth. About the *liṅga*, it is said, 'It lies therein'. And what is it? Conventional truth. 'Placing it', i.e. introducing it into the Clear Light, one should contemplate an image of the Buddha, i.e. Mahāvajradhara. One should make it emerge from Supreme truth. That is the meaning." Ibid., 311. Shendge interprets Kāṇha's commentary to mean that, "Bhagavan Vajradhara occupied the deepest centre of his own being . . . which is endowed with the glory of six types . . ."

Malati J. Shendge, "The Moon and her Reflection in Water: The Sexual Imagery in the Vajrayanic Instruction," *Indian Journal of Buddhist Studies* I.1 (1989): 92.

58 Snellgrove, *Indo-Tibetan Buddhism*, 180-181. See also the comments on the language of the mystic songs in Per Kværne, *An Anthology of Buddhist Tantric Songs: A Study of the Caryāgīti*, Det Norske Videnskaps Akademi Ny Serie no. 14 (Oslo, 1977), 3-4; and, Shendge, *Advayasiddhi*, 13.

59 Tsuda, *Saṁvarodaya-tantra*, 264, VIII.5; 304, XXI.4.

60 *Dohākosha*, trans. Snellgrove in Conze et al, *Buddhist Texts Through the Ages*, 226, no. 19.

61 Snellgrove, "Categories of Buddhist Tantras," 1378-1379. The *Advayasiddhi*, for instance, instructs: "The *Mantrin* (one who practices *Mantracaryā* [sic]) should always glorify himself with the contemplation of the *Tattva*, by means of excreta, urine, seed etc., and the nasal discharge." Shendge, *Advayasiddhi*, 25.

62 B. Bhattacharyya, *Guhyasamāja Tantra*, xiii.

63 George, *Caṇḍamahāroṣaṇa Tantra*, 75.

64 See the discussion of this incident in Chattopadhyaya, *Atiśa*, 134-137.

65 Discussed in Naudou, *Bouddhistes Kasmiriens*, 72.

66 Roberto Vitali, *The Kingdoms of Gu.ge Pu.hrang According to mNga'.ris rgyal.rabs by Gu.ge mkhan.chen Ngag.dbang grags.pa* (Dharamsala, 1996), 112, and the discussion, 214-231, 237-239. The issue is also discussed in Ronald M. Davidson, "Atiśa's *A Lamp for the Path to Awakening*," in *Buddhism in Practice*, ed. Donald S. Lopez, Jr. (Princeton, 1995), 290-301.

67 See Miranda Shaw, *Passionate Enlightenment: Women in Tantric Buddhism* (Princeton: Princeton University Press, 1994). Shaw has exposed the blind androcentrism of many writers on Esoteric Buddhism. She argues convincingly, if somewhat over-emphatically, that women participated fully in the composition and the utilization of Esoteric Buddhist texts. In the present context, it is not surprising that she finds most of her material in what are called here Phase Three texts, such as the *CMT*, *ST* and *dohās*. For another view of these issues, see Adelheid Herrmann-Pfandt, "Yab Yum Iconography and the Role of Women in Tibetan Tantric Buddhism," *Tibet Journal* 22 #1 (1997): 12-34.

68 George, *Caṇḍamahāroṣaṇa Tantra*, 81-85.

69 Tsuda, "A Critical Tantrism," 208, 213-215.

70 George, *Caṇḍamahāroṣaṇa Tantra*, 82, VIII.29-30.

71 Notably Maṇibhadrā, Mekhalā, Kanakhalā and Lakṣmīnkarādevī. See James B. Robinson, *Buddha's Lions: The Lives of the Eighty-four Siddha* (Berkeley, 1979). See the fascinating correlation between Kanakhalā, Lakṣmīnkarādevī, Mekhalā and Vajravārāhī and inner *yoga* in Elisabeth Anne Benard, *Chinnamastā: The Aweful Buddhist and Hindu Tantric Goddess*, (Delhi, 1994).

72 Besides authorship of the *Advaya-siddhi*, Laksmīnkarādevī (ca. 9th c.) is credited with passing on the teachings to Lilavajra, a male *vajracāryā*, who wrote on the *GST* and Yamāri texts. See Benoytosh Bhattacharyya, *An Introduction to Buddhist Esoterism* (New Delhi, 1931), 76-78; and, Shendge, *Advayasiddhi*, 10-11. Shendge expected a female perspective from this work, "but in reality all her teachings in no way differ from those preached by the male practicants of the doctrine." Ibid., 11.

73 *Dohākosha*, trans. Snellgrove in Conze et al, *Buddhist Texts Through the Ages*, 237, no. 94-95.

74 "Goddess Vārāhī who represents Prajñā is spoken of as of the nature of knowledge, whereas god Heruka representing Upāya is spoken of as the knowable, and the *Avadhuti-maṇḍala* (the circle of perfect purification) is formed by the combination of both this knowledge and of the knowable." Dasgupta, *Introduction to Tantric Buddhism*, 96. Also, José Ignacio Cabezón, "Mother Widsom, Father Love: Gender-Based Imagery in Mahāyāna Buddhist Thought," in *Buddhist, Sexuality and Gender*, ed. José Ignacio Cabezón (Albany: SUNY, 1992), 181-199.

75 Snellgrove, *Hevajra Tantra*, 1:23-24.

76 Tsuda, *Saṁvarodaya-tantra*, 331, XXX.17-18.

77 Wayman, *Guhyasamājatantra*, 294.

78 Snellgrove, *Indo-Tibetan Buddhism*, 280. Also see the discussion on 278-288.

79 Knowledge of these practices is attributed to others as well. For instance, the ca. 7th c. logician Dharmakirti, author of the *Pramāṇavarttika*, is supposed to have advocated or known of Buddhist practices which "contradict *dharma* such as cruelty, stealing, sexual intercourse and so forth." Davidson, "'Litany of Names of Mañjuśrī'," 8, note 21. Davidson sagely adds, "The precise significance, however, of this passage is unclear."

80 R.A. Stein, "Nouveaux problèmes du tantrisme sino-japonais," *Annuaire du Collège de France* 75 (1975): 481-488. The sexual rites performed by the Tachikawa sect in Japan claim authority from Amoghavajra and Yixing, but the practices seem to owe as much to Daoist, shamanist and Japanese folk beliefs as to Esoteric Buddhism of either the Phase Two or Phase Three variety. See James H. Sanford, "The Abominable Tachikawa Skull Ritual," *Monumenta Nipponica* 46 (1991): 1-20; and, Michel Strickmann, *Mantras et mandarins: Le bouddhisme tantrique en Chine* (Paris, 1996).

81 H. Hunter, "Five Secrets maṇḍala," in *Function and Meaning in Buddhist Art*, ed. K.R. van Kooij and H. van der Veere (Groningen: Egbert Forsten, 1995), 111-124.

82 Snellgrove, "Introduction," 63.

83 Lo Bue, "*Dharmamaṇḍala-Sūtra* by Buddhaguhya," 789.

84 Ibid., 789, 796, 799, 801.

85 George, *Caṇḍamahāroṣaṇa Tantra*, 67.

86 Astley-Kristensen also mounts evidence for the explicitly sexual interpretation of the Phase Two *Arhyardhaśatikāprajñāpāramitā Sūtra* in Japanese Shingon. That is certainly how the 20th c. scholars he follows understand it, and he traces the belief back to Amoghavajra. But there sexual references are metaphorical: "*Surata* [exquisite bliss] is like the mistaken bliss of Nara and Narī." Astley-Kristensen, *The Rishukyō*, 89.

87 Guenther presses for a symbolic interpretation of sexual imagery in Phase Three texts, turning the discussion immediately to a philosophical level whenever sexuality as "aesthetic experience" appears, without denying the literal interpretation. "The unmistakably erotic language must not deceive us. As embodied beings we use symbols derived from the phenomenal world and from fundamental, human experience. Man's sexuality is but one among the many 'expressions' of his Being and of what is 'expressed' in the body which is mind as well." Guenther, *Tantric View of Life*, 69.

88 Snellgrove, *Indo-Tibetan Buddhism*, 127-128.

89 Already by 1933 Winternitz had criticized Sylvain Levi's use of Asaṅga's verse as "an allusion to 'mystic couples of Buddhas and Bodhisattvas which are of such importance in Tantrism'." Winternitz, "Notes on the *Guhyasamāja-Tantra*," 7-8.

90 Shendge argues all suggestive passages are veiled references to inner yoga. Shendge, "Moon and her Reflection," 89-107. Shendge believes the language was "deliberately inaccessible except to the initiate," which may or may not imply a unique ability on the part of Shendge to pierce this screen, perhaps due to initiation. Shendge seems intent on clearing medieval India of charges that "very grave and unhealthy" practices were performed. "It is doubtful if any society should allow such a cult within itself, knowing fully well its moral and ethical implications, and therefore we should first examine if our understanding of this system is correct at all." Ibid., 91.

91 See Snellgrove, *Indo-Tibetan Buddhism*, 262-264.

92 See Kværne, *Buddhist Tantric Songs*; and, Nilratan Sen, ed., *Caryāgītikośa: Facsimile Edition* (Simla, 1977).

93 B. Bhattacharyya, *Guhyasamāja Tantra*, xii.

94 George, *Caṇḍamahāroṣaṇa Tantra*, 77, VI.182-3.

95 Ibid., 79. Similar sentiments are expressed by Laksmīnkarādevī: "The knower of *mantra* should not feel disgust about anything and should think that *Vajrasattva* himself is physically present in all forms. The possessor of *mantra* should not worry about whatever is approachable or non-approachable, neither about eatables and non-eatables nor about drinkables or non-drinkables. . . . He should not feel disgust for a woman born in any caste as she is Bhagavatī Prajñā (Blessed Gnosis), who has assumed a physical body in this conventional world."

Shendge, *Advayasiddhi*, 29.

96 See Tsuda, *Saṁvarodaya-tantra*, 70-71.

97 Tucci, *Tsaparang*, 20. For the Phase Two conception of *bodhicitta*, particularly as understood in Japan based on the *MVS*, see Minoru, *Bodhicitta*.

98 Kværne, *Buddhist Tantric Songs*, 30-31.

99 This brief summation is based on a number of sources. Details can be found in the *HT*, the *ST* (esp. Chapters 5 and 7), and in Bharati, *Tantric Tradition*; Shashibhusan Dasgupta, *Obscure Religious Cults*, 3rd ed. (Calcutta, 1969), 87-109; Vidya Dehejia, *Yoginī Cult and Temples: A Tantric Tradition* (New Delhi, 1986), 11-64; Kværne, *Buddhist Tantric Songs*, 30-36; Pott, *Yoga and Yantra*, 1-50; Shendge, "Moon and her Reflection," 93-104; Ray, "*Maṇḍala* Symbolism," 297-311; Tsuda, "Critical Tantrism," 213-214; Snellgrove, *Indo-Tibetan Buddhism*, 288-294; idem, "Categories of Buddhist Tantras," 1371-1378; Tucci, *Tibetan Painted Scrolls*, 241-245; Kalff, "Abhidhānottara-Tantra." Shendge calls this form of yoga "*nāḍi*-yoga," or Caṇḍāli-yoga, and argues that the philosophical and ritual aspects of Phase Three can only be interpreted in the light of this. Snellgrove argues once again that this type of yoga had been part of Mahāyāna Buddhism much earlier and, because it is a practice and not a theory, it was not discussed in texts. Even if this is so, Phase Three texts are markedly different from those of earlier Esoteric or exoteric Buddhism in mentioning the topic openly.

100 See Snellgrove, *Hevajra Tantra*, 105-106, 1:II.iv.48ff.; Willemen, *Chinese Hevajratantra*, 97-99; Tsuda, *Saṁvarodaya-tantra*, 49-50, 61.

101 Tsuda, *Saṁvarodaya-tantra*, 69-70. Also see Kalff, "Abhidhānottara-Tantra," 97-107, 157-160, 228 -231.

102 See Snellgrove, *Hevajra Tantra*, 68-70, 1:I.vii.10-18; Willemen, *Chinese Hevajratantra*, 60-61; Tsuda, *Saṁvarodaya-tantra*, Chapter 7 and 60-62; idem, "A Critical Tantrism," 174-175, 215-219.

103 Tucci, *Tsaparang*, 42. Also see the discussion on the "twenty-four vīrās and the cosmic man," 38-44.

104 Snellgrove, *Hevajra Tantra*, 66-72, 1:I.vii. A number of identical signs are given in the *ST*. Tsuda, *Saṁvarodaya Tantra*, 269.

105 See Tsuda, "Critical Tantrism," 172-176; Dehejia, *Yoginī Cult*, 11-64; Snellgrove, *Indo-Tibetan Buddhism*, 160-170; Dasgupta, *Obscure Religious Cults*; Kalff, "Abhidhānottara-Tantra," 153-252.

106 Shendge, "Moon and Her Reflection,"95-102. Guenther is more circumspect, refuting "the impression . . . that orgies and Tantrism in some way or other belonged together," by differentiating "orgies as outgrowth of sexuality and sexual relationship as a means of self-growth." Guenther, *Tantric View of Life*, 97.

107 For a list of cemeteries, see Tsuda, *Saṁvarodaya-tantra*, 292, XVII.36-37; Tucci, *Tsaparang*, 50-54, 180-181; Dawa-Samdup, *Shrīchakrasambhāra*, 91-92; and, Pott, "The Sacred Cemeteries of Nepal," Chapter IV of *Yoga and Yantra*, 76-101. Also see Richard Meisezahl, "L'Étude iconographique des huit Cimetières d'après le traité Śmaśânavidhi de Luyi," in *Geist und Ikonographie des Vajrayâna-Buddhismus: Hommage à Marie-Thérèse de Mallmann* (St. Augustin, 1980), 3-123.

108 See Per Kværne, "On the Concept of Sahaja in Indian Buddhist Tantric Literature," *Temenos* 11 (1975): 88-135; Snellgrove, "Divine Kingship," 204-218; idem, *Buddhist Himalaya*, 68-80; idem, *Indo-Tibetan Buddhism*, 213-277; idem, "Categories of Buddhist Tantras," 1369-1371; Tsuda, *Saṁvarodaya-Tantra*, 294-299, XVIII; idem, "Critical Tantrism," 212-215; George, *Caṇḍamahāroṣaṇa Tantra*, 52-57, III; Carelli, *Sekoddeśatikā* (itself "a commentary on the treatise of tantric baptism"); Alex Wayman, "Preparation of Disciples; the Meaning of Initiation," in *The Buddhist Tantras: Light on Indo-Tibetan Esotericism* (New York, 1973), 54-70; idem, *Guhyasamājatantra*, 146-151; Lessing and Wayman, *Mkhas-grub-rje's*, 271-331.

109 The *STTS* speaks of "The reverend Lord Mahāvairocana, who is the adamantine (aggregate of) body, speech and mind . . . who is, as the complete aggregate of all the tathāgatas . . ." Tsuda, "Critical Tantrism," 197.

110 The sixth Buddha is called Vajrasattva in the *HT* and in the Saṃvara cycle. Snellgrove, *Hevajra Tantra*, 119, 1:109; Dawa-Samdup, *Shrīchakrasambhāra*, 79; and, Tucci, *Tsaparang*, 56-57. He is called Vajradhara in the *GST*. Ibid., 63; and, Wayman, *Guhyasamājatantra*, 26. Vajradhara is the same as Mahāvairocana, as opposed to Vairocana, who is the Tathāgata of the east in the *GST* system. See Snellgrove, *Indo-Tibetan Buddhism*, 204; and, idem, "Categories of Buddhist Tantras," 1366.

111 "[A]ll these later tantras refer to a 6th supreme Buddha who unites the fivefold set within himself and is at the same time identical with the particular tutelary divinity of any particular tantra, Hevajra or any other." Snellgrove, "Categories of Buddhist Tantras," 1366.

112 Dawa-Samdup, *Shrīchakrasambhāra*, 79. Tucci writes of the Saṃvara shrine at Tsaparang, "As in the Guhyasamāja the series of the Buddhas is of six, the five traditional Buddhas running around their source Mahāvajradhara; in the same manner according to these schools of Saṃvara, Heruka is the centre of the five Buddhas and their essence and also their point of origin, that is the matrix of all the Buddhas ensuing therefrom. In fact, it is a new symbol of the same essence and therefore, according to some texts, Heruka, Hevajra, Kālacakra and Guhyasamāja, are always special manifestations whereby the supreme being conveniently called Vajradhara, appears in the individual creatures according to their ability and their karmic preparations." Tucci, *Tsaparang*, 63.

113 Carelli, *Sekoddeśatikā*, 20-23.

114 Tsuda, "Critical Tantrism," 211-212.

115 Snellgrove, *Indo-Tibetan Buddhism*, 207.

116 "The whole universe, that is to say the three worlds, is endowed with the *Sahaja* (Innate). That universe, which is of no other nature, is pervaded by it (i.e. the *Sahaja*) alone." Malati Shendge, "Śrīsahajasiddhi," *Indo-Iranian Journal* 10 (1967): 147.

117 Tsuda, *Saṁvarodaya-tantra*, 51.

118 This reference to Sukhāvatī in a late Esoteric Buddhist text confirms Gregory Schopen's argument that Sukhāvatī was used outside the Amitābha cult "as a generalized religious goal open to the Mahāyāna community as a whole." Schopen, "Sukhāvatı,"177-210.

119 Snellgrove, *Hevajra Tantra*, 92. Modification found in idem, *Indo-Tibetan Buddhism*, 289. Also see Willemen, *Chinese Hevajratantra*, 84.

120 George, *Caṇḍamahāroṣaṇa Tantra*, 67.

121 Snellgrove, *Hevajra Tantra*, 1:117.

122 Snellgrove, "Preface," in Ricca and Lo Bue, *Gyantse*, 9.

123 See Tucci, *Gyantse and Its Monasteries, Part I*, 292-300; idem, *Gyantse and Its Monasteries, Part III*, figs. 388-391; Ricca and Lo Bue, *Gyantse*, 312-313, pls. 64-67.

124 The rise in status sometimes has an effect on the performance of the rites which follow the Phase Two pattern. In Phase Two, the wrathful deity subordinate to the Tathāgata performed preliminary cleansing and guarding functions; in some Phase Three contexts they continue to do so. In other cases, however, it is the main deity himself who is invoked for these preliminary functions. See Tsuda, *Saṁvarodaya-tantra*, 289, XVII.8-11; 289-290, XVII.14-15.

125 Nāropa is known to have been born in Bengal. See Guenther, *Teaching of Nāropa*, 7. For the Mahāsiddhas, see Tucci, *Tibetan Painted Scrolls*, 226-233. The contribution of Bengal to later Buddhism is pointed out in De, "Buddhist Tantric Literature," 1-23. The Orissan connections are presented in a partisan but still valuable treatment in Sahu, *Buddhism in Orissa*, 156-180. The language of the yogic songs, such as the *Caryāgīti*, is characterized as "Old Bengali," "Old Maithili," "Old Bihari" or "Old Oriya." Kværne, *Buddhist Tantric Songs*, 3-4.

126 Snellgrove, *Buddhist Himalaya*, 204.

127 For a discussion of this area as a source of Esoteric Buddhism, though he groups Kashmir with the northwest (Gandhara and Swat), see Ray, "*Maṇḍala* Symbolism," 404-405 . There have been generally unconvincing attempts to suggest sources as far afield as China and Tibet. See P.C. Bagchi, "On Foreign Element in the Tantra," *Indian Historical Quarterly* 7 (1931): 1-16.

128 See the discussion of southern India in section two of Chapter One. Also see Nakamura, *Indian Buddhism*, 323-324, 341; and, L.M. Joshi, "Original Homes of Tantrika Buddhism," *Journal of the Oriental Institute (Baroda)* 16 (1976): 223-232. Joshi comes to the "irresistible historical

conclusion that Mahāyāna as well as Vajrayāna originated in South India, in Andhradesa, around Nagarjunakonda and Amaravati, anciently known as Sri Parvata and Dhanyakataka, respectively."

129 Tsuda, "A Critical Tantrism," 171-172.

130 Snellgrove, *Indo-Tibetan Buddhism*, 157. On the milieu of yogins who shared Buddhist and Hindu affiliations, see K. R. van Kooij, "Some Iconographical Data from the Kālikāpurāṇa with Special Reference to Heruka and Ekajāta," in *South Asian Archaeology 1973*, ed. J. E. van Lohuizen-de Leeuw and J. M. M. Ubaghs (Leiden, 1974), 161-170.

131 Snellgrove, *Indo-Tibetan Buddhism*, 186.

132 Ibid., 181.

133 In his textual analysis of the *Mañjuśrīnāmasaṁgīti* Davidson suggests "the earliest coherent stratum of the text . . . represents a basic meditative form. . . . The next stratum certainly represents an attempt to display in canonical form what began as the instructions of a *vajrācaryā*." Davidson, "'Litany of Names of Mañjuśrī'," 3.

134 Snellgrove, *Hevajra Tantra*, 113, 1:II.v.57. This passage shows that the *STTS* was accepted as an authority on ritual instructions and was part of the foundation of Phase Three.

135 Davidson, "'Litany of Names of Mañjuśrī'," 2-3.

136 This argument is maintained by representatives of the living Tibetan tradition, who accept Buddhist texts as revelation hidden until the climate is ready for their acceptance. The Nyingma school in particular has a tradition of *gterma* (treasures), texts hidden by Padmasambhava or other great teachers, and rediscovered later. See Samten G. Karmay, "King Tsa/Dza and Vajrayāna," in *Tantric and Taoist Studies in Honour of R.A. Stein*, ed. Michel Strickmann (Brussels, 1981), 1:192-211. It is also found in Tāranātha. B. Bhattacharyya, *Guhyasamāja Tantra*, xxxv. Snellgrove also comments, "Tibetan tradition would in general consider the *tantras* as old as the *sūtras*, explaining their relatively late appearance by the secrecy with which they were transmitted. This, however, is unconvincing, for these texts only began to have importance for Buddhism when they were brought into the open, and one may err as much by laying stress on their secrecy as their supposed popularity." Snellgrove, *Hevajra Tantra*, 1:18.

137 Ray, "*Maṇḍala* Symbolism," 401.

138 B. Bhattacharyya, *Guhyasamāja Tantra*, xxxii, xxiv.

139 Winternitz, "Notes on the Guhyasamāja-Tantra," 8.

140 Snellgrove, *Indo-Tibetan Buddhism*, 184.

141 Wayman, *Guhyasamājatantra*, 99. Wayman places the verses inspired by the *GST* to the 5th c. Ibid., 102. Also see idem, "Early Literary History of the Buddhist Tantras, especially the Guhyasamāja-tantra," *Annals of the Bhandarkar Oriental Research Institute* 48-49 (1968): 100-106; and, idem, *Analysis of the Śrāvakabhūmi Manuscript*, University of California Publications in Classical Philology no. 17 (Berkeley, 1961), 39.

142 Davidson, "'Litany of Names of Mañjuśrī'," 4-5.

143 Yukei Matsunaga, "Some Problems of the *Guhyasamāja-Tantra*," *Studies in Indo-Asian Art and Culture* 5 (1972): 109-119.

144 Matsunaga, "Some Problems," 113-114. Also see idem, "Indian Esoteric Buddhism," 239.

145 Matsunaga, "Some Problems," 109.

146 S. Karmay, "King Tsa/Dza and Vajrayāna," 193, note 4.

147 Snellgrove, *Hevajra Tantra*, 1:12-14; Willemen, *Chinese Hevajratantra*, 20-22.

148 Snellgrove, *Hevajra Tantra*, 1:14.

149 Snellgrove, "Categories of Buddhist Tantras," 1383.

150 Snellgrove, *Hevajra Tantra*, 1:14-19; Willemen, *Chinese Hevajratantra*, 20-22. Śāntigupta's commentary, the *Hevajrapiṇḍārthaprakāśa*, dates to the 12th century. Nakamura notes only that the *HT* is posterior to Amoghavajra (705-774 CE). Nakamura, *Indian Buddhism*, 335.

151 Willemen, *Chinese Hevajratantra*, 28. Also see Terry Abbott, "The Chinese Version of the Hevajra Tantra," *Transactions of the International Conference of Orientalists in Japan* 23 (1978): 99-103.

152 Willemen, *Chinese Hevajratantra*, 21-22.

153 Tsuda, *Saṁvarodaya-tantra*, vii. Also see idem, "Critical Tantrism," 174. Citing Tsuda, Nakamura writes that the *ST* was composed at the end of the 8th c. Nakamura, *Indian Buddhism*, 338. Kalff also discusses the question of dates for the Saṃvara texts. After careful consideration, he concludes that no precise date can be accepted presently, though he links the practices to the Kāpālika movement, and suggests a relative chronology may be derived from the study of its history. Kalff, "Abhidhānottara-Tantra," 115-118.

154 Nakamura, *Indian Buddhism*, 339. See also John Newman, "Eschatology in the Wheel of Time Tantra," in *Buddhism in Practice*, ed. Donald S. Lopez, Jr. (Princeton, 1995), 284-289.

155 Carelli, *Sekoddeśatikā*.

156 Tucci, *Tibetan Painted Scrolls*, 212; and, Stanley Wolpert, *A New History of India*, 2nd ed. (Oxford/New York, 1982), 106-108.

157 George, *Caṇḍamahāroṣaṇa Tantra*, 5.

158 R. A. Stein, "Nouveaux problèmes du tantrisme sino-japonais," 484.

159 Snellgrove, *Indo-Tibetan Buddhism*, 184.

175. *Heruka, Nalanda (Bihar), ca. 11th century, Nalanda Museum, same as* **9**

15
Heruka Imagery

Fearful am I to fear itself,/ with my necklace made of a string of heads, and dancing furiously on a solar disk. Black am I and terrible . . . /But my inner nature is tranquil, and holding Nairātmyā in loving embrace, I am possessed of tranquil bliss.
Hevajra Tantra

1 The Iconography of Heruka

Our study of Phase Three ideology revealed that Heruka is the name of the ultimate *tattva*, the sixth Buddha and the experience of absolute reality.[1] We saw that Hevajra and Saṃvara are different forms of this same absolute.[2] Heruka is a type, as affirmed by Snellgrove and van Kooij.[3] But at the same time that Heruka is the ultimate *krodha-vighnāntaka*, he is also an individual deity, who is represented in specific iconographic forms distinct from those of Saṃvara or Hevajra.[4] These special forms have long been associated with Heruka and can be identified in iconographic compendia such as the *Sādhanamālā* and *Niṣpannayogāvalī*. The *Abhidhānottara-sādhana Tantra* and the *Hevajra-sādhana Tantra* also give a number of descriptions of Heruka.[5]

Surviving examples suggest that the most common Heruka form is a two- or four-armed *vīra*-Yakṣa. Usually he holds a *khatvāṅga*-staff, a *vajra*, a skull cup or a *ḍamaru*-drum and stands in a distinctive dancing posture upon a corpse. The texts also list a number of features (skull-cups, ornaments of bone, animal skins, ash-smeared skin) which reinforce a connection with the yogins, among whom Heruka was especially revered. In a circular fashion, the yogins sought to imitate the attributes, attitudes and activities of Heruka, all of which was modeled largely on the idealized yogin.[6] Heruka's is an iconography applicable to both deity and human practitioner.

The *HT* provides descriptions of Heruka-Hevajra relevant to the mutually reflective relationship between Heruka and the yogin:

> *The yogin must wear the sacred ear-rings, and the circlet on his head; on his wrists the bracelets, and the girdle round his waist, rings around his ankles, bangles round his arms; he wears the bone-necklace and for his dress a tiger-skin, and his food must be the five ambrosias.*[7]

The yogin is to conform literally to these instructions, but the forms have symbolic meaning as well:

> *Akṣobhya is symbolized by the circlet, Amitābha by the ear-rings, Ratneśa by the necklace, and Vairocana (by the rings) upon the wrists. Amogha is symbolized by the girdle, Wisdom by the khatvāṅga and Means by the drum, while the yogin represents the Wrathful One himself. Song symbolizes mantra, dance symbolizes meditation, and so singing and dancing the yogin always acts.*[8]

Heruka is almost invariably portrayed with the *khatvāṅga*, an attribute again significant to yogins. Rolf Stein interprets holding it as symbolic possession, equivalent to the mastery of the triple world. In terms of inner yoga, this means raising the *bodhicitta* up the *avadhūtī*, the central channel in the spine.[9] The posture assumed by the deity is a "dance" posture, with the left knee slightly bent and the right foot placed on the inside of the left thigh. This joyful posture is a reminder that *mahāsukha* (great bliss) is Heruka's essence in all his forms, as well as being the product of the ecstatic rituals of yogins and *yoginī* at the *pīṭha*. Van Kooij concludes that "Heruka's iconography gives support to the observation . . . that Heruka is more or less a deified hypostasis of the . . . yogin himself."[10]

2 Eastern Indian Images of Heruka

Beginning in the eleventh century, Heruka images appear simultaneously in Bihar, Bengal and Orissa. Though they continue to appear in these same regions during the twelfth century, few Esoteric Buddhist images remain from the later centuries. For the most part these images were found in monastic contexts, but a few unprovenanced finds survive as well. Continuing our practice for *krodha-vighnāntaka* images of Phases One and Two, we will order our examination of the surviving images based on their geographical provenance.

176. *Heruka, Ratnagiri (Orissa), ca. 11th century, same as* **1**

2.1 Heruka Images of Orissa

Several Orissan sites yielded images of Heruka. A relative concentration of Heruka sculptures was recovered at Ratnagiri, which seems to have undergone periods of renewal even after nearby Lalitagiri and Udayagiri were in decline. Phase One imagery [**121, 124**] and Phase Three imagery were represented simultaneously in the eleventh and twelfth centuries at Ratnagiri. Heruka images at Ratnagiri can be divided into two types: free-standing sculpture and sculpture attached to funerary *stūpas*.

The freestanding Heruka at Ratnagiri

In the banyan grove about thirty meters south-east of Monastery One, archaeologists discovered a large (ht. 161 cm) free-standing stone image of Heruka.[11] [**176**] Mitra does not specify a date, Hock suggests the tenth or eleventh century, and Donaldson places it in the tenth century.[12] Based on the tall and flat nimbus-like hair and the regularized design and carving of the jewelry (necklaces and girdle loops), I would place the sculpture in the eleventh century.

Heruka's smiling countenance is belied by his fangs. The backdrop is incised with flame patterns which echo on a broader scale the wavy patterns of the hair.

The low crown carries skulls, and scarf ends tied above the ears billow upwards. In his raised right hand he holds a *vajra*. The left hand is broken off, but it may have held a skull-cup. The *khatvāṅga* has a *vajra* finial and waving pennons. Heruka holds the staff in the crook of his left elbow, allowing it to rest on the inside of his right ankle. The *vanamālā* is strung with neither skulls nor Tathāgata images but is simply a garland of heads. He stands in what we may call "dancing" *ardha-paryaṇkāsaṇa*, with only the toes of his left foot touching the lower chest of a stiff recumbent male figure. The iconographic characteristics conform well to the description of Jñānavisuddha-Heruka in the *Hevajra-sādhana Tantra*.[13]

Heruka is described in the *Sādhanamālā* and in several other sources as dancing on a corpse.[14] The Hevajra-Heruka of the *HT* stands on a corpse "who represents the threefold world."[15] It seems likely that the stiff-limbed figure beneath the lightly dancing Heruka is a corpse, though the male figure pillows his head with his right hand. One hardly expects a dead body to be making itself more comfortable, but the stiff extension of the legs and proper right arm convince us that, despite the one curious gesture, it is indeed a corpse. Corpses were integral elements of yogic ritual and used for a variety of purposes, including as a dais for the yogin:

> *Going this way and that in the dance, we give no thought to what is chaste or unchaste,/ Adorning our limbs with bone-ornaments, we place the corpse in position,/Union takes place at that meeting, for Dombī is not there rejected.// Dancing as Śrī Heruka with mindful application, undistracted . . .*[16]

Yet we have learned through the study of Phase Two *krodha-vighnāntaka* imagery and of Phase Three texts that to understand such passages literally is unproductive. Since most of the Heruka images we will examine include the corpse underfoot, it is necessary briefly to explore its form and possible meanings in more detail. The long hair of the recumbent figure is tied up like a yogin's or like Śiva. His hair and nakedness fit the stereotypical form of both the wandering yogin and of Śiva. Śiva, the ascetic Hindu deity, is often depicted as *ūrdha linga* (erect); the penis of the recumbent figure is notably limp. The portrayal of a flaccid Śiva may have been a visual means to signify his submission, reinforcing the symbolism of overcoming the threefold world.

Shiníchi Tsuda has made a somewhat analogous suggestion. It will be recalled that Tsuda argues that Phase Three ideology forsakes Buddhism in favor of a Shaivite outlook. He suggests that Buddhist yogins, discouraged by the unsuccessful methods propounded in the *STTS* and the *HT*, adopted the *śmaśāna*-cemetery cult of Hindu yogins:

> *The Buddhist immigrants to the cult of cemetery tried to take the place of these Śaivaite yogins leaving the basic structure of the cult, that is, the group of yoginīs (yoginī-cakra) untouched. Preserving almost all the elements of Bhairava, the god of śmaśāna, adding only trivial elements, they created a new demonic God Heruka, alias Hevajra, who stands trampling his own father Bhairava under foot assuming almost an identical form.*[17]

Tsuda interprets this corpse as Bhairava-Śiva. In the context of the present study it should be obvious that the Esoteric Buddhist *krodha-vighnāntaka* imagery of Phases One and Two provides considerable precedent for images of symbolic conquest and transformation. Well before the *HT* was written, deities were visually conquering their pre-Buddhist progenitors, notably Yamāntaka (destroyer of Yama), Bhūtaḍāmara (trampling Aparājitā), and Trailokyavijaya (trampling Maheśvara-Śiva). The tradition cannot be divorced from the evolution of *krodha-vighnāntaka*, of which Heruka is merely the latest development in a trend we have followed since the late sixth century. One wonders if the well-established metaphor of a wrathful deity trampling on the transformed self might not itself have helped to validate the new paradigm which continued to utilize it. It would appear that the type of appropriation and transformation Tsuda discusses may not be as radical as it seems to him. There is also no need to postulate, as he does, that practitioners lost their Buddhist identity by creating and meditating upon images which depict Heruka becoming Śiva in order to overcome him.

Considering the resemblance among all three of the characters (Heruka, Bhairava-Śiva and the yogin), it is equally possible to interpret the corpse as generally representative of the yogin. Hock observes of the Ratnagiri Heruka that "[the] corpse wears the hat generally worn in painted versions of *ācāryas*."[18] She does not cite a particular painting of an *ācārya* (adept) and no hat is apparent atop the corpse's long hair, but I believe Hock must be responding to the corpse's general resemblance to the yogin. If we accept the spirit of Hock's interpretation, the trampled figure is meant, not as a sectarian insult to Śiva or to Hindu yogins, but as a symbol once again of the transformation of the self. The poisons transmuted by inner blissful experience recreate the human aspirant who, as Heruka, leaves behind the old understanding of impurity to decay like a corpse.

It is interesting that this and several other Phase Three works are found in monasteries, where they must have been part of the meditation rituals of monks. They form a minority among a larger quantity of orthodox Mahāyāna images, Phase One bodhisattva cult imagery **[121, 124]** and a few Phase Two sculptures. It seems doubtful that the monks who desired to have Phase Three images openly practiced the rituals espoused in the texts, risking expulsion. Esoteric rituals in the monastery must have been carried out internally, in which case understanding the body beneath the deity's foot as a pre-enlightenment self-image would be particularly valid.

The Heruka images on funerary stūpa at Ratnagiri

It is not exactly clear how many examples of Heruka on a funerary *stūpa* there are at Ratnagiri. Mitra states there are only two *stūpa* with Heruka images, but elsewhere she describes three. Hock records two in her visits to Ratnagiri; Bénisti discusses only one; I photographed four there, and Donaldson also notes that there are at least four. It may be that when Mitra states, "there are two *stūpas* with the reliefs of the two-armed Heruka," she refers only to the funerary *stūpa* found near Stūpa I, while the three *stūpa* she numbers 49, 64 and 124 are those associated with the area near Monastery II.[19] That would make five such *stūpa* in all.

Three examples will suffice here to represent the group. The first **[177]** depicts Mitra's *stūpa* 124. I believe the second **[180]** belongs to *stūpa* number 49, but the *stūpa* number corresponding to the last sculpture of Heruka is unknown. **[178]** Heruka is portrayed almost identically on all three, waving the *vajra* in the raised proper right hand and holding a skull-cup in the left, while he clasps the *khatvāṅga* with the left elbow. In two cases **[177-178]** the *khatvāṅga* is held against the left thigh by the right ankle. Heruka's high flame-shaped hair, his grin and the garland of heads are prominent. The size and condition of the sculptures make it difficult to do more than to confirm that a figure of some kind lays underneath each dancing Heruka.

Such images are very difficult to date on the basis of style due to their small size, the roughness of the carving and their damaged condition. Debala Mitra, the

177. *Heruka, funerary stūpa, Ratnagiri (Orissa), ca. 11th century*

178. *Heruka, funerary stūpa, Ratnagiri (Orissa), ca. 11th century, detail of* **179**, *same as* **4**

179. *Funerary stūpa, Ratnagiri (Orissa), ca. 11th century*

180. *Heruka, funerary stūpa, Ratnagiri (Orissa), ca. 11th century, detail of* **181**

181. *Funerary stūpa, Ratnagiri (Orissa), ca. 11th century*

excavator, places all seven hundred funerary *stūpa* roughly between the ninth and thirteenth centuries CE.[20] We may place them in the eleventh century, if we allow for some overlap into the early twelfth.

Other Orissan Heruka images

A small (12.2 cm.) metalwork Heruka was found among the hoard of images at Achutrajpur.[21] It is now kept in the Orissa State Museum in Bhubaneswar (no. 296). It closely resembles others so far discussed in terms of attributes and posture. The skull-cup in the left hand is clearly visible, as are three skulls just beneath the *vajra* finial of the *khatvāṅga*. One minor variation is that the lower end of the diagonally held *khatvāṅga* passes on the outside of the lifted right leg. **[180]** Donaldson dates the metal Heruka to the late tenth or early eleventh century, while Mitra ascribes it the eleventh century.[22]

Another Heruka image, probably from the Chaudwar, in the same district as Ratnagiri (Cuttack), was formerly in the local collection of Lakshminarayana Sahu.[23] Descriptions correspond closely with the standard type recovered at Ratnagiri and Achutrajpur. Finally, N.K. Sahu mentions another Heruka image near Kanpur in Balasore District.[24]

At least seven Orissan Heruka sculptures have been identified from the late tenth (at the earliest) through the twelfth centuries. A relatively broad area of coastal and inner Orissa is represented. The format and the media are equally varied. There is a considerable range in size, and both stone and metalwork images survive. Phase Three ideology and practice penetrated Orissan monasteries on a sufficiently significant scale to produce small images for personal meditation (the Achutrajpur metalwork), *stūpa* for funereal commemoration **[177-178, 180]** and large images which were no doubt placed at the center of a shrine. **[176]**

In contrast to the varied provenance and format, the iconographic character of the images is remarkably consistent. By the eleventh century a standard type of Heruka image was accepted in Orissa, and it was shared throughout much of eastern India as a whole.

2.2. Heruka Images of Bihar

Few Heruka images are known to survive from Bihar. Some which were not archaeologically excavated may be from either Bihar or Bengal. The only Heruka image which can be securely placed in Bihar is one discovered in Nalanda. **[182-183]** Fortunately, this single example is a monumental piece, whose power is muted only by the damage it has sustained.

The Nalanda Heruka

The Nalanda Heruka sculpture is 1.75 meters in height. Originally the backdrop of the sculpture was cut out, a feature typical sculpture of the eleventh and twelfth centuries. **[108-109, 184]** It has been since filled in with cement. Heruka's legs are lost, but enough of his left thigh remains to show that the leg was bent and rested on the torso of the prostrate body at the base. The right leg was no doubt bent and lifted, like the Orissan Heruka images. **[176-178, 180]** The same pose is made by the

182. Heruka, Nalanda (Bihar), ca. 11th century, Nalanda Museum, same as **175**

six surviving female *yoginī* attendants placed on the backdrop. They too each trample on a figure.

The wavy hair of Heruka is gathered into a flame-shaped chignon, which forms the nimbus in the skull-ornamented crown for a small image of Akṣobhya Tathāgata. Long tendrils of hair curl over Heruka's shoulders, and regular curled locks escape from the crown on the forehead. Twisting ribbons fly up from the knot above the ears, which bear heavy jewelry from elongated lobes. Heruka has an enlarged pair of eyes and a third eye between the pair. His face is relatively placid, but his grin reveals fangs. His *vanamālā* consists of heads tied onto a rope by their long hair. Elaborate jewelry covers his limbs and torso, neck and head. Faint markings on his short *dhoti* suggest it was meant to depict an animal skin.

The proper right hand was held up above his head, and probably held a *vajra*. The left arm broke at the elbow, causing damage to the midriff. The missing hand probably held a skull-cup. Traces of the short *khatvāṅga* are also visible in the linear scar at the belt and in the crescent of broken stone at his left shoulder. The top of the *khatvāṅga* probably had flaring pennons on it and was short like those held by his *yoginī* attendants.

The figure on which Heruka stands is once again ambiguous. He is naked and stiff, but his eyes are open. **[183]** He rests his left hand, palm out and fingers extended, on his chest, as if making the *abhaya* (fear-not) gesture, or one of surrender. His hair is extremely long, like an ascetic's, and both a mustache and a beard are apparent. The third eye is scored, along with a wheel in his palm. His genitals are once again prominent, his penis lying flaccid over his scrotum. The same iconologic meaning suggested by the figure underneath the Ratnagiri freestanding Heruka **[176]** applies to this one as well.

Accompanied by his *yoginī* consorts, the main figure closely resembles a description of Hevajra-Heruka found in the *HT*, there called Trailokyākṣepa:[25]

> *Dark blue and like the sun in colour with reddened and extended eyes, his yellow hair twisted upwards, and adorned with the five symbolic adornments,/ the circlet, the ear-rings and necklace, the bracelets and belt. These five symbols are well known for the purificatory power of the Five Buddhas./ He has the form of a sixteen-year-old youth and is clad in a tiger-skin. His gaze is wrathful. In his left hand he holds a vajra-skull, and a khatvāṅga likewise in his left, while in his right is a vajra of dark hue . . . /This Lord plays in the cemetery surrounded by his eight yoginīs.*[26]

183. Two yoginī and trampled figure, detail of **182**

It is very likely then that originally Hevajra-Heruka was accompanied by eight *yoginī*, two more than now survive. His troupe is set out in detail in the third chapter of the *HT*. Each of the eight is described holding a different object with which she is identified. Unfortunately, of the six surviving on the sculpture, only the middle one on the left holds an object distinct enough to be identified with a measure of confidence. She holds a *vajra* and thus can be identified as Pukkasī.[27]

The high wavy chignon and the insistent swaying rhythm of body, jewelry and scarves mark this sculpture stylistically as relatively late. A date in the eleventh century, possibly late eleventh, seems most acceptable. Once again we must point out that at Nalanda monastery a Phase Three image was relatively rare. The Heruka sculpture would have been one aspect of a larger artistic and religous context made up of monks informed and images inspired by different schools of Buddhism,

184. Avalokiteśvara with Hayagrīva, Rohoi (Bihar), ca. early 12th century, same as **110**

Esoteric and otherwise. Some Phase One sculptures from the same period and region document the bodhisattva cult at Nalanda and at neighboring sites in Bihar. [**105, 107-109, 112, 184**] A survey of the distribution of surviving Phase Two *krodha-vighnāntaka* images reveals that the majority remain from a slightly earlier period, roughly the ninth and tenth centuries. [**148, 156, 160, 167**] Very few survive from the eleventh century. By contrast, surviving Phase Three images follow the opposite pattern, remaining largely from the eleventh and twelfth centuries. This suggests that at least some Phase Two *krodha-vighnāntaka* may have been supplanted by Phase Three representations within continuous lineages of monks. Phase One works continued to be produced alongside Phase Three imagery among related but possibly distinct groups of monks.[28]

The Heruka images of Sarnath

Sarnath is associated with Śākyamuni Buddha's first preaching. He walked there from Bodh Gaya in order to find his previous yogin colleagues and reveal his newly found enlightenment. The site became an important Buddhist center, and the Dhamekh and Dharmarajika *stūpa* were continually enlarged from foundations at least as early as Aśoka (ca. third century BCE). Smaller shrines and funerary *stūpa*s were built nearby, along with *vihāra* to house a thriving monastic community.[29]

Sarnath is not part of modern Bihar state, but it lays very close to the border with Bihar in eastern-most Uttar Pradesh. Within the sphere of ancient Magadha, it was linked to Bodh Gaya, Rajagriha, Nalanda and other sites along the main Buddhist pilgrimage routes. Sarnath also had political ties with eastern India. The area was briefly ruled by the Pāla kings in the early eleventh century, and the twelfth-century Queen Kumāradevī, who was the principal donor of Monastery One, was the granddaughter of the princely ruler of a region in Bengal, as well as being related to the Pāla monarchs.[30] This explains, I hope, why two of Sarnath's rare Phase Three images are discussed here under the heading of Bihar.

In discussing an eighth-century sculpture of Yamāntaka [**39, 41**], we had occasion to discuss Sarnath's stylistic influence on Nalanda. Sarnath maintained its own school of sculpture into the twelfth century, distinct from Bihar and Bengal, but continued to participate in broad trends of style and iconography. Later sculptures include a few images of Phase Two deities, notably a ca. tenth-century Vajrasattva (ASI Museum, Sarnath, no. 6637) and a Mārīcī fragment. Phase Three imagery is also represented at Sarnath by at least three ca. twelfth-century sculptures. One depicts Mahākāla or Kālajambhala, skull-cup in hand and accompanied by his consort, trampling a royal corpse.[31] More important for this study, however, are the two stone images of Heruka.

The first Sarnath Heruka [**185**] was excavated in 1906-07. It was found as an image placed on *stūpa* 40, northeast of the main shrine, and is now on display in the site museum.[32] The rough quality of the sculpture indicates it may be unfinished. A number of features are nonetheless identifiable, most obviously the *vanamālā*. Heruka dances on the usual stiff corpse-like figure, with his right leg lifted up so that he rests his weight on the ball of his left foot. A high chignon now broken off provided the backdrop for a Buddha image. Heruka's bulging eyes are open wide, and his grin bares fangs. The *khatvāṅga* passes diagonally outside the lifted leg, unlike most of the Orissan examples. [**176, 178**] Both hands are broken off, but from the remains it is evident that they made the standard gestures associated with this common form of Heruka: the right hand is lifted up and probably held a *vajra*,

185. Heruka, Sarnath (Uttar Pradesh), ca. 12th century, Sarnath Museum

while the left held a skull-cup against the midriff and cradled the *khatvāṅga* in the crook of the elbow.

Though severely damaged, a larger and more finished example from approximately the same period survives. [186] The head is completely broken off, and the hands and legs are partial. The figure underfoot is missing, though it too may have been originally present. The intricate carving which remains provides a number of details. The *vanamālā* is made up of cubic, bead-like heads. The lower end of the relatively short *khatvāṅga* bears a finial and passes to the outside of the right ankle. Pennons drape from the top of the staff. The flat backdrop is incised with flame patterns. At the base of the backdrop two donor figures are carved in low relief, one a male yogin with long hair and a beard, and the other a young female figure holding a lotus, either a *yoginī* or patron.

186. *Heruka, Sarnath (Uttar Pradesh), ca. 12th century, Sarnath Museum*

The headless Heruka was kept in the Sarnath site museum's storage shed in 1990. [186] According to museum and archaeological records, the sculpture was unearthed in 1907-08 in the second outer court of Monastery I.[33] The site of discovery helps to confirm its stylistic dating of the twelfth century. As mentioned above, Queen Kumāradevī is considered the patroness of Monastery I because of a long dedicatory inscription found near the gate. Queen Kumāradevī was the royal consort of a Gahadavala king whose inscriptions date from 1114 to 1154.[34] Without mentioning this sculpture, Hiram Woodward suggests the possibility that the entire monastery has an Esoteric Buddhist agenda. He acknowledges problems of interpretation, but sees the *vihāra* as a nine-membered *maṇḍala* of Vajra-tārā.[35] Without accepting or rejecting his reading, we can confidently date this Phase Three Heruka [186], to the early or middle twelfth century. This in turn helps to establish a similar date for a double image of Heruka and his consort now in the Newark Museum. [187] Details of jewelry and the distinctive inscribed flames on the backdrop suggest a related origin for this small sculpture.

187. *Heruka with consort, eastern India, ca. 12th century, The Newark Museum*

2.3 A Sculpture of Heruka from Bengal

188. *Heruka, Comilla, Subhapur (Bengal), ca. 11th century*

In the Dacca Museum, Bangladesh, a fine stone sculpture of Heruka is preserved. [188] Originally found in Subhapur of Comilla District, in what is now southeastern Bangladesh, it is nearly as large as the Nalanda Heruka [182-183], with which it shares an eleventh-century date.[36] The flame-shaped chignon on the Bengali sculpture [188] is even higher and more elaborately layered than its Nalanda counterpart. The scarves, girdle loops, tilt of the head and the garland of severed heads tied to the *vanamālā* by their hair are all comparable. In this case more of the *khatvāṅga* survives, including the long pennons attached to the head. A bell is tied to the *khatvāṅga*, just as a bell is tied to one of the girdle loops on the Nalanda sculpture. [182] Both hands are broken, but they are held in the standard positions. The one unique iconographic characteristic is the lack of the corpse-like figure underfoot. Heruka dances on a lotus pedestal instead of a human.

As Bhattacharyya points out, this image of Heruka closely corresponds to a description of Heruka found in the *Sādhanamālā*, which is itself a late work. In Bhattacharyya's account:

> *In another Sādhana for the worship of this particular kind of Heruka the Khatvāṅga is described as being marked with a Vajra of five thongs [sic] and decorated with a banner with jingling bells . . . His left leg rests on the double lotus (and not on the corpse) while the right in placed on the left thigh in a dancing attitude. The image discovered by Mr. N.K. Bhattasali and deposited in the Dacca Museum, agrees in all details with the description given above.*[37]

2.4 Unprovenanced Eastern Indian Heruka Images

Several images of Heruka appear in manuscripts, the provenance of which is undetermined. They are variously assigned to Bihar or to Bengal. Consensus has been reached that they derive from eastern India, so here they will be discussed together, along with three unprovenanced metalwork images.

Two Manuscript Heruka

Two painted twelfth-century Heruka images correspond iconographically to the same type we have seen in various eleventh-century examples from Orissa, Bihar and Bengal. One, in the Musée Guimet, features a lithe figure before a brilliant nimbus of flames. [COLOR PLATE 13] The second belongs to an illuminated manuscript of the *Prajñāpāramitā* text which Pal has described as "In some ways . . . the most sumptuously illuminated Buddhist manuscript to have survived from the Indian subcontinent."[38] Now in a private collection, Pal dates it to the early twelfth century and concludes that it was painted in West Bengal by an artist familiar with Bihar illuminations.

The Bombay Asiatic Society manuscript Heruka

An article published in the late eighties brought to light a manuscript from the Asiatic Society, Bombay, dated thirty-nine years after the Pāla king Govindapāla, who reigned during the second half of the twelfth century.[39] Gorakshkar and Desai reason that the manuscript must come from Bihar on the grounds of an iconographic argument: only Bihar produced images of adorned Buddha during this period, and one is depicted in the same manuscript. While this is probably too narrow and totalizing a view, a Bihar provenance is still not unlikely, as is a date of the late twelfth or early thirteenth century.

The Heruka figure is matched with an image of his consort Nairātmyā.[40] Both dance on yogins, and Heruka raises his right arm while his left cradles the staff and holds a skull-cup. The context provided by the other images in the manuscript is strongly Phase Three in flavor. We will return to this piece for its Saṃvara image, which is placed on the other side of an adorned Akṣobhya to form a grouping ingeniously identified by John Newman.[41] This image demonstrates that the standard two-armed form of Trailokyākṣepa, or Jñānavisuddha Heruka, which appeared in images of the late tenth or early eleventh century throughout eastern India, maintained its relevance into the thirteenth century.[42]

2.5 Special forms of Heruka in eastern India

The two-armed Heruka, holding a *vajra*, *kapāla* and *khatvāṅga*, was the standard in eastern India. By a significant majority, most surviving images represent this type. Phase Three texts, however, describe more than two dozen different forms.[43] Textual sources help to identify a few stray images of *krodha-vighnāntaka* which resemble Heruka but deviate in one or another way from the standard image. The most helpful identifying attributes are combinations of the special "dancing" *ardhaparyaṇkāsaṇa* posture and the *khatvāṅga* held in the left arm.

189. Heruka, gilt copper alloy, Bengal, ca. 11th century, Los Angeles County Museum of Art

The Los Angeles Heruka

In 1985 the Los Angeles County Museum of Art acquired a very fine, small (15.9 cm) gilt copper-alloy image of a *krodha-vighnāntaka* in dancing *ardhaparyaṇkāsaṇa.* [**189**] Pal suggests a date of the eleventh century and a provenance of Bengal, both supportable attributions. Despite the fact that "this image does not precisely agree with known iconographic descriptions" of Heruka, Pal rightly proposes that "very likely the figure represents Heruka or Hevajra."[44]

Several important features differentiate this image from the standard form. First of all, he has three heads instead of one, and though he still carries the *vajra*, it is not held aloft. Instead, with the *ghaṇṭa*-bell in the left hand, he crosses his wrists in front of his chest, holding the palms inward. This gesture is similar to, but distinct from, the one made by Trailokyavijaya, in which the same implements are sometimes held, but the wrists are turned out, the index fingers extended and the little fingers intertwined. (Compare **158, 160-164**.) The gesture Heruka makes, here referred to as *vajrahūṃkāra mudrā*, is most commonly made by deities embracing a consort. In this case the consort seems to be replaced by the *khatvāṅga*. Stein has explicated the complex symbolism of Heruka and determined that the *khatvāṅga* may symbolize *prajñā*, or wisdom, typically personified by the deity's consort.[45]

More than one of the textual descriptions of Heruka's forms account for features like the three heads and the bell and *vajra* held in the hands as he embraces the consort. However, texts prescribe more than two hands. For instance, the form known as Vikṛtānana:

> *is described as three-faced and six-armed. He bears the Vajra, the Ghaṇṭā [and four other attributes]. . . . The Khātvanga hangs from his left shoulder, and the hands that bear the Vajra and the Ghaṇṭā are, presumably, also engaged in clasping the Śakti [sic].*[46]

Another form is three-headed and four-armed, and carries the *vajra* and *ghaṇṭā* in the right and left hands respectively; the consort is again absent. [47] One major variation between this sculpture and the standard form of Heruka is that he is standing on a stack of four male "corpses" instead of one. This too is easily accommodated with Heruka's iconography as described in the *HT*. There we read that Hevajra-Heruka, in a sixteen-armed form, tramples the four Māra underfoot.[48] In another section of the *HT*, "the four-armed form [of Hevajra-Heruka] symbolizes the destruction of the four Māras." In explaining the characteristics of Nairātmyā, Hevajra-Heruka's consort who holds a knife, a skull and the *khatvāṅga*, the *HT* explains that from the skull, "one drinks the blood of the Four Māras."[49] What are the four Māras, so closely bound up with Heruka's iconography? Representative of the fourfold obstacles to enlightenment, they include Skandamāra (the obstacle of the aggregated constituent elements of existence), Kleśamāra (the obstacle of ego-istic entanglements), Mṛtyumāra (the obstacle of death) and Devaputramāra (the obstacle of rebirth in the form of gods).[50] According to a commentary of the *HT* translated by Snellgrove, the four Māras are personified as Brahmanical gods: Skandamāra is Brahma (god of creation), Kleśamāra is a Yakṣa, Mṛtyumāra is Yama (god of death) and Devaputramāra is Indra.[51] These four personified obstacles to enlightenment are surely intended by the four figures under Heruka's foot. [**189**] He dances ecstatically over their prostrate forms, celebrating his victory and that of the yogin, who "embraces" the *avadhūti* symbolized by the *khatvāṅga*, over the threefold world.

The Metropolitan Museum's Heruka

Twenty palm leaves of the *Aṣṭasāhasrikā Prajñāpāramitā* from eastern India were acquired in 1985 and 1986 by the Metropolitan Museum in New York.[52] The Museum considers the palm leaves to date from the twelfth century and to have possibly originated in Bihar.

Most of the illustrations are of *stūpa* and bodhisattva, but three are of *krodha-vighnāntaka*, and one of these seems to be a form of Heruka. [**190**] The dark-blue Heruka stands in the dancing *ardhaparyaṅkāsana*, embracing his four-armed lighter blue consort. Heruka is three- (or four-) headed and four-armed. He holds the *khatvāṅga* in the lower left hand, and raises the right in the gesture typical of the standard Heruka. Whatever attributes were held in the hand are not discernible, nor can his dais be made out. His *vanamālā* is quite clear, however, as is the flaming background.

190. *Heruka with consort, painting on palm leaf, Bihar (?), ca. 12th century, Metropolitan Museum of Art, New York*

This image of Heruka has much in common with a four-armed form of Hevajra-Heruka described in the *Sādhanamālā*. Bhattacharyya summarizes the latter as follows:

> *[Hevajra-Heruka] is four-armed and is embraced by his Śakti [sic] who is identical with him in all respects. Hevajra[-Heruka] carries in his four hands the blue Vajra, the sword, the Khatvanga and the jewel. The Khatvanga does not however hang from his shoulder but is carried in one of his hands.*[53]

The *khatvāṅga* is indeed held in one of the hands, but the other attributes are not clear. His consort, who should resemble him, also has four arms, and she mirrors his gestures and posture. The description does not specify how many heads Hevajra-Heruka is to have, though generally three heads are matched with six or more arms. Nevertheless, there seem to be sufficient similarities to justify our identification of the painted image as Hevajra-Heruka.

3 Pre-14th Century Heruka Images Outside of Eastern India

Phase Three Esoteric Buddhist imagery spread from eastern India to other parts of India, to Kashmir,[54] and also to Nepal and Tibet. It did not find a direct way from India to China or Japan. China did receive Phase Three texts in the tenth and eleventh centuries, but they had little influence beyond the walls of the translation bureau sponsored by the court. Eventually Phase Three imagery was brought to China through the Tibetans, but we cannot follow these later forms here. Instead we will mention briefly one example in each of three regions which at a relatively early period were introduced to Heruka imagery.

Amaravati, on the Krishna river in Andhra Pradesh, the province south of Orissa, is best known for its early (ca. second century CE) Buddhist art. That it "remained a flourishing Buddhist centre" from the third century BCE through the thirteenth century CE, however, "is attested to by a large number of inscriptions found at the site itself."[55] In the digging season of 1958-59 a few later stone images, described as "slabs" in relatively low relief, were discovered at Amaravati. Included were several late images of Maitreya, Tārā, a wrathful female and Heruka. The statue of Heruka is a rather crude piece but is relatively complete. The iconography corresponds to the standard image of eastern India **[177-187]** in most particulars: the right hand grasps the *vajra* and is raised above the head, the skull-cup is held at the chest in the left hand, the *khatvāṅga* is cradled by the left arm, and the deity poses in the dancing *ardhaparyaṇkāsaṇa*. The date of this piece is difficult to determine, but anytime between the eleventh and thirteenth centuries is possible. The standard Heruka form was spread in many directions, and the south, with its maritime links to Southeast Asia, may have contributed to the spread of Phase Three to Indonesia, where we turn for our next example.

In north central Sumatra, the brick temple of Bahal II at Padang Lawas was dedicated to Heruka. A large stone sculpture of Heruka was found in the central chamber. Although it was broken into pieces and the facial features obliterated, it is still identifiable as closely following the standard two-armed form. Inscriptions were found at the site from 1245 and 1372 CE, though construction of shrines at the site seems to have begun in the eleventh or twelfth century.[56] A date of the ca. thirteenth century seems suitable for the Heruka. There are certain features which reflect a cultural inclination toward a more dance-like posture, but overall, the Sumatran allegiance to eastern Indian Phase Three models can hardly be doubted. It helps confirm the temporal dominance of Phase Three imagery during the thirteenth century.

4 Heruka Imagery: Conclusions

Our examination of surviving images supports Heruka's exalted station in Phase Three Esoteric Buddhism. Five large-scale images including the Sumatran example were likely to have been the central images of shrines. **[176, 175, 186, 188]** In addition, smaller images in stone and metal were relatively plentiful. Painted images appear in significant numbers, and no doubt a more thorough search in manuscript collections will reveal many more. The variety of size and format suggests that Heruka images fulfilled the types of functions which earlier we found for Trailokyavijaya and his Phase Two peers. They provided the principal images to shrines and private altars and were integrated into three dimensional *maṇḍala*.

It should be acknowledged that we have ignored many images which belong within the orbit of Heruka iconography. Because it was our intention to be representative and not comprehensive, we have left out of the discussion works which seem to be variants of Heruka.[57] Nor have we followed Heruka into Nepal or Tibet. Finally, we have neglected the many independent images of Heruka's consorts from the same eleventh to twelfth century period. Besides occurring in some of the same manuscripts in which one finds Heruka images, sculptures of his consorts (and related female *krodha-vighnāntaka*) are found throughout eastern India. These include Nairātmyā sculptures in the West Bengal State Archaeological Museum (no. 04.8), the Indian Museum of Calcutta (no. 5608), Asutosh Museum (no. SC.406.5072) and Bodh Gaya Museum (no. 23); a Sarvabuddhaḍākinī in the Patna Museum (no. A10540), a Vajravārāhī in the Eilenberg collection, and a *yoginī* in the Musée Guimet (no. M.A.652). Outside of India, to mention just a few of the most extraordinary examples, a striking Nairātmyā painting in a Tibeto-Chinese style is dated by Chinese inscription to 1479 CE in the Boston Museum of Fine Arts; Sven Hedin found an ivory image of Nairātmyā in Khotan; and numerous *yoginī* are preserved in the National Museum and in private collections in Bangkok.[58]

The surviving visual evidence is significant collectively in ways other than quantity, size and quality. Notably, all Heruka images fall between the late tenth and the twelfth centuries. By contrast, Phase Two *krodha-vighnāntaka* imagery is concentrated in the ninth and tenth centuries, with a few later examples. This alone suggests that Phase Three imagery developed after the maturation of Phase Two. Additionally, we can see that Phase Three imagery eventually replaced that of Phase Two in the very sites where both were espoused, the monastic centers of eastern India. Our examinations of the imagery of Hevajra and Saṃvara will support this preliminary conclusion based on our examination of Heruka images.

Notes to Chapter Fifteen

1 Jean Przyluski believes that just as Bhairava derives from *bhīru* (dreadful, terrible), so too the name Heruka may have derived from *bhīru* and from *bhīruka* (timid), which became **bheruka* in middle Indian. Further, he holds that this is an instance in which an antonym was used as the appelation of a wrathful deity. Jean Przyluski, "Heruka-Śambara," *Polski Biuletyn Orientalistyczny* 1 (1937): 42-45.

2 Recently John Newman has made an interesting argument that forms of Hevajra and Saṃvara appear together in a 12th c. eastern Indian manuscript as part of a coherent program of iconography which represents both *utpatti krama* and *sampanna krama* modes of Phase Three practice. John Newman, "Vajrayāna Deities in an Illustrated Indian Manuscript of the *Aṣṭasāhasrikā-prajñāpāramitā*," *Journal of the International Association of Buddhist Studies* 13, no. 2 (1990): 117-132.

3 Snellgrove, *Buddhist Himalaya*, 205; van Kooij, "Some Iconographical Data," 161-170. Also see de Mallmann, *Introduction a l'iconographie*, 182-186.

4 Lokesh Chandra recognizes this distinction in his preface to Tucci, *Tsaparang*, xv-xvi. Van Kooij also acknowledges the typological and individual aspects of Heruka in "Some Iconographical Data," 162.

5 See B. Bhattacharyya, *Indian Buddhist Iconography*, 155-156; idem, *Niṣpannayogāvali*, 40-41; idem, "Iconography of Heruka," *Indian Culture* 2 (1935): 23-35; and, K. Krishna Murthy, *Iconography of Buddhist Deity Heruka* (Delhi, 1988).

6 The Heruka *maṇḍala*, "far from being schematic groupings of divinities . . . appear to be forms of real flesh and blood. The central figure of the circle is the yogin himself, whose intention must be to partake of the nature of Heruka." Snellgrove, *Buddhist Himalaya*, 206.

7 Snellgrove, *Hevajra Tantra*, 63, 1:I.vi.2-6; Willemen, *Chinese Hevajratantra*, 55.

8 Snellgrove, *Hevajra Tantra*, 64, 1:I.vi.11-13; Willemen, *Chinese Hevajratantra*, 56-57. According to the *Abhidhānottara-Tantra*, the *khatvāṅga* is the *devatāmūrtiḥ* (which Kalff translates as "embodiment of the godhead"), while the sound of the *ḍamaru* is *prajñā* ("insight"). Kalff, "Abhidhānottara-Tantra,"215 (Sanskrit version, 327).

9 See R. A. Stein, "Les objets rituels de transmutation dans le tantrisme tibétain," *Annuaire du Collège de France* 77 (1977): 488-495.

10 Van Kooij, "Some Iconographical Data," 163.

11 D. Mitra, *Ratnagiri*, 438, 443, pl. CCCXXXVI.B.

12 Hock, "Buddhist ideology," 156; Donaldson, "Buddhist Sculpture of Orissa," 369. Compare the hair with **116** and **118**.

13 Benoytosh Bhattacharyya, "Iconography of Heruka," *Indian Culture* 2 (1935): 24.

14 B. Bhattacharyya, *Indian Buddhist Iconography*, 156.

15 Snellgrove, *Hevajra Tantra*, 1:59.

16 Ibid., 1:101-102. Also see 1:57, 73, 114, 115.

17 Tsuda, "Critical Tantrism," 173.

18 Hock, "Buddhist ideology," 156.

19 Ibid., 152, n. 64. Hock lists *stūpa* 49, 124 and 65 on 156 (the last is a mistake for 64, correctly listed on 152). See Mireille Bénisti, *Contribution l'Étude du Stupa Bouddhique Indien: Les Stupa Mineurs de Bodh-Gaya et de Ratnagiri*, Publications de L'École Française d'Extrême-Orient, no. 125 (Paris, 1981), 115-117, fig. 138, which corresponds to Mitra's no. 64, but offers no possible date.) Also see Donaldson, "Buddhist Sculpture of Orissa," 369; D. Mitra, *Ratnagiri*, 126, 318, 325, 338. On these *stūpa*, which are properly "funerary" and not "votive," see Gregory Schopen, *Bones, Stones, and Buddhist Monks: Collected Papers on the Archaeology, Epigraphy, and Texts of Monastic Buddhism in India* (Honolulu: University of Hawai'i, 1997), 120.

20 D. Mitra, *Ratnagiri*, 28.

21 D. Mitra, *Achutrajpur*, 85-86, fig. 77.

22 Donaldson, "Buddhist Sculpture of Orissa," 370; D. Mitra, *Achutrajpur*, 85.

23 See Sahu, *Buddhism in Orissa*, 208; R.P. Mohapatra, *Archaeology in Orissa (Sites and Monuments)*, 2 vols. (Delhi, 1986), 2:21; and, Donaldson, "Buddhist Sculpture of Orissa," 370. Donaldson identifies this image with one now in the Sambalpur University Museum.

24 Sahu, *Buddhism in Orissa*, 221.

25 Snellgrove, *Hevajra Tantra*, 51, 1:I.ii.7.

26 Ibid., 59, 1:I.iii.13-16; Willemen, *Chinese Hevajratantra*, 49.

27 Snellgrove, *Hevajra Tantra*, 58, 1:I.iii.10. Also see Kāṇha's commentary on "Bhūcarī." Ibid., 55, note 1 (no. vii); Willemen, *Chinese Hevajratantra*, 48. The other *yoginī* and their attributes are Gaurī (moon), Chaurī (sun), Vetālī (water), Ghasmarī (medicament), Śavarī (*amrit*) and Caṇḍālī (*ḍamaru*-drum).

28 The exception may be Mahākāla, who seems to have had a different history than Hayagrīva, Yamāntaka and Trailokyavijaya.

29 See V.S. Agarwala, *A Guide to Sārnāth*, 3rd ed. (New Delhi, 1980); Krishna Kumar, "A Circular Caitya-Gṛha at Sārnāth," *Journal of the Indian Society of Oriental Art* ns 11 (1980): 63-70; J.H. Marshall and Sten Konow, "Sārnāth," *ASI Annual Report 1906 -7* (Calcutta, 1909): 81-85; idem, "Excavations at Sarnath, 1908," *Archaeological Survey of India, Annual Report 1907-8* (Calcutta, 1911): 43-54; and, D. Mitra, *Buddhist Monuments*, 66-69.

30 Hiram W. Woodward, Jr., "Queen Kumāradevī and Twelfth-Century Sārnāth," *Journal of the Indian Society of Oriental Art* ns 12/13 (1981-83): 9-10.

31 Sarnath ASI Museum, no. B(e)i (ht. 60 cm). See Daya Ram Sahni, *Catalogue of the Museum of Archaeology at Sārnāth* (Calcutta, 1914), 135-136, pl. XV.a; also illustrated in Agarwala, *Sārnāth*, pl. X.B.

32 "An unfinished figure of Śiva dancing on a demon lying full length on the base." No. 19(B[H]4), ht. 39 cm. Sahni, *Museum of Archaeology at Sārnāth*, 166.

33 I am grateful to the Assistant Superintendent D.P. Sinha and the Librarian/Keeper Brij Raj Singh, who arranged for me to examine this piece. The museum records identify it as "Śiva Nataraj," which can be disregarded. "A figure of Śiva engaged in a wild dance." Sahni, *Museum of Archaeology at Sārnāth*, 165.

34 Woodward, "Queen Kumāradevī," 9.

35 Ibid., 8-24.

36 Ahmad Hasan Dani, *Buddhist Sculpture in East Pakistan* (Karachi, 1959), no. 34. S. Huntington dates the piece to the early 11th c. in "*Pāla-Sena*," 172-173, fig. 215; and in idem, *Art of Ancient India*, 398-399, fig. 18.13.

37 B. Bhattacharyya, *Indian Buddhist Iconography*, 156. The earliest extant manuscript of the *Sādhanamālā* is dated to 1165 CE.

38 The first [COLOR PLATE 13] is part of the Lionel Fournier collection donated to the Musée Guimet, Paris, published in Gilles Béguin, *Art ésotérique de l'Himālaya: Catalogue de la donation Lionel Fournier* (Paris, 1990), no. 1 (captioned "Inde du Nord-Est, vers 1114"). The second is published in Pradapaditya Pal and Julia Meech-Pekarik, *Buddhist Book Illuminations* (New York, 1988), 92.

39 Sadashiv Gorakshkar and Kalpana Desai, "An Illustrated Manuscript of *Aṣṭasāhasrikā Prajñāpāramitā* in the Asiatic Society of Bombay," in *Orientalia Iosephi Tucci Memoriae Dicata Serie Orientale Roma* no. 56 (Rome, 1987) 2: 561-568; and, Newman, "Vajrayāna Deities," 117-132.

40 Here I accept Newman's corrections of Gorakshkar and Desai's earlier identifications of the two images as Nairātmya (male) and Nairātmyā (female). Newman specifies "Trailokyākṣepa-Heruka/Hevajra." Newman, "Vajrayāna Deities," 118-119.

41 Ibid., 122-124.

42 One other Heruka miniature of this type illuminating *Prajñāpāramitā* is in the British Library, London, mss. Or.14282, 229r (right), published in Losty, "Bengal, Bihar, Nepal?," part one, fig. 9, lower. Losty suggests a date of ca. 1130, and the provenance as Vikramaśila monastery, between modern Bengal and Bihar, but with a predominance of Bengali stylistic traits. No doubt many other examples also exist. Other unprovenanced metalwork Heruka images include a small image in an Amsterdam collection illustrated in Von Schroeder, *Indo-Tibetan Bronzes*, no. 70H; two images from the Heeramaneck collection sold at Sotheby's in 1985 and illustrated in Sotheby's, New York, *Indian,*

Himalayan, South-East Asian Art and Indian Miniatures (New York, 1985), no. 138, no. 76 (color photo).

43 See B. Bhattacharyya, "Iconography of Heruka," 23-35; idem, *Indian Buddhist Iconography*, 155-156; Murthy, *Buddhist Deity Heruka*; and, Newman, "Vajrayāna Deities," 121-122.

44 Pal, *Indian Sculpture*, 197-198, no. 96.

45 R. Stein, "Les objets rituels de transmutation," 488-495.

46 B. Bhattacharyya, "Iconography of Heruka," 27.

47 Ibid., 25 (Satpāramitāvisuddha).

48 Snellgrove, *Hevajra Tantra*, 80, 1:I.ix.15; 110, II.v.8; Willemen, *Chinese Hevajratantra*, 71, 103.

49 Ibid., 59, 1:I.iii.17; 1:75; ibid., 49, 65.

50 "Kleśamāra misleads sentient beings and creates obstacles to the aspirants by making them confused through countless subtle and coarse emotional upsets due to the wrong belief in that which is not a self as being a self. Skandhamāra blocks the way which does not arouse emotive responses and immerses beings in the misery of the three realms in Saṁsāra . . . by letting them believe in the five psychophysical constitutents as a self and become involved in Samsāra through the affect-arousing organization of these constitutents. Mṛtyumāra deprives beings of their life and at improper times and through death interrupts development, studying, thinking about that which one studies, and contemplating it as it bears on one's life not being allowed to come to its end. Devaputramāra comprises Cupid and others." Yangdzogpay, quoted in Herbert V. Guenther, *Treasures on the Tibetan Middle Way* (Berkeley, 1976), 23-24, note 2.

51 Snellgrove, *Hevajra Tantra*, 80, note 2.

52 Metropolitan Museum acquisition no. 1985.400.1-14; and 1986.25.1-6. I would like to thank Martin Lerner and Steven M. Kossak for allowing me to examine and photograph these leaves in storage.

53 B. Bhattacharyya, *Indian Buddhist Iconography*, 158.

54 Naudou points out that Kashmiri Buddhists, including Somanātha (Candranātha), came to eastern India in the 11th c. to seek teachers for the Kālacakra system. Naudou, *Bouddhistes Kasmiriens*, 161-162.

55 D. Mitra, *Buddhist Monuments*, 200. See also H. Sarkar and S.P. Nainar, *Amaravati* (New Delhi, 1980), 17-18; ASI, *Indian Archaeology*, 5, pl. I.b; and a nearly illegible illustration without attribution in Murthy, *Buddhist Deity Heruka*, pl. II.

56 See F.D.K. Bosch, "Verslag van een reis door Sumatra," *Oudheidkundig Verslag* (1930): 133-157, pl. 41a,b; Bernet Kempers, *Ancient Indonesian Art*, 75-77, pls. 223-228; R. Soekmono, "Indonesian Architecture of the Classical Period: A Brief Survey," in *The Sculpture of Indonesia*, ed. and trans. Jan Fontein (New York, 1990), 86-87.

57 For example, the figure in the Zimmerman collection usually identified as Vajrapāṇi, despite the dancing pose on a prostrate corpse and the *vajra* in the raised right hand. It does not have skull cup or, at present, a *khatvāṅga*. See Pratapaditya Pal, *Art of the Himalayas: Treasures from Nepal and Tibet* (New York, 1991), no. 9.

58 Pratapaditya Pal, *The Art of Tibet* (New York, 1969), no. 10. Gösta Montell, "Sven Hedin's Archaeological Collections from Khotan," *The Museum of Far Eastern Antiquities* 10 (1938): 98-99, pl. III.6. Montell rightly suggested that the figure "brings to mind a Lamaistic *maṇḍala*. The central figure might be interpreted as a *ḍākinī*, e.g. Siṁhavaktra." Ibid., 99. It is Nairātmyā, however, not Siṁhavaktra. See J. J. Boeles, "Two Yoginis of Hevajra from Thailand," in *Essays offered to G. H. Luce Vol. 2*, ed. Ba Shin et al (Ascona, 1966).

191. *Hevajra, eastern India (Bengal?), leaf from a manuscript of Aṣṭasāhasrikā Prajñāpāramitā, ca. 1150-1200, Virginia Museum of Fine Arts*

16

Hevajra Imagery

1 The Iconography of Hevajra

The images of Heruka we have just examined could equally well be considered images of Hevajra. Indeed, the *HT* was used in the case of several examples in order to make sense of certain iconographic elements. Hevajra is a form of Heruka, and, at an ultimate level, the two cannot be distinguished. Just as there was throughout the Phase Three Esoteric Buddhist world a standard form with which Heruka was associated, however, certain characteristics came to denote the figure of Hevajra. Some latitude was permitted within these sets of attributes. Regional variations were restricted to posture, which could be either the dancing *ardhaparyaṇkāsaṇa*, *ālīḍha* or *pratyālīḍha*, and the presence or absence of a consort. Otherwise, Hevajra was uniformly depicted with four legs, eight heads and sixteen *kapāla*-bearing arms.

Four forms of Hevajra-Heruka are described in the *HT*. The first is the two-armed form adopted by Eastern India as its standard. **[177-189]** A four-armed **[190]** and a six-armed form, both with three faces, were also produced. By far the most references and the longest descriptions of the *HT* concern the sixteen-armed deity, and the majority of Hevajra images conform to this type.[1]

Before examining the images themselves, the comments of the *HT* on the meaning of this favored and most elaborate form provide a valuable perspective. There we learn:

> *The purificatory significance of the sixteen arms [of Hevajra] is the sixteen kinds of voidness. The four legs signify the crushing of the four Māras,/ The faces the eight releases,/ The eyes the three adamantine ones . . . .*
>
> *[Hevajra's] eyes are red from compassion; his body is black to indicate his sentiments of friendliness; his four legs symbolize the four means of conversion,/ his eight faces the eight releases and his sixteen arms the sixteen voids . . . .*
>
> *[The] Adamantine One, the mighty King and Lord Hevajra . . . discourses on the maṇḍala./ He reposes there in bliss as the essence of all forms, for he is Lord of the maṇḍala. . . . /He*

has sixteen arms and eight faces and four legs, and is terrible in appearance with his garland of skulls and he wears the five symbolic adornments. Nairātmyā, clinging round the neck of this hero and god, addresses him. . . . [He replies:]/ There at [the maṇḍala's] centre am I, O Fair One, together with you. . . . / I have eight faces, four legs, and sixteen arms, and trample the four Māras under foot. Fearful am I to fear itself,/ with my necklace made of a string of heads, and dancing furiously on a solar disk. Black am I and terrible with a crossed vajra *on my head,/ my body smeared with ashes, and my mouths sending forth the sound HŪṂ. But my inner nature is tranquil, and holding Nairātmyā in loving embrace, I am possessed of tranquil bliss.*

The contents of the skull-cups he holds in his hands are also specified:

The skulls in his right hands contain these things in this order: an elephant, a horse, an ass, an ox, a camel, a man, a lion, and a cat./ Those in the left are: Earth, Water, Air, Fire, Moon, Sun, Yama, and Vaiśravana.[2]

Hevajra's selection of objects symbolize his universal mastery over all matter and beings, alive and dead, on earth, in the underworld, on the planets and in the heavens.

2 Eastern Indian Images of Hevajra

Orissa may not have produced images of Hevajra; apparently none survive. There are several unprovenanced images which may either be from Bihar or Bengal. We start with two archaeologically excavated objects from Bengal.

2.1 The Paharpur stone Hevajra

In Paharpur, in the Rajshahi district of what is now Bangladesh, a Buddhist monastery was excavated in the 1920s and 1930s. The monastery has been identified as Somapura, built in the late eighth or early ninth century and continuing to be an important Buddhist center through at least the twelfth century. In the 1927-28 digging season, during excavation of a tank close to the north gate area, a fragmentary grey stone Hevajra embracing his consort was found. [**192**] Digging during 1931-32 on the north side of the steps to the main temple produced a fragment with seven of the proper left hands missing from the previously unearthed sculpture. Now reassembled and displayed in the Indian Museum, Calcutta, it is datable to the twelfth century.[3]

Hevajra has leering grins on all eight faces of the small stone fragment. A *viśvavajra* surmounts the wide flame-shaped chignon on the main head. Each of the eight faces has a third eye in the middle of the forehead below the crown. Hevajra stands in the *ardhaparyaṅkāsaṇa* posture, but damage makes it hard to confirm that he has four legs. A *vanamālā* of heads is visible. The sixteen arms supported a flame-bordered pierced nimbus around the two figures. The sixteen skull cups are empty, probably because the small size of the sculpture (approx. 7.5 cm) prohibits the miniscule detail that would be required for them to contain the objects prescribed in the *HT*.

192. *Hevajra, Paharpur (Bengal), ca. 12th century, Indian Museum, Calcutta*

Nairātmyā wraps her left leg around Hevajra's right leg. She curls both arms around Hevajra's formidable neck, and from the rear she can be seen clenching a broad knife or chopper in her right hand and a skull-cup in her left. Her girdle has slipped from her hips. Were it not for the objects missing from the skull-cups and the doubts about whether he had two or four legs, this object would precisely corresponds to the sixteen-armed form of Hevajra dictated by the *HT*.

193. *Hevajra and Consort, eastern India, 12th century, The Newark Museum*

194. *(below right) Hevajra, Dharmanagar, Tripura (Bengal), metalwork, ca. 12th century*

2.2 Two Hevajra from Bengal

The same year the stone Hevajra was found in Paharpur, a gilt bronze Hevajra was found in the Dharmanagar subdivision of Tripura state. [**194**] This region is on modern Bangladesh's eastern border. The restless, baroque surface of the metalwork figure, base and nimbus reveals its affiliation with twelfth-century sculpture of Bengal.[4] Hevajra stands in *pratyālīḍha*, though the second right leg is lifted up as if in *ardhaparyaṇkāsaṇa*. He has eight heads and sixteen arms, each holding a skull cup. Hevajra is accompanied by eight *yoginī* but not his consort. Of the eight, seven are arranged on the backdrop and one is attached to the base. Each stands in a "dancing" pose. The sculpture encapsulates the *maṇḍala* described in the *HT* consisting of Hevajra and his troupe of *yoginī*.

Somewhat akin to the florid late Bengal style is a fragmentary sculpture of Hevajra with Nairātmyā in the Newark Museum. [**193**] There are remnants of the full set of arms on both sides, and the two main arms clasp his consort and hold skull cups. His head bears the high flame-shaped chignon characteristic of late eastern Indian *krodha-vighnāntaka*.

2.3 A painted Hevajra

Sculptors and painters followed an identical iconographic tradition as far as Hevajra is concerned. A twelfth-century illuminated manuscript from eastern India [**191**] features a representation of Hevajra very similar to the one from Tripura. [**194**] The legs are in the same positions, and the two central arms make the gesture of embrace despite the absence of the consort. The artist has painted in the objects specified by the text for the skull-cups. Despite their diminutive size, one can identify a number of them, including the sun and moon, elephant, ass and ox. The "four Māras" are also present, in absolute surrender before the gigantic Hevajra.

The painting [**191**] is part of an illuminationed manuscript in the Virginia Museum of Fine Arts, and apparently it belongs to the *Prajñāpāramitā* cycle of texts. The Huntingtons assert that the leaves in the Asia Society, New York are part of the same group. They argue strongly for a date of the twelfth century but prefer Bengal rather than Bihar as the provenance.[5]

Most of the themes in this manuscript belong ideologically to Phase Three. In addition to Hevajra and Vajravarahi, the Tathāgata are featured in their adorned multi-armed forms. The exception is an Asia Society leaf depicting Bhūtaḍāmara, a Phase Two *krodha-vighnāntaka* who provides another example of the occasional extension of a Phase Two *krodha-vighnāntaka* into a Phase Three context. In rare instances Phase Two deities appear in Phase Three contexts, but the reverse never occurs, demonstrating again that Phase Three began later in time, overlapped and then largely supplanted Phase Two *krodha-vighnāntaka*.

2.4 Other eastern Indian Hevajra

The Philadelphia Museum owns an image of Hevajra embracing his consort, solid cast in brass with silver alloy inlay.[6] The arrangement of heads closely resemble the stone Hevajra from Paharpur. [**192**] Also similar are the *viśvavajra* crest at the top of the flame-shaped hair, the way the girdle falls off the hips of the consort and the disposition of the hands. The requisite animals, gods, planets and humans are depicted in the skull-cups. The four Māras are aligned in a cruciform beneath Hevajra, and at least three of his four legs are visible frontally. Considering the similarities with the Paharpur Hevajra, perhaps a Bengal provenance should be entertained, along with the twelfth-century date von Schroeder proposes.

An extraordinary three-dimensional Hevajra *maṇḍala* from eastern India serves as a final example. A metalwork lotus opens to reveal Hevajra, who embraces his consort at the center of the pericarp, and eight *yoginī*, who are attached to the inside of the petals.[7] The Hevajra image once again follows the standard form: four legs, sixteen arms holding skull cups, eight heads. On the outside of each lotus petal are scenes which Pal has identified as the eight cemeteries, a prominent motif of Phase Three Esoteric Buddhism.

Pal suggests the piece is once again from Bengal, though his eleventh century date may be slightly early. It is remarkable that, unlike Heruka and Saṃvara images, which are widely spread over eastern India, most (if not all) surviving eastern Indian Hevajra images are associated with Bengal. They are also concentrated in the twelfth century. One can speculate on the reasons for Hevajra's geographical isolation. Perhaps the disciples of the Mahāsiddhas who taught the Hevajra practices were especially prevalent in Bengal. It is also possible that the archaeological record is misleading.

195. Hevajra, Tibet, metalwork, ca. 14th century, Doris Wiener Gallery

3 Early Hevajra Images Outside Eastern India

Although a cursory survey of Nepalese art turns up images of Hevajra, most of them were made after the twelfth century. Some of these closely follow the eastern Indian prototype, though there are variations.[8] Most early Tibetan images of Hevajra are closely related to the eastern Indian standard found at Paharpur [192] and Tripura [194], as well as to the eastern Indian painted example. [191] Hevajra's iconography was the focus of considerable study and comment by Tibetan scholastics, and examples of images are relatively plentiful from the fifteenth century until the present.[9] Here we will cite only a few representative examples.

A ca. thirteenth or fourteenth-century metal Hevajra embracing his consort is probably one of the earliest extant Tibetan metal images of Hevajra.[10] [195] The ca. twelfth-century Hevajra in the Philadelphia Museum of Art referred to above provides a fairly close iconographic prototype. Minor differences are visible, and the Tibetan piece is less accomplished, but it seems clear that the Tibetan artists were faithful to the same eastern Indian model. The Huntingtons are no doubt correct in assigning this piece to "gTsang," or central Tibet.

196. Hevajra with consort, Chuchikjyal Temple, Karsha (Zangskar), wall painting, ca. 14th century

197. Hevajra with consort, Saspol cave (Ladakh), wall painting, ca. 14th century same as 174

Western Tibetan painting between the thirteenth and fourteenth centuries also features Hevjara, as at Karsha and Saspol. At Karsha, in Zangskar, western Tibet, a gorge separates the current monastery buildings from the oldest buildings at the site, which are no longer used. Newer buildings inhabited by nuns have been built around them. Snellgrove and Skorupski mention that one of the old temple buildings houses an important inscription and belongs to the "earlier Ka-dam-pa period," that is, the twelfth or thirteenth century.[11] In the same temple dedicated to Avalokiteśvara, known locally as the Chuchikjyal Temple, there is a wall-painting of Hevajra. **[196]** Embracing his consort, Hevajra is surrounded by his troupe of *yoginī*, other forms of himself, *krodha-vighnāntaka* colleagues, Mahāsiddhas and Indian and Tibetan monks, presumably of the Kadampa lineage. The mural features Heruka between a Saṃvara *maṇḍala* on Hevajra's right and a Vajrabhairava *maṇḍala* on his left.

Another painting of Hevajra in a similar though perhaps slightly later style is found inside a cave above the village of Saspol on the north bank of the Indus River. **[197]** The schematized modeling of the variegated lotus leaves on the dais, the shapes of the backdrop and nimbi, and the simplified treatment of volumes in these two paintings recall painting of the "post-Pāla" style.[12] The Karsha painting is not as sophisticated as the best of the Khara Khoto painting,[13] but neither is it as simplified or naive as the Hevajra painting in the Lhakhang Soma at Alchi. Pal argues that the Lhakhang Soma paintings are contemporary with the Khara Khoto paintings, dating no later than the thirteenth century.[14] Fournier also considers that the paintings of the Lhakhang Soma should be placed around the mid-thirteenth century. [15] Perhaps one can regard the Karsha Hevajra as fourteenth century. After that time there are a large number of Tibetan Hevajra images in painting and metal which maintain the standard eastern Indian model.[16] Probably the most important benchmark for the Tibet's integrated absorption of eastern Indian Esoteric Buddhism is the fifteenth-century Great Stūpa at Gyantse. Predictably, Hevajra is featured there in the highest and most important realms of the *yidam*. [COLOR PLATE 14]

A few early images of Hevajra appear in China during the Yuan Dynasty. Though they must be attributed to the presence of Tibetans within the Mongol empire, these images are also absolutely faithful to the standard found in eleventh or twelfth-century eastern India. One example is an image of Hevajra in Cave 465 at Dunhuang, datable to the late thirteenth or early fourteenth century.[17] Another is a silk tapestry weaving probably produced in the court-administered Palace workshop in Beijing.[18] Thus we have an example of Hevajra from the distant western province of Gansu and one from the capital. Other later Chinese examples of Hevajra exist, but like the two early ones, they were all made under direct or indirect Tibetan influence. They further underscore how powerful the *krodha-vighnāntaka* were in the Phase Three system that engaged the Tibetans.

Continental Southeast Asia is also an important source of Hevajra imagery. Examples from this area corroborate our dating of the spread of the Phase Three style, since none precede the second half of the eleventh century. Thai and Khmer images of Hevajra all follow more or less closely the same eastern Indian prototype. A fine example is a ca. twelfth or thirteenth-century Hevajra in the National Museum of Bangkok.[19] Hevajra usually appears in Southeast Asia in the form Tibetans call "solitary hero," that is, without clasping Nairātmyā. She and the other *yoginī* are frequently depicted independently, also in dancing *ardhaparyaṇkāsaṇa*, with one arm raised and the other at the chest.[20] At least one complete and one partial metalwork *maṇḍala* with Hevajra surrounded by his troupe of eight *yoginī* are known to exist.[21] A large number of other stone and metal images of Hevajra from Thailand and Cambodia survive; one estimate suggests more than forty remain from Cambodia alone.[22] Casts of metal or stone molds depict Hevajra in *maṇḍala* or other groupings.[23]

Larger stone sculptures have also been found at some of the Buddhist sites of ancient Thailand and Cambodia and can be associated with royal cults. At the early twelfth-century site of Phimai, both Hevajra and his attendant *yoginī* are well represented on reliefs, and a number of Hevajra and *yoginī* metalworks have been recovered from the environs.[24] Hiram Woodward has argued that a large stone bust found at Angkor Thom and acquired by the Metropolitan Museum of Art, New York is Hevajra. He believes Hevajra was a deity favored at the site and in Jayavarman VII's pantheon.[25] The bust would have had a commemorative function within the royal funerary cult. Hevajra images are found in a variety of sizes, formats and media, suggesting a widespread penetration of Phase Three practice and imagery into Southeast Asian culture, at least as far as the royal cult could utilize it.

4 Hevajra: Final Considerations

We have seen that Bengal was an important area for Hevajra teachings in the twelfth century. Though the teachings sprang from mixed yogic and monastic roots in eastern India, Hevajra imagery survived mostly in monastic contexts. Presumably solitary wandering yogins also produced images, but they would have had the resources to produce only or mostly perishable ones. The mature Phase Three Hevajra travelled from eastern India to Nepal and to Tibet. From Tibet it spread to Mongolia and northern China. In each of those places Hevajra imagery was an important aspect of Esoteric Buddhist teachings, but there is little to suggest a popular cultic phenomenon, in the manner of Avalokiteśvara or Maitreya. In China there seems to have been minimal appreciation of Phase Three philosophy and practice outside of courts that had direct contacts with Tibetan and Mongolian Buddhists.

If there was a Hevajra cult, it seems to have thrived in Southeast Asia. Hevajra imagery may have come overland to Thailand from eastern India, directly from Bengal via Burma. The transmission of Hevajra teachings was probably reinforced through contacts along the maritime routes from island Southeast Asia and eastern India. Whatever the exact route, it clearly had considerable influence in the highest levels of society. Seemingly removed from his yogic and monastic origins, Hevajra was utilized in the royal cult, not, as with the Ming court, to improve relations with Tibet, but as part of an attempt at local political legitimization. "The cult of the God-King was the central fact of Khmer life, the object of vast programs of temple-building, the spiritual power that held the kingdom together."[26] The compelling power of the Hevajra image seems to have contributed to the cult, which sponsored commemorative monuments more so than monasteries.

The timing of the spread of Hevajra is worth summarizing. Surviving images from eastern India date to the twelfth century. Khmer and Thai examples are nearly coeval, dating from the late twelfth and thirteenth centuries. Tibetan images survive from at least the thirteenth to the present, though it is likely that images were made from the twelfth century on. The mural of Cave 465 at Dunhuang similarly dates to ca. early fourteenth century CE. It appears that despite the earlier origin of the texts and ideas behind the Hevajra imagery, they were not influential enough to generate a lasting impact until the late eleventh or early twelfth century. By that time, however, the ideas and images quickly flowed in eastern, southern and northern directions. Islam alone proved an impenetrable barrier.

Notes to Chapter 16

1 Snellgrove, *Hevajra Tantra*, 51, 1:I.ii.20; 80, I.ix.15; 109-110, II.v.1-11; 111, II.v.24-27; 117, II.ix.10-13.

2 Ibid., 80, 1:I.ix.15; II.ix.11-12; 109-110, II.v.1-11; 111, II.v.24-25; Willemen, *Chinese Hevajratantra*, 71, 103-106, 117.

3 K.N. Dikshit, *Paharpur*, ASI Memoirs no. 55 (Delhi, 1938); Nazimuddin Ahmed and John Sanday, "The ruins of Paharpur," *Arts Asiatiques* 41 (1986): 22-35; and Maulvi A.A. Qadir, *A Guide to Paharpur* (Karachi, 1963). The initial finds were reported in ASI, *Annual Report 1927-28* (Calcutta, 1931), 107 and pl. XLIX.a; and, ASI, *Annual Report 1930-34*, 122 and pl. LV.c-d (front and back views of the restored Hevajra). For confirmation of the date, see S. Huntington, "*Pāla-Sena*," 164; and, idem, *Art of Ancient India*, 399.

4 ASI, *Annual Report 1927-28*, 184-185, pl. XLIX.f. It was removed at that time to the "state Cutchery at Agartala." For the date, see S. Huntington, "*Pāla-Sena*," figs. 77, 280 and 282.

5 S. and J. Huntington, *Leaves*, 191-194. An iconographically similar Hevajra figure is found on an *Aṣṭasāhasrikā Prajñāpāramitā Sūtra* in the British Library, London, Or.14282, 110r, published in Losty, "Bengal, Bihar, Nepal?" (part one), fig. 4, lower. Losty suggests a date of ca. 1130, and places the provenance as Vikramaśila monastery, between modern Bihar and Bengal, but with a greater Bengali character.

6 Von Schroeder, *Indo-Tibetan Bronzes*, no. 66A. Size unknown. Philadelphia Museum of Art no. 68-164-2. Von Schroeder places it in the 12th century, as "late Pāla style."

7 Pratapaditya Pal, *The Sensuous Immortals: A Selection of Sculptures from the Pan-Asian Collection* (Los Angeles, 1977), 96-97, no. 57. One of the 8 petals is lost, so only 7 *yoginī* remain. A recent sale included a metalwork Hevajra and consort. Sotheby's, New York, *Indian and Southeast Asian Art, Sale 7108* (New York, 1998) no. 312, ex. LeRoy Davidson Collection.

8 Béguin, *Art ésotérique de l'Himâlaya*, no. 14; also, Ian Alsop, "Metal Sculpture of the Khasa Mallas," in *Tibetan Art: Towards a Definition of Style*, ed. Jane Casey Singer and Philip Denwood (London, 1997) figs. 54 -55; Pal, *Tibetan Paintings* (London, 1984), 64, no. 23. For variants, see ibid., no. 25; the putatively 12th-13th c. Hevajra in Pal, *Nepal, Where the Gods are Young* (New York, 1975), no. 31; and the similar but much later Hevajra in Macdonald and Stahl, *Newar Art*, fig. 40 (captioned: "Gilt bronze of Hevajra at Patan Museum. Height ca. 35 cm. 17th century"). The variants find counterparts in later Tibetan painting, but the eastern Indian type is more common. Pal, *Tibetan Paintings* pls. 64, 81, 82.

9 L.W.J. van de Kuijp, "Ngor-chen kun-dga'bzangpo on the Posture of Hevajra," in *Investigating Indian Art* (Berlin, 1987), 173-177. An early Hevajra *maṇḍala* belongs to the Michael J. and Beata McCormick Collection, illustrated in Denise Patry Leidy and Robert A.F. Thurman, *Maṇḍala: The Architecture of Enlightenment* (New York, 1997), no. 15, where it is dated to the early 13th c.

10 S. and J. Huntington, *Leaves*, 385-386.

11 Snellgrove and Skorupski, *Cultural Heritage of Ladakh*, 2:41, 48. For Saspol, see ibid., 79-81 and Genoud, *Buddhist Wall-Painting of Ladakh*, 58-61. Kim Gutschow has been working with the Karsha Lonpo on a history of the older temple. A description of contemporary rituals inside the temple is found in Kim Gutschow, "Unfocussed Merit-Making in Zangskar: A Socio-Economic Account of Karsha Nunnery," *Tibet Journal* (in press); and idem, "The *Smyung gnas* Fast in Zanskar: How Liminality Depends on Structure," *Recent Research in Ladakh no. 8* (in press).

12 For a treatment of five modes of "post-Pāla" painting, see Gilles Béguin and Lionel Fournier, "Un sanctuarie méconnu de la région d'Alchi," *Oriental Art* ns 32 (1986/87): 373-387.

13 See Rhie and Thurman, *Wisdom and Compassion*, no. 92; Piotrovsky, *Lost Empire of the Silk Road*, 4, 7, 9-12, 26ff.

14 Pal, *Buddhist Paradise*, LS15, 22.

15 Personal communication, 10 March 1998. This is a revision of the date suggested in Béguin and Fournier, "Un sanctuarie méconnu," 385.

16 Note the ca. 16th c. *maṇḍala* in the John Gilmore Ford collection in S. and J. Huntington, *Leaves*, no. 118; three ca. 17th c. Hevajra *maṇḍala* illustrated in Pal, *Tibetan Paintings*, pls. 64, 81-82; the 19th c. *maṇḍala* of Ngor monastery, in Ngor Thar rtse mKhan po, *Tibetan Maṇḍalas*, nos. 99, 105, 107, 109; 17th and 18th c. metalwork Hevajra illustrated in von Schroeder, *Indo-Tibetan Bronzes*, nos. 121C, 124C, 125D-E; and, Gilles Béguin, *Dieux et démons de l'Himâlaya* (Paris, 1990), nos. 103, 241.

17 Illustrated in Dunhuang Wenwu Yanjiusuo, *Dunhuang Mogaoku* (Dunhuang Mogao Caves), 6 vols. (Tokyo/Beijing 1979-87) 5: pl. 156; and in Dunhuang Institute for Cultural Relics, *The Art Treasures of Dunhuang* (New York, 1991), no. 113, captioned "Image of Pleasure" (i.e., Hevajra in union with Nairātmyā) and described 236.

18 In the National Palace Museum, Taiwan collection. Published in Ge Wanzhang, "Qiantan Xizang Fohua" (An informal discussion of Tibetan Buddhist imagery), *Gugong Wenwu Yuekan* (The National Palace Museum Monthly) 5.8 (1983): 89-98, color pl. 16. For *kesi*, see James C.Y. Watt and Anne E. Wardwell, *When Silk Was Gold: Central Asian and Chinese Textiles* (New York, 1997), 52-105; John E. Vollmer, "Chinese Tapestry Weaving: K'o-ssu," *Hali: The International Journal of Oriental Carpets and Textiles* 5.1 (1982): 36-43; Jean Mailey, *Chinese Silk Tapestry: K'o-ssu* (New York, 1981); and, Schuyler V.R. Cammann, "Notes on the Origin of Chinese K'o-ssu Tapestry," *Artibus Asiae* 11 (1948): 90-109.

19 Illustrated in Chira Chongkol, *Guide to the National Museum Bangkok*, 2nd. ed. (Bangkok, 1986), 46 (bronze, ht. 16.5 cm.). Also see Piriya Krairiksh, *Sculptures from Thailand* (Hong Kong, 1982), no. 22, captioned: "Hevajra, Khmer period, circa 950-1250 AD, Bayon style, circa 1177-1230 AD, found in Kampuchea;" Theodore Bowie, ed., *The Sculpture of Thailand* (New York, 1972), no. 35 (12th-13th century); and, Wolfgang Felten and Martin Lerner, *Thai and Cambodian Sculpture from the 6th to the 14th centuries* (London, 1989), 229.

20 See Boeles, "Two Yoginis of Hevajra," figs. 1-4, 7-11; George Coedès, *Bronzes Khmèrs*, Ars Asiatica, no. 5, pl. XIX.1-3; Felten and Lerner, *Thai and Cambodian Sculpture*, no. 34: "Heads of Hevajra and four Yoginis;" and, James W. Thompson Foundation, *The House on the Klong* (Tokyo, 1968), fig. 25.

21 Felten and Lerner, *Thai and Cambodian Sculpture*, 228-230. The incomplete set is ca. 12th c.; the complete set, unpublished, is described as ca. 12th-13th c.

22 See Wibke Lobo, "The Figure of Hevajra and Tantric Buddhism," in *Sculpture of Angkor and Ancient Cambodia: Millennium of Glory*, ed. H.I. Jessup and T. Zephir (Washington D.C., 1997), 73; three metalwork Hevajra in Coedès, *Bronzes Khmèrs*, pl. XXXI.1-3, which at that time (1923) were in private and royal collections in Bangkok; and another metal Hevajra in the National Museum, Bangkok, illustrated in Hiram W. Woodward, Jr., "Tantric Buddhism at Angkor Thom," *Ars Orientalis* 12 (1981): fig. 5.

23 Boeles, "Two Yoginis of Hevajra," fig. 4; Woodward, "Tantric Buddhism at Angkor Thom," fig. 6. This figure holds his hands slightly differently from the others, touching his wrists in front of his chest. As of 1990, there were four Hevajra on permanent display in the National Museum, Bangkok. Also see Felten and Lerner, *Thai and Cambodian Sculpture*, no. 34 (heads of Hevajra) and no. 35 (a complete Hevajra; 41 cm). For an image from Bantay Kdei, illustrated in front, rear and side views in *Les Collections Khmères du Musée Albert Sarraut a Phnom-Penh* (Paris, 1931), pl. XII., see George Groslier, *La Sculpture Khmère ancienne* (Paris, 1925), pl. 85.

24 See Boeles, "Two Yoginis of Hevajra," 14-29; George Coedès, "L'épigraphie du temple de Phimai," *Bulletin de l'École Française d'Extrême-Orient* 24 (1924): 345-358; Krairiksh, *Sculptures from Thailand*, 26-27; Donatella Mazzeo and Chiara Silvi Antonini, *Monuments of Civilization: Ancient Cambodia* (New York, 1978), 127-128; Theodore Bowie et al, *Arts of Thailand* (Bloomington, 1960), 72-75.

25 Woodward, "Tantric Buddhism at Angkor Thom," 57-71.

26 Bowie et al, *Arts of Thailand*, 72.

198. *Saṃvara, Ratnagiri (Orissa), ca. 11th century, Patna Museum*

17

Samvara Imagery

It will be apparent that Sambara is none other than Śiva in a Buddhist guise. The crescent, the third eye, the trident, the skull-cup are obviously borrowed from Śaiva iconography. Even more pertinent is the presence of the elephant skin, which Śiva proudly exhibits after destroying the elephant demon Gajāsura. . . . Sambara not only holds the decapitated heads of Brahma with one of his left hands, but tramples upon Bhairava and Kālarātri, who are none other than Śiva and Kālī or Chāmuṇḍā.

Pratapaditya Pal, *Bronzes of Kashmir*

Saṃvara's importance in Phase Three Esoteric Buddhism is underscored by the substantial number of extant images from eastern India and the large body of images from Tibet. Saṃvara is a fitting topic with which to conclude because his formal and ideational origins return us to two consequential themes developed earlier. As with the histories of Hayagrīva and Yamāntaka, Saṃvara's roots may be traced to a pre-Buddhist deity. The reformulation of non-Buddhist figures was an aspect of *krodha-vighnāntaka* iconography which occupied our attention in defining the first phase of development of Esoteric Buddhist imagery. The second theme concerns his formal parallels with Śiva, a topic covered in detail with reference to the Phase Two *krodha-vighnāntaka* Trailokyavijaya. In fact, Saṃvara appears just as Trailokyavijaya disappears, and he has so much in common with Trailokyavijaya that Saṃvara may be considered the Phase Three reincarnation of Trailokyavijaya.

1 The Iconography of Samvara

We have already confirmed that Saṃvara and Hevajra are both forms of Heruka. It was shown that Saṃvara-Heruka was among the most important personages of Phase Three Esoteric Buddhism, one of the *krodha-vighnāntaka* who personify *yuganaddha*, the union of wisdom and compassion and absolute reality. As we will see, he is referred to as Paramasukha (Supreme Bliss) Saṃvara, and also as Cakrasaṃvara. Tucci has shown that Saṃvara and Cakrasaṃvara descend in two lineages in Tibetan traditions, but stem from the same Indian source. Their *maṇḍala* and iconography are coterminous.[1]

1.1 A Vedic Saṃvara

As was indicated in the introduction to Phase Three, the text of the *ST* was probably produced slightly later than the *HT*. In its last chapter, the *ST* refers to the *Śriherukābhidāna tantra* and defines itself as a *kalpa* (ritual practice) text extracted from the *Śriherukābhidhāna-mahātantra-rāja*.[2] Evidently by the ninth century Saṃvara was recognized in the *ST* as a powerful *krodha-vighnāntaka* at the forefront of the new Esoteric Buddhist paradigm. We will refer to the *ST* shortly for its descriptions of various forms of Phase Three Saṃvara.

The formulators of Phase Three Esoteric Buddhism apparently drew on a pre-Buddhist Saṃvara. Jean Przyluski points out that a Saṃvara can be traced to the *Rig Veda*. Based on our earlier exploration of the roots of Yamāntaka, Hayagrīva, Śumbha and Niśumbha, it should come as no surprise that the *Rig Veda* casts Saṃvara as a demonic enemy of the gods, "un démon qu'Indra précipite d'en haut, et dont ce dieu brise les 99 ou 100 forteresses."[3] Wendy Doniger explains that Saṃvara was a demon who kept the Soma, the ecstatic ambrosia of the gods, in mountain fortresses, out of the reach of Indra.[4]

Przyluski also suggests that Saṃvara was venerated in India prior to the Aryan invasion, interpreting the destruction of his fortresses by Indra as a metaphor for the Aryan invasion itself. Snellgrove concurs with this analysis of Saṃvara. He writes, "Sambara . . . is probably derived from the pre-Aryan god of that name, so taking us back to the subsoil of Indian religious experience."[5] Tucci has also expressed an opinion concerning Saṃvara's origin: "[Saṃvara-Heruka], before assuming the form as represented by the tantric mystic, was nothing else than a local deity of some ethnic group not well definable."[6]

1.2 The word saṃvara

The etymology of the word *saṃvara* reveals how peculiarly suitable the name of the Vedic demon is for a Phase Three *krodha-vighnāntaka*. Snellgrove takes it to mean "a vow or a bond."[7] The definition is supported by Tsuda's understanding of the *ST*, where it is used in the sense of a bond or "'union' of aspects of the world fused into one."[8] Because the value system of Phase Three equates union with bliss, *saṃvara* was translated into Tibetan in two ways: as "union" and literally as "supreme bliss."[9] According to Thurman and Rhie, Saṃvara's full title is Paramasukha Cakrasaṃvara (Supreme Bliss Wheel Integration):

> *Western scholars have become accustomed to call this deity Samvara or Chakrasamvara, but the Tibetans always prefer bDe-mchog, which translates the Supreme Bliss (Paramasukha) part of his name. The confusion arose perhaps because the word shamvara (not samvara) can be a synonym of paramasukha.*[10]

2.3 Forms of Saṃvara

There are three principal forms of Saṃvara as described in texts: two-armed, six-armed, and twelve-armed forms. Most extant eastern Indian and early Tibetan Saṃvara images fall into the two-armed and twelve-armed categories, but a few examples of the six-armed type can be identified as well.

The two-armed Saṃvara in the ST

The two-armed form of Saṃvara is briefly referred to in the *ST* but not described, at least in the portions of the text edited and translated by Shiníchi Tsuda. In a ritual described in Chapter Ten, the following instructions are given: "[The yogin] should imagine his own body to possess the aspect of the two-armed Heruka." Chapter Thirteen adds: "Possessing the *yoga* of the two-armed *Heruka*, he [the *ācārya*] will have the self-consciousness of five *skandhas* and so on."[11]

Since the *ST* succeeds the *HT*, we might expect the two-armed Saṃvara-Heruka to appear in the form of the standard two-armed Heruka. [**176-189**] Instead we see that the two-armed Saṃvara holds the bell and *vajra* and crosses the wrists in front of the chest, while standing in *ālīḍha*. He does resemble Heruka, however, in that he usually carries a *khatvāṅga*. But for his posture, one would identify the Los Angeles metal sculpture [**189**] as Saṃvara and not Heruka. It should be remembered that such minute distinctions among Heruka, Hevajra and Saṃvara are meaningless in the realm of the absolute identity of the deity, but at a provisional level iconographic details are generally maintained.

The *Sādhanamālā*, which frequently provides more accurate descriptions of Phase Three deities than those of Phase Two, features this description:

> *[Saṃvara has] a string of skulls over his forehead and the crescent moon on the top. . . . He shows the Viśvavajra (on his head-dress) and is three-eyed. He stands in the Ālīdha attitude. . . . He carries the Vajra and the Ghaṇṭa[-bell] . . . and is embraced by his Śakti [sic] Vajravārāhī.*[12]

That the two-armed Saṃvara-Heruka is visualized as holding a *vajra* and bell rather than the *vajra* and skull-cup of Heruka is also confirmed by another passage of the *ST*:

> *The teacher (ācārya), whose nature consists of the deity, who manifests himself in the nature of all buddhas, the hero holding a vajra and a bell . . ./ The wise man, wielding the vajra and occupied in clanging the bell . . .*[13]

The six-armed Saṃvara

Ironically, the most specific description of Saṃvara in the *ST* is devoted to his rarest form. Only a few images of the six-armed deity may be identified securely.[14]

> *[The yogin] should imagine the auspicious Heruka situated in the midst of the solar disc. He is the hero, three-faced, six-armed and standing in the posture of ālīḍha. His central face is deep black; his right face is like a kunda-flower; and his left face is red and very terrible, and is adorned with a crest of twisted hair. Treading on Bhairava and Kālarātri, he abides in the great pleasure (mahāsukha), embracing Vajravairocanī in great rejoicing of desire of compassion. He has attained concentration of mind through the union of a vajra and a bell, embracing (the goddess) with his (first) two arms, and holding a garment of an elephant-skin with his second two arms. He holds in the right hand of his third pair (of arms) a ḍamaruka-drum to be sounded according to the nature of all the dharmas, and he has a khatvāṅga-staff and a kapāla-vessel in his third left hand. His crown is decorated with a wreath of skulls, and is adorned with a crescent moon. He is marked with a cross-vajra on his head and has the lord of the family [i.e., Akṣobhya] on the top of his head. His face is distorted; he is very terrible and assumes the erotic-rasa. He has a tigerskin as his garment, and is adorned with fifty human heads.*[15]

The *Sādhanamālā* description of Vajradāka echoes many of these particulars. They include the three faces, six arms, *ālīḍha*, gods underfoot, the *khatvāṅga*, *vajra* and bell, the crescent moon and the crossed-*vajra* in the hair. The colors of the faces differ, the elephant skin is traded for that of a human, and the drum exchanged for a *triśūla*.[16] The two latter implements are equally characteristic of Śiva, as is the crescent moon. Both the six-armed form and Vajradāka are strongly marked by Shaivite characteristics, a theme to which we will return once we have examined the images themselves.

The twelve-armed Saṃvara

Twelve-armed Saṃvara is the form most commonly found in extant images. There are extensive Tibetan descriptions and interpretations of the multi-armed Saṃvara,[17] and these generally correspond to eastern Indian images, as well as to the account given in the *Niṣpannayogāvalī*:

> *[Saṃvara] stands in the Ālīdha posture on the prostrate forms of Bhairava and Kālarātri. He is blue in colour and his four faces on the east, south, west and north are blue, green, red and yellow in colour . . . He is twelve-armed. With the two principal hands carrying the Vajra and Vajra-marked bell, he embraces his Śakti [sic] Vajravārāhī. With the second pair . . . he carries the elephant skin from which blood trickles down. In the remaining four right hands he holds the Ḍamaru[-drum], the axe, the [karttikā-chopper] and the trident. The four left hands show the Vajra-marked Khaṭvāṅga, the skull cup full of blood, the Vajra-marked noose and the severed head of Brahma.*[18]

Having introduced the three ideal types of Saṃvara in Phase Three literature of eastern India, we will now proceed to examine images. We will reverse the order, however, by beginning with the twelve-armed Saṃvara.

2 Eastern and Northern Indian Twelve-armed Samvara Images

Extant sculptures and paintings of the four-headed, twelve-armed Saṃvara are perhaps slightly less common in eastern India than Heruka or Hevajra, but they are more evenly distributed. We find two Saṃvara images from Orissa and at least one confirmed example from Bihar, Bengal and Kashmir. Due to the present limitations of our knowledge, several other examples still must be considered generally as eastern Indian, from either Bengal or Bihar. All derive from the eleventh and twelfth centuries.

2.1 Orissan Saṃvara images

Two Saṃvara images from Orissa have been identified. One is in the National Museum, New Delhi and another larger image is in the Patna Museum. **[198-202]** The provenance of the Patna image is known to be Ratnagiri, and given close similarities we may assume the same origin for the New Delhi sculpture as well.[19] The necklaces and girdle loops of the New Delhi sculpture are chunkier and executed with less methodical precision than that of the Patna Saṃvara; this may indicate that the New Delhi piece was made slightly earlier. The necklaces, anklets, armlets and triangular shape of the face of the Patna sculpture are comparable to those on

199. *Saṃvara, Orissa (Ratnagiri?), ca. 11th century, National Museum, New Delhi*

200. *Detail of* **199**

a seated Avalokiteśvara from Orissa in the Indian Museum [**122, 125**] and may be dated similarly to the ca. eleventh century. I can find no mention of either Saṃvara image in Hock's work on Ratnagiri, but Mitra suggests a date of the tenth or eleventh century. Donaldson also assigns both images to the late tenth or early eleventh century.[20] I maintain a roughly eleventh century date.

As the two images are iconographically identical, a single description will suffice for both. The damage to one is in some areas complemented by the better condition of the other. Three heads, each with three eyes, wear low crowns ornamented with skulls and beaded bands. The two side heads are more wrathful than the tranquil central face. In the high chignon of the central head is a crescent moon, conventionally a Shaivite symbol. [**198, 201**]

An elephant skin, also held by certain forms of Śiva to be discussed below, is held aloft in the upper pair of hands, creating a symmetrical arch over Saṃvara's head. He grasps the right front and rear legs of the elephant, while the left legs jut out at the level of his hips. The head and eyes of the elephant, with its tusks and trunk hanging down, can be seen from the proper right side.

Each of the twelve wrists wears a wide beaded bracelet, each band of beads separated by twelve to fourteen striations. Three bells hang from the center of the belt, the outer ones flaring slightly. The *vanamālā* is once again made up of heads tied by their hair.

201. *Saṃvara, Ratnagiri (Orissa), ca. 11th century, Patna Museum, same as* **198**

The first pair of hands hold the *vajra* and bell and cross wrists at the chest, keeping the palms in and crossing the right hand outside of the left. On the proper right side, below the elephant leg, the other hands hold a *ḍamaru*-drum, a *triśūla*, a triangular-bladed chopper and a long-handled axe. On the left side, he holds a noose with a *vajra*-finial, the fourfold head of Brahma, a skull-cup and the *khatvāṅga*. The *khatvāṅga* is steadied by the crook of the left elbow, recalling Heruka images. [**176**] These *āyudha* correspond to all those described in the *Niṣpannayogāvalī*. The absence of Saṃvara's consort, Vajravārāhī, is notable.

Saṃvara stands in *āliḍha*, the mirror opposite of Trailokyavijaya's *pratyālidhā*. Here the proper left leg is bent and the right outstretched. As in Trailokyavijaya images, a male form of Śiva lies under the left foot, and Śiva's consort lies under the right. [**200, 202**] The present Śiva is unlike those typically portrayed with Trailokyavijaya. He takes the form of a wrathful or *ugra*-Śiva, more commonly known as Rudra or Bhairava-Śiva. [**118-119**] He is *vāmana*-Yakṣa, with a high chignon, a beard and mustache, and a garland of heads. He holds a *triśūla* and *ḍamaru*-drum in his two left hands and a skull-cup and *mālā*-rosary in his two right hands. Interestingly, Saṃvara himself wears the garland of heads and carries the drum, *triśūla* and skull-cup, but in opposite hands.

Beneath Saṃvara's right leg is Bhairava's consort, Kālarātri ("night of all-destroying time"), rather than Umādevā or Pārvati as with Trailokyavijaya. The cognate of Chāmuṇḍā, who figured in the earlier myth of Śumbha and Niśumbha, Kālarātri is quite unlike the winsome Umādevā. She is a frightful deity who haunts the cemeteries and demands blood sacrifices. The artists graphically depict her

202. *Detail of* **198**

emaciated state with sunken eyes, withered dugs and a convention of lines on her limbs and rib-cage to suggest stringy tendons. She also has a high rounded chignon, big earrings and a garland. With her right hand she holds a *karttikā*-chopper and with her left a skull cup.

In the case of the Patna Museum sculpture [**202**] the feet of both Bhairava and Kālarātri touch a curious raised square in the middle of the dais on which they lay. The lower *vajra*-tipped skull finial of Saṃvara's *khatvāṅga* rests on this platform. A male figure kneels below, offering an unidentifiable object. Beneath the lotus dais of the New Delhi image [**200**] are two kneeling females (proper right) and three lamps or offerings (proper left). Between them a vine curls around two pairs of symmetrical medallions with *cintāmani* and lotus motifs. The back slabs of both sculptures are squared off, as is characteristic of Orissa sculpture [**198, 199, 201**], and inscribed with flames. At the upper corners two *gandharva* offer reverence.

Two large Saṃvara images [**198, 199**], a large Heruka [**176**] and several small Heruka images [**177-181**] constitute a substantial representation of Phase Three *krodha-vighnāntaka* at Ratnagiri. Admittedly, in the context of the sum of tenth and eleventh century images at Ratnagiri, Phase Three imagery is still in the minority. Nevertheless, there unquestionably were practitioners within the monastery gates influential enough to erect large-scale images like the two Saṃvara sculptures, which must have dominated shrines or niches.

2.2 A Saṃvara from North Bengal

Another impressive Saṃvara stone sculpture in excellent condition was found in Bengal. [**203-204**] It is part of a group of eight sculptures from northern Bengal presented in 1934-35 to the Indian Museum, Calcutta by Dr. B.C. Law. The high chignon and stylized eyebrows suggest a date no earlier than the eleventh century, the same date supported by Mitra.[21]

In addition to its concurrence with *Niṣpannayogāvalī* descriptions, this figure shares iconographic characteristics with Orissan Saṃvara sculptures. [**198-202**] Saṃvara's consort is again missing. Nevertheless, he makes the same *vajrahūṃkāra* gesture as the Orissan sculptures with his first pair of arms, as if embracing her. The head of the elephant skin, similarly raised aloft, can be seen just between the second and third outstretched proper right hands. The other right hands carry the *ḍamaru*-drum, an axe, a chopper and a reversed short-handled *triśūla*. The corresponding left hands carry the skull-cup uppermost, the noose, the head of Brahma

203. *Saṃvara, Bengal, ca. 11th century, Indian Museum, Calcutta*

and the *khatvāṅga*. The *vajra* finial crowns the three heads on the shaft of the *khatvāṅga*, symbolizing the three worlds.

Saṃvara's elaborate hair does not appear to include a crescent moon. Skulls are lodged in his low crown, and the tips of *vajra*-prongs emerge from the top of the high-piled hair. Two garland-bearing *gandharva* hover against clouds above him, while flames create an upper-body nimbus.

Strangely, Bhairava and Kālarātri are not underfoot. This recalls a similar anomaly in another Bengali sculpture, the Dacca Museum's Heruka [**188**], where the corpse is absent underfoot. Saṃvara stands again in *ālīḍha* and is surrounded by four *yoginī*, three on the base and one above his head. The *yoginī* stand in similar poses, are four-armed, and each holds a *khatvāṅga* in the manner of her lord. According to Mitra they correspond to Ḍākinī, Lāmā, Khaṇḍarohā and Rupiṇī, "who as required in the Sambara Maṇḍala, surrounded the deity in the four cardinal directions."[22]

The scene below the lotus dais is of considerable interest. [**204**] The central figure stands stiffly, flanked by two animals. The seated figure to the immediate proper right holds a *vajra* and bell in the manner of Vajrasattva. Mitra's judgement that a "horrid scene" is being acted out becomes understandable when one realizes the central figure is being attacked by a jackal and other animals.[23] To elaborate on this interpretation, I believe the scene takes place in a cemetery, and the "upright" figure is a corpse being eaten by jackals. The scene is depicted in multiple perspective, most of the figures seen from the side and the corpse from above. The other figures are yogins who meditate, visualize, dance ecstatically and identify with Vajrasattva.[24] The absence of Bhairava and Kālarātri is more than made up for by this charnel ground vignette.

2.3 A Saṃvara pedestal

Whereas the stone Saṃvara in the Indian Museum [**203-204**] fails to depict Bhairava and Kālarātri under Saṃvara's feet, a pedestal in the National Museum, New Delhi, preserves little else. [**205**] Its provenance is suggested by comparison with Bihar sculptures of the late eleventh and

204. *Detail of 203*

205. *Pedestal for Saṃvara, Bihar (?), ca. late 11th-12th century, National Museum, New Delhi*

early twelfth centuries.[25] On the level surface of the dais the emaciated Kālarātri lays on her back, holding a chopper and a skull cup. Bhairava is in a contorted position, facing forward, holding a *triśūla* and an unidentified object. Below center stands a four-armed *yoginī* in *ālīḍha*, trampling a stiff recumbent figure against a flaming backdrop. She holds a skull-cup and *khatvāṅga* with her left hands and a *ḍamaru*-drum and chopper in her right. To her left is a short dedicatory inscription which mentions Vajravārāhī.[26] The inscription implies that the missing Saṃvara was in the embrace of his consort, Vajravārāhī, and surrounded by the four *yoginī*. This is the form followed by twelfth-century painted images from eastern India, and one adopted in Tibetan art. We can at least be fairly confident that in Bihar between the late eleventh and early twelfth centuries Saṃvara was depicted trampling on Bhairava and Kālarātri, as he did in Orissan images **[198-202]**, and was surrounded by one or more *yoginī*, as he was in Bengal. **[203-204]**

2.4 A metalwork Saṃvara from Vikramaśīla

A metalwork Saṃvara was discovered at Patharghata and placed in the Indian Museum. **[206-207]** The statue is made of a coppery-looking alloy and has copper inlay on the main face's three eyes and mouth. Susan Huntington's suggestion of a date in the eleventh century is followed here.[27] Patharghata is in the neighborhood of the ruins of Vikramaśīla monastery, in Bhagalpur district of modern Bihar near the border with Bengal.

206. *Saṃvara, metalwork, Patharghata (Bihar), ca. 11th century, Indian Museum, Calcutta*

Sculpted fully in the round, Saṃvara is equipped with four faces, twelve arms and a garland of severed heads tied by the hair. He holds above his head a very stylized slender elephant skin, which is almost unrecognizable except for the characteristic ears and trunk near Saṃvara's upper right hand. The primary pair of hands make the *vajrahūṃkāra mudrā*, and Saṃvara is once again deployed in the "solitary hero" mode, without Vajravārāhī. His proper right hands hold the *ḍamaru*-drum, axe, knife and *triśūla*, while the left holds a skull-cup, noose, head of Brahma and a *khatvāṅga*. The *āyudha* correspond exactly with those of the stone Saṃvara from Bengal **[203-204]** and very nearly with the Orissan examples. **[198-202]** A standard type had clearly been rapidly accepted, one which closely approximates the textual *sādhana* as well.

A notable characteristic of the metal image is the crescent moon Saṃvara bears in his hair (not visible in **206-207**), above and to the proper left of a central crest in the form of a *triśūla*. Both symbols are particularly associated with Śiva. Surmounting his *jatāmukuta* is a *viśvavajra*. Another point to be observed is that the two trampled figures are reversed. Under Saṃvara's proper left leg, where we would expect Bhairava, we find Kālarātri,

207. *Rear view of* **206**

with a skull-cup in her left hand and chopper in her right. She has emaciated arms and legs and a skull-like face. Four-armed Bhairava is on the other side, holding the *triśūla*, skull-cup, chopper and *mālā*-rosary. His high flame-shaped chignon helps to define his Shaivite identity. It does not appear that the base has been mis-assembled since recovery. A few other metalwork Saṃvara images discussed below reverse the trampled figures as well, but the arrangement remains unusual and does not seem to reflect a regional pattern.

2.5 Twelfth century metalwork Saṃvara

Several relatively similar eastern Indian metalwork Saṃvara testify to his importance in late Indian Esoteric Buddhism. One was catalogued by the British Museum in 1976. [**208**] Made of brass with copper and silver inlay, this four-headed, twelve-armed Saṃvara image corresponds to the standard type with little or no variation. He holds the elephant skin along with the drum, chopper, short *khatvāṅga*, skull-cup, noose and the head of Brahma. Like the stone Saṃvara in the Indian Museum [**203**], the *triśūla* in a proper right hand is held upside down. A *vāmana*-Yakṣa Bhairava is under the proper left foot, and a glaring Kālarātri with a scored rib-cage is under the right. The only minor variations I detect are the hatchet in a right hand, and the fact that Saṃvara crosses his left arm outside of the right while making the *vajrahūṃkāra* gesture with his primary pair of hands. Nearly all other Saṃvara images do the reverse.

The British Museum Saṃvara is accepted as a twelfth-century work.[28] A photograph of a second Saṃvara bears such a likeness to this sculpture one suspects it is the same work before cleaning. The Archaeological Survey of India, however, lists the second work as belonging to Tabo monastery, in the Spiti area of western Tibet.[29] Two other metal Saṃvara images conform to the iconographic type, though one embraces his consort, an unusual feature in surviving metal and stone images of eastern India.[30]

208. *Saṃvara, eastern India, metalwork, ca. 12th century, British Museum*

2.6 Orissan (?) metalwork Saṃvara

A metalwork image of the four-headed, twelve-armed Saṃvara in *ālīḍha* trampling on Bhairava and Kālarātri belongs to the National Museum in New Delhi. Shashi Asthana suggests the image is from Orissa and datable to the thirteenth or fourteenth century.[31] The thirteenth century is most plausible, and the Orissan provenance is worth considering, despite the dearth of late Buddhist metalwork images available for comparison. The four heads are painted in gold. The painted eyes recall folk paintings of Orissa, rather than those of Nepal or Tibet. The piece is notable because the figure embraces his consort. In addition, like the Vikramaśīla Saṃvara [**206**], Saṃvara tramples on Bhairava and Kālarātri with the proper right and left feet respectively.

209. Saṃvara, Orissa (?), metalwork, ca. 11th-13th century, Indian Museum, Calcutta

210. (right) Rear view of **209**

Another Saṃvara image is apparently unnoticed and unpublished. **[209-210]** Presently in the Indian Museum, Calcutta, the tiny size and somewhat unusual base of the piece makes attribution difficult. Saṃvara embraces his consort Vajravārāhī, whose hand can be seen holding a skull-cup on the back. **[210]** The trunk of the elephant is also visible at the back. In most respects Saṃvara relates to the standard four-headed, twelve-armed type. An Orissan origin is probable.

2.7 Painted Saṃvara images

Like Heruka and Hevajra, Saṃvara also appears in illuminated manuscripts of the twelfth century. One example in a private collection is, according to Pratapaditya Pal, "among the finest covers of the Pāla period now known."[32] Pal assigns it to Bengal and posits an early twelfth-century date. One of the pair of covers depicts Kālacakra with eight consorts, and the other displays nine forms presumably of Saṃvara, with the twelve-armed form to the right of center. This images appears to follow the same iconographic type as stone and metal images, but I have not personally examined the painted wood cover.

2.8 A Kashmiri twelve-armed Saṃvara

Kashmir was also an important Esoteric Buddhist center, which, as we have seen, had an important role in the transmission of Phase Two art and teachings to western Tibet. Phase Three is not well documented until the eleventh and twelfth centuries, but Kashmiri monks traveled to and from eastern India, bringing the Phase Three teachings back to Kashmir. Evidence suggests that the Kālacakra teachings were not received in Kashmir until Somanātha returned there after having studied with masters in eastern India in the third quarter of the eleventh century. Similarly, if one examines the list of writings and translations by Rinchen Zangpo's Kashmiri collaborators, painstakingly assembled by Jean Naudou,[33] more texts relating to deities and practices of Phases One and Two than of Phase Three will be found. By the eleventh century Saṃvara texts and the *GST* (the earliest Phase Three text) were known in Kashmir. The new dispensation was evidently a little slower in Kashmir to overtake Phase Two as the dominant ideology than it was in eastern India. Furthermore, the murals in the early temples of Spiti and Ladakh, which are related stylistically and iconographically to Kashmiri art, belong to Phase Two, though they were painted as late as the end of the twelfth century.

Thus it is hard to accept the earlier range of the ninth to twelfth century which has been applied to a particularly fine Kashmiri brass Saṃvara.[34] [**211**] Perhaps a date of late tenth or early eleventh is acceptable for the brass sculpture. The iconographic characteristics are rendered with superb clarity. Four-headed and twelve-armed, Saṃvara stands in *āliḍha* on Bhairava and Kālarātri. The latter are rendered with considerable detail. Bhairava is four-armed and avidly holds aloft the *triśūla*. He shies away as if in terror. Kālarātri sits upright, her scored arms, ribs, neck and pointed breasts defining her emaciated state. She holds a chopper and a *triśūla* and cups Saṃvara's right foot, as Umādevā touched Trailokyavijaya's. [**163**]

211. *Saṃvara,Kashmir, brass inlaid with silver, ca. late 10th-11th century, Los Angeles County Museum of Art*

Saṃvara's other attributes are equally clear and familiar. The elephant-skin, held buoyantly aloft by the upper arms, is easily identified. The *triśūla* of an upper right hand is mated with the short *khatvāṅga* in a left, the latter with the addition of a skull before the finial. Other hands hold a chopper, a skull-cup, a noose with *vajra*-finials and the head of Brahma. Śiva's crescent moon is also prominently displayed on the proper right in the crown above the Buddha figure and skulls. The Kashmiri artists were employing the same iconographic standard as the artists from Bengal, Bihar and Orissa. For this reason alone it is illogical to isolate this piece by presuming for it a ninth-century date, since, as we have tried to show, nearly all the eastern Indian images date to the eleventh and twelfth centuries.

3 Eastern Indian Two-armed Samvara Images

The two-armed form of Saṃvara appears in eastern Indian images. We have already discussed descriptions of it in eastern Indian texts. The two-armed form is decidedly in the minority among surviving stone and metal images. The two-armed form is not infrequently met with, however, in manuscript illustration.

212. Saṃvara, eastern Indian, metalwork, ca. late 11th-12th century

3.1 A twelfth century two-armed Saṃvara

One of the rare eastern Indian metalwork images of the two-armed Saṃvara was sold at Sotheby and Company's sale of 10 July 1973.[35] **[212]** It would appear to be from Bengal or Bihar, dating to the late eleventh or twelfth century. Saṃvara stands in *ālīḍha*, making the *vajrahūṃkāra* gesture. He wears the garland of heads and tramples on Bhairava, who contorts beneath his proper left foot, and Kālarātri, who cups Saṃvara's right foot, again as Umādevā does. **[163]** The *khatvāṅga* is cradled in Saṃvara's left forearm. This is one of few eastern Indian images in which Saṃvara wears jeweled shin bands, a trait which is much more common in early Tibetan imagery. The two-armed Saṃvara is effectively identical to the twelve-armed form, stripped of the other ten arms.

3.2 Painted two-armed Saṃvara images

The manuscript cover in a private collection discussed above (see 2.7) includes more than one form of the two-armed Saṃvara embracing Vajravārāhī to both sides of the central twelve-armed Saṃvara.[36] The *Aṣṭasāhasrikā Prajñāpāramitā* manuscript in the Asiatic Society of Bombay in which we found a Heruka image also contains a two-armed Saṃvara.[37] The manuscript is attributed to the twelfth or thirteenth century, perhaps from Bihar. Saṃvara tramples on Bhairava and a gaunt Kālarātri, makes the *vajrahūṃkāra* gesture and holds a *khatvāṅga*. Vajravārāhī is not embraced; she appears in a separate illustration that is positioned to pair her with Saṃvara. She also tramples on the identical figures. The only variation in the iconography is that Saṃvara stands in *pratyālīḍha* instead of *ālīḍha*. Thus, except for the *khatvāṅga* and the fact that he holds his crossed palms in instead of out, this image is very close to the two-armed form of Trailokyavijaya. **[156, 158]**

The *Prajñāpāramitā* text donated to the Musée Guimet by Lionel Fournier also contains a very fine image of the two-armed Saṃvara.[38] [COLOR PLATE 15] The manuscript illustrates three pairs of male and female deities on six leaves. The Buddha is paired with Prajñāpāramitā, Heruka with Nairatmya, and Saṃvara with Vajravārāhī. Saṃvara is in *ālīḍha*, making the *vajrahūṃkāra* gesture and cradling the *khatvāṅga* in his left elbow. Against the fiery backdrop his blue body and red-lined eyes create a startling image, quite powerful for its size. The contexts of all three of these examples of two-armed Saṃvara images once again provide evidence of the connections among Phase Three *krodha-vighnāntaka*, who are generally found with one another in later works of art, not mixed with earlier Phase Two *krodha-vighnāntaka*.

4 Early Samvara Images Outside India

After the fourteenth century surviving metal and painted images of Saṃvara in Nepal and Tibet are relatively plentiful. There are too many examples of both the two-armed and twelve-armed forms to do more than cite a few which demonstrate the standard we found in the earliest images in eastern India.[39] Some particularly important images from Tangut and Chinese contexts will be mentioned as well.

A two-armed Saṃvara with Vajravārāhī in the Zimmerman collection is especially notable. **[213]** "This unusual and powerful sculpture is one of the rarest to survive from the early period of Tibetan art."[40] Pal dates it to the twelfth century,

213. *Two-armed Saṃvara, Tibet, metalwork, ca. 12th-13th century, Zimmerman Family Collection*

while Rhie and Thurman suggest a date between the twelfth and early thirteenth centuries, largely on the basis of similarities with the Saṃvara in the Lhakhang Soma in Alchi.

Saṃvara is prominent in western Tibet only after the period which saw the building of Tabo, the Dukhang and Sumtsek of Alchi, Sumda and Mangyu. Besides the Lhakhang Soma Saṃvara just mentioned, the ca. fourteenth-century Saspol cave, which provided an image of Hevajra **[197]**, also contains murals of the two- and twelve-armed forms. **[215, 216]** Their presence together confirms the contemporaneity of their parallel lineages, and the cave as whole reinforces the notion that Phase Three *krodha-vighnāntaka* are generally found apart from Phase Two contexts.

The fidelity of the Tibetan artists to their eastern Indian models is demonstrated by a striking small stone carving of the twelve-armed Saṃvara with consort, acquired by the Metropolitan Museum of New York. **[214]** In truth, the work is difficult to differentiate from eastern Indian sculptures, and its re-attribution to eastern India has recently been put forward by the Museum curator, Steven M. Kossak.[41] Bhairava twists as he is being crushed underfoot, holding a chopper and the *ḍamaru*-drum. Kālarātri is scored with parallel lines, the convention for emaciation seen in eastern Indian sculpture. It is a fine little piece of carving which must have been prized on a personal altar in Tibet. A ca. thirteenth or fourteenth-century date is probably appropriate.

In Nepal and Tibet Saṃvara inspired large shrines to house his image and *maṇḍala*, as well as small-scale objects for personal meditations. As one of the preeminent *krodha-vighnāntaka* of Phase Three Buddhism, his image was painted several times in the highest storey of the Great Stupa at Gyantse [COLOR PLATE 16], and he is still one of the most frequently encountered images in Tibetan Buddhist contexts. Very little tampering with his iconographic characteristics was done in Nepal and Tibet, so that images made as late as the present century can be traced directly back to the characteristics which coalesced around his figure in the tenth and eleventh centuries in eastern India.

There are additionally quite a few Saṃvara images from twelfth and thirteenth-century Tangut Xia sites. From the number of images recovered from *stūpa*s in Khara Khoto and near Yinchuan, it seems there was something of a cult of Saṃvara among the Tanguts. A two-armed sculpture was recovered by Stein at Khara Khoto, and paintings of two-armed Saṃvaras were recovered from Khara Khoto and the Baisikou west *stūpa*.[42] An equal number of twelve-armed Saṃvara images appear in both paintings and wooden sculptures.[43] The tendency to balance four- and twelve-armed forms of Saṃvara at a single site is also maintained in the cave above Saspol village in Ladakh.

During the Yuan period, Cave 465 at Dunhuang was also endowed with a Saṃvara image.[44] The Esoteric Buddhist art of both the Yuan at Dunhuang and of the earlier Tanguts can be related iconographically to eastern Indian forms through the agency of contacts with Tibet. Later Chinese images of Saṃvara are likewise dependent on Tibetan materials.[45] In the eighteenth-century Chinese pantheon associated with Rolpa Dorje (Lalitavajra, 1717-1786 CE), the fifteenth Changkya Hutukhtu, Saṃvara is on the first leaf of *yidam* figures, appearing with Vajrabhairava and Guhyasamāja; the next leaf depicts Kālacakra and Hevajra.[46] In other words, as one would expect, Saṃvara is privileged as one of the primary deities of Phase Three Esoteric Buddhism. To reinforce the importance afforded him in Phase Three texts, we find him given prominence in Tibetan Buddhist contexts of northern China during the Qing dynasty. At the Yonghe Gong, the chief Lamaist temple in Beijing, the first floor of Hall II houses a variety of deities of diverse status, but the

214. *Twelve-armed Saṃvara, Tibet or eastern India, ca. 13th-14th century, The Metropolitan Musem of Art, New York*

215. *Twelve-armed Saṃvara, Saspol cave (Ladakh) wall painting, ca. 14th century*

216. *Two-armed Saṃvara (above right), Saspol cave (Ladakh) wall painting, ca. 14th century*

second floor has only three large shrines. Each shrine contains a sizeable wooden sculpture: Vajradhara inhabits the center shrine and Vajrabhairava and Saṃvara the side shrines.[47]

This rough sketch should serve as an index of the two main forms of Saṃvara as developed in eastern India and Kashmir and transmitted to Nepal, Tibet, the Tangut Xia state and Tibetanized China. The two-armed and the twelve-armed forms were followed with great fidelity throughout the area where Phase Three Esoteric Buddhism was practiced. One assumes that the lack of variation reflects Saṃvara's position of centrality with respect to doctrine. His image was too crucial for details to be left to the preferences of artists. Although there were certain identifying characteristics which became codified, Phase One *krodha-vighnāntaka* like Hayagrīva and Yamāntaka were comparatively more varied and related to no single written prescription. Perhaps fewer inconsistencies were encountered with the Phase Two *krodha-vighnāntaka* Trailokyavijaya, but his status within Phase Two had already risen, and it is my contention he was the model or prototype from which Saṃvara was developed. As Trailokyavijaya's image was itself intertwined with that of Maheśvara-Śiva, Saṃvara's essence is equally so. Now that we have explored the textual doctrines surrounding Saṃvara and are familiar with the visual expressions of these doctrines, we can finally look beneath the surface of his form at the underlying determinative structures.

Notes to Chapter Seventeen

1 Tucci, *Tsaparang*, 17-18. The epigraph for this chapter comes from Pal, *Bronzes of Kashmir*, 173. Vajradāka seems to be another name applied to the 6-armed form of Saṃvara. According to the *Sādhanamālā*, Vajraḍāka holds the *vajra* and bell in his two main hands, embraces his consort Vajravārāhī, and treads on Bhairava and Kālarātri, all characteristics of Saṃvara.

2 Tsuda, *Saṁvarodaya-tantra*, 37.

3 Przyluski, "Heruka-Sambara," 44.

4 O'Flaherty, *Rig Veda*, 162, note 5; nos. 2.12 and 4.26-27.

5 Snellgrove, *Buddhist Himalaya*, 205.

6 Tucci, *Tsaparang*, 22.

7 Snellgrove, *Indo-Tibetan Buddhism*, 153. Lokesh Chandra also suggests "obligation, vow," in his preface to Dawa-Samdup, *Shrīchakrasambhāra Tantra*, 33. See also "sambhāra" in Monier-Williams, *Sanskrit-English Dictionary*, 1179.

8 Tsuda, *Saṁvarodaya-tantra*, 55, 57.

9 See Tucci, *Tsaparang*, 18-20; Snellgrove, *Hevajra Tantra*, 1:138; and, idem, *Indo-Tibetan Buddhism*, 153-154.

10 Rhie and Thurman, *Wisdom and Compassion*, 215.

11 Tsuda, *Saṁvarodaya-tantra*, 277, X.29; and 281, XIII.2.

12 B. Bhattacharyya, *Indian Buddhist Iconography*, 161.

13 Tsuda, *Saṁvarodaya-tantra*, 289, XVII.8-9.

14 One example seems to be in the "campana" of the Kumbum at Gyantse. See Giuseppe Tucci, *Gyantse and its Monasteries*, Vol. 3, fig. 391. It is also described in Ricca and Lo Bue, *Gyantse*, 310, no. 1.

15 Tsuda, *Saṁvarodaya-tantra*, 283-284, XIII.15-20.

16 Translated in Snellgrove, *Buddhist Himalaya*, 207-211.

17 See Dawa-Samdup, *Shrīchakrasambhāra Tantra*, 93-101; Snellgrove, *Indo-Tibetan Buddhism*, 154-155; and, Tucci, *Tsaparang*, 22-27, 48.

18 B. Bhattacharyya, *Indian Buddhist Iconography*, 162. For other descriptions of the 12-armed Saṃvara, 4-headed and 6-headed, see Kalff, "Abhidhānottara-Tantra," 154-156, 188.

19 See Ramaprasad Chandra, *Exploration in Orissa*, ASI Memoirs, no. 44, 12-13, pl. iv.3, captioned "Bhairava, Ratnagiri;" Patna Museum, *Catalogue of Buddhist Sculptures*, 32, captioned "Saptakhasara;" Debala Mitra, "An Image of Sambara in the Patna Museum," *The Orissa Historical Research Journal* 9.3-4 (1960): 43-46; idem, *Ratnagiri*, 426, 429-430. Mitra reports that Sripati Jena, the former *zamindar* of Ratnagiri donated the sculpture in 1929. Shashi Asthana identifies the provenance of the National Museum sculpture as "from Orissa . . . dated to the 11th century." Shashi Asthana, "A Controversial Buddhist Tantrik deity: Trailokya-Vijaya vis-a-vis Sambara," in *History and Culture: B.P. Sinha Felicitation Volume*, ed. Bhagwant Sahai (Delhi, 1987), 168.

20 D. Mitra, *Ratnagiri*, 430; Donaldson, "Buddhist sculpture of Orissa," 372-374.

21 ASI, *Annual Report 1934-35*, 80, 111, pl. XXIV.c; D. Mitra, "Sambara in the Patna Museum," 46.

22 D. Mitra, "Sambara in the Patna Museum," 46.

23 Ibid.

24 Kalff, "Abhidhānottara-Tantra," 181-185. See the cemetery scenes surrounding contemporary (late 12th-early 13th c.) Khara Khoto Saṃvara images, including *maṇḍala* in Piotrovsky, *Lost Empire*, nos. 26, 28, and 29.

25 See S. Huntington, *"Pāla-Sena,"* figs. 136-138.

26 I am indebted to Jacob Kinnard for this information.

27 S. Huntington, *"Pāla-Sena,"* 153, where a history of its discovery by P.C. Mukherji in the "Batsvara" cave is described, with the proviso that Huntington has "seen no record of the specific findspot of the image, which is from Patharghata, but I assume that it is one of the ones collected by Mukherji."

28 Von Schroeder, *Indo-Tibetan Bronzes*, no.73B, captioned, "Saṃvara, Pāla Style, 12th century;" Zwalf, *Buddhism: Art and Faith*, no. 152, captioned, "Saṃvara, Eastern India. 12th century."

29 ASI, New Delhi , neg. 2793/65 (front) and 2794/65 (reverse).

30 For other ca. 12th c. 12-armed metalworks, see the Saṃvara with consort in the Alsdorf collection, illustrated in von Schroeder, *Indo-Tibetan Bronzes*, no. 66c. Von Schroeder mistakenly attributes the piece to the 10th c., which is highly unrealistic on stylistic grounds. Also see Pradapaditya Pal with Stephen Little, *A Collecting Odyssey: Indian, Himalayan, and Southeast Asian Art from the James and Marilynn Alsdorf Collection* (Chicago, The Art Institute of Chicago, 1997), no. 193. Pal and Little designate the sculpture as 12th c. from Bengal. A Saṃvara in the Pan-Asian collection is published in ibid., no. 70D, captioned, "Saṃvara, Pāla style, 12th century." Earlier this image was published by Gilles Béguin as a Tibetan copy of a pre-13th c. Indian example in Béguin, *Dieux et demons*, no. 14; also published in Pratapaditya Pal, "Kashmiri-Style Bronzes and Tantric Buddhism," *Annali dell'Isituto Orientale di Napoli* ns 39 (1979): figs 23-24. Pal describes it as from eastern India, probably Bengal, though no date is suggested. Ibid., 268.

31 National Museum, New Delhi, no. 82.221 (ht. 12 cm.). Asthana, "Controversial Buddhist Tantrik deity," 169, pl. LXX-II.

32 Pal and Meech-Pekarik, *Buddhist Book Illuminations*, 93, illustrated color pl. 19b. Pal mistakes Kālacakra with 8 consorts for Hevajra in pl. 19a.

33 Naudou, *Bouddhistes Kasmiriens*, 156-158, 161-162.

34 See Pal, *Indian Sculpture*, no. 16, captioned, "Kashmir; ninth or tenth century." The late end of the dating spectrum is represented by Béguin, who suggests 11th-12th c. or later. Béguin, *Dieux et démons*, 88, no. 38. Pal has written that "the Kashmiri Sambara is given ten arms, following the *Niṣpannayogāvalī*." Pal, "Kashmiri-Style Bronzes," 268. One of the proper right arms has broken off, which probably misled Pal.

35 Sotheby and Company, *Catalogue of Tibetan, Sino-Tibetan, Nepalese and Indian Art* (London, 1973), no. 189, 77-78.

36 Pal and Meech-Pekarik, *Buddhist Book Illuminations*, 93, color pl. 19b.

37 Gorakshkar and Desai, "An Illustrated Manuscript," pl. V.a; and, Newman, "Vajrayāna Deities," 130, upper.

38 Béguin, *Art ésotérique de l'Himâlaya*, 18-20.

39 For a 13th-14th c. silver twelve-armed Saṃvara embracing his consort, see Alsop, "Metal Sculpture of the Khasa Mallas," fig. 53; for 15th and 16th c. Nepalese metalwork of both forms, see von Schroeder, *Indo-Tibetan Bronzes*, nos. 98D, 98F, 100D, 100E. For Tibetan metalworks of the same or earlier dates, see ibid., nos. 115C, 118F, 128D, 129E. For Nepalese paintings, refer to the extraordinary ca. early 12th c. *maṇḍala* in The Metropolitan Museum of Art, New York, illustrated in Leidy and Thurman, *Maṇḍala*, no. 13; the Ford Saṃvara illustrated in S. and J. Huntington, *Leaves*, no. 92; and the brilliantly colored Nepalese Saṃvara in the Los Angeles County Museum of Art, illustrated in Pal, *Nepal, Where the Gods are Young*, no. 32. Important Tibetan paintings include the 2-armed Saṃvara mural in the Lhakhang Soma of Alchi illustrated in Pal, *Buddhist Paradise*, no. LS16; and the Ford collection's 14th c. Saṃvara *maṇḍala* in Leidy and Thurman, *Maṇḍala*, no. 20. Other early paintings may be found in Rhie and Thurman, *Wisdom and Compassion*, nos. 69-70; and, S. and J. Huntington, *Leaves*, no. 117.

40 Rhie and Thurman, *Wisdom and Compassion*, 215, no. 63. The sculpture is dated to the 12th c. and tentatively identified as Hevajra and Nairātmyā in Pal, *Art of the Himalayas*, no. 53. Another 2-armed Saṃvara sculpture, this one without his consort, was auctioned at Sotheby's, New York, 27 March 1991. It was described as a western Tibetan bronze of the ca. 12/13th c., a reasonable attribution based on the photograph. Sotheby's, *New York, Indian and Southeast Asian Art* (New York, 1991), no. 115.

41 Personal communication, February, 1998.

42 A wooden Saṃvara was recovered by Sir Aurel Stein at Khara Khoto. See Sir Mark Aurel Stein, *Innermost Asia: Detailed report of archaeological explorations in Chinese Turkestan*, 3 vols. (Oxford, 1928), 429-453; idem, *On Ancient Central-Asian Tracks* (London, 1933), 246-251; Fred H. Andrews, *Descriptive Catalogue of Antiquities Recovered by Sir Aurel Stein . . . During His Exploration in Central Asia, Kansu and Eastern Iran* (Delhi, 1935), 246; Amarendra Nath, *Buddhist Images and Narratives* (New Delhi, 1986), 67-73 (misidentified as Trailokyavijaya). The Khara Khoto painting is illustrated in Piotrovsky, *Lost Empire*, no. 27. For the finds in

the Baisikou, see Lei Runze et al, *Xixia Fota* (Beijing: Wenwu Chuban She, 1995), 251.

43 Lei Runze et al, *Xixia Fota*, 183, 253; Piotrovsky, *Lost Empire*, nos. 26, 28, 29.

44 Dunhuang Wenwu Yanjiusuo, *Dunhuang Bihua*, 2: pl. 191.

45 Eugen Pander, "Das Lamaische Pantheon," *Zeitschrift für Ethnologie* 21 (1889): 44-78, fig. 11; Clark, *Two Lamaistic Pantheons*, 80, 90, 93, 233, 234; Raghu Vira and Lokesh Chandra, *A New Tibeto-Mongol Pantheon Part I* (New Delhi, 1961), no. 5.

46 See the xylograph edition of Rolpa Dorje Changkya Hutukhtu, University Chicago Tibetan mss. T-5 no. 20, leaves 21 and 22 (Chinese numbering), as listed in Chang Kun, *Descriptive Account of the Collection of Tibetan Books from the Newberry Library, now in the Far Eastern Library* (Chicago, n.d.); Blanche Christine Olschak with Geshé Thupten Wangyal, *Mystic Art of Ancient Tibet* (London, 1973), icons 61-66; Lohia, *Lalitavajra's Manual*, 106-109.

47 Lessing, *Yong-ho-kung*, 113 and pl. XXV.1.

217. *Andhakārimūrti-Śiva, Salas (Bengal), ca. 11th-12th century, Asutosh Museum, Calcutta*

18

An Iconology of Samvara

In contrast to [endogenous demons] are those demonized others which are depicted as . . . exogenous in terms of a particular religious structure. Surely transgressive, for they embody the alternative values of an alternative structure, they are either exorcised from the dominant structure or conscripted into that structure as tutelary deities. . . . As such, when reeled into the dominant structure, these exogenous mediators can work to reinforce that structure in a variety of ways . . . or they can subvert that structure from the inside as they display the relative nature of the dominant structure along with the individualized merits of a religio/ethical alternative.

Laurie Cozad, "Reeling in the Demon"

Texts dealing with Saṃvara accumulated subsequent to primary Phase Two texts such as the *STTS* and were developed from a Phase Two platform. Makers of Phase Three images accordingly had at their disposal a visual language developed by Phase Two. Therefore it should come as no surprise that Phase Three *krodha-vighnāntaka* images are in many ways the derivatives of earlier images. The connection is particularly marked in relation to Saṃvara and his predecessor Trailokyavijaya, and a structural comparison of the two deities is instructive. Attributes of both strongly parallel Shaivite imagery as well. We will first outline a number of similarities between Trailokyavijaya and Saṃvara and then turn to the meanings implied by the relationship to Śiva.

Samvara and Trailokyavijaya

It has just been shown that Saṃvara images endure in two forms: the four-headed twelve-armed form and the single-headed two-armed form. Trailokyavijaya, Saṃvara's Phase Two model, also takes one of two forms: the four-headed eight-armed form or the single-headed two-armed form. The two-armed forms of Saṃvara and Trailokyavijaya bear special comparison. Both Saṃvara types make a two-handed gesture which is very similar to Trailokyavijaya's namesake *mudrā*. The posture of Saṃvara is the mirror-image of Trailokyavijaya, and both trample Śiva and his consort. The two *krodha-vighnāntaka* are *vira*-Yakṣa, wrathful but not grotesque. Both are considered emanations of Akṣobhya, though in the time of Saṃvara the association became more important as Akṣobhya became central to Phase Three.

The similarities between Trailokyavijaya and Saṃvara have consistently led to confusion. The risk of misidentification is particularly acute when Saṃvara is without his consort, for Trailokyavijaya is invariably depicted alone.[1] Shashi Asthana was confronted with the issue when she encountered two images of Saṃvara which had been identified as Trailokyavijaya.[2] Some of the differences are so subtle, however, that though Asthana corrected the misidentification, even she does not distinguish between the *mudrā* made by Trailokyavijaya, in which the palms are turned outward, and that of Saṃvara, in which the palms are consistently turned in.

The similarity between Saṃvara and Trailokyavijaya figures into Marie-Thérèse de Mallmann's treatment of Trailokyavijaya.[3] She feels that Trailokyavijaya is, like Saṃvara, a form of Heruka, but ultimately she decides against classifying Trailokyavijaya as Heruka because he is never described as such in texts. She instead assumes the two are no more than coevals. Our clearer conception of the historical development of the wrathful deities helps us to understand why the names of related Phase Two and Phase Three *krodha-vighnāntaka* are not used interchangeably in Phase Two texts. Saṃvara belongs to a later stage of development, but that does not preclude his historical connection with a Phase Two deity. De Mallmann's insight into the connection between them should not be ignored.

Hiram W. Woodward Jr. also notes the relationship between Trailokyavijaya and later Phase Three wrathful deities. He sees the connection more in terms of Hevajra but holds a clearer picture of the context. He observes:

> *Trailokyavijaya, the quintessential vajra-family krodha, gave birth to new divinities - Heruka, Hevajra, Saṃvara, and others - who became so important as high patron deities that they were almost never classified as mere krodhas. . . . Once it is understood that Trailokyavijaya is the historical predecessor of Hevajra and his equivalents, however, the relationship can be seen in proper perspective. . . . The Hevajra-tantra, in which Hevajra is a supreme divinity . . . represents a development later than that of Shingon Buddhism . . . Both Hevajra's appearance and his importance, however, would be inexplicable had he not usurped the place and incorporated the qualities of the vajra-family krodha Trailokyavijaya.*[4]

Woodward has understood and articulated the situation more precisely than anyone previously. The only refinements of his position I might suggest is that the Phase Three *krodha-vighnāntaka* have somewhat broader roots in Phase Two *krodha-vighnāntaka* imagery as a whole, and not with Trailokyavijaya alone. The specific formal and doctrinal links between Saṃvara and Trailokyavijaya are more direct than those between Hevajra and Trailokyavijaya. Though sharing much with Trailokyavijaya, Hevajra stands on the "Four Māras" rather than a form of Śiva and consort. In standard Hevajra images the number of arms, heads and legs far outnumber those of Saṃvara and Trailokyavijaya, so that the correspondence with Trailokyavijaya is not obvious.

As de Mallmann points out, texts discussing Trailokyavijaya do not offer explicit affirmations of his identification with Saṃvara. There is a simple explanation for this. No such affirmation could exist, for Phase Two texts could not prophesy Trailokyavijaya would be reincarnated as Saṃvara. Phase Three texts naturally also do not conceive of or discuss Saṃvara's antecedents in the ways we do. However, one Phase Three text does offer convincing evidence of the relationship between the two *krodha-vighnāntaka*.

218. Saṃvara, painting on palm leaf, Eastern India, ca. 12th century, British Library

A passage of the *ST* directs the yogin to take on the form of the two-armed Saṃvara-Heruka and then to recite the following *dhāraṇī*: "*Om śumbha niśumbha hūṃ hūṃ phaṭ*."[5] We have demonstrated the close association between Śumbha and Niśumbha and Trailokyavijaya in the *STTS*. There Mahāvairocana pronounces Trailokyavijaya's secret *dhāraṇī*: "*Om śumbha niśumbha hūṃ gṛhṇa gṛhṇa . . . bhagavan vajra hūṃ phaṭ*,"[6] followed by a shortened version, "*Om niśumbha vajra hūṃ phaṭ*."[7] We proposed that these two demon-enemies of Śiva and his consort were actually depicted on a stone image of Trailokyavijaya from Nalanda. [**167-168**] They appear there as Trailokyavijaya's assistants, and the *ST* instructs the yogin (as Saṃvara) to call on them, as Trailokyavijaya does in the *STTS*.

Saṃvara has come to supplant Trailokyavijaya as the master of Śumbha and Niśumbha, or Trailokyavijaya has been transformed into Saṃvara. There is an image of Saṃvara which seems to combine the attributes of both Saṃvara and Trailokyavijaya, perhaps reflecting a consciousness of their fusing. The image is in an *Aṣṭasāhasrikā Prajñāpāramitā* illuminated manuscript in the British Library [**218**]; its painting of Hevajra was mentioned earlier.[8] The eighteen illuminations are equally divided among male and female deities who are once again exclusively paired: Buddha with Prajñāpāramitā, four pacific male bodhisattva with four female bodhisattva, Hevajra with Nairātmyā, and so forth. Saṃvara is paired with Vajravārāhī, who makes his identification conclusive. Saṃvara makes his usual *vajrahūṃkāra mudrā* with palms facing in. Like Trailokyavijaya, he stands in *pratyālīḍha* instead of *ālīḍha* and has only eight instead of twelve arms. The hands which hold identifiable objects include the sword held in the upper right hand and a bow in one of the left hands. Comparison with intact Trailokyavijaya images (e.g., **162**) demonstrate how closely the illumination of Saṃvara corresponds to Trailokyavijaya's standard eight-armed form standing in *pratyālīḍha* and holding a sword and bow in oppposite hands. It would appear that in this instance the artists were affirming, consciously or not, the common structural identity of Trailokyavijaya and Saṃvara.

Composite images of the two deities, together with the similarities between their iconography (conquering forms of Śiva), form (*vīra*-Yakṣa, *mudrā*, *āsana*) and *dhāraṇī*, constitute considerable evidence that Saṃvara is a Phase Three reformulation of Trailokyavijaya. The historical picture provides additional evidence which, though insufficient by itself, is nevertheless consistent with my hypothesis. Phase Two imagery wanes just as Phase Three imagery emerges. Hayagrīva and Bhūtaḍāmara are adopted into Phase Three imagery as virtually unchanged Dharmapāla, while Yamāntaka is transformed into Yamāri and Vajrabhairava. Yet Trailokyavijaya, arguably the most important Phase Two *krodha-vighnāntaka*, seems to nearly disappear during Phase Three. Why? I maintain it is because he is subsumed into the character of Saṃvara. Once Saṃvara appears, there is no need for Trailokyavijaya, for Saṃvara embodies Trailokyavijaya's essential image and role.

The essential connection between Saṃvara and Trailokyavijaya is their common relationship with Shaivite imagery. Trailokyavijaya's name, form and function were all affected at a deep level by forms of Śiva, notably Tripurāntaka and Andhakamūrti. Trailokyavijaya resembles the Śiva under his foot, creating a visible metaphor of the destruction of the poisons and the enlightened state which is thereby induced. Śiva and Trailokyavijaya are yoked together in one image to represent simultaneously two stages on the path to enlightenment. Subtle clues embedded in the images themselves are the sturdiest props to the thesis. If Trailokyavijaya was indeed reshaped in Phase Three Esoteric Buddhism, one would expect to find his principal aspects at the core of Saṃvara imagery, naturally recast in Phase Three terms.

Phase Three was in many ways more overt about its beliefs and practices than was Phase One or Two. The directness of Phase Three texts is particularly obvious in its use of symbols simultaneously unabashed and abstract. The symbolism ostensibly is explained in the primary texts themselves, as interpretations are not left to commentaries.[9] Phase One *krodha-vighnāntaka* were concentrated on mostly physical obstacles, such as demons who cause sickness. Phase Two *krodha-vighnāntaka* began to assist in the destruction of internal obstacles to enlightenment, and this focus climaxes during Phase Three. For the symbolic transformation of poison into antidote, the shadow of Śiva cast by Saṃvara was bolder and darker than was Trailokyavijaya's.

Samvara and Siva

Before comparing the image of Saṃvara to Hindu images of Śiva, the similarity between Bhairava portrayed under the foot of Saṃvara and Hindu depictions of Bhairava is worth pointing out. The Ratnagiri and Kashmiri sculptures of Saṃvara **[198-202, 211]** provide the clearest images of the trampled Bhairava for comparison with the eleventh-century sculpture of Bhairava from Bihar. **[118-119]** The trampled Bhairava is four-armed, he wears a prominent garland of heads and invariably holds the *triśūla*, perhaps his most important emblem. In the case of the Ratnagiri sculptures he also holds a skull-cup. The same *āyudha* (*triśūla*, skull-cup and garland of skulls) appear also in two- and four-armed Bhairava sculptures, which also carry a chopper or sword and have the same kind of high-piled hair and large circular earrings.

If we now closely compare the Saṃvara images with the trampled Bhairava, it is clear that the artist intended legible correspondence. The garland worn by the Kashmiri Bhairava **[211]** is reproduced on the larger Saṃvara down to the most particular details of the pattern. The Ratnagiri Bhairava sculptures hold the drum and skull-cup in the left and right hands respectively. Saṃvara holds them in precisely the opposite hands. The *triśūla* and the head of Brahma are also traits of Śiva carried by Saṃvara, who is Śiva in a transformed and more powerful form.

Yet Saṃvara is also Chāmuṇḍā, or Kālarātri, who is crushed beneath his other foot. She too wears the garland of heads, and she too holds a *triśūla* and chopper. Fuller images of Chāmuṇḍā share a number of striking traits with Saṃvara images. She also holds an elephant skin above her head and carries a severed head, along with the *triśūla*, skull-cup and drum.[10] As already noted, Kālarātri sometimes caresses Saṃvara with cupped hand **[211-212]**, the same way Umādevā touches Trailokyavijaya. **[162]**

219. *Andhakārimūrti-Śiva, Salas (Bengal), ca. 11th-12th century, Asutosh Museum, Calcutta, detail of* **217**

220. *Bhairava, Bairhatta (Bengal), second half of 12th century, Indian Museum, Calcutta*

Connections run simultaneously between Saṃvara and the deities he subjugates, between Saṃvara and Trailokyavijaya, and between the deities subjugated by Saṃvara and those by Trailokyavijaya. But it is necessary to examine a few important images of Śiva to see just how closely Saṃvara's iconography is linked to that of Śiva.

A ca. eleventh or twelfth-century sculpture in the Asutosh Museum [**219**], like the Śiva from the Konch Mandir [**166-169**], depicts Andhakārimūrti, the form of Śiva who destroys the demon Andhaka with his *triśūla*. Andhakārimūrti is *urdhaliṅga* and ten-armed, that is, he has two more arms than Trailokyavijaya and two less than Saṃvara. At first glance there are a number of similarities to Trailokyavijaya. Comparison with the Bodh Gaya sculpture [**162**] is quite arresting. The posture, the position of the sword, the arrow pulled from a quiver (on the proper right of Śiva's head in **219**), the bow, a shield instead of a wheel and a snake instead of a noose comprise a catalogue of similarities. The drum and chopper in the proper right hands of Śiva are more closely linked to Saṃvara, as is the prominence of the *triśūla*, which for Saṃvara becomes the *khatvāṅga*, held on the reverse side and in the opposite direction. The images to either side of Śiva are also interesting. They resemble the *vāmana*-Yakṣa Bhairava and Kālarātri under Saṃvara's feet. One can see the creators of Trailokyavijaya or Saṃvara drawing on such an image, though of course Trailokyavijaya's images were made considerably earlier, while the Śiva [**219**] and Saṃvara examples [**198-211**] are contemporaries.

A Bhairava sculpture in the Indian Museum, Calcutta also pertains to the discussion.[11] [**220**] This stunning piece of sculpture transforms Bhairava's frequently ponderous stance into the light dance of Heruka and Natarāja images. He carries a combination of *āyudha* belonging properly to Bhairava (the *triśūla* and skull-cup) and those of Andhakamūrti (sword, shield, bow and arrow and snake).[12] [**166**, **219**] A crescent moon adorns his high chignon, a feature echoed by Saṃvara. As are some Saṃvara images from eastern India [**203-205**], Bhairava is accompanied by his eight consorts, the Sapta-Mātṛkā (Seven Mothers) plus one.[13] Among these eight is Chāmuṇḍā. Each is four-armed and carries a *khatvāṅga* and skull-cup, but the other attributes vary. Comparison with the Saṃvara surrounded by his consorts from Bengal is revealing. [**203**] Yet given that these images are contemporaneous and that the Phase Three texts go back two centuries earlier, it is difficult to dismiss such images as merely Buddhist copies of Śiva images. The interchange was surely mutual.[14] Regardless, there is no question that Śiva, Saṃvara and Heruka images share a common vocabulary.

One of Saṃvara's distinguishing attributes is the elephant skin he holds over his head like a trophy. This too is shared with Śiva. Gajāsuramūrti-Śiva is the form of Śiva most closely associated with the elephant skin. Having defeated this prideful demon in the form of an elephant:

> *Gajāsura prayed to Śiva and asked to make the elephant skin his garment and to assume the name of Kṛttivāsa (one who has a skin for a garment, an elephant skin in this case) for himself. Śiva, pleased with him, granted both wishes.*[15]

Gajāsuramūrti-Śiva also often holds the elephant skin aloft in the manner of Saṃvara. The elephant skin is also related to the story of Andhakāsura, and thus images of Andhakamūrti sometimes include the elephant skin.[16]

221. *Bhairava, Balurghat (Bengal), ca. 11th-12th century, Indian Museum, Calcutta*

A final Śiva image is another syncretic form of Bhairava, one in which the elephant skin is prominent. [**221**] Bhairava is twelve-armed like Saṃvara. He carries the elephant skin as a garment so that the head of the elephant is just visible above his own. There is a crescent moon in his hair, and he holds a severed head, along with a skull-tipped *daṇḍa* and *aṅkuśa*-hook, a sword, shield, chopper, skull-cup and a snake. The *āyudha* that overlap with those of Saṃvara are too numerous to be only coincidental: elephant skin, crescent in hair, skull cup, chopper, severed head, club with skull-finial, skull crown and garland of skulls.

The Buddhist interpretation of "Shaivite" Samvara imagery

It will take a specialized study to elucidate the exact set of relationships among Śiva's various forms and those of Trailokyavijaya and particularly Saṃvara. It is not possible for me to pursue this topic beyond a few obvious correspondences. Fortunately, we know how these features, which were clearly related to Shaivite imagery, were understood by a few prominent practitioners of Phase Three Esoteric Buddhism. These scholars include Śūraṅgavajra, the pre-twelfth century author of a Sanskrit commentary on the *Abhidhānottara-tantra*, and two Tibetans, Buton Rinpoche (1290-1364), the renowned exegete, and Phagpa (1235-1280), the powerful Sakya hierarch known for his role in Yuan China.

Śūraṅgavajra understood the symbolism of Saṃvara with his consort Vajravārāhī within a dual framework of conventional Mahāyāna and Phase Three inner yoga. On the one hand the trampling of Bhairava and Kālarātrī represents the overcoming of the duality of *saṁsāra* and *nirvāṇa*. But from the yogic perspective, Saṃvara's four heads, for example, refer to the inner channels related to the four elements, while the trampling of Bhairava and Kālarātrī "represents the blocking of the veins of the two lower orifices."[17] Any sectarian antagonism is thoroughly masked by such an interpretation.

Buton's more extensive explication, for which I am dependent on Kalff's translation and discussion, assumes a mythic tone reminiscent of the *STTS*'s account of the taming of Maheśvara. According to Buton, the gods who worshipped Maheśvara engage in acts of excessive desire, hatred and ignorance. Vajradhara manifests himself as Cakrasaṃvara, who tramples and subdues Bhairava and Kālarātrī. But this method of "taming" is given a very non-sectarian interpretation. The "subduing of the body" is accomplished by Saṃvara, "having changed into (deities) similar in name and external appearance (as those to be tamed)" and trampling them under foot. The subjugation speech is similarly accomplished by changing the *mantras* of the gods into Buddhist *mantras* by inserting them between familiar syllables of *OṂ* and *Hūṃ Hūṃ Phaṭ*. The conquering of the mind "consists in causing it to expire (lit. faint) into the competely non-conceptual sphere."[18] The bone ornaments, the *āyudha* and other possessions are taken from Bhairava and enjoyed by the other gods. Finally, the subjugation of Bhairava and Kālarātrī is a matter of the "absorbing of their life-force" and:

> *the perfection of the complete purification and abandoning of their obscurations. The absorbing of their mind consists in the perfection of fusing the mind with the clear light and then realizing (its) emergence in the pairwise union (yuganaddha).*[19]

Phagpa also compiled interpretations of Saṃvara's iconography.[20] In his work we find Buddhist explanations for many of the *āyudha* which various forms of Śiva and Kālarātri/Chāmuṇḍā hold. Besides the obvious Phase Three Esoteric Buddhist symbols of *vajra*, bell and the embrace of the consort, we find that the elephant hide refers to tearing away the veil of ignorance or illusion. The drum evokes a joyous, resounding voice; the axe a cutting off of the roots of birth and death; the dagger the destruction of pride and the six poisons. The *triśūla* is a sign of overcoming the triple world. The *khatvāṅga* represents the *bodhicitta*, an interpretation we already encounted for Hevajra and Heruka. The skull-cup signifies discrimination between existence and nonexistence while the noose refers to tying off the living nature of beings. Brahma, the "creator god," is the Hindu personification of the creation of life. In holding Brahma's severed head, Saṃvara proclaims all delusions, all the illusions of *saṁsāra* have been cut off. Saṃvara's long hair is tied up on top of his head like a yogin to signify his meritorious accomplishments, presumably through yogic *tapa*s. The lunar crescent shows that the *bodhicitta* grows like the waxing moon; it is surmounted by the *viśvavajra* (pointing in the four directions) to demonstrate that Saṃvara's actions move in all directions to help all people.

Phagpa also offers a symbolic interpretation of Bhairava and Kālarātri. Kālarātri ("Night of Time") represents the extreme position of *nirvāṇa*, while Bhairava represents the extreme position of *saṁsāra*. Saṃvara thus in typical Buddhist fashion avoids either extreme.

> *Indicating that through his great compassion he remains in the realm of living beings, with his outstretched right foot he treads on the supine figure of the Night of Time (who represents) the extremity of nirvāṇa. She is red and emaciated and holds a sacrificial knife and a skull cup. Indicating that through his great wisdom he holds neither to the idea of a person nor of any real element, with his left foot which is drawn back he treads face-downward the figure of Bhairava (who represents) the extremity of saṁsāra.*[21]

It would seem that the Tibetan scholastics of the thirteenth century have been as faithful to eastern Indian Saṃvara teachings as thirteenth and fourteenth century Tibetan artists were to eastern Indian iconographic models. Phagpa's interpretation is surely related to Śuraṅgavajra's and not a Tibetan invention. It seems likely that the eastern Indian artists had these or similar values in mind when they drew on the symbolic forms which were available to them. Yogic and Shaivite symbols were part of the hybrid religious culture in which the formulators of Phase Three Esoteric Buddhism in eastern India participated. Using principles of inversion, they transformed Śiva's symbols into Buddhist ones. Śiva's *triśūla*, a scepter signifying his lordship over the three worlds, is inverted literally in some images of Saṃvara. **[208]** More commonly the *triśūla* is changed into the *khatvāṅga*, retaining the three skulls and fusing the points of the *triśūla* into a *vajra* finial. **[203, 213, 214]**

Bhairava-Śiva cut off Brahma's heads because Brahma addressed him haughtily and insulted his dignity.[22] Bhairava performs penance for his patricide, but the Buddhists take this well-known example of Śiva's impulsive and prideful behavior to represent Saṃvara cutting off creation itself, an action with connotations on philosophical, meditational and inner-yoga levels. A twentieth-century Tibetan master, the late Chögyam Trungpa Rinpoche, describes the symbolism:

> *In the tantric tradition, ego or confusion or ignorance is personified as Rudra [i.e., Śiva]. All the tantric traditions of Buddhism are concerned with the taming of Rudra, the Rudra of ego.*[23]

The undisguised nature of Shaivite elements in Saṃvara imagery recalls the explicit content of Phase Three texts. Like the other symbolic modes within Phase

Three Esoteric Buddhism, the superimposition of Saṃvara onto the image of Śiva involves levels of symbolism we cannot hope to explicate but only to recognize. A passage in Tāranātha's seventeenth-century description of the life of the Mahāsiddha Krishnācārya documents the sectarian rivalry between Indian followers of Saṃvara and Śiva. The conflict is resolved with the determination that "Maheśvara and the goddess Umā had been transformed into Śrī Heruka [i.e., Saṃvara], who had indeed crushed them."[24]

I am not qualified to assert that the living tradition of Tibetan scholarship and religious practice has never sustained a sectarian-rivalry interpretation of the Buddhist Saṃvara's humiliation of the Hindu Bhairava. However, in an admittedly token attempt to compare my outsider's findings with contemporary insiders' understanding, I took my questions to a Tibetan scholar. In Dharmasala, on 20 June 1990, I had the good fortune to interview the impressively learned and equally kind Tibetan Lama, Kirti Tsenshap Rinpoche.[25] He explained that Saṃvara holding the elephant skin represents overcoming the mind's graspingness and the tenacious belief in the reality of things. Śiva underfoot is by no means to be thought of as a figure dragged in from another religion to be humiliated. Both Saṃvara and Śiva are to be recognized as enlightened beings. Bewilderment and attachment, the basis of transmigration, must be overcome through wisdom and *upāya*. Wisdom is represented by Saṃvara's right leg (trampling on the female) and *upāya* (compassionate means) by the left leg, which together overcome great desire, ignorance and attachment.

The discussion then turned to the relationship of Trailokyavijaya and Saṃvara. After consulting texts, the Rinpoche concluded that though the names are different, Trailokyavijaya and Saṃvara carry the same meaning. In his interpretation, deities like Trailokyavijaya are for aspirants with lesser capacity, while deities like Saṃvara are for those of sharper faculties. The two types of deities are not understood as having developed temporally, one after the other; they are considered to have appeared simultaneously and are ranked on the basis of profundity and subtlety. For the Rinpoche, there lies the only difference between Trailokyavijaya and Saṃvara. While the Rinpoche does not "represent" the Tibetan understanding *in toto*, his expressed opinion does suggest that for at least some living Tibetans, the underlying meaning is more important than the superficial (if overt) Indian sectarian symbolism, and that the hieratic ranking of the deities is emphasized more than their historical relationship.

We may conclude that Trailokyavijaya and Saṃvara are linked across the lines of a historical development from Phase Two to Phase Three. Saṃvara shares many of the functions with which Trailokyavijaya was charged earlier, and his links with Shaivite imagery are equally determinative and complex. We have seen that in Trailokyavijaya images the trampled Maheśvara symbolizes the transformation of the self. The identification of the "corpse" in Phase Three images of Heruka with the yogin's unenlightened self can be used to decode the presence of Bhairava and Kālarātri beneath Saṃvara's feet. Kalff similarly concludes that "The taming of Bhairava and Kālarātrī by Saṃvara and Vajravārāhī becomes in that sense also the model for the taming of the practitioner's own defilements."[26] Our analysis of the structure of Saṃvara's iconography confirms that there is a strong continuity of symbolic language between Phases Two and Three. The main difference between the two stages is that the processes symbolized by the subjugated forms of Śiva are expressed more forcefully in Phase Three in order to indicate the increased centrality of *krodha-vighnāntaka* in the system as a whole.

Conclusions

In tracking the careers of a trio of Phase Three *krodha-vighnāntaka*, we have watched them fulfill the developmental trajectory begun in Phase One. Throughout Phase Two the wrathful deities are brought ever higher, rising to a paramount position during Phase Three in the system as a whole and in its concrete expressions, shrines and *maṇḍala*. No doubt there are a host of factors to explain this development. One has to do with the Phase Three conception of enlightenment and the obstacles to enlightenment. The *HT* explains the basis for Phase Three enlightenment in terms which draw on Mahāyāna philosophy:

> *The six faculties of sense, their six spheres of operation, the five skandhas and the five elements are pure in essence, but* they are obstructed by ignorance *[avidyā]* and emotional disturbance *(kleśa). Their purification consists in self-experience, and by no other means of purification may one be released. This self-experiencing, this supreme bliss, arises from the pure condition of the sense-spheres. Form and so on, and whatever other sense-spheres there are, all these appear to the yogin in their purified condition, for of Buddha-nature is this world.*[27]

Since all the faculties and elements are pure in essence, only the obstructions of *avidyā* and *kleśa* intervene between the experience of *saṁsāra* and the experience of *nirvāṇa*. The *krodha-vighnāntaka* symbolizes the critical work of the elimination of these barriers to induce realization. This is no different in essence from the Phase Two understanding of the *krodha-vighnāntaka*, nor even, ultimately, from that of Phase One. The objectification of *avidyā* and *kleśa* as demons in Phase One Esoteric Buddhism demanded a similar relative/mundane conception of the *krodha-vighnāntaka* and his task of subjugation. Beginning in Phase Two and culminating in Phase Three, the objectified mythological stock of the *krodha-vighnāntaka* was transformed. The process was internalized so that, as the above passage from the *HT* explains, the process was self-experience, not other-directed. *Kleśa* and *avidyā* are experienced by Phase Three practitioners also as pure.

The *krodha-vighnāntaka* emblematize the transformation of consciousness, the turning of what Snellgrove calls the "psychophysical switch,"[28] since they take on the qualities of ignorance, anger and passion in order to conquer them. From the beginning, the early *krodha-vighnāntaka* echo the formal appearance of the Yakṣa-demons they overcome. Phase One Yamāntaka looks at times like a reluctant oath-bound Yakṣa. Trailokyavijaya picks up the same *āyudha* that Maheśvara lays down. Saṃvara does the same in a Phase Three context. The formal similarities between the *krodha-vighnāntaka*, who symbolize the destruction of obstacles to enlightenment, and their foes, the symbols of those obstructions, is a perfect embodiment of the central Esoteric Buddhist experience: *saṁsāra* and *nirvāṇa* are "not two."

Notes to Chapter Eighteen

1 The exception to this general rule occurs in late Tibetan contexts, where he is a tertiary guardian figure in Phase Three *maṇḍala*, such as the Ṣaṭchakravartī *maṇḍala*. See B. Bhattacharyya, *Niṣpannayogāvalī*, 75, where Vajrahūṃkāra is accompanied by Surābhakṣi. The epigraph for this chapter comes from Laurie Cozad, "Reeling in the Demon: An Exploration into the Category of the Demonized Other as Portrayed in *The Journey to the West*," *Journal of the American Academy of Religion* 66, no. 1 (1998): 120.

2 Asthana, "Controversial Buddhist Tantrik deity," 167-172.

3 De Mallmann, *Introduction a l'iconographie*, 381.

4 Woodward, "Tantric Buddhism at Angkor Thom," 60.

5 Tsuda, *Saṁvarodaya-tantra*, 281, XIII.3.

6 T.18.882.370b-c.

7 T.18.882.371b.

8 British Library, London, Or.14282, 110r, published in Losty, "Bengal, Bihar, Nepal?," part one, fig. 6, lower. Losty suggest a date of ca. 1130 and places the provenance as Vikramaśila monastery, between modern Bihar and Bengal, but with a greater Bengali stylistic character. Losty's identifications are fairly accurate, except that the figure is identified as Mahākāla, and Hevajra is mentioned as a possibility in a footnote. He also identifies the Saṃvara figure as Mahākāla, and then acknowledges this as problematic in footnote 21.

9 Refer to passages of the *HT* quoted above in which the symbolism of colors, jewelry, etc. is explicated.

10 Note the 12th c. Chāmuṇḍā from Daharol, Dinajpur District of West Bengal, in the Asutosh Museum, Calcutta, no. 407.5084; two late Chāmuṇḍā images in the same museum, nos. 489.5866 and T.3263; the Chāmuṇḍā from Dharmasala, Cuttack District of Orissa, no. AY66 in the Orissa State Museum, Bhubaneswar; and a Chāmuṇḍā image in the Bharat Kala Bhavan, no. 199.

11 Published by Claudine Bautze-Picron, "Bhairava et les Mères au Bengale septentrional," *Arts Asiatiques* 45 (1990): 61-66. She dates it to the second half of the 11th c., largely on the grounds of the form of the inscription on the socle, which mentions Bhairava by name.

12 Syncretic forms of Śiva joining Gajāsura, Andhaka and Bhairava Śiva are mentioned in Goswami, "Ugra-Mūrtis of Śiva," 103.

13 For identification, see Bautze-Picron, "Bhairava et les Mères," 64-64.

14 B. Bhattacharyya argues strongly for the dependence of later Hindu "tantric" imagery on earlier Esoteric Buddhist imagery, in Benoytosh Bhattacharyya, "The Cult of Bhūtaḍāmara," *Proceedings and Transactions of the 6th All India Conference, Patna, Dec. 1930* (Patna, 1933): 349-370; and idem, "Buddhist Deities in Hindu Garb," *Proceedings and Transactions of the Fifth All Indian Oriental Conference* (Lahore, 1930): 1277-1298. It seems that his points, which unfortunately are embedded in a clearly prejudicial presentation, have been largely ignored. It may be time for a specialist in eastern Indian art to reconsider this topic.

15 Goswami, "Ugra-Mūrtis of Śiva," 107-108.

16 Note the ca. 10th c. over-lifesize Gajāsuramūrti from Puri now in the Indian Museum, Calcutta, no. A241278/NS3363; and Chola 9th c. Gajāsuramūrti in the Cleveland Museum published in Kramrisch, *Manifestations of Śiva*, no. 39. Also see Gayatri Akhouri, *Śaivism in Ancient Bihar* (Patna, 1988), 170-171; Goswami, "Ugra-Mūrtis of Śiva," 108-109; and the ca. 11th c. Andhakāsuramūrti in the Bharat Kala Bhavan, Benares, no. 172.

17 Kalff, "Abhidhānottara-Tantra," 125, 140.

18 Ibid., 73.

19 Ibid. Also see the discussion on ibid., 67-76.

20 Translated in Dawa-Samdup, *Shrichakrasambhāra Tantra*, 1-68, with the section pertinent to our discussion on 21-29. A revised translation is in Snellgrove, *Indo-Tibetan Buddhism*, 154-155. For the confirmed attribution to Phagpa, see David Reigle, "New Preface, 1984," in Kazi Dawa-Samdup, *Shrichakrasambhāra Tantra: A Buddhist Tantra*, reprint ed. (Talent, 1984), i-iii.

21 Snellgrove, *Indo-Tibetan Buddhism*, 154.

22 Goswami, "Ugra-Mūrtis of Śiva," 115-118.

23 Herbert V. Guenther and Chögyam Trungpa, *The Dawn of Tantra* (Berkeley, 1974), 8.

24 David Templeman, trans., *Tāranātha's Life of Krsnācārya/Kānha* (Dharamsala, 1989), 36.

25 I am indebted to Dr. Gareth Sparham for sharing his deep knowledge of the Tibetan language, Tibetan Buddhist texts and scholars; for arranging meetings with several Tibetan scholars; and for acting as interpreter for my unusual and specific questions.

26 Kalff, "Abhidhānottara-Tantra," 143.

27 Snellgrove, *Indo-Tibetan Buddhism*, 125 (emphasis added).

28 Ibid., 123.

Afterword

1 Historical Models of Esoteric Buddhism

This study of wrathful deities in Esoteric Buddhist art has been necessarily also a history of Esoteric Buddhism itself. To understand the wrathful deities, one must view their place in Esoteric Buddhism. In a circular manner, however, the study of the *krodha-vighnāntaka* has proved to be an instrument by which a certain meaningful order may be imposed upon a heterogenous mix of historical materials (archaeological, artistic and textual) and living traditions, which shape our views of the movement as a whole. The study graphically demonstrates the growing importance of the *krodha-vighnāntaka* in Esoteric Buddhism. The wrathful deity theme acts as an instructive yardstick for measuring change in doctrinal development.

In the context of the study of Esoteric Buddhism, the scrutiny of Esoteric Buddhism under the light cast by the *krodha-vighnāntaka* theme has been productive mainly because the wrathful deities have not been utilized to this extent in previous studies. Without doubt this study has benefited tremendously from prior scholarship, some of which concerns individual wrathful deities. Japanese secondary sources have admittedly been underutilized, and there is no question that the results of ongoing investigations of East Asian Esoteric Buddhism will clarify and extend the understanding of the situation in Tibet and India as well. Yet this attempt yielded its fruit mainly because the trans-cultural field as it is most broadly conceived has been left fallow for so long.

There have, of course, been other more learned and in some ways more inclusive models of the development of Esoteric Buddhism. The primary studies are oriented much more toward philosophical doctrines gleaned from texts with debatable degrees of intelligibility. Such scholarship has been keyed fundamentally to texts. Systems for classifying texts are accepted almost axiomatically as developmental models for Esoteric Buddhism itself. The present study has tried to widen the focus beyond texts to incorporate a segment of the visible expressions of ideas, including those which may or may not have been afforded importance in written texts as well.

Limiting the scope of inquiry to wrathful deities in all periods of Esoteric Buddhist art is like digging a trial trench at an archaeological site. The aim is to reveal the stratigraphy of successive stages of development. Until the entire site is uncovered there is no way of knowing whether the trench is representative. Once dug, however, the findings may be calibrated with other trenches repeatedly sunk, as it were, into the library of the site. It is thus necessary to compare the stratigraphy of my narrow trench with the results of analyses made using different criteria.

1.1 Comparison with Snellgrove's Model and the Relationship between Mahāyāna and Early Esoteric Buddhism

Krodha-vighnāntaka images resolve into three stages, each of which can be tied to broader developments in Esoteric Buddhism. How do these stages compare with other models? One attempt at broad classification is found in the works of David Snellgrove, on which I have relied heavily. Better than anyone, Snellgrove fulfills the commonly shared intention of modern scholarship to approach the subject of conflicting Esoteric Buddhist texts from an historical viewpoint.[1] A historical approach is in contradistinction to scholars working within the tradition, who regard all such texts as timeless expressions of truth and consequently arrange them on the basis of Buddhistic function, or correlate them to the various abilities of aspirants along a scale of graduated value. Snellgrove divides Esoteric Buddhist texts into those which correspond in outlook and practice to Mahāyāna Buddhism and those which present a distinct attitude.[2] The classification I have proposed as Phase One, comprised of wrathful deities as attendants to bodhisattva, closely dovetails with Snellgrove's mixed Mahāyāna-Esoteric Buddhism and confirms his judgement that there is considerable overlap during the earliest era of Esoteric Buddhism. The point is of some importance. As was discussed in Section One, there is presently a tendency among some scholars to separate Mahāyāna from Esoteric Buddhism at an early stage and also to project the origins of Esoteric Buddhism back to a very early date.

Mahāyāna Buddhism, into which the *krodha-vighnāntaka* were first born, may be characterized as a religion focusing on the accumulation of merit through acts done for the benefit of all sentient beings. The *Lotus Sūtra* recommends the propagation of itself and the creation of images of the Buddha as the most effective means to develop a fund of merit. In ritual practice this involves the offering of flowers, lamps, incense and the "seven treasures"[3] to the Buddhas, bodhisattva and their images. Devotion is considered to serve Buddhist ends. Abhayamitra, a monk of the late fifth century, for example, "caused to be made for worship" at least three standing Buddha figures at Sarnath, and in one inscription he calls himself "a monk with mind subdued through devotion."[4] Early (or Phase One) Esoteric Buddhism continued in this vein by encouraging rituals, image-making and devotion to particular forms of the Buddhas and bodhisattva.

Phase One *krodha-vighnāntaka* attend the same bodhisattva who are prominent in cultic Mahāyāna. Images of these bodhisattva, which include attendant *krodha-vighnāntaka*, seem to have provided the focus for devotions. This in itself is consonant with Mahāyāna cult practice, and, other than the use of *mantra* and *dhāraṇī*, there is very little additional evidence of exclusively Esoteric Buddhist intentions or practices. The early *krodha-vighnāntaka* personify the attributes and powers of the bodhisattva and are dependent on the bodhisattva with whom they are associated. Certain of the *krodha-vighnāntaka*, like Hayagrīva and Yamāntaka, are of more ancient origin, descended from Vedic and chthonic spirits, demons or gods. While one can distinguish philosophical *pāramitā* Mahāyāna from cultic Mahāyāna, at the stage of early Phase One imagery it is premature to distinguish Esoteric Buddhism from cultic Mahāyāna. The blurred line between Mahāyāna and Phase One Esoteric Buddhism continues throughout the medieval period in India until the destruction of the Buddhist establishments.

The most substantial doctrinal and ritual shift occurs between Phase One and the combination of Phases Two and Three. The transformation manifests visibly in the treatment of the *krodha-vighnāntaka*. We can point to a rather sharp dividing line between Phase One subsidiary *krodha-vighnāntaka* and the independent deities of Phases Two and Three. The division represents an altered attitude, which, without rejecting the Mahāyāna method of the accumulation of merit, considers it a method unnecessarily limiting and sluggish. The new intention instead was to swiftly cut through the bonds of *karma*, *kleśa*, *avidyā* and *saṁsāra* that keep one revolving in unenlightened habits of mind, rather than merely to outgrow them gradually through the accumulation of merit.

The concept of an inner power to cut through these obstructions is at the heart of the rising status of the *krodha-vighnāntaka*, who begin to personify this power. At first the power is attributed to the main bodhisattva of Phase One, and the *krodha-vighnāntaka* are merely the personifications of the bodhisattva's ability to perform this *karma*-dissolving function. As Phase Two Esoteric Buddhism stresses the new methods over and above the older practices of devotion and merit-production, naturally these personifications are featured increasingly and removed from their subordinate contexts. Power is no longer an aspect of the bodhisattva, but a personification of the strength which could be tapped within the adept.

The evidence of the *krodha-vighnāntaka* substantiates Snellgrove's observation of two categories within Esoteric Buddhism. The wrathful deities who are the subordinates of the major Mahāyāna bodhisattva correspond to texts, practices and images closely related to cultic Mahāyāna; the independently represented wrathful deities correspond to distinctly recognizable characteristics of Esoteric Buddhism. We will return to a refinement of Snellgrove's broadest distinction below.

1.2 Comparison with Tsuda's Model

Shiníchi Tsuda's system of classification also has many continuities with that generated by a study of *krodha-vighnāntaka* images. He postulates three major divisions, instead of just two.[5] The basis for his classification is, once again, primarily doctrinal positions espoused in texts. He sees the first stage, exemplified by the *MVS*, not merely contiguous with Mahāyāna, but the crowning fulfillment of Mahāyāna. Obviously there is a great deal of overlap among Snellgrove's mixed Mahāyāna-Esoteric Buddhism, Tsuda's "Vairocana" Mahāyāna, and my own Phase One. For Tsuda, the border of "Tantrism," or Esoteric Buddhism, was crossed by the *STTS* with the articulation of an "easy" or "quick" method of yoga. The *STTS* stage balances Mahāyāna Buddhism and yogic techniques, he feels, but this balance is lost with post-*STTS* Esoteric Buddhism. According to Tsuda, the emergence of the "cemetery" cult eliminated all Buddhist character from Esoteric Buddhism.

Tsuda's system creates a hierarchy by ranking each stage of development on the basis of its correspondence to "true" Buddhism. The value attached to each stage is determined by its temporal distance from the origin of Buddhism.[6] The further a movement is in time from "true" Buddhism, the less worthy it is. The present study by contrast accepts as genuine the claim to Buddhism made by writers, artists and practitioners of all three stages. In other respects, however, my

PLATE 1. *Acala, eastern India (?), painting on cloth, ca. 11th - 12th century, Shelley and Donald Rubin Collection*

PLATE 2. *Four deity thangka, central Tibet, painting on cloth, ca. 14th century, Musée Guimet*

PLATE 3. *Acala, detail of* PLATE 2

PLATE 4. *Hayagrīva, Ratnagiri (Orissa), ca. 9th century, detail of* **2, 70**

PLATE 5. *Avalokiteśvara, Dunhuang (western China), painting on cloth, ca. 12th century, Musée Guimet*

PLATE 6. *Hayagriva, detail of* PLATE 5

PLATE 7. *Amitāyus, central Tibet, painting on cloth, ca. 12th century, Los Angeles County Museum of Art*

PLATE 8. *Deities in Hayagrīva chapel, Gyantse (Tibet), wall painting, 15th century*

PLATE 9. *Hayagrīva, Gyantse (Tibet), wall painting, 15th century*

PLATE 10. *Yamāntaka, Alchi Sumtsek (Ladakh), wall painting, ca. 12th- 13th century*

PLATE 11. *Yamāntaka, Gyantse (Tibet), wall painting, 15th century*

PLATE 12. Trailokyavijaya, Gyantse (Tibet), wall painting, 15th century

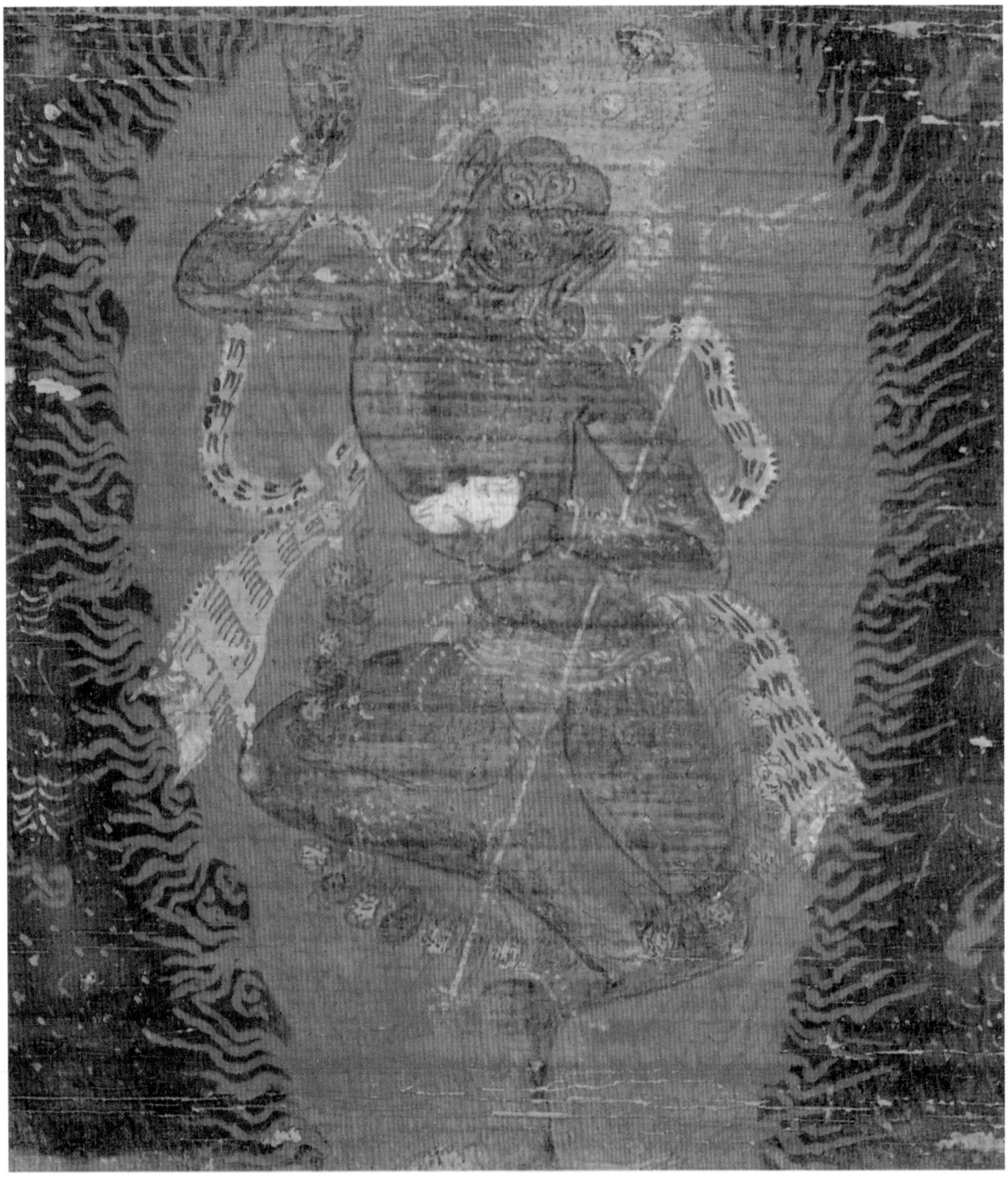

PLATE 13. Heruka, eastern India, painting on palm leaf, ca. early 12th century, Musée Guimet

PLATE 14. Hevajra Kapaladhara, Gyantse (Tibet), wall painting, 15th century

PLATE 15. *Samvara, eastern India, painting on palm leaf, ca. early 12th century, Musée Guimet*

PLATE 16. *Cakrasamvara, Gyantse (Tibet), wall painting, 15th century*

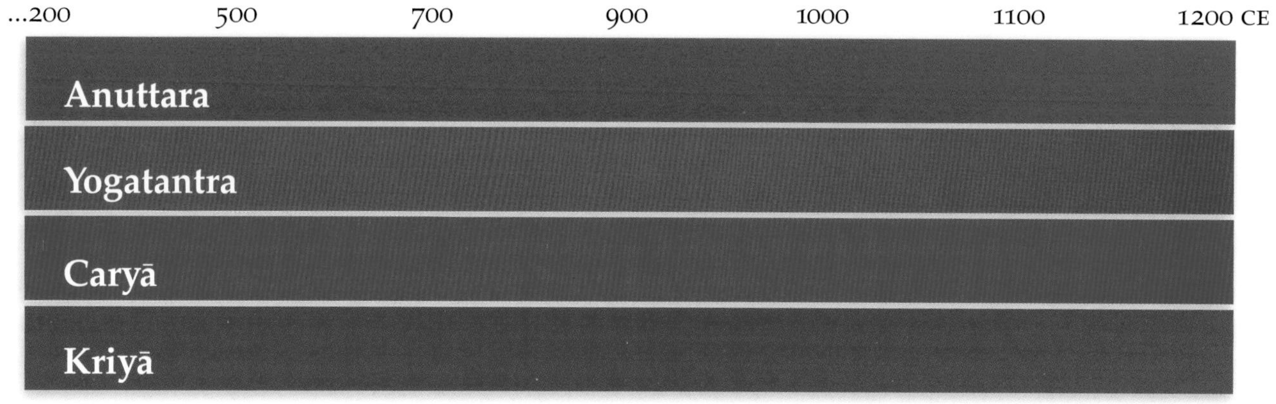

Graph 2 Schematic model of Esoteric Buddhism in eastern India based on Tibetan revelatory exegesis

Graph 3 Schematic model of the historical development of Esoteric Buddhism in eastern India adapted from the Tibetan text-classification system

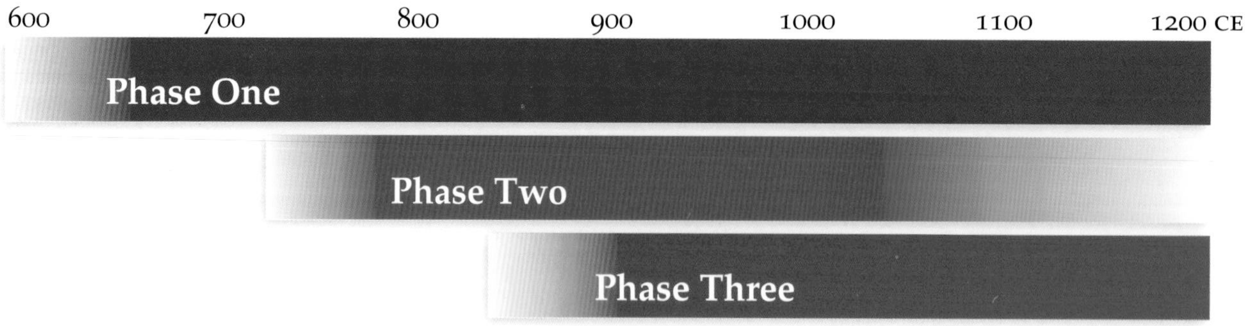

Graph 4 Schematic model of the historical development of Esoteric Buddhism in eastern India based on the study of krodha-vighnāntaka imagery

study of *krodha-vighnāntaka* agrees with Tsuda's categories in broad outline, but not in detail. For instance, the wrathful deity images related to the *MVS* clearly fall into the middle category of Phase Two; Tsuda would place them in Phase One. We do find though, like Tsuda, that Phase Two and Phase Three diverge. The distinction in the treatment of Phase Two and Phase Three *krodha-vighnāntaka*, though not as dramatic as that between Phase One and Phases Two and Three, is noteworthy.

To be sure, Snellgrove also recognizes that texts (and by extension images) within the orbit of the *STTS* are distinct from those of the Phase Three class. Still he prefers to emphasize commonalities, reducing differences to nuances due primarily to social milieu. I find with Tsuda, however, that the difference between Esoteric Buddhism of the *STTS* and post-*STTS* practice is categorical. Although differences in the morphological characteristics between Phase Two and Phase Three *krodha-vighnāntaka* are minimal, the two groups are composed of distinct members of different sets. Only a small number overlap. Equally important is the consistency with which their roles in larger compositions are distinguished. Phase Two wrathful deities (e.g., Trailokyavijaya and Bhūtaḍāmara) are depicted independently and in either supporting roles or at the center of *maṇḍala*. By contrast, Phase Three *krodha-vighnāntaka* (e.g., Saṃvara, Heruka and Hevajra), are depicted either independently or at the center of the *maṇḍala*, and rarely, if ever, as subordinates. Phase Three *krodha-vighnāntaka* are also the primary speakers in Phase Three texts, a privilege not granted Phase Two deities.

1.3 The Tibetan Text-classification Model

The most pervasive model of the development of Esoteric Buddhism in modern scholarship is adopted out of convenience from the Tibetan text classification system, standardized at least by the time of Buton (1290 - 1364 C.E.).[7] Other systems existed prior to standardization, and various sub-systems within the broadest and most common classification of the four types of Esoteric Buddhist texts survive to the present day.[8] I am not qualified to enter into a scholarly analysis or critique of this system (or systems) as it developed in Tibet. Nonetheless, it is necessary to briefly sketch the most prevalent scheme and acknowledge the wisdom with which it was formulated, as well as its influence on modern scholarship.

The Tibetan system divides texts into four categories: *kriyā* (action), *caryā* (performance), yoga and *anuttarayoga* (peerless yoga) texts. It also ranks them based on profundity and efficacy for Buddhist tasks. For instance, Guenther quotes from *sNgags-kyi spyi-don tzhangs-dbyangs 'brug-sgra*:

> *The Kriyātantras are for the dull; the Caryātantras for those of medium intelligence, the Yogatantras for those of superior and the Anuttarayogatantras for those of highest intellectual capabilities.*[9]

The Tibetan tradition considers all four *tantra*s to be timeless and therefore contemporaneous. Tāranātha writes:

> *Long ago, when the Mahāyāna teachings first came to the earth, it seems that the Kriyā, Caryā and Yoga Tantras also emerged, at least speaking in general terms. The Guhyasamāja and others of the Anuttarayogatantra collection also appeared in one group.*[10]

(The Tibetan revalatory model of the development of Esoteric Buddhism is represented by Graph 2. [COLOR PLATE 17])

The four categories belong to a series of progressive stages, "beginning from the level of a child related to its parents and developing to the level of complete maturity."[11] The four are also compared to phases of courtship:

> *Those who can identify their desire to look at the goddess of their contemplation with the path of their spiritual development are taught the Kriyātantra; those who, in addition, are able to smile at their partner, but cannot do more than this, are given the Caryātantra; those who can hold the hands of the inspiring female or desire bodily contact, but are unable to proceed further towards the consummatory act, are taught the Yogatantra; and those who not only stay with contemplation but make the desire to copulate with a real woman the path of their spiritual growth, are taught the Anuttarayogatantra.*[12]

It is no coincidence that the terms used in this last analogy recall the language of Phase Three *anuttarayoga tantra*. Without negating the validity of its predecessors, the latest form of Esoteric Buddhism to develop naturally cast itself as the most profound, suitable for the most proficient candidates. The criteria governing the final form and ranks of the system were derived from the latest stage of development to cast itself in the most favorable light. In other words, the Tibetan system enshrines Phase Three values above historical ones.

The four types of texts may be correlated generally to the three phases of the model propounded here. The ideals embedded in texts classified as *kriyā* and *caryā*, as well as the treatment of the *krodha-vighnāntaka* found therein, correspond to Phase One, as exemplified by the *MMK*. The *MVS*, however, is usually considered a *caryā* text, which points up the inherent ambiguities in the Tibetan system.[13] The *STTS* is an example of a *yoga tantra*, belonging in my formulation to Phase Two. The *anuttarayoga tantra* and related *atiyoga* teachings are found in images and texts belonging to Phase Three.

Thus, when the first two categories of *kriyā* and *caryā* are collapsed into one, there is a rough correspondence between the Tibetan classification system and the one derived from the study of *krodha-vighnāntaka*. One can note with Strickmann that the "quadripartite schema" by which "[most] modern exegetes are as if bewitched . . . . clearly suggests that the four classes of Tantra represent successive stages in an historical development, with a consequent relegation of earlier works to the lower steps in a hierarchy of spiritual values."[14] However, as already noted, the historical implications of the four-fold scheme are downplayed or ignored in the Tibetan system.[15] Nevertheless, the Tibetan system is made up of categories which do reflect historical origins, even if the Tibetan scholastics did (and do) not choose to understand them in historical terms. Indeed, they are bound not to, given their acceptance of the texts as revelation.

Graph 3 [COLOR PLATE 17] schematically represents the historical model adapted from the Tibetan classification system. The Tibetan model often has been adopt- into academic discourse without sufficient self-consciousness. Without going into a full history of its penetration, a few examples are in order. Already in the nineteenth century the four-fold classification system of the Tibetans was reported and discussed by scholars.[16] Winternitz accepts the classifications, Matsunaga uses the classification to order his discussion of Indian Esoteric Buddhism as a whole, and Malandra speaks of the "*kriyātantra* tradition" and "*kriyātantric* Buddhism."[17] Tucci concurs that the Tibetan classification is "right, in the sense that it is based on an actual difference of contents and of trends."[18] Most recently, Snellgrove acknowledges how pervasive the model has been in scholarly literature when, in his introduction to Esoteric Buddhism, he states:

> *[F]or the convenience of readers who are already acquainted with it, it seems best to accept provisionally this convenient fourfold arrangement, leaving its rather arbitrary nature to be clarified later.*[19]

Both Snellgrove and Strickmann have pointed out the "inherent ambiguities" and inadequacies in the system of literary classification, as well as its limited utility for greater historical purposes.

I would argue that there are several advantages to rejecting the traditional Tibetan scheme as a model of the historical development of South and East Asian Esoteric Buddhism. First, it is asking too much of a system designed to classify texts to double as a historical model. Second, doing so only reinforces the unfortunate emphasis on texts as the primary, if not exclusive, source of evidence for or expression of doctrinal development. Third, as it is understood today, the system is colored by the evaluative ranking of the four categories. Valid as the Tibetan evaluation may be in terms of spiritual efficacy, it is as inappropriate to historical considerations as Tsuda's model, which merely reverses the priorities of ranking. Fourth and finally, the tacit acceptance of the Tibetan system inhibits the creation of different thematic ordering systems, such as the one structured around the *krodha-vighnāntaka*. (The historical model of the development of Esoteric Buddhism in India derived from this study appears in Graph 4. [COLOR PLATE 17])

2 Perspectives Gained from the Study of *Krodha-vighnantaka* Images

2.1 The Problem of Dates

A critical contribution of this study is toward the resolution of problems of periodization. Unambiguous evidence of the dates of broad movements has been provided by isolating the major themes proper to distinct stages in the evolution of Esoteric Buddhism and then grouping together the execution of those themes in visual art. The value of these dates is not in their potential to direct us to the elusive "ultimate origin" of a specific text or idea. Monuments to individual creative acts or enlightenment experiences cannot be expected in this context. Instead, grouping works of art which reflect the same stage can help us date the period of a paradigmatic shift accepted at a collective level. It is consistently true that the period when images begin to appear falls after the dates attributed to the earliest layer of relevant texts, though the texts are often accepted as the exclusive markers of the beginning of each movement. Sculpted and painted images are more accurate gauges than texts to identify the period when a substantial community of practitioners engaged in the ritual activity described in a text. No doubt both types of dates need to be taken into account when delineating the history of Esoteric Buddhism.

Phase One

The periods indicated by the treatment of works of art do not fall into a simple linear progression. Phase One overlaps with both Phases Two and Three. The *krodha-vighnāntaka*, however, are incorporated into Mahāyāna art as early as Phase One. In eastern India the incorporation took place in the sixth and seventh century. We were able to follow Phase One imagery in eastern India through to the thirteenth century, when Buddhist institutions were for all intents and purposes extinguished in that area. Within this enduring path of Phase One imagery we saw not stasis but change in the treatment of the *krodha-vighnāntaka*. The wrathful deity increases in size and importance relative to the bodhisattva until about the tenth century. The ninth and tenth centuries constitute the richest period of growth for Phase Two *krodha-vighnāntaka* imagery. The decline of the Phase One wrathful deity in the tenth century and the contemporary florescence of Phase Two imagery are likely to be related.

After the tenth century, the wrathful attendants in Phase One imagery are included even more often in the groupings of the primary bodhisattva. But with repetition comes reduced significance. The *krodha-vighnāntaka* generally loses importance, as measured by size, variety and visual interest. The wrathful deity degenerates into a customary motif, approaching the status of decorative appendage. It is almost as if the vitality of the image abandons the Phase One format once the wrathful deity has an outlet apart from the bodhisattva.

Phase Two

Phase Two has a much more limited life-span than Phase One in eastern India and in China. East Asian Phase Two imagery begins in the late eighth century. Chinese interest in Phase Two Buddhism peaks in the ninth century, the time of early Phase Two images in eastern India. Japanese Esoteric Buddhists, on the other hand, continued to produce Phase Two images into the twentieth century. After the tenth century, Japan was nearly completely unaffected by eastern Indian developments. Eastern Indian Phase Two wrathful imagery is clustered quite consistently in the ninth and tenth centuries. Its survival somewhat later in pockets such as Kashmir is demonstrated by the dominance of Phase Two imagery in western Tibetan shrines (Tabo, Alchi, Sumda, and Mangyu) datable between the eleventh and early thirteenth centuries and derived from Kashmiri Buddhist art.

Phase Three

Phase Three *krodha-vighnāntaka* imagery of eastern India is concentrated in the eleventh and twelfth centuries. Many Phase Three images come from the same eastern Indian centers which earlier produced Phase Two wrathful deities. Images in the mode of Phase One continue to be produced alongside images of both Phase Two and Phase Three, its Mahāyānic essence not in direct "competition" with either of the later Phases; but it is apparent that Phase Three supplanted Phase Two.

Naturally the Tibetan, East and Southeast Asian evidence for dates of the development of Esoteric Buddhism is somewhat more complicated. Other factors are involved in the transmission of Buddhism to these areas. Nevertheless, they provide confirmation for both the relative and the absolute chronology of the evolution of Esoteric Buddhism in South Asia. Phase Two wrathful deities dating from the ninth century are found in Java, while Phase Three images of Heruka and Hevajra date from considerably later. Both types may be accommodated without violating the scheme just outlined. In Thailand and in Tibet, a few isolated Phase Two deities survived in a predominantly Phase Three context, preserved in a kind of spiritual suspended animation. However, no Phase Three images of earlier than the tenth century survive from India or any other place, which convincingly suggests no such images were made until after the ninth century.

2.2 The Origin and Nature of the Krodha-vighnāntaka

A few principles of image-creation have been particularly evident in the study of the origins of Esoteric Buddhist wrathful deities. One is personification. The earliest *krodha-vighnāntaka*s are personified aspects or powers of the bodhisattva they attended. In Phase One, Vajrapuruṣa is the personification of Vajrapāṇi's principal emblem and instrument of power, the *vajra*. At times it emerges from Vajrapuruṣa's head as he stands next to the much larger Vajrapāṇi. Instead of holding the *vajra* in his hand, Vajrapāṇi places his hand on the head of its personification. Yamāntaka is also the personification of Mañjusri's power to speedily locate and round up various types of deities in the chiliocosm. Hayagrīva is the personification of Avalokiteśvara's powers to transform recalcitrant beings with the sound of his voice.

By the time of Phase Two the personifications are no longer confined to the bodhisattva. Sometimes they belong to a Buddha, or, in cases like Bhūtaḍāmara, the wrathful deity is no longer conceived as the embodiment of a narrow aspect of the bodhisattva, but of his essence. Bhūtaḍāmara is Vajrapāṇi himself. The wrathful deities are still personifications in some sense, but they become the embodiments of less literal and more abstract concepts. Trailokyavijaya represents the personification of the compassionate destruction of inner obstacles. Again, he is a form of Vajrapāṇi, and if he is linked to superior deities, it is to Akṣobhya Buddha, to Mahāvairocana Buddha or to all the Tathāgata Buddha together.

In Phase Three, the idea of personification becomes less distinct, or else so broad it is practically meaningless. *Krodha-vighnāntaka* like Heruka, Hevajra and Saṃvara are embodiments of the ultimate bliss, the *dharmakaya* and the "Sixth" or "Ādi" Buddha. As such the wrathful deities, who were once personifications of aspects of bodhisattva, now themselves spawn subsidiary forms.

Another principle of image-making that affects the form of the *krodha-vighnāntaka* is the notion of regeneration. This is clearly articulated during all three phases. Even as Yamāntaka is a personification of an aspect of a bodhisattva, older non-Buddhist iconographic forms are drawn on to give him shape, substance and personality. He and Hayagrīva are converted adversaries of the gods and become identified with Buddhism. Even the Phase Three *krodha-vighnāntaka* Saṃvara has hoary pre-Buddhist roots. Not only are names and roles adapted or inverted from Vedic or other chthonic layers of ancient Indian religious belief; such adaptations govern the forms first given to the *krodha-vighnāntaka* as well.

The earliest wrathful figures are nearly indistinguishable from converted Yakṣas attending the bodhisattva. The conflation of visual forms reveals the ideological fusion of the early *krodha-vighnāntaka* with pre-Buddhist beings of similar name and character, as discovered by textual studies. It is also worth pointing out that during much of Phase One there is something of a generic quality to the images of *krodha-vighnāntaka*. The body-type, gestures and *āyudha* - in short, the forms, if not the iconographic significance - of Hayagrīva and Yamāntaka, for instance, are virtually interchangeable. An increasing specificity of iconography develops in Phases Two and Three. This tendency toward iconographic clarity is intensified for all phases as Esoteric Buddhism expands out of South Asia. There is a discernible trend abroad toward the literal in depictions of iconographic characteristics which had not been emphasized in South Asian imagery.

Regeneration also occurs across the three phases. We followed Yamāntaka through his Phase One and Phase Two incarnations. Although there is substantial consistency between the two incarnations, certain alterations in treatment, form and integration into compositions occur with the transition from Phase to Phase. For example, while a late Phase One Yamāntaka of the twelfth century might still be two-armed, as he was in an early Phase One image of the eighth century, Phase Two Yamāntaka images of the ninth or tenth century were consistently six-armed. It was not possible to follow Yamāntaka into Phase Three (or Hayagrīva into Phase Two) because of material constraints on this study. It is a matter for regret that it was also not possible to explore in detail the Phase Three transformation of Yamāntaka into Yamāri and Vajrabhairava. His adaptation is particularly well-documented in both images and texts, at least in the Tibetan tradition. We were, however, able to suggest that the Phase Two Trailokyavijaya is regenerated as Saṃvara in Phase Three.

Regeneration applies at still another level. If the Yakṣa image-making tradition determines to a large degree the form of early Phase One imagery, Shaivite imagery has the same effect on prominent *krodha-vighnāntaka* of Phases Two and Three. Forms of Śiva are simultaneously subjugated and glorified by the *krodha-vighnāntaka* image as it absorbs the identity of the converted Śiva. Regeneration in this sense impacted both Phase Two Trailokyavijaya and the Phase Three Saṃvara.

The principles of personification, inversion and regeneration, and the transformation of non-Buddhist deities into Buddhist ones at work in several different layers of the wrathful deity image over a long period should not suggest that there were no fundamental changes over time in the conception of the *krodha-vighnāntaka*. We must understand the *krodha-vighnāntaka,* not merely as a Yakṣa recycled for Esoteric Buddhism, but as an entity carrying its own significance as an aspect of the "demonic divine." We will briefly recapitulate the essential doctrines embodied in the wrathful deities at different stages.

Phase One wrathful deities are objectified powers of the bodhisattva and are able to govern obstacles pertaining to the mundane realm. They cure snake bites, headaches, injuries and disease caused by demons, bring rain, arouse love, vanquish armies, convert the enemies of Buddhism and so on. These obstacles prevent the aspirant from taking advantage of human rebirth to fulfill the Mahāyāna path. Phase Two *krodha-vighnāntaka* symbolize inner transformations and help to conquer hardened patterns of *karma* and thought which produce egoism, anger and lust. Signification takes place on a mythic level, through dialects of power, submission and regeneration of archetypal forms. This transmundane approach is brought to fruition in Phase Three, when the inherent paradox of a spiritual goal attained with immediate, physical praxis finds astonishing expression in the wrathful image that fuses compassionate intentions with malevolent forms. Terrifying deities in sexual embrace expose the enigma at the heart of Phase Three Esoteric Buddhism: poison as its own antidote, harnessed obstacles as the liberating force.

The history of the *krodha-vighnāntaka* follows the trajectory of the apotheosis of obstacles. Non-Buddhist forms and meanings are adopted initially as subsidiary correlates to a primary Buddhist ideology. Subsequently, there is a transformation from within, and an outward expression of Buddhist values. Finally, there occurs the ultimate epiphany of these agents as the essence of *tathata* (suchness). The development of the *krodha-vighnāntaka* away from the mundane and physical and toward inner transcendence culminates in a reaffirmation of the sensual. Salvation achieved in this body is expressed, if not attained, through an exalted sensuality, itself an obstacle when experienced from a mundane perspective. Like Uroborus, the end meets the beginning.

The potential for expressing the transcendent reality of the *coincidential oppositorum* in the early *krodha-vighnāntaka* is realized gradually in more and more powerful forms. Contrary to what one might expect, the most advanced practitioners depended on physical representations as critical to successful practice. Some of the greatest Esoteric Buddhist masters, Amoghavajra, Kōbō Daishi, Rinchen Zangpo and Atiśa, produced or inspired the greatest art of the *krodha-vighnāntaka*.

2.3 Final Remarks

The analysis of a narrowly defined theme found repeatedly in visual imagery over a wide area and period has allowed us to boldly assign relatively specific dates to developments. The success of the model remains to be seen, but at the very least we have unified a significant number of geographically scattered images by their Esoteric Buddhist character. Analyzed as groups, they can be used by more skillful interpreters in tandem with other types of evidence. The sheer number of images of *krodha-vighnāntaka* argues against the assessment of Nalanda, for instance, as:

> *a vast tragic ruin with little to show in the local museum . . . [More generally, it] is perhaps interesting to note how very scanty is any form of tantric imagery amongst the little that does survive here and there in situ in sufficient quantity for one to gain at least an impression of the iconographic predilections of the later inmates. The Indian Museum at Calcutta has received Buddhist remains from all over eastern India, but here too there is very little which does not belong to the more conventional Buddhist world of Buddhas and Great Bodhisattvas.*[20]

Hopefully, the present study has gathered together a sufficient quantity of images to overturn this impression. However flawed my analysis may prove to be, I have endeavored to clear a space in the study of Esoteric Buddhism for the evidence provided by works of visual art. I respectfully suggest that what Snellgrove characterizes as "inevitably a form of academic reconstruction drawing upon a vast quantity of literary materials"[21] needs to solidify its foundations with concrete imagery, literally lying all around it.

Notes to Afterword

1 Snellgrove, "Categories of Buddhist Tantras," 1353.

2 Snellgrove, *Indo-Tibetan Buddhism*, 279; idem, "Categories of Buddhist Tantras," 1364.

3 Liu Xinru, *Ancient India and Ancient China* (Oxford, 1988), 92-102. The seven treasures, which stimulated the trade between Buddhist nations, were gold, silver, lapis lazuli, quartz crystal, pearl, red coral and agate.

4 John M. Rosenfield, "On the Dated Carvings of Sārnāth," *Artibus Asiae* 26 (1963): 10.

5 Tsuda, "A Critical Tantrism."

6 In Tsuda's privileging of the "Vairocana" Esoteric Buddhism of Kūkai at the expense of later Esoteric Buddhism in India and Tibet, one is tempted to see a more sophisticated version of the implicit ethnocentrism which has led some — but by no means all — Japanese scholars to see Shingon as pure and subsequent developments as degenerate. See the discussion of this attitude in Snellgrove, *Indo-Tibetan Buddhism*, 117, 152.

7 Alex Wayman, "Analysis of the Tantric Section of the Kanjur Correlated to Tanjur Exegesis," *Indo-Asian Studies, Part 1* (New Delhi, 1963), 118. An even greater antiquity of the Tibetan classification system seems to be supported by one of the Tibetan manuscripts found at Dunhuang which asks, in R.A. Stein's translation, "A quelle catégorie (de *tantra; mchams*) est-il rattaché?" The answer the text provides is that the teaching in question belongs to the Mahāyoga, one of the four standard categories. R.A. Stein, "Un Genre Particulier d'Exposés du Tantrisme Ancien Tibétain et Khotanais," *Journal Asiatique* 275.3-4 (1987): 266.

8 See Snellgrove, "Categories of Buddhist Tantras," 1353-1357; Alex Wayman, "Outline of the Thob Yig Gsal Bahi Me Lon," in *Indo-Asian Studies*, Part 1, ed. Raghu Vira (New Delhi, 1963), 117; and, Lessing and Wayman, *Mkhas-grub-rje's*.

9 Guenther, *Tantric View of Life*, 141. Tsongkhapa also quotes the *Vajrapanjara*: "Action Tantras are for the inferior./Yoga without actions is for those above them./The supreme Yoga is for supreme beings./ The Highest Yoga is for those above them." Tsong-ka-pa, *Tantra in Tibet*, 151.

10 Templeman, *Tāranātha's Life of Krsnācārya/Kānha*, 92.

11 Guenther and Trungpa, *The Dawn of Tantra*, 4.

12 Sang ngag dorje tegpay salamgi namshag rinpochay temkay, quoted in Guenther, *Treasures*, 66.

13 Snellgrove also recognizes that the *MVS*, despite its traditional Tibetan classification as a *caryā* text, is a "presumably early tantra of the Yoga Tantra class." Snellgrove, *Indo-Tibetan Buddhism*, 196.

14 Michel Strickmann, "A Survey of Tibetan Buddhist Studies," *The Eastern Buddhist* 10, no. 1 (1977): 140-141.

15 On the other hand, there is no question that the Tibetans are quite interested in the history of the transmission of Esoteric Buddhism to Tibet. To mention a single example, the 15th c. Shakya mchog ldan divides this transmission into three periods: early translations (Padmasambhava), middle translations (Rinchen Zangpo, including texts on Cakrasamvara, Hevajra, Guhyasamaja) and later translations (Kalacakra). Jose Ignacio Cabezon, "Experience and Reason: Shakya mchog-ldan's History of Madhyamaka," paper presented at the Twentieth Annual Conference on South Asia, Madison, Wisconsin, 2 November 1991.

16 See Waddell, *Tibetan Buddhism*, 152; Louis de la Vallée Poussin, "The Four Classes of Buddhist Tantras," *Journal of the Royal Asiatic Society* (1901): 900-901.

17 Winternitz, *History of Indian Literature*, 327-331; Matsunaga, "Indian Esoteric Buddhism," 229-242; Malandra, *Unfolding a Maṇḍala*, 21.

18 Tucci, *Tibetan Painted Scrolls*, 220.

19 Snellgrove, *Indo-Tibetan Buddhism*, 119, note 5.

20 Ibid., 185.

21 Ibid.

Glossary of Sanskrit Terms

abhaya: gesture of greeting, "fear not" with the palm out.
abhicāraka: ritual for suppression or exorcism.
abhiṣeka: ritual initiation.
ācarya: adept, initiated practitioner.
adhiṣṭhāna: empowerment; surrender to mystic grace.
ahamkāra: realization of the practioner's identity with the deity.
ālīḍha: archer's posture, with one leg bent at the knee, the other straight; interpretations differ, but here it designates the proper left leg bent and the right straight. Contrast *pratyālīdha*.
amṛit: nectar, ambrosia; elixir.
añjali: two-handed gesture in which the palms are brought together in front of the chest, signifying reverence or submission.
aṅkuśa: hook or elephant-keeper's goad.
anuttara: peerless, none higher.
anuttara yoga tantra: "Supreme yoga *tantra;*" most esteemed in the Tibetan fourfold classification of Esoteric Buddhist texts, refers to texts which describe rites of supreme culmination yoga; these include texts which describe developments covered here under the rubric of Phase Three.
ardhaparyaṇkāsaṇa: in its dancing, or *tandava*, form the weight of the body is carried by one leg (usually the left) while the right leg is drawn up, the right foot resting on the left thigh; especially associated with Heruka.
avadhūti: central nerve channel in Buddhist inner yoga; called the *sushumnā* in Hindu yoga.
avidyā: ignorance, unenlightened state.
āyudha: weapon, trophy (such as an animal skin) or emblem (such as a *vajra*) held by a deity.
āyudhapurusa: personification of an attribute held by a deity.
bandhaya-sīman: preliminary stage in Esoteric Buddhist ritual; establishes, purifies and protects the ritual arena.
bhaga: vagina.
bhavana: visualization ritual.
bodhicitta: seed of enlightenment; thought of enlightenment; has both Mahāyana and Phase Three usages.
bodhyagri: (alt. *bodhyangir*) gesture performed by Mahāvairocana, in which the left forefinger is grasped by the right fist; sometimes interpreted as the union of wisdom and compassion.
cakra: wheel; in inner yoga, one of four (or seven) energy centers.
caryā: performance; ranked second in the Tibetan fourfold classification of Esoteric Buddhist texts; refers to *tantras* which describe rites of religious practice; these include texts covered here under the rubric of Phase One.
chauryi: fly whisk, usually made of a yak or buffalo tail.
ḍākinī: female accomplished yoga practioner in Phase Three contexts who acts as an initiation-giving deity and consort.
ḍamaru: two-sided drum made of human cranium.
daṇḍa: club-like weapon; common *āyudha* of Yamāntaka and other *krodha-vighnāntaka*.
dhāraṇī: magical invocation and prayer.
dharmapāla: broad category of guardian deities who protect the Buddhist teachings, rather than a specific locale, as Lokapāla or *dvārapāla*.
dhoti: skirt-like garment wrapped around the waist; in *krodha-vighnāntaka* sometimes replaced or supplemented by an animal skin.
dhyāna: meditation *mudrā*, hands resting on each other in the lap.
dikpāla: guardians of the eight directions, mainly in Hindu formulations.
dohā: ecstatic songs of Mahāsiddhas.
dvārapāla: class of minor guardians deities; sometimes encountered as paired gate guardians.
Gaṇa: impish demon who attends Śiva.
ghaṇṭā: ritual bell, which can symbolize wisdom; embodied by the female.
guhya: secret, veiled, innermost.
homa: fire rituals in which sacrifices and obstacles are burned up.
jaṭāmukuṭa: high-piled chignon.
kalpa: ritual manual text.
kapāla: skull cup.
karuṇa: compassion
khatvāṅga: long staff which may symbolize the *avadhūti* or the consort.
kleśa: poison of human desire and attachment.
kriyā: action; ranked lowest in the Tibetan fourfold classification of Esoteric Buddhist texts, referring to *tantras* which describe rites of magic; these include texts covered here under the rubric of Phase One.
krodha: wrath.
kṣetrapāla: guardians of fields or territories; a kind of *dvārapāla*.
kula: family; deity grouping.
lambodara: big-bellied.
laukika: mundane in orientation; compare *lokottara*.
liṅga: phallus; or Shaivite phallic symbol of Śiva.
Lokapāla: Kings of the Four Directions who wear armor; protectors.
lokottara: supramundane in orientation; compare *laukika*.
mahāsukha: great bliss; ecstatic experience of the union of wisdom and compassion.
mālā: bead rosary
maṇḍala: psycho-cosmic diagram ordering deities symmetrically within the "palace" of the central deity.
mantra: sound-form which both represents and *is* the deity, and thus has transformative powers; *mantra* are linked together to form *dhāraṇī*.
Mantranaya: practice of *mantra*; alternative name for mixed Mahāyāna /early Esoteric Buddhism, sometimes referred to as *Mantrayāna* and designated here Phase One Esoteric Buddhism.
Mantrayāna: vehicle of *mantra*; name used to designate (somewhat misleadingly) early Esoteric Buddhism based on the prominence of *mantra* and *dhāraṇi* recitation; actually a movement situated entirely within cultic Mahāyāna.
mudrā: symbolic hand gesture.
nādi: nerve channel in inner yoga.
nāga: serpent deity.
pañcakula: five-family system of middle and later Esoteric Buddhism, prominent in Phase Two; applied to the five directions of the *maṇḍala*, five Tathāgata, etc.
padma: lotus; one of the three and five *kula*; family associated with Hayagriva.
pāramitā: perfection.
parivāra: the entourage of a Buddhist deity, emanations, attendants, etc.
pāśa: rope, cord, or noose.
pitha: a pilgrimage site where secret yogic practices occur.
prajñā: wisdom; also, female consort of Buddhist deity.
pralambapada āsana: seated with both legs hanging down off the dais.
pratyālīḍha: posture with proper right leg bent at the knee, left extended straight. Contrast *ālīḍha*.
preta: hungry ghost; suffering hell being.
śakti: Hindu term for consort of Śiva; connotes active energy; mistakenly used to refer to Buddhist consorts, or *prajñā*.
sādhana: ritual prescription for visualization of a deity, including a description of the deity's form and attributes.
samādhi: enlightened blissful state of integration.
saṁsāra: phenomenal experience in the contingent world.
samyak sambodhi: absolute, transcendent enlightenment.
siddhi: (magical) power, ability
skandha: one of the five constituent "heaps" which arise codependently to give rise to streams of consciousness.
śmaśāna: cemetery; charnel ground.
śukra: "unclean" fluids such as semen and menses.
śūnyatā: emptiness/nothingness as ultimate state of reality.
tantra: refers to Esoteric Buddhist texts; has come to loosely designate the movement as a whole.
tapas: ascetic practice, renunciation of sensual comforts or pleasure.

tarjanī: gesture of admonition or threat, with forefinger raised, other fingers curled into the palm.

Tathāgata*:* refers to one or another form of the Buddha; the five Tathāgata are sometimes wrongly refered to as *dhyāni* Buddhas.

trailokyavijaya: two-handed *mudrā* in which the wrists are crossed in front of the chest, palms held outward, little fingers entwined, forefingers erect; also, the proper name of a Phase Two deity.

trikula: three-family system of early Esoteric Buddhism and cultic Mahāyāna; prominent in Phase One.

triśūla: trident-like emblem associated with Śiva.

upavita: sacred thread of Brahmins, sometimes transformed into a string of pearls or a snake when worn by *krodha-vighnāntaka*.

upāya: skillful means; associated with compassion and the worldly work of leading sentient beings towards elightement.

ūrdha-liṅga: ithyphallic.

uttarīya: upper garment or scarf worn diagonally across the torso.

vāhana: mount or vehicle of a deity; may be an animal (such as the buffalo), a Hindu god (such as Maheśvara), a corpse or human devotee.

vajra: diamond-wisdom sceptre; adamantine thunderbolt representing wisdom; also one of the five families, particularly associated with the *krodha-vighnāntaka*.

vajrahūṃkara: two-handed gesture in which the wrists are crossed at the chest (right over left) and the palms turned in while holding the *vajra* and bell in right and left hands respectively; associated with Saṃvara and Hevajra; also the proper name of a Phase Two deity.

vāmana: dwarfish body type of *krodha-vighnāntaka*. Contrast *vīra*.

vanamālā: long looping scarf or garland, often hanging below the knees.

vandana mudrā: gesture of salutation with arm raised, hand out, fingers pointing toward the greeted deity.

vara (alt. *varada*)*:* gesture of gift-giving with palm out, fingertips pointing down.

vidyā: light, knowledge, and/or words expressing knowledge and power in the form of *dhāraṇī*.

vighna: obstacles to enlightenment, variously considered as human, natural and supernatural, inner or outer.

vighnāntaka: destroyer of obstacles; also the proper name of a *krodha-vighnāntaka* who tramples on the elephant-headed personification of obstacles, Vināyaka.

vihāra: residential monastic complex.

vinayahasta: two-handed gesture made by crossing the two arms in front of the chest, palms inward; signifies submission, surrender or humility; primary *mudrā* of Phase One *krodha-vighnāntaka*

vīra: hero; a *krodha-vighnāntaka* body type characterized by a graceful form and a warrior-like, heroic aspect. Contrast *vāmana.*

viśvavajra: universal *vajra*; ritual implement comprised of two *vajra* crossed perpendicularly.

Yakṣa: an ancient India nature spirit with invisible powers; gradually subordinated to Śiva as Gaṇa; contributes to the development of the *āyudhapuruṣa* image and thus the *krodha-vighnāntaka* image.

yoginī: female yoga practitioner; sometimes applied to class of female adepts or deities attending Phase Three *krodha-vighnāntaka* such as Heruka and Hevajra.

yoga tantra: rites of yoga; ranked third in the Tibetan fourfold classification of Esoteric Buddhist texts, referring to texts such as the *STTS,* included here under the rubric of Phase Two.

yuganaddha: blissful union combining widsom and compassion

Tibetan terms and names

Buton Rinpoche = Bu ston rin po che
Changkya = Lcang skya
chörten = stūpa
Demchog = bDem mchog
Drigung = 'Bri gung
Drogmi = Hbrog mi
Gyantse = rGyal rtse
Drogmi = Hbrog-mi
Kadampa = bKa' gdams pa
Kagyupa = bKa' brgyud pa
Kaygrubjay = mKhas grub rje
Nyingmapa = rNying ma pa
Peltseg = dPal brtsegs
Phagpa = 'Phags pa
Rinchen Zangpo = Rin chen bzang po
Sang ngag dorje tegpay salamgi namshag rinpochay temkay = gsang ngag rdo rje theg pa'i sa lam gyi rnam bzhag rin po che them skas
terma = gter ma
Tsongkhapa = Tsong kha pa
Yangdzogpay = Yongs rdzogs bstan pa'i
Yeshe Day = Ye ses sde
Yeshe Ö = Yeshes 'Od
yidam = class of initiatory or tutelary deities including Buddhas and *krodha-vighnāntaka*

Select Bibliography

Abe, Stanley. "Inside the Wonder House: Buddhist Art and the West." In *Curators of the Buddha: The Study of Buddhism under Colonialism*, edited by Donald S. Lopez, Jr., pp. 63-106. Chicago, 1995.

Abbott, Terry. "The Chinese Version of the Hevajra Tantra." *Transactions of the International Conference of Orientalists in Japan* 23 (1978): 99-103.

Abhayadatta. *Caturaśiti-siddha-pravrtti.* Translated by James B. Robinson, under the title *Buddha's Lions: The Lives of the Eighty-Four Siddhas*. Berkeley, 1979.

Acharya, Padmasri P. "Varieties of Stones Used in Building Temples and Making Images in Orissa (Quarries and Method of Transport)." *The Orissa Historical Research Society* 13, no. 2 (1965): 9-20.

Acker, W.R.B. *Some T'ang and Pre-T'ang Texts on Chinese Painting*. Leyden, 1954.

Advayavajra. *Advayavajrasamgraha*. Edited by H. Sastri. Gaekwad's Oriental Series, no. 40. Baroda, 1927.

Agarwala, V.S. *A Guide to Sārnāth*. 3rd ed. New Delhi, 1980.

Agrawala, Prithvi Kumar. "The Kumbhanda Figures in Sanchi Sculpture." *East and West* 37 (1987): 179-189.

Agrawala, R.C. "Trisula Purusa in Indian Sculpture." *Indian Historical Quarterly* 36 (1960): 186-188.

Ahmed, Nazimuddin, and John Sanday. "The Ruins of Paharpur." *Arts Asiatiques* 41 (1986): 22-35.

Akiyama Terukazu, and S. Matsubara. *Arts of China: Buddhist Cave Temples, New Researches.* Translated by A.C. Soper. Tokyo, 1969.

Akhouri, Gayatri. *Śaivism in Ancient Bihar*. Patna, 1988.

Almond, Philip C. *The British Discovery of Buddhism*. Cambridge, 1988.

Andrews, Fred H. *Descriptive Catalogue of Antiquities Recovered by Sir Aurel Stein ... During His Exploration in Central Asia, Kansu and Eastern Iran.* Delhi, 1935.

Archaeological Survey of India. *Annual Report 1927-28*. Calcutta, 1931.

______. *Annual Report 1930-34*. Delhi, 1936.

______. *Annual Report 1934-35*. Delhi, 1937.

______. *Eastern Circle: Annual Report 1920-21*. Patna, 1921.

______. (Department of Archaeology, Government of India). *Indian Archaeology 1958-59: Review*. New Delhi, 1959.

Argan, Giulio Carlo. "Ideology and Iconology." In *The Language of Images*, edited by W.J.T. Mitchell, pp. 15-23. Chicago, 1980.

"Arts of Asia Recently Acquired by American Museums." *Archives of Asian Art* 26 (1972-73): 77-106.

Asher, Frederick. *The Art of Eastern India, 300-800*. Minneapolis, 1980.

______. "The Former Broadley Collection, Bihar Sharif." *Artibus Asiae* 32 (1970): 105-24.

Asia Society, The. *Handbook of the Mr. and Mrs. John D. Rockefeller 3rd Collection*. New York, 1981.

Asthana, Shashi. "A Controversial Buddhist Tantrik deity: Trailokya-Vijaya vis-a-vis Sambara." In *History and Culture: B.P. Sinha Felicitation Volume*, edited by Bhagwant Sahai, pp. 167-172. Delhi, 1987.

Astley-Kristensen, Ian. *The Rishukyō: The Sino-Japanese Tantric Prajñāpāramitā in 150 Verses (Amoghavajra's Version)*. Buddhica Britannica Series Continua III. Tring, 1991.

Auboyer, Jeannine. *Rarities of the Musée Guimet*. New York, 1975.

Backus, Charles. *The Nan-chao kingdom and T'ang China's Southwestern Frontier*. Cambridge, 1981.

Bagchi, P.C. "On Foreign Element in the Tantra." *Indian Historical Quarterly* 7 (1931): 1-16.

Bailey, H.W. "Hvatanica IV." *Bulletin of the School of Oriental and African Studies* 10 (1942): 886-924.

Bakshi, Dwijendra Nath. *Hindu Divinities in Japanese Buddhist Pantheon*. Calcutta, 1979.

Barthes, Roland. *Mythologies*. New York, 1972.

Barua, Dipak K. *Buddha Gaya Temple: Its History*. 2nd ed. Buddha Gaya, 1981.

Bautze-Picron, Claudine. "Between men and gods: small motifs in the Buddhist art of eastern India, an interpretation." In *Function and Meaning in Buddhist Art*, edited by K.R. van Kooij and H. van der Veere, pp. 60-79. Groningen, 1995.

______. "Bhairava et les Mères au Bengale septentrional." *Arts Asiatiques* 45 (1990): 61-66.

______. "Lakhi Sarai, An Indian Site of Late Buddhist Iconography and Its Position within the Asian Buddhist World." *Silk Road Art and Archaeology* 1 (1990): 123-176.

______. "Śākyamuni in Eastern India and Tibet in the 11th to the 13th Centuries." *Silk Road Art and Archaeology* 4 (1995/96): 355-408.

Beckwith, Christopher I. *The Tibetan Empire in Central Asia: A History of the Struggle for Great Power among Tibetans, Turks, Arabs, and Chinese during the Early Middle Ages*. Princeton, 1987.

Beglar, J.D. *Report of A Tour Through the Bengal Provinces . . . in 1872-73*. Archaeological Survey of India, no. 7. Calcutta, 1878.

Begley, Wayne E. *Pāla Art: Buddhist and Hindu Sculpture from Eastern India, ca. 800-1200 ad*. Iowa City, 1969.

______. *Visnu's Flaming Wheel: The Iconography of the* Sudarśana-Cakra. New York, 1973.

Béguin, Gilles. *Art ésotérique de l'Himâlaya: Catalogue de la donation Lionel Fournier*. Paris, 1990.

______. *Dieux et démons de l'Himâlaya: Art du Bouddhisme lamaïque*. Paris, 1977.

Béguin, Gilles, and Lionel Fournier. "Un sanctuarie méconnu de la région d'Alchi." *Oriental Art* ns 32 (1986/87): 373-387.

Benard, Elisabeth Anne. *Chinnamastā: The Aweful Buddhist and Hindu Tantric Goddess*. Delhi, 1994.

Bendall, Cecil. "The Megha-Sūtra." *Journal of the Royal Asiatic Society*, ns 12 (1880): 286-311.

Benisti, Mireille. *Contribution a l'Étude du Stupa Bouddhique Indien: Les Stupa Mineurs de Bodh-Gaya et de Ratnagiri*. Publications de L'École Française d'Extrême-Orient, no. 125. Paris, 1981.

Berkson, Carmel. *The Caves at Aurangabad: Early Buddhist Tantric Art in India*. New York/Ahmedabad, 1986.

______. *Ellora: Concept and Style*. New Delhi, 1992.

Berlin, Museum für Indische Kunst. *Museum für Indische Kunst, Berlin: Katalog 1976 Ausgestellte Werke*. Berlin, 1976.

Bernet Kempers, August Johan. *Ancient Indonesian Art*. Cambridge, 1959.

______. "The Bronzes of Nālandā and Hindu-Javanese Art." *Bijdragen tot de Taal-, Land-, en Volkenkunde van Nederlandsch-Indie* 90 (1933): 1-88.

______. "De Beelden van Tjandi Djago en hun Voor-Indisch Prototype." *Maandblad voor Beeldende Kunsten* 10 (1933): 173-179.

______. "Nālandā Bronzes." *Nederlandsch-Indië Oud en Nieuw* 18 (1933): 347-354; 393-400.

______. "Raffles' Bronscollectie in Het Britsch Museum." *Maandblad voor Beeldende Kunsten* 12 (1935): 99-113.

Bethlenfalvy, Géze. "Alexander Csoma de Körös in Ladakh." In *Proceedings of the Csoma de Körös Memorial Symposium*, edited by Louis Ligeti, pp. 7-26. Budapest, 1978.

Beyer, Stephen. *The Cult of Tārā*. Berkeley, 1973.

Bharati, Agehananda. "Śakta and Vajrayāna: Their Place in Indian Thought." In *Studies of Esoteric Buddhism and Tantrism*, edited by Matsunaga Yukei, pp. 73-99. Koyasan, 1965.

______. *The Tantric Tradition*. London, 1965; reprint ed., New Delhi, 1976.

Bhattacharya, Gouriswar. "A Second Dated Tārā Image of the Reign of Devapāla." *Indian Museum Bulletin* 17 (1982): 21-23.

______. "The Buddhist Deity Vajrapāṇi." *Silk Road Art and Archaeology* 4 (1995/96): 323-354

Bhattacharyya, Benoytosh. "Buddhist Deities in Hindu Garb." In *Proceedings and Transactions of the Fifth All Indian Oriental Conference*, pp. 1277-1298. Lahore, 1930.

______. "The Cult of Bhūtaḍāmara." In *Proceedings and Transactions of the 6th All India Conference, Patna, Dec. 1930*, pp. 349-370. Patna, 1933.

______. *Guhyasamāja Tantra or Tathāgataguhyaka*. Gaekwad's Oriental Series, no. 53. Baroda, 1931.

______. "The Iconography of Heruka." *Indian Culture* 2 (1935): 23-35

______. *The Indian Buddhist Iconography, Mainly based on the Sādhanamālā and Cognate Tantric Texts of Rituals*. 2nd rev. ed. Calcutta, 1968.

______. *An Introduction to Buddhist Esoterism*. New Delhi, 1931.

______. *Niṣpannayogāvali of Mahāpandita Abhayākaragupta*. Gaekwad's Oriental Series, no. 109. Baroda, 1949; reprint ed., 1972.

______. *Sādhanamālā*, Gaekwad's Oriental Series, no. 26 and 41. Baroda, 1925 and 1928.

______. *Two Vajrayāna Works*. Gaekwad's Oriental Series, no. 44. Baroda, 1929.

Bhattacharyya, D.G. "On Buddhist Mudrās." *Bulletin of the Baroda Museum* 28 (1978-79): 205-214

Bills, Sheila Coffin. "A Chronological Study of Sino-Tibetan Metal Sculpture (1260-1450)." Ph.D. dissertation, Case Western Reserve University, 1983.

Birnbaum, Raoul. *Studies on the Mysteries of Mañjuśri: A Group of East Asian Maṇḍalas and their Traditional Symbolism*. Society for the Study of Chinese Religions, Monograph, no. 2. Boulder, 1983.

Bischoff, Frédéric A. "The First Chapter of the Legend of Padmasambhava - A Translation." In *Serta Tibeto-Mongolica: Festschrift für Walther Heissig*, edited by R. Kaschewsky, Klaus Sagaster, and M. Weiers, pp. 33-46. Wiesbaden, 1973.

______. Arya Mahabala-Nama-Mahayanasutra, *Tibétain (MSS. de Touen-Houang) et Chinois: Contribution à l'étude des divinités mineures du bouddhisme tantrique*. Buddhica, no. 10. Paris, 1956.

Bischoff, Frédéric A. and Charles Hartman. "Padmasambhava's Invention of the Phur-Bu: Ms. Pelliot Tibétain 44." In *Études Tibétaines: Dédiées à la mémoire de Marcelle Lalou*, pp. 11-28. Paris, 1971.

Blacker, Carmen. "Methods of Yoga in Japanese Buddhism." *MILLA wa-MILLA* 8 (1968): 31-46.

Bloss, Lowell W. "The Taming of Māra: Witnessing to the Buddha's Virtues." *History of Religions* 18.2 (1978): 156-176.

Bodrogi, Tibor. *Art of Indonesia*. Greenwich, 1972.

Boeles, J.J. "Two Yoginis of Hevajra from Thailand." In *Essays offered to G.H. Luce Vol. 2*, edited by Ba Shin et al, pp. 14-29. Ascona, 1966.

Bolle, Kees W. "Devotion and Tantra." In *Studies of Esoteric Buddhism and Tantrism*, edited by Matsunaga Yukei, pp. 217-228. Koyasan, 1965.

Boord, Martin J. *The Cult of the Deity Vajrakīla: According to the Texts of the Northern Treasures Tradition of Tibet (Byang-gter phur-ba)*. Tring, 1993.

Bosch, F.D.K. "Buddhistische Gegevens uit Balische Handscriften." *Mededelingen der Kon. Nederl. Akad. van Wetenschappen* 68B, no. 3 (1929): 43-77; English translation in *Selected Studies in Indonesian Archaeology*, pp. 109-133. The Hague, 1961.

______. "Inventaris der Hindoe-oudheden." *Rapporten van den Oudheidkundigen Dienst in Nederlandsch-Indië* (1915): 1-376.

______. "Verslag van een reis door Sumatra." *Oudheidkundig Verslag* (1930): 133-157.

van den Bosch, Lourens P. "Yama: The God on the Black Buffalo." *Visible Religion: Annual for Religious Iconography* 1 (1982): 21-64.

Boston, Museum of Fine Arts. *Courtly Splendor: Twelve Centuries of Treasures from Japan*. Boston, 1990.

Bowie, Theodore et al. *The Arts of Thailand*. Bloomington, 1960.

Bowie, Theodore, ed. *The Sculpture of Thailand*. New York, 1972.

Brandes, J.L.A. *Beschrijving van de ruïne bij de desa Toempang genaamd Tjandi Djago, in de Residentie Pasoeroean*. The Hague, 1904.

Brandon, S.G.F. *Man and God in Art and Ritual: A Study of Iconography, Architecture and Ritual Action as Primary Evidence of Religious Belief and Practice*. New York, 1975.

Bravmann, René. *Islam and Tribal Art in West Africa*. Cambridge, 1974.

Brinker, Helmut. "Ch'an Portraits in a Landscape." *Archives of Asian Art* 27 (1973-74): 8-29.

______. "Shussan Shaka in Sung and Yüan Painting." *Ars Orientalis* 9 (1973): 21-39.

Brinker, Helmut, and Roger Goepper. *Kunstschätze aus China*. Zurich/Berlin, 1980.

Brooks, Douglas Renfrew. *The Secret of the Three Cities: An Introduction to Hindu Śākta Tantrism*. Chicago, 1990.

Brough, John. "The Language of the Buddhist Sanskrit Texts." *Bulletin of the School of Oriental and African Studies* 16 (1954): 351-375.

Buchanan, Francis. *Journal of Francis Buchanan (Afterwards Hamilton) Kept During the Survey of the Districts of Patna and Gaya in 1811-1812*. Edited by V.H. Jackson. Patna, 1925.

Buchanan, Francis, and R. M. Martin. *The History, Antiquities, Topography, and Statistics of Eastern India*. London, 1938.

Burnouf, Eugène. *Introduction a l'histoire du Buddhisme indien*. Paris, 1844.

Bussagli, Mario. *Central Asian Painting*. New York, 1979.

Buswell, Robert E., Jr. "Introduction: Prolegomenon to the Study of Buddhist Apocryphal Scriptures." In *Chinese Buddhist Apocrypha*, edited by Robert Buswell, Jr., pp. 1-30. Honolulu, 1990.

Cabezon, Jose Ignacio. "Experience and Reason: Shakya mchog-ldan's History of Mādhyamika." Paper presented at Twentieth Annual Conference on South Asia, Madison, Wisconsin, 2 November 1991.

______. "Mother Widsom, Father Love: Gender-Based Imagery in Mahayana Buddhist Thought." In *Buddhist, Sexuality and Gender*, edited by José Ignacio Cabezón, pp. 181-199. Albany, 1992.

Cammann, Schuyler V.R. "Notes on the Origin of Chinese K'o-ssu Tapestry." *Artibus Asiae* 11 (1948): 90-109.

______. "Religious Symbolism in Persian Art." *History of Religions* 15 (1976): 193-208.

______. "Symbolic Meanings in Oriental Rug Patterns." *Textile Museum Journal* 3 (1972): 5-54.

Carelli, Mario E., ed. and trans. *The Sekoddeśatika of Nadapāda (Nāropā)*. Goekwad's Oriental Series, no. 90. Baroda, 1941.

Carter, Thomas Francis. *The Invention of Printing in China and its Spread Westward*. Revised by L. Carrington Goodrich. New York, 1955.

Chakravarti, H. "The Śaivite Deity Ksetrapāla." *Indian Historical Quarterly* 9 (1933): 237-243.

Chandra, Ramaprasad. *Exploration in Orissa*. Archaeological Survey of India Memoirs, no. 44. Calcutta, 1930.

Chandra, Pramod. *Stone Sculpture in the Allahabad Museum: A Descriptive Catalogue*. Poona, 1970.

Chang Chen Chi, trans. *Esoteric Teachings of the Tibetan Tantra: Including Seven Initiation Rituals and the Six Yogas of Naropa*. Edited by C.A. Muses. n.p., 1961; reprint ed., York Beach, 1982.

Chang Kun. *Descriptive Account of the Collection of Tibetan Books from the Newberry Library, now in the Far Eastern Library*. Chicago, n.d.

Chapin, Helen. "A Long Roll of Buddhist Images." Revised by Alexander C.

Soper. *Artibus Asiae* 32, nos. 1-3 (1970): 1-41, 157-199, 259-306; 33, no. 1/2 (1971): 75-142.

Chattopadhyaya, Alaka, with Lama Chimpa. *AtiŚa and Tibet: Life and Works of Dīpaṃkara Śrījñāna*. Calcutta, 1967; reprint ed., Delhi, 1981.

Chen Guoying. "Xian dongjiao sanzuo Tangmu qingli ji" (Inventory Record of three Tang tombs from the eastern suburbs of Xian). *Kaogu yu Wenwu* 2 (1981):25-31.

Ch'en, Kenneth. *Buddhism in China: A Historical Survey*. Princeton, 1964.

______. "The economic background of the Hui-ch'ang suppression of Buddhism." *Harvard Journal of Asiatic Studies* 19 (1956): 67-105.

______. *The Chinese Transformation of Buddhism*. Princeton, 1973.

Cheng Xuehua. "Tang tiejin huacai shike zao xiang" (Tang Dynasty gilt and polychromed statuary). *Wenwu* 7 (1961): 61-63.

Chia Chung-Yao, "The Church-State Conflict in the T'ang Dynasty." *Chinese Social History: Translations of Selected Studies*. Washington D.C., 1956.

Chongkol, Chira. *Guide to the National Museum Bangkok*. 2nd ed. Bangkok, 1986.

Chou I-liang. "Tantrism in China." *Harvard Journal of Asiatic Studies* 8 (1944-45): 241-331.

Clark, Walter Eugene. *Two Lamaistic Pantheons*. Cambridge, 1937.

Clauson, Gerard. "Reviews." *Bulletin of the School of Oriental and African Studies* 32 (1969): 416-419.

Clifford, James. *The Predicament of Culture*. Cambridge, 1988.

Coedès, George. *Bronzes Khmèrs*. Ars Asiatica, no. 5. Paris, 1923.

______. "L'épigraphie du temple de Phimai." *Bulletin de l'École Française d'Extrême-Orient* 24 (1924): 345-358.

______. "Les inscriptions malaises de Çrivijaya." *Bulletin de l'École Française d'Extrême-Orient* 30 (1930): 56-57.

Cohn, Bernard S. "The Transformation of Objects into Artifacts, Antiquities, and Art in Nineteenth-Century India." In *Colonialism and Its Forms of Knowledge: The British in India*, pp. 76-105. Princeton, 1996.

Conze, Edward. "The Adhyardhaśatikā Prajñāpāramitā." In *Studies of Esoteric Buddhism and Tantrism*, edited by Matsunaga Yukei, pp. 101-115. Koyasan, 1965.

______. "The Iconography of the Prajñāpāramitā." In *Thirty Years of Buddhist Studies, Selected Essays*, pp. 258-260. Columbia, 1968.

______. "Tantric Prajñāpāramitā Texts." *Sino-Indian Studies* 5, no. 2 (1956): 100-122.

Conze, Edward; I.B. Horner; D. Snellgrove; and A. Waley. *Buddhist Texts Through the Ages*. New York, 1954.

Coomaraswamy, Ananda. *Yakṣas*. Washington D.C., 1928, 1930; reprint ed., 2 parts in one; New Delhi, 1971.

Colpe, Carsten. "Syncretism." Translated by Matthew J. O'Connell. *The Encyclopedia of Religion*. 14: 218-227. Chief editor, Mircea Eliade. New York, 1987.

Corbin, Henry. *Spiritual Body and Celestial Earth: From Mazdean Iran to Shi`ite Iran*. Translated by Nancy Pearson. Princeton, 1977.

Cozad, Laurie. "Reeling in the Demon: An Exploration into the Category of the Demonized Other as Portrayed in *The Journey to the West*." *Journal of the American Academy of Religion* 66, no. 1 (1998): 117-145.

Cunningham A. and Garrick, H.B.W. *Report of tours in North and South Bihar in 1880-81*. Archaeological Survey of India, no. 16. Calcutta, 1883.

Czuma, Stanislaw J. with Morris, Rekha. *Kushan Sculpture: Images from Early India*. Cleveland, 1985.

Dagyab, Loden Sherap. *Ikonographie und Symbolik Des Tibetischen Buddhismus*. Asiatische Forschungen, no. 77. Wiesbaden, 1983.

______. *Tibetan Religious Art*. Wiesbaden, 1977.

Daizōkyō Gakujutsu Yōgo Kenkyukai (Research Association for the Terminology of the Taishō Tripitaka). *Taishō Shinshū Daizokyō Sakuin: Mikkyō* (Index to the Taishō Tripitaka: Esoteric Buddhism section). Vols. 10-11. Tokyo 1964, 1971.

Dalai Lama, H.H. the Fourteenth, and Jeffrey Hopkins. *The Kālachakra Tantra: Rite of Initiation for the Stage of Generation*. London, 1985.

Dani, Ahmad Hasan. *Buddhist Sculpture in East Pakistan*. Karachi, 1959.

Daniélou, Alain. *Hindu Polytheism*. New York, 1964.

Darain, Steven. "Buddhism in Bihar from the Eighth to the Twelfth Century with Special Reference to Nalandā." *Asiatische Studien* 25 (1971): 335-352.

Das, D.R. "Semi-Cave Shrines of Orissa." In *Ratna-Chandrik: Panorama of Oriental Studies (Shri R.C. Arawala Festschrift)*, edited by Devendra Handa and Ashvini Agrawal, pp. 291-304. New Delhi, 1989.

Dasgupta, K.K. "Iconography of Tārā." In *The Śakti Cult and Tārā*, edited by D.C. Sircar, pp. 115-127. Calcutta, 1967.

Dasgupta, Shashibhusan. *An Introduction to Tantric Buddhism*. 3rd ed. Calcutta, 1974.

______. *Obscure Religious Cults*. 3rd ed. Calcutta 1969.

Davidson, Ronald M. "Appendix: An Introduction to the Standards of Scriptural Authenticity in Indian Buddhism." In *Chinese Buddhist Apocrypha*, edited by Robert E. Buswell, Jr., pp. 291-325. Honolulu, 1990.

______. "The *Litany of Names of Mañjuśrī*: Text and Translation of the *Mañjuśrīnāmasaṃgīti*." In *Tantric and Taoist Studies in Honour of R.A. Stein*, edited by Michel Strickmann, pp. 1-69. Brussels, 1981.

______. "Reflections on the Maheśvara Subjugation Myth: Indic Materials, Sa-skya-pa Apologetics, and the Birth of Heruka." *JIABS* 14, no. 2 (1991): 197-235.

Dawa-Samdup, Lama Kazi. *Shrīchakrasambhāra Tantra*. Tantrik Texts no. 7. Edited by John Woodroffe [Arthur Avalon]. London/Calcutta, 1919; reprint ed., New Delhi, 1987.

De, S.K. "Buddhist Tantric Literature (Sanskrit) of Bengal." *New Indian Antiquary* 1 (1938-39): 1-23.

Dehejia, Vidya. *Yoginī Cult and Temples: A Tantric Tradition*. New Delhi, 1986.

Demiéville, Paul. Abstract of *Rishukyō no kenkyū* by S. Toganoo. *Bibliographie Bouddhique* 4-5 (1931-33): 96-98.

______. "Les éditions imprimées du Canon bouddhique." In *Choix d'Études Bouddhiques (1929-1970)*, pp. 223-240. Leiden, 1973.

______. "Sources chinoises sur le bouddhisme." In *Choix d'Études Bouddhiques (1929-1970)*, pp. 157-222. Leiden, 1973.

Demiéville, Paul; Hubert Durt; and Anna Seidel. *Repertoire du Canon Bouddhique Sino-Japonais, Édition de Taishō (Taishō Shinshū Daizokyō)*. Fascicule Annexe du Hōbōgirin, Édition Révisée et Augmentée. Paris/Tokyo, 1978.

Deshpande, M.N. *The Caves of Panhāle-Kāji (Ancient Pranālaka)*. Memoirs of the Archaeological Survey of India, no. 84. New Delhi, 1986.

______. "The Panhāle Kāji Caves: A Hinayāna and Tantric Vajrayānic Centre, with caves of Nātha *Sampradāya*." In *Facets of Indian Art: A Symposium*, edited by R. Skelton et al, pp. 14-17. London, 1986.

Deva, Krishna. "Significance of Pratītya-Samutpāda-Sūtra in Buddhist Art and Thought." In *Buddhist Iconography*, pp. 42-46. New Delhi, 1989.

Dikshit, K.N. *Paharpur*. Archaeological Survey of India Memoirs, no. 55. Delhi, 1938.

Diskul, M.C. Subhadradis, ed. *The Art of Srivijaya*. Paris, 1980.

Diskul, M.C. Subhadradis, and A.B. Griswald. *The Sculpture of Thailand*. New York, 1972.

Dohanian, Diran Kavork. *The Mahāyāna Buddhist Sculpture of Ceylon*. New York, 1977.

Donaldson, Thomas. *Hindu Temple Art Of Orissa*. 3 vols. Leiden, 1985-86.

______. "Iconography of the Buddhist Sculpture of Orissa." Cleveland, 1990. (Typewritten.)

______. "Orissan Images of Aṣṭabhujāpīta Marīcī." *Journal of the Orissa Research Society* 3 (1985):35-44.

______. "Sculptural Maṇḍalas of Eight Bodhisattvas." Paper presented at the Madison conference on South Asian studies, Fall 1990.

Dowman, Keith. "The Maṇḍalas of the Lo Jampa Lhakhang." In *Tibetan Art: Towards a definition of style*, edited by Jane Casey Singer and Philip Denwood, pp. 186-195. London, 1997.

Dunhuang Institute for Cultural Relics. *The Art Treasures of Dunhuang*. New York, 1991.

Dunhuang Wenwu Yanjiusuo (Dunhuang Research Institute). *Duhuang Mogaoku* (Dunhuang Mogao Caves). 5 Vols. Tokyo/Beijing, 1980-82; Japanese Edition: *Chūgoku Sekkutsu: Tonkōga Bakkōtsu* (Chinese Cave Temples: Dunhuang). 5 vols. Tokyo/Beijing, 1979-87.

Dunhuang Yanjiu Yuan. *Zhongguo Meishu Quanji 15: Dunhuang Bihua* (Chinese Fine Arts Collection: Dunhuang mural painting). 2 vols. Shanghai, 1985.

Dunhuang Yanjiu Yuan and Sun Xiushen. *Mogao ku bihua yishu: Yuandai* (The art of mural painting in the Mogao caves: Yuan dynasty). Dunhuang Art Booklet Series, no. 13. Lanzhou, 1986.

Dunnell, Ruth W. *The Great State of White and High: Buddhism and state formation in eleventh-century Xia*. Honolulu, 1996.

Duquenne, Robert. "Daiitoku Myōō." In *Hōbōgirin: Dictionnaire Encyclopédique du Bouddhisme D'Après Les Sources Chinoises et Japonaises Fasc. 6: Da-Daijizaiten*, edited by Hubert Durt, pp. 652-670. Tokyo/Paris, 1983.

______. "On Realizing Buddhahood in One's Body." *Transactions of the International Conference of Orientalists in Japan* 26 (1981): 148-149.

Dutt, Nalinaksha, ed. *Gilgit Manuscripts Vol.1*. Srinagar, 1939.

Eastman, Kenneth W. "Summary Report: The Eighteen Tantras of the *Tattvasaṃgrha/Māyājāla*." *Transactions of the International Conference of Orientalists in Japan* 26 (1981): 95-96.

Eberhard, Wolfram. *A History of China*. 2nd ed. Berkeley, 1960.

Edwards, Richard. "Pu-tai-Maitreya and a Reintroduction to Hangchou's Fei-lai-feng." *Ars Orientalis* 14 (1984): 5-50.

Eliade, Mircea. "Methodological Remarks on the Study of Religious Symbolism." In *The History of Religions: Essays in Methodology*, edited by Mircea Eliade and Joseph M. Kitagawa, pp. 86-107. Chicago, 1959.

______. *The Sacred and the Profane: The Nature of Religion*. New York, 1959.

______. "Survivals and Camouflages of Myths." In *Symbolism, the Sacred, and the Arts*, edited by Diane Apostolos-Cappadona, pp. 32-52. New York, 1988.

______. *Yoga: Immortality and Freedom*. 2nd ed. Princeton, 1969.

Ennin, *Ennin's Diary: The Record of a Pilgrimage to China in Search of the Law*. Translated by Edwin O. Reischauer. New York, 1955.

Essen, Gerd-Wolfgang, and Tsering Tashi Thingo. *Die Götter des Himalaya: Buddhistische Kunst Tibets, Die Sammlung Gerd-Wolfgang Essen*. 2 vols. Munich, 1989.

Everding, Karl-Heinz. *Die Präexistenzen der lCan skya Qutuqtus*. Asiatische Forschungen, no. 104. Wiesbaden, 1988.

Fabri, Charles. *History of the Art of Orissa*. New Delhi, 1974.

Farmer, Edward; G.R.G. Hambly; D. Kopf; B.K. Marshall; and Romeyn Taylor. *Comparative History of Civilizations in Asia*. 2 vols. Menlo Park, 1977.

Felten, Wolfgang, and Martin Lerner. *Thai and Cambodian Sculpture from the 6th to the 14th centuries*. London, 1989.

Fergusson, James and James Burgess. *The Cave Temples of India*. Reprint ed. Delhi, 1969.

Feugère, Laure. "The Pelliot Collection from Dunhuang." *Orientations* 20, no. 3 (1989): 41-52.

Fickle, Dorothy H. "Crowned Buddha Images in Southeast Asia." In *Art and Archaeology in Thailand*, pp. 85-120. Bangkok, 1974.

Filliozat, Jean. "Le Complexe d'oedipe dans un tantra Bouddhique." In *Études Tibétaines dédiées à la mémoire de Marcelle Lalou*, pp. 142-148. Paris, 1971.

Finot, Louis. "Lokeçvara en Indochine." In *Études Asiatique publiées à l'occasion du vingt-cinquième anniversaire de l'École Française d'Extrême-Orient*, pp. 1:227-256. Paris, 1925.

Fisher, Philip. *Making and Effacing Art: Modern American Art in a Culture of Museums*. New York, 1991.

Fontein, Jan. *The Sculpture of Indonesia*. New York, 1990.

______. "Relics and reliquaries, texts and artefacts." In *Function and Meaning in Buddhist Art*, edited by K.R. van Kooij and H. van der Veere, pp. 21-31. Groningen, 1995.

Fontein, Jan, and Money L. Hickman. *Zen Painting and Calligraphy*. Boston, 1970.

Fontein, Jan, and Wu Tung. *Unearthing China's Past*. Boston, 1973.

Forte, Antonino. "The Activities in China of the Tantric Master Manicintana (Pao-ssu-wei: ?-721 AD) from Kashmir and of his Northern Indian Collaborators." *East and West* ns 34 (1984):301-345.

______. *Mingtang and Buddhist Utopias in the History of the Astronomical Clock: the Tower, Statue and Armillary Sphere Constructed by Empress Wu*. Serie Orientale Roma, no. 59. Rome, 1988.

______. *Political Propaganda and Ideology in China at the End of the Seventh Century. Inquiry into the Nature, Authors and Function of the Tun-huang Document S.6502, Followed by an Annotated Translation*. Naples, 1976.

Foucault, Michel. *Madness and Civilization: A History of Insanity in the Age of Reason*. Translated by Richard Howard. New York, 1973.

Foucher, Alfred. *Étude sur l'iconographie Bouddhique de l'inde, d'après des textes inédits*. Paris, 1905.

Franke, Herbert. "Some Remarks on the Interpretation of Chinese Dynastic Histories." *Oriens* 3 (1950): 113-122.

Friedlaender, Walter. *Mannerism and Anti-Mannerism in Italian Painting*. New York, 1965.

Fujieda, Akira and Murata, Jiro. *Chü-yung kuan: The Buddhist Arch of the 14th c. AD at the Pass of the Great Wall, North-west of Peking*. 2 vols. Translated by Leon Hurwitz. Kyoto, 1955.

Gail, Adalbert. "Mañjuśrī and his sword." In *Function and Meaning in Buddhist Art*, edited by K.R. van Kooij and H. van der Veere, pp. 135-138. Groningen, 1995.

Gaulier, Simone; Robert Jera-Bezard; and Monique Maillard. *Buddhism in Afghanistan and Central Asia*. 2 vols. Iconography of Religions, no. 13. Leiden, 1976.

Ge Wanzhang. "Qiantan Xizang Fohua" (An informal discussion of Tibetan Buddhist imagery). *Gugong Wenwu Yuekan* 1.8 (1983): 87-98.

Geertz, Clifford. "Art as a Cultural System." In *Local Knowledge: Further Essays in Interpretive Anthropology*, pp. 94-120. New York, 1983.

______. "Religion As a Cultural System." In *The Interpretation of Cultures*, pp. 87-125. New York, 1973.

Gelfman, Wayne. "Kukai's Interpretation of the *Rishukyō*." *Transactions of the International Conference of Orientalists in Japan* 23 (1978): 103-104.

Genoud, Charles; with photographs by Inoue Takao. *Buddhist Wall-painting of Ladakh*. Geneva, 1982.

George, Christopher S. *The Caṇḍamahāroṣaṇa Tantra: Chapters I-VIII; A Critical Edition and English Translation*. American Oriental Series, no. 56. New Haven, 1974.

Gernet, Jacques. *Les aspects économiques du bouddhisme dans la sociéte chinoise du V' et X' siècle*. Saigon, 1956.

Giles, Lionel. "Dated Chinese Manuscripts in the Stein Collection, part VI. 10th century (AD 947-995)." *Bulletin of the School of Oriental And African Studies* 11 (1943-46): 148-149.

von Glasenapp, Helmuth. "Buddhism and Comparative Religion." *Sino-Indian Studies (Liebenthal Festschrift)* 5, nos. 3-4 (1957): 47-52.

Goepper, Roger. *Aizen-Myōō, The Esoteric King of Lust: An Iconographic Study*.

Artibus Asiae. Zurich, 1993.

______. *Alchi: Buddhas, Göttinnen, Maṇḍalas; Wandmalerei in einem Himalaya-Kloster*. Photgraphs by Jaro Poncar. Köln, 1982; English revised ed., *Alchi: Buddhas, Goddesses, Maṇḍalas*. Köln, 1984.

______. *Alchi, Ladakh's Hidden Buddhist Sanctuary: The Sumtsek*. London, 1996.

______. "Clues for a Dating of the Three-Storeyed Temple (Sumtsek) in Alchi, Ladakh." *Asiatische Studien* 44.2 (1990): 159-169.

______. *Shingon: Die Kunst des Geheimen Buddhismus in Japan*. Köln, 1988.

Goetz, H. "An Imperial Incense Burner from Taranatha's Monastery." *Bulletin of the Baroda State Museum* 4, no. 1-2 (1949): 57-60.

Gombrich, E.H. *The Sense of Order*. Ithaca, 1979.

Gómez, Luis O. "Buddhism in India." In *The Encyclopedia of Religion*, edited by Mircea Eliade, 2:351-385. New York, 1987.

______. "A Mahāyāna Liturgy." In *Buddhism in Practice*, edited by Donald S. Lopez, Jr., pp. 183-196. Princeton, 1995.

______. "Observations of the Role of the *Gandavyuha* in the Design of Barabudur." In *Barabudur: History and Significance of a Buddhist Monument*, edited by Luis O. Gómez and Hiram W. Woodward, Jr., pp. 173-194. Berkeley, 1981.

Gómez, Luis O., and Hiram W. Woodward, Jr. "Introduction." In *Barabudur: History and Significance of a Buddhist Monument*, edited by Luis O. Gómez and Hiram W. Woodward, Jr., pp. 1-14. Berkeley, 1981.

Gonda, Jan. "The Absence of vahanas in the Veda and their occurrence in Hindu art and literature." In *Change and Continuity in Indian Religion*, pp. 71-114. The Hague, 1965.

Gorakshkar, Sadashiv and Desai, Kalpana. "An Illustrated Manuscript of *Aṣṭasāhasrikā Prajñāpāramitā* in the Asiatic Society of Bombay." In *Orientalia Iosephi Tucci Memoriae Dicata*, edited by G. Gnoli and L. Lanciotti, pp. 561-568. Serie Orientale Roma no. 56.2. Rome, 1987.

Goswami, Niranjan. "A Study of the Ugra-Mūrtis of Śiva." Ph.D. dissertation, University of Pennsylvania, 1972.

Govinda, Lama Anagarika. "Tantric Buddhism." In *2500 Years of Buddhism*, edited by P.V.Bapat, pp. 312-328. New Delhi, 1956.

Grabar, Oleg. *The Formation of Islamic Art*. New Haven, 1973.

Granoff, Phyllis. "Maheśvara/Mahākāla: A Unique Buddhist Image from Kasmir." *Artibus Asiae* 41 (1979): 64-82.

______. "Tobatsu Bishamon: Three Japanese Statues in the United States and an Outline of the Rise of This Cult in East Asia." *East and West* 20 (1970): 144-167.

Gredzens, David. *Visions from the Top of the World: The Art of Tibet and the Himalayas*. Minneapolis, 1983.

Grinstead, Eric D. "The Dragon King of the Sea." *The British Museum Quarterly* 31 (1967): 96-100.

______. "Tangut Fragments in the British Museum." *The British Museum Quarterly* 24 (1961): 82-87.

______. "The Tangut Tripitaka, Background Notes." *Sung Studies Newsletter* 6 (1972): 19-23.

Groslier, George. *Les Collections Khmères du Musée Albert Sarraut a Phnom-Penh*. Paris, 1931.

______. *La Sculpture Khmère Ancienne*. Paris, 1925.

Grünwedel, Albert. *Buddhistische Kunst in Indien*. Berlin, 1893; English translation, *Buddhist Art in India*. Translated by Agnes C. Gibson. Edited by James Burgess. London, 1900.

Guenther, Herbert V. *The Life and Teaching of Nāropā: Translated from the original Tibetan with a Philosophical Commentary based on the Oral Transmission*. Oxford, 1963.

______. *The Tantric View of Life*. Berkeley/London, 1972.

______. *Treasures On the Tibetan Middle Way*. Berkeley, 1976.

Guenther, Herbert V,. and Chögyam Trungpa. *The Dawn of Tantra*. Berkeley, 1974.

van Gulik, Robert Hans. *Hayagrīva: The Mantrayānic Aspect of Horse-Cult in China and Japan*. Leiden, 1935.

______. *Siddham: An Essay on the History of Sanskrit Studies in China and Japan*. New Delhi, 1980.

Gupte, Ramesh Shankar. *The Iconography of the Buddhist Sculptures (Caves) of Ellora*. Aurangabad, 1964.

______. *Iconography of the Hindus, Buddhists and Jains*. Bombay, 1972.

Gupte, Ramesh Shankar, and B.D. Mahajan. *Ajanta. Ellora and Aurangabad Caves*. Bombay, 1962.

Gutschow, Kim. "Unfocussed Merit-Making in Zangskar: A Socio-Economic Account of Karsha Nunnery." *Tibet Journal*. In press.

______. "The *Smyung gnas* Fast in Zanskar: How Liminality Depends on Structure." *Recent Research in Ladakh no. 8*. In press.

Haarh, Erik. "Contributions to the Study of Maṇḍala and Mudrā: Analysis of Two Tibetan Manuscripts in the Royal Library in Copenhagen." *Acta Orientalia* 23 (1959): 57-91.

Hadjinicolaou, Nicos. *Art History and Class Struggle*. London, 1978.

Hakeda, Yoshito S. *Kūkai: Major Works*. New York, 1972.

Harle, J.C. "Remarks on *Ālīdha*." In *Mahāyānist Art After AD 900*, edited by William Watson, pp. 10-14. Colloquies on Art and Archaeology in Asia, no. 2. London, 1972.

Haque, Enamul. *Treasures in the Dacca Museum*. Dacca, 1963.

Harpham, Geoffrey. *On the Grotesque: Strategies of Contradiction in Art and Literature*. Princeton, 1982.

Havell, E.B. *Indian Sculpture and Painting*. London, 1908.

Hedin, Sven. *Jehol: City of Emperors*. New York, 1933.

Heller, Amy. "Early Ninth Century Images of Vairochana from Eastern Tibet." *Orientations* 25, no. 6 (1994): 74-79.

______. "Eighth- and Ninth-Century Temples and Rock Carvings of Eastern Tibet." In *Tibetan Art: Towards a definition of style*, edited by Jane Casey Singer and Philip Denwood, pp. 86-103. London, 1997.

Heller, Amy, and Thomas Marcotty. "Phur-pa: Tibetan Ritual Daggers." *Arts of Asia* 17, no. 4 (1987): 69-77.

Herrmann-Pfandt, Adelheid. "Yab Yum Iconography and the Role of Women in Tibetan Tantric Buddhism." *Tibet Journal* 22, no. 1 (1997): 12-34.

Hesse, Hermann. *The Glass Bead Game (Magister Ludi)*. Translated by Richard and Clara Winston. New York, 1969.

Hirakawa, Akira. "The Rise of Mahāyāna Buddhism and its Relationship to the Worship of Stūpas." *Memoirs of the Research Department of the Toyo Bunko* 22 (1963): 57-106.

Hobbs, Edward. "Prologue: An Introduction to Methods of Textual Criticism." In *The Critical Study of Sacred Texts*, edited by Wendy Doniger O'Flaherty, pp. 1-27. Berkeley, 1979.

Hōbōgirin: Dictionnaire Encyclopédique du Bouddhisme D'Après les Sources Chinoises et Japonaises; Premier Fascicule: A-Bombai. Edited by Paul Demiéville. Tokyo, 1929.

Hock, Nancy. "Buddhist ideology and the sculpture of Ratnagiri, seventh through thirteenth centuries." Ph.D. dissertation, University of California, Berkeley, 1987.

Hong Huizhen. "Hangzhou Feilai feng 'Fan shi' zaoxiang chutan" (Preliminary Investigation of the "Buddhist style" sculptures of Hangzhou's Feilai feng). *Wenwu*, no. 1 (1986): 50-61.

Hooykaas, C. *A Balinese Temple Festival*. The Hague, 1977.

Howard, Angela F. "Buddhist Sculpture of Pujiang, Sichuan: A Mirror of the Direct Link Between Southwest China and India in High Tang." *Archives of Asian Art* 42 (1989): 49-61.

Hucker, Charles O. *A Dictionary of Official Titles in Imperial China*. Stanford, 1985.

Hunter, H. "Five Secrets maṇḍala." In *Function and Meaning in Buddhist Art*, edited by K.R. van Kooij and H. van der Veere, pp. 111-124. Groningen, 1995.

Hunter, W.W. "Csoma de Koros: A Pilgrim Scholar." In Alexander Csoma Korosi [sic], *The Life and Teachings of Buddha*, pp. 1-24. Calcutta, 1957.

Huntington, John. "Cave Six at Aurangabad: A Tantrayāna Monument?" In *Kaladarsana: American Studies in the Art of India*, edited by Joanna Williams, pp. 47-55. New Delhi, 1981.

______. "Gu-ge bris: A Stylistic Amalgam." In *Aspects of Indian Art*, edited by Pratapaditya Pal, pp. 105-117. Leiden, 1972.

______. "Origin of the Buddha Image, Early Image Traditions and the Concept of *Buddhadarśanapunya*." In *Studies in Buddhist Art of South Asia*, edited by A.K. Narain, pp. 23-58. New Delhi, 1985.

______. *The Phur-pa, Tibetan Ritual Daggers*. Ascona, 1975.

Huntington, Susan. *The Art of Ancient India*. New York/Tokyo, 1985.

______. *The "Pāla-Sena" Schools of Sculpture*. Leiden, 1984.

Huntington, Susan and John. *Leaves from the* Bodhi *Tree: The Art of Pāla India (8th-12th centuries) and Its International Legacy*. Dayton, 1990.

Iida, Shotaro. "Towards a Second Look at Visual Mode in Buddhist Tradition." In *Facets of Buddhism*, pp. 43-64. Delhi, 1991.

Indian Antiquary 9 (1890): 113-116, 142-144.

Ishida, Hisatoyo. *Esoteric Buddhist Painting*. Translated and adapted by E. Dale Saunders. Tokyo, 1987.

________. *Mandara no kenkyū* (A Study of Maṇḍala). 2 vols. Tokyo, 1975.

Ishimoto Yasuhiro. *Kyōō-gokokuji zō den Shingon'in ryōkai mandara* (The Maṇḍalas of the Two Worlds in the Shingon-in of the Kyōō-gokokuji). Tokyo, 1977.

Iyanaga Nobumi. "Daijizaiten." *Hōbōgirin* 6 (1983): 713-765.

______. "Récits de la soumission de Maheśvara par Trailokyavijaya." In *Tantric and Taoist Studies III*, edited by Michel Strickmann, pp. 633-745. Brussels, 1985.

Jan Yün-hua. "Buddhist Relations Between India and Sung China." *History of Religions* 6 (1966): 24-42, 135-168.

______. *A Chronicle of Buddhism in China 581-960 AD, Translations from Monk Chih-p'an's* Fo-tsu T'ung-chi. Santiniketan, 1966.

Jao Tsung-i. "The Vedas and the Murals of Dunhuang." *Orientations* 20, no. 3 (1989): 71-76.

Jasper, J.E., and Mas Pirngadie. "Beeldjes van Goden en Dieren." In *De Inlandsche Kunstnijverheid in Nederlandsch Indië, V. De Bewerking van Niet-Edele Metalen*, pp. 45-62. 's-Gravenhage, 1930.

Jayaswal, K.P. *An Imperial History of India in a Sanskrit Text [c. 700 BC-c. 770 AD]*. Lahore, 1934; reprint ed., Patna, 1988.

______. "Metal Images of Kurkihar Monastery." *Journal of the Indian Society of Oriental Art* 2, no. 2 (1934): 70-83.

Johnstone, Marea A. *Borobudur: An Analysis of the Gallery 1 Reliefs*. Pelita Borobudur Series C, no. 3. Borobudur, 1981.

Jones, Ernest. *The Life and Work of Sigmund Freud*. Abridged ed. New York, 1961.

de Jong, J.W. "The Background of Early Buddhism." *Journal of Indian and Buddhist Studies (Indogaku Bukkyogaku Kenkyu)* 12, no. 1 (1964): 34-47

______. "A Brief History of Buddhist Studies in Europe and America." *Eastern Buddhist* 7, no. 1 (1974): 49-82; 7, no. 2 (1974): 55-106; 17, no. 1 (1984) 79-107. 2nd ed., revised and enlarged. Delhi, 1987.

______. "Notes on the Sources and the Text of the Sang Hyang Kamahayanan Mantranaya." In *Buddhist Studies*, edited by Gregory Schopen, pp. 619-636. Berkeley, 1979.

______. Review of *Die Präexistenzen der lCan skya Qutuqtus*, by Karl-Heinz Everding. *Indo-Iranian Journal* 34 (1991): 149-152.

Joshi, L.M. "Original Homes of Tantrika Buddhism." *Journal of the Oriental Institute (Baroda)* 16 (1976): 223-232.

Joshi, N.P. "Hayagrīva in Brahmanical Iconography." *Journal of the Indian Society of Oriental Art* ns 5 (1972-73): 36-42.

______. "A Note on Triśūla-Purusha." *Journal of the U.P. Historical Society* ns 8 (1960): 79-81.

Kahn, Harold L. *Monarchy in the Emperor's Eyes: Image and Reality in the Ch'ien-lung Reign*. Cambridge, 1971.

Kalff, Martin Michael. "Selected Chapters from the Abhidhānottara-Tantra: The Union of Female and Male Deities." Ph. D. dissertation, Columbia University, 1979.

Kalsang, Ladrang. *The Guardian Deities of Tibet*. Dharmsala, 1996.

Kanazawa, Hiroshi. *Japanese Ink Painting: Early Zen Masterpieces*. Tokyo/New York, 1979.

Kandaswamy, S.N. "Tantric Buddhism in Tamil Literature." *Tamil Civilization* 4.1-2 (1986): 86-99.

Kapstein, Matthew. "Samantabhadra and Rudra: Innate Englightenment and Radical Evil in Rnying-ma-pa-Buddhism." In *Discourse and Practice*, edited by Frank Reynolds and David Tracy, pp. 51-82. Albany, 1992.

Karmay, Heather. *Early Sino-Tibetan Art*. Warminster, 1975.

Karmay, Samten G. "King Tsa/Dza and Vajrayāna." In *Tantric and Taoist Studies in Honour of R.A. Stein, 1*, pp. 192-211. Edited by Michel Strickmann. Brussels, 1981.

Kenney, E.J. "Textual Criticism." In *The New Encyclopœdia Britannica*, 15th ed. 18: 189-195.

Khandalavala, Karl. Review of *Yakṣa Cult and Iconography*, by Ram Nath Misra. Lalit Kala 22 (1985): 39-40.

Khosla, Romi. *Buddhist Monasteries in the Western Himalaya*. Kathmandu, 1979.

Kim, Hongnam. "The Divine Triad." In *The Story of a Painting: A Korean Buddhist Treasure from the Mary and Jackson Burke Foundation*, pp. 2-3. New York, 1991.

Kiyota Jakuun. "Kongōchōkyō no Bon-Kan taisho ni tsuite" (Comparison between the Sanskrit and Chinese texts of the Tattvasaṃgraha). *Indogaku Bukkyōgaku kenkyū* 4.1 (1956): 89-92.

Klimburg-Salter, Deborah E. "Reformation and Renaissance: A Study of Indo-Tibetan Monasteries in the Eleventh Century." In *Orientalia Iosephi Tucci Memoriae Dicata*, edited by G. Gnoli and L. Lanciotti, pp. 683-702. Serie Orientale Roma 56.2. Rome, 1987.

______. *The Silk Route and the Diamond Path*. Los Angeles, 1982.

______. *Tabo A Lamp for the Kingdom: Early Indo-Tibetan Buddhist Art in the Western Himalaya*. New York, 1997.

van Kooij, K.R. "Some Iconographical Data from the Kālikāpurāṇa with Special Reference to Heruka and Ekajatā." In *South Asian Archaeology 1973*, edited by J.E. van Lohuizen-de Leeuw and J.M.M. Ubaghs, pp. 161-170. Leiden, 1974.

Krairiksh, Piriya. *Sculptures from Thailand*. Hong Kong, 1982.

Kramrisch, Stella. *Indian Sculpture in the Philadelphia Museum of Art*. Philadelphia, 1960.

______. *Manifestations of Shiva*. Philadelphia, 1981.

______. *The Presence of Śiva*. Princeton, 1981.

Krom, N.J. "De Buddhistische Bronzen in het Museum te Batavia." In *Rapporten der Commissie voor Oudheidkundig Onderzoek op Java en Madoera*, pp. 1-83. Batavia (?), 1912.

______. "De Bronsvondst van Ngandjoek." *Rapporten van den Oudheidkundige Dienst in Nederlandsch-Indie* (1913): 59 -72.

______. *Inleiding tot de Hindoe-Javaansche Kunst*. 3 vols. The Hague, 1923.

______. *The Life of the Buddha on the Stupa of Barabudur*. London, 1925; reprint ed., Varanasi, 1974.

Kuhn, Thomas S. *The Structure of Scientific Revolutions*. 2nd enlarged ed. Chicago, 1970.

van der Kuijp, L.W.J. "Ngor-chen kun-dga'bzang-po on the Posture of Hevajra: A Note on the Relationship between Text, Iconography and Spiritual Praxis." In *Investigating Indian Art*, pp. 173-177. Berlin, 1987.

Kukai. *Kōbō daishi zenshū* (Collected works of Kobo Daishi). 7 vols. Kyoto, 1965.

Kumar, Krishna. "A Circular Caitya-Grha at Sārnāth." *Journal of the Indian Society of Oriental Art* ns 11 (1980): 63-70.

Kuraishi, Muhammad Hamid. *List of Ancient Monuments Protected Under Act VII of 1904 in the Province of Bihar and Orissa*. Archaeological Survey of India, New Imperial Series, no. 51. Calcutta, 1931.

Kværne, Per. *An Anthology of Buddhist Tantric Songs: A Study of the Caryagiti*. Det Norske Videnskaps Akademi Ny Serie, no. 14. Oslo, 1977.

_____. "On the Concept of Sahaja in Indian Buddhist Tantric Literature." *Temenos* 11 (1975): 88-135.

Kwanten, Luc. "Chio-ssu-lo (997-1065): A Tibetan Ally of the Sung." *Rocznik Orientalistyczny* 39 (1978): 97-105.

_____. *Imperial Nomads, A History of Central Asia, 500-1500*. Philadelphia, 1979.

_____. "The Role of the Tangut in Chinese-Inner Asian Relations." *Acta Orientalia* 39 (1978): 191-198.

Kwanten, Luc, and Susan Hesse. *Tangut (Hsi Hsia) Studies: A Bibliography*. Indiana University Uralic and Altai Series, no. 137. Bloomington, 1980.

Kyacanov, E.I. "Monuments of Tangut Legislation (12th-13th Centuries)." In *Études Tibétaines*, edited by Ariane Macdonald, pp. 29-42. Paris, 1976.

_____. "A Tangut Document of 1224 from Khara Khoto." *Acta Orientalia Hungaricae* 24 (1971): 189-201.

_____. "Tibetans and Tibetan Culture in the Tangut State Hsi Hsia (982-1227)." In *Proceedings of the Csoma de Körös Memorial Symposium*, edited by Louis Ligeti, pp. 205-211. Budapest, 1978.

Kyoto Kyōōgokokuji. *Godai Myōō* (Five Great Kings of Wisdom). Tokyo, 1987.

Lal, Shyam Kishore. *Female Divinities in Hindu Mythology and Ritual*. Puna, 1980.

Lalou, Marcelle. "Documents de Touen-Houang: I. Deux Prières de Caravaniers Tibétains." *Mélanges chinois et bouddhiques* 8 (1946/47): 217-223.

_____. "Four Notes on Vajrapāṇi." *Adyar Library Bulletin* 20 (1956): 287-93.

_____. "A Fifth Note on Vajrapāṇi." *Adyar Library Bulletin* 25 (1961): 242-249.

_____. *Iconographie des Étoffes Peintes (pata) dans le* Mañjuśrimūlakalpa. Paris, 1930.

_____. "*Mañjuśrimūlakalpa* and *Tārāmūlakalpa*." *Harvard Journal of Asiatic Studies* 1 (1936): 327-349.

_____. "Les Textes Bouddhiques au temps du roi Khri-Sron-Lde-Bcan: contribution à la Bibiliographie du Kanjur et du Tanjur." *Journal Asiatique* 241 (1953): 313-353.

_____. "Un Traité de Magie Bouddhique." In *Études d'orientalisme publiées par le Musée Guimet à la memoire de Raymond Linossier Vol. 2*, pp. 303-322. Paris, 1932.

Lamotte, Étienne. *History of Indian Buddhism From the Origins to the Saka Era*. Translated by Sara Webb-Boin. Louvain, 1988.

_____. "Vajrapāṇi en Inde." In *Mélanges de Sinologie offerts à Monsieur Paul Demiéville*, pp. 113-161. Bibliothèque de l'Institut des Hautes Études Chinoises, no. 20. Paris, 1966.

Lancaster, Lewis R. "Buddhist Literature: Its Canons, Scribes, and Editors." In *The Critical Study of Sacred Texts*, edited by Wendy Doniger O'Flaherty, pp. 215-229. Berkeley, 1979.

_____. "The Editing of Buddhist Texts. In *Buddhist Thought and Asian Civilization: Essays in Honor of Herbert V. Guenther on His Sixtieth Birthday*, edited by Leslie S. Kawamura and Keith Scott, pp. 145-151. Emeryville, 1977.

_____. *The Korean Buddhist Canon: A Descriptive Catalogue*. Berkeley, 1979.

Langer, Susanne K. *Feeling and Form: A Theory of Art*. New York, 1953.

LaPlante, John D. "A Pre-Pāla Sculpture and its Significance for the International Bodhisattva Style in Asia." *Artibus Asiae* 26 (1963): 247-284.

Lavine, Steven D., and Ivan Karp, eds. *Exhibiting Cultures: The Poetics and Politics of Museum Display*. Washington, 1991.

Ledderose, Lothar. *Im Schatter hoher Bäume: Malerei der Ming- und Qing-Dynastien (1368-1911) aus der Volksrepublik China*. Baden-Baden, 1985.

Lee Yu-min. "The Maitreya Cult and its Art in Early China." Ph.D. dissertation, Ohio State University, 1983.

Lei Runze; Yu Cunhai; and He Jiying, eds. *Xixia Fota* (Buddhist Pagodas of Western Xia). Beijing, 1995.

Leidy, Denise Patry, and Robert A. F. Thurman. *Maṇḍala: The Architecture of Enlightenment*. New York, 1997.

Leoshko, Janice. "The Appearance of Amoghapāśa in Pāla Period Art." In *Studies in Buddhist Art of South Asia*, edited by A.K Narain, pp. 127-135. New Delhi, 1985.

_____. "Buddhist Art of Northern India." In *Asian Art: Selections from the Norton Simon Museum*, edited by Pratapaditya Pal, pp. 20-33. Pasadena, 1988. Adapted from *Orientations* 19, no. 7 (1988): 30-43.

_____. "Buddhist Images from Telhara, a Site in Eastern India." *South Asian Studies* 4 (1988): 89-97.

_____. "Buddhist Sculptures from Bodhgaya." In *Bodhgaya, the site of enlightenment*, edited by Janice Leoshko, pp. 45-60. Bombay, 1988.

_____. "The Case of the Two Witnesses to the Buddha's Enlightenment." *Marg* 39 (1988): 40-52.

_____. "The Implications of Bodhgaya's Sūrya." In *Aksayanīvi: Essays presented to Dr. Debala Mitra*, pp. 231-234. Delhi, 1991.

_____. "Pilgrimage and the evidence of Bodhgaya's images." In *Function and Meaning in Buddhist Art*, edited by K.R. van Kooij and H. van der Veere, pp. 45-57. Groningen, 1995.

Lerner, Martin. *The Flame and the Lotus: Indian and Southeast Asian Art from the Kronos Collection*. New York, 1984.

Lessing, Ferdinand D. *Yung-Ho-Kung: An Iconography of the Lamaist Cathedral in Peking, With Notes on Lamaist Mythology and Cult*. Stockholm, 1942.

Lessing, Ferdinand D., and Alex Wayman. *Introduction to the Buddhist Tantric Systems, translated from Mkhas-grub-rje's* Rgyud sde spyihi rnam par gzag pa rgyas par brjod. 2nd ed. Delhi, 1978.

Lévi, Sylvain. *The Mission of Wang Hiuen-ts'e in India*. Translated by S.P. Chatterjee. Calcutta, 1967.

_____. *Sanskrit Texts from Bali*. Gaekwad's Oriental Series, no. 68. Baroda, 1933.

Levinson, Susan B. "Discovering an Important Mongol Silk Textile." *Hali: The International Journal of Oriental Carpets and Textiles* 5.4 (1983): 496-497.

Li Lincan. *Gugong Zhixiu Xuancui* (Masterpieces of Chinese Silk Tapestry and Embroidery in the National Palace Museum). Taipei, 1971.

_____. *Nanzhao Daliguo xin cailiao de zonghe yanjiu* (A study of the Nan-chao and Ta-li kingdoms in the light of art materials found in various museums). Taipei, 1982.

Liebert, Gösta. *Iconographic Dictionary of the Indian Religions: Hinduism-Buddhism Jainism*. Studies in South Asian Culture, no. 5. Leiden, 1976.

Lim, K.W. "Studies in Later Buddhist Iconography." *Bijdragen Tot de Taal-, Land- en Volkenkunde van Nederlandsch-Indie* 120 (1964): 327-341.

Lin Likouang, "Punyodaya (Na-t'i), un propagateur du Tantrisme en Chine et au Cambodge à l'Époque de Hiuan-Tsang." *Journal Asiatique* 227 (1935): 83-100.

Linrothe, Rob. "Beyond Sectarianism: Towards Reinterpreting the Iconography of Esoteric Buddhist Deities Trampling Hindu Gods." *Indian Journal of Buddhist Studies* 2, no. 2 (1990): 16-25.

Linrothe, Rob. "Compassionate Malevolence: Wrathful Deities in Esoteric Buddhist Art." Ph.D. dissertation, University of Chicago, 1992.

_____. "Mapping the Iconographic Programme of the Sumtsek." In Roger Goepper, *Alchi, Ladakh's Hidden Sanctuary: The Sumtsek*, pp. 269-272.

London, 1996.
______. "The Murals of Mangyu: A Distillation of Mature Esoteric Buddhist Iconography." *Orientations* 25, no. 11 (1994): 92-102.
______. "New Delhi and New England: Old Collections of Tangut Art." *Orientations* 27, no. 4 (1996): 32-41.
______. "Peripheral Visions: On Recent Finds of Tangut Buddhist Art." *Monumenta Serica* 43 (1995): 235-62.
______. "Provincial or Providential: Reassessment of an Esoteric Buddhist 'Treasure.'" *Monumenta Serica* 37 (1986-87): 197-225.
de Lippe, Aschwin. *Indian Mediaeval Sculpture*. Amsterdam, 1978.
Liu Xinru. *Ancient India and Ancient China*. Oxford, 1988.
Lo Bue, Eberto. "The Dharmamaṇḍala-Sutra by Buddhaguhya." In *Orientalia Iosephi Tucci Memoriae Dicata*, edited by G. Gnoli and L. Lanciotti, pp. 787-818. Serie Orientale Roma no. 56.2. Rome, 1987.
Lo Hsiang-lin. *Tang dai Guangzhou Guangxiao si yu Zhong-Yin jiaotong zhi guanxi* (Guangxiao Monastery of Canton during the Tang with reference to Sino-Indian relations). Hong Kong, 1960.
Lobo, Wibke. "The Figure of Hevajra and Tantric Buddhism." In *Sculpture of Angkor and Ancient Cambodia: Millennium of Glory*, edited by Helen I. Jessup and Thierry Zephir, pp. 71-78. Washington D.C., 1997.
Lohia, Sushama. *Lalitavajra's Manual of Buddhist Iconography*. New Delhi, 1994.
Lohuizen-de Leeuw, Johanna E. van. *Indische skulpturen der Sammlung Eduard von der Heydt*. Zurich, 1964.
Lokesh Chandra. "The Iconography of Uma and Maheśvara in Japanese Art." *Annals of the Bhandarkar Oriental Research Institute* 58/59 (1977-78): 733-744.
______. "Identification of the Nañjuk Bronzes" and "The Bronze-find of Nañjuk." In *Cultural Horizons of India* Volume IV (New Delhi: Aditya Prakashan, 1995), 97-120.
______. *Materials for a History of Tibetan Literature*. New Delhi, 1963.
______. *A Ninth Century Scroll of the Vajradhātu Maṇḍala*. New Delhi, 1986.
______. "Oddiyāna: A New Interpretation." In *Tibetan Studies in Honour of Hugh Richardson*, edited by Michael Aris and Aung San Suu Kyi, pp. 73-78. Oxford, 1979.
______. "The Role of *Tantras* in the Defence Strategy of T'ang China." In *Kusumanjali*, edited by M.S. Nagaraja Rao, pp. 53-59. Delhi, 1987.
______. "The Tripitaka-Translator Pao-ssu-Wei (Cintāmani)." In *Śramana Vidyā Studies in Buddhism, Prof. Jagannath Upadhyaya Commemoration Volume*, pp. 283-286. Sarnath, 1987.
Lokesh Chandra, and David L. Snellgrove, eds. *Sarva-tathāgata-tattva-sangraha*. New Delhi, 1981.
Lokesh Chandra, and Chikyō Yamamoto. *The Esoteric Iconography of Japanese Maṇḍalas*. New Delhi, 1971.
Lopez, Donald S., Jr., ed. *Buddhism in Practice*. Princeton, 1995.
Lorenzen, David N. *The Kāpālikas and Kālāmukhas, Two Lost Saivite Sects*. New Delhi, 1972.
Losty, J.P. "Bengal, Bihar, Nepal? Problems of Provenance in 12th-Century Illuminated Buddhist Manuscripts, Part One." *Oriental Art*, ns 35, no. 2 (1989): 86-96; Part Two, *Oriental Art* ns 35, no. 3 (1989): 140-149.
Lutz, Albert. *Der Tempel der Drei Pagoden*. Zürich, 1991.
Macdonald, Alexander W., and Anne Vergati Stahl. *Newar Art: Nepalese Art During the Malla Period*. Warminster, 1979.
Macdonald, Ariane. *Le Maṇḍala du Mañjuśrīmūlakalpa*. Paris, 1962.
McGuiness, Stephen, and Ogasawara Sae. *Chinese Textile Masterpieces: Sung, Yuan and Ming Dynasties*. Hong Kong, 1988.
Magurn, Blanche W. "Daiitoku Myō-ō, A Japanese Buddhist Deity." *Bulletin of the Fogg Museum of Art* 10 (November 1942): 14-23.
Mailey, Jean. *Chinese Silk Tapestry: K'o-ssu*. New York, 1981.
Malandra, Geri Hockfield. "Ellora: The 'Archaeology of a *Maṇḍala*'." *Ars Orientalis* 15 (1985): 67-94.
______. "The Buddhist Caves at Ellora." Ph.D. dissertation, University of Minnesota, 1983.
______. *Unfolding a Maṇḍala: The Buddhist Cave Temples at Ellora*. Albany, 1993.
Malla, Bansi Lal. "A Note on Vaishnavite Āyudhapuruṣas in Mediaeval Kashmiri Sculptures." *Indian Museum Bulletin* 20 (1985): 28-31.
______. *Sculptures of Kashmir (600-1200 AD)*. Delhi, 1990.
de Mallmann, Marie-Thérèse. *Étude Iconographique sur Mañjuśrī*. Paris, 1964.
______. *Introduction a l'étude d'Avalokiteśvara*. Paris, 1948.
______. *Introduction a l'iconographie du tantrisme bouddhique*. Paris, 1975.
______. "Un manuscrit illustré du Devī-Mahātmya." *Arts Asiatiques* 2 (1955): 178-196.
______. "Un point d'iconographie indo-javanaise: Khaśarpana et Amoghapāśa." *Artibus Asiae* 11 (1948): 176-188.
Manabe, Shunsho. "The Expression of Elimination of Devils in the Iconographic Texts of the T'ang Period and its Background." *Indogaku bukkyōgaku kenkyū* 12.2 (1967): 907-914.
Mani, V.R. *The Cult of Weapons: The Iconography of the Āyudhapuruṣas*. Delhi, 1985.
Marshall, Sir John. "Excavations at Sahêth-Mahêth." In *Archaeological Survey of India, Annual Report 1910-11*, pp. 1-24. Calcutta, 1914.
Marshall, Sir John, and Alfred Foucher. *The Monuments of Sañchi*. 3 vols. London, 1940.
Marshall, Sir John, and Sten Konow. "Excavations at Sarnath, 1908." In *Archaeological Survey of India, Annual Report 1907-8*, pp. 43-54. Calcutta, 1911.
______. "Sārnāth." In *Archaeological Survey of India, Annual Report 1906 -07*, pp. 81-85. Calcutta, 1909.
Martin, H. Desmond. "The Mongol Wars with Hsi Hsia (1205-27)." *Journal of the Royal Asiatic Society* (1942): 195-228.
Marzuki, Yazir, and Toeti Heraty. *Borobudur*. Yogyakarta(?), 1985.
Matsumoto Eiichi. *Tonkōga no Kenkyū* (Research on Dunhuang Paintings). 2 vols. Tokyo, 1937.
Matsumoto, Moritaka. "Chang Sheng-wen's Long Roll of Buddhist Images: A Reconstruction and Iconology." Ph.D. dissertation, Princeton University, 1976.
Matsunaga, Alicia. *The Buddhist Philosophy of Assimilation: The Historical Development of the* Honji-Suijaku *Theory*. Tokyo, 1969.
Matsunaga, Yukei. "Indian Esoteric Buddhism as Studied in Japan." In *Studies of Esoteric Buddhism and Tantrism in Commemoration of the 1150th Anniversary of the founding of Koyasan University*, edited by Matsunaga Yukei, pp. 229-242. Koyasan, 1965.
______. "On the Date of the *Mañjuśrīmūlakalpa*." In *Tantric and Taoist Studies in Honor of R.A. Stein Vol. 3*, edited by Michel Strickmann, pp. 882-893. Brussels, 1985.
______. "Some Problems of the *Guhyasamāja-Tantra*." *Studies in Indo-Asian Art and Culture* 5 (1972): 109-119.
______. "Tantric Buddhism and Shingon Buddhism." *The Eastern Buddhist* 2, no. 2 (1969): 5-7.
Matsunaga Yukei and Kei Kato. *Maṇḍala: Buddhist Art of Western Tibet*. 2 vols. Tokyo, 1981.
Mazzeo, Donatella, and Chiara Silvi Antonini. *Monuments of Civilization: Ancient Cambodia*. New York, 1978.
Meech, Julia. "A Painting of Daiitoku from the Bigelow Collection." *Bulletin, Museum of Fine Arts, Boston* 67, no. 37 (1969): 18-43.
Meisezahl, Richard O. "Amoghapāśa: Some Nepalese Representations and Their Vajrayānic Aspects." *Monumenta Serica* 26 (1967): 494-496.

______. "The Amoghapāśahrdaya-dhāraṇi: The Early Sanskrit Manuscript of the Reiunji Critically Edited and Translated." *Monumenta Nipponica* 17 (1962): 265-328.

______. "L'Étude iconographique des huit Cimetières d'après le traité Śmaśānavidhi de Luyi." In *Geist und Ikonographie des Vajrayâna-Buddhismus: Hommage à Marie-Thérèse de Mallmann*, pp. 3-123. St. Augustin, 1980.

Minoru, Kiyota. *Shingon Buddhism: Theory and Practice*. Los Angeles/Tokyo, 1978.

______. *Tantric Concept of Bodhicitta: A Buddhist Experiential Philosophy*. Madison, 1982.

Misra, Ram Nath. "Yakṣa, A Linguistic Complex." *Journal of the U.P. Historical Society* ns 9 (1961): 74-75.

______. *Yakṣa Cult and Iconography*. New Delhi, 1981.

Mitra, Debala. *Bronzes from Achutrajpur, Orissa*. Delhi, 1978.

______. *Buddhist Monuments*. Calcutta, 1971.

______. "An Image of Sambara in the Patna Museum." *The Orissa Historical Research Journal* 9, no. 3-4 (1960): 43-46.

______. *Ratnagiri (1958-61)*. 2 vols. Archaeological Survey of India Memoirs, no. 80. New Delhi, 1981-83.

Mitra, Rajendralala. *Buddha Gaya: The Great Buddhist Temple, the Hermitage of Śakya Muni*. Calcutta, 1878; reprint ed., Delhi, 1972.

Mitter, Partha. *Much Maligned Monsters: History of European Reactions to Indian Art*. Oxford, 1977.

Miyasaka, Yūshō. "Yamantaka." *Indogaku Bukkyōgaku Kenkyū* 19, no. 2 (1971): 504-512.

Mochizuki Shinkō, with Tsukamoto Zenryū. *Bukkyō daijiten*. 10 vols. 4th ed. Tokyo, 1958-1963.

Mohapatra, R.P. *Archaeology in Orissa (Sites and Monuments)*. 2 vols. Delhi, 1986.

Moharana, Surendra Kumar. "Development of Tantric Buddhism in Orissa." Ph.D. dissertation, Utkal University, Bhubaneswar 1985.

Monier-Williams, Sir Monier. *Sanskrit-English Dictionary*. Oxford, 1899; reprint ed., New Delhi, 1988.

Montell, Gösta. "Sven Hedin's Archaeological Collections from Khotan." *The Museum of Far Eastern Antiquities* 10 (1938): 145-221.

Mukherjee, Prabhat. *Lalitagiri, Udayagiri and Ratnagiri*. Madras, 1984.

Murthy, K. Krishna. *Iconography of Buddhist Deity Heruka*. Delhi, 1988.

Mus, Paul. "Le buddha paré, son origine indienne, Cakyamuni dans le Mahāyānisme moyen." *Bulletin de l'École Française d'Extrême-Orient* 28 (1928): 1-2, 153-278.

Nakamura, Hajime. *Indian Buddhism: A Survey with Bibliographical Notes*. Buddhist Traditions, no. 1. Delhi, 1987.

Nanjio, Bunyiu. *A Catalogue of the Chinese Translation of the Buddhist Tripitaka (A Translation of the* Ta ming san tsang sheng chiao mu lu*)*. Oxford, 1883.

______. *A Catalogue of the Buddhist Tripitaka, with additions and corrections by Lokesh Chandra*. New Delhi, 1980.

Nara National Museum. *The Grand Exhibition of Silk Road Civilizations Volume Three: The Route of Buddhist Art*. Nara, 1988.

Nath, Amarendra. *Buddhist Images and Narratives*. New Delhi, 1986.

Naudou, Jean. *Les Bouddhistes Kasmiriens Au Moyen Age*. Paris, 1968.

______. *Buddhists of Kasmir*. Translated by Brereton and Picron [sic]. Delhi, 1980.

de Nebesky-Wojkowitz, René. *Oracles and Demons of Tibet: The Cult and Iconography of the Tibetan Protective Deities*. 'S-Gravenhage, 1956.

Newman, John. "On Recent Studies in Buddhist Architecture of Western India: A Review." *Indian Journal of Buddhist Studies* 1 (1989): 108-112.

______. "Vajrayāna Deities in an Illustrated Indian Manuscript of the *Aṣṭasāhasrikā-prajñāpāramitā*." *Journal of the International Association of Buddhist Studies* 13, no. 2 (1990): 117-132.

Ngor Thar rtse mkhan po. *Tibetan Maṇḍalas: The Ngor Collection*. 2 vols. Tokyo, 1983.

Nicolas-Vandier, Nicole; Simone Gaulier; Françoise Leblond; Monique Maillard; and Robert Jera-Bezard. *Bannières et Peintures de Touen-Houang Conservées au Musée Guimet*. 2 vols. Mission Paul Pelliot, nos. 14-15. Paris, 1974-76.

Nihon Bijutsu Zenshu (Japanese fine art collections) *Vol. 6: Mikkyō no Bijutsu: Tōji/Jingōji/Murōji* (Esoteric Buddhist Art of Tōji, Jingōji and Murōji temples). Edited by Uehara Shoichi. Tokyo, 1980.

Ningxia Huizu Zizhi Qu Wenwu Guanli Weiyuan Hui Bangong Shi, Helan xian Wenwu Ju (Office of Helan County Cultural Relics, Branch of the Ningxia Huizu Autonomous Region and Cultural Relics Bureau). "Ningxia Helan xian Baisikou Shuangta kance weixiu jianbo" (Preliminary report on the Survey and Maintenance of the Baisikou Twin Pagodas in Ningxia's Helan County). *Wenwu* 8 (1991): 14-26.

______. "Ningxia Helan xian Hongfo Ta qingli Jianbao" (Excavation Report on the Ningxia Helan County's Hongfo Stupa). *Wenwu* 8 (1991): 1-13, 26.

Niyogi, Pushpa. "Organisation of Buddhist Monasteries in Ancient Bengal and Bihar." *Journal of Indian History* 51 (1973): 531-557.

______. "Some Buddhist Monasteries in Ancient Bengal and Bihar." *Journal of Indian History* 54 (1976): 273-298.

Obeyesekere, Gananath. *Medusa's Hair: An Essay on Personal Symbols and Religious Experience*. Chicago, 1981.

Oda, Jishu. "Acalāgra Vidyārāja." In *Encyclopaedia of Buddhism, Fascicle: Acala-Akankheyya Sutta*, edited by G.P. Malalasekera, pp. 155-161. Colombo, 1963.

O'Flaherty, Wendy Doniger. *The Origins of Evil in Hindu Mythology*. Berkeley, 1976.

______. *The Rig Veda, An Anthology*. New York, 1981.

Okazaki Jōji. "Butsuzō rinshoken no godai myōō" (Godai Myō-ō images on an esoteric Buddhist bell). *Bijutsushi* 16, no. 1 (1966): 18-32.

Olschak, Blanche Christine, with Geshé Thupten Wangyal. *Mystic Art of Ancient Tibet*. London, 1973.

Olson, Eleanor. *Tantric Buddhist Art*. New York, 1974.

Omura Seigai. *Mikkyō hattatsu-shi* (The History of Esoteric Buddhism). Tokyo, 1918.

Orlando, Raffaello. "A Study of Chinese Documents Concerning the Life of the Tantric Buddhist Patriarch Amoghavajra (AD 705-774)." Ph.D. dissertation, Princeton, 1981.

Otto, Rudolph. *The Idea of the Holy*. 2nd ed. London, 1950.

Pal, Pratapaditya. "An Addorsed Śaiva Image From Kashmir and Its Cultural Significance." *Art International* 24, no. 5-6 (1981): 6-60.

______. *Art of Nepal*. Los Angeles, 1985.

______. *Art of the Himalayas: Treasures from Nepal and Tibet*. New York, 1991.

______. *The Art of Tibet*. New York, 1969.

______. *Art of Tibet*. Los Angeles, 1983.

______. *The Arts of Nepal: Part I, Sculpture*. Leiden/Köln, 1974.

______. *The Arts of Nepal: Part II, Painting*. Leiden/Köln, 1978.

______. *Bronzes of Kashmir*. New York, 1975.

______. "Bronzes of Kashmir: Their Sources and Influences." *Journal of the Royal Society of Arts* 121 (1973): 726-749.

______. *A Buddhist Paradise: the Murals of Alchi, Western Himalayas*. Basel/Hong Kong, 1982.

______. "Cosmic Vision and Buddhist Images." *Art International* 25 (1982): 8-40.

______. *Hindu Religion and Iconology According to the* Tantrasara. Los Angeles, 1981.

______. "The Iconography of Amoghapāśa Lokeśvara. Part One." *Oriental Art* 12 (1966): 234-239; Part Two: *Oriental Art* 13 (1967): 20-28.

______. *The Ideal Image: The Gupta Sculptural Tradition and Its Influence*. New York, 1978.
______. *Indian Sculpture: A Catalogue of the Los Angeles County Museum of Art Collection; Vol. II, 700-1800*. Los Angeles, 1988.
______. "Kashmir and the Tibetan Connection." *Marg* 40, no. 2 (nd): 57-75.
______. "Kashmiri-Style Bronzes and Tantric Buddhism." *Annali dell'Istituto Orientale di Napoli* ns 39 (1979): 253-73.
______, ed. *Light of Asia: Buddha Śākyamuni in Asian Art*. Los Angeles, 1984.
______. "The Lord of the Tent in Tibetan Paintings." *Pantheon* 35, no. 2 (1977):97-102.
______. *Nepal, Where the Gods Are Young*. New York, 1975.
______. *The Sensuous Immortals: A Selection of Sculptures from the Pan-Asian Collection*. Los Angeles, 1977.
______. *Tibetan Paintings*. London, 1984.
Pal, Pratapaditya, and Julia Meech-Pekarik. *Buddhist Book Illuminations*. New York, 1988.
Pal, Pradapaditya, with Stephen Little. *A Collecting Odyssey: Indian, Himalayan, and Southeast Asian Art from the James and Marilynn Alsdorf Collection*. Chicago, 1997.
Pander, Eugen. "Das Lamaische Pantheon." *Zeitschrift für Ethnologie* 21 (1889): 44-78.
______. *Das Pantheon des Tschangstscha Hutuktu: ein Beitrag zur Iconographie des Lamaismus*. Edited by Albert Grünwedel. Veröffentlichungen aus dem Königlichen Museum für Völkerkunde, no. 1.2/3. Berlin, 1890.
Panofsky, Erwin. "Iconography and Iconology: An Introduction to the Study of Renaissance Art." In *Meaning in the Visual Arts*, pp. 26-54. Chicago, 1955.
______. *Perspective as Symbolic Form*. New York, 1991.
Patel, Prabhubhai. "Cittaviśuddhiprakaranam of Āryadeva." *Indian Historical Quarterly* 9 (1933): 705-721.
Patil, D.R. *The Antiquarian Remains in Bihar*. Patna, 1963.
Patna Museum. *Catalogue of Buddhist Sculptures in the Patna Museum*. Edited by S.A. Shere. Patna, 1957.
______. *Patna Museum Catalogue of Antiquities*. Edited by Parmeshwari Lal Gupta. Patna, 1965.
Pattnaik, Shyam Sundar. "Trailokya Vijaya Images from the Banpur Bronzes." *The Orissa Historical Research Journal* 16, no. 1-2 (1967): 82-87.
Paul, Debjani. *The Art of Nālandā: Development of Buddhist Sculpture AD 600-1200*. New Delhi, 1995.
Pelliot, Paul. *Les Grottes de Touen-houang*. Paris, 1914-24.
Petech, Luciano. "The 'Bri-gun-pa Sect in Western Tibet and Ladakh." In *Proceedings of the Csoma de Körös Memorial Symposium*, edited by Louis Ligeti, pp. 313-325. Budapest, 1978.
______. "Tibetan Relations with Sung China and with the Mongols." In *China Among Equals: The Middle Kingdom and its Neighbors, 10th-14th Centuries*, edited by Morris Rossabi, pp. 181-188. Berkeley, 1983.
Piotrovsky, Mikhail. *Lost Empire of the Silk Road: Buddhist Art from Khara Khoto (X-XIIIth century)*. Milan, 1993.
Pletye. C.M. "Bijdrage tot de kennis van het Mahayana op Java." *Bijdragen tot de Taal-, Land- en Volkenkunde* 52 (1901): 362-378; Part Two: 54 (1902): 195-202.
Poongundran, R. "Tantric Buddhism in Tamil Nadu." *Tamil Civilization* 4, no. 1-2 (1986): 180-185.
Pott, P.H. "The Amoghapāśa from Bhatgaon and its Parivara." *Journal of the Indian Society of Oriental Art* ns 4 (1971-72): 63-65.
______. "Plural Forms of Buddhist Iconography." In *India Antiqua*, pp. 284-290. Leyden, 1947.
______. "Some Remarks on the `Terrific Deities' in Tibetan `Devil Dances'." In *Studies of Esoteric Buddhism and Tantrism*, edited by Matsunaga Yukei, pp. 269-278. Koyasan, 1965.
______. *Yoga and Yantra: Their Interrelation and their Significance for Indian Archaeology*. Translated by Rodney Needham. The Hague, 1966.
Przyluski, Jean. "Le Bouddhisme Tantrique à Bali, d'après une publication récente." *Journal Asiatique* 218 (1931): 159-167.
______. "Heruka-Śambara." *Polski Biuletyn Orientalistyczny* 1 (1937): 42-45.
______. "Les Vidyārāja: Contribution a l'Histoire de la Magie dans les Sectes Mahāyānistes." *Bulletin de l'École Francaise d'Extrême-Orient* 23 (1923): 301-318.
Qadir, A.A. *A Guide to Paharpur*. Karachi, 1963.
Raffles, Sir Thomas Stamford. *Antiquarian, Architectural, and Landscape Illustrations of the History of Java*. London, 1844.
______. *History of Java*. 2nd ed. London, 1830.
Raghu Vira, and Lokesh Chandra. *A New Tibeto-Mongol Pantheon Part I*. New Delhi, 1961.
Rao, Gopinatha. *Elements of Hindu Iconography*. Madras, 1914-16; reprint ed., 4 vols. in 2, New York, 1968.
Ray, P.K. "Kuruma, an Ancient Buddhist Site." *The Orissa Historical Research Journal* 24-26 (1980): 93-96.
Ray, Reginald Alden. "*Maṇḍala* Symbolism in Tantric Buddhism." Ph.D. dissertation, University of Chicago, 1973.
Reigle, David. "New Preface, 1984." In Dawa-Samdup, Lama Kazi, *Shrichakrasambhāra Tantra: A Buddhist Tantra*, pp. i-iii. Talent (Oregon), 1984.
Reis, Maria Dorothea. "*The Great Compassion Dhāraṇī* of the Thousand-armed Avalokiteśvara: its Scriptural Source and Cult in China." Kyoto, 1989. (Typewritten.)
Reischauer, Edwin O. *Ennin's Travels in T'ang China*. New York, 1955.
Rhie, Marylin M. *The Fo-Kuang Ssu: Literary Evidences and Buddhist Images*. New York, 1977.
______. *Interrelationships Between the Buddhist Art of China and the Art of India and Central Asia from 618-755 AD*. Naples, 1988.
______. "A Study of the Historical Literary Evidences and Stylistic Chronological Dating of the Buddhist Images in the Main Shrine Hall of the Fo-Kuang Monastery at Wu-T'ai Shan." Ph.D. dissertation, University of Chicago, 1970.
Rhie, Marylin, and Robert Thurman. *Wisdom and Compassion: The Sacred Art of Tibet*. New York, 1991.
Ricca, Franco, and Erberto Lo Bue. *The Great Stupa of Gyantse: A Complete Tibetan Pantheon of the Fifteenth Century*. London, 1993.
Ricoeur, Paul. *Interpretation Theory: Discourse and the Surplus of Meaning*. Fort Worth, 1976.
Robinson, James B. *Buddha's Lions: The Lives of the Eight-four Siddha*. Berkeley, 1979.
Roerich, George. *Biography of Dharmasvāmin (Chag lo tsa-ba Chos-rje-dpal), A Tibetan Monk Pilgrim*. Patna, 1959.
Rosenfield, John M. "On the Dated Carvings of Sārnāth." *Artibus Asiae* 26 (1963): 10-26.
Rosenfield, John M., and Elizabeth ten Grotenhuis. *Journey of the Three Jewels: Japanese Buddhist Paintings from Western Collections*. New York, 1979.
Ruegg, D. Seyfort. "La Traduction du Canon Bouddhique Selon Une Source Tibéto-Mongole." In *Études Tibétaines*, edited by Ariane Macdonald, pp. 61-64. Paris, 1976.
Sagaster, Klaus. *Subud Erike, Ein Rosenkranz aus Perlen: Die Biographie des 1. Pekinker lCan skya Khutukhtu Nag dban blo bzan c'os ldan*. Asiatische Forschungen, no. 20. Wiesbaden, 1967.
Sahni, Daya Ram. *Catalogue of the Museum of Archaeology at Sārnāth*. Calcutta, 1914.
Sahu, N.K. *Buddhism in Orissa*. Cuttack, 1958.

Said, Edward W. *Orientalism*. New York, 1978.

Sakai Shinten, and Shiraishi Shindo."Two Ślokas in the Sanskrit Text of Tattva-saṃgraha-tantra, Chapter of (Vidyārāja) Trailokyavijaya, with a Commentary and Indices." *Indogaku bukkyōgaku kenkyū* 7, no. 2 (1959): 722-728.

Samanta, Suchitra. "Transformation and Alimentation: An Interpretation of Sacrificial Blood Offerings (Balidan) to the Śakti Goddess Kali." Paper presented at the 20th Annual Conference on South Asia, Madison, Wisconsin, 1 November 1991.

Sanford, James H. "The Abominable Tachikawa Skull Ritual." *Monumenta Nipponica* 46 (1991): 1-20.

Saraswati, S.K. *Tantrayana Art: An Album*. Calcutta, 1977.

Sarkar, H., and S.P. Nainar. *Amaravati*. New Delhi, 1980.

Saso, Michael. "The Goma Fire Rite: A Step-by-Step Translation and Interpretation of the Ju-Hachi-Dō and Goma Ritual." Kyoto, 1986. (Typewritten.)

Sastri, Ganapati, ed. *Āryamañjuśrīmūlakalpa*. 3 vols. Trivandrum Sanskrit Series, nos. 70, 76, 84. Trivandrum, 1920-1925.

Sastri, Hirananda. *Nālandā and Its Epigraphic Material*. Archaeological Survey of India Memoirs, no. 66. Delhi, 1942.

Sato, Sotaro. *Ellora Cave Temples*. Tokyo, 1977.

Saunders, E. Dale. Mudrā*: A Study of Symbolic Gestures in Japanese Buddhist Sculpture*. New York, 1960.

______. "Some Tantric Techniques." In *Studies of Esoteric Buddhism and Tantrism*, edited by Matsunaga Yukei, pp. 167-177. Koyasan, 1965.

Sawa Ryūken. *Sōran Fudō Myōō* (Comprehensive investigation of Acala Vidyārāja). Kyoto, 1984.

Schapiro, Meyer. *Words and Pictures: On the Literal and the Symbolic in the Illustration of a Text*. The Hague/Paris, 1973.

Scheurleer, Pauline Lunsingh, and Marijke J. Klokke. *Ancient Indonesian Bronzes: A Catalogue of the Exhibition in the Rijksmuseum Amsterdam*. Leiden, 1988.

______. *Divine Bronze: Ancient Indonesian Bronzes from* AD *600 to 1600*. Leiden, 1988.

Schnitger, F.M. *Hindoe-Oudheden aan de Batang Hari*. Utrecht, 1936.

Schopen, Gregory. "Archaeology and Protestant Presuppositions in the Study of Indian Buddhism." *History of Religions* 31, no. 1 (1991): 1-23.

______. "Burial `*Ad Sanctos*' and the Physical Presence of the Buddha in Early Indian Buddhism: A Study in the Archaeology of Religions." *Religion* 17 (1987): 193-225.

______. "The Bodhigarbhālaṅkāralakṣa and Vimaloṣṇīsa Dhāraṇīs in Indian Inscriptions." *The Journal of the International Association of Buddhist Studies* 3 (1980): 119-149.

______. *Bones, Stones, and Buddhist Monks: Collected Papers on the Archaeology, Epigraphy, and Texts of Monastic Buddhism in India*. Honolulu, 1997.

______. "The Five Leaves of the Buddhabalādhānaprātihāryavikurvāṇanirdeśa-sūtra found at Gilgit." *Journal of Indian Philosophy* 5 (1978): 319-336.

______. "The Generalization of an Old Yogic Attainment in Medieval Mahāyāna Sūtra Literature: Some Notes on *Jātismara*." *Journal of the International Association of Buddhist Studies* 6 (1983): 109-47.

______. "On Monks, Nuns and `Vulgar' Practices: The Introduction of the Image Cult into Indian Buddhism." *Artibus Asiae* 49 (1988/89): 153-168.

______. "The Phrase `sa pṛthivīpradeśaś caityabhūto bhavet' in the *Vajracchedikā*: Notes on the Cult of the Book in Mahāyāna." *Indo-Iranian Journal* 17 (1975): 147-81.

______. "Sukhāvatī as a Generalized Religious Goal in Sanskrit Mahāyāna Sūtra Literature." *Indo-Iranian Journal* 19 (1977): 177-210.

______. "The Text on the `Dhāraṇī Stones from Abhayagiriya': A Minor Contribution to the Study of Mahāyāna Literature in Ceylon." *Journal of the International Association of Buddhist Studies* 5 (1982): 100-108.

______. "Two Problems in the History of Indian Buddhism: The Layman/Monk Distinction and the Doctrines of the Transference of Merit." *Studien zur Indologie und Iranistik* 10 (1985): 9-47.

Schoterman, J.A. "A surviving Amoghapāśa sādhana: Its relation to the five main statues of Candi Jago." In *Ancient Indonesian Sculpture*, edited by Marijke J. Klokke and Pauline Lunsingh Scheurleer, pp.154-177. Leiden, 1994.

Schram, Louis M.J. "The Monguors of the Kansu-Tibetan Border; Part II. Their Religious Life." *Transactions of the American Philosophical Society* ns 47 (1957): 1-164.

von Schroeder, Ulrich. *Buddhist Sculptures of Sri Lanka*. Hong Kong, 1990.

______. *The Golden Age of Sculpture in Sri Lanka*. Hong Kong, 1992.

______. *Indo-Tibetan Bronzes*. Hong Kong, 1981.

Seckel, Dietrich. *The Art of Buddhism*. Revised ed. New York, 1968.

Sedyawati, Edi. "The Making of Indonesian Art." In Jan Fontein, *The Sculpture of Indonesia*, pp. 97-111. Washington, 1990.

Seidenfaden, Erik. "An Excursion to Phimai, a temple city in the Khotar province." *Journal of the Siam Society* 17 (1923): 1-19.

Sen, Nilratan, ed. *Caryāgītikośa: Facsimile Edition*. Simla, 1977.

Sharpa Tulku, and Michael Perrot. *A Manual of Ritual Fire Offerings*. Dharamsala, 1987.

Shaw, Miranda. *Passionate Enlightenment: Women in Tantric Buddhism*. Princeton, 1994.

Shendge, Malati J. *Advayasiddhi, Edited with an Introduction*. Baroda, 1964.

______. "The Literary Forms of Tantra." *Transactions of the International Conference of Orientalists in Japan* 12 (1967): 37-46.

______. "The Moon and her Reflection in Water: The Sexual Imagery in the Vajrayānic Instruction." *Indian Journal of Buddhist Studies* 1, no. 1 (1989):89-107.

______. "Śrisahajasiddhi." *Indo-Iranian Journal* 10 (1967): 126-149.

Shiba Yoshinobu. "Sung Foreign Trade: Its Scope and Organization." In *China Among Equals: The Middle Kingdom and its Neighbors, 10th-14th Centuries*, edited by Morris Rossabi, pp. 89-115. Berkeley, 1983.

Siklós, Bulcsu. *The Vajrabhairava Tantras: Tibetan and Mongolian Versions, English Translation and Annotations*. Tring, 1996.

______. "The Evolution of the Buddhist Yama." In *The Buddhist Forum* 4 (1996): 165-189.

Singer, Jane Casey. "Early Thankas: Eleventh-Thirteenth Centuries." In *On the Path to the Void: Buddhist Art of the Tibetan Realm*, edited by Pratapditya Pal, pp. 180-195. Mumbai, 1996.

______. "Painting in Central Tibet c. 950-1400." *Artibus Asiae* 54, no. 1/2 (1994): 87-136.

Singh, Madanjeet. *Himalayan Art*. Greenwich, 1968.

Sinha, B.P. "Representations of the Buddhist Deities Trampling Hindu Deities." In *Indian History Congress: Proceedings of the 21st Session, 1958 Trivandrum*, pp. 225-227. Bombay, 1959.

______. "Some Reflections on Indian Sculpture (Stone or Bronze) of Buddhist Deities Trampling on Hindu Deities." In *Dr. Satkari Mookerji Felicitation Volume*, edited by B.P. Sinha et al, pp. 97-107. Varanasi, 1969.

Śivaramamurti, C. "The Weapons of Viṣṇu" *Artibus Asiae* 18 (1955): 128-136.

Skorupski, Tadeusz. *The Sarvadurgatipariśodhana Tantra: Elimination of all Evil Destinies*. New Delhi, 1983.

______. "Tibetan Homa Rites." In *Agni: The Vedic Ritual of the Fire Altar*, edited by Fritz Staal, pp. 2: 403-417. 3 vols. Berkeley, 1983.

Slusser, Mary S. *Nepal Maṇḍala: A Cultural Study of the Kathmandu Valley*. 2 vols. Princeton, 1982.

Snellgrove, David L. *Buddhist Himalaya: Travels and Studies in quest of the origins and nature of Tibetan Religion*. Oxford, 1957.

______. "Categories of Buddhist Tantras." In *Orientalia Iosephi Tucci Memoriae Dicata*, edited by G. Gnoli and L. Lanciotti, pp. 1353-1384. Serie Orientale Roma, no. 56.3. Rome, 1988.

______. *The Hevajra Tantra*. 2 vols. London, 1959.

______, ed. *The Image of the Buddha*. Paris, 1978.

______. *Indo-Tibetan Buddhism: Indian Buddhists and their Tibetan Successors*. 2 vols. Boston, 1987.

______. "Indo-Tibetan Liturgy and its Relationship to Iconography." In *Mahāyānist Art After AD 900*, edited by William Watson, pp. 36-46. Colloquies on Art and Archaeology in Asia, no. 2. London, 1972.

______. "Introduction." In *Sarva-tathāgata-tattva-sangraha: Facsimile reproduction of a Tenth Century Sanskrit Manuscript from Nepal*, edited by Lokesh Chandra and David L. Snellgrove, pp. 5-67. New Delhi, 1981.

______. "The Notion of Divine Kingship in Tantric Buddhism." *Studies in the History of Religions: Sacral Kingship* 4 (1959): 204-218.

______. "Śakyamuni's Final *Nirvāna*." *Bulletin of the School of Oriental and African Studies (University of London)* 36 (1973): 399-411.

Snellgrove, David L., and Tadeusz Skorupski. *The Cultural Heritage of Ladakh*. 2 vols. Warminster, 1979-80.

Snodgrass, Adrian. *The Matrix and Diamond World Maṇḍalas in Shingon Buddhism*. 2 vols. New Delhi, 1988.

______. *The Symbolism of the Stūpa*. Ithaca, 1985.

Soekmono, R. "Indonesian Architecture of the Classical Period: A Brief Survey." In *The Sculpture of Indonesia*, edited and translated by Jan Fontein, pp. 64-95. New York, 1990.

Sofronov, M.V. "The Tangut Text of the Chü-yung-kuan Polyglot Inscription." *Acta Orientalia (Hung.)* 23 (1970): 297-326.

Soothill, W.E., and Lewis Hodous. *A Dictionary of Chinese Buddhist Terms*. London, 1937.

Soper, Alexander C. *Chinese, Korean and Japanese Bronzes: A Catalogue of the Auriti Collection*. Serie Orientale Roma, no. 35. Rome, 1966.

______. *Literary Evidence for Early Buddhist Art in China*. Ascona, 1959.

______. "A Vacation Glimpse of the T'ang Temples of Ch'ang-an: The *Ssu-T'a Chi* by Tuan Ch'eng-shih." *Artibus Asiae* 23 (1960): 15-40.

Sotheby and Company. *Catalogue of Tibetan, Sino-Tibetan, Nepalese and Indian Art*. London, 1973.

Sotheby's, New York. *Indian and Southeast Asian Art*. New York, 1991.

______. *Indian and Southeast Asian Art, Sale 7108*. (New York, 1998)

______. *Indian, Himalayan, South-East Asian Art and Indian Miniatures*. New York, 1985.

Soymié, Michel. "Notes D'Iconographie Bouddhique: Des Vidyārāja et Vajradhara de Touen-Houang." *Cahiers d'Extrême-Asie* 3 (1987): 9-26.

Spiro, Melford E. "Religion: Problems of Definition and Explanation." In *Anthropological Approaches to the Study of Religion*, edited by Michael Banton, pp. 85-126. London, 1966.

Srivastava, K.M. "The Lost University of Vikramaśila." *Arts of Asia* 17.4 (1987): 44-55.

von Staël-Holstein, Baron A. "Remarks on the Chu Fo P'u Sa Shêng Hsiang Tsan." *National Library of Peiping Bulletin* 1 (1928): 1-9.

Stein, Sir Mark Aurel. *Innermost Asia: Detailed report of archaeological explorations in Chinese Turkestan*. 3 vols. Oxford, 1928.

______. *On Ancient Central-Asian Tracks*. London, 1933.

Stein, Rolf A. "Avalokiteśvara/Kouan-Yin: Exemple de Transformation d'un Dieu en Déesse." *Cahiers d'Extrême-Asie* 2 (1986): 17-80.

______. "La soumission de Rudra et autres contes tantriques." *Journal Asiatiques* 283 ,no. 1 (1995): 121-160.

______. "Un Genre Particulier d'Exposés du Tantrisme Ancient Tibétain et Khotanais." *Journal Asiatique* 275, no. 3-4 (1987): 265-282.

______. "Mi-ñag et Si-hia: Géographie Historique et Légendes Ancestrales." *Bulletin de l'École Française d'Extrême-Orient* 44 (1947-1950): 223-265.

______. "Nouveaux problèmes du tantrisme sino-japonais." *Annuaire du Collège de France* 75 (1975): 481-488.

______. "Les objets rituels de transmutation dans le tantrisme tibétain." *Annuaire du Collège de France* 75 (1975): 488-495.

______. "Le Phur-bu du tantrisme tibétain." *Annuaire du Collège de France* 77 (1977): 607-615.

______. "Problèmes de mythologie et de rituel tantriques (Tibet)." *Annuaire du Collège de France* 73 (1973): 463-470.

______. "Quelques problèmes du tantrisme chinois." *Annuaire du Collège de France* 74 (1974): 499-508.

______. "Recherches autour du récit de Rudra (Tibet)." *Annuaire du Collège de France* 74 (1974): 508-517.

______. "Recherches sur le *phur-bu* (suite)." *Annuaire du Collège de France* 78 (1977-78): 647-654.

Steinkellner, Ernst. "Remarks on Tantristic Hermeneutics." In *Proceedings of the Csoma de Körös Memorial Symposium*, edited by Louis Ligeti, pp. 445-458. Budapest, 1978.

Stewart, Mary L. *Nālandā Mahāvihāra: A Study of an Indian Pāla Period Buddhist Site and British Historical Archaeology, 1861-1938*. Oxford, 1989.

Stoddard, Heather. "A Stone Sculpture of mGur mGon-po, Mahākāla of the Tent, Dated 1292." *Oriental Art* 31 (1985): 278-282.

Strickmann, Michel. "The *Consecration Sūtra*: A Buddhist Book of Spells." In *Chinese Buddhist Apocrypha*, edited by Robert E. Buswell, Jr., pp. 75-118. Honolulu, 1990.

______. "Heralds of Maitreya." Paper presented at the Princeton Conference on Maitreya Studies, 1- 3 May 1983.

______. "Homa in East Asia." *Agni: The Vedic Ritual of the Fire Altar*, pp. 2:418-455. Edited by Fritz Staal. 3 vols. Berkeley, 1983.

______. *Mantras et mandarins: Le bouddhisme tantrique en Chine*. Paris, 1996.

______. "A Survey of Tibetan Buddhist Studies." *The Eastern Buddhist* 10, no. 1 (1977): 128-149.

Strong, John S. *The Legend of King Aśoka: A Study and Translation of the Aśokāvadāna*. Princeton, 1983.

Sugimura, Yuzo. *Chinese Sculptures, Bronzes and Jades in Japanese Collections*. Honolulu, 1966.

Sutherland, Gail Hinich. "The Demon and His Disguises: The Yakṣa in Hindu and Buddhist Art and Literature." Ph.D. Dissertation, University of Chicago, 1988.

______. *Yakṣa in Hinduism and Buddhism: The Disguises of the Demon*. Albany, 1991.

Taishō shinshū daizōkyō (Buddhist canon newly compiled in the Taishō era [1912-1925]). Edited by Takakusu Junjirō and Watanabe Kaikyoku. 88 vols. Tokyo, 1924-34.

Taishō shinshū daizōkyō zuzō (Illustrated Section of the Buddhist canon newly compiled in the Taisho Period [1912-26]). Edited by Takakusu Junjirō and Ono Gemmyō. 12 vols. Tokyo, 1932-34.

Tajima, Ryujun. "Les Deux Grand Maṇḍalas et la Doctrine de l'Ésotérisme Shingon." *Bulletin de la Maison Franco-Japonaise* ns 6 (1959): 1-353.

______. *Étude sur le* Mahāvairocanasūtra. Paris, 1937.

Takata Osamu; Akiyama Terukazu; and Yanagisawa Taka. *Takao Mandara* (The Ryōkai Mandara of the Jingōji, Kyoto: Garbhadhātu Maṇḍala and Vajradhātu Maṇḍala, the Oldest Maṇḍala Paintings of Esoteric Buddhism in Japan). Tokyo, 1967.

Takata Osamu, and Yanagisawa Taka. *Genshoku Nihon no bijutsu: Butsuga* (Primary Japanese art: Buddhist painting). Tokyo, 1969.

Takáts, Zoltán V. "Abhanga Motives in the Art of Ajanta and Wu Tao-tzu." *Wissenschaftliche Zeitschrift der Karl-Marx-Universität, Leipzig* 9, no. 4 (1959/60): 641-648.

Tartakov, Gary, and Vidya Dehejia. "Sharing, Intrusion and Influence: The Mahiśāsuramardinī Imagery of the Calukyas and Pallavas." *Artibus Asiae* 45, no. 4 (1984): 287-345.

Templeman, David, trans. *Tāranātha's Life of Krsnācāarya/Kānha*. Dharamsala, 1989.

Tenzin, Khempo Sangay, and Gomchen Oleshey. *Deities and Divinities of Tibet: The Nyingma Icons*. Translated by Keith Dowman. Kathmandu, 1988.

Tewari, Ramesh Chandra. "Pre-Buddhist Elements in Himalayan Buddhism: The Institution of Oracles." *Journal of the International Association of Buddhist Studies* 10 (1987): 142-143.

Thingo, Tsering Tashi. *Leidraad Bij de Meditatie Over de Sarvavid-Vairocana-Maṇḍala*. Antwerp, 1980.

Thompson Foundation, The James W. *The House on the Klong*. Tokyo, 1968.

Tibet House Museum, *Inaugural Exhibition Catalogue*. New Delhi, 1965.

Till, Barry, and Paula Swart. *Images from the Tomb: Chinese Burial Figurines*. Victoria, 1988.

Tiwari, Arya Ramchandra. "Rare Image of the Tripurāntaka in the Watson Museum, Rajkot." *Bulletin of the Baroda Museum* 28 (1978-79): 221-234.

Tobi, A.C. "De Buddhistische Bronzen in het Museum te Leiden." *Oudheidkundig Verslag* (1930): 158-201.

Toganoo Shōun. *Mandara no Kenkyū* (A Study of the *maṇḍala*). Koyasan, 1927.

______. *Rishukyō no kenkyū* (Researches on the Nayasutra). Koyasan, 1930.

Tokuno, Kyoko. "The Evaluation of Indigenous Scriptures in Chinese Buddhist Bibliographical Catalogues." In *Chinese Buddhist Apocrypha*, edited by Robert E. Buswell, Jr., pp. 31-74. Honolulu, 1990.

Tokyo National Museum. *Kōbō Daishi and the Art of Esoteric Buddhism*. Tokyo, 1983.

Toyka-Fuong, Ursula. *Ikonographie und Symbolik des Tibetischen Buddhismus: Die Kultplastiken der Sammlung Werner Schulemann im Museum für Asiatische Kunst, Köln*. Asiatische Forschungen, no. 78B. Wiesbaden, 1983.

Tripathy, Kunja Behari. "Banpur Copperplate Inscription of Somavamsi Indrarātha." *Journal of the Asiatic Society* 8.4 (1966): 271-276.

Trungpa, Chögyam. *Crazy Wisdom*. Boston, 1991.

Tsonkhapa. *Tantra in Tibet: The Great Exposition of Secret Mantra*. Translated and edited by Jeffrey Hopkins. London, 1977.

Tsuda, Shiníchi. "A Critical Tantrism." *Memoirs of the Research Department of the Toyō Bunkō* 36 (1978): 167-231.

______. *The Saṁvarodaya-Tantra: Selected Chapters*. Tokyo, 1974.

Tucci, Giuseppe. "Animadversiones Indicae." *Journal of the Asiatic Society of Bengal* ns 26 (1930): 128-132.

______. *Gyantse and Its Monasteries: Part 1, General description of the Temples (Indo-Tibetica IV.1)*. Translated by Uma Marina Vesci. Edited by Lokesh Chandra. New Delhi, 1989.

______. *Gyantse and Its Monasteries: Part 2, Inscriptions, Texts and Translations (Indo-Tibetica IV.2)*. Translated by Uma Marina Vesci. Edited by Lokesh Chandra. New Delhi, 1989.

______. *Gyantse and Its Monasteries: Part 3, Plates (Indo-Tibetica IV.3)*. Translated by Uma Marina Vesci. Edited by Lokesh Chandra. New Delhi, 1989.

______. *Indo-Tibetica*. 4 vols. Rome, 1932-41.

______. "Preliminary report on an archaeological survey in Swat." *East and West* ns 9 (1958): 279-328.

______. *Rin-chen-bzan-po and the Renaissance of Buddhism in Tibet around the Millennium (Indo-Tibetica II)*. Translated by Nancy Kipp Smitth. Edited by Lokesh Chandra. New Delhi, 1988.

______. *Stūpa: art, architectonics and symbolism (Indo-Tibetica I)*. Translated by Uma Marina Vesci. Edited by Lokesh Chandra. New Delhi, 1988.

______. *The Temples of Western Tibet and Their Artistic Symbolism: The Monasteries of Spiti and Kunavar (Indo-Tibetica III.1)*. Translated by Uma Marina Vesci et al. Edited by Lokesh Chandra. New Delhi, 1988.

______. *The Temples of Western Tibet and their Artistic Symbolism: Tsaparang (Indo-Tibetica III.2)*. Translated by Uma Marina Vesci. Edited by Lokesh Chandra. New Delhi, 1989.

______. *The Theory and Practice of the Maṇḍala*. Translated by A.H. Broderick. New York, 1969.

______. *Tibetan Painted Scrolls*. 2 vols. Rome, 1949.

Twitchett, Denis, ed. *The Cambridge History of China: Volume 3, Sui and T'ang China, 589-906, Part I*. Cambridge, 1979.

Uhlig, Helmut, ed. *Tantrische Kunst des Buddhismus*. Berlin, 1981.

Ui Hakuju; Suzuki Munetada; Yenshō Kanakura; and Tada Tokan. *Chibetto daizōkyō somokurōkū* (A Complete Catalogue of the Tibetan Buddhist Canons [*bka'-'gyur* and *bstan-'gyur*]). Sendai, 1934.

Upadhyay, G.P. "Reappraisal of the Myth of Tripurādahana." *Journal of Indian History* 54 (1976): 539-546.

Upasak, C.S., ed. *Nālandā: Past and Present*. Nalanda, 1977.

de La Vallée Poussin, Louis. *Bouddhisme: Études et Matériaux*. London, 1898.

______. *Bouddhisme: Opinions sur l'histoire de la dogmatique*. Paris, 1909.

______. "The Buddhist `Wheel of Life' from a New Source." *Journal of the Royal Asiatic Society* (1897) 463-470.

______. "The Four Classes of Buddhist Tantras." *Journal of the Royal Asiatic Society* (1901): 900-901.

______. "Tantrism." In *Encyclopædia of Religion and Ethics* 12: 193-197. Edited by James Hastings. New York, 1922.

Vasu, N.N. *The Archaeological Survey of Mayurbhanja*. 2 vols. Calcutta, 1912.

Visser, H.F.E. *Asiatic Art in Private Collections in Holland and Belgium*. Amsterdam, 1948.

de Visser, M.W. *Ancient Buddhism in Japan*. 2 vols. Leiden/Paris, 1928-1935.

______. *The Bodhisattva Ākāśgarbha (Kokūzō) in China and Japan*. Amsterdam, 1931.

Vitali, Roberto. *Early Temples of Central Tibet*. London, 1990.

______. *The Kingdoms of Gu.ge Pu.hrang According to mNga'.ris rgyal.rabs by Gu.ge mkhan.chen Ngag.dbang grags.pa*. Dharamsala, 1996.

Vogel, J. Ph. *Buddhist Art in India, Ceylon and Java*. Translated by A.J. Barnouw. Oxford, 1935; reprint ed., New Delhi, 1977.

Vollmer, John E. "Chinese Tapestry Weaving: K'o-ssu." *Hali: The International Journal of Oriental Carpets and Textiles* 5, no. 1 (1982): 36-43.

Waddell, L. Austine. *The Buddhism of Tibet, or Lamaism*. London, 1895; reprint ed., under the title, *Tibetan Buddhism, with Its Mystic Cults, Symbolism and Mythology*. New York, 1972.

Waldschmidt, Ernst, and Rose Leonore. *Nepal: Art Treasures from the Himalayas*. London, 1969.

Waley, Arthur. *A Catalogue of Paintings Recovered from Tun-huang by Sir Aurel Stein, K.C.I.E.* London, 1931.

Watt, James C.Y., and Anne E. Wardwell. *When Silk Was Gold: Central Asian and Chinese Textiles*. New York, 1997.

Wayman, Alex. "Analysis of the Tantric Section of the Kanjur Correlated to Tanjur Exegesis." In *Indo-Asian Studies, Part 1*, edited by Raghu Vira, pp. 118-125. New Delhi, 1963.

______. *Analysis of the Śrāvakabhūmi Manuscript*. University of California Publications in Classical Philology, no. 17. Berkeley, 1961.

______. *The Buddhist Tantras: Light on Indo-Tibetan Esotericism*. New York, 1973.

______. *Chanting the Names of Mañjuśrī: The* Mañjuśrī nāma-samgīti*: Sanskrit and Tibetan Texts*. Boston, 1985.

______. "Contributions on the Symbolism of the Maṇḍala-Palace." In *Études Tibétaines dédiées à la mémoire de Marcelle Lalou*, pp. 557-566. Paris, 1971.

______. "Early Literary History of the Buddhist Tantras, especially the Guhyasamāja-tantra." *Annals of the Bhandarkar Oriental Research Institute* 48-49 (1968): 100-106.

______. "Outline of the Thob Yig Gsal Bahi Me Lon." In *Indo-Asian Studies, Part 1*, edited by Raghu Vira, pp. 109-117. New Delhi, 1963.

______. "Preparation of Disciples; the Meaning of Initiation." In *The Buddhist Tantras: Light on Indo-Tibetan Esotericism*, pp. 54-70. New York, 1973.

______. "Received Teachings of Tibet and Analysis of the Tantric Canon." In *The Buddhist Tantras: Light on Indo-Tibetan Esotericism*, pp. 225-239. New York, 1973.

______. "Reflections on the Theory of Barabudur as a *Maṇḍala*." In *Barabudur: History and Significance of a Buddhist Monument*, edited by Luis O. Gómez and Hiram W. Woodward, Jr., pp. 139-172. Berkeley, 1981.

______. "Studies in Yama and Māra." *Indo-Iranian Journal* 3 (1959): 44-73, 112-131.

______. "Totemic Beliefs in the Buddhist Tantras." *History of Religions* 1.1 (1961): 81-94.

______. *Yoga of the Guhyasamājatantra: The Arcane Lore of Forty Verses, A Buddhist Tantra Commentary*. Delhi, 1977.

Wayman, Alex, and R. Tajima. *The Enlightenment of Vairocana*. Delhi, 1992.

Weiner, Sheila L. *Ajanta: Its Place in Buddhist Art*. Los Angeles, 1977.

Weinstein, Stanley. *Buddhism under the T'ang*. Cambridge, 1987.

Welch, Claude. *Protestant Thought in the Nineteenth Century, Vol. 1, 1799-1870*. New Haven, 1972.

Whitfield, Roderick. *The Art of Central Asia: The Stein collection in the British Museum*. 3 vols. Tokyo, 1982-85.

Whitfield, Roderick, and Anne Farrer. *Caves of the Thousand Buddhas: Chinese Art from the Silk Route*. London, 1990.

Wiesner, Ulrich. "Report from Europe." *Oriental Art* ns 37 (1991): 171-176.

Willemen, Charles. *The Chinese Hevajratantra*. Orientalia Gandensia, no. 8. Leuven, 1983.

______. "A Tantric `Heart-Sutra'." *Samādhi: Cahiers d'Études Bouddhiques* 7, no. 1 (1973): 2-11.

______. "Tripitaka Shan-wu-wei's Name: A Chinese Translation from Prakrit." *T'oung Pao* 67, no. 3-5 (1981): 362 -365.

Williams, Joanna. "The Iconography of Khotanese Painting." *East and West* ns 23 (1973): 109-154.

______. "The Sculpture of Mandasor." *Archives of Asian Art* 26 (1972-73): 50-66.

Winternitz, Moriz. *History of Indian Literature vol. II, Part I: Buddhist Literature*. Translated by Bhaskara Jha. Delhi, 1987.

______. "Notes on the Guhyasamāja-Tantra and the Age of the Tantras." *The Indian Historical Quarterly* 9 (1933): 1-10.

With, Karl. *Java: Brahmansche, Buddhistische und Eigenlebige Architektur und Plastik auf Java*. The Hague, 1920.

Wolpert, Stanley. *A New History of India*. 2nd ed. Oxford/New York, 1982.

Woodroffe, Sir John [Arthur Avalon]. *Principles of Tantra*. 2nd ed. Madras, 1955.

______. *Shakti and Shakta*. Madras, 1955.

Woodward, Hiram W., Jr. "Queen Kumāradevī and Twelfth-Century Sārnāth." *Journal of the Indian Society of OrientalArt* ns 12/13 (1981-83): 8-24.

______. "Tantric Buddhism at Angkor Thom." *Ars Orientalis* 12 (1981): 57-71.

Wu, K.T. "Chinese Printing Under Four Alien Dynasties." *Harvard Journal of Asiatic Studies* 13 (1950): 447-523.

Wu Tung, and Denise Patry Leidy. "Recent Archaeological Contributions to the Study of Chinese Ceramics." In *Imperial Taste: Chinese Ceramics from the Percival David Foundation*, edited by Suzanne Kotz, pp. 93-102. Los Angeles, 1989.

Yamada, Ishi. *Sarvatathāgatatattvasaṃgraha*. New Delhi, 1981.

Yamamoto, Chikyō. *Introduction to the Maṇḍala*. Kyoto, 1980.

______. "List of Ritual Texts and Figures of Esoteric Buddhism in Japan Contained in the Iconographic Section of the Taishō Edition of the Chinese Buddhist Tripitaka." In *The Esoteric Iconography of Japanese Maṇḍalas*, edited by Lokesh Chandra, pp. 55-117. New Delhi, 1971.

______, trans. *Mahavairocana-Sutra: translated into English from Ta-p'i-lu-che-na ch'eng-fo shen-pien chia-ch'ih ching, the Chinese version of Śubhākarasiṁha and I-hsing (AD 725)*. New Delhi, 1990.

Yamasaki, Taikō. *Shingon: Japanese Esoteric Buddhism*. Translated and adapted by Richard and Cynthia Peterson. Edited by Yasuyoshi Morimoto and David Kidd. Boston/London, 1988.

Yanagisawa Taka. *Nippon no butsuga: Takao mandara, Jingō-ji* (Japanese Buddhist painting: the Takao *maṇḍala* in Jingōji temple). Tokyo, 1976-87.

Yashiro Yukio. "To Sekicho Fudō Myōōzo" (A carved stone statue of Āryacalanātha of the Tang period). *Bijutsu kenkyū* 71 (1937): 441-459.

Yijing. *Chinese Monks in India: Biography of eminent monks who went to the Western world in search of the Law during the great T'ang Dynasty*. Translated by Latika Lahiri. Delhi, 1986.

______. *A Record of the Buddhist Religion as Practiced in India and the Malay Archipelago*. Translated by J. Takakusu. Oxford, 1896; reprint ed., Taipei, 1970.

Ying Chiang. *Gugong Tushu Wenxian Xuancui* (Select Chinese rare Books and Historical Documents in the National Palace Museum). Taipei, 1971.

Yoritomi Motohiro. *Mandara no hotoketachi* (The Buddhas of the *Maṇḍala*). Tokyo, 1985.

Young, G.M. "A Journey to Toling and Tsaparang in Western Tibet." *Journal of the Panjab Historical Society* 7, no. 2 (1919): 177-198.

Yu, K. "Amoghavajra (2)." In *Encyclopaedia of Buddhism, Fascicle: Akankheyya Sutta-Anabhirati*, pp. 482-487. Edited by G.P. Malalasekera. Colombo, 1964.

Yunnan sheng wenwu gongzuo dui (Archaeological Team of Yunnan Province). "Dali Chongsheng si santa zhuta de shice he qingli" (Survey and Renovation of the Main Pagoda at the Chongsheng Temple in Dali). *Kaogu xuebao*, no. 2 (1981): 245-67.

Zhu Qixin. "Bronze Buddhist Figures of the Late Western Xia Dynasty." *Orientations* 22, no. 10 (1991): 62-64.

Zimmer, Heinrich. *The Art of Indian Asia*. 2 vols. Princeton, 1955; reprint ed., Delhi, 1983.

______. *Myths and Symbols in Indian Art and Civilization*. Princeton, 1972.

Zürcher, Erik. "`Prince Moonlight': Messianism and Eschatology in Early Medieval Chinese Buddhism." *T'oung Pao* 68 (1982): 1-75.

Zwalf, W. *Buddhism: Art and Faith*. New York, 1985.

Works Found in the *Taishō Shinshū Daizōkyō* and *Taishō Shinshū Daizōkyō Zuzō*

Works are cited according to the standard numbers of the *Taishō* printed edition (T) and those found in the index volume of the "Hōbōgirin": Paul Demiéville et al, *Répertoire du Canon Bouddhique Sino-Japonais, Édition de Taishō (Taishō Shinshū Daizōkyō)*, Fascicule Annexe du Hōbōgirin, Édition Révisée et Augmentée (Paris/Tokyo, 1978). The index number is followed by the Sanskrit title (romanized), as given in the Hōbōgirin index, in Bunyiu Nanjio *A Catalogue of the Chinese Translation of the Buddhist Tripitaka*, Lewis Lancaster, *Korean Buddhist Canon*, or Bunyiu Nanjio, *A Catalogue of the Buddhist Tripitaka with additions and corrections by Lokesh Chandra*. Otherwise no Sanskrit title is reconstructed. The translator (or compiler) and date of translation is provided where known. Please refer to the Hōbōgirin index for the Chinese characters.

T.8.243. *Adhyardhaśatikā Prajñāpāramitā*. Amoghavajra, before 774 CE

T.8.245. *Kārunikarāja-rashtrapāla-prajñāpāramitā-sūtra*. Kumārajiva, attributed; 5th century?

T.8.246. *Kārunikarāja-rashtrapāla-prajñāpāramitā-sūtra*. Amoghavajra, 765 CE

T.8.258. *Svalpākṣarā Prajñāpāramitā Sūtra*. Devaśānti (?), 982 CE

T.9.262. *Saddharmapundarīka sūtra*. Kumārajiva, 406 CE

T.13.397. *Mahāvaipulyamahāsamnipātasūtra*. Dharmaksema et al; 414-426 CE

T.13.405. *Ākāśagarbhasūtra*. Buddhayaśas, 408-413 CE

T.18.848. *Mahāvairocana abhisambodhi vikurvitādhisthāna vaipulya sūtra* (*MVS*). Śubhakarasiṁha and Yixing, 725 CE

T.18.849. Section of T.18.849. Vajrabodhi, 1st half of 8th c.

T.18.865. *Sarva-tathāgata-tattva-samgraha mahāyānabhi-samaya-mahākalpa-rāja* (*STTS*). Amoghavajra, 753 CE

T.18.866. *STTS*. Vajrabodhi, 723 CE

T.18.869. "Synopsis of the 18 Assemblies of the Vajraśekhara." Amoghavajra, 746-774 CE

T.18.882. *STTS*. Dānapāla, 1012-1015 CE

T.18.885. *Guhyasamāja tantra* (*GST*). Dānapāla, 1002 CE

T.18.890. *Māyājāla Mahātantra*. Dharmabhadra, ca. 989-999 CE

T.18.891. *Māyājāla mahāyoga tantra dasakrodha vidyārāja mahāvidyā dhyāna kalpa sūtra*. Dharmabhadra, ca. 989-999 CE

T.18.892. *Hevajra Tantra*. Dharmapāla, 1054-1055.

T.18.893. *Susiddhikara sūtra*. Śubhakarasiṁha, 726 CE

T.18.901. *Dhāraṇisamuccaya sūtra*. Atigupta, 654 CE

T.18.903. Amoghavajra, 746-774 CE

T.19.965. Dharmasena, before 847 CE

T.19.967. *Sarva-durgati-pariśodhana* (*SDPS*) *usnīsavijayā dhāraṇi*. Buddhapāli, 683 CE

T.19.968. *SDPS*. Du Xingkai, 679 CE

T.19.969. *SDPS*. Divākara, 682 CE

T.19.970. *SDPS*. Divākara, 676-688.

T.19.971. *SDPS*. Yijing, 710 CE

T.19.972. Amoghavajra, 746-774 CE

T.19.974A. *SDPS*. Dharmadeva, 988 CE

T.19.981. Yixing, early eighth c.

T.19.985. *Mahāmāyūrī vidyārājñī sūtra*. Yijing, 705 CE

T.19.994. *Kārunikarāja-rāshtrapāla-prajñāpāramitā-sūtra-bodhimanda-dhyāya-kalpa*. Amoghavajra, pre-774 CE

T.20.1056. *Sahasra-bhuja-sahasra-netra-Avalokiteśvara-sādhana-vidhi* from the *Vajraśekhara-tantra*. Amoghavajra, 746-774 CE

T.20.1057. *Nīlakantha sūtra*. Zhitong, 627-649 CE

T.20.1068. *Sahasra-bhuja-sahasra-netra . . . kalpa*. Śubhakarasiṁha, early eighth century.

T.20.1092. *Amoghapāśa-kalpa-rāja sūtra*. Bodhiruci, 707 CE

T.20.1093. *Amoghapāśa-hrdaya-dhāraṇī*. Jñānagupta, 587 CE

T.20.1094. *Amoghapāśa-hrdaya*. Xuanzang, 659 CE

T.20.1095. *Amoghapāśahrdaya*. Bodhiruci, pre-727 CE

T.20.1096. *Amoghapāśa-dhāraṇi*. Li Wuchan, 700 CE

T.20.1097. *Amoghapāśa-hrdaya-dhāraṇī sūtra*. Manicintana, 693 CE

T.20.1101. *Mahāvaipulya-Mañjuśrī-sūtra (Tārā-kalpa)*. Amoghavajra, 746-774 CE

T.20.1106. *Ārya Tārābhattārikāyā-nāmāstottaraśataka*. Tian Xizai, 985 CE

T.20.1129. *Śrī-sarva-Bhūtaḍāmara Tantra*. Dharmadeva, 994 CE

T.20.1133. *Vajrayūh-dhāraṇī-adhyāya-kalpa*. Amoghavajra, pre-774 CE

T.20.1134A,B. *Vajrayūh-dhāraṇi-adhyāya-kalpa*. Amoghavajra, pre-774 CE

T.20.1141. *Maitreya bodhisattva yoga (kalpa)*. Śubhakarasiṁha, early 8th c.

T.20.1180. *Sadakṣara-vidyā-mantra sūtra*. Bodhiruci, 693 CE

T.20.1188. *Mañjuśrīnāmasamgīti*. Suvarnadhāraṇī, 1111-1117 CE

T.20.1189. *Mañjuśrīnāmasamgīti*. Sharapa (Tangut Xia), 1259.

T.20.1190. *Mañjuśrīnāmasamglti*. Prajñā (? Tibetan), 14th c.

T.20.1191. *Mañjuśrīmūlakalpa* (*MMK*). Tian Xizai, ca. 983 CE

T.21.1199. *Canda-mahārosana-Acala-vidhī* and *Usnīsavijayā-mudra-opadeśa* from *Vajrapāṇi-abhiṣeka-uttara-tantra* (Sanskrit reconstructed from title of Tibetan version). Amoghavajra, pre. 774 CE

T.21.1200. *Trisamaya-rāja-krodharāja-Acala-dūta-sādhana-vidhi*. Amoghavajra, pre-774 CE

T.21.1205. *Acala-vidyārāja. . . guhya-siddhi-kalpa*. Amoghavajra and Bianzhi, pre-774 CE

T.21.1209. *Trailokyavijaya-sādhana-vidhi-atigihya-dvāra* from the *Vajraśekhara-tantra*. Amoghavajra, 446-774 CE (?)

T.21.1210. *Trailokyavijaya-krodha-vidyarāja . . . kalpa*. Amoghavajra, pre-774 CE

T.21.1214. *Yamāntaka-ādhyāya-kalpa*. Amoghavajra, pre-774 CE

T.21.1215. *Mahāyāna-vaipulya-mañjuśrī-bodhisattvāvatamsaka-mūlatantra-Yamāntaka-krodharāja-mantra-mahābālaguna-kalpa-varga*. Amoghavajra, pre-774 CE

T.21.1216. *Mahāvaipulya-Mañjuśrī-kumarabhūta-bodhisattvāvatamsaka-mūlatantra-Yamāntaka-krodharāja-prasmasā-mantra-abhicaruka-kalpavarga*. Amoghavajra, pre-774 CE

T.21.1217. *Yamāntaka-krodha-vidyārāja-siddhi-kalpa*. Dharmabhadra, 989-999 CE

T.21.1220. Vajrabodhi, pre-732 CE

T.21.1243. *Mahābala sūtra*. Dharmapāla, 983 CE

T.21.1276. *Garudapatalaparivarta* (Chapter from *MMK*) Amoghavajra, 746-774 CE

T.39.1796. *MVS*, commentary. Yixing (and Śubhakarasiṁha), 683-727 CE

T.52.2120. *Taizongchao zeng sikong dabian zheng guangzhi sanzang heshang biaozhi ji*. Compiled by Yuanzhao, 719-800 CE

T.55.2157. *Zhenyuan xinding shijiao mulu*. Compiled by Yuanzhao, 800 CE

T.85.2879. *Fugen-bosatsu-setsushō-myōgyō*.

T.86.2921. *Hizōki*. Kukai and Wenbi, 774-835 CE

T.87.2974. *Ritasōgyara-gobushinkan*.

T.87.2975. *Ritasōgyara-gobushinkan*.

T.87.2976. *Ritasōgyara-gobushinkan*.

T.87.2977. *Taizōzuzō*.

T.87.2978. *Taizōzuzō*.

T.87.2981. *Taizōkyūzuyō*. Compiled by Enchin.

T.88.3007. *Besson-zakki*. Complied by Shinkaku, 1117-1180 CE

T.89.3022. *Kakuzenshō*. Complied by Kakuzen, ca. 1217 CE

T.90.3022A. *Kakuzenshō*, cont. Compiled by Kakuzen, ca. 1217 CE

T.91.3083. *Godaisonzuzō*. Kōgon, 1250 CE

T.91.3100. *Myōōbuzuzō*.

T.97.3231. *Ninnōkyō-mandara*.

T.97.3264. *Gōzanze-myōō-zuzōshū*.

INDEX

(Note: words appear in order of the English alphabet.)

T

U

V

W

Y

Z